T0255560

Lecture Notes in Computer Science   10000

More information about this series at http://www.springer.com/series/7407

Bernhard Steffen · Gerhard Woeginger (Eds.)

Computing and Software Science

State of the Art and Perspectives

 Springer

Editors
Bernhard Steffen
Technical University of Dortmund
Dortmund, Germany

Gerhard Woeginger
RWTH Aachen
Aachen, Germany

ISSN 0302-9743   ISSN 1611-3349   (electronic)
Lecture Notes in Computer Science
ISBN 978-3-319-91907-2   ISBN 978-3-319-91908-9   (eBook)
https://doi.org/10.1007/978-3-319-91908-9

LNCS Sublibrary: SL1 – Theoretical Computer Science and General Issues

Cover illustration: The tag cloud shown on the cover, provided by Markus Frohme, Stefan Naujokat, and Bernhard Steffen (TU Dortmund, Germany), visualizes the topical coverage of the articles included. Used with permission.

This Springer imprint is published by the registered company Springer Nature Switzerland AG
The registered company address is: Gewerbestrasse 11, 6330 Cham, Switzerland

Geleitwort

Quoting the introductory sentence of the preface Jan van Leeuwen wrote in September 1995 in [1], it is my pleasure to state mutatis mutandis: "This volume of the series Lecture Notes in Computer Science (including its subseries Lecture Notes in Artificial Intelligence and Lecture Notes in Bioinformatics) marks a truly unique and festive moment: it is the 10,000th volume that appears in the series."

Indeed, during the 46 years since the launch of the LNCS series in 1973 more than 10,000 volumes have been published in LNCS as of today, roughly 1000 volumes during the first half of this 45-year period and more than 9000 volumes since 1995. The 10,000 volumes published constitute a treasure of around 350,000 research papers and make the series an indispensable resource for computer scientists and an outstanding bibliographic entity across all disciplines of scientific research as well.

In the aforementioned preface of LNCS 1000, a short overview of the beginnings of the series and of its history up to 1995 is presented, also by pointing to some key publications. While it is too demanding to survey the developments in and around LNCS since then at the same level of depth within the limitations of a "Geleitwort", we make an attempt to briefly summarize some major developments and accomplishments of LNCS.

The vast majority of the volumes published in LNCS have always been proceedings or post-proceedings drawing together the research papers or revised versions of work presented at conferences or workshops, thus providing an archival documentation of the scientific outcome of the underlying meetings. However, even in its early years, LNCS included course notes, monographs, and advanced school lectures as well, several of which were among the bestselling and most broadly known ones of their times.

Not least because of the steep growth in the number of LNCS volumes published annually since the early 1990s, exceeding 100 volumes published in 1993, and in order to visually distinguish the non-proceedings literature from proceedings content and post-proceedings content, starting in 1995 we introduced several LNCS color-cover sublines: the Tutorials, the State-of-the-Art Surveys, the Hot Topics, and later on, the Festschrifts. Initially, these books came with a color jacket cover wrapped around the red-and-silver standard cover (blue-and-silver for LNAI). However, we soon learnt that librarians didn't like the jacket covers and mostly removed them before putting the books on the shelves so we then printed the actual softcover in full color.

The LNCS color cover subline volumes include many nice and widely used volumes covering a broad variety of topics. An outstanding Tutorial is MMIXware – A RISC Computer for the Third Millennium by Don E. Knuth [2]. Among the LNCS State-of-the-Art Surveys, it is Neural Networks: Tricks of the Trade by Grégoire Montavon, Genevieve B. Orr, and Klaus-Robert Müller (Eds.) [3] which stands out, not only because of its extremely high number of chapter downloads in SpringerLink. After year-long discussions back and forth with the LNCS series editors on how to deal with proposals for collections of articles honoring an individual scientist or the anniversary of a result or of an institution, we introduced the LNCS Festschrift subline; here a remarkable one is the volume for Zohar Manna on the occasion of his 64th birthday edited by Nachum Dershowitz [4]. At a time when LNCS was still covered by Thompson ISI's Science Citation Index (Expanded), we established the LNCS Transactions sublines, publishing journal content while using LNCS as the production and distribution machinery, thus providing a direct inroad for ISI indexing. Unfortunately and without any prior indication, ISI stopped indexing LNCS in SCI(E) meaning that the formula didn't work any longer and most of the LNCS Transactions then had trouble attracting submissions for publication.

With around 600 volumes published annually, LNCS had reached a critical size, e.g., with regard to subscriptions by institutions. We therefore decided to source out growth by establishing the Lecture Notes in Business Information Processing, LNBIP, and the proceedings series Communications in Computer and Information Science, CCIS, which also allows for the publication of content from more applied or regional conferences and which serves as an incubator environment for LNCS. Internally at Springer, other editorial groups beyond computer science tried to adapt the LNCS publication model and workflow for their audiences and especially the engineering colleagues succeeded in establishing several successful proceedings series.

In the second half of the 1990s, when electronic publishing had already been established for scientific journals, we realized that for the future success of a proceedings series like LNCS, besides printed content distribution, availability of the content in electronic version as part of a digital library would become crucial. Unfortunately, the workflow for feeding, and the structure of, the digital library established at Springer for electronic journal publishing could not be used for the production and presentation of electronic LNCS proceedings in a straightforward manner, mainly because the journal article files processed by professional typesetters were clean and uniform and included carefully structured metadata in HTML, whereas the proceedings article files we received in "camera-ready" fashion were prepared by authors individually using various text processing systems for typesetting on different machine configurations.

As our digital library colleagues were busy with optimizing electronic journal publishing, we in editorial had to take the lead in the development of electronic proceedings publishing at Springer, also in response to a demand expressed by conference organizers and proceedings volume editors more and more urgently. With the help of our colleague Antje Endemann, as well as with the essential contribution of a freelance technical consultant, Markus Richter, and in cooperation with in-house digital library colleagues, we succeeded in 1998 to shoot the first two LNCS volumes onto SpringerLink: FSE 1997, volume 1267 [5], for which we received the complete collection of article files from Eli Biham, and IDA 1997, volume 1280 [6], with all files received from Michael Berthold. A few years later, all LNCS volumes, previously published in print version only, were re-digitized and included in the digital library. LNCS Online has since survived several platform and provider changes and, with well over 100 million article downloads annually, has become the most highly used content item in SpringerLink.

The LNCS publication workflow was further refined, e.g., by sending the proofs of the papers, once they had passed through the light typesetting and normalization process at our end, to the corresponding paper author for approval. Moreover, in parallel to the PDF article files, we now produce full-text HTML and offer both versions in the digital library. Videos can be seamlessly embedded in an LNCS paper and other files can be provided as electronic supplementary material. We have experimented and now offer data/code publishing services and systematically offer the inclusion of author ORCIDs. And, last but not least, already back in 2011 [7], we started publishing in the Gold Open Access mode.

When I took over LNCS in early 1991, Gerhard Goos and Juris Hartmanis had been onboard as LNCS series editors already since the formation of the series in 1973, also drawing advice from an Editorial Board made up of internationally highly reputed computer scientists. The LNCS subseries Lecture Notes in Artificial Intelligence with Joerg Siekmann as series editor had published its first volume, LNCS/LNAI 345 [8], in 1988. Initially all proposals were evaluated and decided upon by the series editors, based on the proposal information received and the context information prepared by Springer, often relating the proposal to predecessor publications with us. Most often proposal decisions were taken unanimously and this didn't change much when Jan van Leeuwen joined as third LNCS series editor in 1994 and when we gave up the Editorial Board. However, occasionally we got stuck with the evaluation of proposals, even when taking into account external expert advice. Once, in such a deadlock situation, Juris Hartmanis stated: "Thinking back on what we were allowed to publish when we were young I feel we should give them a try" (and he authorized me to quote him on this statement). And indeed, looking at some of the very early volumes published in LNCS, one can find articles published even in the German language, which up to now haven't received significant numbers of citations.

With the expansion of the topical coverage of LNCS and the steadily and rapidly increasing number of proposals received, especially from China, the need to ask for external expert advice became more urgent than before and this put me more and more into a position of managing series editor. Repeat proposals, e.g., conference series successfully publishing in LNCS for years, were granted default acceptance status and weren't evaluated in depth each year anew. In 2004, when reaching volume number 3000, a new group of 14 outstanding computer scientists took over as LNCS series editors providing valuable advice during the years of accelerated growth of the series and essentially acting as an Advisory Board.

The Lecture Notes in Bioinformatics, LNBI, commenced publication as a subseries of LNCS in 2005, with Sorin Istrail, Pavel Pevzner, and Mike Waterman as series editors and LNBI 3500 [9] as the first volume. In an attempt to structure and classify the huge amount of content published, topical sublibraries and sublines were intro- duced such as the Advanced Research in Computing and Software Science, ARCoSS, as a quality and relevance focused subline headed by Giorgio Ausiello and Vladimiro Sassone, or, later on, the Formal Methods subline headed by Ana Cavalcanti and Marie-Claude Gaudel. Conference communities and learned societies, like the International Association for Cryptologic Research, IACR, whose proceedings we published from as early on as 1984 and which had developed a bundle of conferences and workshops held each year, sought a publication package deal that would avoid formal evaluation of individual proposals with its delays and uncertainties each year anew. In a certain sense, LNCS developed into a holding in which various conference communities and learned societies had their share and their sheltered place for the publication of their proceedings and post-proceedings.

For me personally, the delayed publication of this anniversary volume coincides with a major change in my (professional) life: after having been in charge of LNCS since 1991, I am approaching my legal retirement age and have now handed over responsibility for the series to my successor Aliaksandr Birukou. Having worked with Alex for more than seven years, I am absolutely convinced that he will do an excellent job continuing and further developing LNCS by bringing in fresh ideas. Given this closing aspect of my involvement with Springer and LNCS, this is a unique opportunity to express my sincere gratitude, externally as well as internally, for a wonderful professional life often overgrowing my private life:

Firstly, special thanks, as well as my sincere apologies, go to Bernhard Steffen and Gerhard Woeginger as the editors of the present book and to the authors whose articles are included here: thank you for delivering such a nice thought-provoking collection of expository articles, providing a highly relevant snapshot of the state of the art of foundational aspects of computer science, and please accept my apologies for delaying this project.

Internally, I am reporting my gratitude to several generations of management: some of the direct and higher-up line managers under whom I worked actively provided recognition and support, while others at least let me do my thing – and this is by no means self-evident. And then there is, of course, the entire LNCS Team, now headed by Aliaksandr Birukou, to whom I want to express my gratitude: first and foremost, to Anna Kramer as my long-year right hand, the team's soul and pacemaker, and our external communication center; and to Christine Reiss as the technical innovation expert, workflow specialist and Anna's substitute; as well as to Nicole Sator as personal/team assistant. However, each of the LNCS assistant editors working with us in the past and now deserves a big thank you for dealing as project managers with hundreds of, or even a thousand, LNCS projects during the publication stage and typically under very tight schedules. Presently, the LNCS assistant editors (in order of time working for us) are: Erika Siebert-Cole, Peter Strasser, Ingrid Haas, Elke Werner, Abier El-Saeidi, Miriam Costales, Sanja Evenson, Alla Serikova, and Lauren Perkins. Posthumously and in deep gratitude, I acknowledge the essential contribution of fellow editor Frank Holzwarth, who for many years was our LaTeX-wizard and IT-factotum and who prematurely passed away in January 2018. A special thank you goes to colleague editors Ralf Gerstner and Ronan Nugent, around the corner here in Heidelberg, for their input, advice, and help on many proposals and projects, as well as to Beijing colleague editor Celine Chang, who, besides running her own publication program, as the LNCS bridgehead in China has been of invaluable help in the success of LNCS in this booming country. Finally, my gratitude extends to the production department, especially to colleagues Viktoria Dobisch and Anja Seibold here in Heidelberg and to their counterpart, Julia Pressels Loyola, who runs the LNCS group of well over 200 people at Scientific Publishing Services Pvt Ltd in Chennai, India, for always being cooperative in incorporating our special requirements into their workflows and for turning around a vast number of projects under extremely tight schedules.

Interacting with the computer science research and development community for almost three decades, I met excellent scientists and outstanding characters, many of them working extremely hard. Of course, like in real life, there were also conflicts and battles to be fought, some even at the kindergarten level of interaction. However, overall, at home, in the office, on the phone, and in email, as well as in personal meetings at conferences and during campus visits, I experienced the computer science research community as a wonderful working environment. The success Springer had in computer science publishing during the past few decades is all due to the authors' community in the field, to whom I shall remain connected in deep gratitude.

September 2019   Alfred Hofmann

References

1. van Leeuwen, J. (ed.): Computer Science Today: Recent Trends and Developments, LNCS, vol. 1000. Springer, Heidelberg (1995). https://doi.org/10.1007/BFb0015232
2. Knuth, D.E. (ed.): MMIXware: A RISC Computer for the Third Millennium, LNCS, vol. 1750. Springer, Heidelberg (1999). https://doi.org/10.1007/3-540-46611-8
3. Montavon, G., Orr, G.B., Müller, K.R. (eds.): Neural Networks: Tricks of the Trade, 2nd edn., LNCS, vol. 7700. Springer, Heidelberg (2012). https://doi.org/10.1007/978-3-642-35289-8
4. Dershowitz, N. (ed.): Verification: Theory and Practice, Essays Dedicated to Zohar Manna on the Occasion of His 64th Birthday, LNCS, vol. 2772. Springer, Heidelberg (2003). https://doi.org/10.1007/b12001
5. Biham, E. (ed.): Fast Software Encryption, 4th International Workshop, FSE 1997, Haifa, Israel, January 20–22, 1997, Proceedings, LNCS, vol. 1267. Springer, Heidelberg (1997). https://doi.org/10.1007/BFb0052329
6. Liu, X., Cohen, P., Berthold, M. (eds.): Advances in Intelligent Data Analysis: Reasoning about Data, Second International Symposium, IDA-1997, London, UK, August 4–6, 1997, Proceedings, LNCS, vol. 1280. Springer, Heidelberg (1997). https://doi.org/10.1007/BFb0052824
7. Domingue, J.D., et al. (ed.): The Future Internet, Future Internet Assembly 2011: Achievements and Technological Promises, LNCS, vol. 6656. Springer, Heidelberg (2011). https://doi.org/10.1007/978-3-642-20898-0
8. Nossum, R.T. (ed.): Advanced Topics in Artificial Intelligence, 2nd Advanced Course, ACAI '87, Oslo, Norway, July 28 – August 7, 1987, LNCS, vol. 345. Springer, Heidelberg (1988). https://doi.org/10.1007/3-540-50676-4
9. Miyano, S., Mesirov, J., Kasif, S., Istrail, S., Pevzner, P.A., Waterman, M. (eds.): Research in Computational Molecular Biology, 9th International Conference, RECOMB 2005, Cambridge, MA, USA, May 14–18, 2005, Proceedings, LNCS/LNBI, vol. 3500. Springer, Heidelberg (2005). https://doi.org/10.1007/b135594

Preface

The first volume of the Springer LNCS series appeared back in the year 1973, and in the meantime more than 10000 volumes have been published. LNCS proceedings have accompanied and helped to shape our scientific life. The book series has formed the knowledge backbone for generations of computer scientists. It was therefore a special honor for us to accept Alfred Hofmann's invitation to cooperatively edit the 10000th volume. We are very proud that we could win world-leading experts to share their specific views and visions with us in this book.

The contributions in this volume focus on the foundational aspects of computer science, the thematic origin and stronghold of LNCS, under the title *"Computing and Software Science: State of the Art and Perspectives"*. They are organized in two parts.

The first part, *Computation and Complexity*, presents a collection of expository papers on fashionable themes in algorithmics, optimization, and complexity. The topics cover a wide territory, ranging from efficient algorithms in areas like social choice, graph drawing, and wireless networks to knowledge harvesting, green computing, chess programs, and brain computation. The introduction to this part presents a brief overview of the 12 contributions.

The second part, *Methods, Languages and Tools for Future System Development*, aims at sketching the methodological evolution that helps to guarantee that future systems meet their increasingly critical requirements. To understand how far today's ambitions reach, one must only think of challenges like automotive driving and traffic control, secure communications and business transactions, knowledge and process management in healthcare, and robotic systems and digital manufacturing, where autonomic systems closely cooperate with humans. The introduction to this topical part provides an overview of its 12 contributions structured in the three sections *The Power of Languages; Validation: Testing and Beyond;* and *Verification Methods and Tools*.

We are very grateful to the authors for their exceptional contributions and their reviewing support. Their constructive mutual feedback turned the development of this volume into a collaborative effort. In fact, the second topical part used zero-blind reviewing to explicitly encourage discussion and cross referencing. We are also very grateful to Springer, and here in particular to Alfred Hofmann, for his initiative and continuous support, and to Markus Frohme for his help with the OCS (in particular during the production phase).

March 2019

Bernhard Steffen
Gerhard Woeginger

Organization

Reviewing Committee (Computation and Complexity)

Pankaj K. Agarwal	Duke University, USA
Haris Aziz	UNSW Sydney, Australia
Rene Bekker	Vrije Universiteit Amsterdam, The Netherlands
Carla Binucci	University of Perugia, Italy
Ulrik Brandes	ETH Zürich, Switzerland
Felix Brandt	Technische Universität München, Germany
William Cook	University of Waterloo, Canada
Tim Dwyer	Monash University Melbourne, Australia
Edith Elkind	University of Oxford, UK
Esther Ezra	Georgia Tech, USA
Kyle Fox	The University of Texas at Dallas, USA
Martin Gronemann	Universität zu Köln, Germany
Magnus Halldorsson	Reykjavik University, Iceland
Johannes Hoffart	Max-Planck-Institut für Informatik, Saarbrücken, Germany
Robert Legenstein	Graz University of Technology, Austria
Wolfgang Maass	Graz University of Technology, Austria
Michel Mandjes	Universiteit van Amsterdam, The Netherlands
Petra Mutzel	TU Dortmund, Germany
Christos H. Papadimitriou	Columbia University New York, USA
Kirk Pruhs	University of Pittsburgh, USA
Kenneth Regan	University at Buffalo, The State University of New York, USA
Dana Ron	Tel Aviv University, Israel
Marcus Schaefer	DePaul University Chicago, USA
Falk Schreiber	Univesität Konstanz, Germany
Piotr Skowron	University of Warsaw, Poland
Bettina Speckmann	Eindhoven University of Technology, The Netherlands
Peter Spreij	Universiteit van Amsterdam, Radboud University Nijmegen, The Netherlands
Nicos Starreveld	Korteweg-de-Vries Instituut, Amsterdam, The Netherlands
Fabian Suchanek	Télécom Paris University, France
Luca Trevisan	U.C. Berkeley, USA
Santosh Vempala	Georgia Tech College of Computing, USA
Roger Wattenhofer	ETH Zürich, Switzerland
Gerhard Weikum	Max Planck Institute for Informatics, Germany
Ryan Williams	MIT, USA

Gerhard Woeginger	RWTH Aachen, Germany
Michael Wooldridge	University of Oxford, UK
Marc van Krefeld	Universiteit Utrecht, The Netherlands
Reinhard von Hanxleden	CAU Kiel, Germany

Reviewing Committee (Methods, Languages and Tools for Future System Development)

Rajeev Alur	University of Pennsylvania, USA
Christel Baier	TU Dresden, Germany
Albert Benveniste	Inria, France
George Candea	EPFL, Switzerland
Alastair Donaldson	Imperial College London, UK
Hilding Elmqvist	Mogram AB, Sweden
Patrice Godefroid	Microsoft Research, USA
Radu Grosu	Technische Universität Wien, Austria
Klaus Havelund	Jet Propulsion Laboratory/NASA, USA
Thomas A. Henzinger	IST, Austria
Holger Hermanns	Saarland University, Germany
Falk Howar	Dortmund University of Technology and Fraunhofer ISST, Germany
Marieke Huisman	University of Twente, The Netherlands
Michael Huth	Imperial College London, UK
Reiner Hähnle	TU Darmstadt, Germany
Bengt Jonsson	Uppsala University, Sweden
Joost-Pieter Katoen	RWTH Aachen University, Germany
Fabrice Kordon	Sorbonne Université, France
Kim Larsen	University of Southern Denmark, Denmark
Axel Legay	Inria, France
Michael Leuschel	University of Düsseldorf, Germany
Tiziana Margaria	University of Limerick and Lero, Ireland
Petra Mutzel	TU Dortmund, Germany
Alan Mycroft	University of Cambridge, UK
Flemming Nielson	Technical University of Denmark
Grigore Rosu	University of Illinois at Urbana-Champaign, USA
Scott Smolka	Stony Brook University, USA
Bernhard Steffen	TU Dortmund University, Germany
Frits Vaandrager	Radboud University, The Netherlands
Jaco van de Pol	University of Twente, The Netherlands

Reviewers

Eranda Cela	TU Graz, Austria
Janosch Fuchs	RWTH Aachen, Germany
Tim Hartmann	RWTH Aachen, Germany

Contents

Methods, Languages and Tools for Future System Development

Computation and Complexity

Computation and Complexity

Gerhard J. Woeginger[(⊠)]

Department of Computer Science, RWTH Aachen, 52074 Aachen, Germany
woeginger@algo.rwth-aachen.de

Abstract. Algorithmics, computation, optimization, complexity, combinatorics and knowledge representation are closely related sub-areas of Theoretical Computer Science. The following summary presents short descriptions of the twelve chapters in this topical part.

This first part of the book covers a wide range of topics that may roughly be summarized under the words *"computation"* and *"complexity"*. The choice of topics reflects the massive developments in computer science over recent decades. Many research areas that used to be outside of traditional computer science have been conquered and attacked with computer science tools. For example, classical Euclidean geometry has led to the area *computational geometry*, classical graph theory has led to *algorithmic graph theory*, biology gave us the area of *computational biology*, from the social sciences we got *computational social choice*, and economics delivered the areas of *algorithmic game theory* and *computational economics*. Computer science has always been very successful in modelling communication systems, for example *wireless networks*. One of the biggest challenges in neuroscience consists in understanding how the human brain works and how the *brain performs computations*. The internet (as a gigantic decentralized computing system) has led to the areas *data mining* and *knowledge harvesting*.

The first part of the book deals with some of these challenges and trends, and the following twelve chapters analyze some aspects of these developments. We present short descriptions of these chapters.

The chapter **"Some Estimated Likelihoods for Computational Complexity"** by Williams [16] addresses some of the most fundamental open problems in computational complexity theory. Of course, we would like to know the answer to the P versus NP question (Is P = NP?). A slightly easier problem asks whether P = PSPACE (this statement should at least be easier to disprove than P = NP, as NP⊆PSPACE holds). Other central open questions in complexity theory concern the so-called Exponential Time Hypothesis (ETH) of Impagliazzo and Paturi [9], the Strong Exponential Time Hypothesis (SETH), and the Nondeterministic Strong Exponential Time Hypothesis (NSETH), which all form strengthenings of the statement P ≠ NP. In his chapter, Ryan Williams states concrete probabilities with which he believes that the various open problems have positive answers: P ≠ NP with probability 80%, ETH should hold with probability 70%, SETH with probability 25%, and so on. The body of the chapter deals with the reasons why and how Ryan arrived at these probabilities, with technical possibilities and impossibilities, and many other things.

ⓒ Springer Nature Switzerland AG 2019
B. Steffen and G. Woeginger (Eds.): Computing and Software Science, LNCS 10000, pp. 3–8, 2019.
https://doi.org/10.1007/978-3-319-91908-9_1

The chapter **"Computing in Combinatorial Optimization"** by Cook [5] summarizes some of the history of algorithms for combinatorial optimization problems. One of the most prominent problems in this area is the Travelling Salesman Problem (TSP): Given a finite number of points with pairwise distances, find a shortest path connecting all points. William Cook traces the problem back to the year 1930, when Karl Menger described the problem in a colloquium held in Vienna; Menger used the German word "Botenproblem" ("postman problem") for the TSP, as the problem is faced in practice by every postman. Starting from the TSP, the chapter walks through a variety of other fundamental problems and algorithms. The reader learns many surprising facts on the history of the assignment problem, the Hungarian algorithm, dynamic programming, linear programming, cutting planes, matchings, the simplex method, CPLEX, and the reader meets Kurt Gödel, Julia Robinson, Richard Karp, George Dantzig, Michel Balinski, Richard Bellman, Jack Edmonds, Lex Schrijver, and many other superstars of the area.

The chapter **"Computational Social Choice: The First Ten Years and Beyond"** by Aziz et al. [2] introduces the reader to a relatively new subarea of theoretical computer science. Computational social choice lies at the intersection between social choice theory (a subarea of economics and political science) and computer science. As a typical application, we want to mention *Dodgson's method* which is an electoral system that was proposed in 1876 by the British mathematician Charles Dodgson (who is much better known under the name Lewis Carroll, the author of Alice in Wonderland). On the positive side, *Dodgson's method* yields an electoral system that is very safe and extremely difficult to manipulate. On the negative side, Bartholdi et al. [3] have shown that even determining the winner of an election under Dodgson's method is an NP-hard problem. Other popular topics in computational social choice concern voting, coalition formation, matching markets, market equilibria, fair division, and cake cutting protocols. The chapter authors highlight several representative research areas in contemporary computational social choice, and also hint at future developments of the field.

The chapter **"Geometric Optimization Revisited"** by Agarwal et al. [1] deals with the area of computational geometry. Computational geometry is devoted to the study of algorithms that deal with points, lines, circles, triangles, polytopes, spheres, and other geometric objects. The area was triggered by computer graphics and computer-aided design, and more recently by geographic information systems, robotics, and computer vision. Typical problems studied in computational geometry concern motion planning, visibility problems, geometric location, geometric search, route planning, and mesh generation. Computational geometry forms an old and very mature part of algorithmics, and there are entire books available that summarize the main results [6,7]. The chapter concentrates on three concrete problems that have been very active in recent years: Geometric set cover problems; geometric independent set problems; and computing maps between point sets. These problems are typically hard to solve, and the chapter discusses various ways of working around this hardness.

The chapter **"Ten Reasons to Get Interested in Graph Drawing"** by Binucci et al. [4] introduces the reader to the area of graph drawing. (Note that there are ten authors who present ten reasons.) Graph drawing combines methods from geometry, graph theory, algorithmics, and information visualization to derive nice two-dimensional pictures of graphs that arise in application areas such as cartography, social network analysis and bioinformatics. A standard example is how to get a nice drawing of a subway network, with clearly readable names of subway stations and clearly recognizable changeover points. The chapter highlights ten concrete topics in graph drawing, four from theory (computational geometry; canonical orderings; the existential theory of the reals; SPQR-trees) and six from applications (information visualization; software engineering; model-based design; automated cartography; social sciences; molecular biology).

The chapter **"Sublinear-Time Algorithms for Approximating Graph Parameters"** by Ron [14] surveys the field of sublinear-time algorithms. For decades, researchers in algorithmics have been aiming for *linear-time* algorithms and considered them as the best-possible type of result that one can hope for. After all, it is hard to imagine that one could do better than linear-time: For any non-trivial problem, an algorithm should at least read and consider all of the input before making a qualified decision. However, (very) large data sets have become prevalent in a wide variety of settings, and it is natural to wonder what one can actually do in sublinear-time. With sublinear-time, one obviously can only read a miniscule fraction of the input. Typically, sublinear-time algorithms must use randomization and must give an answer which is (in some sense) approximate. Dana Ron discusses a variety of results on the sublinear approximation of certain graph parameters (average degree; higher moments of the degree distribution; number of connected components; vertex cover number; the weight of minimum spanning trees).

The chapter **"Dynamic Erdős-Rényi graphs"** by Mandjes et al. [11] deals with dynamic versions of the classical random graph model. Transportation networks, traffic networks, communication networks, and energy networks form the backbone of our modern society. Networks and graphs are used to model social, physical, chemical, biological, and technological phenomena. The existing literature predominantly focuses on static graphs: A random graph is drawn just once, and does not change over time. In many real-life situations, however, the network structure temporally evolves, with edges appearing and disappearing over time. The chapter discusses two dynamic versions of the classical Erdős-Rényi random graph. In the first version, the transition rates are governed by an external regime process, and in the second version the transition rates are periodically resampled. The chapter analyzes the corresponding moments, derives central limit theorems and investigates the large deviations asymptotics.

The chapter **"Wireless Network Algorithmics"** by Halldorsson and Wattenhofer [8] provides an introduction to algorithmic models for wireless networks. While wireless networks save us the costly process of introducing cables and make our lives easier, they also create new problems, as wireless transmission may suffer from interference. To prevent interference, we could carefully schedule all transmissions so that concurrent transmissions are separated in space or time; however, scheduling a transmission at a different time might create new interferences at the newly chosen time slot. Another possibility would be to increase the transmission power in order to reduce interference; however, by increasing the transmission power, we may also create new interferences with other transmissions. The chapter presents the most popular mathematical models for wireless networks. It discusses a number of central results on link scheduling algorithms and on power control algorithms, it states future directions and poses several major open questions.

The chapter **"Green Computing Algorithmics"** by Pruhs [12] surveys the relatively new field of green computing, which perhaps could as well be called energy-aware computing. Nowadays one of the main problems in the design of new and faster VLSI chips is the generated heat, as it requires expensive (and noisy) cooling systems for computers. For instance, CEO Eric Schmidt from Google says: *"What matters most to the computer designers at Google is not speed, but power, low power, because data centers can consume as much electricity as a city."* Power consumption has led us to rethink and to redesign algorithmics from scratch, now with the minimization of energy as our top design constraint (instead of the somewhat outdated maximization of speed). The chapter explains why a theory of energy as a computational resource will look very different from the established theory of time or space as computational resources. Kirk Pruhs discusses various optimization problems under energy constraints, such as circuit routing in a network, scheduling on heterogeneous processors, and finding schedules that optimally trade off energy and performance.

The chapter **"Brain Computation: A Computer Science Perspective"** by Maass et al. [10] gives an introduction for computer scientists into brain computation. The human brain carries out tasks that are very demanding from a computational point of view, and apparently it is powered by a mere 20 Watts. The computational neuroscience pioneer David Marr has proposed a three-level approach to understanding brain computation: The behavioral level identifies the input-output behavior of the system, the algorithmic level analyzes the processes and representations used in the system, and the hardware level studies the biophysical elements and the molecular mechanisms used by the system to implement the algorithm. The chapter provides an overview of interactions between computer science and the study of computational aspects of the brain. The authors discuss the methodology of the computational study of the brain, while focusing on algorithms of the brain, on abstract and simplified models of brain systems, and on learning.

The chapter **"Rating Computer Science Via Chess"** by Regan [13] provides an introduction to (certain aspects of) computer chess. The chapter author Ken Regan is not only a well-known authority in theoretical computer science, but also a top notch chess player: In the 1970s he was one of the youngest chess masters since Bobby Fischer, and in 1980 he reached the international master (IM) level. In recent years Ken has also served as a member of the anti-cheating committee of the World Chess Federation (FIDE), where he has been pivotal in writing the guidelines to prevent cheating in professional chess. By using his database with tens of thousands of top-level games, Ken has devised computer programs that can help to determine whether a player is playing more like a human or rather more like a computer. The chapter provides insight into the intersection between chess and computer science. Among other things, it discusses the complexity of endgames, the ways chess computers work, and it analyzes rating systems for the strength of chess players and chess programs.

The chapter **"Knowledge Harvesting: Achievements and Challenges"** by Weikum et al. [15] gives an overview on recent developments in the area of knowledge bases and knowledge harvesting. Knowledge bases are a technology used to store complex structured and unstructured information used by a computer system. Knowledge harvesting designs approaches for turning noisy Internet content into clearly structured information on entities and relations. Prominent examples of knowledge bases are the *Google* Knowledge Graph, the *True Knowledge Answer Engine* of Amazon, the semantic search engine *Facebook Graph Search*, and *Wolfram Alpha*. Prominent examples of knowledge harvesting are search engines like *Google* or *Bing*, semantic search, aggregating by entities, recommendations and data integration. The chapter surveys key principles of knowledge harvesting, summarizes the state of the art, discusses strategic challenges, and points out opportunities for future research.

References

1. Agarwal, P., Ezra, E., Fox, K.: Geometric optimization revisited. In: Steffen, B., Woeginger, G. (eds.) Computing and Software Science. LNCS, vol. 10000, pp. 66–84. Springer, Cham (2018)
2. Aziz, H., Brandt, F., Elkind, E., Skowron, P.: Computational social choice: the first ten years and beyond. In: Steffen, B., Woeginger, G. (eds.) Computing and Software Science. LNCS, vol. 10000, pp. 48–65. Springer, Cham (2018)
3. Bartholdi, J., Tovey, C.A., Trick, M.A.: Voting schemes for which it can be difficult to tell who won the election. Soc. Choice Welf. **6**, 157–165 (1989)
4. Binucci, C., et al.: Ten reasons to get interested in graph drawing. In: Steffen, B., Woeginger, G. (eds.) Computing and Software Science. LNCS, vol. 10000, pp. 85–104. Springer, Cham (2018)
5. Cook, W.: Computing in combinatorial optimization. In: Steffen, B., Woeginger, G. (eds.) Computing and Software Science. LNCS, vol. 10000, pp. 27–47. Springer, Cham (2018)
6. de Berg, M., Cheong, O., van Kreveld, M.J., Overmars, M.H.: Computational Geometry: Algorithms and Applications. Springer, Heidelberg (2008). https://doi.org/10.1007/978-3-540-77974-2
7. Edelsbrunner, H.: Algorithms in Combinatorial Geometry. Springer, Heidelberg (1987). https://doi.org/10.1007/978-3-642-61568-9
8. Halldorsson, M., Wattenhofer, R.: Wireless network algorithmics. In: Steffen, B., Woeginger, G. (eds.) Computing and Software Science. LNCS, vol. 10000, pp. 141–160. Springer, Cham (2018)
9. Impagliazzo, R., Paturi, R.: The complexity of k-SAT. In: Proceedings of the 14th IEEE Conference on Computational Complexity, pp. 237–240 (1999)

10. Maass, W., Papadimitriou, C., Vempala, S., Legenstein, R.: Brain computation: a computer science perspective. In: Steffen, B., Woeginger, G. (eds.) Computing and Software Science. LNCS, vol. 10000, pp. 184–199. Springer, Cham (2018)
11. Mandjes, M., Starreveld, N., Bekker, R., Spreij, P.: Dynamic Erdős-Rényi graphs. In: Steffen, B., Woeginger, G. (eds.) Computing and Software Science. LNCS, vol. 10000, pp. 123–140. Springer, Cham (2018)
12. Pruhs, K.: Green computing algorithmics. In: Steffen, B., Woeginger, G. (eds.) Computing and Software Science. LNCS, vol. 10000, pp. 161–183. Springer, Cham (2018)
13. Regan, K.: Rating computer science via chess. In: Steffen, B., Woeginger, G. (eds.) Computing and Software Science. LNCS, vol. 10000, pp. 200–216. Springer, Cham (2018)
14. Ron, D.: Sublinear-time algorithms for approximating graph parameters. In: Steffen, B., Woeginger, G. (eds.) Computing and Software Science. LNCS, vol. 10000, pp. 105–122. Springer, Cham (2018)
15. Weikum, G., Hoffart, J., Suchanek, F.: Knowledge harvesting: achievements and challenges. In: Steffen, B., Woeginger, G. (eds.) Computing and Software Science. LNCS, vol. 10000, pp. 217–235. Springer, Cham (2018)
16. Williams, R.: Some estimated likelihoods for computational complexity. In: Steffen, B., Woeginger, G. (eds.) Computing and Software Science. LNCS, vol. 10000, pp. 9–26. Springer, Cham (2018)

Some Estimated Likelihoods
for Computational Complexity

R. Ryan Williams[(✉)]

MIT CSAIL & EECS, Cambridge, MA 02138, USA
rrw@mit.edu

Abstract. The editors of this LNCS volume asked me to speculate on open problems: out of the prominent conjectures in computational complexity, which of them might be true, and why?

I hope the reader is entertained.

1 Introduction

Computational complexity is considered to be a notoriously difficult subject. To its practitioners, there is a clear sense of *annoying* difficulty in complexity. Complexity theorists generally have many intuitions about what is "obviously" true. Everywhere we look, for every new complexity class that turns up, there's another conjectured lower bound separation, another evidently intractable problem, another apparent hardness with which we must learn to cope. We are surrounded by spectacular consequences of all these obviously true things, a sharp coherent world-view with a wonderfully broad theory of hardness and cryptography available to us, but—*gosh, it's so annoying!*—we don't have a clue about how we might prove any of these obviously true things. But we try anyway.

Much of the present cluelessness can be blamed on well-known "barriers" in complexity theory, such as relativization [BGS75], natural properties [RR97], and algebrization [AW09]. Informally, these are collections of theorems which demonstrate strongly how the popular and intuitive ways that many theorems were proved in the past are fundamentally too weak to prove the lower bounds of the future.

- Relativization and algebrization show that proof methods in complexity theory which are "invariant" under certain high-level modifications to the computational model (access to arbitrary oracles, or low-degree extensions thereof) are not "fine-grained enough" to distinguish (even) pairs of classes that seem to be obviously different, such as NEXP and BPP.
- Natural properties also show how the generality of many circuit complexity lower bound proofs can limit their scope: if a method of proving circuit complexity lower bounds applies equally well to proving lower bounds against *random* functions, then it had better not be a highly constructive argument, where one can feasibly discern the circuit complexity of a simple function. Otherwise, our method for proving circuit lower bounds also proves an upper

© Springer Nature Switzerland AG 2019
B. Steffen and G. Woeginger (Eds.): Computing and Software Science, LNCS 10000, pp. 9–26, 2019.
https://doi.org/10.1007/978-3-319-91908-9_2

bound, showing that pseudorandom functions cannot be implemented in the circuit class.

In any case, these barriers show that many known proof methods have so much slack in their arguments that, when it comes to questions like P versus NP, the method will simply hang itself. To make further progress on complexity class separations and prove these obviously-true theorems, we need to dig into computation deeper, and find less superficial methods of argument which speak about computation on a finer level.

I think it is highly probable that a decent level of cluelessness is due to simply being *wrong* about some of these obviously true things. I'm certainly not the first to proclaim such an opinion; Lipton and Regan's blog and books [Lip10, LR13] have spoken at length about how everyone was wrong about X for all sorts of X, and other "contrarian" opinions about complexity can be found in Gasarch's polls on P vs NP [Gas02, Gas12]. The idea that complexity theorists can be very wrong is certainly not in doubt.[1] The fact that it happens at a non-trivial frequency is enough that (I think) folks should periodically reconsider the conjectured complexity separations they have pondered over the years, and update their thoughts on them as new information arises. Regardless of one's opinions about how wrong we may or may not be, I think it is an important exercise to review the major problems in one's field once a year, and seriously check if you got any smarter about them over the previous year.

Moreover, I claim that complexity theorists are more often wrong about their lower bound conjectures than their upper bound conjectures. (Two recent occurrences are the non-rigidity of Hadamard/Sylvester matrices [AW17] which had been conjectured for decades to be rigid, along with the construction of good linear codes that are also not rigid [Dvi17].) This observation is quite probably due to the extremely useful and natural (conservative) heuristic that:

> *If a bunch of smart people could not figure out how to do it, then it probably cannot be done.*

So, when no good upper bound (i.e., algorithm) is attained for a problem, even after a bunch of smart people have thought about it, the inclination is to conclude that the upper bound does not exist (i.e., a lower bound). Hence it is natural that beliefs about lower bounds tend to be refuted more often than those about upper bounds: we rarely assert that interesting upper bounds exist, unless we already know how to attain them. (An interesting exception is that of matrix multiplication over a field; researchers in that area tend to believe that nearly-optimal running time is possible for the problem.) There seems to be an additional belief in the justification of the above heuristic:

> *As the bunch of smart people who cannot find a good algorithm increases over time, we get closer to a universal quantifier over all good algorithms.*

---

[1] Just ask my students!

For example, our collective inability to find an efficient SAT algorithm, even over decades of thought about the problem, even though all the other thousands of NP-complete problems are *really only SAT in disguise*, suggests to many that P ≠ NP.

Unfortunately, I do not believe that the "bunch of smart people" living in the present time covers this sort of quantifier well, and I am not sure how we will raise the next generation of smart people to cover it more thoroughly (other than teaching them to be skeptical, and providing them a vastly-thicker literature of algorithms and complexity than what we had). For this reason, I am probably less dogmatic than a "typical" complexity theorist regarding questions such as P versus NP.

1.1   Some Estimated Likelihoods for Some Major Open Problems

I decided to present my perspective on some well-known open problems in complexity theory with a table of my personal "estimated likelihood" values for each one. Here is the table:

Table 1. What you receive, when you ask for my opinions on some open problems in complexity theory.

Proposition	RW's estimated likelihood
TRUE	100%
$\text{EXP}^{\text{NP}} \neq \text{BPP}$	99%
NEXP $\not\subset$ P/poly	97%
L ≠ NP	95%
NP $\not\subset$ SIZE(n^k)	93%
BPP ⊆ SUBEXP	90%
P ≠ PSPACE	90%
P ≠ NP	80%
ETH	70%
NC1 ≠ TC0	50%
NEXP ≠ EXP	45%
SETH	25%
NEXP ≠ coNEXP	20%
NSETH	15%
L ≠ RL	5%
FALSE	0%

The numerical values of my "estimated likelihoods" are (obviously) nothing too rigorous. What is more important is the relative measure between problems. I did want the measures to be "consistent" in some simple senses. For example, if we know that A implies B, then B should not be (much) less likely to be true than A. I will give some explanations for my likelihoods in the next section.

There are many other open problems for which I could have put a likelihood, but I wanted to focus on problems where I thought I had something interesting to say along with my measure of likelihood. I deliberately refrained from putting a measure on conjectures which I do not feel that I am very knowledgeable on the state-of-the-art, such as the famous Unique Games Conjecture of Khot [Kho02]. For the record, the present state of knowledge suggests to me that Unique Games (as usually stated) is probably *intractable*, but perhaps not NP-hard. But what do I know? A very recent line of work [KMS17, KMS18] claims to settle the 2-to-2 conjecture, a close relative of Unique Games.

2   Thoughts on Various Separations

I will discuss the separations mentioned in Table 1, starting with those that I think are most likely to be true.

2.1   EXP with an NP Oracle Versus BPP

Recall that BPP is the class of problems solvable in randomized polynomial time (with two-sided error), and EXP^{NP} is the class of problems solvable in (deterministic) exponential time with access to an oracle for the SAT problem (note that exponentially-long SAT instances can be solved in one step with such a model). I put 99% on the likelihood of $EXP^{NP} \neq BPP$, for several reasons. One reason is that everything we know indicates that randomized computation is *far, far* weaker than deterministic exponential time, and exponential time with an NP oracle should be only more powerful. Another reason is that the open problem becomes trivially closed (separating the two classes) if one makes various small changes in the problem statement. Change the "two-sided error" to "one-sided error" (the class RP) and it is easy to separate them. Change the EXP to ZPEXP (randomized exponential time with "zero-error") and it is again easy to separate them. For a third reason, $EXP^{NP} \neq BPP$ is implied by very weak circuit lower bounds (such as $NEXP \not\subset P/poly$) that I am also very confident are true (they will be discussed later).

It appears to me that $EXP^{NP} \neq BPP$ is primarily still open because there are oracles making them equal [Hel86], so one will need to use the right sort of non-relativizing argument to get the job done. I do not view the existence of oracles as a significant barrier, but rather a caution sign that we will need to dig into the guts of Turing machines (or equivalent formalizations) in order to separate the classes. Some potential approaches to (weak) lower bounds against BPP are outlined in an earlier article of mine [Wil13b].

2.2   NEXP vs P/poly

Recall that NEXP is the class of problems solvable in nondeterministic exponential time: a huge complexity class. The class P/poly is a special kind of class: it consists of those problems over $\{0,1\}^\star$ which can be solved by an *infinite family* of polynomial-size circuits $\{C_n\}$. Intuitively, this is a computational model with an infinitely-long description (a so-called *non-uniform* model), but for any particular input length n, the description of the computer solving the problem on all inputs of length n (and the running time of this computer) is a fixed polynomial of n. I put 97% likelihood on NEXP $\not\subset$ P/poly. Note that this lower bound would imply $EXP^{NP} \neq BPP$.

I can think of two major reasons why this separation is almost certainly true.

2.2.1 Why Would Non-uniformity Help Here?

I can see no reason why the non-uniform circuit model should let us significantly speed-up the solution to every NEXP problem (or to every EXP problem, for that matter). Having a distinct algorithm for each input length does not intuitively seem to be very helpful: how could it be that every input length n allows for some special hyper-optimization on that particular n, yielding an exponentially faster solution to an NEXP problem? And how could this happen to be true for *every* individual length n? In this light, it feels remarkable to me that this separation problem is still open at all.

Note that there are still oracles relative to which NEXP is contained in P/poly, even in the algebrization sense [AW09]. It is known that there are *undecidable* problems in P/poly, but this is because we can concoct undecidable problems out of *unary* (or more generally, sparse) languages.

I am willing to entertain the possibility that there are *infinitely many* input lengths for which NEXP problems are easy: perhaps NEXP is contained *infinitely often* in P/poly. For example, the "good" input lengths could have the form $2^{2^{\cdot^{\cdot^{2}}}}$, or something more bizarre. This would be an amazing result, but because we only require infinitely many input lengths to work, perhaps some hyper-optimization of certain strange input lengths is possible in this setting. There are oracles relative to which NEXP is contained infinitely often in NP [For15], which shows that infinitely-often simulations can be very tricky to rule out. Still, this also seems unlikely.

2.2.2 Extremely Weak Derandomization.

If the first reason was not already enough, the second reason for believing NEXP $\not\subset$ P/poly is that extremely weak derandomization results would already imply the result. More precisely, it is generally believed that P = BPP. A productive way to think about P = BPP is to study a particular approximation problem, often called CAPP:

Circuit Approximation Probability Problem (CAPP)
Input: A Boolean circuit C
Output: The quantity $\Pr_{x \in \{0,1\}^n}[C(x) = 1]$, to within $\pm 1/10$.

(Note the choice of $1/10$ is arbitrary, and could be any constant in $(0, 1/2)$.) It is known that a deterministic polynomial time algorithm for CAPP would imply

P = BPP. From the work of Impagliazzo and Wigderson [IW97] on pseudorandom generators, such an algorithm follows from assuming that $\mathsf{TIME}[2^{O(n)}]$ does not (infinitely often) have $2^{\delta n}$-size circuits, for some $\delta > 0$. It was shown by Impagliazzo, Kabanets, and Wigderson [IKW02] that a deterministic $2^{n^{\varepsilon}}$-time algorithm for CAPP, for every $\varepsilon > 0$ would already imply $\mathsf{NEXP} \not\subset \mathsf{P/poly}$.[2] So, sub-exponential time deterministic algorithms for CAPP imply the NEXP circuit lower bound.

But in fact something even stronger can be said. For a circuit C with n inputs and size s, the brute-force algorithm for deciding CAPP takes no more than $2^n \cdot \mathsf{poly}(s)$ time. I showed [Wil10] that deciding CAPP in deterministic time

$$O(2^n \cdot \mathsf{poly}(s)/\alpha(n)),$$

for any super-polynomial function $\alpha(n)$, would already imply $\mathsf{NEXP} \not\subset \mathsf{P/poly}$. That is, *any* significant improvement over exhaustive search for CAPP would imply the lower bound we seek.[3] I strongly believe that such an algorithm exists, but it may be tough to find. Several circuit lower bounds against NEXP have indeed been proved by giving non-trivial SAT algorithms for various circuit classes [Wil11, Wil14, Tam16, ACW16, COS17].

2.3   LOGSPACE vs NP

I also believe that $\mathsf{L} \neq \mathsf{NP}$ is extremely likely: that (for example) the Vertex Cover problem on m-edge graphs cannot be solved by any algorithm that uses only m^k time (for some constant k) and $O(\log m)$ additional space (beyond the $O(m \log(n))$ bits of input that lists the edges of the graph). This is far from a controversial position; $O(\log m)$ space is not enough to even store a subset of nodes from the graph (a candidate vertex cover), and it is widely believed that this tiny space requirement is a severe restriction on computational power. In particular it is also widely believed that $\mathsf{L} \neq \mathsf{P}$ (which I would put less likelihood on, but not much less).

I mainly want to highlight $\mathsf{L} \neq \mathsf{NP}$ because (unlike the situation of $\mathsf{P} \neq \mathsf{NP}$, which is murkier) I believe that substantial progress has already been made on the problem. Significant combinatorial approaches to space lower bounds (such as [BJS98, Ajt99, BSSV00, BV02]) have yielded model-independent superlinear time lower bounds on decision problems in P, when the space usage is $n^{1-\varepsilon}$ or less. (In fact, these results hold in a non-uniform version of time-space bounded computation.) Approaches based on diagonalization/simulation methods, aimed at proving lower bounds on NP-hard decision problems such as SAT, include [For00, FLvMV05, Wil08a, Wil13a, BW12] and show that problems such as SAT, Vertex Cover, and Independent Set require $n^{2\cos(\pi/7)}$ time to be solved

---

[2] In fact, a "nondeterministic" algorithm for CAPP of this form would be enough. I will refrain here from defining what such an algorithm means, and refer the reader to the paper [IKW02].

[3] Again, a "nondeterministic" CAPP algorithm with this property would already be enough.

when the space usage of the algorithm is $n^{o(1)}$. Unfortunately, $2\cos(\pi/7) < 1.81$, and in fact the last reference above shows that current techniques cannot improve this curious exponent. So in a quantitative sense, we have a long way to go before $\mathsf{L} \neq \mathsf{NP}$.

After studying these methods for years now, I am more-or-less convinced of $\mathsf{L} \neq \mathsf{NP}$ and that it will be proved, possibly long before P vs NP is resolved. In fact I believe that only a few new ideas will be required to yield enough "bootstrapping" to separate L and NP. The catch is that I am afraid the missing ideas will need to be extraordinarily clever, unlike anything seen before in mathematics (at least a Gödel-incompleteness-level of cleverness, relative to the age in which he proved those famous theorems). In the meantime, we do what we can.

2.4   NP Does Not Have Fixed Polynomial-Size Circuits

Recall that $\mathsf{SIZE}(n^k)$ is the class of problems solvable with Boolean circuits (of fan-in two) with $O(n^k)$ gates. Here we are investigating the likelihood of the proposition

$$\forall k \in \mathbb{N}, \mathsf{NP} \not\subset \mathsf{SIZE}(n^k).$$

That is, for every k, there is some problem in NP that doesn't have $O(n^k)$-size circuits.

First, I put a bit less likelihood (93%) on $\mathsf{NP} \not\subset \mathsf{SIZE}(n^k)$ for some constant k, because it implies $\mathsf{NEXP} \not\subset \mathsf{P/poly}$ (and they don't seem to be equivalent), so it is stronger than the other circuit lower bound problems that have been mentioned so far.

There is a considerable history of results in this direction. Kannan [Kan82] proved "fixed polynomial" circuit lower bounds for the class $\mathsf{NP}^{\mathsf{NP}}$ (a.k.a. $\Sigma_2\mathsf{P}$): for every constant $k \geq 1$, there is a problem in $\mathsf{NP}^{\mathsf{NP}}$ that does not have n^k size Boolean circuits (over any gate basis that you like). Over time, his fixed-polynomial lower bound has been improved several times, from $\mathsf{NP}^{\mathsf{NP}}$ to seemingly smaller complexity classes such as $\mathsf{ZPP}^{\mathsf{NP}}$ [KW98]. It is known that $\mathsf{MA/1}$ (Merlin-Arthur with one bit of advice) is not in $\mathsf{SIZE}(n^k)$ for each k [San07], and due to our beliefs about circuit lower bounds [IW97] it is believed that $\mathsf{MA} = \mathsf{NP}$ (i.e., it is believed that randomness doesn't help much with non-interactive verification of proofs). This looks like strong evidence in favor of $\mathsf{NP} \not\subset \mathsf{SIZE}(n^k)$, besides the intuition that NP problems that require $n^{100000k}$ nondeterministic time probably can't be "compressed" to n^k-size circuits.

The problems of proving that classes such as P, NP, and P^{NP} have fixed polynomial-size circuits are discussed in [Lip94, FSW09, GM15, Din15], and many absurd-looking consequences have been derived from propositions such as $\mathsf{NP} \subset \mathsf{SIZE}(n^k)$ (of course, none of these have been proved to be actually contradictory).

Here's an example from [FSW09]. $\mathsf{P}^{\mathsf{NP}} \subset \mathsf{SIZE}(n^k)$ implies that for **every** NP verifier V, and every yes-instance x for the verifier V, there is a witness y_x that is extremely compressible: it can be represented by a circuit of only $O(|x|^k)$ size. To see this, note that the problem

Given an x and an integer i, print the ith bit of the lexicographically first y such that $V(x,y)$ accepts (or print 0 if no such y exists)

is in P^{NP}, and therefore has $O(n^k)$-size circuits under the hypothesis. Thus the witnesses printed by these circuits have low circuit complexity, for every x.

2.5   BPP is in Sub-Exponential Time

Recall $\mathsf{SUBEXP} = \cap_{k\in\mathbb{N}}\mathsf{TIME}(2^{n^{1/k}})$, i.e., it is the class of problems solvable in $O(2^{n^{\varepsilon}})$ time, for any $\varepsilon > 0$ as close to zero as you like.

The main reason for putting a high likelihood on $\mathsf{BPP} \subseteq \mathsf{SUBEXP}$ is that it is implied by $\mathsf{EXP} \not\subset io\text{-}\mathsf{P}/\mathsf{poly}$ [NW94, BFNW93], which I also believe to be true, although perhaps not quite as strongly as $\mathsf{NEXP} \not\subset \mathsf{P}/\mathsf{poly}$. (The "io" part stands for "infinitely often" and it means that there is a function EXP which, for almost every input length n, fails to have circuits of size $\mathsf{poly}(n)$.) The intuition for why $\mathsf{EXP} \not\subset io\text{-}\mathsf{P}/\mathsf{poly}$ is similar to the intuition for why $\mathsf{NEXP} \not\subset \mathsf{P}/\mathsf{poly}$. As a starting point, one can easily prove results like $\mathsf{EXP} \not\subset io\text{-}\mathsf{TIME}[2^{n^k}]$ for every constant k, by diagonalization. It would be very surprising, even magical, if one could take a problem that cannot be solved infinitely-often in 2^{n^k} time and solve it infinitely-often in polynomial time, simply because one got a separate algorithm and received polynomially-long extra advice for each input length. Intuitively, to solve the hardest problems in EXP, the only advice that could truly help you solve the problem quickly (on all inputs of length n) would be the entire 2^n-bit truth table for length n, and for such problems it is not clear why some input lengths would ever be easier than others. (Aside: it is interesting to note that $\mathsf{P} = \mathsf{NP}$ implies circuit lower bounds such as $\mathsf{EXP} \not\subset io\text{-}\mathsf{P}/\mathsf{poly}$.)

For what it's worth, I would put about 87% likelihood on $\mathsf{P} = \mathsf{BPP}$: a bit lower than the 90% BPP in sub-exponential time (for good reason), but not significantly less. These two likelihoods aren't substantially different for me, because I tend to believe that non-trivial derandomizations of BPP are likely to imply much more efficient derandomizations, along the lines of Theorems 1.4 and 1.5 in [Wil10].

2.6   P vs PSPACE

I have put a little less likelihood (90%) on $\mathsf{P} \neq \mathsf{PSPACE}$ than the previous lower bounds mentioned such as $\mathsf{L} \neq \mathsf{NP}$. I feel that less intellectual progress has been made on separating P from PSPACE, and so the extent to which we should believe $\mathsf{P} \neq \mathsf{PSPACE}$ is less understood. For example, we don't know an $n^{1.0001}$ time lower bound against any PSPACE-hard problem solvable in linear space, such as quantified Boolean formula satisfiability (but we do know a few non-trivial-but-not-so-great lower bounds [HPV77, Wil08b, LW13]). The reminder that such a time lower bound is still open should signal a call-to-arms for complexity theorists:

If PSPACE *is so large, why can't we prove an* $n^{1.0001}$ *time lower bound against solving QBF? What are the obstacles? Can we articulate some interesting tools that would suffice to prove the lower bound, if we had them?*

Nevertheless, P $=$ PSACE *does look extremely unlikely*: the idea that PSPACE corresponds to computing winning strategies in two-player games makes it clear that our world would be extremely weird and wonderful if P $=$ PSPACE and we discovered a fast algorithm for solving quantified Boolean formulas.

2.7   P vs NP

I do not have much to say about P versus NP beyond what has already been said, over many decades, by many researchers (a notable example is Aaronson's astounding recent survey [Aar16]). But I do only give 80% likelihood of P $\neq$ NP being true. Why only 80%? Because the more I think about P versus NP, the less I understand about it, so why should I be so confident in its answer? Because ETH is less likely to be true than P $\neq$ NP, and I feel like the truth of ETH is not so far from a coin toss. Because it is not hard, when you squint, to view incredible achievements like the PCP theorem [AS98, ALM+98] as progress towards P $=$ NP (one only has to satisfy $7/8 + \varepsilon$ of the clauses in a MAX-3-SAT instance! [Hås01]) instead of hardness for approximately solving NP problems.

Yes, intuitively and obviously P $\neq$ NP—but only intuitively and obviously. (Incidentally, I put about the same likelihood on the existence of one-way functions; I tend to believe in strong worst-case to average-case reductions.)

2.8   ETH: The Exponential Time Hypothesis

Recall that ETH asserts that

3SAT on n variables cannot be solved in $2^{\varepsilon n}$ time, for some $\varepsilon > 0$.

I put only 70% likelihood on ETH. My chief reason (which will also appear later when I discuss NEXP and EXP) is that we simply do not yet have a somewhat-comprehensive understanding of what can be solved via sub-exponential time algorithms. That is not for a lack of trying: it is a very active subject (see for example [FK10]). Our understanding of polynomial-time algorithms is fairly deep, but even there we have very few lower bounds: we know a lot less about what *cannot* be done.

Although I give it only 70% likelihood, I do not think it is necessarily presumptuous to base a research program on ETH being true, but I do think researchers should be a little more skeptical of ETH, and periodically think seriously about how it might be refuted. (As Russell Impagliazzo often reminds me: "It's not a Conjecture, it's a Hypothesis! We chose that word for a reason.") More points along these lines will be given when SETH (the Stronger ETH) is discussed.

2.9   NC1 versus TC0

Recall that NC^1 ("Nick's Class 1") is the class of problems solvable with $O(\log n)$-depth circuits of polynomial size and constant fan-in for each gate. The class TC^0 contains problems solvable with $O(1)$-depth fan-in circuits of polynomial size with unbounded fan-in MAJORITY gates along with inverters. (The T stands for "Threshold"—without loss of generality, the gates could be arbitrary linear threshold functions.) It is well-known that $TC^0 \subseteq NC^1$, and $NC^1 \neq TC^0$ is sometimes used as a working hypothesis.

Upon reflection, I have possibly put significantly less weight on $NC^1 \neq TC^0$ (only 50% likelihood) than one might expect. (I know of at least one complexity theorist who has worked for years to prove that $NC^1 = TC^0$. No, it's not me.) One not-terribly-serious reason for doubting $NC^1 \neq TC^0$ is that TC^0 is (as far as we know) the class of circuits most closely resembling the human brain, and we are all familiar with how unexpectedly powerful that sort of computational device can be.

A more serious reason for doubting $NC^1 \neq TC^0$ is that NC^1 has proven to be surprisingly easier than expected, and TC^0 has been surprisingly powerful (in a formal sense). Barrington's amazing theorem [Bar89] shows that NC^1 corresponds to only "$O(1)$-space computation" in a computational model that has random access to the input. One corollary is that the word problem over the group S_5 (given a sequence of group elements, is its product the identity?) is already NC^1-complete: solving it in TC^0 would prove $NC^1 = TC^0$.

The circuit complexity literature shows that many problems known to be in NC^1 were systematically placed later in TC^0; a nice example is integer division [BCH86, RT92] but many other interesting numerical and algebraic tasks also turn out to be in TC^0 (such as the pseudorandom function constructions of Naor and Reingold [NR04]). For many different types of groups (but not S_5, as far as we know) their word problems are known to be in TC^0 (see [MVW17] for very recent work, with references). In fact, every natural problem that I know in NC^1 is either already NC^1-complete under TC^0 reductions, or is already in TC^0 (there are no good candidate problems which are neither). So perhaps we are one smart threshold circuit away from making the two classes equal.

An argument leaning towards $NC^1 \neq TC^0$ may be found in Allender and Koucky [AK10] who show that if $NC^1 = TC^0$, then there are $n^{1+\varepsilon}$-size $O(1/\varepsilon)$-depth TC^0 circuits for certain NC^1-complete problems, for every $\varepsilon > 0$. Another point is that, if $NC^1 = TC^0$, then (by a padding argument) the class PSPACE lies in the so-called "polynomial-time counting hierarchy" which intuitively seems smaller. Maybe multiple layers of oracle calls to counting solutions are powerful, and such circuits exist? To me, it's a coin flip.

2.10   EXP vs NEXP

Many may wonder why I put only 45% likelihood on $EXP \neq NEXP$. (I suspect the others will, instead of wondering, just assume that I'm out of my mind.) Well, for one, we do have that $EXP \neq NEXP$ implies $P \neq NP$, and the other direction (at least from a provability standpoint) does not seem to hold, so it is natural to consider $\mathsf{EXP} \neq \mathsf{NEXP}$ to be not as likely as $\mathsf{P} \neq \mathsf{NP}$.

To make the percentage dip below 50%, there are other reasons. For one, if we think we're ignorant about what is impossible in P, then we are total idiots about what is impossible in EXP. The scope of what can be done in exponential time has been barely scratched, I believe, and many improved exponential time algorithms in the literature are mainly applications of known polynomial-time strategies to exponential-sized instances. That is, we generally don't know how to construct algorithms that take advantage of the additional structure provided by succinctly-represented inputs—which are the defining feature of many NEXP-complete problems [PY86, GW83])—and I am inclined to believe that non-trivial algorithms for solving problems on succinct inputs should exist. Arora et al. [ASW09] study exponentially-large graphs whose edge relations are defined by small weak circuits such as AC^0, and give several interesting algorithms for solving problems on such graphs. They also show how the usual NP-complete problems cannot be solved on graphs defined by AC^0 circuits unless $\mathsf{NEXP} = \mathsf{EXP}$.

Let me give a concrete example of the knife edge that NEXP versus EXP sits upon. Let $f : \{0,1\}^{2n} \to \{0,1\}$ be a Boolean function, and define the *graph of f* to be the 2^n-node graph with vertex set $\{0,1\}^n$ and edge set $\{(u,v) \mid f(uv) = 1\}$. Define the Max-Clique-CNF problem to be:

Given a CNF F on 2n variables and m clauses, and an integer $k \in [2^n]$, is there a clique in the graph of F of size at least k?

One can define the Max-Clique-DNF problem in an analogous way. In unpublished work, Josh Alman and I noticed that Max-Clique-CNF is solvable in $2^{O(m+n)}$ time, but Max-Clique-DNF is already NEXP-complete, even for constant-width DNFs of n variables and $\mathsf{poly}(n)$ terms! Das et al. [DST17] make similar observations for the CNF and DNF versions of other NP-hard problems.

I would be very surprised if the hardest cases of the Max-Clique problem (or even the somewhat-hardest cases) can be generated by tiny DNF formulas of constant width. I predict that problems solvable in $2^{O(n)}$ time can be solved faster than the naive $2^{2^{O(n)}}$ deterministic running time; perhaps even in $2^{O(n^k)}$ time for some large constant k.

2.11   SETH: The Strong Exponential Time Hypothesis

Recall that SETH asserts that

For all $\delta < 1$, there is k such that k-SAT on n variables is not in $2^{\delta n}$ time.

So SETH says there is no universal $\delta < 1$ and algorithm solving constant-width CNF SAT instances in $2^{\delta n}$ time. I am generally considered to be a skeptic of SETH (due to work such as [Wil16]), but I am not completely convinced that SETH is false: I put 25% likelihood.

The main reason for skepticism is that the area of exponential-time algorithms has produced *many* results where the naive running time of c^n for an NP-complete problem was reduced to $O((c - \delta)^n)$ for some $\delta > 0$ (see the textbook of Fomin and Kratsch for examples [FK10]). I do not see a good reason for believing that k-SAT is immune to such improvements. But people have tried hard to solve the problem, especially over the last 10 years, so there is some reason to believe SETH. Personally, I have benefited from believing it is false: trying to solve SAT faster has led me down several fruit-bearing paths that I would have never explored otherwise. I believe that contentious conjectures/hypotheses like SETH need to exist, to keep a research area vibrant and active.

I should stress that a large chunk of recent work of the form *SETH implies X* (such as [AVW14, BI15, ABV15, Bri14, BM16, BI16]) does not actually require SETH to be true. In fact, their hardness rests on the following basic *Orthogonal Vectors* (or *Disjoint Sets*) problem.

Orthogonal Vectors: *Given n Boolean vectors in $c \log(n)$ dimensions (for some constant parameter c), are there two which are orthogonal?*

The *Orthogonal Vectors Conjecture* (OVC) is that for every $\varepsilon > 0$, there is a (potentially large) $c \geq 1$ such that no algorithm solves Orthogonal Vectors in $n^{2-\varepsilon}$ time. It is known that OVC implies SETH [Wil04, WY14], and many SETH-hardness results are actually OVC-hard. It looks very plausible to me that OVC is true but SETH is false.

It is useful to think of the Orthogonal Vectors problem as an interesting detection version of rectangular matrix multiplication: *given a "skinny" Boolean matrix A, does $A \cdot A^T$ contain a zero entry?* Note that detecting if there is a *non-zero* can be done in randomized linear time, by Freivalds' checker for matrix multiplication [Fre77]. So the OVC asks whether matrix multiplication checking in the Boolean domain can be extended to checking for a zero entry, without (essentially) multiplying the two matrices.

2.12 NEXP vs CoNEXP

According to Table 1, I am putting 80% likelihood on NEXP = coNEXP. Why would a self-respecting complexity theorist do that? Here are a few reasons:

1. **It is true with small advice.** First, it is known that coNEXP is already contained in NEXP *with $O(n)$ bits of advice*, as reported by Buhrman, Fortnow, and Santhanam [BFS09]. Given a language $L \in$ coNEXP, for inputs of length n, the advice encodes the number of strings of length n which are in L. Then in nondeterministic exponential time, one can guess the inputs that are *not* in L, guess witnesses for each of them, and verify all of this information. Thus in order to put coNEXP in NEXP without advice, it would suffice to be able to count (in NEXP) the number of accepted strings of length n for an NEXP machine. Note how the power of exponential time is being used: coNP $\subset$ NP/poly seems very unlikely in comparison. This proof looks to be inspired by the inductive counting technique in the

proof of $\mathsf{NSPACE}[S(n)] = \mathsf{coNSPACE}[S(n)]$, due to Immerman [Imm88] and Szelepcsényi [Sze88].

2. **The Spectrum Problem.** A stronger result than $\mathsf{NEXP} = \mathsf{coNEXP}$ would be implied by an expected resolution of the *spectrum problem*. In finite model theory, the *spectrum* of a first-order sentence ϕ is the set of all finite cardinalities of models of ϕ. For example, if ϕ is a sentence that defines the axioms of a field, then its spectrum is the set of all prime powers. In the 1950s, Asser (see [DJMM12] for a comprehensive survey) asked whether the complement of a spectrum is always a spectrum itself: i.e.,

> The Spectrum Problem: *Given a first-order sentence ϕ, is there another sentence ψ whose spectrum is the complement of ϕ's spectrum?*

This question has a long rich history, and some working in finite model theory believe the answer to be yes. Jones and Selman [JS74] showed that the spectrum problem has a yes answer if and only if $\mathsf{NTIME}[2^{O(n)}] = \mathsf{coNTIME}[2^{O(n)}]$, since in fact the class of all spectra (where the numbers are encoded in some finite alphabet) equals $\mathsf{NTIME}[2^{O(n)}]$. There are several interesting conjectures regarding spectra, any of which would imply a yes-answer [Ash94, CM06], and the conclusion would be stronger than proving $\mathsf{NEXP} = \mathsf{coNEXP}$. (For instance, one could have nondeterministic $2^{O(n^9)}$-time algorithms for deciding the complements of nondeterministic $O(2^n)$-time problems, and this would still imply $\mathsf{NEXP} = \mathsf{coNEXP}$, but not necessarily the spectrum conjecture.)

3. **Max-Clique-DNF.** From the section on EXP vs NEXP (Sect. 2.10), the following would imply $\mathsf{NEXP} = \mathsf{coNEXP}$: Given a DNF formula F of constant width, $2n$ variables, and $\mathsf{poly}(n)$ terms, there is a nondeterministic algorithm running in $2^{\mathsf{poly}(n)}$ time which accepts F if and only if the graph of F does not have a clique of a certain desired size. (Recall we said that the corresponding problem for CNF is solvable exactly in $2^{\mathsf{poly}(n)}$ time.)

4. **Why not?** I don't know of any truly counter-intuitive consequences of $\mathsf{NEXP} = \mathsf{coNEXP}$. Because one can enumerate over all inputs of length n in exponential time, and in nondeterministic exponential time one can even guess witnesses of exponential length for each input of length n, I think these classes will behave differently than our intuition about lower complexity classes.

2.13 NSETH: Nondeterministic SETH

The NSETH, introduced by Carmosino *et al.* [CGI+16] recently, states:

> For all $\delta < 1$, there is a k such that k-UNSAT on n variables is not in nondeterministic in $2^{\delta n}$ time.

So NSETH proposes that there is no proof system which can refute unsatisfiable $\omega(1)$-width CNFs in $2^{\delta n}$ steps, for any $\delta < 1$.

I put 15% likelihood on NSETH being true. The most obvious reason for skepticism is that the mild extension to Merlin-Arthur proof systems is very false: Formula-UNSAT for $2^{o(n)}$-size formulas can be proved with a probabilistic verifier in only $2^{n/2+o(n)}$ time [Wil16].

Since it is generally believed that $\mathsf{MA} = \mathsf{NP}$, one might think the story is essentially over, and that I should have a much lower likelihood for NSETH. That is not quite the case: while MA may well equal NP, it is not clear how a $2^{n/2}$-time MA algorithm could be simulated in 1.999^n nondeterministic time. It's not even clear that the (one-round) Arthur-Merlin version of SETH is false, because the inclusion of MA in AM takes quadratic overhead. Refuting the one-round Arthur-Merlin SETH (where Arthur tosses coins, then Merlin sends a message based on the coins, then an accept/reject decision is made, and we want Merlin to prove that a given formula is UNSAT in 1.999^n time) would probably imply that a non-uniform variant of NSETH is false.

2.14   L vs RL

I put 95% likelihood on $\mathsf{L} = \mathsf{RL}$, that is, the problems solvable in randomized logarithmic space equals the problems solvable in (deterministic) logspace. At this moment in time, it feels like this problem has "almost" been solved. Intuitively, there are two factors in favor of $\mathsf{L} = \mathsf{RL}$: (1) we already believe that randomness generally does not help solve problems much more efficiently than deterministic algorithms, and (2) space-bounded computation appears to be fairly robust under modifications to the acceptance conditions of the model (think of $\mathsf{NL} \subseteq \mathsf{SPACE}[\log^2 n]$ [Sav70] and $\mathsf{NL} = \mathsf{coNL}$ [Imm88, Sze88]).

As far as I know, the main problem that was thought to be a potential separator of RL and L was undirected s-t connectivity [AKL+79]. However this problem was shown to be in L by a remarkable algorithm of Reingold [Rei08]. In follow-up work, Reingold et al. [RTV06] showed how to solve s-t connectivity in Eulerian directed graphs in L, and show that a logspace algorithm for a seemingly slight generalization of their problem would imply $\mathsf{L} = \mathsf{RL}$. My personal interpretation of these results is that $\mathsf{L} = \mathsf{RL}$ is true, and is only one really good idea away from being resolved.

Acknowledgment. I appreciate Gerhard Woeginger's considerable patience with me during the writing of this article, and Scott Aaronson, Josh Alman, Boaz Barak, Greg Bodwin, Sam Buss, Lance Fortnow, Richard Lipton, Kenneth Regan, Omer Reingold, Rahul Santhanam, and Madhu Sudan for helpful comments on a draft, some of which led me to adjust my likelihoods by a few percentage points.

References

[Aar16] Aaronson, S.: $P \overset{?}{=} NP$. In: Nash Jr., J.F.F., Rassias, M.T.T. (eds.) Open Problems in Mathematics, pp. 1–122. Springer, Cham (2016). https://doi.org/10.1007/978-3-319-32162-2_1

[ABV15] Abboud, A., Backurs, A., Williams, V.V.: Tight hardness results for LCS and other sequence similarity measures. In: FOCS, pp. 59–78 (2015)

[ACW16] Alman, J., Chan, T.M., Williams, R.R.: Polynomial representations of threshold functions and algorithmic applications. In: FOCS, pp. 467–476 (2016)

[Ajt99] Ajtai, M.: A non-linear time lower bound for Boolean branching programs. Theory Comput. **1**(1), 149–176 (2005). Preliminary version in FOCS'99

[AK10] Allender, E., Koucký, M.: Amplifying lower bounds by means of self-reducibility. J. ACM **57**(3), 14 (2010)

[AKL+79] Aleliunas, R., Karp, R.M., Lipton, R.J., Lovász, L., Rackoff, C.: Random walks, universal traversal sequences, and the complexity of maze problems. In: FOCS, pp. 218–223 (1979)

[ALM+98] Arora, S., Lund, C., Motwani, R., Sudan, M., Szegedy, M.: Proof verification and the hardness of approximation problems. J. ACM **45**(3), 501–555 (1998)

[AS98] Arora, S., Safra, S.: Probabilistic checking of proofs: a new characterization of NP. J. ACM **45**(1), 70–122 (1998)

[Ash94] Ash, C.J.: A conjecture concerning the spectrum of a sentence. Math. Log. Q. **40**, 393–397 (1994)

[ASW09] Arora, S., Steurer, D., Wigderson, A.: Towards a study of low-complexity graphs. In: Albers, S., Marchetti-Spaccamela, A., Matias, Y., Nikoletseas, S., Thomas, W. (eds.) ICALP 2009, Part I. LNCS, vol. 5555, pp. 119–131. Springer, Heidelberg (2009). https://doi.org/10.1007/978-3-642-02927-1_12

[AVW14] Abboud, A., Williams, V.V., Weimann, O.: Consequences of faster alignment of sequences. In: Esparza, J., Fraigniaud, P., Husfeldt, T., Koutsoupias, E. (eds.) ICALP 2014. LNCS, vol. 8572, pp. 39–51. Springer, Heidelberg (2014). https://doi.org/10.1007/978-3-662-43948-7_4

[AW09] Aaronson, S., Wigderson, A.: Algebrization: a new barrier in complexity theory. ACM TOCT **1**(1), 2 (2009)

[AW17] Alman, J., Williams, R.: Probabilistic rank and matrix rigidity. In: STOC, pp. 641–652 (2017)

[Bar89] Barrington, D.A.M.: Bounded-width polynomial-size branching programs recognize exactly those languages in NC^1. J. Comput. Syst. Sci. **38**(1), 150–164 (1989)

[BCH86] Beame, P.W., Cook, S.A., Hoover, H.J.: Log depth circuits for division and related problems. SIAM J. Comput. **15**(4), 994–1003 (1986)

[BFNW93] Babai, L., Fortnow, L., Nisan, N., Wigderson, A.: BPP has subexponential time simulations unless EXPTIME has publishable proofs. Comput. Complex. **3**(4), 307–318 (1993)

[BFS09] Buhrman, H., Fortnow, L., Santhanam, R.: Unconditional lower bounds against advice. In: Albers, S., Marchetti-Spaccamela, A., Matias, Y., Nikoletseas, S., Thomas, W. (eds.) ICALP 2009, Part I. LNCS, vol. 5555, pp. 195–209. Springer, Heidelberg (2009). https://doi.org/10.1007/978-3-642-02927-1_18

[BGS75] Baker, T., Gill, J., Solovay, R.: Relativizations of the P =? NP question. SIAM J. Comput. **4**(4), 431–442 (1975)

[BI15] Backurs, A., Indyk, P.: Edit distance cannot be computed in strongly subquadratic time (unless SETH is false). In: STOC, pp. 51–58 (2015)

[BI16] Backurs, A., Indyk, P.: Which regular expression patterns are hard to match? In: FOCS, pp. 457–466 (2016)

[BJS98]   Beame, P., Thathachar, J.S., Saks, M.: Time-space tradeoffs for branching programs. J. Comput. Syst. Sci. **63**(4), 542–572 (2001). Preliminary version in FOCS'98

[BM16]   Bringmann, K., Mulzer, W.: Approximability of the discrete Fréchet distance. JoCG **7**(2), 46–76 (2016)

[Bri14]   Bringmann, K.: Why walking the dog takes time: frechet distance has no strongly subquadratic algorithms unless SETH fails. In: FOCS, pp. 661–670 (2014)

[BSSV00] Beame, P., Saks, M., Sun, X., Vee, E.: Time-space trade-off lower bounds for randomized computation of decision problems. J. ACM **50**(2), 154–195 (2003). Preliminary version in FOCS'00

[BV02]   Beame, P., Vee, E.: Time-space tradeoffs, multiparty communication complexity, and nearest-neighbor problems, pp. 688–697 (2002)

[BW12]   Buss, S.R., Williams, R.: Limits on alternation trading proofs for time-space lower bounds. Comput. Complex. **24**(3), 533–600 (2015). Preliminary version in CCC'12

[CGI+16] Carmosino, M., Gao, J., Impagliazzo, R., Mikhailin, I., Paturi, R., Schneider, S.: Nondeterministic extensions of the strong exponential time hypothesis and consequences for non-reducibility. In: ACM Conference on Innovations in Theoretical Computer Science (ITCS), pp. 261–270 (2016)

[CM06]   Chateau, A., More, M.: The ultra-weak Ash conjecture and some particular cases. Math. Log. Q. **52**(1), 4–13 (2006)

[COS17]   Chen, R., Oliveira, I.C., Santhanam, R.: An average-case lower bound against ACC0. In: Electronic Colloquium on Computational Complexity (ECCC), vol. 24, no. 173 (2017)

[Din15]   Ding, N.: Some new consequences of the hypothesis that P has fixed polynomial-size circuits. In: Jain, R., Jain, S., Stephan, F. (eds.) TAMC 2015. LNCS, vol. 9076, pp. 75–86. Springer, Cham (2015). https://doi.org/10.1007/978-3-319-17142-5_8

[DJMM12] Durand, A., Jones, N.D., Makowsky, J.A., More, M.: Fifty years of the spectrum problem: survey and new results. Bull. Symb. Logic **18**(4), 505–553 (2012)

[DST17]   Das, B., Scharpfenecker, P., Torán, J.: CNF and DNF succinct graph encodings. Inf. Comput. **253**(3), 436–447 (2017)

[Dvi17]   Dvir, Z.: A generating matrix of a good code may have low rigidity. Written by Oded Goldreich (2017). http://www.wisdom.weizmann.ac.il/~oded/MC/209.pdf

[FK10]   Fomin, F.V., Kratsch, D.: Exact Exponential Algorithms. Springer, Heidelberg (2010). https://doi.org/10.1007/978-3-642-16533-7

[FLvMV05] Fortnow, L., Lipton, R.J., van Melkebeek, D., Viglas, A.: Time-space lower bounds for satisfiability. J. ACM **52**(6), 835–865 (2005)

[For00]   Fortnow, L.: Time-space tradeoffs for satisfiability. J. Comput. Syst. Sci. **60**(2), 337–353 (2000)

[For15]   Fortnow, L.: Nondeterministic separations. In: Theory and Applications of Models of Computation (TAMC), pp. 10–17 (2015)

[Fre77]   Freivalds, R.: Probabilistic machines can use less running time. In: IFIP Congress, pp. 839–842 (1977)

[FSW09]   Fortnow, L., Santhanam, R., Williams, R.: Fixed-polynomial size circuit bounds. In: CCC, pp. 19–26. IEEE (2009)

[Gas02]   Gasarch, W.I.: The P =? NP poll. ACM SIGACT News **33**(2), 34–47 (2002)

[Gas12]   Gasarch, W.I.: Guest column: the second P=? NP poll. ACM SIGACT News **43**(2), 53–77 (2012)

[GM15]   Goldreich, O., Meir, O.: Input-oblivious proof systems and a uniform complexity perspective on P/poly. ACM Trans. Comput. Theory (TOCT) **7**(4), 16 (2015)

[GW83]   Galperin, H., Wigderson, A.: Succinct representations of graphs. Inf. Control **56**(3), 183–198 (1983)

[Hås01]   Håstad, J.: Some optimal inapproximability results. J. ACM **48**(4), 798–859 (2001)

[Hel86]   Heller, H.: On relativized exponential and probabilistic complexity classes. Inf. Control **71**(3), 231–243 (1986)

[HPV77]   Hopcroft, J., Paul, W., Valiant, L.G.: On time versus space. J. ACM **24**(2), 332–337 (1977)

[IKW02]   Impagliazzo, R., Kabanets, V., Wigderson, A.: In search of an easy witness: exponential time vs. probabilistic polynomial time. J. Comput. Syst. Sci. **65**(4), 672–694 (2002)

[Imm88]   Immerman, N.: Nondeterministic space is closed under complement. SIAM J. Comput. **17**, 935–938 (1988)

[IW97]   Impagliazzo, R., Wigderson, A.: P = BPP if E requires exponential circuits: derandomizing the XOR lemma. In: STOC, pp. 220–229 (1997)

[JS74]   Jones, N.D., Selman, A.L.: Turing machines and the spectra of first-order formulas. J. Symb. Log. **39**(1), 139–150 (1974)

[Kan82]   Kannan, R.: Circuit-size lower bounds and non-reducibility to sparse sets. Inf. Control **55**(1), 40–56 (1982)

[Kho02]   Khot, S.: On the power of unique 2-prover 1-round games. In: STOC, pp. 767–775. ACM (2002)

[KMS17]   Khot, S., Minzer, D., Safra, M.: On independent sets, 2-to-2 games, and grassmann graphs. In: STOC, pp. 576–589 (2017)

[KMS18]   Khot, S., Minzer, D., Safra, M.: Pseudorandom sets in Grassmann graph have near-perfect expansion. In: Electronic Colloquium on Computational Complexity (ECCC), vol. 18, no. 6 (2018)

[KW98]   Kobler, J., Watanabe, O.: New collapse consequences of NP having small circuits. SIAM J. Comput. **28**(1), 311–324 (1998)

[Lip94]   Lipton, R.J.: Some consequences of our failure to prove non-linear lower bounds on explicit functions. In: Structure in Complexity Theory Conference, pp. 79–87 (1994)

[Lip10]   Lipton, R.J.: The P=NP Question and Gödel's Lost Letter. Springer, Heidelberg (2010). https://doi.org/10.1007/978-1-4419-7155-5. http://rjlipton.wordpress.com

[LR13]   Lipton, R.J., Regan, K.W.: People, Problems, and Proofs. Springer, Heidelberg (2013). https://doi.org/10.1007/978-3-642-41422-0. http://rjlipton.wordpress.com

[LW13]   Lipton, R.J., Williams, R.: Amplifying circuit lower bounds against polynomial time, with applications. Comput. Complex. **22**(2), 311–343 (2013)

[MVW17]   Miasnikov, A., Vassileva, S., Weiß, A.: The conjugacy problem in free solvable groups and wreath products of abelian groups is in TC^0. In: Weil, P. (ed.) CSR 2017. LNCS, vol. 10304, pp. 217–231. Springer, Cham (2017). https://doi.org/10.1007/978-3-319-58747-9_20

[NR04]   Naor, M., Reingold, O.: Number-theoretic constructions of efficient pseudo-random functions. J. ACM **51**(2), 231–262 (2004)

[NW94] Nisan, N., Wigderson, A.: Hardness vs randomness. J. Comput. Syst. Sci. **49**(2), 149–167 (1994)

[PY86] Papadimitriou, C.H., Yannakakis, M.: A note on succinct representations of graphs. Inf. Control **71**(3), 181–185 (1986)

[Rei08] Reingold, O.: Undirected connectivity in log-space. J. ACM **55**(4), 17:1–17:24 (2008)

[RR97] Razborov, A., Rudich, S.: Natural proofs. J. Comput. Syst. Sci. **55**(1), 24–35 (1997)

[RT92] Reif, J.H., Tate, S.R.: On threshold circuits and polynomial computation. SIAM J. Comput. **21**(5), 896–908 (1992)

[RTV06] Reingold, O., Trevisan, L., Vadhan, S.: Pseudorandom walks on regular digraphs and the RL vs L problem. In: STOC, pp. 457–466. ACM (2006)

[San07] Santhanam, R.: Circuit lower bounds for Merlin-Arthur classes. SIAM J. Comput. **39**(3), 1038–1061 (2009). Preliminary version in STOC'07

[Sav70] Savitch, W.J.: Relationships between nondeterministic and deterministic tape complexities. J. Comput. Syst. Sci. **4**(2), 177–192 (1970)

[Sze88] Szelepcsényi, R.: The method of forced enumeration for nondeterministic automata. Acta Informatica **26**(3), 279–284 (1988)

[Tam16] Tamaki, S.: A satisfiability algorithm for depth two circuits with a sub-quadratic number of symmetric and threshold gates. In: Electronic Colloquium on Computational Complexity (ECCC), vol. 23, no. 100 (2016)

[Wil08a] Williams, R.R.: Time-space tradeoffs for counting NP solutions modulo integers. Comput. Complex. **17**(2), 179–219 (2008)

[Wil08b] Williams, R.: Non-linear time lower bound for (succinct) quantified Boolean formulas. In: Electronic Colloquium on Computational Complexity (ECCC), (TR08-076) (2008)

[Wil13a] Williams, R.: Alternation-trading proofs, linear programming, and lower bounds. TOCT **5**(2), 6 (2013)

[Wil13b] Williams, R.: Towards NEXP versus BPP? In: Bulatov, A.A., Shur, A.M. (eds.) CSR 2013. LNCS, vol. 7913, pp. 174–182. Springer, Heidelberg (2013). https://doi.org/10.1007/978-3-642-38536-0_15

[Wil14] Williams, R.: New algorithms and lower bounds for circuits with linear threshold gates. In: STOC, pp. 194–202 (2014)

[Wil16] Williams, R.R.: Strong ETH breaks with Merlin and Arthur: short non-interactive proofs of batch evaluation. In: CCC, pp. 2:1–2:17 (2016)

[Wil11] Williams, R.: Nonuniform ACC circuit lower bounds. JACM **61**(1), 2 (2014). Preliminary version in CCC'11

[Wil04] Williams, R.: A new algorithm for optimal 2-constraint satisfaction and its implications. Theor. Comput. Sci. **348**(2–3), 357–365 (2005). Preliminary version in ICALP'04

[Wil10] Williams, R.: Improving exhaustive search implies superpolynomial lower bounds. SIAM J. Comput. **42**(3), 1218–1244 (2013). Preliminary version in STOC'10

[WY14] Williams, R., Yu, H.: Finding orthogonal vectors in discrete structures. In: SODA, pp. 1867–1877 (2014)

Computing in Combinatorial Optimization

William Cook$^{(\boxtimes)}$

University of Waterloo, Waterloo, Canada
bico@uwaterloo.ca

Abstract. Research in combinatorial optimization successfully combines diverse ideas drawn from computer science, mathematics, and operations research. We give a tour of this work, focusing on the early development of the subject and the central role played by linear programming. The paper concludes with a short wish list of future research directions.

Keywords: Combinatorial optimization · Linear programming
Traveling salesman problem

1 In the Beginning was n Factorial

The design of efficient algorithms for combinatorial problems has long been a target of computer science research. Natural combinatorial models, such as shortest paths, graph coloring, network connectivity and others, come equipped with a wide array of applications as well as direct visual appeal. The discrete nature of the models allows them to be solved in finite time by listing candidate solutions one by one and selecting the best, but the number of such candidates typically grows extremely fast with the input size, putting optimization problems out of reach for simple enumeration schemes.

A central model is the *traveling salesman problem*, or TSP for short. It is simple to state. Given a set of cities, together with the distance between each pair, find the shortest way to visit all of them and return to the starting point, that is, find the shortest circuit containing every city in the specified set.

The TSP has its own array of applications, but its prominence is more due to its success as an engine of discovery than it is to miles saved by travelers. The cutting-plane method [20], branch-and-bound [22], local search [32], Lagrangian relaxation [53], and simulated annealing [65], to name just a few, were all developed with the salesman problem as the initial target. This success, coupled with the simplicity of the model, has made the TSP the poster child for the $\mathcal{NP}$-hard class of problems.

It was Karl Menger who first brought the algorithmic challenge of the TSP to the attention of the mathematics community, describing the model in a colloquium held in Vienna in 1930 [76].

B. Steffen and G. Woeginger (Eds.): Computing and Software Science, LNCS 10000, pp. 27–47, 2019.
https://doi.org/10.1007/978-3-319-91908-9_3

We use the term *Botenproblem* (because this question is faced in practice by every postman, and, by the way, also by many travelers) for the task, given a finite number of points with known pairwise distances, to find the shortest path connecting the points. This problem is of course solvable by finitely many trials. Rules that give a number of trials below the number of permutations of the given points are not known.

Menger was quite informal about the notion of an algorithm, speaking of "rules". (He used the German word "Regeln".) Keep in mind that at the time Alan Turing was an undergraduate student at Cambridge and still several years away from his breakthrough concept of general-purpose computing machines [87].

Menger's call for a better-than-finite TSP algorithm arose at an important period of mathematical research, where fundamental issues in logic and computability were being explored. Indeed, the published statement of Menger's problem appears in the same volume as Gödel's paper [37] on incompleteness theorems. This is not entirely a coincidence, since Gödel and Menger were both Ph.D. students of Hans Hahn and active members of the Vienna Circle. Being a great fan of the salesman problem, I'd like to think Gödel and Menger spent time discussing TSP complexity in Viennese coffee houses, but there is no indication of that.

His challenge did however capture the imagination of the mathematics community. Denoting by n the number of cities to visit, beating $n!$ in a race to the optimal TSP tour became a well-established research topic by the late 1940s.

The first major paper was written by Robinson [82] in 1949, while she was a post-doctoral fellow at the RAND Corporation. Her Ph.D. thesis, *Definability and Decision Problems in Arithmetic* [81], placed her firmly on Gödel's side of the Vienna Circle activities, but the TSP proved hard to resist while she was at RAND as part of "what may have been the most remarkable group of mathematicians working on optimization every assembled" [50].

When we today read the statement of Menger's problem, we immediately think of it in terms of establishing an asymptotic complexity bound. But early researchers considered it not as an asymptotic challenge, but rather as a call for mathematical methods to handle modest-sized instances. The following passage is Robinson's description [82] of her research target.

> Since there are only a finite number of paths to consider, the problem consists in finding a method for picking out the optimal path when n is moderately large, say $n = 50$. In this case there are more than 10^{62} possible paths, so we can not simply try them all. Even for as few as 10 points, some short cuts are desirable.

Her approach towards a 50-point algorithm was to consider a relaxation of the TSP where each city is assigned to another (and no two cities are assigned to the same target city), so as to minimize the total distance between pairs of cities in the assignments. A solution to this relaxation gives a set of disjoint directed circuits (possibly including circuits having only two points) such that every city is contained in exactly one of them. The total length of the solution provides a lower bound on the length of any TSP tour.

Robinson's relaxation is known as the *assignment problem*, where we typically think of assigning n workers to n tasks, rather than assigning cities to cities. Her solution method is an iterative approach, moving step by step towards the optimal assignment via a cycle-canceling operation (that later became a standard technique for minimum-cost flow problems).

> The method presented here of handling this problem will enable us to check whether a given system of circuits is optimal or, if not, to find a better one. I believe it would be feasible to apply it to as many as 50 points provided suitable calculating equipment is available.

She mentions again the specific target of 50-point problems, but the paper does not provide an analysis of the algorithm's running time.

Several years later, in 1956, Flood [32] wrote the following in a survey paper on TSP methods.

> It seems very likely that quite a different approach from any yet used may be required for successful treatment of the problem. In fact, there may well be no general method for treating the problem and impossibility results would also be valuable.

It is not clear what he meant by "impossible", but Flood may have had in mind the notion of polynomial time and was thus speculating that the TSP had no solution method with the number of steps bounded above by n^k for some constant k. Such an algorithm would certainly have been viewed as a major breakthrough at the time, possibly permitting the solution of the target-sized instances.

An argument for suggesting Flood was hoping to replace Menger's $n!$ by a more tidy n^k can be seen in Schrijver's beautifully detailed history of combinatorial optimization [84, Chap. 3]. Schrijver cites several examples from the early 1950s where authors point out polynomial running-time bounds. The earliest of these is the following passage from a lecture given by von Neumann [78] in 1951, concerning the assignment problem.

> We shall now construct a certain related 2-person game and we shall show that the extreme optimal strategies can be expressed in terms of the optimal permutation matrices in the assignment problem. (The game matrix for this game will be $2n \times n^2$. From this it is not difficult to infer how many steps are needed to get significant approximate solutions with the method of G. W. Brown and J. von Neumann. It turns out that this number is a moderate power of n, i.e. considerably smaller than the "obvious" estimate $n!$ mentioned earlier.)

Details are not provided in the transcript, but the use of the phrase "moderate power of n" fits with the overall theme of developing methods for use in practice.

An explicit running-time bound for solving the assignment problem was given by Munkres [77] in 1957, making use of a variant of the Hungarian algorithm.

The final maximum on the number of operations needed is

$$(11n^3 + 12n^2 + 31n)/6.$$

This maximum is of theoretical interest since it is so much smaller than the $n!$ operations necessary in the most straightforward attack on the problem.

Munkres's paper is entirely analysis; there is no mention of target applications or possible computational testing. Indeed, his use of the phrase "theoretical interest" is striking, making an early claim for the mathematics of algorithmic complexity.

From Menger to Robinson to von Neumann to Munkres, we see the modern treatment of combinatorial algorithms starting to take shape. But back in the TSP camp, the obvious $n!$ bound for worst-case complexity remained the state of the art through the 1930s, 40s, and 50s. This finally changed in 1962 with the publication of papers by Bellman [5] and Held and Karp [52], describing an elegant method for solving any n-city TSP in time proportional to $n^2 2^n$. Not the dreamed-for n^k, but still an answer to Menger's challenge.

The Bellman-Held-Karp algorithm adopts Bellman's general tool of dynamic programming [4], building an optimal tour from shortest paths through each of the 2^n subsets of points. Both teams were well aware of the asymptotic limitations of the algorithm. In a section titled "Computational Feasibility", Bellman gives estimates of the memory requirement (which also grows exponentially with n) for 11, 17, and 21 cities. He goes on to write the following passage [5].

> It follows that the case of 11 cities can be treated routinely, that 17 cities requires the largest of current fast memory computers, but that problems involving 21 cities are a few years at least beyond our reach. One can improve upon these numbers by taking advantage of the fact that the distances will be integers and that we need not use all the digits of one word to specify a distance, but this requires some fancy programming.

This is an interesting display of mathematical analysis with real-world computing in mind.

Held and Karp take this a step further, giving explicit computational results on IBM hardware: "An IBM 7090 program can solve any 13-city traveling-salesman problem in 17 seconds." And they describe how the exact algorithm can be used as a tool for high-quality solutions for larger instances [52].

> It is characteristic of the algorithms under discussion that their complexity, measured by numbers of arithmetic operations and storage requirements, grows quite rapidly. They are, however, a vast improvement over complete enumeration, and permit the rapid solution of problems of moderate size. In this section we show how the algorithms can be combined with a method of successive approximations to provide a systematic procedure for treating large problems. This procedure yields a sequence of permutations, each obtained from its predecessor by the solution of a derived subproblem of moderate size having the same structure as the given problem. The

associated costs form a monotone nonincreasing sequence which may not converge to the optimum solution; however, computer experimentation has yielded excellent results in a variety of cases.

Again, a fantastic combination of theory and practice. Their computer code, developed together with Richard Shareshian, was made available to users of IBM's hardware; an image of the 1964 press release is displayed in Fig. 1.

FOR RELEASE:

A. M's, Thursday
January 2, 1964

FROM: International Business Machines Corp.
Data Processing Division
112 East Post Road
White Plains, New York

Bert Reisman
914 WHite Plains 9-1900

WHITE PLAINS, N.Y., Jan. 2 . . . . IBM mathematicians

(left to right) Michael Held, Richard Shareshian and Richard M. Karp

review the manual describing a new computer program which provides

business and industry with a practical scientific method for handling a

wide variety of complex scheduling tasks. The program, available to

users of the IBM 7090 and 7094 data processing systems, consists of a

set of 4,500 instructions which tell the computer what to do with data fed

into it. It grew out of the trio's efforts to find solutions for a classic

mathematical problem -- the "Traveling Salesman" problem -- which has

long defied solution by man, or by the fastest computers he uses.

Fig. 1. Michael Held, Richard Shareshian and Richard Karp, 1964. Courtesy of IBM Corporate Archives.

2 Dantzig, Linear Programming, and Cutting Planes

We mentioned that Julia Robinson was a post-doc at the RAND Corporation, a think tank for the United States government. Another member of the RAND group was the remarkable George Dantzig. His name is forever associated with his life's work: the creation of the linear programming model, the simplex method for its solution, and its application to problems far and wide. Grötschel [44] gave the following powerful summary.

The development of linear programming is—in my opinion—the most important contribution of the mathematics of the 20th century to the solution of practical problems arising in industry and commerce.

This is from the operations research perspective, but Dantzig's LP model was also a bombshell for the general theory and practice of computing in combinatorial optimization.

Linear programming was introduced to the world in a lecture given by Dantzig on September 9, 1948, at an economics meeting at the University of Wisconsin in Madison [18].

The basic assumptions of the model lead to a fundamental set of linear equations expressing the conditions which much be satisfied by the various levels of activity, X_i, in the dynamic system. These variables are subject to the further restriction $X_i \geq 0$. The determination of the "best" choice of X_i is made to depend on the maximization (or minimization) of linear form in X_i. ... It is proposed that computational techniques developed by J. von Neumann and by the author be used in connection with large scale digital computers to implement the solution of programming problems.

This last point, concerning digital computers, is important. Dantzig was working to get linear programming at the head of the queue for implementation on the first generation of electronic hardware. Computation pioneers Hoffman and Wolfe [57] write the following.

Linear programming was an important force in sponsoring the early UNIVAC computers, as well as the SEAC at the National Bureau of Standards, because of U.S. Air Force funding in support of computations required by it and other planning tools developed by Dantzig and his associates in the Office of the Air Controller.

The computers were lined up and ready to go. And, indeed, extensive LP tests were made as early as 1952 [56,79].

The general LP model is to optimize a linear function $c^T x$ subject to constraints $Ax = b, x \geq 0$, where matrix A, vector b, and vector c are data and $x = (x_1, x_2, \ldots, x_n)$ is a vector of variables. Note that each x_i can be assigned possibly a fractional value. This makes the connection to combinatorial optimization subtle, since combinatorial objects, such as paths, correspond to integer-valued solutions. Indeed, most often in combinatorial models we have a logical choice for each variable, either we use it or we do not, $x_i = 1$ or $x_i = 0$.

In some basic cases, like the assignment problem, it can be shown there exists always an optimal LP solution that is integer valued. Geometrically, this means all vertices of the polyhedral set $\{x : Ax = b, x \geq 0\}$ have integer components. There are beautiful theorems in combinatorics that can be described in this way, but, for optimization models, such naturally-integer examples are the exception, rather than the rule.

The TSP is not one of the exceptional cases. That said, it is also true that any combinatorial problem is, in principle, an LP problem. Take the example of the salesman. A tour through n cities selects n direct point-to-point links, that is, n edges in the complete graph on n points. So a tour can be specified as a 0-1 vector indexed by the edges of the complete graph, where a 1 means we include the edge in the tour. The TSP is to minimize the total travel distance, which is a linear function, over these $(n-1)!$ vectors. That sounds unpleasant, but, for any finite set of vectors S, a classic result of Minkowski states that there exists a convex polytope P such that S is precisely the set of vertices of P, that is, P is the convex hull of S. For our set of tour vectors, by taking the linear constraints that describe the corresponding polytope P, we have formulated the TSP as an LP problem.

Cheers for Minkowski, but actually solving the LP problem could be difficult. Indeed, following up on Robinson's work, Heller [54] and Kuhn [68] presented results showing the number of linear constraints needed to describe the TSP polytope grows exponentially fast with the number of cities. This is not a trivial statement. For example, there are $n!$ solutions to the n-dimensional assignment problem and yet its corresponding polytope is described by only $2n + 2n^2$ constraints. But not so for the TSP.

Dantzig brushed aside this concern. He was willing to gamble that only a small number of these exponentially many constraints would be needed to solve a target instance that was making the rounds of the US mathematics community, namely to visit one city chosen in each of the 48 states plus Washington, DC.[1] He and his RAND colleagues Ray Fulkerson and Selmer Johnson settled the challenge, finding a tour through the 49 cities together with an LP proof that it was the shortest possible.

The approach they invented in this TSP work is called the *cutting-plane method*. Rather than taking the full polytope as envisioned by Heller and Kuhn, they instead take a simple polytope that includes all of the tours, and refine it step by step, adding in each step constraints that are satisfied by all tours but violated by the optimal solution to the current LP relaxation. At the end of their computation, they have an LP relaxation of the TSP that has as an optimal solution a TSP tour. Game over.

In the research-report version of their paper, Dantzig et al. [19] wrote the following line to start a section titled "The method".

The title of this section is perhaps pretentious, as we don't have a method in a precise sense.

This is typical of the modest style of writing at the time, but there were indeed certain ad hoc aspects to their work.

1. They did not know explicitly the full set of inequalities that define the TSP polytope for $n = 49$ points. Indeed, even today the full description is known only for $n \leq 9$. So it was possible they could reach an LP relaxation having a non-tour optimal solution and not have any means to refine their relaxation with an additional constraint.

2. Even for the classes of constraints they did know, they did not have available exact algorithms to test whether or not the current LP solution satisfies all member constraints of each class. In the computation, they relied on their own creativity to locate a violated constraint.

3. Despite Dantzig's willingness to place a wager, they had no upper bound on the number of iterations that might be needed to reach an LP optimal solution that was a tour. Indeed, without further restrictions on the constraints to be considered (such as defining facets of the TSP polytope) the process is not guaranteed to be finite.

That is three strikes. Nonetheless, Dantzig's team accomplished the task described in their abstract [20]: "It is shown that a certain tour of 49 cities, one

---

[1] This is literally true. Dantzig wagered Fulkerson one dollar that at most 25 inequalities would be needed on top of the assignment problem constraints [57].

in each of the 48 states and Washington, DC, has the shortest road distance." A feat no team would surpass until the 1970s.

Interestingly, rather than unleash the new electronic computers that Dantzig secured for LP testing, the TSP team carried out all computations by hand. This was due to the shear size of their model. The 1,176 variables in the 49-city example put it far beyond the capabilities of available hardware and software. In the long run this proved to be a good thing—the specialized techniques they developed to short-cut the computations provided a template for large-scale computing in the following decades.

The computation by Dantzig's team was an amazing accomplishment, but, due to the three strikes, the work made no direct contribution to the asymptotic complexity of the TSP. Here is the concluding paragraph of their paper [20].

> It is clear that we have left unanswered practically any question one might pose of a theoretical nature concerning the traveling-salesman problem; however, we hope that the feasibility of attacking problems involving a moderate number of points has been successfully demonstrated, and that perhaps some of the ideas can be used in problems of similar nature.

That is marvelous in its modesty. The team may not have given Karl Menger a satisfactory answer, but they showed us how to use LP to attack seemingly intractable problems.

The cutting-plane method is far and away the most successful technique for the exact solution of $\mathcal{NP}$-hard models in combinatorial optimization; a nice survey can be found in Jünger et al. [60].

For the TSP itself, it took twenty years for the community to catch up to the by-hand computations of Dantzig's team. But starting in the 1970s, led

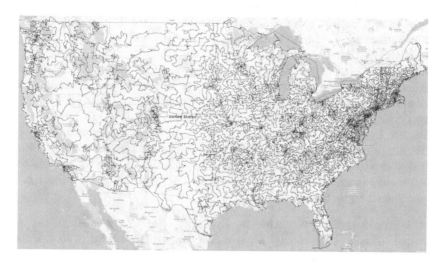

Fig. 2. Optimal walking tour to 49,603 sites from the National Register of Historic Places. Image Google Maps ©.

by Martin Grötschel and Manfred Padberg and aided by increasingly powerful computing platforms, great progress was made in exact methods [1,17,43,45,80]. It is now routine to exactly solve problems with many hundreds of cities.

The most recent study [15] reports the optimal solution of a 49,603-city USA instance with point-to-point distances measured by walking directions provided by Google Maps. I like to think Dantzig, Fulkerson, and Johnson would be proud (Fig. 2).

3 Edmonds, Matchings, and Polynomial Time

Following the success of Bellman, Held and Karp, the stage in the 1960s look set for the jump to an n^k algorithm for the TSP. And the best hope for making such a breakthrough was Jack Edmonds, a mathematician who brought the theory of combinatorial optimization into the modern era.

The 28-year-old Edmonds burst onto the scene in 1961, at a summer workshop held at the RAND Corporation. At the time, he was working for the National Bureau of Standards, having obtained a Master's degree at the University of Maryland. Balinsky, Edmonds, and several other young researchers had been invited to join a who-is-who list of stars from the field of combinatorics. He described his talk as follows [26].

> At this lecture, everybody I'd ever heard of was there. Gomory and Dantzig and Tutte and Fulkerson and Hoffman ... And I gave this grand philosophical speech ... Here is a good algorithm, here is a solved integer program. This was a sermon, this was a real sermon. Here is a solved integer program. It was my first glimpse of heaven.

This was a report on a polynomial-time algorithm for the matching problem in general graphs, a difficult generalization of the assignment problem. Along the way, he made a strong case for the mathematical importance of such *good algorithms*.

Edmonds' paper on these topics was written in 1963 and appeared in journal form [24] in 1965, the same year as Alan Cobham's paper on machine-independent computation [13]. Both authors present the notion of polynomial-time algorithms, but they emphasize different aspects of the theory. In his Turing Award lecture [14], Stephen Cook summarized the work as follows.

> Cobham pointed out that the class was well defined, independent of which computer model was chosen, and gave it a characterization in the spirit of recursive function theory. The idea that polynomial time computability roughly corresponds to tractability was first expressed in print by Edmonds.

It was certainly a great year for computational complexity—the classic paper by Hartmanis and Stearns [51] also appeared in journal form in 1965.

If you are a card-carrying complexity theorist, then you almost certainly turn to Cobham's elegant paper for an explanation of the class $\mathcal{P}$. For a combinatorial optimizer, however, Edmonds is the polynomial-time champion (Fig. 3). His description is less formal, but he brings the topic to life, showing by example how to put combinatorial problems into $\mathcal{P}$. It is his glimpse of algorithmic heaven.

Fig. 3. Jack Edmonds, 2015. Photograph courtesy of Kathie Cameron.

The center piece of Edmonds' paper is his *blossom algorithm* for matching in a general graph. A *matching* is a set of edges that have no common end points. Unlike the assignment problem, the natural LP relaxation for matchings may have optimal solutions that are not integer valued. For this problem, however, Edmonds was able to describe explicitly the full set of linear inequalities that define the polytope promised by Minkowski. He thus obtained an LP model that returns always a matching as an optimal solution. The LP has exponentially many constraints, but he was able to devise a primal-dual algorithm to handle them all in polynomial time. And his algorithm was not just good in theory, but also in practice: careful implementations are able to handle graphs with a million or more points [2,16,66,75].

In his work, Edmonds was able to overcome all three strikes we had against the cutting-plane method. So the big question was whether or not his methodology would also give a means to devise a polynomial-time algorithm for the TSP. Edmonds writes that he did indeed follow up his success with matchings by taking a crack at the salesman problem [27].

Inspired by Dantzig, Fulkerson, Johnson (1954), I became excited in 1961 to show that TSP is co-$\mathcal{NP}$ by finding an $\mathcal{NP}$ description of a set of inequalities whose solution set is the convex hull of all the 0,1 incidence vectors of tours in G. I failed, and so in 1966 I conjectured that TSP is not in $\mathcal{P}$.

Sadly, he became convinced we will never see an n^k algorithm for the TSP. He stated this explicitly in a paper [28] published in 1967: "I conjecture that there is no good algorithm for the traveling salesman problem." Bad luck for all fans of the TSP. And the news got even worse when both the directed and undirected versions of the TSP appeared on Karp's famous list [62] of 21 $\mathcal{NP}$-hard problems in 1972.

So the fate of the TSP is now tied to the great $\mathcal{P}$ versus $\mathcal{NP}$ question. But, along the way, Edmonds provided an important insight into possible solution methods. He made the following remark during a discussion that took place after a TSP lecture by Gomory [42] in 1964.

> For the traveling salesman problem, the vertices of the associated polyhedron have a simple characterization despite their number—so might the bounding inequalities have a simple characterization despite their number. At least we should hope they have, because finding a really good traveling salesman algorithm is undoubtedly equivalent to finding such a characterization.

Edmonds' thesis was that polynomial-time algorithms go hand-in-hand with polyhedral characterizations.

And he was right. Some twenty years later, Edmonds' thesis was proven in a deep result by Grötschel et al. [49]. The theorem is based on the ellipsoid algorithm for linear programming and it goes by the slogan *optimization ≡ separation*. Roughly speaking, if we can solve an optimization problem in polynomial time, then we have an implicit description of the corresponding polytope, and, the other way around, if we understand the polytope then we have a polynomial-time algorithm for the optimization problem.

Beautiful! The new work brought together combinatorial-optimization theory, practice, algorithms, and complexity, all united via linear programming.

4   Sixty-Three Years of Progress

Let's take a step back to fill in other research highlights, before jumping ahead to current topics. In this quick survey, we start the combinatorial-optimization clock ticking with the 1954 publication of the Dantzig-Fulkerson-Johnson paper on the TSP.

Despite the ringing success of their cutting-plane method, the research carried out by Dantzig's team did not have an immediate impact on the computational side of the field. They were simply too far ahead of their time, both in the sophisticated use of LP theory and in their ability to perform by-hand calculations that were out of reach for existing computing platforms.

But the clock did not stand still in the 1950s. Led by Hoffman's min-max theorems [55], Ford and Fulkerson's network-flow algorithms [33], Gomory's cutting planes [41], and Eastman [22] and Land and Doig's [69] branch-and-bound method, the overall field advanced quickly. This work, particularly by Hoffman, showed further the central role that was to be played by linear programming.

The following decade was dominated by Edmonds on the algorithmic side, including polynomial-time results for matchings [23], matroid intersection [25], optimal branchings [28], Gaussian elimination [29] and, together with Karp, maximum flow and minimum-cost flow [30]. On the computational side, Lin and Kernighan's introduction of powerful heuristic methods for graph partitioning [64] and the TSP [72,73] established the study of heuristic search as an important and sophisticated component of combinatorial optimization.

The 1970s saw the introduction of the formal study of α-approximation algorithms by Johnson [58], where he considers polynomial-time methods that produce solutions guaranteed to have value no greater than α times that of an optimal solution. His paper was quickly followed by Christofides' 1.5-approximation for the TSP [11], and the sub-discipline was off and running. A highlight here is the spectacular result on approximating the maximum-cut problem by Goemans and Williamson [39] in 1995, where they use semi-definite programming to move beyond what can be obtained with the natural LP relaxation. Texts by Vazirani [88] and Williamson and Shmoys [89] provide great coverage of the area.

We have already discussed the iconic result of the 1980s, the decade of optimization ≡ separation. But these years also saw, on the applied/computational side, the start of a great expansion of the use of the cutting-plane method. This work goes well beyond the confines of the TSP, led by successful projects by Grötschel et al. [46–48] and others. A huge boost to this computational area was the arrival of robust LP solvers that could be called as functions from within a cutting-plane code, in particular the CPLEX library created by Bixby [6].

Moving to the 1990s, a major development was the introduction of new hierarchical relaxations of combinatorial optimization models by Lovász and Schrijver [74], Sherali and Adams [85], and Lasserre [70]. The template for this line of work was the classic paper on cutting planes by Chvátal [12], where he shows that the convex hull associated with any combinatorial problem can be obtained by iteratively applying a simple rounding process. The new procedures expand on this idea, by considering the problem in higher-dimensional spaces (obtained by adding variables to the initial relaxation) where it can be easier to enforce integrality conditions.

I've been skipping over important work by a host of researchers, so with the field getting ever broader and more active, I prefer not to try for a two-line summary of the 2000s. But let me point out a clear highlight, the publication of Schrijver's monograph *Combinatorial Optimization: Polyhedra and Efficiency* [84]. His work, published in 2003, covers 1881 pages in three volumes and includes over 4,000 references. Schrijver's scholarly writing is amazing. And to bring you forward from 2003, there are excellent recent texts by Frank [35] and Korte and Vygen [67]. If you want to study the first sixty-three years of combinatorial optimization, these three books contain all the material you need.

5   Wish List of Research Directions

A good sign of the health of a field of study is the ease in which it is possible to list future research directions. Combinatorial optimization looks great under this metric. I could have started with any of the seventy-five open problems and conjectures listed in Schrijver's monograph [84]. But I decided to go with only a short wish list of five topics, all aimed at pushing forward the intersection of computation, algorithms, and theory.

5.1   Improving the Simplex Method

Perhaps the most important contribution the computer-science algorithms community could make to the field of operations research would be the delivery of ideas to improve the practical performance of the simplex method for solving linear programming problems. The simplex method was named one of the top ten algorithms of the century [21], but it needs help to continue to drive progress in OR applications. The steepest-edge pivot rules that are the state of the art in simplex implementations date back to the 1970s [40], and the best known methods for implementing these rules go back to the early 1990s [34]. Moreover, there currently are no implementations of the simplex method that make effective use of multi-core processors, GPUs, or other parallel computing platforms.

For solving any single large-scale LP model, the simplex method has a serious competitor in the class of polynomial-time algorithms called interior-point methods, that parallelize nicely. But for solving a sequence of closely related LP models, such as those that arise in the cutting-plane method or in a branch-and-bound search, the simplex method is the only game in town. This comes from the fact that the simplex method can be set up to start its search at the optimal solution to the previously solved model, dramatically decreasing the number of steps needed to reach an optimal solution to the new model. Interior-point methods are not able to do this effectively.

Here is the context. Over a broad class of models and considering the commercial software libraries CPLEX 1.0 to 11.0 and Gurobi 1.0 to 7.0, Bixby [7] reports a machine-independent speed-up in mixed-integer programming (MIP) codes of a factor over 1.3 million in the past 25 years, roughly a factor of 1.75 each year. That is amazing progress in practical computing and it has been a driving force in the growth of successful OR applications. But Bixby also reports that, with continued increases in model sizes, linear programming has become a roadblock towards solutions in a substantial fraction of MIP settings. Help is needed.

The big ticket item, from the CS theory side, is the fact that there is no known polynomial-time variant of the simplex method. Avis [3] sums things up nicely in a short note marking the 100th anniversary of the birth of George Dantzig.

Surely the close collaboration of TCS and the optimization community would be able to settle this question: is there or is there not a polynomial time pivot selection rule for the simplex method? Of course I think all of us, including George, hope for a positive answer that is both strongly polynomial time and a winner in practice!

Settling this question may be difficult, but there has been progress in understanding the complexity of Dantzig's algorithm, including a long line of award winning papers from the OR, CS, optimization, and mathematics communities.

- Borgwardt [8], average-case analysis of the simplex method, Lanchester Prize 1982 (INFORMS).
- Kalai [61], quasi-polynomial bound on diameter of polyhedra, Fulkerson Prize 1994 (MOS and AMS).
- Spielman and Teng [86], smoothed analysis of the simplex method, Gödel Prize 2008 (ACM) and Fulkerson Prize 2009 (MOS and AMS).
- Friedmann [36], super-polynomial lower bounds for simplex pivot rules, Tucker Prize 2012 (MOS).
- Santos [83], counterexample to the Hirsh conjecture, Fulkerson Prize 2015 (MOS and AMS).

Each of these results concerns analysis of the simplex method or the paths it takes along the edges of polyhedra. What I'd like to emphasize is the need for turning analytical insights, such as these, into recommendations for improving the simplex method in practice.

For example, can machine-learning techniques be used to build pivot-selection rules that adapt to the properties of the input polyhedra? In this area, every saved pivot helps.

5.2 Language of Algorithms

I'd like to draw attention to a research direction that is more of a dream than a specific problem. Namely, the development and adoption of a more nuanced way of expressing accomplishments in the analysis of algorithms.

Avis [3] gives a dramatic example. Suppose history was reversed and Dantzig announced a polynomial-time interior-point algorithm in his 1948 talk in Madison. Would a paper today on a newly invented, exponential-time simplex method have a chance of being accepted into a major conference? Would it even be coded for testing? One might hope the operations research community would handle the task, but it takes an exceptional amount of care to implement the simplex method in a way that makes it competitive with interior-point codes. Without guidance from the algorithms community, it seems unlikely the necessary time and energy would be devoted to building the expertise needed to bring the simplex method into practical use.

I do not mean to criticize the focus on asymptotic analysis and polynomial-time results. Indeed, this focus drives CS theory, and CS theory has long supplied a lifeline of techniques for everyone in the business of attacking large-scale optimization models. But this focus, together with the use of big-oh notation and the hiding of logarithmic factors, can sometimes make it difficult to tap into ideas that can have a major impact in computational studies. And, more importantly, it may sometimes hinder the creation of techniques that could have dramatic impact on computational practice, such as the simplex method in Avis's fable.

5.3   Understanding Heuristic Algorithms

The term *heuristic* is sometimes used to describe both non-exact techniques, such as simulated annealing, as well as exact, but exponential-time, techniques, such as the cutting-plane method. In my discussion I refer only to the first meaning. That is, a *heuristic algorithm* is one designed to find a hopefully good solution, but comes without a performance guarantee.

Heuristic algorithms are widely used in operations research and many other areas. They are used, but not understood. The success of these techniques far outstrips our ability to explain and evaluate analytically.

In his 2010 Knuth Prize lecture [59], David Johnson discussed the theme of how best to increase the impact of theoretical computer science research. His first rule was "Study problems people might actually want to solve" and his top open question in this regard was the following.

When (and why) do metaheuristc approaches work well?

Just so. Computer science is the research community best equipped with analytic tools to address this issue.

And Johnson is not the only giant of computer science to bring up this topic. Richard Karp, in a lecture given at Harvard University in 2011 [63], made the following statement.

Heuristics are often "unreasonably effective," for reasons not well understood.

This is certainly the case. Recall that I mentioned the report of an optimal TSP tour to visit 49,603 sites with distance measured by Google walking routes. To solve this instance, the total computing time for the cutting-plane method and branch-and-bound search was 178.9 years (on a network of processors). That is a great deal of computing power, but it turned out that the heuristic tour we had at the start of the search was in fact optimal. All of the computation was to verify there was no better solution. It is definitely unreasonable that a combination of local search and genetic algorithms was able to produce an optimal solution for such a complex optimization problem. Unreasonable and unexplained.

5.4   Analysis of Exact Algorithms for Hard Problems

Facing an $\mathcal{NP}$-hard optimization problem, the main targets for study are approximation methods and computational methods, combining heuristic search with lower-bound techniques like cutting planes. A third option is the study of exponential-time exact solution algorithms. Research in this direction can provide effective means to handle small problem instances (and these can in turn be used to solve larger examples, using techniques such as the local-cuts procedure described in [1]), as well as providing insights that can be adopted in branch-and-bound and other computational methods.

A nice survey of this area, together with a list of open problems, is given in Woeginger [90]. Prominent among these is the challenge of improving the Bellman-Held-Karp $n^2 2^n$ bound for solving an n-city TSP, possibly replacing the exponential term by c^n for a constant $c < 2$. It has been 55 years since the publication of the BHK algorithm, but there has been no improvement for general instances. This is likely one of the longest-standing, non-trivial, complexity bounds for any combinatorial model.

5.5 Complexity of Cutting-Plane Methods

The cutting-plane method is a well-established computational technique, with successful application to a broad range of combinatorial models. As such, it is a good target for investigation from a computer science theory perspective. Possible topics include examining bounds on the complexity of the overall method, investigating algorithms for separation problems to deliver cutting planes for particular models, and obtaining insights into the selection of cutting planes to speed the convergence of the process.

A nice result of the first type was given recently by Chandrasekaran et al. [10], establishing a polynomial-time cutting-plane method for the matching problem. A direct challenge here would be to establish a similar bound for the subtour relaxation of the TSP.

For the second type of problem, there are interesting results for the separation of TSP inequalities by Carr [9], Fleischer and Tardos [31], Letchford [71] and others. But, even for this intensely studied model, there are far more open questions than results. For example, the comb-separation problem (the most basic question for TSP inequalities) is not known to be $\mathcal{NP}$-hard and also not known to be polynomial-time solvable. It would be interesting to see non-trivial approximation results in this area.

The third type of problem, the selection of cutting planes, is critical in practice. It would be great to see analysis for well-known models, such at the TSP, the maximum-cut problem, and the maximum stable-set problem. A nice paper here is an initial study of TSP inequalities by Goemans [38]. His results are worst-case comparisons, but they predict well the performance seen in computational studies (see [1, p. 524]).

References

1. Applegate, D.L., Bixby, R.E., Chvátal, V., Cook, W.: The Traveling Salesman Problem: A Computational Study. Princeton University Press, Princeton (2006)
2. Applegate, D.L., Cook, W.: Solving large-scale matching problems. In: Johnson, D.S., McGeoch, C.C. (eds.) Algorithms for Network Flows and Matching. DIMACS Series in Discrete Mathematics and Theoretical Computer Science, vol. 12, pp. 557–576. American Mathematical Society, Providence (1993)

3. Avis, D.: George Dantzig: father of the simplex method. Bull. EATCS **116** (2015)
4. Bellman, R.: Dynamic Programming. Princeton University Press, Princeton (1957)
5. Bellman, R.: Dynamic programming treatment of the travelling salesman problem. J. ACM **9**, 61–63 (1962)
6. Bixby, R.: You have to figure out who your customer is going to be. Optima **101**, 1–6 (2016)
7. Bixby, R.: A saga of 25 years of progress in optimization. Lecture at the University of Tokyo, 1 December 2016
8. Borgwardt, K.-H.: Some distribution-independent results about the asymptotic order of the average number of pivot steps of the simplex-method. Math. Oper. Res. **7**, 441–462 (1983)
9. Carr, R.: Separating clique trees and bipartition inequalities having a fixed number of handles and teeth in polynomial time. Math. Oper. Res. **22**, 257–265 (1997)
10. Chandrasekaran, K., Végh, L.A., Vempala, S.S.: The cutting plane method is polynomial for perfect matchings. Math. Oper. Res. **41**, 23–48 (2015)
11. Christofides, N.: Worst-case analysis of a new heuristic for the travelling salesman problem. Report no. 388, Graduate School of Industrial Administration, Carnegie Mellon University, Pittsburgh (1976)
12. Chvátal, V.: Edmonds polytopes and a hierarchy of combinatorial problems. Discret. Math. **4**, 305–337 (1973)
13. Cobham, A.: The intrinsic computational difficulty of functions. In: Proceedings of the 1964 International Congress for Logic, Methodology, and Philosophy of Sciences, pp. 24–30. North Holland, Amsterdam (1965)
14. Cook, S.A.: An overview of computational complexity. Commun. ACM **26**, 401–408 (1983)
15. Cook, W., Espinoza, D., Goycoolea, M., Helsgaun, K.: US50K (2016). http://www.math.uwaterloo.ca/tsp/us/index.html
16. Cook, W., Rohe, A.: Computing minimum-weight perfect matchings. INFORMS J. Comput. **11**, 138–148 (1999)
17. Crowder, H., Padberg, M.W.: Solving large-scale symmetric travelling salesman problems to optimality. Manag. Sci. **26**, 495–509 (1980)
18. Dantzig, G.: Programming in a linear structure. Econometrica **17**, 73–74 (1948)
19. Dantzig, G., Fulkerson, R., Johnson, S.: Solution of a large scale traveling salesman problem. Technical report P-510. RAND Corporation, Santa Monica (1954)
20. Dantzig, G., Fulkerson, R., Johnson, S.: Solution of a large-scale traveling-salesman problem. Oper. Res. **2**, 393–410 (1954)
21. Dongara, J., Sullivan, F.: The top 10 algorithms. IEEE Comput. Sci. Eng. **2**, 22–23 (2000)
22. Eastman, W.L.: Linear programming with pattern constraints. Ph.D. thesis, Department of Economics, Harvard University, Cambridge (1958)
23. Edmonds, J.: Maximum matching and a polyhedron with 0,1-vertices. J. Res. Nat. Bur. Stan. **69B**, 125–130 (1965)
24. Edmonds, J.: Paths, trees, and flowers. Can. J. Math. **17**, 449–467 (1965)
25. Edmonds, J.: Submodular functions, matroids, and certain polyhedra. In: Guy, R., Hanani, H., Sauer, N., Schönheim, J. (eds.) Combinatorial Structures and Their Applications, pp. 69–87. Gordon and Breach, New York (1970)
26. Edmonds, J.: A glimpse of heaven. In: Lenstra, J.K., et al. (eds.) History of Mathematical Programming-A Collection of Personal Reminiscences, pp. 32–54. North-Holland, Amsterdam (1991)

27. Edmonds, J.: EP and PPA: can it be hard to find if it's easy to recognize and you know it's there? Lecture at the 21st Combinatorial Optimization Workshop, Aussois, France, 13 January 2017
28. Edmonds, J.: Optimum branchings. J. Res. Nat. Bur. Stan. **71B**, 233–240 (1967)
29. Edmonds, J.: Systems of distinct representatives and linear algebra. J. Res. Nat. Bur. Stan. **71B**, 241–245 (1967)
30. Edmonds, J., Karp, R.M.: Theoretical improvements in algorithmic efficiency for network flow problems. J. ACM **19**, 248–264 (1972)
31. Fleischer, L., Tardos, É.: Separating maximally violated comb inequalities in planar graphs. Math. Oper. Res. **24**, 130–148 (1999)
32. Flood, M.M.: The traveling-salesman problem. Oper. Res. **4**, 61–75 (1956)
33. Ford, L.R., Fulkerson, D.R.: Flows in Networks. Princeton University Press, Princeton (1962)
34. Forrest, J.J., Goldfarb, D.: Steepest-edge simplex algorithms for linear programming. Math. Program. **57**, 341–274 (1992)
35. Frank, A.: Connections in Combinatorial Optimization. Oxford University Press, Oxford (2011)
36. Friedmann, O.: Exponential lower bounds for solving infinitary payoff games and linear programs. Ph.D. thesis, Ludwig-Maximilians-Universität München (2011)
37. Gödel, K.: Über formal unentscheidbare Sätze der Principia Mathematica und verwandter Systeme, I. Monats-hefte für Mathematik und Physik **38**, 173–198 (1931)
38. Goemans, M.: Worst-case comparison of valid inequalities for the TSP. Math. Program. **69**, 335–349 (1995)
39. Goemans, M., Williamson, D.: Improved approximation algorithms for maximum cut and satisfiability problems. J. ACM **42**, 1115–1145 (1995)
40. Goldfarb, D., Reid, J.K.: A practicable steepest-edge simplex algorithm. Math. Program. **1**, 361–371 (1977)
41. Gomory, R.E.: Outline of an algorithm for integer solutions to linear programs. Bull. Am. Math. Soc. **64**, 275–278 (1958)
42. Gomory, R.E.: The traveling salesman problem. In: Proceedings of the IBM Scientific Computing Symposium on Combinatorial Problems, pp. 93–121. IBM, White Plains (1996)
43. Grötschel, M.: On the symmetric travelling salesman problem: solution of a 120-city problem. Math. Program. Study **12**, 61–77 (1980)
44. Grötschel, M.: Notes for a Berlin Mathematical School (2006)
45. Grötschel, M., Holland, O.: Solution of large-scale symmetric travelling salesman problems. Math. Program. **51**, 141–202 (1991)
46. Grötschel, M., Jünger, M., Reinelt, G.: A cutting plane algorithm for the linear ordering problem. Oper. Res. **32**, 1195–1220 (1984)
47. Grötschel, M., Jünger, M., Reinelt, G.: On the acyclic subgraph polytope. Math. Program. **33**, 28–42 (1985)
48. Grötschel, M., Jünger, M., Reinelt, G.: Facets of the linear ordering polytope. Math. Program. **33**, 43–60 (1985)
49. Grötschel, M., Lovász, L., Schrijver, A.: Geometric Algorithms and Combinatorial Optimization. Springer, Berlin (1988). https://doi.org/10.1007/978-3-642-97881-4
50. Grötschel, M., Nemhauser, G.L.: George Dantzig's contributions to integer programming. Discret. Optim. **5**, 168–173 (2008)
51. Hartmanis, J., Stearns, R.E.: On the computational complexity of algorithms. Trans. Am. Math. Soc. **117**, 285–306 (1965)

52. Held, M., Karp, R.M.: A dynamic programming approach to sequencing problems. J. Soc. Ind. Appl. Math. **10**, 196–210 (1962)
53. Held, M., Karp, R.M.: The traveling-salesman problem and minimum spanning trees: Part II. Math. Program. **1**, 6–25 (1971)
54. Heller, I.: On the problem of the shortest path between points. I. Abstract 664t. Bull. Am. Math. Soc. **59**, 551 (1953)
55. Hoffman, A.J.: Generalization of a theorem of Konig. J. Wash. Acad. Sci. **46**, 211–212 (1956)
56. Hoffman, A., Mannos, M., Sokolowsky, D., Wiegmann, N.: Computational experience in solving linear programs. J. Soc. Ind. Appl. Math. **1**, 17–33 (1953)
57. Hoffman, A.J., Wolfe, P.: History. In: Lawler, E.L., Lenstra, J.K., Rinnooy Kan, A.H.G., Shmoys, D.B. (eds.) The Traveling Salesman Problem, pp. 1–15. Wiley, Chichester (1985)
58. Johnson, D.S.: Approximation algorithms for combinatorial problems. J. Comput. Syst. Sci. **9**, 256–278 (1974)
59. Johnson, D.S.: Knuth Prize Lecture (2010)
60. Jünger, M., Reinelt, G., Thienel, S.: Practical problem solving with cutting plane algorithms. In: Cook, W., Lovász, L., Seymour, P. (eds.) Combinatorial Optimization. DIMACS Series in Discrete Mathematics and Theoretical Computer Science, vol. 20, pp. 111–152. American Mathematical Society, Providence (1995)
61. Kalai, G.: Upper bounds for the diameter and height of graphs of the convex polyhedra. Discret. Comput. Geom. **8**, 363–372 (1992)
62. Karp, R.M.: Reducibility among combinatorial problems. In: Miller, R.E., Thatcher, J.W. (eds.) Complexity of Computer Computations, pp. 85–103. Plenum Press, New York (1972)
63. Karp, R.M.: Implicit hitting set problems. Lecture at Harvard University, 29 August 2011
64. Kernighan, B.W., Lin, S.: An efficient heuristic procedure for partitioning graphs. Bell Syst. Tech. J. **49**, 291–307 (1970)
65. Kirkpatrick, S., Gelatt Jr., C.D., Vecchi, M.P.: Optimization by simulated annealing. Science **220**, 671–680 (1983)
66. Kolmogorov, V.: Blossom V: a new implementation of a minimum cost perfect matching algorithm. Math. Program. Comput. **1**, 43–67 (2009)
67. Korte, B., Vygen, J.: Combinatorial Optimization: Theory and Algorithms. Springer, Berlin (2012). https://doi.org/10.1007/978-3-642-24488-9
68. Kuhn, H.W.: On certain convex polyhedra. Abstract 799t. Bull. Am. Math. Soc. **61**, 557–558 (1955)
69. Land, A.H., Doig, A.G.: An automatic method of solving discrete programming problems. Econometrica **28**, 497–520 (1960)
70. Lasserre, J.B.: Global optimization with polynomials and the problem of moments. SIAM J. Optim. **11**, 796–817 (2001)
71. Letchford, A.N.: Separating a superclass of comb inequalities in planar graphs. Math. Oper. Res. **25**, 443–454 (2000)
72. Lin, S.: Computer solutions of the traveling salesman problem. Bell Syst. Tech. J. **44**, 2245–2269 (1965)
73. Lin, S., Kernighan, B.W.: An effective heuristic algorithm for the traveling-salesman problem. Oper. Res. **21**, 498–516 (1973)
74. Lovász, L., Schrijver, A.: Cones of matrices and set-functions, and 0–1 optimization. SIAM J. Optim. **1**, 166–190 (1991)

75. Mehlhorn, K., Schäfer, G.: Implementation of $O(nm \log n)$ weighted matchings in general graphs: the power of data structures. J. Exp. Algorithmics **7**, Article 4 (2002)

76. Menger, K.: Bericht über ein mathematisches Kolloquium. Monats-hefte für Mathematik und Physik **38**, 17–38 (1931)

77. Munkres, J.: Algorithms for the assignment and transportation problems. J. Soc. Ind. Appl. Math. **5**, 32–38 (1957)

78. von Neumann, J.: A certain zero-sum two-person game equivalent to the optimal assignment problem. In: Kuhn, H.W., Tucker, A.W. (eds.) Contributions to the Theory of Games, pp. 5–12. Princeton University Press, Princeton (1953). (Transcript of a seminar talk given by Professor von Neumann at Princeton University, 26 October 1951)

79. Orden, A.: Solution of systems of linear inequalities on a digital computer. In: Proceedings of the 1952 ACM National Meeting, pp. 91–95 (1952)

80. Padberg, M., Rinaldi, G.: A branch-and-cut algorithm for the resolution of large-scale symmetric traveling salesman problems. SIAM Rev. **33**, 60–100 (1991)

81. Robinson, J.: Definability and decision problems in arithmetic. Ph.D. thesis, University of California, Berkeley (1948)

82. Robinson, J.: On the Hamiltonian game (a traveling salesman problem). RAND Research Memorandum RM-303. RAND Corporation, Santa Monica (1949)

83. Santos, F.: A counterexample to the Hirsh conjecture. Ann. Math. **176**, 383–412 (2011)

84. Schrijver, A.: Combinatorial Optimization. Springer, Berlin (2003)

85. Sherali, H.D., Adams, W.P.: A Reformulation-Linearization Technique for Solving Discrete and Continuous Nonconvex Problems. Springer, Berlin (2013). https://doi.org/10.1007/978-1-4757-4388-3

86. Spielman, D.A., Teng, S.-H.: Smoothed analysis of algorithms: why the simplex algorithm usually takes polynomial time. J. ACM **51**, 385–463 (2004)

87. Turing, A.M.: On computable numbers, with an application to the Entscheidungsproblem. Proc. London Math. Soc. **s2-42**, 230–265 (1937)

88. Vazirani, V.V.: Approximation Algorithms. Springer, Heidelberg (2003). https://doi.org/10.1007/978-3-662-04565-7

89. Williamson, D.P., Shmoys, D.B.: The Design of Approximation Algorithms. Cambridge University Press, Cambridge (2011)

90. Woeginger, G.J.: Exact algorithms for NP-hard problems: a survey. In: Jünger, M., Reinelt, G., Rinaldi, G. (eds.) Combinatorial Optimization — Eureka, You Shrink!. LNCS, vol. 2570, pp. 185–207. Springer, Heidelberg (2003). https://doi.org/10.1007/3-540-36478-1_17

Computational Social Choice: The First Ten Years and Beyond

Haris Aziz[1], Felix Brandt[2(✉)], Edith Elkind[3], and Piotr Skowron[4]

[1] UNSW Sydney and Data61 (CSIRO), Sydney, Australia
[2] Technische Universität München, Munich, Germany
brandtf@in.tum.de
[3] University of Oxford, Oxford, UK
[4] Technische Universität Berlin, Berlin, Germany

Abstract. Computational social choice is a research area at the intersection of computer science, mathematics, and economics that is concerned with aggregation of preferences of multiple agents. Typical applications include voting, resource allocation, and fair division. This chapter highlights six representative research areas in contemporary computational social choice: restricted preference domains, voting equilibria and iterative voting, multiwinner voting, probabilistic social choice, random assignment, and computer-aided theorem proving.

1 Introduction

Within the past few decades there has been a lively exchange of ideas between computer science, in particular artificial intelligence, algorithms and complexity theory, on the one hand, and economics, in particular game theory and social choice, on the other hand. This exchange goes in both directions, and is largely motivated by the emergence and the growing ubiquity of the Internet, which created a need for concepts concerning social interaction and cooperation provided by economics as well as for the algorithmic tools of computer science.

A recent example of this trend is the formation of the inter-disciplinary research area known as *computational social choice*, which combines ideas, models, and techniques from social choice theory with those of computer science. Social choice theory, which itself is already a multi-disciplinary area with contributions from economics, mathematics, political science, and philosophy, concerns the formal analysis and design of methods for aggregating the preferences of multiple agents. Typical applications include voting, resource allocation, and fair division. Computer science offers several powerful tools such as algorithm design, complexity theory, and communication complexity for analyzing such problems. At the same time, computer science has produced new application areas for social choice such as webpage ranking or collective decision-making in computational multi-agent systems.

In its most general form, social choice theory is concerned with a set of alternatives and a set of agents who possess binary preference relations (typically

B. Steffen and G. Woeginger (Eds.): Computing and Software Science, LNCS 10000, pp. 48–65, 2019.
https://doi.org/10.1007/978-3-319-91908-9_4

assumed to be complete and transitive) over the alternatives; a collection of agents' preference relations is called a preference profile. Problems of interest then include how to define (and find) a collective choice in form of a set of alternatives, a ranking of alternatives, or a lottery over alternatives that appropriately reflect the agents' individual preferences. Collective outcomes and aggregation functions that return these outcomes are usually evaluated and compared by verifying whether they satisfy desirable properties, so-called axioms. Classic results in social choice—the most famous of which is certainly Arrow's impossibility theorem [2]—have shown the incompatibility of certain sets of axioms, or characterized specific aggregation functions in terms of axioms they satisfy.

Most subareas of social choice (e.g., coalition formation, matching markets, and fair division) can be obtained as special cases of the general model described above by imposing structure on the set of alternatives and restricting the domain of preference relations accordingly. For example, in assignment problems, the goal is to find a fair and efficient assignment of objects to agents based on the agents' preferences over objects. To cast an assignment problem as a social choice problem, we let the set of alternatives be the set of all possible allocations and postulate that agents are indifferent among all allocations in which they receive the same object. This conceptual insight is useful because it sometimes allows the transfer of positive results from superdomains to subdomains and that of negative results from subdomains to superdomains. However, most statements require a specific analysis of the domain in question and are often based on axioms that can only be meaningfully defined within this domain. Moreover, computational statements usually do not carry over from one domain to another due to the different representations.

Initial results in computational social choice focused on the computational complexity of aggregation functions that were proposed in the social choice literature. For example, it was shown that computing Kemeny's rule, which returns collective consensus rankings and satisfies many desirable axioms, is NP-hard [23], and deciding whether a given alternative is on top of a consensus ranking is Θ_2^p-complete [85]. This and similar hardness results were followed by the analysis of heuristics, approximation algorithms, and fixed-parameter tractable algorithms for these problems. At the same time, new interesting computational problems concerning various ways of manipulating the election outcome were defined and investigated. Here, computational hardness is desirable and meant to serve as a shield against strategic behavior (see, e.g., [55, 70–72]). The contributions of contemporary computational social choice go far beyond purely algorithmic questions, and it has been claimed that computational social choice has revitalized the entire field of social choice theory. For instance, a recent result in computational social choice resolved a long-standing open problem in the cake cutting literature: Aziz and Mackenzie [6] proposed the first envy-free cake cutting protocol that requires a bounded number of queries and cuts. Even though the number of cuts is astronomically large, this result is surprising because experts believed that no such protocol exists.[1]

---

[1] The number of cuts is upper bounded by $n^{n^{n^{n^{n^{n}}}}}$ where n is the number of agents.

Computational social choice is much too broad to be covered in its entirety in this chapter. We will therefore discuss a handful of new exciting research directions within computational social choice that have not been comprehensively addressed so far and that we consider to be particularly promising: restricted preference domains, voting equilibria and iterative voting, multiwinner voting, probabilistic social choice, random assignment, and computer-aided theorem proving.

2   Restricted Preference Domains

It is well known that when we aggregate the preferences of a group of agents by taking a majority vote over each pair of alternatives, we cannot ensure a rational outcome: the collective preference relation may fail to be transitive even if individual preferences are. This observation goes back to Condorcet (1785), and can be seen as the root cause for many impossibility results such as those of Arrow [2] or Gibbard [82] and Satterthwaite [120].

Black [26] was the first to observe that this issue does not arise if the voters' preferences are essentially one-dimensional: he defined the domain of *single-peaked preferences* and showed that for preference profiles that belong to this domain, the majority preference relation is necessarily transitive for an odd number of voters; this implies the existence of a Condorcet winner (an alternative that is preferred to every other alternative by a majority of voters). Informally, a preference profile is said to be single-peaked if the alternatives can be ordered on a line so that each voter has a favorite point (peak) on this line and his affinity for the alternatives declines as one moves away from the peak in either direction.

Single-peaked preferences have received a considerable amount of attention from social choice researchers since Black's pioneering work (e.g., [100]). More recently, it has been observed that restricting attention to such preferences can also simplify many problems in computational social choice. For instance, there are several voting rules that return a Condorcet winner whenever it exists and otherwise have to solve an NP-hard optimization problem. For any such rule computing the winner is easy if the number of voters is odd and their preferences are single-peaked: by Black's result, we can simply return the Condorcet winner. For some of these rules, further effort yields polynomial-time algorithms for single-peaked profiles with an even number of voters [39]. The single-peaked ordering of the alternatives can also be used as a basis for a dynamic program; intuitively, one proceeds by computing a partial solution for each prefix of the alternative ordering. This approach leads, e.g., to a polynomial-time algorithm for computing the outcome of the Chamberlin–Courant multiwinner voting rule (see Sect. 4) for single-peaked profiles [24]. In recent years, many other computational social choice problems were shown to become easier for single-peaked preferences: examples include various forms of strategic behavior in elections (see, e.g., [74, 75]) and preference elicitation [52]. Some of these easiness results extend to preference profiles that are nearly single-peaked, i.e., can be made single-peaked by a small number of modifications (such as deleting a few voters or collapsing or swapping a few alternatives) (see, e.g., [56, 57, 75, 134]).

In single-peaked profiles, alternatives can be positioned on a line in a way that respects the voters' preferences. We can also obtain positive algorithmic results if alternatives can be mapped to a tree [109, 137] or a cycle [110]. Another approach is based on ordering voters rather than alternatives; the resulting domain of *single-crossing preferences* also admits efficient algorithms for a number of problems that are otherwise computationally hard (see, e.g., [95, 125]).

An interesting class of algorithmic problems associated with restricted preference domains is to determine whether a given profile belongs to a particular domain. For single-peaked and single-crossing preferences, these problems admit efficient algorithms [59] as well as elegant characterizations in terms of forbidden substructures [21, 44]. By contrast, for trees, the complexity depends on whether we are satisfied with any tree, in which case there is an efficient algorithm [130], or whether we want to construct a tree that satisfies additional constraints, in which case the answer depends on the nature of the constraints [109]. A related question is whether voters and alternatives can be embedded into a d-dimensional space so that the preferences are driven by distances: for $d = 1$ the existence of such an embedding can be determined in polynomial time [59], but for $d > 1$ this problem is equivalent to the existential theory of reals (and thus, in particular, NP-hard) [107]. It is also hard to determine whether a preference profile is close to being single-peaked or single-crossing for many distance measures (with some notable exceptions) [45, 57, 69].

A more extensive survey of recent computational results for restricted domains is provided by Elkind et al. [66].

3   Voting Equilibria and Iterative Voting

In many voting scenarios, a voter or a group of voters can alter an election outcome to their benefit by misrepresenting their preferences; indeed, no reasonable voting rule is immune to this problem [82, 120]. As a consequence, understanding the complexity of finding a manipulative vote under various voting rules has been a prominent research topic in computational social choice since the inception of the area (see, e.g., the survey by Conitzer and Walsh [55]). However, the standard setting of voting manipulation assumes that only some of the voters are strategic, and the interests of all strategic voters are aligned.

When *all* voters act strategically, it is natural to assume that their behavior is governed by a game-theoretic solution concept, such as Nash equilibrium. However, it is not easy to identify an appropriate solution concept: voting games rarely admit dominant strategies, and they often have many Nash equilibria. For instance, under plurality voting with at least three voters, the situation where all voters vote for the same alternative is a Nash equilibrium, even if this alternative is universally hated, as no voter can unilaterally change the election outcome.

One can eliminate some of these equilibria by assuming that, in addition to preferences over alternatives, voters also have secondary preferences: e.g., they may prefer not to lie unless a lie is clearly beneficial (such voters are called *truth-biased*), or they may prefer not to participate at all if their vote cannot influence the election outcome (such voters are called *lazy*). Either assumption eliminates many unrealistic Nash equilibria; the properties of the surviving equilibria and their computational complexity have been investigated by a number of authors [62,63,103,129]. Another useful technique to get rid of many of the unintuitive outcomes is to focus on trembling-hand Nash equilibria [106].

An alternative approach is to move away from the assumption that all voters submit their ballots simultaneously. For instance, one can consider settings where voters submit their ballots one by one; the appropriate solution concept is then subgame-perfect Nash equilibrium [58,133]. Alternatively, one can consider dynamic mechanisms, where voters take turns changing their ballots in response to the observed outcome, until no voter has an incentive to make a change: this line of work was initiated by Meir et al. [97], who focused on better/best-response dynamics of plurality voting, and has been subsequently extended to other voting rules (see, e.g., [84,93,104,116]). Convergence and complexity of iterative voting depends on whether voters get to observe the full set of current ballots or just some aggregated information about the ballot profile [68,98,115], whether voters compute their best responses at each step, or may use other heuristics [84,105], and whether voters exhibit secondary preferences, such as laziness or truth bias [113]; see the recent survey by Meir [96].

4   Multiwinner Voting

In multiwinner voting, the goal is to select not just a single winner, but a fixed-size set of winners (a *committee*). Multiwinner voting has a diverse set of applications, which include electing parliaments, shortlisting candidates for a job, selecting locations for public facilities, or deciding which products to advertise to customers. As a consequence, there is a wide variety of multiwinner voting rules, and the research challenge is to formulate desirable properties (axioms) for such rules so as to decide which rules are more suitable for each application, as well as to develop efficient algorithms for computing the outputs of such rules.

Multiwinner voting rules can be broadly classified according to their inputs; while most of the research so far focused on rules where voters have to rank the alternatives, there is also a substantial body of work on multiwinner rules that merely ask each voter to indicate which alternatives they approve.

For ranked ballots, an important class of multiwinner rules is that of *committee scoring rules* [65], which can be seen as analogues of the classic single-winner scoring rules. In more detail, under single-winner scoring rules, each voter assigns a certain number of points to each alternative, based on that alternative's position in her ranking. A typical example is the Borda rule: the Borda score assigned by voter v to alternative c is given by $m - j$, where j is the position of c in v's ranking and m is the number of alternatives; the winner(s) are the alternatives with the highest total Borda score (summed over all voters). Similarly, under committee scoring rules, each voter assigns a score to each *committee*, based on the set of positions of committee members in her preference order. For instance, the score that voter v assigns to a committee S can be the sum of Borda scores of all members of S, or the Borda score of v's most preferred member of S; under the former approach, the winning size-k committee consists of k alternatives with the highest Borda score, and under the latter approach we get the well-known Chamberlin–Courant rule [50].

An alternative approach is based on extending Condorcet's principle to the multiwinner setting. There are several ways to implement this idea: one can directly compare committees and ask for a committee that is preferred to every other committee by a majority of voters, or one can compare committees and individual alternatives, and require that each committee member is preferred to each non-member by a majority of voters [22,80,114], or, alternatively, that no 'large' group of voters prefers a non-member of the committee to each committee member [20,61]. Yet another class of voting rules, which includes the popular single transferable vote rule, is based on iteratively adding alternatives to the committee and removing or reweighting the voters who approve these alternatives. The seemingly simpler setting of multiwinner voting with approval ballots also admits a variety of interesting voting rules; in fact, there are sophisticated approval-based multiwinner rules that date back to 19th century such as those due to Thiele and Phragmén. This area also has connections to the literature on apportionment [46].

Unfortunately, for many appealing multiwinner rules it is NP-hard to find a winning committee [15,92,94,112,126]. To circumvent these hardness results, researchers have developed approximation algorithms and used techniques of fixed-parameter tractability (see, e.g., [24,48,94,124,126]); also, it has been shown that many multiwinner voting rules become easier when voters' preferences belong to a restricted domain (see Sect. 2) [24,60,108,110,125,137].

Computational social choice researchers have also contributed to understanding multiwinner voting rules from a normative perspective. For ranked ballots, Elkind et al. [65] put together a list of prominent multiwinner rules, formulated a number of desirable properties of such rules, and determined which of the rules in their list satisfied each property. Interestingly, they observed that an approximation algorithm for an NP-hard voting rule, when interpreted as a voting rule in its own right, may perform better according to these criteria than the rule it was meant to approximate; this is the case, for instance, for the Greedy Monroe rule of Skowron et al. [124]. For approval-based ballots, the *justified representation* axiom and its extensions have been used to explain some features of the important Proportional Approval Voting (PAV) rule [19,119]. The class of committee scoring rules discussed in the beginning of this section was shown to admit an axiomatic characterization [127] that is reminiscent of Young's famous characterization of single-winner scoring rules [136]; the structure of this class and axiomatic properties of individual rules within this class are a subject of ongoing research (see, e.g., [49,64,76,77,123,126]). We refer the reader to the recent survey by Faliszewski et al. [78] for further details on axiomatic and computational properties of multiwinner rules.

5 Probabilistic Social Choice

Randomization plays an important role in social choice theory. It is easily seen that deterministically picking a single winner is at variance with basic fairness principles (for example, when there are two alternatives and two voters such that each voter prefers a different alternative). In the past few years, there has been refreshed interest in voting rules that return probability distributions over alternatives (so-called lotteries) (e.g., [11,13,14,31,32,34]). Often, the outcomes of these rules can also be interpreted as fractional shares of the alternatives.

Randomization may provide a way to circumvent classic impossibility results because the design space of probabilistic voting rules is much richer than that of deterministic ones. Since it is impractical to ask voters for their complete preferences over all lotteries, a common approach is to systematically extend preferences over alternatives to (possibly incomplete) preferences over lotteries via so-called preference extensions. There are various sensible preference extensions, which in turn lead to different generalizations of standard properties such as strategyproofness (no voter is better off by misrepresenting his preferences) and Pareto efficiency (no voter can be made better off without making another one worse off). A very influential preference extension is based on first-order stochastic dominance (SD). According to this extension, lottery p is preferred to lottery q if and only if, for every alternative x, the probability that p selects an alternative that is at least as good as x is greater or equal than the probability that q selects such an alternative. Equivalently, p is preferred to q if and only if, for every utility function consistent with the preferences over alternatives, p yields at least as much expected utility as q. A series of increasingly difficult theorems has recently culminated in a sweeping computer-aided impossibility, showing that there is no randomized rule that simultaneously satisfies SD-efficiency and weak SD-strategyproofness [32], see also Sect. 7.

Of course, every set-valued voting rule can be straightforwardly turned into a randomized rule by returning the uniform lottery over all winners. Randomization, however, allows for more elaborate rules that satisfy properties unmatched by deterministic rules. Particularly noteworthy in this context are *random serial dictatorship* (RSD) and *maximal lotteries* (ML).

RSD is defined by picking a sequence of the voters uniformly at random and then invoking *serial dictatorship* where voters proceed in a sequence, and each voter narrows down the set of alternatives by picking his most preferred alternatives among the ones selected by previous voters. RSD enjoys strong SD-strategyproofness, but violates SD-efficiency. It is often used in the domain of assignment where it is also referred to as *random priority* (see Sect. 6). While implementing RSD by uniformly selecting a sequence of agents and then running serial dictatorship is straightforward, it was shown that computing the resulting RSD probabilities is #P-complete [10], but fixed parameter tractable for parameters such as the number of voters or the number of alternatives [7].

ML is defined as the rule that returns all lotteries that are at least as good as any other lottery in a well-defined way. Maximal lotteries can thus be viewed as a probabilistic generalization of the notion of a Condorcet winner. However, in contrast to deterministic Condorcet winners which often fail to exist, existence of maximal lotteries is guaranteed by the *Minimax Theorem*. ML satisfies a very strong notion of efficiency (stronger than *SD*-efficiency), but fails to be even weakly *SD*-strategyproof. Maximal lotteries are equivalent to mixed maximin strategies in a symmetric zero-sum game induced by the voters' preferences and can be computed in polynomial time via linear programming. ML has been characterized as the only randomized voting rule that satisfies two fairly natural consistency conditions and it has been repeatedly recommended for practical use (see [33]).[2]

Other computational work on probabilistic social choice deals with establishing hardness of manipulation via randomization (e.g., [54, 102, 132]), approximating deterministic voting rules (e.g., [25, 111, 122]), defining new randomized rules (e.g., [4, 8]), and measuring the worst-case utilitarian performance of randomized voting rules (e.g., [1]). A more comprehensive overview of recent trends in probabilistic social choice is provided by Brandt [36].

6 Random Assignment

Random assignment is concerned with the probabilistic assignment of m objects to n agents. Each agent specifies transitive and complete preferences over the objects, and the goal is to allocate the objects among the agents in a fair, efficient, and strategyproof manner. When fairly assigning indivisible objects, randomization is necessary in order to satisfy agents with identical preferences. Possible applications include assigning dormitories to students, jobs to applicants, rooms to housemates, processor time slots to jobs, parking spaces to employees, offices to workers, kidneys to patients, etc.

For simplicity, it is often assumed that $m = n$, that each agent has demand for exactly one object (unit demand), and that individual preferences are strict. A *random assignment* is a probability distribution over deterministic assignments and can be represented by a matrix that specifies, for each agent and each object, the probability with which the agent receives the object. The matrix is bistochastic, which means that all row sums and all column sums are equal to 1.[3] A *random assignment rule* maps each preference profile to a random assignment. It is assumed that agents are only concerned about their individual random assignment, given by the corresponding row of the bistochastic matrix. In order to reason about the axiomatic properties of random assignments and random assignment rules, preferences over objects can be extended to preferences over lotteries just as described in Sect. 5. It is then possible to define efficiency, strategyproofness, and envy-freeness (no agent prefers another agent's random assignment) based on the *SD* preference extension. Bogomolnaia and Moulin [29] have shown that no random assignment rule satisfies *SD*-efficiency, strong

---

[2] ML is one of several voting rules used by the online voting tool Pnyx (https://pnyx.dss.in.tum.de).

[3] By the *Birkhoff-von Neumann Theorem*, any random assignment can be represented by a (not necessarily unique) convex combination over discrete assignments.

SD-strategyproofness and equal treatments of equals (agents with identical preferences receive identical individual random assignments), even when individual preferences are strict. The tradeoff among these properties is the subject of ongoing research (e.g., [5,99]).

RSD, as described in Sect. 5, has a particularly natural interpretation in random assignment: a sequence of agents is picked uniformly at random and then one agent after another picks his most preferred of the remaining objects. RSD inherits strategyproofness from the more general voting domain, but still violates *SD*-efficiency and only satisfies a weak notion of *SD*-envy-freeness. The computational properties of RSD mentioned in Sect. 5 also hold within the domain of assignment [7,10,118].

A well-studied alternative to RSD is the probabilistic serial (PS) rule, which is *SD*-efficient, strongly *SD*-envy-free, and weakly *SD*-strategyproof (as long as individual preferences are strict).[4] Under *PS*, agents 'eat' the most preferred available object at an equal rate until all objects are consumed. When a most preferred object is completely consumed, agents eat their next most preferred object that is still available. The fraction of any object consumed by an agent is the probability of the agent receiving that object. There have been a number of appealing axiomatic characterizations of PS using *SD*-efficiency, *SD*-envy-freeness, and additional properties [27,28,131]. Furthermore, PS has been extended in a number of ways (e.g., [3,47,88,121,135]). In particular, there is a natural extension to the more general case of multi-unit demand [29,86,91]. Just as in the case of ties in the preferences, weak *SD*-strategyproofness breaks down when allowing multi-unit demand. However, it has been shown that the problem of manipulating PS to increase one's expected utility is NP-hard [16].

Maximal lotteries, as described in Sect. 5, are known as *popular* random assignments within the domain of assignment [12,89]. In contrast to the voting domain, however, popular random assignments are rarely unique and popularity can be seen as a property of random assignment rules rather than a rule by itself. In this sense, popularity is stronger than *SD*-efficiency and it is violated by both RSD and PS. Moreover, popularity has been shown to be incompatible with each of weak *SD*-strategyproofness and weak *SD*-envy-freeness [42]. Kavitha et al. [89] have shown that popular random assignments can be computed in polynomial time via linear programming.

Apart from examining existing rules, the structure and computational complexity of efficiency notions constitutes an interesting research area [14,17]. There is a close connection between probabilistic assignment of indivisible objects and deterministic allocation of divisible objects (see, e.g., [9]). Other recent work has focused on theoretically and experimentally analyzing the performance of random assignment rules (e.g., [18,79,87]) and extending the model to allow for other richer features such as incorporating side constraints [47], priorities of objects over agents [90], endowments [3], or optional participation [35].

---

[4] No rule satisfies these conditions when ties are allowed in the agents' preferences [88].

7   Computer-Aided Theorem Proving

Due to its rigorous axiomatic foundation and its emphasis on impossibility results, social choice theory is particularly well-suited for computer-aided theorem proving techniques. Apart from work that is directed towards formalizing and verifying existing results (see, e.g., [83, 101]), a number of recent papers have proved new theorems with the help of computers [30, 32, 37, 41, 43]. This branch of research was initiated by Tang and Lin [128], who reduced well-known impossibility results such as Arrow's theorem to finite instances, which could then be checked by SAT solvers.

In more detail, the approach for these proofs usually goes along the following lines:[5] First, it is manually proven that if there exists a voting rule that satisfies a given set of axioms for $m+1$ alternatives and $n+1$ voters, then we can also find a voting rule that satisfies the same set of axioms for m alternatives and n voters. The contrapositive of this statement can serve as an induction step for impossibility theorems: If there is *no* voting rule satisfying some axioms for fixed m and n, then there is no such rule for any larger m and n either. Thus, it suffices to prove the impossibility for fixed—and ideally small—m and n. Checking whether there *exists* a voting rule that satisfies certain axioms even for small m and n can be very difficult and is obviously a much more complex task than checking whether a *given* voting rule satisfies the axioms. Exhaustive search is infeasible because the number of possible voting rules is prohibitively large. These problems are therefore typically tackled using general problem solvers such as SAT (propositional satisfiability), SMT (satisfiability modulo theories), ASP (answer set programming), or MIP (mixed integer programming). In most cases, the axioms are encoded as a propositional formula and a SAT solver is asked whether this formula has a satisfying assignment. If it does, the satisfying assignment can be translated back to a concrete voting rule that satisfies the given axioms. If the formula is unsatisfiable, no such voting rule exists. Many SAT instances are initially computationally infeasible and can only be solved after leveraging insights into the axioms and finding a restricted domain of preference profiles sufficient for the impossibility. A common criticism of computer-aided proving methods is that the verdict of the computer usually stands without human-readable proof. Fortunately, when relying on SAT solving, this criticism can be addressed by extracting a human-readable proof from an inclusion-minimal unsatisfiable set of clauses returned by the SAT solver. This approach, pioneered by Brandt and Geist [37], has been successfully applied in several recent papers [30, 32, 41, 43].

Two representative results in this branch of research are an improved computer-aided proof of Moulin's *No-Show Paradox* and an impossibility for randomized voting rules mentioned in Sect. 5. The first proof requires only 12 voters (instead of Moulin's 25) and this bound is furthermore shown to be tight [41]. The computer proof (unexpectedly) exploits certain automorphisms in preference profiles, which makes the proof easier to verify and arguably more elegant

---

[5] This section focuses on voting, but all techniques can be similarly applied to other social choice domains such as assignment or coalition formation.

than Moulin's proof. The second result shows the incompatibility of *SD*-efficiency and weak *SD*-strategyproofness and strengthens a number of previous impossibilities [32]. Since working with lotteries requires real-valued arithmetic (rather than only Boolean logic), the statement was obtained via an SMT solver. The resulting proof is rather complex and difficult to verify for humans. It was therefore translated back into a proof in higher-order logic, which was in turn verified via the interactive theorem prover Isabelle/HOL.[6]

An important benefit of the described approach is its universality and flexibility. As soon as a problem has been formalized, it is straightforward to adapt individual axioms or alter the encoding so that related problems can be solved, too. For a more comprehensive account of computed-aided theorem proving in social choice theory, the reader is referred to the survey by Geist and Peters [81].

8 Further Reading

There are various excellent sources that extensively cover the existing literature, most notably the *Handbook of Computational Social Choice* [40] and a recently released book on trends in computational social choice [67]. Further overviews and introductions were provided by Rothe [117], Brandt et al. [38], Conitzer [53], Faliszewski and Procaccia [70], Faliszewski et al. [73], and Chevaleyre et al. [51].

Acknowledgements. Haris Aziz is supported by a Julius Career Award. Felix Brandt is supported by the DFG under grant BR 2312/11-1. Edith Elkind and Piotr Skowron are supported by the ERC under grant 639945 (ACCORD). Piotr Skowron is also supported by a Humboldt Research Fellowship for Postdoctoral Researchers. The authors thank Florian Brandl and Dominik Peters for helpful feedback.

References

1. Anshelevich, E., Postl, J.: Randomized social choice functions under metric preferences. J. AI Res. **58**, 797–827 (2017)
2. Arrow, K.J.: Social Choice and Individual Values, 1st edn. Cowles Foundation, New Haven (1951)
3. Athanassoglou, S., Sethuraman, J.: House allocation with fractional endowments. Int. J. Game Theory **40**(3), 481–513 (2011)
4. Aziz, H.: Maximal recursive rule: a new social decision scheme. In: Proceedings of 23rd IJCAI, pp. 34–40 (2013)
5. Aziz, H., Kasajima, Y.: Impossibilities for probabilistic assignment. Soc. Choice Welf. **49**(2), 255–275 (2017)
6. Aziz, H., Mackenzie, S.: A discrete and bounded envy-free cake cutting protocol for any number of agents. In: Proceedings of 57th FOCS, pp. 416–427 (2016)
7. Aziz, H., Mestre, J.: Parametrized algorithms for random serial dictatorship. Math. Soc. Sci. **72**, 1–6 (2014)

---

[6] Unfortunately, the theorems considered in this context are much too complex to be proven directly by higher-order theorem provers.

8. Aziz, H., Stursberg, P.: A generalization of probabilistic serial to randomized social choice. In: Proceedings of 28th AAAI, pp. 559–565 (2014)

9. Aziz, H., Ye, C.: Cake cutting algorithms for piecewise constant and piecewise uniform valuations. In: Liu, T.-Y., Qi, Q., Ye, Y. (eds.) WINE 2014. LNCS, vol. 8877, pp. 1–14. Springer, Cham (2014). https://doi.org/10.1007/978-3-319-13129-0_1

10. Aziz, H., Brandt, F., Brill, M.: The computational complexity of random serial dictatorship. Econ. Lett. **121**(3), 341–345 (2013)

11. Aziz, H., Brandt, F., Brill, M.: On the tradeoff between economic efficiency and strategyproofness in randomized social choice. In: Proceedings of 12th AAMAS, pp. 455–462 (2013)

12. Aziz, H., Brandt, F., Stursberg, P.: On popular random assignments. In: Vöcking, B. (ed.) SAGT 2013. LNCS, vol. 8146, pp. 183–194. Springer, Heidelberg (2013). https://doi.org/10.1007/978-3-642-41392-6_16

13. Aziz, H., Brandl, F., Brandt, F.: On the incompatibility of efficiency and strategyproofness in randomized social choice. In: Proceedings of 28th AAAI, pp. 545–551 (2014)

14. Aziz, H., Brandl, F., Brandt, F.: Universal Pareto dominance and welfare for plausible utility functions. J. Math. Econ. **60**, 123–133 (2015)

15. Aziz, H., Gaspers, S., Gudmundsson, J., Mackenzie, S., Mattei, N., Walsh, T.: Computational aspects of multi-winner approval voting. In: Proceedings of 14th AAMAS, pp. 107–115 (2015)

16. Aziz, H., Gaspers, S., Mackenzie, S., Mattei, N., Narodytska, N., Walsh, T.: Manipulating the probabilistic serial rule. In: Proceedings of 14th AAMAS, pp. 1451–1459 (2015)

17. Aziz, H., Mackenzie, S., Xia, L., Ye, C.: Ex post efficiency of random assignments. In: Proceedings of 14th AAMAS, pp. 1639–1640 (2015)

18. Aziz, H., Chen, J., Filos-Ratsikas, A., Mackenzie, S., Mattei, N.: Egalitarianism of random assignment mechanisms. In: Proceedings of 15th AAMAS, pp. 1267–1268 (2016)

19. Aziz, H., Brill, M., Conitzer, V., Elkind, E., Freeman, R., Walsh, T.: Justified representation in approval-based committee voting. Soc. Choice Welf. **48**(2), 461–485 (2017)

20. Aziz, H., Elkind, E., Faliszewski, P., Lackner, M., Skowron, P.: The Condorcet principle for multiwinner elections: from shortlisting to proportionality. In: Proceedings of 26th IJCAI, pp. 84–90 (2017)

21. Ballester, M.A., Haeringer, G.: A characterization of the single-peaked domain. Soc. Choice Welf. **36**(2), 305–322 (2011)

22. Barberà, S., Coelho, D.: How to choose a non-controversial list with k names. Soc. Choice Welf. **31**(1), 79–96 (2008)

23. Bartholdi III, J., Tovey, C.A., Trick, M.A.: The computational difficulty of manipulating an election. Soc. Choice Welf. **6**(3), 227–241 (1989)

24. Betzler, N., Slinko, A., Uhlmann, J.: On the computation of fully proportional representation. J. AI Res. **47**, 475–519 (2013)

25. Birrell, E., Pass, R.: Approximately strategy-proof voting. In: Proceedings of 22nd IJCAI, pp. 67–72 (2011)

26. Black, D.: On the rationale of group decision-making. J. Polit. Econ. **56**(1), 23–34 (1948)

27. Bogomolnaia, A.: Random assignment: redefining the serial rule. J. Econ. Theory **158**, 308–318 (2015)

28. Bogomolnaia, A., Heo, E.J.: Probabilistic assignment of objects: characterizing the serial rule. J. Econ. Theory **147**, 2072–2082 (2012)

29. Bogomolnaia, A., Moulin, H.: A new solution to the random assignment problem. J. Econ. Theory **100**(2), 295–328 (2001)

30. Brandl, F., Brandt, F., Geist, C., Hofbauer, J.: Strategic abstention based on preference extensions: positive results and computer-generated impossibilities. In: Proceedings of 24th IJCAI, pp. 18–24 (2015)

31. Brandl, F., Brandt, F., Hofbauer, J.: Incentives for participation and abstention in probabilistic social choice. In: Proceedings of 14th AAMAS, pp. 1411–1419 (2015)

32. Brandl, F., Brandt, F., Geist, C.: Proving the incompatibility of efficiency and strategyproofness via SMT solving. In: Proceedings of 25th IJCAI, pp. 116–122 (2016)

33. Brandl, F., Brandt, F., Seedig, H.G.: Consistent probabilistic social choice. Econometrica **84**(5), 1839–1880 (2016)

34. Brandl, F., Brandt, F., Suksompong, W.: The impossibility of extending random dictatorship to weak preferences. Econ. Lett. **141**, 44–47 (2016)

35. Brandl, F., Brandt, F., Hofbauer, J.: Random assignment with optional participation. In: Proceedings of 16th AAMAS, pp. 326–334 (2017)

36. Brandt, F.: Rolling the dice: recent results in probabilistic social choice. In: Endriss, U. (ed.) Trends in Computational Social Choice. AI Access (2017)

37. Brandt, F., Geist, C.: Finding strategyproof social choice functions via SAT solving. J. AI Res. **55**, 565–602 (2016)

38. Brandt, F., Conitzer, V., Endriss, U.: Computational social choice. In: Weiß, G. (ed.) Multiagent Systems, 2nd edn, pp. 213–283. MIT Press, Cambridge (2013)

39. Brandt, F., Brill, M., Hemaspaandra, E., Hemaspaandra, L.: Bypassing combinatorial protections: polynomial-time algorithms for single-peaked electorates. J. AI Res. **53**, 439–496 (2015)

40. Brandt, F., Conitzer, V., Endriss, U., Lang, J., Procaccia, A. (eds.): Handbook of Computational Social Choice. Cambridge University Press, Cambridge (2016)

41. Brandt, F., Geist, C., Peters, D.: Optimal bounds for the no-show paradox via SAT solving. Math. Soc. Sci. **90**, 18–27 (2017)

42. Brandt, F., Hofbauer, J., Suderland, M.: Majority graphs of assignment problems and properties of popular random assignments. In: Proceedings of 16th AAMAS, pp. 335–343 (2017)

43. Brandt, F., Saile, C., Stricker, C.: Voting with ties: strong impossibilities via SAT solving. In: Proceedings of 17th AAMAS. IFAAMAS (2018)

44. Bredereck, R., Chen, J., Woeginger, G.J.: A characterization of the single-crossing domain. Soc. Choice Welf. **41**(1), 989–998 (2013)

45. Bredereck, R., Chen, J., Woeginger, G.: Are there any nicely structured preference profiles nearby? Math. Soc. Sci. **79**, 61–73 (2016)

46. Brill, M., Laslier, J.F., Skowron, P.: Multiwinner approval rules as apportionment methods. In: Proceedings of 31st AAAI, pp. 414–420 (2017)

47. Budish, E., Che, Y.-K., Kojima, F., Milgrom, P.: Designing random allocation mechanisms: theory and applications. Am. Econ. Rev. **103**(2), 585–623 (2013)

48. Byrka, J., Sornat, K.: PTAS for minimax approval voting. In: Liu, T.-Y., Qi, Q., Ye, Y. (eds.) WINE 2014. LNCS, vol. 8877, pp. 203–217. Springer, Cham (2014). https://doi.org/10.1007/978-3-319-13129-0_15

49. Caragiannis, I., Nath, S., Procaccia, A.D., Shah, N.: Subset selection via implicit utilitarian voting. J. AI Res. **58**, 123–152 (2017)

50. Chamberlin, J.R., Courant, P.N.: Representative deliberations and representative decisions: proportional representation and the Borda rule. Am. Polit. Sci. Rev. **77**(3), 718–733 (1983)

51. Chevaleyre, Y., Endriss, U., Lang, J., Maudet, N.: A short introduction to computational social choice. In: van Leeuwen, J., Italiano, G.F., van der Hoek, W., Meinel, C., Sack, H., Plášil, F. (eds.) SOFSEM 2007. LNCS, vol. 4362, pp. 51–69. Springer, Heidelberg (2007). https://doi.org/10.1007/978-3-540-69507-3_4

52. Conitzer, V.: Eliciting single-peaked preferences using comparison queries. J. AI Res. **35**, 161–191 (2009)

53. Conitzer, V.: Making decisions based on the preferences of multiple agents. Commun. ACM **53**(3), 84–94 (2010)

54. Conitzer, V., Sandholm, T.: Universal voting protocol tweaks to make manipulation hard. In: Proceedings of 18th IJCAI, pp. 781–788 (2003)

55. Conitzer, V., Walsh, T.: Barriers to manipulation in voting. In: Brandt, F., Conitzer, V., Endriss, U., Lang, J., Procaccia, A.D. (eds.) Handbook of Computational Social Choice. Cambridge University Press, Cambridge (2016)

56. Cornaz, D., Galand, L., Spaajaard, O.: Bounded single-peaked width and proportional representation. In: Proceedings of 20th ECAI, pp. 270–275 (2012)

57. Cornaz, D., Galand, L., Spaajaard, O.: Kemeny elections with bounded single-peaked or single-crossing width. In: Proceedings of 23th IJCAI, pp. 76–82 (2013)

58. Desmedt, Y., Elkind, E.: Equilibria of plurality voting with abstentions. In: Proceedings of 11th ACM-EC, pp. 347–356 (2010)

59. Doignon, J., Falmagne, J.: A polynomial time algorithm for unidimensional unfolding representations. J. Algorithms **16**(2), 218–233 (1994)

60. Elkind, E., Lackner, M.: Structure in dichotomous preferences. In: Proceedings of 24th IJCAI, pp. 2019–2025 (2015)

61. Elkind, E., Lang, J., Saffidine, A.: Condorcet winning sets. Soc. Choice Welf. **44**(3), 493–517 (2015)

62. Elkind, E., Markakis, E., Obraztsova, S., Skowron, P.: Equilibria of plurality voting: lazy and truth-biased voters. In: Hoefer, M. (ed.) SAGT 2015. LNCS, vol. 9347, pp. 110–122. Springer, Heidelberg (2015). https://doi.org/10.1007/978-3-662-48433-3_9

63. Elkind, E., Markakis, E., Obraztsova, S., Skowron, P.: Complexity of finding equilibria of plurality voting under structured preferences. In: Proceedings of 15th AAMAS, pp. 394–401 (2016)

64. Elkind, E., Faliszewski, P., Laslier, J., Skowron, P., Slinko, A., Talmon, N.: What do multiwinner voting rules do? An experiment over the two-dimensional Euclidean domain. In: Proceedings of 31st AAAI, pp. 494–501 (2017)

65. Elkind, E., Faliszewski, P., Skowron, P., Slinko, A.: Properties of multiwinner voting rules. Soc. Choice Welf. **48**(3), 599–632 (2017)

66. Elkind, E. Lackner, M., Peters, D.: Structured preferences. In: Endriss, U. (ed.) Trends in Computational Social Choice. AI Access (2017)

67. Endriss, U. (ed.): Trends in Computational Social Choice. AI Access (2017)

68. Endriss, U., Obraztsova, S., Polukarov, M., Rosenschein, J.S.: Strategic voting with incomplete information. In: Proceedings of 25th IJCAI, pp. 236–242 (2016)

69. Erdélyi, G., Lackner, M., Pfandler, A.: Computational aspects of nearly single-peaked electorates. J. AI Res. **58**, 297–337 (2017)

70. Faliszewski, P., Procaccia, A.D.: AI's war on manipulation: are we winning? AI Mag. **31**(4), 53–64 (2010)

71. Faliszewski, P., Rothe, J.: Control and bribery in voting. In: Brandt, F., Conitzer, V., Endriss, U., Lang, J., Procaccia, A.D. (eds.) Handbook of Computational Social Choice. Cambridge University Press, Cambridge (2016)
72. Faliszewski, P., Hemaspaandra, E., Hemaspaandra, L., Rothe, J.: A richer understanding of the complexity of election systems. In: Ravi, S., Shukla, S. (eds.) Fundamental Problems in Computing: Essays in Honor of Professor Daniel J. Rosenkrantz. Springer, Dordrecht (2009). https://doi.org/10.1007/978-1-4020-9688-4_14
73. Faliszewski, P., Hemaspaandra, E., Hemaspaandra, L.: Using complexity to protect elections. Commun. ACM **53**(11), 74–82 (2010)
74. Faliszewski, P., Hemaspaandra, E., Hemaspaandra, L., Rothe, J.: The shield that never was: societies with single-peaked preferences are more open to manipulation and control. Inf. Comput. **209**(2), 89–107 (2011)
75. Faliszewski, P., Hemaspaandra, E., Hemaspaandra, L.A.: The complexity of manipulative attacks in nearly single-peaked electorates. Artif. Intell. **207**, 69–99 (2014)
76. Faliszewski, P., Skowron, P., Slinko, A., Talmon, N.: Committee scoring rules: axiomatic classification and hierarchy. In: Proceedings of 25th IJCAI, pp. 250–256 (2016)
77. Faliszewski, P., Skowron, P., Slinko, A., Talmon, N.: Multiwinner analogues of the plurality rule: axiomatic and algorithmic views. In: Proceedings of 30th AAAI, pp. 482–488 (2016)
78. Faliszewski, P., Skowron, P., Slinko, A., Talmon, N.: Multiwinner voting: a new challenge for social choice theory. In: Endriss, U. (ed.) Trends in Computational Social Choice. AI Access (2017)
79. Filos-Ratsikas, A., Frederiksen, S.K.S., Zhang, J.: Social welfare in one-sided matchings: random priority and beyond. In: Lavi, R. (ed.) SAGT 2014. LNCS, vol. 8768, pp. 1–12. Springer, Heidelberg (2014). https://doi.org/10.1007/978-3-662-44803-8_1
80. Gehrlein, W.V.: The Condorcet criterion and committee selection. Math. Soc. Sci. **10**(3), 199–209 (1985)
81. Geist, C., Peters, D.: Computer-aided methods for social choice theory. In: Endriss, U. (ed.) Trends in Computational Social Choice. AI Access (2017)
82. Gibbard, A.: Manipulation of voting schemes: a general result. Econometrica **41**(4), 587–601 (1973)
83. Grandi, U., Endriss, U.: First-order logic formalisation of impossibility theorems in preference aggregation. J. Philos. Logic **42**(4), 595–618 (2013)
84. Grandi, U., Loreggia, A., Rossi, F., Venable, K.B., Walsh, T.: Restricted manipulation in iterative voting: condorcet efficiency and borda score. In: Perny, P., Pirlot, M., Tsoukiàs, A. (eds.) ADT 2013. LNCS (LNAI), vol. 8176, pp. 181–192. Springer, Heidelberg (2013). https://doi.org/10.1007/978-3-642-41575-3_14
85. Hemaspaandra, E., Spakowski, H., Vogel, J.: The complexity of Kemeny elections. Theoret. Comput. Sci. **349**(3), 382–391 (2005)
86. Heo, E.J.: Probabilistic assignment with multiple demands: a generalization of the serial rule and and its characterization. J. Math. Econ. **54**, 40–47 (2014)
87. Hosseini, H., Larson, K., Cohen, R.: Investigating the characteristics of one-sided matching mechanisms. In: Proceedings of 15th AAMAS, pp. 1443–1444 (2016)
88. Katta, A.-K., Sethuraman, J.: A solution to the random assignment problem on the full preference domain. J. Econ. Theory **131**(1), 231–250 (2006)
89. Kavitha, T., Mestre, J., Nasre, M.: Popular mixed matchings. Theoret. Comput. Sci. **412**(24), 2679–2690 (2011)

90. Kesten, O., Unver, U.: A theory of school choice lotteries. Theor. Econ. **10**(2), 543–595 (2015)
91. Kojima, F.: Random assignment of multiple indivisible objects. Math. Soc. Sci. **57**(1), 134–142 (2009)
92. LeGrand, R., Markakis, E., Mehta, A.: Some results on approximating the minimax solution in approval voting. In: Proceedings of 6th AAMAS, pp. 1193–1195 (2007)
93. Lev, O., Rosenschein, J.S.: Convergence of iterative scoring rules. J. AI Res. **57**, 573–591 (2016)
94. Lu, T., Boutilier, C.: Budgeted social choice: from consensus to personalized decision making. In: Proceedings of 22nd IJCAI, pp. 280–286 (2011)
95. Magiera, K., Faliszewski, P.: How hard is control in single-crossing elections? In: Proceedings of 21st ECAI, pp. 579–584 (2014)
96. Meir, R.: Iterative voting. In: Endriss, U. (ed.) Trends in Computational Social Choice. AI Access (2017)
97. Meir, R., Polukarov, M., Rosenschein, J.S., Jennings, N.R.: Convergence to equilibria in plurality voting. In: Proceedings of 24th AAAI, pp. 823–828 (2010)
98. Meir, R., Lev, O., Rosenschein, J.S.: A local-dominance theory of voting equilibria. In: Proceedings of 15th ACM-EC, pp. 313–330 (2014)
99. Mennle, T., Seuken, S.: An axiomatic approach to characterizing and relaxing strategyproofness of one-sided matching mechanisms. In: Proceedings of 15th ACM-EC, pp. 37–38 (2014)
100. Moulin, H.: On strategy-proofness and single peakedness. Public Choice **35**(4), 437–455 (1980)
101. Nipkow, T.: Social choice theory in HOL: Arrow and Gibbard-Satterthwaite. J. Automated Reason. **43**, 289–304 (2009)
102. Obraztsova, S., Elkind, E.: On the complexity of voting manipulation under randomized tie-breaking. In: Proceedings of 22nd IJCAI, pp. 319–324 (2011)
103. Obraztsova, S., Markakis, E., Thompson, D.R.M.: Plurality voting with truth-biased agents. In: Vöcking, B. (ed.) SAGT 2013. LNCS, vol. 8146, pp. 26–37. Springer, Heidelberg (2013). https://doi.org/10.1007/978-3-642-41392-6_3
104. Obraztsova, S., Lev, O., Markakis, E., Rabinovich, Z., Rosenschein, J.S.: Beyond plurality: truth-bias in binary scoring rules. In: Proceedings of 14th AAMAS, pp. 1733–1734 (2015)
105. Obraztsova, S., Markakis, E., Polukarov, M., Rabinovich, Z., Jennings, N.R.: On the convergence of iterative voting: how restrictive should restricted dynamics be? In: Proceedings of 29th AAAI, pp. 993–999 (2015)
106. Obraztsova, S., Rabinovich, Z., Elkind, E., Polukarov, M., Jennings, N.R.: Trembling hand equilibria of plurality voting. In: Proceedings of 25th IJCAI, pp. 440–446 (2016)
107. Peters, D.: Recognising multidimensional Euclidean preferences. In: Proceedings of 31st AAAI, pp. 642–648 (2017)
108. Peters, D.: Single-peakedness and total unimodularity: new polynomial-time algorithms for multi-winner elections. In: Proceedings of 32nd AAAI (2018)
109. Peters, D., Elkind, E.: Preferences single-peaked on nice trees. In: Proceedings of 30th AAAI, pp. 594–600 (2016)
110. Peters, D., Lackner, M.: Preferences single-peaked on a circle. In: Proceedings of 31st AAAI, pp. 649–655 (2017)
111. Procaccia, A.D.: Can approximation circumvent Gibbard-Satterthwaite? In: Proceedings of 24th AAAI, pp. 836–841 (2010)

112. Procaccia, A.D., Rosenschein, J.S., Zohar, A.: On the complexity of achieving proportional representation. Soc. Choice Welf. **30**, 353–362 (2008)
113. Rabinovich, Z., Obraztsova, S., Lev, O., Markakis, E., Rosenschein, J.S.: Analysis of equilibria in iterative voting schemes. In: Proceedings of 29th AAAI, pp. 1007–1013 (2015)
114. Ratliff, T.C.: Some startling inconsistencies when electing committees. Soc. Choice Welf. **21**(3), 433–454 (2003)
115. Reijngoud, A., Endriss, U.: Voter response to iterated poll information. In: Proceedings of 11th AAMAS, pp. 635–644 (2012)
116. Reyhani, R., Wilson, M.C.: Best reply dynamics for scoring rules. In: Proceedings of 20th ECAI, pp. 672–677 (2012)
117. Rothe, J. (ed.): Economics and Computation: An Introduction to Algorithmic Game Theory, Computational Social Choice, and Fair Division. Springer, Heidelberg (2015). https://doi.org/10.1007/978-3-662-47904-9
118. Saban, D., Sethuraman, J.: The complexity of computing the random priority allocation matrix. Math. Oper. Res. **40**(4), 1005–1014 (2015)
119. Sánchez-Fernández, L., Elkind, E., Lackner, M., Fernández, N., Fisteus, J.A., Basanta Val, P., Skowron, P.: Proportional justified representation. In: Proceedings of 31st AAAI, pp. 670–676 (2017)
120. Satterthwaite, M.A.: Strategy-proofness and Arrow's conditions: existence and correspondence theorems for voting procedures and social welfare functions. J. Econ. Theory **10**(2), 187–217 (1975)
121. Schulman, L.J., Vazirani, V.V.: Allocation of divisible goods under lexicographic preferences. In: Proceedings of 35th FSTTCS, pp. 543–559 (2015)
122. Service, T.C., Adams, J.A.: Strategyproof approximations of distance rationalizable voting rules. In: Proceedings of 11th AAMAS, pp. 569–576 (2012)
123. Skowron, P.: What do we elect committees for? A voting committee model for multi-winner rules. In: Proceedings of 24th IJCAI, pp. 1141–1148 (2015)
124. Skowron, P., Faliszewski, P., Slinko, A.: Achieving fully proportional representation: approximability result. Artif. Intell. **222**, 67–103 (2015)
125. Skowron, P., Yu, L., Faliszewski, P., Elkind, E.: The complexity of fully proportional representation for single-crossing electorates. Theoret. Comput. Sci. **569**, 43–57 (2015)
126. Skowron, P., Faliszewski, P., Lang, J.: Finding a collective set of items: from proportional multirepresentation to group recommendation. Artif. Intell. **241**, 191–216 (2016)
127. Skowron, P., Faliszewski, P., Slinko, A.: Axiomatic characterization of committee scoring rules. In: Proceedings of 6th COMSOC (2016)
128. Tang, P., Lin, F.: Computer-aided proofs of Arrow's and other impossibility theorems. Artif. Intell. **173**(11), 1041–1053 (2009)
129. Thomson, D.R.M., Lev, O., Leyton-Brown, K., Rosenschein, J.: Empirical analysis of plurality election equilibria. In: Proceedings of 12th AAMAS, pp. 391–398 (2013)
130. Trick, M.A.: Recognizing single-peaked preferences on a tree. Math. Soc. Sci. **17**(3), 329–334 (1989)
131. Ünver, M.U., Kesten, O., Kurino, M., Hashimoto, T., Hirata, D.: Two axiomatic approaches to the probabilistic serial mechanism. Theor. Econ. **9**, 253–277 (2014)
132. Walsh, T., Xia, L.: Lot-based voting rules. In: Proceedings of 11th AAMAS, pp. 603–610 (2012)
133. Xia, L., Conitzer, V.: Stackelberg voting games: computational aspects and paradoxes. In: Proceedings of 24th AAAI, pp. 921–926 (2010)

134. Yang, Y., Guo, J.: The control complexity of r-approval: from the single-peaked case to the general case. In: Proceedings of 13th AAMAS, pp. 621–628 (2014)
135. Yilmaz, O.: Random assignment under weak preferences. Games Econ. Behav. **66**(1), 546–558 (2009)
136. Young, H.P.: Social choice scoring functions. SIAM J. Appl. Math. **28**(4), 824–838 (1975)
137. Yu, L., Chan, H., Elkind, E.: Multiwinner elections under preferences that are single-peaked on a tree. In: Proceedings of 23rd IJCAI, pp. 425–431 (2013)

Geometric Optimization Revisited

Pankaj K. Agarwal[1], Esther Ezra[2,3], and Kyle Fox[4(✉)]

[1] Department of Computer Science, Duke University, Durham, NC 27708-0129, USA
[2] Department of Computer Science, Bar-Ilan University, Ramat Gan, Israel
[3] School of Math, Georgia Institute of Technology, Atlanta, GA 30332, USA
[4] Department of Computer Science, The University of Texas at Dallas, Richardson, TX 75080, USA
kyle.fox@utdallas.edu

Abstract. Many combinatorial optimization problems such as set cover, clustering, and graph matching have been formulated in geometric settings. We review the progress made in recent years on a number of such geometric optimization problems, with an emphasis on how geometry has been exploited to develop better algorithms. Instead of discussing many problems, we focus on a few problems, namely, set cover, hitting set, independent set, and computing maps between point sets.

1 Introduction

A combinatorial optimization problem is often formulated as maximizing or minimizing a function of one or more variables subject to a number of inequality (and equality) constraints. In contrast to continuous optimization, the set of feasible solutions is discrete or can be reduced to discrete. Because several problems in a wide range of fields such as mathematics, operations research, statistics, graph algorithms, machine learning, auction theory, robotics, GIS, computer graphics, and computational geometry can be formulated as combinatorial optimization problems, it has been an active research area for more than seventy years. Many of the combinatorial optimization problems are known to be NP-Hard and thus much attention has focused on fast approximation algorithms. With the increasing size of data sets, faster, say, near-linear-time, approximation algorithms are needed even if polynomial-time exact algorithms exist.

In many applications, the underlying optimization problem involves a large number of constraints that are induced by a set of geometric objects in low dimensions. In fact, one of the earliest combinatorial optimization problems studied was the transportation-plan problem in Euclidean space (see Sect. 4 below for a formal definition), which was first investigated by the French mathematician

P.K. Agarwal and K. Fox are supported in part by NSF under grants CCF-15-13816, CCF-15-46392, and IIS-14-08846, by ARO grant W911NF-15-1-0408, and by grant 2012/229 from the U.S.-Israel Binational Science Foundation. E. Ezra is supported in part by NSF CAREER under grant CCF-15-53354, and by Grant 824/17 from the Israel Science Foundation.

© Springer Nature Switzerland AG 2019
B. Steffen and G. Woeginger (Eds.): Computing and Software Science, LNCS 10000, pp. 66–84, 2019.
https://doi.org/10.1007/978-3-319-91908-9_5

Gaspard Monge in 1784. Furthermore, many classical combinatorial problems have been formulated in geometric settings; e.g., the Euclidean traveling salesperson problem: computing the shortest tour in a set of points in $\mathbb{R}^d$; the k-center problem: covering a set of points by k congruent disks of the smallest radius; and the geometric hitting-set problem: stabbing a set of simple geometric objects (e.g. disks) by the minimum number of points. We refer to such combinatorial optimization problems as *geometric optimization* problems.

A natural question in the context of geometric optimization problems is whether geometry can be exploited to obtain faster algorithms or to improve the approximation factor in the case of approximation algorithms. This question has received much attention over the last forty years and tremendous progress has been made on a large class of problems. For example, faster algorithms have been developed for low-dimensional linear programming [49], and a polynomial-time ε-approximation algorithm is now known for the Euclidean traveling salesperson problem [22,61] while no such algorithm exists for general graphs unless $P = NP$.

A survey paper by Agarwal and Sharir [14] in Vol. 1000 of LNCS (see [15] for an expanded version of this survey) reviews the work on geometric optimization until the early 1990s, including parametric search, prune-and-search, and randomized algorithms for LP-type problems. In the current volume, we discuss some of the main developments in this area over the last two decades, focusing on a few classical combinatorial optimization problems in geometric settings.

The first problem that we discuss (Sect. 2) is the classical set-cover or hitting-set problem in geometric settings, i.e., we have a set system whose elements are simple geometric objects such as points, lines, squares, disks, etc., and each set is a subset of geometric objects that satisfies certain geometric constraints (e.g. input points lying inside a disk). It turns out that both the set-cover and the hitting-set problems are **NP-Complete** even in very simple geometric settings. Therefore, attention has focused on developing fast approximation algorithms with as good an approximation factor as possible, including obtaining a trade-off between the running time and approximation factor. The work on geometric set-cover has also led to some interesting work in combinatorial geometry, including work on ε-nets and discrepancy theory.

A problem closely related to set-cover is the independent-set problem. Although the independent-set problem is intractable even from the approximation point of view for arbitrary graphs [76], it is easier to approximate in many geometric settings. Several interesting results have been obtained, including a quasi-polynomial ε-approximation algorithm that has found applications in many related problems (Sect. 3).

Next, we turn our attention in Sect. 4 to the problem of computing maps between two point sets to identify shared structures between them. We first consider the transportation-map problem mentioned earlier. Next, we discuss the problem of computing maps between two point sequences, which model time-series data or trajectories, and review recent results. We note that polynomial-time algorithms exist for both of these problems even in non-geometric settings.

2   Geometric Set Cover

A *set system* (or range space) $(P, \mathcal{R})$ is a pair consisting of an underlying universe P of *objects* (also called the *space*) and a family $\mathcal{R}$ of subsets of P, referred to as *ranges*. A *set cover* of $(P, \mathcal{R})$ is a subcollection $S \subseteq \mathcal{R}$ such that $\bigcup S = P$. In a typical geometric setting, P is a set of points in $\mathbb{R}^d$, and each set in $\mathcal{R}$ is the intersection of P with a simply-shaped region (e.g., halfspaces, balls, simplices, etc.); with a slight abuse of notation, we will use $\mathcal{R}$ to denote the set of these regions as well. Given this setting, the geometric *set-cover* problem is to find a smallest subcollection of regions that cover the underlying set of points. The dual problem of set-cover is the *hitting-set* problem: find the smallest subset $H \subseteq P$ such that $H \cap R \neq \emptyset$ for all $R \in \mathcal{R}$. The problem of set-cover (resp., hitting-set) can also be formulated where one assigns (non-negative) weights on the regions (resp., points), in which case the objective is to find a coverage (resp., hitting set) of smallest weight.

These problems were among the original NP-Complete problems [56], and the classic greedy approach leads to a $(1 + \ln n)$-approximation algorithm, where $n = |P|$ [74]. Dinur and Steurer [40] showed that a polynomial-time $o(\log n)$-approximation algorithm is infeasible unless $P = NP$. They remain NP-Complete even in simple 2D geometric settings such as when P is a set of points and $\mathcal{R}$ is a set of unit squares or disks [52, Chap. 8]. Nevertheless, the approximation factors achieved in geometric setups are considerably better than those obtained in abstract settings. We present an overview of these results in Sect. 2.2.

2.1   Greedy Algorithms

Let $(P, \mathcal{R})$ be a geometric set system, where $P \subseteq \mathbb{R}^d$ and $\mathcal{R}$ is a set of simply-shaped regions in $\mathbb{R}^d$. For the time being we assume P is finite, and set $n = |P|$, $m = |\mathcal{R}|$. As mentioned above, the standard greedy approach yields a $(1 + \ln n)$-approximation factor, but a naïve implementation of this approach is in general inefficient. By exploiting geometric properties of the set system, considerably faster algorithms can be obtained in many cases. We briefly present such an approach, introduced in [7], when $P \subset \mathbb{R}^2$ and $\mathcal{R}$ is a collection of planar regions with low "union complexity", that is, the number of vertices and arcs appearing along the boundary of $\bigcup S$, for any subset $S \subseteq \mathcal{R}$, is close to linear. This is, e.g., the case for (pseudo-)disks[1] and "fat triangles"[2]; see [19] and the references therein. Here, we focus on the hitting-set problem.

Let Opt be the size of the optimal hitting set of $(P, \mathcal{R})$. The main idea is to construct a set Π of $O(\mathsf{Opt})$ pairwise-disjoint cells (appearing in a plane decomposition induced by a subset of the regions in $\mathcal{R}$) that cover P. Each cell of Π has small complexity (e.g., cells are trapezoids or triangles), and each cell meets only a small fraction of the boundary regions in $\mathcal{R}$. Using the fact that

---

[1] Each of the regions is bounded by a closed Jordan curve, where each pair of boundary curves meet at most twice.

[2] In each triangle, every angle is greater than some constant.

the union complexity of $\mathcal{R}$ is close to linear, Agarwal *et al.* [7] show that such a Π can be constructed in near-linear time. They choose one point of P from each cell of Π, add it to the hitting set, remove the regions of $\mathcal{R}$ hit by the chosen points, and recurse. They show that the procedure terminates after $O(\log n)$ steps, thereby constructing a hitting set of size $O(\mathsf{Opt}\log n)$ in near-linear time.

Greedy algorithms have also been used to approximate the solution of the *art-gallery* problem, that is, the set-up is a polygonal domain P and the goal is to place a smallest number of guards in P, such that any point $p \in P$ is *visible* to at least one of these guards [70]. This problem is an instance of geometric set-cover in which the set $\mathsf{P} = P$ is infinite and so is the set of ranges, one range for each point $p \in P$ (namely, the *visibility polygon* of P). The art-gallery problem is known to be **APX-Hard** [43], and if the guard locations are chosen anywhere in the polygon, no polynomial-time approximation algorithm is known. In such cases, however, one can still obtain efficient approximation algorithms if they are allowed to leave a relatively small portion of P uncovered [6,37]. Very recently, Bonnet and Miltzow [26] showed an $O(\log \mathsf{Opt})$ approximation algorithm assuming the vertices of P have integer coordinates (as well as several general position assumptions). Moreover, they showed in a slightly earlier work [27] that when the guards are selected among the vertices of P (with arbitrary real coordinates), the *exact* problem cannot be solved in time $n^{o(\mathsf{Opt}/\log \mathsf{Opt})}$, unless the *Exponential Time Hypothesis (ETH)* fails.

2.2 Iterative Reweighing Scheme and ε-Nets

Not only can one obtain fast $O(\log n)$-approximation algorithms for hitting-set (or set-cover) in geometric settings, the approximation factor can be improved to $o(\log n)$. One general technique to obtain improved approximations is based on linear programming. Roughly speaking, one (implicitly) formulates the hitting-set problem as a linear program and uses an iterative reweighing scheme, proposed for solving packing and covering linear programs [44], to compute a near-optimal fractional solution. Then, the concept of ε-nets is used to construct an integral solution. We first describe ε-nets and then make the connection to set-cover and hitting-set.

ε-*Nets.* Let $\Sigma = (\mathsf{P}, \mathcal{R})$ be a (discrete) set system, and let $w : \mathsf{P} \to \mathbb{R}_{\geq 0}$ be a weight function. Given a parameter $0 < \varepsilon < 1$, a range $R \in \mathcal{R}$ is called ε-*heavy* if $w(R) \geq \varepsilon w(\mathsf{P})$ and ε-*light* otherwise. A subset $N \subseteq \mathsf{P}$ is called an ε-*net* of $(\mathsf{P}, \mathcal{R})$ if $N \cap R \neq \emptyset$ for every ε-heavy range $R \in \mathcal{R}$. If we flip the roles of P and $\mathcal{R}$, we obtain the so called *dual set system*: $\Sigma^* = (\mathcal{R}, \mathsf{P}^*)$, where $\mathsf{P}^* = \{\{R \in \mathcal{R} \mid p \in R\} \mid p \in \mathsf{P}\}$. We note that a set cover of Σ is a hitting set of Σ^* and vice-versa. In the dual case, an ε-net for $(\mathcal{R}, \mathsf{P}^*)$ is a subset $\mathcal{S} \subseteq \mathcal{R}$ that covers all the ε-heavy points of P, that is, those points that are originally covered by regions whose total weight is at least $\varepsilon w(\mathcal{R})$. Originally introduced as a tool for range-searching data structures in computational geometry, ε-nets have found many applications in computational and combinatorial geometry as well as in learning theory.

By a seminal result of Haussler and Welzl [49, Chap. 5], a geometric set system $(\mathsf{P}, \mathcal{R})$ has an ε-net of size $O(\varepsilon^{-1} \log \varepsilon^{-1})$ (the same asymptotic bound holds in dual set systems). In fact, a random sample of that size is an ε-net with constant probability. More generally, set systems of *VC-dimension* d admit ε-nets of size $O((d/\varepsilon) \log(d/\varepsilon))$; informally, this fact implies that the number of sets in $\mathcal{R}$ is polynomial in $|\mathsf{P}|$ (concretely, $O(|\mathsf{P}|^d)$), and that this property is hereditary for any restriction of the set system onto a subset of P [49, Chap. 5]. In general, it is known that the bound on ε-nets for set systems of finite VC-dimension is tight in the worst case [49, Chap. 5], and recently Pach and Tardos [65] showed that this bound is tight in several geometric settings. Still, there are several favorable geometric scenarios where this bound is smaller, that is, it is very close to $O(1/\varepsilon)$. For example, ε-nets of size $O(1/\varepsilon)$ exist when $\mathcal{R}$ is a set of halfspaces in two or three dimensions, pseudo-disks in the plane, or translates of a fixed convex polytope in 3-space; see, e.g., the references in [20]. The case of axis-parallel boxes in two and three dimensions was addressed by Aronov *et al.* [20], who showed an ε-net bound of $O(\varepsilon^{-1} \log \log \varepsilon^{-1})$; this bound has later been shown to be tight [65]. Additional progress has been made by Clarkson and Varadarajan [39], who introduced a method for constructing small-size ε-nets in several dual set systems. Specifically, they addressed the case where the underlying regions in $\mathcal{R}$ have low union complexity and showed that the resulting ε-nets have complexity $o(\varepsilon^{-1} \log \varepsilon^{-1})$. Later, this bound has further been improved by Aronov *et al.* [20]. For example, for fat triangles the bound is $O(\varepsilon^{-1} \log \log^* \varepsilon^{-1})$, and for more general fat objects the bound becomes $O(\varepsilon^{-1} \log^* \varepsilon^{-1})$.

Iterative Reweighing Scheme. We now describe a simple algorithm, which computes a hitting set of Σ using ε-nets [49, Chap. 6]; the algorithm can compute a set cover of Σ by running it on the dual range space Σ^*. Let k be an integer such that $k/2 < \mathsf{Opt} \le k$. We initialize the weight of each point in P to 1 and repeat the following step until every range is $1/(2k)$-heavy. Let R be a $1/(2k)$-light range. We double the weights of all points in R. We refer to this step as a *weight-doubling* step. When the process stops, we return a $1/(2k)$-net H of Σ (with respect to the final weights), which serves as a hitting set (as at this point all ranges are $1/(2k)$-heavy). If a $1/(2k)$-net of size $O(kg(k))$ can be computed efficiently, we obtain a hitting set of size $O(\mathsf{Opt} \cdot g(\mathsf{Opt}))$.

Using a double-counting argument, it can be shown that if $\mathsf{Opt} \le k$, then the above procedure terminates within $\mu(k) = O(k \log n)$ weight-doubling steps. Therefore, if the algorithm does not terminate within $\mu(k)$ steps, we can conclude that Σ does not have a hitting set of size at most k. An exponential search can then be used to guess the value of k such that $k/2 < \mathsf{Opt} \le k$. Many methods have been proposed to check whether a $1/(2k)$-light range exists at each stage. For example, a $1/(2k)$-net can be computed at each step to detect a light range. Agarwal and Pan [12] described a data structure to detect light ranges, which leads to a near-linear-time implementation of the above algorithm in many cases. Putting these results together, one obtains a near-linear-time $O(1)$-approximation algorithm when ranges are disks in the plane or halfspaces in $\mathbb{R}^3$, and an $O(\log \log \mathsf{Opt})$-approximation algorithm when ranges are rectangles or fat triangles. See [12] for details and concrete results.

As noted above, this algorithm is nothing but the iterative-reweighing algorithm proposed by packing and covering linear programs. The set of final weights that the algorithm computes is a near-optimal fractional solution, and the ε-net is being used to "round" this fractional solution into an integral solution. Agarwal and Pan presented a simpler iterative-reweighing scheme for computing a hitting set or set cover by formulating the problem as 2-player zero-sum game and computing a near-optimal strategy for each of the two players. The strategy for one of the players gives a near-optimal fractional solution for the hitting set, and then they use ε-nets to compute the actual hitting set [12].

2.3   Extensions

Weighted Set-Cover. The above iterative-reweighing technique is in general not extendible to compute a hitting set (or set cover) of smallest weight. Specifically, an $O(\log \mathsf{Opt})$-approximation factor can be obtained when all weights are greater than 1 [44], but the situation is unclear for arbitrary weight functions. Moreover, one may encounter the issue that this latter approximation factor can be arbitrarily larger than $\log n$ (e.g., if the input weights are large), which defeats the advantage geometric settings may have over abstract ones.

Notable progress on this problem was made by Varadarajan [72], who used a *quasi-uniform sampling* approach in order to find an approximately optimal weighted set cover, where the regions in $\mathcal{R}$ have low union complexity. The resulting approximation factors almost match those in the unweighted case. Chan *et al.* [34] later strengthened Varadarajan's technique and obtained asymptotically matching bounds.

Multi-Set-Cover. Another problem of interest is that of *multi-set-cover*, that is, in addition to the set system $(\mathsf{P}, \mathcal{R})$, each point $p \in \mathsf{P}$ has an integer demand $\mathsf{d}(p)$, and the goal is to find a smallest set cover so that each p is covered by $\mathsf{d}(p)$ (distinct) regions of the cover. For abstract set systems, the standard greedy approach results in a $(1 + \ln n)$-approximation factor [74], but the LP-relaxation approach based on ε-nets does not extend to the multi-cover setting. This problem was studied by Chekuri *et al.* [36], who showed similar asymptotic approximation factors as those obtained for the (standard) geometric set-cover. Their proof technique is somewhat intricate and involves a reduction to set cover with objects of one dimensional higher, which is the key to obtain an $O(\log \mathsf{Opt})$-approximation.

PTAS: Shifted Grids and Local Search. Notwithstanding that polynomial-time approximation schemes (PTASes) for the hitting-set/set-cover problem exist in a few cases, including pseudo-disks in the plane and halfspaces in 3-space [63], a PTAS is much more difficult to obtain in general. For instance, even for the cases of fat triangles in the plane (of similar size with angles close to 60 degrees) and fat axis-parallel rectangles (of similar size), the set-cover problem is APX-Hard

[33,51]. In fact, the work in [51] presents several such hardness results, where the overall conclusion is that for "non-shallow" (and even very simple) geometric settings, the hitting-set/set-cover problem tends to be APX-Hard, whereas in *shallow* settings it is more likely to have a PTAS[3].

For the case of points and unit disks in the plane, if only the points are given but the disks can be drawn anywhere in the plane, then one can obtain a PTAS for set cover using a "sliding grid" technique due to Hochbaum and Maas [52, Chap. 9]. The main observation is that in an optimal solution any given point is covered by only a constant number of disks. Therefore, any grid cell in the plane with constant side length must contain only a few disks in the optimal solution. This immediately yields a PTAS for hitting-set of points and unit disks by observing that a disk D covers a point p if and only if the unit disk centered at p is hit by the center of D. Chan [31] addressed the case of disks with arbitrary radii, and presented a PTAS for hitting-set based on *planar separators*. If the disk set is discrete, the problem becomes considerably more difficult; Mustafa and Ray [63] presented a PTAS for hitting set of arbitrary disks exploiting a local-search algorithm. In a more recent paper, Mustafa *et al.* [62] studied the weighted set cover problem for arbitrary disks, where they obtained a quasi-polynomial-time approximation scheme (QPTAS); their technique was inspired by a result of Adamaszek and Wiese [2] for approximating the maximum independent set for axis-parallel rectangles; we review this result is detail in Sect. 3.

3   Geometric Independent Set

Given a collection $\mathcal{R}$ of n (simply-shaped) regions, the geometric *maximum independent-set* problem is to find a maximum-cardinality subset $S \subset \mathcal{R}$ of pairwise disjoint regions. This is the largest independent set in the *intersection graph* of $\mathcal{R}$, and for brevity we just refer to the problem as the *independent-set* problem. When the regions in $\mathcal{R}$ are assigned (non-negative) weights, the *maximum-weight independent-set* problem is to find a maximum-weight subset $S \subseteq \mathcal{R}$ of pairwise-disjoint regions.

In abstract graphs, the independent-set problem is known to be NP-Complete. Unless NP = ZPP, no polynomial-time algorithm with approximation factor better than $n^{1-\varepsilon}$, for any $\varepsilon > 0$, exists [52, Chap. 10], and the currently best known approximation is $O(n(\log \log n)^2/(\log n)^3)$ [45]. Moreover, even when the maximum degree of the graph is 3, a PTAS does not exist. Recently Har-Peled and Quanrud [51] showed that it is possible to construct intersection graphs of triangles in 3-space for which a PTAS does not exist. However, better approximation algorithms have been developed for some geometric settings, and in some cases even a PTAS exists, e.g., the cases of fat objects [31] (such as disks and squares) and pseudo-disks [35].

Of particular interest is the case of axis-parallel rectangles which attracted much attention over the past decade [2,30,35,38] because of its application to

---

[3] A collection of geometric objects is *shallow* if any point in the ambient space is covered by only a few such objects.

"label placement" in a map—place on top of a given map as many labels as possible from a given collection without conflicts; each label is represented as a rectangle, and the rectangles are required to be pairwise disjoint. Nevertheless, there is also a high theoretical interest in this setting since the currently known PTAS techniques for fat objects do not extend to axis-parallel rectangles. In the sequel we describe these techniques and their consequences for different cases.

PTAS for Fat Objects. We begin with reviewing the case of fat objects. First, the case of unit disks is handled using the "sliding grid" technique [52, Chap. 9]. As in set-cover, the main observation is that a grid cell of side-length Δ can contain only $O(\Delta^2)$ pairwise-disjoint unit disks in an optimal solution (but unlike set-cover, the disks here are *given*). If the disks have arbitrary radii, the grid is replaced by a hierarchical spatial subdivision. Specifically, Chan [31] used *randomly shifted quadtrees*, originally proposed for Euclidean TSP [22]. His construction extends to any dimension $d \geq 2$; moreover, this extension applies to any set of fat objects, as the packing argument applied for (unit) disks still holds. An interesting consequence of Chan's algorithm is that it extends to the weighted case as well.

PTAS for Pseudo-Disks. The techniques for fat objects do not extend to pseudo-disks, as they strongly rely on a packing argument exploiting the fatness property. For the unweighted case, Chan and Har-Peled [35] showed a PTAS using a simple local-search approach and exploiting a planar separator theorem. An interesting consequence of their analysis is that a local-search algorithm yields a PTAS for the independent-set problem in planar graphs, giving an alternative approach to existing algorithms [76, Chap. 10]. In the weighted case, Chan and Har-Peled [35] used a clever LP-relaxation approach, where the main idea is to sparsify the intersection graph (which is a consequence of the low union complexity of pseudo-disks), and then apply *Turán's theorem* in order to extract the desired independent set. The latter implies that in every graph on n vertices and average degree d, there is an independent set of size at least $n/(d+1)$.

Axis-Parallel Rectangles. The main difficulty in obtaining small approximation factors for non-fat objects (excluding pseudo-disks) is the fact that their union complexity is typically large, e.g., for axis-parallel rectangles in the plane this complexity is quadratic (realized by a set of long and skinny rectangles forming a grid). It is fairly standard to obtain a logarithmic approximation for axis-parallel rectangles in the plane, using, e.g., a naïve LP-relaxation. However, improving the approximation factor further is considerably more challenging. Chan and Har-Peled [35] showed an $O(\log n/\log\log n)$-approximation for the weighted case, and an intricate LP-relaxation based approach by Chalermsook and Chuzhoy [30] obtains an $O(\log\log n)$-approximation for the unweighted case, which is currently the best known. Although an $O(1)$-approximation algorithm for axis-parallel rectangles has remained elusive, the recent QPTAS for the weighted case by Adamaszek and Wiese [2] is a major step forward. They present a $(1 - \varepsilon)$-approximation algorithm that runs in $n^{O(\operatorname{poly}(\log n)/\varepsilon)}$ time. A key idea in their analysis is a new geometric dynamic programming scheme, which recursively subdivides the plane into polygons of bounded complexity. Chuzhoy and Ene [38] obtained an improved QPTAS for the unweighted case, reducing the running time to $n^{O(\text{poly}(\log\log n)/\varepsilon)}$. These results suggest that the problem is unlikely to be APX-Hard.

Non-rectilinear Non-fat Objects. For arbitrarily oriented non-fat objects such as segments or triangles, the approximation factors are worse, because the structural properties imposed by such objects tend to be weaker. Among these settings is the case of line-segments in the plane, studied by Agarwal and Mustafa [11], who obtained an approximation factor close to $O(\sqrt{\text{Opt}})$ using properties of partially ordered sets. Fox and Pach [46] improved and generalized this bound to curves, each pair of which have a bounded number of intersections. In this case a QPTAS was shown, using the existence of separators in intersection graphs. The case of arbitrary polygons in the plane has been studied by Har-Peled [50], who showed a QPTAS based on the decomposition in [2].

4   Maps Between Point Sets

In this section, we consider the problem of computing a map between two point sets, say, A and B, each representing a geometric object, with the goal of identifying common structure (similarity) between them. This is a central problem in shape analysis, which has been studied extensively in computational geometry, computer vision, computer graphics, molecular biology, and machine learning. For simplicity, we assume A and B to be finite point sets, and in some cases a weight may be associated with each point. We seek a *correspondence* $C \subseteq A \times B$ subject to some restriction on C, e.g., each point of A and B should appear in at least one pair in C or there is some penalty for each point not included in any pair of C. A cost function is defined to measure how well C measures the common structure between A and B, and the goal is to compute a correspondence that minimizes the cost function.

The cost function generally falls under one of two loosely defined categories. *Extrinsic* cost functions are based on the embedding of the points in the ambient space, while *intrinsic* cost functions are based on properties of the objects represented by A and B and not on their embedding in the ambient space. Examples of the former include the Hausdorff distance and the Fréchet distance, and an example of the latter is the Gromov-Hausdorff distance. Extrinsic cost functions are generally easier to optimize using combinatorial algorithms, and many fast algorithms exist; see [17] for a survey of earlier results. Intrinsic cost functions are significantly more difficult and most of the known algorithms rely on numerical methods; see [54] for a survey.

In this section, we will focus on two settings of extrinsic cost functions: transportation maps between two weighted point sets and order preserving maps between point sequences. We will then briefly discuss their extensions and the relatively sparse landscape of combinatorial optimization for intrinsic measures.

4.1   Transportation Maps

Let R and B be two point sets in $\mathbb{R}^d$, and let $|R| = |B| = n$. Let $\lambda : R \cup B \to \mathbb{N}$ denote the *supplies* of points in A and the *demands* of points in B. We assume $\sum_{r \in R} \lambda(r) = \sum_{b \in B} \lambda(b) = U$. A function $\tau : R \times B \to \mathbb{N}$ is a *transportation map* between R and B if $\sum_{b \in B} \tau(r,b) = \lambda(r)$ for all $r \in R$ and $\sum_{r \in R} \tau(r,b) = \lambda(b)$ for all $b \in B$.

Let $\mathrm{d}(\cdot, \cdot)$ be a suitable distance function. We define the cost of a transportation map τ to be $\mu(\tau) = \sum_{(r,b) \in R \times B} \mathrm{d}(r,b)\tau(r,b)$. The *Hitchcock-Koopmans transportation problem* (often referred to simply as the *transportation problem*) is to find a minimum-cost transportation map τ^*. The cost $\mu(\tau^*)$ is called the *transportation distance* or *earth mover's distance*. The transportation problem is a special case of the minimum-cost flow problem in complete bipartite graphs. Similarly, the special case of the transportation problem with all supplies and demands equal to 1 is a special case of the minimum-cost perfect matching problem in complete bipartite graphs. For that reason, we refer to this special case as *geometric bipartite matching*.

The Hitchcock-Koopmans transportation problem as defined above is the discrete version of the *optimal transport* or *Monge-Kantarovich* problem originally proposed by Gaspard Monge in 1784 and studied extensively since the early 20th century. Both the continuous and discrete versions of the transportation problem are used in a wide range of applications, including computing the Barycenter of a family of distributions, matching shapes, matching images, and matching probability distributions. We focus on the discrete transportation problem in this section and refer the reader to the book by Villani [75] for more information on (continuous) optimal transport. We begin by discussing algorithms for *geometric bipartite matching*. We then discuss the case of general supplies and demands.

Geometric Bipartite Matching. For simplicity, we slightly reformulate the geometric bipartite matching problem from the version given above. A *matching* M is a set of point-disjoint pairs or *edges* $(r,b) \in R \times B$. A point is *exposed* with respect to M if it does not belong to any pair of M. A *perfect matching* contains every point in $R \cup B$ exactly once. A minimum cost matching is a perfect matching M^* that minimizes $\sum_{(r,b) \in M^*} \mathrm{d}(r,b)$.

In weighted bipartite graphs with n vertices and m edges, a minimum cost matching can be computed in $O(mn + n^2 \log n)$ time using the Hungarian algorithm [47]. The running time has been improved to $O(m\sqrt{n}\,\mathrm{polylog}(n))$ using an interior-point method [57]. This fact, in turn, implies the existence of an $O(n^{5/2}\,\mathrm{polylog}(n))$-time algorithm for geometric bipartite matching.

In the language of geometric bipartite matching, the Hungarian algorithm works as follows. We maintain a set of potentials $\pi : R \cup B \to \mathbb{R}$ on the points of R and B such that $\pi(r) + \pi(b) \le d(r,b)$ as well as a matching M. Initially, $M = \emptyset$, $\pi(r) = 0$ for all $r \in R$, and $\pi(b) = \min_{r \in R} \mathrm{d}(r,b)$ for all $b \in B$. An edge (r,b) is called *admissible* if $\mathrm{d}(r,b) = \pi(r) + \pi(b)$. The Hungarian algorithm guarantees every edge of M is admissible. An *alternating path* is a sequence that alternates between edges of M and edges outside of M. An alternating path between two exposed points is called an *augmenting path*.

The algorithm iteratively changes potentials in order to create new augmenting paths lying on admissible edges and then augments M by finding such a path P, removing every edge of $P \cap M$, and adding every edge of $P \oplus M$. Each *augmentation* increases the size of M by one, guaranteeing that each edge of M is admissible. Vaidya [71] showed that each iteration can be performed in $O(n\phi(n))$ time in geometric settings (in contrast to $O(m+n \log n)$ time for general graphs), where $\phi(n)$ is the update time to maintain a weighted bichromatic closest pair between two point sets dynamically under insertions and deletions. For $d = 2$, he described such data structures with $\phi(n) = O(\log^3 n)$ if the distance between a pair of points is measured in the L_1 or L_∞ metric, and with $\phi(n) = O(\sqrt{n})$ for any other L_p metric. Agarwal et al. [5] presented an improved data structure for general L_p-metrics with $\phi(n) = O(n^\varepsilon)$, for an arbitrarily small constant $\varepsilon > 0$. The bound was recently improved to $O(\mathrm{polylog}(n))$ by Kaplan et al. [55]. Putting these results together, a minimum-weight matching between two point sets in $\mathbb{R}^2$ of size n each can be computed in $O(n^2 \mathrm{polylog}(n))$ time for any L_p metric. This bound holds for a larger class of well-behaved metrics in the plane; see e.g. [55].

No subquadratic algorithm is known for computing the minimum-weight bipartite matching in the plane except for some very special cases such as when points are in convex position [58] or when points have polynomially bounded integer coordinates [68]. Efrat et al. [42] described an $O(n^{3/2} \log n)$ algorithm to compute the optimal bottleneck matching, i.e., minimizing the maximum length of an edge in the matching, in the plane. Consequently, a series of papers have investigated approximation algorithms for geometric bipartite matching [16,73]. Agarwal and Varadarajan [16] proposed a Monte Carlo algorithm that with high probability computes an $O(\log(1/\varepsilon))$-approximate matching in $O(n^{1+\varepsilon})$ time for any fixed dimension and under any L_p-metric. Their algorithm decomposes space using a large randomly shifted grid. Within each grid cell, they recursively compute a matching using as many points as possible. Some points may be left unmatched due to imbalances between the points of R and B lying within each cell, so they optimally match the leftover points lying in all cells using the Hungarian algorithm. In expectation, the total cost of matching the leftover points within each level of recursion is a constant approximation of the cost of the optimal geometric matching on R and B, so limiting the number of levels to $O(\log(1/\varepsilon))$ gives them their desired approximation factor. Adapting their method, Indyk [53] described a Monte Carlo algorithm that in $O(n \, \mathrm{polylog}(n))$ time approximates the cost of the optimal matching within a constant factor, with high probability. Unfortunately, his approach cannot be extended to compute the matching itself.

The state-of-the-art for geometric bipartite matching is an algorithm of Sharathkumar and Agarwal [69] that computes an ε-approximation under any L_p metric in $O(n \, \mathrm{poly}(\log n, 1/\varepsilon))$ time with high probability. Like the Hungarian algorithm, their algorithm performs a sequence of augmentation steps, each of which increases the size of the matching by one. However, they relax the admissibility condition slightly so that the cost of the matching it computes is at most $(1 + \varepsilon)$ times that of the optimal matching but the total number of edges in all the augmenting paths computed is only $O(n\varepsilon^{-1} \log n)$. Using a data structure based on randomly shifted quadtrees, they compute the augmenting path at each step in time proportional to the length of the augmenting path. An interesting question is whether their approach yields an ε-approximation algorithm for the bottleneck matching or the root-mean-square Euclidean matching (i.e., minimize the sum of squares of Euclidean lengths of the matching edges). Agarwal and Sharathkumar [13] presented an algorithm that uses dynamic nearest neighbor data structure and obtains a $O((1/\delta)^{\log_2(1/\delta)})$-approximate matching in $O(n^{1+\delta})$ time. This is the first sub-quadratic $O(1)$-approximation algorithm in high dimensional spaces. For fixed dimensions, they also developed an $O((1/\varepsilon^{O(d)})n^{3/2} \log^5(n/\varepsilon))$-time deterministic algorithm that computes an ε-approximate bipartite matching.

Transportation. We now return to transportation problems with arbitrary integer supplies and demands, with U being the total demand (or supply). As mentioned earlier, the transportation problem can be formulated as an instance of minimum-cost flow in a complete bipartite graph. Using the currently best-known algorithm for minimum cost flow by Lee and Sidford [57], optimal transportation maps can be computed in $O(n^{5/2} \text{polylog}(n) \text{polylog}(U))$ time, assuming the demand and supply of each point is an integer and the total demand is U. Extending Vaidya's matching algorithm, Atkinson and Vaidya [24] had shown that the optimal transportation map can be computed in $O(n^2 \phi(n) \log(U))$ time, where $\phi(n)$ is again the update time for maintaining the weighted bichromatic closest pair. The above discussion implies that the optimal transportation map can be computed in $O(n^2 \text{polylog}(n) \log(U))$ time under any L_p metric in $\mathbb{R}^2$. Recently, Agarwal *et al.* [10] improved the running time to $O(n^2 \text{polylog}(n))$ by adapting a strongly polynomial-time minimum-cost flow algorithm by Orlin [64] for general graphs.

Sharathkumar and Agarwal [68] describe an algorithm that computes, in $O((n\sqrt{U} \log^2 n + U \log U)\phi(n) \log(\Delta U/\varepsilon))$ time, where Δ is the diameter of $R \cup B$, a transportation map that is optimal within an additive error of ε. Andoni *et al.* [18] describe a result similar to Indyk's [53] in that they can estimate the *cost* of the optimal transportation map within an ε factor in $n^{1+o_\varepsilon(1)}$ time (here, the constant in the little-o depends upon ε) assuming $U = n^{O(1)}$.

Agarwal *et al.* [10] describe two approximation algorithms for the transportation problem. The first is a Monte Carlo algorithm that computes in $O(n^{1+\varepsilon})$ time a transportation map with expected cost $O(\log^2(1/\varepsilon))$ of the optimal. This algorithm is an extension of the one by Agarwal and Varadarajan [16] for geometric bipartite matching, but a number of new ideas are needed to handle arbitrary demand and supply values. Their other algorithm gives an ε-approximation in $O(n^{3/2}\varepsilon^{-d} \text{polylog}(n) \text{polylog}(U))$ time. For this algorithm, they construct a graph of $O(n/\varepsilon^d)$ edges over $R \cup B$ for which the optimal transportation distance is at most $(1 + \varepsilon)\mu(\tau^*)$ and then run the minimum cost flow algorithm of Lee and Sidford [57].

4.2   Order Preserving Maps

Let $P = \langle p_1, \ldots, p_n \rangle$ and $Q = \langle q_1, \ldots, q_n \rangle$ be two sequences of points in $\mathbb{R}^d$. Recall, a *correspondence* between P and Q is a set of pairs $C \subseteq P \times Q$. A correspondence C is *monotone* if for any two pairs $(p_i, q_j), (p_{i'}, q_{j'}) \in C$ with $i' \geq i$, we have $j' \geq j$. The goal is to compute monotone correspondences that have certain properties. While one can imagine many criteria for computing monotone correspondences, we focus on three in this survey; minimizing the discrete Fréchet distance, dynamic time warping (DTW), and minimizing the geometric edit distance (GED). These criteria have been used in many applications such as speech recognition, molecular biology, and trajectory analysis.

Both the discrete Fréchet distance and DTW require C to contain every point in P and Q at least once. However, minimizing the Fréchet distance requires finding such a correspondence C that minimizes the maximum distance between p and q for any $(p, q) \in C$ while DTW minimizes the *sum* of distances. Formally, we define the discrete Fréchet distance as $\mathsf{dfr}(P, Q) = \min_C \max_{(p,q) \in C} \|p - q\|$ and the DTW distance as $\mathsf{dtw}(P, Q) = \min_C \sum_{(p,q) \in C} \|p - q\|$ where both minima are taken over all correspondences C covering points in P and Q. GED requires C to be a matching on P and Q—i.e. each point appears in exactly one pair—and it minimizes the sum of distances between matched points plus an additional gap penalty g for each point in P and Q outside of C. Formally, GED is defined as $\mathsf{ged}(P, Q) = \min_C \sum_{(p,q) \in C} \|p - q\| + g(2n - 2|C|)$ with the minimum taken over all matchings C.

Exact Algorithms. All three criteria can be computed in $O(n^2)$ time using straightforward dynamic programming algorithms, and these algorithms can be interpreted as computing a path through a weighted grid G on $V = \{(i, j) \mid 0 \leq i \leq n, 0 \leq j \leq n\}$ where, in general, each cell (i, j) has weight $\|p_i - q_j\|$. The exact paths allowed and their cost vary by criteria, but generally one takes steps from each position (i, j) to one of $(i + 1, j)$, $(i, j + 1)$, and $(i + 1, j + 1)$ while trying to minimize the maximum cell weight encountered for the discrete Fréchet distance or some function based on the sum of weights for DTW or GED. For the remainder of this section, we focus on attempts to improve the running times for computing these criteria both exactly and approximately.

Progress on exact algorithms with worst-case guarantees was only made recently. Agarwal *et al.* [4] described the first result, an $O(n^2 \log \log n / \log n)$ time algorithm for computing the discrete Fréchet distance. We will briefly describe a *decision procedure* for determining if $\mathsf{dfr}(P, Q) \leq \delta$, for a given parameter δ. Then, using a binary search, the actual Fréchet distance can be found. The main idea in the decision procedure is to partition the dynamic programming grid into *blocks* $B_0, B_1, \ldots$ containing $O(\log n)$ columns each. Then, in each block B_i, one needs to (implicitly) determine which of the cells in its rightmost column are *reachable* by a path through the grid touching cells of weight at most δ.

Subsequently, Gold and Sharir [48] described $O(n^2 \log \log \log(n) / \log \log(n))$ time algorithms for computing DTW and GED when $d = 1$. Their approach is similar to [4], but filling the entries of the right column of each B_i is now more challenging, thereby resulting in a somewhat larger running time. For each B_i, they encode the costs of all the paths between boundary cells as points in high dimensional Euclidean space and use a bichromatic dominating pairs reporting algorithm [32] to compute and encode the cheapest boundary-to-boundary paths.

Recent lower bound results suggest that no significantly faster algorithm can be developed for these problems. In particular, no $O(n^{2-\varepsilon})$-time algorithm exists, for constant ε, assuming the strong exponential time hypothesis (SETH) holds[4]. The strongest of these lower bounds was formulated by Abboud et al. [1].

Approximations. Bringmann and Mulzer [28] have shown that a strongly subquadratic ε-approximation for the discrete Fréchet distance is unlikely assuming SETH, and they have presented an α-approximation algorithm for this problem, for any $\alpha \in [1, n]$, that runs in $O(n \log n + n^2/\alpha)$ time. In contrast, near-linear-time ε-approximation algorthms have been proposed for discrete Fréchet distance and some other related cost functions by restricting the input to certain *natural families* of sequences. Here we focus on κ-packed curves[5]; see [21] for other types of well-behaved curves. Aronov et al. [21] described an ε-approximation for the discrete Fréchet distance that runs in $O((\kappa/\varepsilon)n \log n)$ time on κ-packed sequences (see [9,41]). The key component of their algorithm is an approximate decision procedure that given a value δ, correctly reports, in $O(\kappa n/\varepsilon)$ time, the discrete Fréchet distance to be less than δ if $\mathsf{dfr}(P, Q) < (1 - \varepsilon)\delta$ and correctly reports the distance to be greater than δ if $\mathsf{dfr}(P, Q) > (1 + \varepsilon)\delta$. The decision procedure accomplishes this by constructing simplified sequences P', Q' of P and Q respectively, and then reducing the problem to a reachability problem in a grid graph with $O(\kappa n/\varepsilon)$ cells. Agarwal et al. [9] obtained similar bounds for DTW and GED. Their algorithm computes ε-approximations of those criteria in $O((\kappa/\varepsilon)n \log n)$time for κ-packed curves by covering the dynamic programming grid described above with rectangles of similar weights. Then, using the properties of κ-packed curves, they observe that the overall number of boundary cells, appearing along all the rectangles, is relatively small.

4.3   Extensions

Our use of extrinsic cost functions in defining optimal transportation maps and monotone correspondences is useful for matching of shapes that lie in the same position within their ambient spaces. However, one can still use extrinsic costs to do rigid matching between shapes lying in different positions or even orientations in their ambient space by minimizing the measures under translation or rotation.

---

[4] SETH says that for all $0 < \delta < 1$, there is a $k > 2$ such that k-SAT requires $2^{\delta n}$ time to be solved in the worst-case.

[5] A point sequence is κ-packed if the length of its polygonal chain is at most $\kappa \cdot r$ within any ball of radius r.

One method of finding a good translation/rotation is the iterative closest point (ICP) method [25], wherein one iteratively computes a correspondence between two objects based on an extrinsic measure and then translates/rotates one of the objects to minimize the cost of the correspondence.

Intrinsic costs, mentioned in the beginning of the section, are more useful for applications like non-rigid matching of shapes. Notwithstanding a number of recent results in computer graphics and geometric modeling on methods for intrinsic cost functions—see [54] for a survey—very few combinatorial algorithms are known for them. For example, consider the problem of computing the Gromov-Hausdorff distance between two metric spaces $X_1 = (X_1, \rho_1)$ and $X_2 = (X_2, \rho_2)$, defined as

$$\frac{1}{2} \inf_C \sup_{(x_1,x_2),(x_1',x_2') \in C} |\rho_1(x_1, x_1') - \rho_2(x_2, x_2')|,$$

where the infimum is taken over all correspondences $C \subseteq X_1 \times X_2$ containing each $x_1 \in X_1$ and $x_2 \in X_2$ at least once. Gromov-Hausdorff distance is used in applications such as matching of deformable shapes [29, 60]. The currently known results concerning approximability of computation include a proof that it is NP-Hard to approximate this measure within a factor less than 3, when X_1 and X_2 are metric trees [8, 67], and an $O(\min\{n, \sqrt{rn}\})$-approximation algorithm for that case where r is the ratio of the longest edge length in both trees to the shortest edge length [8]. This problem is an instance of low-distortion embedding between two metric spaces, which has been extensively studied; see [59, Chap. 15] for a survey.

5   Discussion

In this survey, we reviewed recent progress on a few geometric optimization problems, namely, geometric set cover and hitting set, geometric independent set, and computing maps between a pair of point sets. Because of lack of space, there are several major developments in geometric optimization that we did not cover here. Perhaps the most significant among them is the PTAS for Euclidean TSP by Arora [22] and by Mitchell [61]. Their techniques—randomly shifted quadtrees and guillotine subdivisions—have been successfully applied to many geometric optimization problems and have had a profound impact on the field. See [23] for a survey.

Another technique that has become quite popular over the last two decades is the *coreset* based approach. Roughly speaking, a coreset is a small subset of the input set where an optimal solution to a problem on the coreset is a good approximation of the optimal solution on the overall set. Surprisingly, fast algorithms exist for computing coresets for a large class of geometric optimization problems whose sizes depend only on the quality of approximation and not on the input size. See surveys [3, 66].

Other widely-studied topics include optimal path planning, curve/surface simplification, clustering, and network-design problems.

Acknowledgements. We thank Timothy Chan, Sariel Har-Peled, and Micha Sharir for their helpful comments.

References

1. Abboud, A., Hansen, T.D., Williams, V.V., Williams, R.: Simulating branching programs with edit distance and friends: or: a polylog shaved is a lower bound made. In: Proceedings of the 48th Annual ACM Symposium on Theory Computing, pp. 375–388 (2016)
2. Adamaszek, A., Wiese, A.: Approximation schemes for maximum weight independent set of rectangles. In: Proceedings of the 54th IEEE Annual Symposium on Foundations of Computer Science, pp. 400–409 (2013)
3. Agarwal, P.K., Har-Peled, S., Varadarajan, K.R.: Geometricapproximation via coresets. In: Goodman, J.E., Pach, J., Welzl, E. (eds.) Combinatorial and Computational Geometry, pp. 1–30. Cambridge University Press, New York (2005)
4. Agarwal, P.K., Avraham, R.B., Kaplan, H., Sharir, M.: Computing the discrete fréchet distance in subquadratic time. SIAM J. Comput. **43**, 429–449 (2014)
5. Agarwal, P.K., Efrat, A., Sharir, M.: Vertical decomposition of shallow levels in 3-dimensional arrangements and its applications. SIAM J. Comput. **29**(3), 912–953 (1999)
6. Agarwal, P.K., Ezra, E., Ganjugunte, S.K.: Efficient sensor placement for surveillance problems. In: Krishnamachari, B., Suri, S., Heinzelman, W., Mitra, U. (eds.) DCOSS 2009. LNCS, vol. 5516, pp. 301–314. Springer, Heidelberg (2009). https://doi.org/10.1007/978-3-642-02085-8_22
7. Agarwal, P.K., Ezra, E., Sharir, M.: Near-linear approximation algorithms for geometric hitting sets. Algorithmica **63**(1–2), 1–25 (2012)
8. Agarwal, P.K., Fox, K., Nath, A., Sidiropoulos, A., Wang, Y.: Computing the Gromov-Hausdorff distance for metric trees. In: Proceedings of 26th International Symposium on Algorithms and Computation, pp. 529–540 (2015)
9. Agarwal, P.K., Fox, K., Pan, J., Ying, R.: Approximating dynamic time warping and edit distance for a pair of point sequences. In: 32nd International Symposium on Computational Geometry, pp. 6:1–6:16 (2016)
10. Agarwal, P.K., Fox, K., Panigrahi, D., Varadarajan, K., Xiao, A.: Efficient algorithms for the geometric transportation problem. In: 33rd International Symposium on Computational Geometry (2017, to appear)
11. Agarwal, P.K., Mustafa, N.H.: Independent set of intersection graphs of convex objects in 2D. Comput. Geom. **34**(2), 83–95 (2006)
12. Agarwal, P.K., Pan, J.: Near-linear algorithms for geometric hitting sets and set covers. In: Proceedings of the 30th Annual Symposium on Computational Geometry, pp. 271–280 (2014)
13. Agarwal, P.K., Sharathkumar, R.: Approximation algorithms for bipartite matchingwith metric and geometric costs. In: Proceedings of the 46th Annual ACM Symposium on Theory of Computing, pp. 555–564 (2014)
14. Agarwal, P.K., Sharir, M.: Algorithmic techniques for geometric optimization. In: van Leeuwen, J. (ed.) Computer Science Today. LNCS, vol. 1000, pp. 234–253. Springer, Heidelberg (1995). https://doi.org/10.1007/BFb0015247
15. Agarwal, P.K., Sharir, M.: Efficient algorithms for geometric optimization. ACM Comput. Surv. **30**(4), 412–458 (1998)

16. Agarwal, P.K., Varadarajan, K.R.: A near-linear constant-factor approximation for Euclidean bipartite matching? In: Proceedings of the 20th Annual Symposium on Computational Geometry, pp. 247–252 (2004)
17. Alt, H., Guibas, L.J.: Discrete geometric shapes: matching, interpolation, and approximation. In: Sack, J.R., Urrutia, J. (eds.) Handbook of Computational Geometry, pp. 121 – 153. North-Holland, Amsterdam (2000)
18. Andoni, A., Nikolov, A., Onak, K., Yaroslavtsev, G.: Parallel algorithms for geometric graph problems. In: Proceedings of the 46th ACM Symposium on Theory of Computing, pp. 574–583 (2014)
19. Aronov, B., de Berg, M., Ezra, E., Sharir, M.: Improved bounds for the union of locally fat objects in the plane. SIAM J. Comput. **43**(2), 543–572 (2014)
20. Aronov, B., Ezra, E., Sharir, M.: Small-size ε-nets for axis-parallel rectangles and boxes. SIAM J. Comput. **39**, 3248–3282 (2010)
21. Aronov, B., Har-Peled, S., Knauer, C., Wang, Y., Wenk, C.: Fréchet distance for curves, revisited. In: Azar, Y., Erlebach, T. (eds.) ESA 2006. LNCS, vol. 4168, pp. 52–63. Springer, Heidelberg (2006). https://doi.org/10.1007/11841036_8
22. Arora, S.: Polynomial time approximation schemes for euclidean traveling salesman and other geometric problems. J. ACM **45**(5), 753–782 (1998)
23. Arora, S.: Approximation schemes for NP-hard geometric optimization problems: a survey. Math. Program. **97**(1–2), 43–69 (2003)
24. Atkinson, D.S., Vaidya, P.M.: Using geometry to solve the transportation problem in the plane. Algorithmica **13**(5), 442–461 (1995)
25. Besl, P.J., McKay, N.D.: A method for registration of 3-D shapes. IEEE Trans. Pattern Anal. Mach. Intell. **14**, 239–256 (1992)
26. Bonnet, É., Miltzow, T.: An approximation algorithm for the art gallery problem. CoRR abs/1607.05527 (2016). http://arxiv.org/abs/1607.05527
27. Bonnet, É., Miltzow, T.: Parameterized hardness of art gallery problems. In: 24th Annual European Symposium on Algorithms, vol. 57, pp. 19:1–19:17 (2016)
28. Bringmann, K., Mulzer, W.: Approximability of the discrete fréchet distance. J. Comput. Geom. **7**(2), 46–76 (2016)
29. Bronstein, A.M., Bronstein, M.M., Kimmel, R.: Efficient computation of isometry-invariant distances between surfaces. SIAM J. Sci. Comput. **28**(5), 1812–1836 (2006)
30. Chalermsook, P., Chuzhoy, J.: Maximum independent set of rectangles. In: Proceedings of the 20th Annual ACM-SIAM Symposium on Discrete Algorithms, pp. 892–901 (2009)
31. Chan, T.M.: Polynomial-time approximation schemes for packing and piercing fat objects. J. Algorithms **46**(2), 178–189 (2003)
32. Chan, T.M.: All-pairs shortest paths with real weights in $O(n^3/\log n)$ time. Algorithmica **50**(2), 236–243 (2008)
33. Chan, T.M., Grant, E.: Exact algorithms and apx-hardness results for geometric packing and covering problems. Comput. Geom. **47**(2), 112–124 (2014)
34. Chan, T.M., Grant, E., Könemann, J., Sharpe, M.: Weighted capacitated, priority, and geometric set cover via improved quasi-uniform sampling. In: Proceedings of the 23rd ACM-SIAM Symposium on Discrete Algorithms, pp. 1576–1585 (2012)
35. Chan, T.M., Har-Peled, S.: Approximation algorithms for maximum independent set of pseudo-disks. Disc. Comput. Geom. **48**, 373–392 (2012)
36. Chekuri, C., Clarkson, K.L., Har-Peled, S.: On the set multicover problem in geometric settings. ACM Trans. Algorithms **9**(1), 9:1–9:17 (2012)
37. Cheong, O., Efrat, A., Har-Peled, S.: Finding a guard that sees most and a shop that sells most. Disc. Comput. Geom. **37**(4), 545–563 (2007)

38. Chuzhoy, J., Ene, A.: On approximating maximum independent set of rectangles. In: Proceedings of the IEEE 57th Annual Symposium on Foundations of Computer Science, pp. 820–829 (2016)
39. Clarkson, K.L., Varadarajan, K.R.: Improved approximation algorithms for geometric set cover. Disc. Comput. Geom. **37**(1), 43–58 (2007)
40. Dinur, I., Steurer, D.: Analytical approach to parallel repetition. In: Proceedings of the 46th Annual ACM Symposium on Theory of Computing, pp. 624–633 (2014)
41. Driemel, A., Har-Peled, S., Wenk, C.: Approximating the Fréchet distance for realistic curves in near linear time. Disc. Comput. Geom. **48**(1), 94–127 (2012)
42. Efrat, A., Itai, A., Katz, M.J.: Geometry helps in bottleneck matching and related problems. Algorithmica **31**(1), 1–28 (2001)
43. Eidenbenz, S., Stamm, C., Widmayer, P.: Inapproximability results for guarding polygons and terrains. Algorithmica **31**(1), 79–113 (2001)
44. Even, G., Rawitz, D., Shahar, S.: Hitting sets when the VC-dimension is small. Inf. Process. Lett. **95**(2), 358–362 (2005)
45. Feige, U.: Approximating maximum clique by removing subgraphs. SIAM J. Discret. Math. **18**(2), 219–225 (2004)
46. Fox, J., Pach, J.: Computing the independence number of intersection graphs. In: Proceedings of the 22nd Annual ACM-SIAM Symposium on Discrete Algorithms, pp. 1161–1165 (2011)
47. Fredman, M.L., Tarjan, R.E.: Fibonacci heaps and their uses in improved network optimization algorithms. J. ACM **34**(3), 596–615 (1987)
48. Gold, O., Sharir, M.: Dynamic time warping and geometric edit distance: Breaking the quadratic barrier. CoRR abs/1607.05994 (2016)
49. Har-Peled, S.: Geometric Approximation Algorithms. American Mathematical Society, Boston (2011)
50. Har-Peled, S.: Quasi-polynomial time approximation scheme for sparse subsets of polygons. In: Proceedings of the 30th Annual Symposium on Computational Geometry, pp. 120–129 (2014)
51. Har-Peled, S., Quanrud, K.: Approximation algorithms for polynomial-expansion and low-density graphs. In: Bansal, N., Finocchi, I. (eds.) ESA 2015. LNCS, vol. 9294, pp. 717–728. Springer, Heidelberg (2015). https://doi.org/10.1007/978-3-662-48350-3_60
52. Hochbaum, D.S. (ed.): Approximation Algorithms for NP-Hard Problems. PWS Publishing Co., Boston (1997)
53. Indyk, P.: A near linear time constant factor approximation for Euclidean bichromatic matching (cost). In: Proceedings of the 18th Annual ACM-SIAM Symposium on Discrete Algorithms, pp. 39–42 (2007)
54. van Kaick, O., Zhang, H., Hamarneh, G., Cohen-Or, D.: A survey on shape correspondence. Comput. Graph. Forum **30**(6), 1681–1707 (2011)
55. Kaplan, H., Mulzer, W., Roditty, L., Seiferth, P., Sharir, M.: Dynamic planar Voronoi diagrams for general distance functions and their algorithmic applications. In: Proceedings of the 28th Annual ACM-SIAM Symposium on Discrete Algorithms, pp. 2495–2504 (2017)
56. Karp, R.M.: Reducibility among combinatorial problems. In: Miller, R.E., Thatcher, J.W., Bohlinger, J.D. (eds.) Complexity of Computer Computations, pp. 85–103. Springer, Boston (1972). https://doi.org/10.1007/978-1-4684-2001-2_9
57. Lee, Y.T., Sidford, A.: Path finding methods for linear programming: solving linear programs in Õ(vrank) iterations and faster algorithms for maximum flow. In: Proceedings of the 55th Annual IEEE Symposium on Foundations of Computer Science, pp. 424–433 (2014)

58. Marcotte, O., Suri, S.: Fast matching algorithms for points on a polygon. SIAM J. Comput. **20**, 405–422 (1991)
59. Matoušek, J.: Lectures on Discrete Geometry. Springer, New York (2002). https://doi.org/10.1007/978-1-4613-0039-7
60. Mémoli, F., Sapiro, G.: A theoretical and computational framework for isometry invariant recognition of point cloud data. Found. Comput. Math. **5**(3), 313–347 (2005)
61. Mitchell, J.S.B.: Guillotine subdivisions approximate polygonal subdivisions: a simple polynomial-time approximation scheme for geometric TSP, k-MST, and related problems. SIAM J. Comput. **28**(4), 1298–1309 (1999)
62. Mustafa, N.H., Raman, R., Ray, S.: Settling the APX-hardness status for geometric set cover. In: Proceedings of the 55th IEEE Annual Symposium on Foundations of Computer Science, pp. 541–550 (2014)
63. Mustafa, N.H., Ray, S.: Improved results on geometric hitting set problems. Disc. Comput. Geom. **44**(4), 883–895 (2010)
64. Orlin, J.B.: A faster strongly polynomial minimum cost flow algorithm. Oper. Res. **41**(2), 338–350 (1993)
65. Pach, J., Tardos, G.: Tight lower bounds for the size of epsilon-nets. J. Am. Math. Soc. **26**, 645–658 (2013)
66. Phillips, J.M.: Coresets and sketches. CoRR abs/1601.00617 (2016)
67. Schmiedl, F.: Computational aspects of the Gromov-Hausdorff distance and its application in non-rigid shape matching. Disc. Comput. Geom. **57**(4), 854–880 (2017)
68. Sharathkumar, R., Agarwal, P.K.: Algorithms for the transportation problem in geometric settings. In: Proceedings of the 23rd Annual ACM-SIAM Symposium on Discrete Algorithms, pp. 306–317 (2012)
69. Sharathkumar, R., Agarwal, P.K.: A near-linear time ε-approximation algorithm for geometric bipartite matching. In: Proceedings of the 44th Annual ACM Symposium on Theory of Computing, pp. 385–394 (2012)
70. Urrutia, J.: Art gallery and illumination problems. In: Handbook of Computational Geometry, pp. 973–1027. North-Holland (2000)
71. Vaidya, P.M.: Geometry helps in matching. SIAM J. Comput. **18**(6), 1201–1225 (1989)
72. Varadarajan, K.R.: Weighted geometric set cover via quasi-uniform sampling. In: Proceedings of the 42nd ACM Symposium on Theory of Computing, pp. 641–648 (2010)
73. Varadarajan, K.R., Agarwal, P.K.: Approximation algorithms for bipartite and non-bipartite matching in the plane. In: Proceedings of the 10th Annual ACM-SIAM Symposium on Discrete Algorithms, pp. 805–814 (1999)
74. Vazirani, V.V.: Approximation Algorithms. Springer, Heidelberg (2001). https://doi.org/10.1007/978-3-662-04565-7
75. Villani, C.: Optimal Transport: Old and New, vol. 338. Springer, Heidelberg (2008). https://doi.org/10.1007/978-3-540-71050-9
76. Williamson, D.P., Shmoys, D.B.: The Design of Approximation Algorithms. Cambridge University Press, Cambridge (2011)

10 Reasons to Get Interested in Graph Drawing

Carla Binucci[1], Ulrik Brandes[2], Tim Dwyer[3], Martin Gronemann[4],
Reinhard von Hanxleden[5], Marc van Kreveld[6], Petra Mutzel[7(✉)],
Marcus Schaefer[8], Falk Schreiber[9], and Bettina Speckmann[10]

[1] University of Perugia, Perugia, Italy
`carla.binucci@unipg.it`
[2] ETH Zurich, Zurich, Switzerland
`ulrik.brandes@gess.ethz.ch`
[3] Monash University, Melbourne, Australia
`tim.dwyer@monash.edu`
[4] University of Cologne, Cologne, Germany
`gronemann@informatik.uni-koeln.de`
[5] Kiel University, Kiel, Germany
`rvh@informatik.uni-kiel.de`
[6] Utrecht University, Utrecht, The Netherlands
`m.j.vankreveld@uu.nl`
[7] TU Dortmund University, Dortmund, Germany
`petra.mutzel@cs.tu-dortmund.de`
[8] DePaul University, Chicago, USA
`MSchaefer@cdm.depaul.edu`
[9] University of Konstanz, Konstanz, Germany
`falk.schreiber@uni-konstanz.de`
[10] TU Eindhoven, Eindhoven, The Netherlands
`b.speckmann@tue.nl`

Abstract. This is an invitation to the research area of graph drawing. It encompasses basic research such as graph theory, complexity theory, data structures, and graph algorithms as well as applied research such as software libraries, implementations, and applications. Application domains include areas within computer science (e. g., information visualization, software engineering, model-based design, automated cartography) as well as outside (e. g., molecular biology and the social sciences). A selection of results demonstrates the influence of graph drawing on other areas and vice versa.

Keywords: Graph drawing · Visualization · Complexity
Computational geometry · Software engineering

1 Introduction

The ultimate goal of graph drawing is to construct suitable visualizations of graphs and networks. While important contributions date back much further,

© Springer Nature Switzerland AG 2019
B. Steffen and G. Woeginger (Eds.): Computing and Software Science, LNCS 10000, pp. 85–104, 2019.
https://doi.org/10.1007/978-3-319-91908-9_6

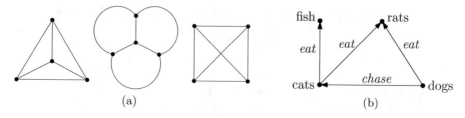

Fig. 1. (a) The graph K_4 in three different styles: planar straight-line, planar with circular arcs, and non-planar straight-line. (b) Graph with vertex and edge labels.

institutionalization began with an *International Work Meeting on Graph Drawing* in 1992. The first published proceedings appeared as *Lecture Notes in Computer Science* vol. 894 in 1994 and have appeared in this series ever since.[1] From the very beginning, the area has featured a unique combination of basic research in, for instance, topological graph theory, complexity, data structures, computational geometry, and optimization, research in various application domains, and practical research on implementations, tools, and usage.

We highlight ten characteristic topics of basic and applied research in graph drawing to incentivize readers to learn more about the area. A comprehensive overview is given in the *Handbook of Graph Drawing and Visualization* [80], and some open problems have been compiled by Brandenburg *et al.* [16].

2   Basic Research

The most common visual representation of a graph is a two-dimensional *drawing* in which points in the plane represent vertices and curves connecting them represent edges.

2.1   Computational Geometry

When drawing a graph we need to give the vertices coordinates and the edges shapes. Computational geometry is the field within algorithms research that is concerned with coordinates and shapes. Most of the aesthetic criteria that assess the quality of a drawing of a graph are geometric, and techniques from computational geometry can be used to compute them.

We call a graph *planar* if it can be drawn in the plane without edge crossings. Suppose we are given a planar straight-line drawing of a graph (see Fig. 1). Its *angular resolution* is the smallest angle in the drawing over any two edges incident to the same vertex. The *graph resolution* is the maximum ratio between the longest edge length and the shortest distance between distinct, non-incident features (two vertices, or a vertex and a non-incident edge). Both resolutions can be computed in linear time.

---

[1] See http://graphdrawing.org/ for a complete list.

The *area requirement* of a graph is the size of the integer grid needed to embed the graph so that all vertices lie on grid points. Commonly, the graph is planar and a planar drawing on the grid is required. The algorithm of de Fraysseix *et al.* [35] shows that any planar graph can be drawn planarly on the $2n - 4$ by $n - 2$ grid (see Fig. 2(b)). This bound was improved by Schnyder [71], who shows that an $n - 2$ by $n - 2$ grid suffices. It is also possible to use quality measures on faces. Since the "best" shape of a face is convex, one may wonder which planar graphs allow drawings where all faces are convex. Chrobak and Kant [24] showed that every triconnected planar graph allows a drawing where all bounded faces are convex. The vertices are chosen on an $n - 2$ by $n - 2$ grid.

The angular resolution of planar graph drawings can often be improved if one is willing to use curved edges; angular resolution must now be defined using tangents of curves at incident vertices. *Lombardi drawings* are plane drawings where all edges are circular and the angular resolution at every vertex is perfect [30]. Not all planar graphs admit a Lombardi drawing. Other variants from the straight-line edge style are edges with bends and thick edges. Especially the former is studied extensively in graph drawing.

For non-planar graphs, intersection angles of edges are important for readable, aesthetic graph drawings. This observation has led to the introduction of right-angle crossing drawings [29] and large angle crossing drawings [37] of nonplanar graphs. How different drawing styles and aesthetic measures relate was investigated by Hoffmann *et al.* [44]. Figure 1(a) shows a K_4 drawing in three different styles, leading to a different optimal angular resolution in each style.

Often drawings also need labels, see Fig. 1(b). Automated label placement has been studied extensively in various research fields. To compute placements, text labels are usually represented by a rectangular bounding box. Labels should be placed close to the features they refer to, and they should not intersect each other, nor any other features. In this setting, label placement can be seen as an optimization problem related to packing; for an overview of results, see [54].

2.2   Graph Theory: Canonical Orderings

One of the most intuitive ways to draw a planar graph by hand is to add elements (vertices, edges, faces, etc.) of the graph in an incremental manner to an already existing drawing. This drawing usually satisfies certain properties that serve as an invariant during this process.

In 1988 de Fraysseix *et al.* [35] took this idea and introduced the so-called *canonical orderings* for maximal planar graphs (graphs to which no edge can be added without losing planarity). They used this order of the vertices in an algorithm to draw every maximal planar graph in a planar straight-line style on a grid of quadratic size (see Sect. 2.1 and Fig. 2). The canonical ordering as described in [35] requires the graph to be maximal planar. In case the input does not satisfy this constraint, one may augment it by simply triangulating it. This step, however, is not advisable for certain applications. A more general variant for triconnected planar graphs has been given by Kant [48]. His definition differs from the original one in that it uses an ordered partition of the vertices instead

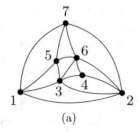
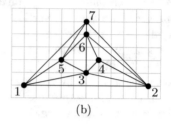

(a)   (b)

Fig. 2. (a) Example for a canonical ordering of a maximal planar graph and (b) incremental construction of a planar straight-line grid drawing using the algorithm in [35].

of a vertex ordering. A more detailed description of a linear-time algorithm to obtain such an ordering is given by Badent *et al.* [5]. They also show that a canonical ordering induces one in the dual of a triconnected planar graph.

Kant's definition has found numerous applications in graph drawing. Although the initial purpose was to draw planar graphs, it has been successfully applied to other graph-related problems. For example, Chiang *et al.* [23] use it to encode planar graphs with as few bits as possible. See [5] for an extensive list of applications.

Gronemann [39] suggested orderings for directed planar graphs based on *st*-orderings. This allows one to use techniques for undirected graphs to construct *upward planar drawings* (all arcs point upward). For undirected triconnected non-planar graphs, Schmidt [70] showed how to efficiently obtain a *Mondshein sequence*, a special non-separating ear decomposition similar to canonical orderings. With this result, Schmidt is able to improve the runtime to linear time for several algorithms, e.g., for finding independent spanning trees in triconnected graphs, which is the preprocessing step for querying internally disjoint paths.

2.3   Complexity: A Real Analogue of NP in Graph Drawing

In this section, we give some intuition for the fact that several problems in graph drawing with a geometric flavor like the rectilinear crossing number are computationally different from NP-complete problems like the crossing number.

The *existential theory of the reals*, ETR, is the set of all true, existential statements over the real numbers, such as $(\exists x, y)[xy = 1 \land x^2 + y^2 = 1]$, stating that the hyperbola intersects the unit circle, or, equivalently, the set of real satisfiable formulas like $[xy = 1 \land x^2 + y^2 = 1]$. ETR is very expressive, particularly for graph drawing problems involving straight lines, convexity, or metric concepts. Take $\overline{cr}$, the *rectilinear crossing number*. Deciding whether a graph has a straight-line drawing with k crossings can be phrased in ETR. Since ETR is decidable in polynomial space, we can compute $\overline{cr}$, at least in principle. A closer study reveals that many problems decidable via ETR are computationally equivalent to it; this implies that solving them is likely hard, much harder than NP-complete problems. Similarly to NP, we can introduce a complexity class

$\exists\mathbb{R}$, the real satisfiability problem, as the set of problems which computationally reduce to ETR. Returning to the $\overline{cr}$-problem: Bienstock [9] showed that it is equivalent to ETR, so $\exists\mathbb{R}$-complete. Since ETR encodes NP-complete problems, this also implies that computing $\overline{cr}$ is NP-hard.

While ETR, like satisfiability for NP, can serve as a starting point to show $\exists\mathbb{R}$-completeness, there are problems closer to graph drawing that can fulfill this role. The two most fundamental ones are *stretchability of pseudoline arrangements*, deciding the question whether a pseudoline arrangement is isomorphic to a straight-line arrangement, a result due to Mnëv, and its projective dual, the realizability of a *chirotope* by a pointset. A promising third problem has been added to the list recently, realizability of an *allowable sequence* [45]. These three problems can serve as the starting point for reductions, like the Clique or Independent set problem for NP.

Intersection graphs, such as *string graphs* (Jordan arcs), and *interval graphs* (intervals on a line), can often be recognized in NP, but convexity seems to escalate the complexity to $\exists\mathbb{R}$. We know that recognizing intersection graphs of line segments (one of the oldest $\exists\mathbb{R}$-results, due to Kratochvíl and Matoušek [53]), rays, convex sets, disks and unit disks is $\exists\mathbb{R}$-complete. There are further $\exists\mathbb{R}$-complete problems in simultaneous graph drawing, visibility graphs, and metric problems such as unit distance and matchstick graphs, Delaunay triangulations, and problems related to angles and slopes. See [53,59] for a survey.

We conclude with some candidates for $\exists\mathbb{R}$-completeness: Does the rectilinear crossing number problem, $\overline{cr}(G) \leq k$, remain $\exists\mathbb{R}$-complete for fixed k? Is calculating the geometric thickness of a graph, or its maximum rectilinear crossing number $\exists\mathbb{R}$-complete? How hard is it to decide whether a graph has a straight-line drawing in which certain edges have to be free of crossings? For puzzle fans: How hard is it to tell whether a set of puzzle pieces can be placed into a given frame without overlapping (see Nagata's Arrow Puzzle)?

2.4 Data Structures: SPQR-Tree

Decomposition techniques often lead to efficient approaches for solving graph problems. The idea of using a decomposition in triconnected components goes back to MacLane (1937) and Tutte (1966) and has been used early in the graph algorithm literature (e. g., Bienstock and Monma [10]), but the methods became much easier using the data structure of SPQR-trees.

The data structure of SPQR-trees was suggested by Di Battista and Tamassia [26] in the context of graph drawing to represent the triconnected decomposition of a biconnected graph using series parts (S-nodes), parallel parts (P-nodes), and triconnected parts (R-nodes). Q-nodes denote single edges. Every node comes with a skeleton describing the whole graph with some parts contracted to an edge. For example, the skeleton of an S-node is a cycle, the skeleton of a P-node is a pair of vertices with some parallel edges, and the skeleton of an R-node is a triconnected component. The data structure combines these nodes in form of a tree (see Fig. 3). Since for planar graphs the skeletons are also planar, a combinatorial embedding of all the skeletons uniquely describes a planar embedding

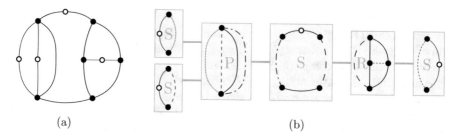

(a)   (b)

Fig. 3. (a) A biconnected graph and (b) its SPQR-tree with the skeletons (Q-nodes skipped). The edges in the skeletons represent either an original edge (solid) or a larger part of the graph (dashed, dotted).

of the whole graph and vice versa. Hence, SPQR-trees can be used to represent the set of all planar embeddings of a biconnected graph. This data structure can be computed in linear time and linear space [40].

SPQR-trees are applicable to problems that are easier to solve for triconnected graphs than for non-triconnected ones. This is particularly true for problems in which combinatorial embeddings play a crucial role. Another example are problems that can be solved in linear time for the class of series-parallel graphs. This data structure also works for problems in which divide-and-conquer methods work well.

SPQR-trees have been used heavily within the graph drawing community, e.g., to elegantly solve variations of planarity testing problems such as on-line, cluster or upward planarity testing, and to efficiently compute layouts (e.g., bend minimization and symmetric planar drawings). A survey on the SPQR tree data structure and its applications can be found in [63].

Outside graph drawing, SPQR-trees have been used for many different graph problems, e.g., for maintaining a minimum spanning tree and for solving triangulation problems. In computer-aided design they are important for solving layout decomposition problems in general multiple patterning lithography [87]. In business process management, the data structure has been used for developing process models and analyzing the control flow of business processes (e.g., [83]). SPQR-trees have also been used outside Computer Science: in electrical engineering for the generation of wave digital structures from reference circuits [34] and in theoretical physics for reducing Feynman integrals in perturbative quantum field theory [58].

3   Applications

3.1   Information Visualization

Information visualization is the research field concerned with all aspects of creating interactive visuals for *abstract* data. Abstract data are any data *without* inherent geometry: whether multivariate *tabular* data or—the chief concern of this article—relational data, where objects (which may have their own

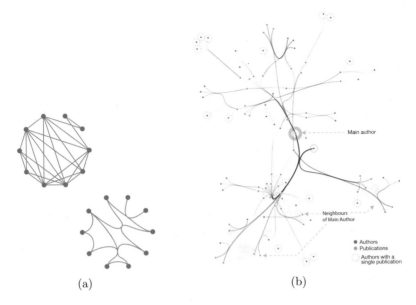

Fig. 4. Investigations of confluent drawing by a graph drawing paper and later by an information visualization paper. (a) Flat and outerplanar strict confluent drawings of the same graph by Eppstein *et al.* [33]. (b) Bach *et al.* [3] apply confluent drawing to a large authorship network.

attributes) are related to one another in various ways. The latter, of course, are networks or graphs. Network visualization has always been a core topic of information visualization. Papers on this topic presented at information visualization forums routinely cite—and are heavily inspired by—material originally presented at graph drawing forums, and vice-versa.

Speaking generally, the graph drawing community tends to be rigorous about developing efficient and correct algorithms and the theory to support these. In information visualization, the focus is more on applications and the human factors or usability of the methods. Just one such example is the idea of *confluent* drawings of graphs in which the edges are drawn in bundles to reduce clutter but in such a way that their connectivity remains clear (see Fig. 4). Confluent drawing was introduced in the graph drawing community first [28] primarily as a theoretical topic. More recently, the practical applications of this idea have been explored at InfoVis [3].

Another area where early work in graph drawing had significant impact upon information visualisation is *force-directed* layout. Graph drawers were the first to make this algorithm scale to large graphs with, for example, the Barnes-Hut cell opening criteria used in physics particle simulations by Tunkelang [82] and the first to make interactive, animated versions for online graph layout [31]. These ideas were later chosen for the force-directed layout implementation in D3, one of the most highly cited and influential InfoVis papers ever [15].

It is also interesting to consider the graph drawing approach to tree comparison, which has focused on crossing minimisation problems, e. g., Tanglegrams. By contrast, an early information visualization approach focused on interaction, e. g., Tree Juxtaposer [62]. Another major theme of tree visualization at InfoVis has been treemaps [76]. This design, developed by InfoVis researchers, inspired graph drawers to tackle the much harder problem of creating space-filling drawings of directed acyclic graphs at Graph Drawing [81]. In summary (and in keeping with the subject of trees), it is an extremely healthy cross-pollination that occurs between these two communities, helping both to grow and prosper.

3.2   Software Engineering

The field of software engineering concerns all the phases of the lifecycle of a software system: design, development, implementation, testing, and maintenance. Each of these phases may involve a large amount of data, thus requiring the use of visualization techniques to help software engineers in carrying out their job. Since the relationships and the interplay between data, objects, procedures, and architectural components of an architectural system are usually modeled as graphs, special attention has been devoted to the study of algorithms and user interfaces for the visualization of graphs in the scientific literature.

In the following we describe interconnections between software engineering and graph drawing. Early works that used graph drawing techniques focused on the automatic layout of Entity-Relationship diagrams [6] and data flow diagrams [7]. These papers are milestones since they are among the first applications of graph drawing to computer-aided software engineering and they devise a new strategy to incrementally build a graph layout. This strategy, called the *topology-shape-metrics (TSM)* approach, has been formally defined and made popular by a work of Tamassia [79] and it aims to compute a drawing of the graph in an *orthogonal* style (vertices are drawn as points or rectangles and edges are drawn as chains of horizontal and vertical segments).

The object-oriented programming paradigm became extremely popular in the late'90s and motivated the introduction of the *Unified Modeling Language (UML)*, a universal formalism intended to visually describe the architecture and the behavior of a software system at different levels of abstractions. In particular, *class diagrams* are among the most adopted types of UML diagrams. They are based on the use of graphs and are helpful in the design of a software architecture in terms of its classes (vertices of the graph) and their relationships (edges of the graph). These class diagrams required new graph drawing research. One of the main challenges for automatic visualization of a class diagram is to clearly show different types of relationships that such a diagram can have: some relationships (e. g., generalizations) correspond to oriented edges that describe the hierarchical structure (inheritance) of the classes, while other types of relationships correspond to non-oriented edges. Moreover, labels (both for the vertices and for the edges) [13,50] and clustering information (to model containment relations) [27,42] must be taken into account in the layout.

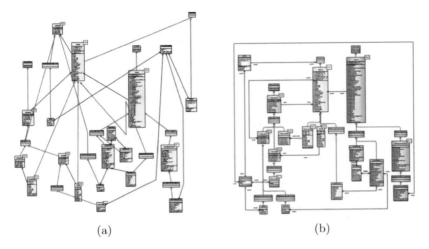

(a)   (b)

Fig. 5. Two layouts of the same UML class diagram taken from [41]: (a) an industrial layout; (b) a layout based on the extended TSM approach (OGDF).

Several techniques have been proposed in the graph drawing literature to automatically visualize a class diagram. The layouts computed by the first commercial tools were mainly based on the well-known *layered* approach of Sugiyama *et al.* [78], without distinguishing between directed and undirected edges. According to this approach vertices are suitably distributed on different horizontal layers. Seemann [75] was the first to propose a modified version of the layered approach, considering separately directed and undirected edges.

The approaches in [32,41] proposed new drawing algorithms that exploit and extend the TSM approach in order to handle *mixed* graphs (i. e., graphs with both directed and undirected edges), vertices of prescribed size, and clusters of vertices. These algorithms produce significant improvements with respect to the layered approach (see Fig. 5) and their implementations are integrated in software libraries and systems, like OGDF and the yFiles library. Alternative techniques have been described for dealing with mixed graphs [12,14], vertices of prescribed size, and orthogonal drawings with prescribed clusters of vertices (see [80]).

We finally mention that some tools for software documentation integrate graph visualization facilities to automatically generate class diagrams of object-oriented software from annotated source code. Among them, Doxygen[2] is widely used and adopts the layered drawing algorithm available in the GraphViz library.

3.3   Model-Based Design

Model-based design (MBD), also referred to as *model-based development* or *model-driven engineering*, is a design methodology where some artefact, referred

---

[2] http://www.stack.nl/~dimitri/doxygen/.

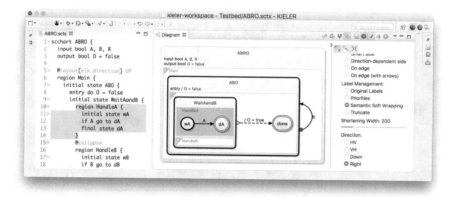

Fig. 6. An SCChart modeled with KIELER. The graphical view (center) is synthesized automatically from the textual **ABRO**.sctx model (left). *Layout directives* (starting with @) govern the filtering and drawing, e.g., region **HandleA** is collapsed. The view also helps to navigate in the model; here, the user has clicked in region **HandleB**, which selects the corresponding part in the text. The control panel (right) gives further options on layout and filtering, concerning for example the shortening of labels.

to as *system under development* (SUD), is created based on some model(s) of it. This model (or collection of models) is initially rather abstract, concentrating on *what* the SUD is supposed to do, and only in later—possibly automated—development stages it is specified *how* the SUD does what it does. The models tend to use a graphical instead of a textual syntax; as Schätz *et al.* put it, "Intuitively, model-based development means to use diagrams instead of code" [69]. As argued in this section, automated graph drawing is not as systematically employed in MBD as it could and should be.

It is common practice especially in the development of cyber-physical systems to start with a graphical model of the SUD and often also its environment, and synthesize (textual) code for generating software or hardware from this model. There are numerous commercially successful tools that support this, such as Matlab/Simulink (from Mathworks), LabVIEW (National Instruments), ASCET (ETAS) or SCADE (Ansys/Esterel Technologies). The typical scenario is that the modeler manually creates a drawing (or *view*) of the model, using an initially empty drawing canvas and a palette from which graphical elements are dragged and dropped onto the canvas. This can be very time consuming; Petre quotes a developer: "I quite often spend an hour or two just moving boxes and wires around, with no change in functionality, to make it that much more comprehensible when I come back to it" [67]. When creating or changing a model, an estimated 30% of a user's time is spent on manual layout adjustments according to Klauske and Dziobek [51]. In particular programmers who are used to powerful text editors and integrated development environments (IDEs) such as Eclipse often find working with today's graphical editors rather cumbersome.

Ideally, one would like that modelers can focus their efforts on the models they work with, and do not have to spend significant time on mechanical drawing activities, just like today's circuit developers leave the place-and-route step typically to automation. This is also advocated in *modeling pragmatics*, which concerns all practical aspects of handling a model in its design process [36]. The separation of *model* and *view* is in fact a classic design principle in software development, known as model-view-controller pattern. Applied to MBD, this means that customized views should be constructed automatically from a model. This, however, requires automated graph drawing capabilities. One modeling tool that follows this approach is KIELER, shown in Fig. 6, which uses the Eclipse Layout Kernel[3] (ELK), an open-source collection of numerous layout algorithms implemented in Java. However, to adapt this approach into common practice, there is a range of obstacles to overcome, ranging from fundamental difficulties and technical problems (such as properly dealing with comments [74]) to psychological issues, concerning various stakeholders in different communities. For example, todays modelers are just accustomed to creating the layout manually, just like early circuit designers were used to do manual placement and routing. Even though there seems to be a pretty clear case for the usage of graph drawing techniques to improve modeler productivity, as argued above, there is little pressure on the tool vendors to provide good solutions. Sometimes, however, there is no way around this; for example, when the visual syntax changes significantly from one tool version to the next, old models must be migrated automatically to the next version [68]. Also, while modelers are often unhappy with automatic layout results applied to "their" finished models that they have hand-crafted before, they seem much more open to automatic layout if it has been applied from the very beginning. But still, mechanisms that let modelers guide the layout and *layout stability*, meaning that small changes in the model should not lead to abrupt changes in the overall drawing, are important issues to be addressed for increasing the acceptance of automated graph drawing in MBD practice.

3.4 Automated Cartography

Graph drawing and cartography both use a certain degree of abstraction when visualizing data. The graph drawing perspective has hence been used to address several questions from automated cartography. Consider, for example, an administrative map of the countries of Europe. Such a map can be viewed as a graph in two ways: (1) the boundaries of the countries can be considered edges, and the three-country points are the most prominent vertices, and (2) the adjacencies of countries can be represented by a graph, dual to the first view. Also the information shown on certain maps can be seen as graphs to be drawn. A prominent example are the weighted trees of flow maps. Below we describe the main map types that relate to graph drawing.

---

[3] http://www.eclipse.org/elk.

(a)   (b)

Fig. 7. (a) Rectangular cartogram of the 2008 US presidential election (from Buchin *et al.* [21]. (b) Flow map showing migration from Colorado (from Verbeek *et al.* [84]).

Cartograms show values for regions by shrinking and expanding those regions, so that the area of each region corresponds to the value represented, for example total population. Necessarily, cartograms show distorted regions.

The first algorithmic study of *rectangular cartograms*, where all regions are rectangles of specified sizes (Fig. 7(a)), is due to van Kreveld and Speckmann [55]; extensions and refinements were presented by Buchin *et al.* [21]. It is not always possible to realize the same rectangle adjacencies as the corresponding region adjacencies on a normal map. To overcome this, *rectilinear cartograms* were introduced, where regions can have more than four corners. De Berg *et al.* [8] showed that only constantly many corners per region are needed in rectilinear cartograms. Alam *et al.* [1] showed that eight corners is always enough. In *linear cartograms*, Euclidean distances between vertices represent values, such as travel time. Vertices must be placed correspondingly and the map will be distorted [11,47]. Alternatively, one can use distorted edges to represent travel time [19].

Flow maps show the movement of objects between geographic locations on a map using thick arrows (Fig. 7(b)). Edge bundling is often used to avoid visual clutter. Using a modification of Steiner trees, Buchin *et al.* [20] modelled this problem and gave an approximation algorithm, since a general formulation is NP-hard.

Schematic maps are commonly used for public transportation systems. Connections between major stations are drawn with polygonal lines that are highly abstracted: they have only a few segments with few orientations (horizontal, vertical, or slope +1 or −1). Cabello *et al.* [22] compute an order of the connections suitable for incremental placement, leading to an $O(n \log n)$ time algorithm. Neyer [64] views the problem as a line simplification problem and approximates each connection with the minimum number of segments in the specified orientations. Nöllenburg and Wolff [66] give an integer programming approach to the problem, respecting multiple constraints. Brandes and Wagner [17] draw connections between stations as circular arcs and address the visualization problem as a graph layout problem.

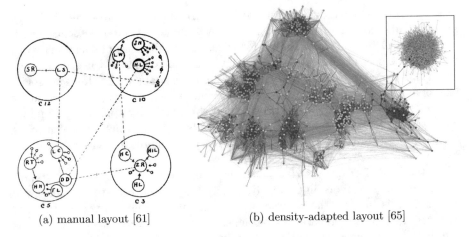

(a) manual layout [61]	(b) density-adapted layout [65]

Fig. 8. Social networks of actors organized into (a) cottages (circles) and (b) dorms (colors). Layout is (a) manual taking known groups into account and (b) with a graph-drawing algorithm based on local density variation not knowing the clusters (inset shows result of straightforward force-directed layout).

3.5   Social Sciences

Graph drawing is relevant to much of the social sciences but its most direct association is with social structure and social relations. The analytic concept of *social networks* has been linked so closely with its representation as a graph that the use of related graph-theoretic techniques in any discipline is often considered an application of social network analysis.

Social networks in the strict sense consist of actors and the social ties that moderate their actions [43,85]. Variant types include affiliation networks (depending on context, represented as hypergraphs or bipartite graphs with a fixed bipartition), ego networks (represented with or without the defining focal actor who is in relationship with everyone else, and with or without relationships between the other actors), and longitudinal networks (given, for instance, as cross-sectional panel data, interval-censored aggregations, or relational events). Descriptive features include macro-level classifications such as being a core-periphery or small-world type network as well as structural properties such as cohesive groups, roles, and actor centralities. Statistical inference is often based on particular families of models for which there is a long history [38].

It was realized early on that visualization is not only for communication but that it can serve as a tool to explore the intricate and a-priori unknown patterns of complex webs of relationships [18]. The first known matrix representation of a graph of social relations goes back to the end of the 19th century [25] and Moreno's influential book [61] is full of hand-made graph drawings such as the one in Fig. 8(a).

While graphs associated with social relations often exhibit certain tendencies such as being sparse with one or more locally dense centers, low average distance, and a skewed degree distribution, there is no guaranteed restriction to any particular class of graphs. Instead, layout problems are often associated with an analytic focus. A rule of thumb for effective visualization of social networks is that the aspect of interest defines layout constraints whereas the objective for the remaining degrees of freedom is to maximize readability. In this way, social networks provide a rich source of graph drawing problems, even if the resulting problems have often been addressed without this particular application in mind. Examples include (straight or radial) layered layout to depict actor centrality and status, clustered layout for (nested or flat) communities, and preprocessing techniques for skewed degree distributions.

Actual use of graph drawing methods is limited, though. A lack of graphical standards and, more importantly, widely known and easy-to-use dedicated software tools hinders the routine practice of purposefully designed graphical illustrations that are prepared with the help of graph drawing algorithms. While the share of network visualization papers in the area of information visualization is increasing, the development of dedicated layout algorithms is lagging behind. Consequently, as in almost any applied area, the most widely used tools are relatively standard implementations of force-directed layout algorithms. Given the rich history of visualization in social network analysis, the variety of layout problems, and its increasing relevance due to the spread of online social networks, there is a lot to be gained by developing – and applying – more sophisticated layout algorithms. An example, a preprocessing technique to untangle small-world networks common in social media [65], is given in Fig. 8(b). Other heavily underexplored areas are network models, ensembles of networks, multilayer networks, and sequences of relational events.

3.6   Molecular Biology

Molecular biology is a subfield of biology which studies structure and function of cells at a molecular level. Cells are living objects composed of molecules such as DNA, proteins, and metabolites, that interact with each other in different ways. *Molecules* and their *interactions* play a central role, and structures based on these elements are commonly referred to as *biological networks*. Examples include gene regulatory and metabolic networks. In addition, there are further graphs derived from those elements such as phylogenetic trees and correlation networks. See [46] for an overview of networks in molecular biology.

These structures are often represented by multivariate networks which differ in both the semantics of vertices and edges as well as the data attached to vertices and edges. Examples are undirected graphs (e. g., for protein interaction networks), rooted trees (phylogenetic trees) and hyper-graphs (metabolic networks), often containing additional attributes attached to vertices and edges. Figure 9 shows some examples, Kohlbacher *et al.* present more information about multivariate networks in the life sciences in [52].

While manual drawings of tree-like information such as the tree of life appeared at least at the beginning of the 19th century [77], the earliest drawings of cellular networks are most likely of metabolic (sub)pathways in the early 20th

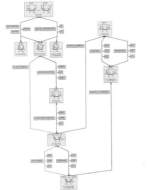

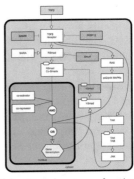

(a) Metabolic network (hyper-graph) visualized with an adapted layered approach [72].

(b) Regulatory network (directed graph) visualized with a hive plot layout [56].

(c) Signal transduction network (directed graph) visualized manually in the SBGN AF standard [60].

Fig. 9. Some biological networks and related layout methods.

century, for example, the glucose fermentation pathway proposed by Wohl in 1907 [86]. A huge number of biological networks have been drawn manually, and manual drawings are still common nowadays for illustrations in publications, in electronic systems such as the well-known KEGG database and so on.

When graph drawing algorithms became available, they were first used to compute visualizations for presentations (e. g., for networks derived from databases as in [49]), later employed to support the discovery process such as to investigate structure, connectivity, or hubs in such networks, and finally novel layout algorithms were developed tailored to specific networks (e. g., see Fig. 9) or—as generic algorithms—for different visualization tasks (e. g. [73]). Applications and specific adaptions of common graph drawing algorithms for the visualization of biological networks are detailed in [4]. Examples for specific layout methods motivated by biological questions or data characteristics are power-graph layout, which reduces the network complexity by explicitly representing re-occurring network motifs, and hive plot layout, which is a parallel coordinate layout of a graph with radially arranged axes, see also Fig. 9.

Standardised representations, ontologies and taxonomies are common in biological sciences, an early example is Linnaeus' taxonomy from 1735 [57]. Recent developments also include graphical standards: SBGN (Systems Biology Graphical Notation) covers the graphical representation of major networks and processes in molecular biology. The specifications of the three SBGN languages not only defines glyphs for vertices and edges, their syntax and semantics, but also contain rules and recommendations for a good layout of these networks.

Graph drawing is well established in molecular biology as method to visualize biological networks. Similar to other areas discussed earlier, molecular biology is not only a field of science which uses and applies graph drawing algorithms, but also an interesting source of new problems in graph drawing. This field offers a broad range of layout problems for multivariate graphs and, given the increasing size, complexity and availability of the data, there is huge interest for better visualization (layout) and exploration methods. Some open problems in biological network visualization are presented by Albrecht *et al.* [2].

Acknowledgements. This work was supported by the DFG under the project *Compact Graph Drawing with Port Constraints* (DFG HA 4407/8-1 and MU 1129/9-1). Marc van Kreveld is supported by the Netherlands Organisation for Scientific Research (NWO) on project no. 612.001.651. Bettina Speckmann is supported by the Netherlands Organisation for Scientific Research (NWO) on project no. 639.023.208.

References

1. Alam, M., Biedl, T., Felsner, S., Kaufmann, M., Kobourov, S., Ueckerdt, T.: Computing cartograms with optimal complexity. Discret. Comput. Geom. **50**(3), 784–810 (2013)
2. Albrecht, M., Kerren, A., Klein, K., Kohlbacher, O., Mutzel, P., Paul, W., Schreiber, F., Wybrow, M.: On open problems in biological network visualization. In: Eppstein, D., Gansner, E.R. (eds.) GD 2009. LNCS, vol. 5849, pp. 256–267. Springer, Heidelberg (2010). https://doi.org/10.1007/978-3-642-11805-0_25
3. Bach, B., Riche, N.H., Hurter, C., Marriott, K., Dwyer, T.: Towards unambiguous edge bundling: investigating confluent drawings for network visualization. IEEE Trans. Vis. Comput. Graph. **23**(1), 541–550 (2017)
4. Bachmaier, C., Brandes, U., Schreiber, F.: Biological networks. In: Handbook of Graph Drawing and Visualization, pp. 621–651. Chapman and Hall/CRC, Boco Raton (2014)
5. Badent, M., Brandes, U., Cornelsen, S.: More canonical ordering. J. Graph Algorithms Appl. **15**(1), 97–126 (2011)
6. Batini, C., Talamo, M., Tamassia, R.: Computer aided layout of entity relationship diagrams. J. Syst. Softw. **4**(2), 163–173 (1984)
7. Batini, C., Nardelli, E., Tamassia, R.: A layout algorithm for data flow diagrams. IEEE Trans. Softw. Eng. **12**(4), 538–546 (1986)
8. de Berg, M., Mumford, E., Speckmann, B.: On rectilinear duals for vertex-weighted plane graphs. Discret. Math. **309**(7), 1794–1812 (2009)
9. Bienstock, D.: Some provably hard crossing number problems. Discret. Comput. Geom. **6**(5), 443–459 (1991)
10. Bienstock, D., Monma, C.: On the complexity of embedding planar graphs to minimize certain distance measures. Algorithmica **5**, 93–109 (1990)
11. Bies, S., van Kreveld, M.: Time-space maps from triangulations. In: Didimo, W., Patrignani, M. (eds.) GD 2012. LNCS, vol. 7704, pp. 511–516. Springer, Heidelberg (2013). https://doi.org/10.1007/978-3-642-36763-2_45
12. Binucci, C., Didimo, W.: Computing quasi-upward planar drawings of mixed graphs. Comput. J. **59**(1), 133–150 (2016)
13. Binucci, C., Didimo, W., Liotta, G., Nonato, M.: Orthogonal drawings of graphs with vertex and edge labels. Comput. Geom. **32**(2), 71–114 (2005)
14. Binucci, C., Didimo, W., Patrignani, M.: Upward and quasi-upward planarity testing of embedded mixed graphs. Theoret. Comput. Sci. **526**, 75–89 (2014)

15. Bostock, M., Ogievetsky, V., Heer, J.: D^3 data-driven documents. IEEE Trans. Vis. Comput. Graph. **17**(12), 2301–2309 (2011)

16. Brandenburg, F., Eppstein, D., Goodrich, M.T., Kobourov, S., Liotta, G., Mutzel, P.: Selected open problems in graph drawing. In: Liotta, G. (ed.) GD 2003. LNCS, vol. 2912, pp. 515–539. Springer, Heidelberg (2004). https://doi.org/10.1007/978-3-540-24595-7_55

17. Brandes, U., Wagner, D.: Using graph layout to visualize train interconnection data. In: Whitesides, S.H. (ed.) GD 1998. LNCS, vol. 1547, pp. 44–56. Springer, Heidelberg (1998). https://doi.org/10.1007/3-540-37623-2_4

18. Brandes, U., Freeman, L.C., Wagner, D.: Social networks. In: Tamassia, R. (ed.) Handbook of Graph Drawing and Visualization, pp. 805–839. Chapman and Hall/CRC, Boca Raton (2013)

19. Buchin, K., van Goethem, A., Hoffmann, M., van Kreveld, M., Speckmann, B.: Travel-time maps: linear cartograms with fixed vertex locations. Geograph. Inf. Sci. (GIScience) **2014**, 18–33 (2014)

20. Buchin, K., Speckmann, B., Verbeek, K.: Angle-restricted Steiner arborescences for flow map layout. Algorithmica **72**(2), 656–685 (2015)

21. Buchin, K., Speckmann, B., Verdonschot, S.: Evolution strategies for optimizing rectangular cartograms. GIScience **2012**, 29–42 (2012)

22. Cabello, S., de Berg, M., van Kreveld, M.: Schematization of networks. Comput. Geom. **30**(3), 223–228 (2005)

23. Chiang, Y.T., Lin, C.C., Lu, H.I.: Orderly spanning trees with applications to graph encoding and graph drawing. In: SODA 2001, pp. 506–515. SIAM (2001)

24. Chrobak, M., Kant, G.: Convex grid drawings of 3-connected planar graphs. Int. J. Comput. Geom. Appl. **7**(3), 211–223 (1997)

25. Delitsch, J.: Über Schülerfreundschaften in einer Volksschulklasse. Zeitschrift für Kinderforschung **5**(4), 150–163 (1900)

26. Di Battista, G., Tamassia, R.: On-line graph algorithms with SPQR-trees. In: Paterson, M.S. (ed.) ICALP 1990. LNCS, vol. 443, pp. 598–611. Springer, Heidelberg (1990). https://doi.org/10.1007/BFb0032061

27. Di Battista, G., Didimo, W., Marcandalli, A.: Planarization of clustered graphs. In: Mutzel, P., Jünger, M., Leipert, S. (eds.) GD 2001. LNCS, vol. 2265, pp. 60–74. Springer, Heidelberg (2002). https://doi.org/10.1007/3-540-45848-4_5

28. Dickerson, M., Eppstein, D., Goodrich, M.T., Meng, J.Y.: Confluent drawings: visualizing non-planar diagrams in a planar way. In: Liotta, G. (ed.) GD 2003. LNCS, vol. 2912, pp. 1–12. Springer, Heidelberg (2004). https://doi.org/10.1007/978-3-540-24595-7_1

29. Didimo, W., Eades, P., Liotta, G.: Drawing graphs with right angle crossings. Theoret. Comput. Sci. **412**(39), 5156–5166 (2011)

30. Duncan, C.A., Eppstein, D., Goodrich, M.T., Kobourov, S.G., Nöllenburg, M.: Lombardi drawings of graphs. J. Graph Algorithms Appl. **16**(1), 85–108 (2012)

31. Eades, P., Cohen, R.F., Huang, M.L.: Online animated graph drawing for web navigation. In: Di Battista, G. (ed.) GD 1997. LNCS, vol. 1353, pp. 330–335. Springer, Heidelberg (1997). https://doi.org/10.1007/3-540-63938-1_77

32. Eiglsperger, M., Gutwenger, C., Kaufmann, M., Kupke, J., Jünger, M., Leipert, S., Klein, K., Mutzel, P., Siebenhaller, M.: Automatic layout of UML class diagrams in orthogonal style. Inf. Visual. **3**(3), 189–208 (2004)

33. Eppstein, D., Holten, D., Löffler, M., Nöllenburg, M., Speckmann, B., Verbeek, K.: Strict confluent drawing. In: Wismath, S., Wolff, A. (eds.) GD 2013. LNCS, vol. 8242, pp. 352–363. Springer, Cham (2013). https://doi.org/10.1007/978-3-319-03841-4_31

34. Franken, D., Ochs, J., Ochs, K.: Generation of wave digital structures for networks containing multiport elements. Trans. Circuits Syst. **52**(3), 586–596 (2005)
35. de Fraysseix, H., Pach, J., Pollack, R.: How to draw a planar graph on a grid. Combinatorica **10**(1), 41–51 (1990)
36. Fuhrmann, H., von Hanxleden, R.: Taming graphical modeling. In: Petriu, D.C., Rouquette, N., Haugen, Ø. (eds.) MODELS 2010. LNCS, vol. 6394, pp. 196–210. Springer, Heidelberg (2010). https://doi.org/10.1007/978-3-642-16145-2_14
37. Giacomo, E.D., Didimo, W., Liotta, G., Meijer, H.: Area, curve complexity, and crossing resolution of non-planar graph drawings. Theory Comput. Syst. **49**(3), 565–575 (2011)
38. Goldenberg, A., Zheng, A.X., Fienberg, S.E., Airoldi, E.M.: A survey of statistical network models. Found. Trends Mach. Learn. **2**(2), 129–233 (2010)
39. Gronemann, M.: Bitonic *st*-orderings for upward planar graphs. In: Hu, Y., Nöllenburg, M. (eds.) GD 2016. LNCS, vol. 9801, pp. 222–235. Springer, Cham (2016). https://doi.org/10.1007/978-3-319-50106-2_18
40. Gutwenger, C., Mutzel, P.: A linear time implementation of SPQR-trees. In: Marks, J. (ed.) GD 2000. LNCS, vol. 1984, pp. 77–90. Springer, Heidelberg (2001). https://doi.org/10.1007/3-540-44541-2_8
41. Gutwenger, C., Jünger, M., Klein, K., Kupke, J., Leipert, S., Mutzel, P.: A new approach for visualizing UML class diagrams. In: Diehl, S., Stasko, J.T., Spencer, S.N. (eds.) Symposium on Software Visualization 2003, pp. 179–188. ACM (2003)
42. Gutwenger, C., Jünger, M., Leipert, S., Mutzel, P., Percan, M., Weiskircher, R.: Advances in *C*-planarity testing of clustered graphs. In: Goodrich, M.T., Kobourov, S.G. (eds.) GD 2002. LNCS, vol. 2528, pp. 220–236. Springer, Heidelberg (2002). https://doi.org/10.1007/3-540-36151-0_21
43. Hennig, M., Brandes, U., Pfeffer, J., Mergel, I.: Studying Social Networks - A Guide to Empirical Research. Campus Frankfurt, New York (2012)
44. Hoffmann, M., van Kreveld, M.J., Kusters, V., Rote, G.: Quality ratios of measures for graph drawing styles. In: 26th Canadian Conference on Computational Geometry, CCCG (2014)
45. Hoffmann, U.: Intersection graphs and geometric objects in the plane. Ph.D. thesis, Technische Universität Berlin, Berlin (2016)
46. Junker, B.H., Schreiber, F.: Analysis of Biological Networks. Wiley Series on Bioinformatics, Computational Techniques and Engineering. Wiley, New York (2008)
47. Kaiser, C., Walsh, F., Farmer, C., Pozdnoukhov, A.: User-centric time-distance representation of road networks. GIScience **2010**, 85–99 (2010)
48. Kant, G.: Drawing planar graphs using the canonical ordering. Algorithmica **16**, 4–32 (1996)
49. Karp, P.D., Paley, S.M.: Automated drawing of metabolic pathways. In: Lim, H., Cantor, C., Bobbins, R. (eds.) International Conference on Bioinformatics and Genome Research, pp. 225–238 (1994)
50. Klau, G.W., Mutzel, P.: Combining graph labeling and compaction. In: Kratochvíl, J. (ed.) GD 1999. LNCS, vol. 1731, pp. 27–37. Springer, Heidelberg (1999). https://doi.org/10.1007/3-540-46648-7_3
51. Klauske, L.K., Dziobek, C.: Improving modeling usability: Automated layout generation for Simulink. In: Proc. MathWorks Automotive Conference (2010)
52. Kohlbacher, O., Schreiber, F., Ward, M.O.: Multivariate networks in the life sciences. In: Kerren, A., Purchase, H.C., Ward, M.O. (eds.) Multivariate Network Visualization. LNCS, vol. 8380, pp. 61–73. Springer, Cham (2014). https://doi.org/10.1007/978-3-319-06793-3_4

53. Kratochvíl, J., Matoušek, J.: Intersection graphs of segments. J. Combin. Theory Ser. B **62**(2), 289–315 (1994)
54. van Kreveld, M.: Geographic information systems (Chap. 59). In: Goodmann, J., O'Rourke, J., Toth, C. (eds.) Handbook of Discrete and Computational Geometry, 3rd edn. Chapman & Hall/CRC, Boca Raton (2017)
55. van Kreveld, M., Speckmann, B.: On rectangular cartograms. Comput. Geom. **37**(3), 175–187 (2007)
56. Krzywinski, M., Birol, I., Jones, S.J., Marra, M.A.: Hive plots - rational approach to visualizing networks. Brief. Bioinform. **13**, 627–644 (2012)
57. Linnaei, C.: Species Plantarum. Holmiae (1735)
58. von Manteuffel, A., Studerus, C.: Reduze 2–distributed Feynman integral reduction. CoRR (2012)
59. Matousek, J.: Intersection graphs of segments and $\exists\mathbb{R}$. arXiv:1406.2636 (2014)
60. Mi, H., Schreiber, F., Moodie, S., Czauderna, T., Demir, E., Haw, R., Luna, A., Novère, N.L., Sorokin, A., Villéger, A.: Systems biology graphical notation: activity flow language level 1 version 1.2. J. Integr. Bioinform. **12**(2), e265 (2015)
61. Moreno, J.L.: Who Shall Survive? Foundations of Sociometry, Group Psychotherapy and Sociodrama. Beacon House, New York (1953). (First published in 1934)
62. Munzner, T., Guimbretière, F., Tasiran, S., Zhang, L., Zhou, Y.: TreeJuxtaposer: scalable tree comparison using focus+ context with guaranteed visibility. ACM Trans. Graph. (TOG) **22**(3), 453–462 (2003)
63. Mutzel, P.: The SPQR-tree data structure in graph drawing. In: Baeten, J.C.M., Lenstra, J.K., Parrow, J., Woeginger, G.J. (eds.) ICALP 2003. LNCS, vol. 2719, pp. 34–46. Springer, Heidelberg (2003). https://doi.org/10.1007/3-540-45061-0_4
64. Neyer, G.: Line simplification with restricted orientations. In: Dehne, F., Sack, J.-R., Gupta, A., Tamassia, R. (eds.) WADS 1999. LNCS, vol. 1663, pp. 13–24. Springer, Heidelberg (1999). https://doi.org/10.1007/3-540-48447-7_2
65. Nocaj, A., Ortmann, M., Brandes, U.: Untangling the hairballs of multi-centered, small-world online social media networks. J. Graph Algorithms Appl. **19**(2), 595–618 (2016)
66. Nöllenburg, M., Wolff, A.: Drawing and labeling high-quality metro maps by mixed-integer programming. IEEE Trans. Vis. Comp. Graph. **17**(5), 626–641 (2011)
67. Petre, M.: Why looking isn't always seeing: readership skills and graphical programming. Commun. ACM **38**(6), 33–44 (1995)
68. Rüegg, U., Lakkundi, R., Prasad, A., Kodaganur, A., Schulze, C.D., von Hanxleden, R.: Incremental diagram layout for automated model migration. In: ACM/IEEE 19th International Conference on Model Driven Engineering Languages and Systems, MODELS 2016, pp. 185–195. ACM, New York (2016)
69. Schätz, B., Pretschner, A., Huber, F., Philipps, J.: Model-based development of embedded systems. In: Bruel, J.-M., Bellahsene, Z. (eds.) OOIS 2002. LNCS, vol. 2426, pp. 298–311. Springer, Heidelberg (2002). https://doi.org/10.1007/3-540-46105-1_34
70. Schmidt, J.M.: The Mondshein sequence. In: Esparza, J., Fraigniaud, P., Husfeldt, T., Koutsoupias, E. (eds.) ICALP 2014. LNCS, vol. 8572, pp. 967–978. Springer, Heidelberg (2014). https://doi.org/10.1007/978-3-662-43948-7_80
71. Schnyder, W.: Embedding planar graphs on the grid. In: Proceedings of 1st Annual ACM-SIAM Symposium on Discrete Algorithms, pp. 138–148 (1990)
72. Schreiber, F.: High quality visualization of biochemical pathways in BioPath. Silico Biol. **2**(2), 59–73 (2002)
73. Schreiber, F., Dwyer, T., Marriott, K., Wybrow, M.: A generic algorithm for layout of biological networks. BMC Bioinform. **10**, 375 (2009)

74. Schulze, C.D., von Hanxleden, R.: Automatic layout in the face of unattached comments. In: Proceedings of Symposium on Visual Languages and Human-Centric Computing (2014)
75. Seemann, J.: Extending the Sugiyama algorithm for drawing UML class diagrams: towards automatic layout of object-oriented software diagrams. In: DiBattista, G. (ed.) GD 1997. LNCS, vol. 1353, pp. 415–424. Springer, Heidelberg (1997). https://doi.org/10.1007/3-540-63938-1_86
76. Shneiderman, B.: Tree visualization with tree-maps: 2-D space-filling approach. ACM Trans. Graph. **11**(1), 92–99 (1992)
77. Stevens, P.: Augustin Augier's "Arbre Botanique" (1801), a remarkable early botanical representation of the natural system. Taxon **32**, 203–211 (1983)
78. Sugiyama, K., Tagawa, S., Toda, M.: Methods for visual understanding of hierarchical system structures. IEEE Trans. Syst. Man. Cybern. **11**(2), 109–125 (1981)
79. Tamassia, R.: On embedding a graph in the grid with the minimum number of bends. SIAM J. Comput. **16**(3), 421–444 (1987)
80. Tamassia, R. (ed.): Handbook of Graph Drawing and Visualization. Chapman and Hall/CRC, Boca Raton (2013)
81. Tsiaras, V., Triantafilou, S., Tollis, I.G.: Treemaps for directed acyclic graphs. In: Hong, S.-H., Nishizeki, T., Quan, W. (eds.) GD 2007. LNCS, vol. 4875, pp. 377–388. Springer, Heidelberg (2008). https://doi.org/10.1007/978-3-540-77537-9_37
82. Tunkelang, D.: JIGGLE: Java interactive graph layout environment. In: Whitesides, S.H. (ed.) GD 1998. LNCS, vol. 1547, pp. 413–422. Springer, Heidelberg (1998). https://doi.org/10.1007/3-540-37623-2_33
83. Vanhatalo, J., Völzer, H., Koehler, J.: The refined process structure tree. Data Knowl.Eng. **68**(9), 793–818 (2009)
84. Verbeek, K., Buchin, K., Speckmann, B.: Flow map layout via spiral trees. IEEE Trans. Vis. Comput. Graph. **17**(12), 2536–2544 (2011)
85. Wasserman, S., Faust, K.: Social Network Aanalysis. Methods and Applications. Cambridge University Press, Cambridge (1994)
86. Wohl, A.: Die neueren Ansichten über den chemischen Verlauf der Gärung. Biochemische Zeitschrift **5**, 45–64 (1907)
87. Zhang, Y., Luk, W.S., Zhou, H., Yan, C., Zeng, X.: Layout decomposition with pairwise coloring for multiple patterning lithography. In: Proceedings of International Conference on Computer-Aided Design, pp. 170–177. IEEE Press (2013)

Sublinear-Time Algorithms
for Approximating Graph Parameters

Dana Ron$^{(\boxtimes)}$

School of Electrical Engineering, Tel Aviv University, 69978 Tel Aviv, Israel
danaron@tau.ac.il

1 Introduction

Given a graph $G = (V, E)$, we may be interested in computing various parameters
that are associated with the graph. Such parameters include the average degree,
the number of connected components, and the size of a minimum vertex cover.
These parameters and many others can be computed (exactly or approximately)
in an efficient manner. That is, in time that is polynomial in the size of the graph,
and possibly even linear in this size. However, for very large graphs, even linear
time may by infeasible. Hence, we need to design more efficient algorithms, that
is, algorithms that run in *sublinear* time.

Given the constraint on their running time, such algorithms cannot read the
entire graph, but can access parts of the graph by performing queries. We mainly
consider two types of queries: degree queries and neighbor queries. In a degree
query the algorithm specifies a vertex $v \in V$, and the answer to the query is
the degree of v in G, denoted $d(v)$. In a neighbor query, the algorithm specifies
a vertex v and an index i. The answer to the query is the ith neighbor of v if
$i \in \{1, \ldots, d(v)\}$, and is a special symbol, $\perp$, otherwise.[1] A third possible type of
query is a vertex-pair query, where the algorithm specifies a pair of vertices $\{u, v\}$
and the answer is 1 if $\{u, v\} \in E$ and 0 otherwise. If the graph is edge weighted,
then the answer to a neighbor query (similarly, a vertex-pair query) also includes
the weight of the corresponding edge. We assume that the algorithm is given the
number of vertices in the graph, denoted n, and, without loss of generality, may
assume that $V = \{1, \ldots, n\}$. In all that follows, unless stated explicitly otherwise,
the algorithm has access to degree queries and neighbor queries.

The algorithms presented in this survey are randomized algorithms that are
allowed a small constant failure probability (e.g., 1/3). This failure probability
can be reduced in a standard manner to any desired value $\delta > 0$ at a multiplicative cost of $\log(1/\delta)$. The algorithms compute approximations of various
graph parameters. Ideally, we would like to design algorithms that, given any
$\epsilon \in (0, 1)$, compute an approximation that is within a multiplicative factor of

---

D. Ron—Research supported by the Israel Science Foundation grant no. 671/13.

[1] Observe that a degree query to a vertex v can be replaced by $O(\log d(v))$ neighbor
queries to v by performing a "doubling" search. For the sake of simplicity we allow
both types of queries.

© Springer Nature Switzerland AG 2019
B. Steffen and G. Woeginger (Eds.): Computing and Software Science, LNCS 10000, pp. 105–122, 2019.
https://doi.org/10.1007/978-3-319-91908-9_7

$(1\pm\epsilon)$ from the exact value of the graph parameter in question, and furthermore, their complexity grows polynomially with $1/\epsilon$. While some of the algorithms have this desired behavior, others provide weaker approximations, as we detail when presenting the corresponding results.

In the rest of this section, we present a variety of results for sublinear approximation of graph parameters. In the sections that follow we give more details for a selection of these results.

1.1 Average Degree and Higher Moments of the Degree Distribution

The Average Degree. The problem of estimating the average degree $\bar{d} = \bar{d}(G)$ of a graph G in sublinear time was first studied by Feige [10]. He considered this problem when the algorithm is allowed only degree queries, so that the problem is a special case of estimating the average value of a function given query access to the function. For a general function $d : \{1, \ldots, n\} \to \{0, \ldots, n-1\}$, obtaining a constant-factor estimate of the average value of the function (with constant success probability) requires $\Omega(n)$ queries to the function (and this remains true even if there is a promise that the average value is at least 1). Feige showed that when d is the degree function of a graph, for any $\epsilon \in (0, 1]$ it is possible to obtain an estimate $\tilde{d}$ such that $\tilde{d} \in [\bar{d}, (2 + \epsilon) \cdot \bar{d}]$ with probability at least $2/3$ by performing $O(\sqrt{n}/\epsilon)$ (uniformly selected) queries. He also showed that in order to go below a factor of 2 in the quality of the estimate, $\Omega(n)$ queries are necessary.

However, given that the object in question is a graph, it is natural to allow the algorithm to query the neighborhood of vertices of its choice and not only their degrees; indeed, the aforementioned problem definition follows this natural convention. Goldreich and Ron [14] showed that by giving the algorithm this extra power, it is possible to break the factor-2 barrier. They provide an algorithm that, given $\epsilon \in (0, 1)$, outputs a $(1 \pm \epsilon)$-factor estimate of the average degree (with probability at least $2/3$) after performing $\tilde{O}_\epsilon(n^{1/2})$ degree and neighbor queries, assuming $\bar{d} \geq 1$. (We use $\tilde{O}_\epsilon(\cdot)$ to suppress both $\mathrm{poly}(\log n)$ factors and $\mathrm{poly}(1/\epsilon)$ factors.) More precisely, the number of queries and the running time are $\tilde{O}_\epsilon((n/\bar{d})^{1/2})$ in expectation. Thus, the complexity decreases as the average degree increases. Furthermore, this result is essentially optimal [14]: a $(1 \pm \epsilon)$-factor estimate requires $\Omega((n/(\epsilon\bar{d}))^{1/2})$ queries.

Higher Moments. For a graph $G = (V, E)$, consider the sum (average) of higher powers of the vertices' degrees: for $s \geq 1$ we let $M_s = M_s(G) \overset{\text{def}}{=} \sum_{v \in V} d(v)^s$ and $\mu_s = \mu_s(G) \overset{\text{def}}{=} \frac{1}{n} \cdot M_s(G)$. Observe that for $s = 1$ we have that $\mu_1 = \bar{d}$ (and $M_1 = 2m$ where m is the number of edges in the graph), while for $s = 2$, the variance of the degree distribution is $\mu_2 - \mu_1^2$.

Gonen et al. [15] gave a sublinear-time algorithm for approximating μ_s. Technically, their algorithm approximates the number of stars in a graph (with a given size s), but a simple modification yields an algorithm for moments estimation. A much simpler algorithm (and analysis) was later given by Eden et al. [9] with essentially the same complexity (the dependence on $1/\epsilon$, s and the poly$(\log n)$ factors are reduced in [9]). Both papers show how to obtain a $(1 \pm \epsilon)$-factor approximation of μ_s by performing $\widetilde{O}_\epsilon \left(\frac{n^{1-\frac{1}{s+1}}}{\mu_s^{\frac{1}{s+1}}} + \min\left\{n^{1-\frac{1}{s}}, \frac{n^{s-1}}{\mu_s^{1-\frac{1}{s}}}\right\} \right)$ queries in expectation, where this bound is essentially optimal [15] (up to a dependence on $1/\epsilon$ and polylogarithmic factors in n). For example, when $s = 2$ this function behaves as follows. For $\mu_2 \leq n^{1/2}$ the bound is $n^{2/3}/\mu_2^{1/3}$, for $n^{1/2} < \mu_2 \leq n$, the bound is $n^{1/2}$, and for $\mu_2 > n$, it is $n/\mu_2^{1/2}$.

Aliakbarpour et al. [1] consider a stronger model that assumes access to uniform random *edges*. They show that in this model $\widetilde{O}_\epsilon \left(\frac{m}{M_s^{1/s}} + n^{1-1/s} \right) = \widetilde{O}_\epsilon \left(n^{1-1/s} \cdot \max\left\{1, \overline{d} \cdot \mu_s^{-\frac{1}{s}}\right\} \right)$ queries suffice for $s > 1$.

The Lower Bound and Graphs with Bounded Arboricity.

The lower bound constructions showing that the complexity of the aforementioned algorithms for approximating μ_s is essentially optimal [15], are based on "locally dense" graphs. In particular, the first (and simpler) lower bound (corresponding to the first term, $n^{1-\frac{1}{s+1}}/\mu_s^{\frac{1}{s+1}} = n/M_s^{\frac{1}{s+1}}$), is simply based on the difficulty of "hitting" a clique of size $M_s^{\frac{1}{s+1}}$, and the second lower bound (corresponding to the second term), is based on a complete bipartite subgraph. A natural question is whether we can get a better upper bound if we know that there are no dense subgraphs. This question was answered affirmatively by Eden et al. [9]. They showed that a significantly improved complexity can be obtained for graphs with bounded arboricity.[2] For precise details see [9].

Number of Triangles and Larger Cliques.

Gonen et al. [15] also considered the problem of approximating the number of triangles in a graph G, denoted $t = t(G)$. They showed a linear lower bound when the algorithm may use degree and neighbor queries and $m = \Theta(n)$. This raises the natural question whether a sublinear bound can be obtained if the algorithm is also allowed pair-queries (which are not helpful in the case of moments estimation). This question was answered affirmatively by Eden et al. [7]. They gave an algorithm whose query complexity and running time are $\widetilde{O}_\epsilon \left(\frac{n}{t^{1/3}} + \frac{m^{3/2}}{t} \right)$ in expectation. To be precise, in the expression for the query complexity, the second term is $\min\{m, m^{3/2}/t\}$ (so that the number of queries is at most linear, and is strictly sublinear as long as $t > m^{1/2}$). This bound on the query complexity is tight (up to factors polynomial in $\log n$ and $1/\epsilon$) [7]. The result was recently extended to approximating the number of k-cliques [8], for any given $k \geq 3$.

---

[2] The *arboricity* of a graph G, denoted $\mathrm{arb}(G)$, is the minimum number of forests into which its edges can be partitioned. It satisfies [20, 21] $\mathrm{arb}(G) = \max_{S \subseteq V} \left\{ \left\lceil \frac{|E(S)|}{|S|-1} \right\rceil \right\}$, where $E(S)$ denotes the set of edges in the subgraph induced by S.

1.2 The Number of Connected Components

The problem of approximating the number of connected components in a graph was addressed by Chazelle et al. [4] in the course of designing an algorithm for approximating the minimum weight of a spanning tree. We discuss the latter problem in Subsect. 1.4. Their algorithm for approximating the number of connected components of a graph G, denoted $cc(G)$, outputs an estimate that with probability at least $2/3$ is within an additive error of ϵn from $cc(G)$ (for any given $\epsilon \in (0,1)$). The query complexity and running time of the algorithm are $\widetilde{O}(\bar{d}/\epsilon^2)$.

1.3 Minimum Vertex Cover and Related Parameters

Let $vc(G)$ denote the minimum size of a vertex cover in a graph G. The problem of approximating $vc(G)$ in sublinear time was first studied by Parnas and Ron [24]. They showed how to obtain an estimate $\widehat{vc}$ that with probability at least $2/3$ satisfies $\widehat{vc} \in [vc(G), 2 \cdot vc(G) + \epsilon n]$. The query complexity and running time of the algorithm are $d^{O(\log d/\epsilon^3)}$ where d is the maximum degree in the graph. The dependence on d can be replaced by a dependence on $\bar{d}/\epsilon$ (recall that $\bar{d}$ denotes the average degree in the graph) [24]. It is also possible to replace the combination of the multiplicative factor of 2 and the additive term of ϵn by a multiplicative factor of $2 + \epsilon$ at a cost that depends on $n/vc(G)$ (and such a cost is unavoidable).

The upper bound of $d^{O(\log d/\epsilon^3)}$ was significantly improved in a sequence of papers [19,22,23,27]. The best result, appearing in [23] (and building on [22] and [27]), gives an upper bound of $\widetilde{O}(\bar{d}/\epsilon^{O(1)})$.

On the negative side, it was also proved in [24] that at least a linear dependence on the average degree, $\bar{d}$, is necessary. Namely, $\Omega(\bar{d})$ queries are necessary for obtaining an estimate $\widehat{vc}$ that satisfies (with probability at least $2/3$) $\widehat{vc} \in [vc(G), \alpha \cdot vc(G) + \epsilon n]$ for any $\alpha \geq 1$ and $\epsilon < 1/4$, provided that $\bar{d} = O(n/\alpha)$. In particular this is true for $\alpha = 2$. We also mention that obtaining such an estimate with $\alpha = 2 - \gamma$ for any constant γ and sufficiently small constant ϵ requires $\Omega(\sqrt{n})$ queries, as shown by Trevisan (see [24]). For $\alpha < 7/6$, the lower bound [3] is $\Omega(n)$.

Improved Approximation for Restricted Families of Graphs. Hassidim et al. [16] introduced the notion of a *Partition Oracle*, and showed how it can be applied to solve a variety of testing and approximation problems in sublinear time (possibly under a promise that the graph belongs to a certain restricted family of graphs). In particular, for graphs with excluded minors[3] (of constant size, e.g., planar graphs), this implies an algorithm that computes an estimate $\widehat{vc}$ that satisfies (with probability at least $2/3$) $\widehat{vc} \in [vc, vc + \epsilon n]$ (i.e., with no multiplicative factor). The query complexity and running time of the algorithm are $O(d^{\mathrm{poly}(1/\epsilon)})$. An improved partition oracle presented in [17] implies that an

---

[3] A graph H is a minor of a graph G if H can be obtained from a subgraph of G by a sequence of edge contractions.

estimate with the same quality can be obtained in time $O((d/\epsilon)^{O(\log(1/\epsilon))}) = O(d^{\log^2(1/\epsilon)})$. Similar results hold for the size of a minimum dominating set and maximum independent set.

Maximum Matching. The aforementioned algorithms for approximating $vc(G)$ work by approximating the size of a maximal matching. Nguyen and Onak [22] showed how such an approximation can be extended and used in a recursive manner (based on *augmenting paths* for matchings) so as to obtain an estimate $\widehat{mm}$ of the *maximum* size of a matching in a graph G, denoted $mm(G)$. The estimate satisfies $\widehat{mm} \in [mm(G) - \epsilon n, mm(G)]$ with probability at least $2/3$. The query complexity of the algorithm is $2^{d^{O(1/\epsilon)}}$ in expectation. This result was improved by Yoshida et al. [27] to $d^{O(1/\epsilon^2)}$.

1.4 Minimum Weight Spanning Tree

Chazelle et al. [4] studied the problem of approximating the minimum weight of a spanning tree in an edge-weighted graph. For a (connected) graph $G = (V, E)$ with an associated weight function w over E, let $st(G, w)$ denote the minimum weight of a spanning tree in G (according to the weight function w). Assuming $w(e) \in \{1, \ldots, W\}$ for an integer W and every $e \in E$, they show how to obtain an estimate $\widehat{st}$ that satisfies $\widehat{st} \in [st(G, w), (1 + \epsilon)st(G, w)]$ with high constant probability by performing $\tilde{O}\left(\frac{\bar{d} \cdot W}{\epsilon^2}\right)$ queries. Here a query for a neighbor of a given vertex v also returns the weight of the corresponding edge. They also give an almost-matching lower bound of $\Omega\left(\frac{\bar{d} \cdot W}{\epsilon^2}\right)$. The algorithm can be extended to the case of non-integer weights in the range $[1, W]$ (by discretization of the edge weights).[4]

The problem of approximating the minimum weight of a spanning tree when the distance function is a metric was studied by Czumaj and Sohler [6], and for the special case of the Euclidean metric, by Czumaj et al. [5].

1.5 Distance to Properties

Another type of graph parameter is the distance of a graph to having a particular property. Distance is measured in terms of the fraction of edges that need to be added and/or removed so that the graph obtains the property. Distance approximation was first explicitly introduced by Parnas et al. [25] (together with tolerant property testing).

In what is known as the *dense-graphs model*, a distance-approximation algorithm for a graph property $\mathcal{P}$ may perform vertex-pair queries, and is given an approximation parameter $\epsilon \in (0, 1)$. It should output an estimate of the distance to the property that is within $\pm \epsilon n^2$ from the true value with probability at least

---

[4] In CRT it was shown how this can be done at a cost of $1/\epsilon$ in the query complexity, and Bansal [2] showed how this cost can be avoided.

2/3. Hence a distance-approximation algorithm is a generalization of a (graph) property-testing algorithm (as defined in [12]). A property-testing algorithm should distinguish between the case that the graph has the property (distance 0), and the case in which it has distance greater than ϵ to the property.

As observed in [25], for some graph properties, known algorithms for property testing in the dense-graphs model presented in [12] immediately imply distance approximation algorithms. In particular this holds for a variety of *Graph Partitioning* properties (such as bipartiteness, and more generally, k-colorability), where the query complexity is polynomial in $1/\epsilon$. (Assuming $\mathcal{P} \neq \mathcal{NP}$, the running time cannot be polynomial in $1/\epsilon$.) Fischer and Newman [11] proved that every property that has a testing algorithm in the dense-graphs model whose query complexity depends only on $1/\epsilon$, has a distance approximation algorithm whose query complexity depends only on $1/\epsilon$ (though the dependence may be quite high (e.g., a tower function)).

Marko and Ron [19] studied distance approximation for bounded-degree and unbounded-degree sparse graphs. In both cases the algorithms can perform neighbor and degree queries. For graphs with a degree bound d, distance is measured with respect to $d \cdot n$, while when there is no bound on the degree, distance is measured with respect to a given upper bound on the number of edges. They present several distance approximation algorithms for properties that have testing algorithms [13], such as k-connectivity and subgraph-freeness.

1.6 Organization

Following a preliminaries section, in Sect. 3 we describe an algorithm for approximating the average degree $\bar{d}$, and more generally, μ_s for $s \geq 1$. In Sect. 4 we give two algorithms for approximating the minimum size of a vertex cover, and in Sect. 5 we describe an algorithm for approximating the minimum weight of a spanning tree. Due to space constraints, some analysis details are omitted.

2 Preliminaries

For an integer s, we let $[s] \overset{\text{def}}{=} \{1, \ldots, s\}$. Let $G = (V, E)$ be an undirected graph, which, unless stated otherwise, is simple and unweighted. We denote the number of vertices in G by n and the number of edges by m. Each vertex $v \in V$ is associated with a unique id, denoted $\text{id}(v)$. For a vertex $v \in V$, we let $\Gamma(v)$ denote its set of neighbors, and let $d(v)$ denote its degree. We denote the maximum degree in the graph by $d = d(G)$, and the average degree by $\bar{d} = \bar{d}(G)$. We assume it is possible to uniformly select a vertex in V, and for any vertex $v \in V$ to obtain its degree $d(v)$ (referred to as a *degree query*), as well as its ith neighbor for any $i \in [d(v)]$ (referred to as a *neighbor query*), all at unit cost.

3   Moments of the Degree Distribution

3.1   Average Degree

We start by considering the average degree, $\bar{d} \overset{\text{def}}{=} \frac{1}{n} \sum_{v \in V} d(v)$. In what follows we present an algorithm due to [9] (which is a variant of the algorithm appearing in [26]).

This algorithm and its analysis are more elegant than what appears in [14], and also serve as an introduction to higher moments. We have chosen to combine the presentation of the algorithm and its analysis, since we believe it better brings out the ideas behind them. The more general algorithm, for higher moments, is presented in a more conventional and formal manner in Subsect. 3.2.

In what follows we assume we have a "rough" constant factor estimate $\tilde{m}$ of the number of edges in the graph. That is, $\tilde{m} = \Theta(m)$. We describe an algorithm that, given such an estimate $\tilde{m}$, computes a "refined" estimate of $\bar{d} = 2m/n$ that is within $(1 \pm \epsilon)$ of $\bar{d}$ (for any given approximation parameter $\epsilon \in (0, 1)$). In fact, to ensure its correctness, the algorithm only requires that $\tilde{m} = O(m)$. Furthermore, if $\tilde{m} = \Omega(m)$, then with high probability it will not overestimate $\bar{d}$ (but may underestimate it). The running time of the algorithm is $\tilde{O}_\epsilon((n/\tilde{m})^{1/2})$. Hence, the assumption regarding $\tilde{m}$ can be removed by a geometric search, as shown in [14, Sect. 3.1.2].

Weight Assignment. Consider assigning each edge $e \in E$ to its endpoint that has *smaller degree*, breaking ties arbitrarily (e.g., by the ids of the vertices). Let the *weight* of vertex v, denoted $w(v)$, be twice[5] the number of edges assigned to v. Observe first that since each edge is assigned to exactly one vertex, $\sum_{v \in V} w(v) = 2m$. Next, observe that $w(u) \leq 2(2m)^{1/2}$ for every vertex u. This is true since $w(u) \leq 2 \cdot d(u)$, and for each of the $w(u)/2$ edges $\{u, v\}$ that are assigned to u, we have that $d(u) \leq d(v)$. Hence, if $w(u) > 2(2m)^{1/2}$ for some u, then $\sum_{v \in V} d(v) > (w(u)/2) \cdot d(u) > 2m$, contradicting the fact that $\sum_{v \in V} d(v) = 2m$.

The algorithm starts by selecting r vertices, uniformly, independently, at random, where $r = \frac{c_r \cdot n}{\tilde{m}^{1/2}} \cdot \frac{1}{\epsilon^2} = \Theta\left(\frac{n^{1/2}}{\bar{d}^{1/2}} \cdot \frac{1}{\epsilon^2}\right)$ and c_r is a (sufficiently large) constant. Let $R = \{u_1, \dots, u_r\}$ denote the multiset of vertices selected, and let $w(R) \overset{\text{def}}{=} \sum_{i=1}^{r} w(u_i)$. By the definition of the weight of vertices, since each u_i is selected uniformly at random, $\text{Exp}[w(u_i)] = 2m/n = \bar{d}$ for each $i \in [r]$, so that $\text{Exp}_R\left[\frac{1}{r} \cdot w(R)\right] = \bar{d}$.

We can now apply the multiplicative Chernoff bound on the sum of the random variables $X_i = w(u_i)$, which satisfy $\text{Exp}[X_i] = \bar{d}$ and $X_i \in [0, 2(2m)^{1/2}]$. By our choice of r and the assumption that $\tilde{m} = \Theta(m) = \Theta(\bar{d} \cdot n)$, we get that

$$\text{Pr}_R\left[\left|\frac{1}{r} \cdot w(R) - \bar{d}\right| > \epsilon \bar{d}\right] < 2 \exp\left(\frac{-r \cdot \bar{d} \cdot \epsilon^2}{3 \cdot 2(2m)^{1/2}}\right) < 1/10,$$

---

[5] The factor of 2 is due to the relation between the number of edges and the average degree, as well as for the sake of consistency with the higher moments algorithm.

where the last inequality is for a sufficiently large constant c_r in the setting of the sample size r. The above implies that if we had an oracle for the weight function over vertices, we could compute $w(R)$ and simply output $\frac{1}{r} \cdot w(R)$. Unfortunately, we do not have such an oracle, and furthermore, it is not even clear how to approximate $w(u_i)$ for all $u \in R$ in an efficient manner. Therefore, we approximate $w(R)$ in a different manner, as described next, conditioning on the event that $w(R) = (1 \pm \epsilon) \cdot \overline{d} \cdot r$ (which holds with probability at least 9/10). In what follows we assume without loss of generality that $\epsilon \leq 1/2$ (or else we set $\epsilon = 1/2$).

Approximating $w(R)$. Let $E(R)$ denote the multiset of *ordered* pairs, (u, v) such that $u \in R$ and $\{u, v\} \in E$. Note that if u and v both belong to R, then $E(R)$ contains both (u, v) and (v, u). Consider next "spreading" the weight of the vertices in R onto $E(R)$. Namely, for each $(u, v) \in E(R)$, if $d(u) < d(v)$ or $d(u) = d(v)$ and $\mathrm{id}(u) < \mathrm{id}(v)$, then $w(u, v) = 2$, and otherwise, $w(u, v) = 0$. By this definition,

$$w(R) = \sum_{(u,v) \in E(R)} w(u, v) .$$

The benefit of moving the assignment of weight from vertices to (ordered) edges, is that for any edge (u, v), we can determine whether $w(u, v) = 2$ or $w(u, v) = 0$ by simply performing two degree queries. Note that $|E(R)| = \sum_{u \in R} d(u)$, which can be computed by performing degree queries on all vertices in R. Also note that we can select a pair $(u, v) \in E(R)$ uniformly at random as follows: Select a vertex $u \in R$ with probability $d(u)/|E(R)|$, select $i \in [d(u)]$ uniformly at random, and query the ith neighbor of u to obtain (u, v). Finally, observe that $\mathrm{Exp}[|E(R)|] = \overline{d} \cdot r$, and by Markov's inequality, $|E(R)| \leq 10 \cdot \overline{d} \cdot r$ with probability at least 9/10. From this point on, we condition on the last event, in addition to $w(R) = (1 \pm \epsilon) \cdot \overline{d} \cdot r$, which gives us that $w(R)/|E(R)| \geq 1/20$.

Armed with the ability to uniformly sample (ordered) edges from $E(R)$ and obtain their weight, the algorithm selects, uniformly, independently, at random, $q = c_q/\epsilon^2$ edges in $E(R)$ (for an appropriate constant c_q), and sums their weights. Let the sum be denoted by X. By the above discussion, the expected value of X/q is $\frac{w(R)}{|E(R)|}$, which is at least 1/20. By applying the multiplicative Chernoff bound, we get that X/q is within $(1 \pm \epsilon)$ from this expected value with probability at last 9/10. Hence, the algorithm outputs $\frac{|E(R)|}{q \cdot r} \cdot X$ as its estimate for $\overline{d}$.

By summing the probabilities of three "bad" events ((1) $w(R)$ deviates from $\overline{d} \cdot r$ by more than a factor of $(1 \pm \epsilon)$; (2) $|E(R)| > 10 \cdot \overline{d} \cdot r$; (3) X/q deviates from $\frac{w(R)}{|E(R)|}$ by more than a factor of $(1 \pm \epsilon)$), we get that

$$\frac{|E(R)|}{q \cdot r} \cdot X = (1 \pm \epsilon) \cdot \frac{w(R)}{r} = (1 \pm 3\epsilon) \cdot \overline{d} ,$$

with probability at least 2/3. By running the algorithm with $\epsilon/3$ instead of ϵ, we obtain the desired accuracy.

Since the geometric search for a "rough" constant factor estimate $\widetilde{m}$ for m increases the complexity of the algorithm by a multiplicative factor of $\text{poly}(\log n)$ (in expectation), we get the following theorem.

Theorem 1. *There exists an algorithm that, given query access to a graph $G = (V, E)$ and an approximation parameter $\epsilon \in (0, 1)$, returns a value that belongs to $[(1 - \epsilon) \cdot \overline{d}, (1 + \epsilon) \cdot \overline{d}]$ with probability at least $2/3$. The expected query complexity and running time of the algorithm are $\widetilde{O}_\epsilon \left(\frac{n^{1/2}}{\overline{d}^{1/2}} \right)$.*

3.2 Higher Moments

For $s \geq 1$, we consider the sum over all vertices, of their degrees to the power of s, denoted $M_s \stackrel{\text{def}}{=} \sum_v d(v)^s$ and let $\mu_s \stackrel{\text{def}}{=} \frac{1}{n} \cdot M_s$ (so that in particular, $M_1 = 2m$ and $\mu_1 = \overline{d}$). As done implicitly in the case of $s = 1$ (described in Subsect. 3.1), we consider an ordering, denoted $\prec$, over the graph vertices, where $u \prec v$ if $d(u) < d(v)$ or $d(u) = d(v)$ and $id(u) < id(v)$. Our algorithm is given in Fig. 1, and as can be seen, generalizes the algorithm described in Subsect. 3.1. The sample sizes r and q will be determined in the analysis (see the statement of Theorem 2).

Algorithm 1 (An algorithm for approximating μ_s)

1. *Select r vertices, uniformly, independently, at random and denote the resulting multi-set by R. Query the degree of each vertex in R, and let $d(R) = \sum_{v \in R} d(v)$.*
2. *For $i = 1, \ldots, q$ do:*
   (a) *Select a vertex $u_i \in R$ with probability proportional to its degree (i.e., with probability $d(u_i)/d(R)$), and query for a random neighbor v_i of u_i.*
   (b) *If $u_i \prec v_i$, then $X_i = (d^{s-1}(u_i) + d^{s-1}(v_i))$, otherwise, $X_i = 0$.*
3. *Return $X = \frac{1}{r} \cdot \frac{d(R)}{q} \cdot \sum_{i=1}^{q} X_i$.*

Fig. 1. An algorithm for approximating μ_s.

Here too we assign weights to vertices (and to edges), so that when summing over the weights of all vertices (similarly, all edges) we get M_s. We first introduce some notations. Let $\Gamma_\succ(u) = \{v \in \Gamma(u) : v \succ u\}$, $\Gamma_\prec(u) = \Gamma(u) \setminus \Gamma_\succ(u)$, $d_\succ(u) = |\Gamma_\succ(u)|$ and $d_\prec(u) = |\Gamma_\prec(u)|$. For each vertex u let

$$w_s(u) \stackrel{\text{def}}{=} \sum_{v \in \Gamma_\succ(u)} \left(d(u)^{s-1} + d(v)^{s-1} \right) ,$$

and observe that for $s = 1$ the weight of a vertex u equals $2d_\succ(u)$, which fits the definition in Subsect. 3.1. Taking the sum over all vertices we get

$$\sum_{u \in V} w_s(u) = \sum_{u \in V} d_\succ(u) \cdot d(u)^{s-1} + \sum_{v \in V} d_\prec(v) \cdot d(v)^{s-1} = M_s. \qquad (1)$$

For a multi-set of vertices R, let $w_s(R) \overset{\text{def}}{=} \sum_{u \in R} w_s(u)$, and let $E(R)$ be as defined in Subsect. 3.1 (i.e., $E(R) \overset{\text{def}}{=} \{(u, v) : u \in R, \{u, v\} \in E\}$). Observe that if for each $(u, v) \in E(R)$ we define $w_s(u, v) = d(u)^{s-1} + d(v)^{s-1}$ when $u \prec v$ and $w_s(u, v) = 0$ otherwise, then $w_s(R) = \sum_{(u,v) \in E(R)} w_s(u, v)$.

The next lemma provides a bound on the maximum weight of a vertex (recall that for $s = 1$ the bound was $O(m^{1/2})$). It is proved by separately considering "low-degree" vertices and "high-degree" vertices, where the degree threshold is $M_s^{\frac{1}{s+1}}$.

Lemma 1. *For every vertex $v \in V$ we have that $w_s(v) \leq 4M_s^{\frac{s}{s+1}}$.*

Lemma 1 is the main ingredient in the proof of the next theorem.

Theorem 2. *If $r = \dfrac{c_r \cdot n}{\epsilon^2 \cdot M_s^{\frac{1}{s+1}}}$ for a sufficiently large constant c_r, and $q = \min\left\{n^{1-\frac{1}{s}}, \dfrac{n^{s-\frac{1}{s}}}{M_s^{1-\frac{1}{s}}}\right\} \cdot \dfrac{c_q}{\epsilon^2}$ for a sufficiently large constant c_q, then for X as defined in Step 3 of Algorithm 1, $X \in [(1 - 2\epsilon)\mu_s, (1 + 3\epsilon)\mu_s]$ with probability at least $2/3$.*

Proof Sketch: Lemma 1 implies that for r as stated in the theorem, with high constant probability, the sample R is such that $w(R)$ is close to its expected value, $r \cdot \mu_s$. The size of r also ensures that with high constant probability $d(R)$ (as defined in Algorithm 1) is not much larger than its expected value, $r \cdot \bar{d}$. Conditioned on these two events we get that $\text{Exp}[X_i] = \frac{w_s(R)}{d(R)} = \Omega\left(\frac{M_s}{m}\right)$, for the random variables X_i defined in Step 2b of Algorithm 1. Since it can be shown that $m \leq M_s^{\frac{1}{s}} \cdot n^{1-\frac{1}{s}}$, we get that $\text{Exp}[X_i] = \Omega\left(\frac{M_s^{1-\frac{1}{s}}}{n^{1-\frac{1}{s}}}\right)$. We also use the fact that each X_i is upper bounded by $2\max_v\{d(v)^{s-1}\} \leq 2\min\{M_s^{1-\frac{1}{s}}, n^{s-1}\}$ (since $d(v) \leq M_s^{1/s}$ and $d(v) < n$). By the multiplicative Chernoff bound we get that for a sufficiently large constant c_q in the setting of q, $\Pr\left[\left|\frac{1}{q}\sum_{i=1}^q X_i - \frac{w(R)}{d(R)}\right| > \epsilon \cdot \frac{w(R)}{d(R)}\right] < \frac{1}{10}$, and the theorem follows. $\qquad \square$

As stated in Theorem 2, the sample sizes r and q used in the algorithm depend on M_s. Similarly to the case of the average degree ($s = 1$), a constant factor estimate suffices, and such an estimate can be found by performing a geometric search (at a multiplicative cost of $\text{poly}(s \log n, 1/\epsilon)$ [9, Sect. 6]), obtaining the following theorem:

Theorem 3. *There exists an algorithm that, given query access to a graph $G = (V, E)$ and an approximation parameter $\epsilon \in (0, 1)$, returns a value that belongs to $[(1 - \epsilon) \cdot \mu_s, (1 + \epsilon) \cdot \mu_s]$ with probability at least*

$2/3$. *The expected query complexity and running time of the algorithm are*

$$O\left(\frac{n^{1-\frac{1}{s+1}}}{\mu_s^{\frac{1}{s+1}}} + \min\left\{n^{1-\frac{1}{s}}, \frac{n^{s-1}}{\mu_s^{\frac{1-\frac{1}{s}}{s}}}\right\} \cdot \mathrm{poly}(s\log n, 1/\epsilon)\right).$$

4 Minimum Vertex Cover and Maximum Matching

There are several approaches to the problem of approximating the size of a minimum vertex cover in sublinear time. Here we present two. Both are based on the relation between vertex covers and matchings. Namely, for any graph $G = (V, E)$ and any matching $M \subseteq E$, the size of a minimum vertex cover of G, denoted $\mathrm{vc}(G)$, satisfies $\mathrm{vc}(G) \geq |M|$ (because any vertex cover must include at least one endpoint of every edge in M). Furthermore, if M is a maximal matching, then $\mathrm{vc}(G) \leq 2|M|$ (because taking both endpoints of each edge in M gives us a vertex cover). Both algorithms provide an estimate $\widehat{\mathrm{vc}}$, that with high constant probability satisfies $\widehat{\mathrm{vc}} \in [\mathrm{vc}(G), 2\mathrm{vc}(G) + \epsilon n]$. The algorithms are described for bounded degree graphs, where their complexity depends on the degree bound, d. They can be adapted to work with bounded average degree, $\bar{d}$, as we discuss shortly following Theorem 5.

4.1 Building on a Distributed Algorithm

In this subsection we describe an algorithm that is due to [19]. The basic underlying idea (first applied in [24]) is to transform a local distributed algorithm into a sublinear algorithm. Recall that in the local distributed model, there is a processor residing on each vertex, and the computation proceeds in rounds. In each round, each vertex can send messages to all its neighbors. When the computation ends, each vertex knows "its part" of the output, where in the case of the computation of a vertex cover, it knows whether or not it belongs to the cover.

The distributed algorithm described in [19] is similar to the $O(\log n)$-rounds distributed algorithm for the maximal independent set of Luby [18]. The algorithm, presented in Fig. 2, is described as if there is a processor assigned to every edge, but clearly this can be emulated by processors that are assigned to the vertices. For an edge $e = \{u, v\}$, we let $d(e) \stackrel{\mathrm{def}}{=} d(u) + d(v)$ denote the number of edges that have a common endpoint with e, which are considered to be its neighbors.

In the course of the algorithm (described in Fig. 2), the edges (processors assigned to them) make various decisions (to activate/inactivate themselves, to select/un-select themselves, and to add their endpoints to the cover). Following each such decision, a corresponding message is sent to all neighboring edges (this notification is not stated explicitly in the algorithm). On a high level, the algorithm works in iterations, where in each iteration a new subset of vertices is added to the cover C (based on a certain (distributed) random process). In each iteration, the vertices added to C constitute endpoints of a matching. After the last iteration, for each edge that has remained uncovered by C, one of its endpoints is added to C. In the analysis of the algorithm, we show that with high probability (over the random selection process), the number of edges remaining in the final stage is small.

Theorem 4. *For every graph $G = (V, E)$ with degree-bound d and every $\delta > 0$, Algorithm 2 constructs a vertex cover $C \subseteq V$ such that with probability at least $5/6$, $|C| \in [\text{vc}(G), 2 \cdot \text{vc}(G) + \delta n]$.*

Algorithm 2 (Distributed approximation for minimum vertex cover)

1. *Each edge initially activates itself.*
2. *From $i = 1$ to $r = 16 \cdot \log(6d/\delta)$:*
   (a) Each active edge e selects itself with probability $\frac{1}{4 \cdot d(e)}$. If $d(e) = 0$ then e is selected with probability 1.
   (b) Every two neighboring edges that were both selected, un-select themselves.
   (c) Each vertex that is incident to a selected edge (that was not un-selected), adds itself to the vertex cover C.
   (d) All selected edges and neighbors of selected edges, inactivate themselves.
   (e) Active edges update their degrees to be the number of their active neighbors.
3. *For every edge that remained active, its endpoint with the smaller id adds itself to the vertex cover C.*

Fig. 2. A distributed algorithm for an approximate minimum vertex cover.

Proof Sketch: Since an edge inactivates itself only when one of its endpoints is added to C, and in Step 3 one endpoint from each edge that is still active is added to C, all edges are covered by the end of the algorithm. Hence C is a vertex cover, and this implies the lower bound on its size.

By the definition of the algorithm, the vertices that are added to C in the r iterations of Step 2 are endpoints of a matching. Hence, their number is at most $2 \cdot \text{vc}(G)$. It remains to show that with probability at least $5/6$, the number of edges that remain active at the start of Step 3 is at most δn. To this end we introduce the following notation: for each $i \in [r]$, let m_i be the number of active edges remaining at the end of the ith iteration of Step 2. For $i = 0$ let $m_0 = m$. It can be shown, that given the process by which the algorithm selects and de-activates edges,

$$\text{Exp}\,[m_i \mid m_{i-1}] \leq \left(1 - \frac{1}{16}\right) m_{i-1} . \tag{2}$$

The heart of the argument for establishing Eq. (2) is that the following holds for each iteration i and integer $j > 0$. If we consider at the start of iteration i an active edge e that has j active neighbors, then the probability that e is selected in iteration i and remains selected (since none of its active neighbors is selected), is $\Omega(1/j)$. But if e remains selected, then it, as well as its j active neighbors, are inactivated. The inactivation of an edge can be caused by more than one selected neighbor, but since the selected edges do not neighbor each other, an edge can be inactivated due to at most two of its neighbors. Equation (2) follows by summing the "inactivation contribution" of edges with varying numbers of (active) neighbors.

Equation (2) in turn implies that for $r = 16\log(6d/\delta)$, $\text{Exp}[m_r] \leq (1-1/16)^r \cdot m < (\delta/6)n$. By Markov's inequality, $m_r \leq \delta n$ with probability at least $5/6$, as desired. $\qquad\square$

In order to estimate the size of a minimum vertex cover we apply the observation that it is possible to emulate the outcome of the distributed algorithm (Algorithm 2) at any vertex v of our choice by considering the subgraph induced by all vertices at distance at most $r+1$ from v. Since the distributed algorithm is randomized, we only need to take care to use the same coin-flips if we encounter the same vertex u in the neighborhoods of two different vertices v_1 and v_2. The sublinear approximation algorithm is given in Fig. 3.

Algorithm 3 (Sublinear Approximation for $\text{vc}(G)$, Version I)

1. *Uniformly and independently sample $s = 2/\epsilon^2$ vertices from G. Let $S = \{v_1, \ldots, v_s\}$ be the multiset of the sampled vertices.*
2. *For each $v_i \in S$, query G in order to obtain the subgraph $G_r(v_i)$ induced by the $(r+1)$-neighborhood of v_i, where $r = 16\log(6d/\delta)$ is as in Algorithm 2, and $\delta = \epsilon/2$.*
3. *Run Algorithm 2 on the graph that is the union of all subgraphs $G_r(v_i)$ for $v_i \in S$ (in a sequential manner). For each $i \in [s]$, let $\chi_i = 1$ if the algorithm adds v_i to the cover, otherwise $\chi_i = 0$.*
4. *Output $\widehat{vc} = \frac{n}{s}\sum_{i=1}^{s}\chi_i + (\epsilon/2)n$.*

Fig. 3. A sublinear algorithm for approximating the minimum size of a vertex cover.

The next theorem follows by applying Theorem 4 together with the multiplicative Chernoff bound.

Theorem 5. *For every graph G with degree bound d, and every $\epsilon \in (0, 1]$, Algorithm 3 outputs an estimate $\widehat{vc}$, that with probability at least $2/3$ satisfies $\widehat{vc} \in [\text{vc}(G), 2 \cdot \text{vc}(G) + \epsilon n]$. The query and time complexity of the algorithm are $d^{O(\log(d/\epsilon))}$.*

We remark that the same modifications of the algorithm in [24] can be applied here to achieve a dependence on $\Theta(\overline{d}/\epsilon)$ instead of d in the query complexity. The idea is to slightly modify the distributed algorithm so that initially, each vertex with degree greater than $2\overline{d}/\epsilon$ is added to the cover, and all edges incident to these vertices are inactivated. This increases the size of the cover by an additive term of at most $\epsilon n/2$, and reduces the maximum degree in the graph induced by active edges to $2\overline{d}/\epsilon$.

4.2   Building on a Random Ordering

The local emulation of the distributed algorithm described in the previous subsection can be viewed as an *oracle* (which is randomized) for a vertex cover C.

Namely, the cover C is defined by the protocol of the distributed algorithm, and the coin flips used in the course of the execution of the distributed algorithm (that determine which edges are selected in each iteration). The oracle is given a vertex v and should answer whether $v \in C$. To this end it emulates the execution of the distributed algorithm in the neighborhood of v (flipping coins "on the fly", while keeping track of previous coin flips if needed). The sublinear algorithm for approximating the size of a minimum vertex cover can now be viewed as simply querying the oracle on $\Theta(1/\epsilon^2)$ uniformly selected vertices, and using the fraction of sampled vertices that belong to the cover to determine its estimate.

Nguyen and Onak [22] also design such a randomized oracle for a vertex cover, but their oracle is not based on a distributed algorithm but rather on the greedy *sequential* algorithm for constructing a maximal matching (and adding to the cover both endpoints of each edge in the matching). This algorithm considers an arbitrary ranking $\pi : E \to [m]$ of the edges of the graph (where each edge is given a unique rank). In each step the algorithm checks whether the next edge according to this ranking neighbors any edge that was already added to the matching M_π (initially, M_π is empty). If not, then the new edge is added to M_π. While for different rankings π we may get a different matching M_π, we always obtain a maximal matching (and hence $|M_\pi| \in [\text{vc}(G), 2\text{vc}(G)]$).

Suppose we are given an edge e, and would like to determine whether $e \in M_\pi$ (without necessarily constructing the entire matching M_π). Consider the edges that neighbor e. Observe that in order to decide whether $e \in M_\pi$, it suffices to know whether any of its neighbors with *lower rank* (according to π) is in M_π. If at least one of them is, then $e \notin M_\pi$, and if none of them belong to M_π, then $e \in M_\pi$. This gives rise to the (recursively defined) oracle in Fig. 4.

Algorithm 4 (Oracle for M_π, given an edge e as input)

1. *For each edge e' neighboring e such that $\pi(e') < \pi(e)$, recursively call the oracle (Algorithm 4) on e'.*
2. *If the oracle returns TRUE for one of these neighbors, then return FALSE, else return TRUE.*

Fig. 4. An oracle of a maximal matching M_π

The first question that arises is what is the number of recursive calls that the oracle needs to perform in order to decide whether e belongs to M_π. This of course depends on $\pi(e)$ (e.g., if $\pi(e) = 1$ then there are no recursive calls) and more generally on the ranking of edges in the neighborhood of e. To be precise, if we consider the tree of recursive calls, then the paths in the tree correspond to edges with decreasing ranks. Nguyen and Onak consider a random choice of π, and analyze the expected number of recursive calls, where the expectation is taken both over the choice of π and the choice of a random edge e. Observe that if we increase the range of π from $[m]$ to $[\text{poly}(m)]$, then $\pi(e)$ can be selected on-the-fly (that is, independently for each encountered edge), with only a small probability of a collision (i.e., $\pi(e) = \pi(e')$ for $e \neq e'$).

The next lemma directly follows from Lemma 12 in [22] (a more general *Locality Lemma* regarding random rankings of edges is Lemma 4 in [22]).

Lemma 2. *Let $G = (V, E)$ be any graph with maximum degree bounded by d. For a uniformly selected ranking π over E and a uniformly selected edge $e \in E$, the expected number of recursive calls made by Algorithm 4 when called on e is $2^{O(d)}$.*

The resulting sublinear approximation algorithm for the size of a minimum vertex cover is similar to Algorithm 3, and is provided in Fig. 5.

Algorithm 5 (Sublinear Approximation for $\mathrm{vc}(G)$, Version II)

1. *Uniformly and independently sample $s = 2/\epsilon^2$ vertices from G. Let S be the multiset of the sampled vertices.*
2. *For each $v \in S$, query the maximal matching oracle (Algorithm 4) on all edges incident to v (where π is a random ranking selected on the fly by Algorithm 4). If the oracle returns TRUE on one of these edges, then set $\chi_v = 1$, otherwise $\chi_v = 0$.*
3. *Output $\widehat{\mathrm{vc}} = \frac{n}{s}\sum_{v \in S}\chi_v + (\epsilon/2)n$.*

Fig. 5. A sublinear algorithm for approximating the minimum size of a vertex cover.

The proof of the correctness of Algorithm 5, stated next, is essentially the same as the proof of Theorem 5, and the bound on the query complexity follows from Lemma 2.

Theorem 6. *For every $\epsilon > 0$, and every graph G, Algorithm 5 outputs an estimate $\widehat{\mathrm{vc}}$, that with probability at least $2/3$ satisfies $\widehat{\mathrm{vc}} \in [\mathrm{vc}(G), 2 \cdot \mathrm{vc}(G) + \epsilon n]$. The query complexity of the algorithm is $2^{O(d)}/\epsilon^2$.*

Comparing the bound in Theorem 6 to the bound in Theorem 5 we see that while the dependence on d is larger, the dependence on $1/\epsilon$ is improved. More importantly, the approach suggested in [22] led to a significant improvement in the complexity, as we discuss shortly next. Here too we remark that it is possible to achieve a dependence on $\Theta(\bar{d}/\epsilon)$ instead of d in the complexity of the algorithm.

Reducing the Query Complexity. Nguyen and Onak [22] also suggested the following variant of their algorithm. When making recursive calls on edges neighboring an edge e, perform the calls from the smallest to the largest rank. Since once some neighboring edge of e returns TRUE, we know that e should return FALSE (so that there is no need to make calls on the other neighboring edges), they asked whether it can be proved that this variant has smaller query complexity (in expectation). A very clever analysis of Yoshida et al. [27] showed that indeed the expected number of recursive calls can be upper bounded by a polynomial in d. This yields an algorithm for approximating the size of a minimum vertex cover whose query complexity is $O(d^4/\epsilon^2)$, or $O(\overline{d}^4/\epsilon^4)$ in terms of the average degree $\overline{d}$. Onak et al. [23] showed how to further modify the algorithm so as to obtain an algorithm whose query complexity is $\widetilde{O}(\overline{d}) \cdot \mathrm{poly}(1/\epsilon))$, which almost matches the lower bound of $\Omega(\overline{d})$ for constant ϵ [24].

5   Minimum Weight Spanning Tree

In this section we present a slight variant of Chazelle et al. [4] algorithm for approximating the minimum weight of a spanning tree in an edge weighted graph with weights in $[W]$ for an integer W. We denote the minimum weight of a spanning tree by $\mathrm{st}(G, w)$ where $G = (V, E)$ is the underlying graph and $w : E \to [W]$ is the weight function.

The first idea underlying the algorithm is to reduce the problem of approximating $\mathrm{st}(G, w)$ to that of approximating the number of connected components in a graph. Specifically, for each $j \in [W]$, let $G_j = (V, E_j)$ for $E_j \overset{\text{def}}{=} \{e \in E : w(e) \leq j\}$, and let cc_j denote the number of connected components in G_j. The next lemma relates between $\mathrm{st}(G, w)$ and $\mathrm{cc}_1, \ldots, \mathrm{cc}_{W-1}$. It can be established by recalling Kruskal's algorithm for finding a minimum-weight spanning tree.

Lemma 3. $\mathrm{st}(G, w) = n - W + \sum_{j=1}^{W-1} \mathrm{cc}_j$.

Armed with Lemma 3 it remains to show how to obtain an approximation of the number of connected components $\mathrm{cc}(H)$ of a graph H (and to apply this to the graphs $G_1, \ldots, G_{W-1}$). For the sake of simplicity, in what follows we describe an algorithm whose complexity depends on the maximum degree d (rather than the average degree $\overline{d}$, as done in [4]). The algorithm, which is due to Czumaj

---

Algorithm 6 (Sublinear Approximation for $\mathrm{cc}(H)$)

1. *Repeat the following $s = 1/\gamma^2$ times:*
   (a) *Select a vertex $v_i \in V$ uniformly at random.*
   (b) *Pick a random integer X_i according to the probability distribution* $\Pr[X_i \geq k] = 1/k$.
   (c) *If $X_i > B$ then set $\chi_i = 0$.*
   (d) *Else, perform a Breadth First Search (BFS) from v_i until $X_i + 1$ vertices are reached, or the BFS can reach at most X_i vertices (since v_i belongs to a connected component with at most X_i vertices). In the former case set $\chi_i = 0$ and in the latter case set $\chi_i = 1$.*
2. *Output $\widehat{cc} = \frac{n}{s} \sum_{i=1}^{s} \chi_i$.*

Fig. 6. A sublinear algorithm for approximating the number of connected components in a graph H.

and Sohler [6], receives both an approximation parameter γ and a size bound B (and its performance is analyzed as a function of these two parameters).

Lemma 4. *For every graph G with degree bounded by d and for every $\gamma \in (0, 1]$ and integer B, $\mathrm{Exp}[\widehat{cc}] \in [cc(H) - n/B, cc(H)]$ and $\mathrm{Var}[\widehat{cc}] \leq \gamma^2 \cdot n \cdot cc(H)$. The expected number of queries performed by Algorithm 6 is $O\left(\frac{d}{\gamma^2} \log B\right)$.*

Lemma 4 can be established by a fairly standard probabilistic analysis.

In Fig. 7 we give an algorithm for approximating the minimum weight of a spanning tree by using Algorithm 6 as a subroutine.

Algorithm 7 (Sublinear Approximation for $st(G, w)$)

1. *For $j = 1$ to $W - 1$:*
   (a) *Run Algorithm 6 on G_j with parameters $\gamma = \epsilon/8$ and $B = 4W/\epsilon$ (the degree bound d is the maximum degree in G).*
   (b) *Let $\widehat{cc}_j$ be the estimate it returns.*
2. *Output $\widehat{st} = n - W + \sum_{j=1}^{W-1} \widehat{cc}_j$.*

Fig. 7. A sublinear algorithm for approximating the minimum weight of a spanning tree.

The next theorem follows by applying Lemmas 3 and 4 and Chebishev's inequality.

Theorem 7. *For every edge-weighted graph G with degree bounded by d and weights in $[W]$, and for every $\epsilon \in (0, 1]$ Algorithm 7 returns an estimate $\widehat{st}$ that satisfies $\widehat{st} \in [(1 - \epsilon) \cdot st(G, w), (1 + \epsilon) \cdot st(G, w)]$ with probability at least $2/3$. Its expected query complexity is $O\left(\frac{d \cdot W}{\epsilon^2} \log \frac{W}{\epsilon}\right)$.*

References

1. Aliakbarpour, M., Biswas, A.S., Gouleakis, T., Peebles, J., Rubinfeld, R., Yodpinyanee, A.: Sublinear-time algorithms for counting star subgraphs with applications to join selectivity estimation. Technical report 1601.04233, Arxiv (2016). To appear in Algorithmica. 107
2. Bansal, V.: Sublinear-time algorithms for estimating the weight of minimum spanning trees. Unpublished manuscript (2003). 109
3. Bogdanov, A., Obata, K., Trevisan, L.: A lower bound for testing 3-colorability in bounded-degree graphs. In: Proceedings of FOCS, Los Alamitos, CA, pp. 93–102 (2002). 108
4. Chazelle, B., Rubinfeld, R., Trevisan, L.: Approximating the minimum spanning tree weight in sublinear time. SIAM J. Comput. **34**(6), 1370–1379 (2005). 108, 109, 120
5. Czumaj, A., Ergun, F., Fortnow, L., Magen, A., Newman, I., Rubinfeld, R., Sohler, C.: Approximating the weight of the euclidean minimum spanning tree in sublinear time. SIAM J. Comput. **35**(1), 91–109 (2005). 109

6. Czumaj, A., Sohler, C.: Estimating the weight of metric minimum spanning trees in sublinear time. SIAM J. Comput. **39**(3), 904–922 (2009). 109, 120
7. Eden, T., Levi, A., Ron, D., Seshadhri, C.: Approximately counting triangles in sublinear time. SIAM J. Comput. **46**(5), 1603–1646 (2017). 107
8. Eden, T., Ron, D., Seshadhri, C.: On approximating the number of k-cliques in sublinear time. CoRR, abs/1707.04858 (2017). 107
9. Eden, T., Ron, D., Seshadhri, C.: Sublinear time estimation of degree distribution moments: the arboricity connection. In: Proceedings of ICALP, pp. 7:1–7:13 (2017). 106, 107, 110, 114
10. Feige, U.: On sums of independent random variables with unbounded variance, and estimating the average degree in a graph. SIAM J. Comput. **35**(4), 964–984 (2006). 106
11. Fischer, E., Newman, I.: Testing versus estimation of graph properties. SIAM J. Comput. **37**(2), 482–501 (2007). 110
12. Goldreich, O., Goldwasser, S., Ron, D.: Property testing and its connections to learning and approximation. J. ACM **45**, 653–750 (1998). 110
13. Goldreich, O., Ron, D.: Property testing in bounded degree graphs. Algorithmica **32**, 302–343 (2002). 110
14. Goldreich, O., Ron, D.: Approximating average parameters of graphs. Random Struct. Algorithms **32**(4), 473–493 (2008). 106, 111
15. Gonen, M., Ron, D., Shavitt, Y.: Counting stars and other small subgraphs in sublinear time. SIAM J. Discret. Math. **25**(3), 1365–1411 (2011). 106, 107
16. Hassidim, A., Kelner, J.A., Nguyen, H.N., Onak, K.: Local graph partitions for approximation and testing. In: Proceedings of FOCS, pp. 22–31 (2009). 108
17. Levi, R., Ron, D.: A quasi-polynomial time partition oracle for graphs with an excluded minor. ACM Trans. Algorithms **11**(3), 24 (2015). 109
18. Luby, M.: A simple parallel algorithm for the maximal independent set problem. SIAM J. Comput. **15**(2), 1036–1055 (1986). 115
19. Marko, S., Ron, D.: Distance approximation in bounded-degree and general sparse graphs. ACM Trans. Algorithms **5**(2), 22 (2009). 108, 110, 115
20. Nash-Williams, C.S.J.A.: Edge-disjoint spanning trees of finite graphs. J. Lond. Math. Soc. **1**(1), 445–450 (1961). 107
21. Nash-Williams, C.S.J.A.: Decomposition of finite graphs into forests. J. Lond. Math. Soc. **1**(1), 12 (1964). 107
22. Nguyen, H.N., Onak, K.: Constant-time approximation algorithms via local improvements. In: Proceedings of FOCS, pp. 327–336 (2008). 108, 109, 118, 119
23. Onak, K., Ron, D., Rosen, M., Rubinfeld, R.: A near-optimal sublinear-time algorithm for approximating the minimum vertex cover size. In: Proceedings of SODA, pp. 1123–1131 (2012). 108, 119
24. Parnas, M., Ron, D.: Approximating the minimum vertex cover in sublinear time and a connection to distributed algorithms. Theoret. Comput. Sci. **381**(1–3), 183–196 (2007). 108, 115, 117, 120
25. Parnas, M., Ron, D., Rubinfeld, R.: Tolerant property testing and distance approximation. J. Comput. Syst. Sci. **72**(6), 1012–1042 (2006). 109, 110
26. Seshadhri. C.: A simpler sublinear algorithm for approximating the triangle count. CoRR, abs/1505.01927 (2015). 111
27. Yoshida, Y., Yamamoto, M., Ito, H.: An improved constant-time approximation algorithm for maximum matchings and other optimization problems. SIAM J. Comput. **41**(4), 1074–1093 (2012). 108, 109, 119

Dynamic Erdős-Rényi Graphs

Michel Mandjes[1]([envelope]), Nicos Starreveld[1], René Bekker[2], and Peter Spreij[1]

[1] Korteweg-de Vries Institute for Mathematics, University of Amsterdam,
Amsterdam, The Netherlands
m.r.h.mandjes@uva.nl
[2] Department of Mathematics, VU University, Amsterdam, The Netherlands

Abstract. We propose two classes of dynamic versions of the classical Erdős-Rényi graph: one in which the transition rates are governed by an external regime process, and one in which the transition rates are periodically resampled. For both models we consider the evolution of the number of edges present, with explicit results for the corresponding moments, functional central limit theorems and large deviations asymptotics.

Keywords: Random graphs · Dynamics · Scaling limits

1   Introduction

Over the past decades, networks have been the subject of an intensive research effort. As networks offer the right framework to model e.g. social, physical, chemical, biological and technological phenomena, various specific aspects have been studied in depth. Arguably among the most studied objects is the *Erdős-Rényi graph* [6,7]. In such a random graph $G(n,p)$ there are n vertices, and each of the $N = \binom{n}{2}$ edges is 'up' with a fixed probability $p \in (0,1)$ or 'down' otherwise. By now there is a sizeable literature on this type of graph, providing detailed insight into its probabilistic properties, an example of a key result being that if the 'up-probability' p is larger than $\log n/n$, then the resulting graph is almost surely connected.

The existing literature predominantly focuses on *static* graphs: the random graph is drawn just once, and does not change over time. In many real-life situations, however, the network structure temporally evolves, with edges appearing and disappearing. In a few recent contributions, first results on such dynamic random graphs have been reported, but the analysis of this class of models is still in its infancy; see e.g. [8,9,15], and [1] for an illustration of its use in engineering.

In [15] various dynamic random graph models are discussed, among them a dynamic Erdős-Rényi graph in which all N edges evolve independently. In this model, each edge makes transitions from present to absent and vice versa in a Markovian manner: it exists for an exponential time with parameter μ (which we refer to as the 'up-rate'), and disappears for an exponential time with parameter λ (the 'down-rate'). For this model various metrics can be analyzed in closed

© Springer Nature Switzerland AG 2019
B. Steffen and G. Woeginger (Eds.): Computing and Software Science, LNCS 10000, pp. 123–140, 2019.
https://doi.org/10.1007/978-3-319-91908-9_8

form. In particular the distribution of the number of edges at time t, throughout this paper denoted by $Y(t)$, can be explicitly computed. A special case is that in which no edges exist at $t = 0$: then the distribution of $Y(t)$ coincides with the number of edges in a static Erdős-Rényi graph $G(n, p(t))$ (with an up-probability that depends on t).

In many applications the model that we just sketched is of limited relevance, as various features that play a role in real-life networks are not covered. To remedy this, in [15] alternative random graph processes were proposed, such as the dynamic counterparts of the configuration model and the stochastic block model. It is noted that a specific property that is often not fulfilled in real networks is that of the edges evolving independently; in practice likely there will be 'external' factors that affect all these N processes simultaneously, rendering them dependent. An example is a dynamic random graph in which the values of the up-rate and down-rate are determined by an independent stochastic process (think of temperature in a chemical network, weather conditions in a road traffic network, economic conditions in a financial network, etc.).

Motivated by the above considerations, the focus of this paper is on models in which the edges evolve *dependently*; the main contribution is that we propose and analyze two such models. In the first model, studied in Sect. 2, the up-rate and the down-rate of each of the edges are determined by an external, autonomously evolving Markov process $X(t)$, in the sense that at time t these rates (for all edges) are λ_i and μ_i if $X(t) = i$; this mechanism is usually referred to as *regime switching*. In the second model, which is analyzed in Sect. 3, the up-rate and the down-rate (say, Λ and M) are resampled every $\Delta > 0$ time units (and these sampled values then apply to all edges).

In more detail, our findings are the following. The focus is on the probabilistic properties of the process $Y(t)$ that records the number of edges present as a function of time. For both models mentioned above we manage to uniquely characterize its transient and stationary behavior, albeit in a somewhat implicit way: for the first model in terms of a PDE for the corresponding probability generating function (PGF), for the second model in terms of a recursion for the PGF. Then we use these characterizations to point out how transient and stationary means can be computed. The next step is to consider scaling limits; under a particular scaling, the process $Y(t)$ satisfies a functional central limit theorem. More specifically, after centering and scaling it converges to an Ornstein-Uhlenbeck (OU) process; interestingly, in [13] it is shown that for certain dynamic Erdős-Rényi graphs that a particular clique-complex related quantity (the 'Betti number') is described by an OU process as well. Finally we discuss for both models the corresponding sample-path large deviations, characterizing the models' rare-event behavior. In Sect. 4, the results are illustrated by numerical examples.

2   Erdős-Rényi Graphs Under Regime Switching

In this section we consider the following model. Let $(X(t))_{t \geqslant 0}$ be an irreducible continuous-time Markov process, typically referred to as the *regime process* or *background process*, living on the state space $\{1, \ldots, d\}$. The transition rate matrix corresponding to $(X(t))_{t \geqslant 0}$ is denoted by $Q = (q_{ij})_{i,j=1}^d$ and the corresponding invariant distribution by the (column) vector $\boldsymbol{\pi}$. As before, we consider the situation of N possible edges. Let $\mu_i \geqslant 0$ be the hazard rate of an existing edge becoming inactive when the regime process is in state i; likewise, $\lambda_i \geqslant 0$ is the hazard rate corresponding with a non-existing edge becoming active. Due to the common regime process the edges are reacting to, the number of links present (denoted by $(Y(t))_{t \geqslant 0}$) evolves according to an interesting dynamic structure.

2.1 Generating Function

We start our exposition by studying the (transient and stationary) PGFs

$$\phi_i(t, z) := \mathbb{E}\left(z^{Y(t)} 1_{\{X(t) = i\}}\right), \quad \phi_i(z) := \mathbb{E}\left(z^Y 1_{\{X = i\}}\right).$$

We do so by first analyzing $p_i(m, t) := \mathbb{P}(Y(t) = m, X(t) = i)$, by following classical procedures; later we also point out how $p_i(m) := \mathbb{P}(Y = m, X = i)$ can be found. Setting up the Kolmogorov equations, with $q_i := -q_{ii} > 0$,

$$p_i(m, t + \Delta t) = \sum_{j \neq i} p_j(m, t) q_{ji}\, \Delta t$$
$$+ p_i(m+1, t)\mu_i(m+1)\Delta t + p_i(m-1, t)\lambda_i(N-m+1)\Delta t$$
$$+ p_i(m, t)\left(1 - q_i \Delta t - \mu_i\, m\, \Delta t - \lambda_i\,(N-m)\,\Delta t\right) + o(\Delta t),$$

leading to the linear system of differential equations

$$p_i'(m, t) = \sum_{j=1}^d p_j(m, t) q_{ji} + p_i(m+1, t)\mu_i\,(m+1)$$
$$+ p_i(m-1, t)\lambda_i\,(N-m+1) - p_i(m, t)\mu_i\,m - p_i(m, t)\lambda_i\,(N-m),$$

where $p_i(-1, t)$ and $p_i(N+1, t)$ are set to 0. Multiplying by z^m and summing over $m = 0$ up to N, we arrive at the PDE

$$\frac{\partial}{\partial t}\phi_i(t, z) = \sum_{j=1}^d \phi_j(t, z) q_{ji} + \mu_i(1-z)\frac{\partial}{\partial z}\phi_i(t, z) +$$
$$\lambda_i N(z-1)\phi_i(t, z) + \lambda_i z(1-z)\frac{\partial}{\partial z}\phi_i(t, z).$$

In stationarity, the left-hand side of the previous display can be equated to 0, thus leading to an ODE. We obtain

$$0 = \sum_{j=1}^d \phi_j(z) q_{ji} + \mu_i(1-z)\phi_i'(z) + \lambda_i N(z-1)\phi_i(z) + \lambda_i z(1-z)\phi_i'(z).$$

2.2 Moments

Following a standard procedure, we can find explicit expressions for all (factorial) moments. To this end, we define $e_{i,k} := \mathbb{E}((Y)_k 1_{\{X=i\}})$, with $(x)_k$ denoting $x(x-1)\cdots(x-k+1)$. We obtain the factorial moments by differentiating with respect to z and plugging in $z = 1$: in self-evident matrix/vector notation, with $\Lambda := \mathrm{diag}\{\boldsymbol{\lambda}\}$ and $M := \mathrm{diag}\{\boldsymbol{\mu}\}$,

$$\mathbf{0}^{\mathrm{T}} = e_1^{\mathrm{T}} Q - e_1^{\mathrm{T}} M + \boldsymbol{\pi}^{\mathrm{T}} \Lambda N - e_1^{\mathrm{T}} \Lambda.$$

This leads to $\mathbb{E}Y = e_1^{\mathrm{T}} \mathbf{1}$, with $e_1^{\mathrm{T}} = N \cdot \boldsymbol{\pi}^{\mathrm{T}} \Lambda (\Lambda + M - Q)^{-1}$; observe that the mean is proportional to N, as expected. This procedure provides a recursion for all factorial moments: by differentiating k times and inserting $z = 1$, we obtain, for $k = 2, 3, \ldots, N$,

$$\mathbf{0}^{\mathrm{T}} = e_k^{\mathrm{T}} Q - k\, e_k^{\mathrm{T}} M + kN\, e_{k-1}^{\mathrm{T}} \Lambda - k\, e_k^{\mathrm{T}} \Lambda - k(k-1)\, e_{k-1}^{\mathrm{T}} \Lambda,$$

and consequently

$$e_k^{\mathrm{T}} = k\,(N - k + 1) \cdot e_{k-1}^{\mathrm{T}} \Lambda (k\Lambda + kM - Q)^{-1}.$$

Observe that this recursion can be explicitly solved, as we know e_1^{T}; the following result now straightforwardly follows.

Proposition 1. *For $k = 1, \ldots, N$,*

$$e_k^{\mathrm{T}} = k!\,(N)_k \cdot \boldsymbol{\pi}^{\mathrm{T}} \Lambda (\Lambda + M - Q)^{-1} \Lambda (2\Lambda + 2M - Q)^{-1} \cdots \Lambda (k\Lambda + kM - Q)^{-1},$$

whereas $e_k^{\mathrm{T}} = 0$ for $k = N + 1, N + 2, \ldots$.

Following standard techniques, we can now evaluate all stationary probabilities as well. First, $p_i(N)$ follows from the identity $e_{i,N} = \mathbb{E}((Y)_N 1_{\{X=i\}}) = N!\, p_i(N)$. We can recursively find the other probabilities $p_i(m)$; applying

$$e_{i,N-1} = \mathbb{E}((Y)_{N-1} 1_{\{X=i\}}) = (N-1)!\, p_i(N-1) + N!\, p_i(N),$$

we can express $p_i(N - 1)$ in terms of $p_i(N)$ (and $e_{i,N-1}$ and $e_{i,N}$). In general $p_i(m)$ can be found from $p_i(m + 1), \ldots, p_i(N)$ using

$$e_{i,m} = \sum_{k=m}^{N} (k)_m p_i(k).$$

Remark 1. In addition, the *transient* factorial moments $\mathbb{E}((Y(t))_k\, 1_{\{X(t)=i\}})$ can be (recursively) found; in every step of the recursion a system of linear differential equations (rather than a linear-algebraic equation) needs to be solved; see [12] for a similar procedure in the context of infinite-server queues under regime switching.

2.3   Diffusion Results Under Scaling

In this subsection we impose the scaling $Q \mapsto N^\delta Q$, entailing that the regime process is sped up by a factor N^δ, with the objective to prove a functional central limit theorem for the resulting limiting process. To get a feeling for how this scaling affects the system's behavior, we first compute the mean and variance of the stationary number of edges. To this end, we use the following lemma, which is proven in the appendix. In the sequel $D := (\mathbf{1}\boldsymbol{\pi}^T - Q)^{-1} - \mathbf{1}\boldsymbol{\pi}^T$ denotes the *deviation matrix*. Also $x^\star := \boldsymbol{x}^T\boldsymbol{\pi}$ for $\boldsymbol{x} \in \mathbb{R}^d$ and $\Gamma := \mathrm{diag}\{\boldsymbol{\gamma}\} = \Lambda + M$. Let $\boldsymbol{\gamma} := \boldsymbol{\lambda} + \boldsymbol{\mu}$ be componentwise positive.

Lemma 1. *Define* $F_{N,k} := (k\,\Gamma - NQ)^{-1}$ *for* $k \in \mathbb{N}$. *Then, as* $N \to \infty$,

$$F_{N,k} = \frac{1}{k}\frac{1}{\gamma^\star}\mathbf{1}\,\boldsymbol{\pi}^T + \frac{1}{N}E + O(N^{-2}), \quad E := \left(I - \frac{1}{\gamma^\star}\mathbf{1}\,\boldsymbol{\pi}^T\Gamma\right)D\left(I - \frac{1}{\gamma^\star}\boldsymbol{\gamma}\,\boldsymbol{\pi}^T\right).$$

Let us first evaluate the mean of Y under this scaling; in the steps below we use $\boldsymbol{\pi}^T\Lambda\mathbf{1} = \lambda^\star$ and $D\mathbf{1} = \mathbf{0}$. From the above lemma, we find, with $\bar{\varrho} := \lambda^\star/\gamma^\star$,

$$\mathbb{E}\,Y = N\boldsymbol{\pi}^T\Lambda(\Lambda + M - N^\delta Q)^{-1}\mathbf{1} = N\boldsymbol{\pi}^T\Lambda F_{N^\delta,1}\mathbf{1}$$
$$= N\boldsymbol{\pi}^T\Lambda\left(\frac{1}{\gamma^\star}\mathbf{1}\boldsymbol{\pi}^T\mathbf{1} + N^{-\delta}E\mathbf{1} + O(N^{-2\delta})\right) = N\,\bar{\varrho} + O(N^{1-\delta}).$$

Along the same lines,

$$(\mathbb{E}\,Y)^2 = N^2\bar{\varrho}^{\,2} - N^{2-\delta}\frac{2}{\gamma^\star}\boldsymbol{\pi}^T(\Lambda - \bar{\varrho}\,\Gamma)D\,\bar{\varrho}\,\Gamma\mathbf{1} + o(N^{\max\{1,2-\delta\}}).$$

In addition, ignoring sublinear terms,

$$\mathbb{E}\,Y(Y-1) = 2N(N-1)\,\boldsymbol{\pi}^T\Lambda(\Lambda + M - N^\delta Q)^{-1}\Lambda(2\Lambda + 2M - N^\delta Q)^{-1}\mathbf{1}$$
$$= 2N(N-1)\,\boldsymbol{\pi}^T\Lambda\,F_{N^\delta,1}\,\Lambda\,F_{N^\delta,2}\mathbf{1}$$
$$= 2N(N-1)\,\boldsymbol{\pi}^T\Lambda\left(\frac{1}{\gamma^\star}\mathbf{1}\,\boldsymbol{\pi}^T + \frac{1}{N^\delta}E\right)\Lambda\left(\frac{1}{2\gamma^\star}\mathbf{1}\,\boldsymbol{\pi}^T + \frac{1}{N^\delta}E\right)\mathbf{1}.$$

Using the following equalities

$$\boldsymbol{\pi}^T\Lambda\left(\frac{1}{\gamma^\star}\mathbf{1}\,\boldsymbol{\pi}^T\right)\Lambda\left(\frac{1}{2\gamma^\star}\mathbf{1}\,\boldsymbol{\pi}^T\right)\mathbf{1} = \frac{\bar{\varrho}^{\,2}}{2},$$

$$\boldsymbol{\pi}^T\Lambda\,E\Lambda\left(\frac{1}{2\gamma^\star}\mathbf{1}\,\boldsymbol{\pi}^T\right)\mathbf{1} = \frac{1}{2\gamma^\star}\boldsymbol{\pi}^T(\Lambda - \bar{\varrho}\,\Gamma)D(\Lambda - \bar{\varrho}\,\Gamma)\mathbf{1},$$

$$\boldsymbol{\pi}^T\Lambda\left(\frac{1}{\gamma^\star}\mathbf{1}\,\boldsymbol{\pi}^T\right)\Lambda E\mathbf{1} = -\frac{1}{\gamma^\star}\boldsymbol{\pi}^T(\Lambda - \bar{\varrho}\,\Gamma)D\,\bar{\varrho}\,\Gamma\mathbf{1},$$

we arrive at

$$\mathbb{E}\,Y(Y-1) = N(N-1)\,\bar{\varrho}^{\,2} + N^{2-\delta}\frac{1}{\gamma^\star}\boldsymbol{\pi}^T(\Lambda - \bar{\varrho}\,\Gamma)D(\Lambda - 3\,\bar{\varrho}\,\Gamma)\mathbf{1} + o(N^{\max\{1,2-\delta\}}).$$

By virtue of the identity $\operatorname{Var} Y = \mathbb{E}Y(Y-1) + \mathbb{E}Y - (\mathbb{E}Y)^2$, we thus find

$$\operatorname{Var} Y = N\,\bar\varrho(1-\bar\varrho) + N^{2-\delta}\,v + o(N^{\max\{1,2-\delta\}}), \tag{1}$$

with

$$v := \frac{1}{\gamma^\star}\boldsymbol{\pi}^{\mathrm{T}}(\Lambda - \bar\varrho\,\Gamma)D(\Lambda - \bar\varrho\,\Gamma)\mathbf{1}.$$

It can be checked that this formula is symmetric, in the sense that it is invariant under swapping $\boldsymbol{\lambda}$ and $\boldsymbol{\mu}$, which is in line with $\operatorname{Var} Y = \operatorname{Var}(N-Y)$; note that $\Lambda - \bar\varrho\,\Gamma = (1-\bar\varrho)\Lambda - \bar\varrho M$.

Upon inspecting the asymptotic shape of $\operatorname{Var} Y$, we observe a dichotomy. For $\delta > 1$ the regime process jumps so fast that all edges essentially behave independently, experiencing an 'effective up-rate' of $\lambda^\star$, and an 'effective down-rate' of $\mu^\star$, so that in this regime Y is approximated with a Binomial random variable with parameters N and $\bar\varrho$. For $\delta < 1$ the regime process is relatively slow, and hence affects the variance (which is, as a result, superlinear in N).

We now prove a functional central limit theorem. For the moment we focus on the case $\delta = 1$; in Remark 3 we comment on what happens when $\delta > 1$ or $\delta < 1$. Let $P_1(\cdot)$ and $P_2(\cdot)$ be two independent unit-rate Poisson processes. With $Z_i(s) := 1_{\{X(s)=i\}}$, and $Y(0) = 0$ (remarking that any other starting point can be dealt with similarly),

$$Y(t) = P_1\left(\sum_{i=1}^{d}\int_0^t \lambda_i Z_i(s)(N-Y(s))\mathrm{d}s\right) - P_2\left(\sum_{i=1}^{d}\int_0^t \mu_i Z_i(s)Y(s)\mathrm{d}s\right). \tag{2}$$

The first step is to verify that $Y(t)/N$ converges to $y(t)$, defined as the solution of the integral equation

$$y(t) = \lambda^\star\int_0^t (1 - y(s))\mathrm{d}s - \mu^\star\int_0^t y(s)\mathrm{d}s,$$

i.e., $y(t) = \varrho(t) := \bar\varrho\cdot(1 - e^{-\gamma^\star t})$. Define

$$\bar Y(t) := \frac{Y(t) - N\varrho(t)}{\sqrt{N}}; \tag{3}$$

our objective is to prove that $\bar Y(\cdot)$ converges to a Gaussian process (and we identify this process). As we follow [2, Sect. 5], which in turn uses intermediate results of [10], we restrict ourselves to the most important steps.

We know from (2) that, for some martingale $K(t)$,

$$\mathrm{d}Y(t) = \boldsymbol{\lambda}^T \boldsymbol{Z}(t)(N-Y(t))\mathrm{d}t - \boldsymbol{\mu}^T \boldsymbol{Z}(t)Y(t)\mathrm{d}t + \mathrm{d}K(t),$$

and therefore

$$\mathrm{d}\bar Y(t) = \sqrt{N}\big((1-\varrho(t))\boldsymbol{\lambda}^{\mathrm{T}} - \varrho(t)\boldsymbol{\mu}^{\mathrm{T}}\big)\boldsymbol{Z}(t)\mathrm{d}t - \boldsymbol{\gamma}^{\mathrm{T}}\boldsymbol{Z}(t)\bar Y(t)\mathrm{d}t + \frac{\mathrm{d}K(t)}{\sqrt{N}} - \sqrt{N}\varrho'(t)\mathrm{d}t.$$

Now define $W(t) := e^{Z_+(t)}\bar{Y}(t)$, where $Z_+(t) := \int_0^t \boldsymbol{\gamma}^{\mathrm{T}} \boldsymbol{Z}(s)\mathrm{d}s$, so that,

$$\mathrm{d}W(t) = e^{Z_+(t)}\left(\sqrt{N}\big((1-\varrho(t))\boldsymbol{\lambda}^{\mathrm{T}} - \varrho(t)\boldsymbol{\mu}^{\mathrm{T}}\big)\boldsymbol{Z}(t)\mathrm{d}t + \frac{\mathrm{d}K(t)}{\sqrt{N}} - \sqrt{N}\varrho'(t)\mathrm{d}t\right).$$

Observing that $\big((1-\varrho(t))\boldsymbol{\lambda}^{\mathrm{T}} - \varrho(t)\boldsymbol{\mu}^{\mathrm{T}}\big)\boldsymbol{\pi} = \varrho'(t)$, and recalling that $\boldsymbol{\gamma} = \boldsymbol{\lambda} + \boldsymbol{\mu}$, the equality in the previous display simplifies to

$$\mathrm{d}W(t) = e^{Z_+(t)}\left(\sqrt{N}\big(\boldsymbol{\lambda}^{\mathrm{T}} - \varrho(t)\boldsymbol{\gamma}^{\mathrm{T}}\big)\big(\boldsymbol{Z}(t) - \boldsymbol{\pi}\big)\mathrm{d}t + \frac{\mathrm{d}K(t)}{\sqrt{N}}\right).$$

We now consider the two terms in the previous display separately. As was established in [2, 10], for the first term, as $N \to \infty$,

$$\int_0^{\cdot} \sqrt{N}e^{Z_+(s)}\big(\boldsymbol{\lambda}^{\mathrm{T}} - \varrho(s)\boldsymbol{\gamma}^{\mathrm{T}}\big)\big(\boldsymbol{Z}(s) - \boldsymbol{\pi}\big)\mathrm{d}s \to \int_0^{\cdot} e^{\gamma^\star s}\mathrm{d}G(s),$$

where $G(\cdot)$ satisfies

$$\langle G\rangle_t = g(t) := 2\int_0^t \boldsymbol{\pi}^{\mathrm{T}}(\Lambda - \varrho(s)\Gamma)D(\Lambda - \varrho(s)\Gamma)\mathbf{1}\mathrm{d}s. \tag{4}$$

Also as in [2, 10], the second term obeys, as $N \to \infty$,

$$\int_0^{\cdot} \frac{1}{\sqrt{N}}e^{Z_+(s)}\mathrm{d}K(s) \to \int_0^{\cdot} e^{\gamma^\star s}\mathrm{d}H(s),$$

where $H(\cdot)$ satisfies (using the relation between $K(\cdot)$ and the Poisson processes $P_1(\cdot)$ and $P_2(\cdot)$)

$$\langle H\rangle_t = h(t) := \int_0^t \lambda^\star(1-\varrho(s))\mathrm{d}s + \int_0^t \mu^\star\varrho(s)\mathrm{d}s. \tag{5}$$

Combining the two terms studied above, it thus follows that, as $N \to \infty$, $W(\cdot)$ weakly converges to $W_\infty(\cdot)$, which is the solution to the stochastic differential equation, with $B(\cdot)$ a standard Brownian motion,

$$\mathrm{d}W_\infty(t) = e^{\gamma^\star t}\sqrt{g'(t) + h'(t)}\,\mathrm{d}B(t). \tag{6}$$

Translating this back in terms of a stochastic differential equation, again mimicking the line of reasoning of [2, 10], we obtain the following result.

Theorem 1. *$\bar{Y}(\cdot)$ converges weakly to $\bar{Y}_\infty(\cdot)$, which is the solution to the stochastic differential equation*

$$\mathrm{d}\bar{Y}_\infty(t) = -\gamma^\star\bar{Y}_\infty(t)\,\mathrm{d}t + \sqrt{g'(t) + h'(t)}\,\mathrm{d}B(t), \tag{7}$$

with $g(\cdot)$ and $h(\cdot)$ given by (4) and (5), respectively.

Remark 2. Using the behavior of $g'(t)$ and $h'(t)$ for t large, we conclude that for large values of t ('in stationarity'), this stochastic differential equation reads

$$d\bar{Y}_\infty(t) = -\gamma^\star \bar{Y}_\infty(t)\,dt + \sqrt{2\gamma^\star \bar{\varrho}\,(1 - \bar{\varrho}) + 2\gamma^\star v}\,dB(t),$$

which defines an OU process with mean 0 and variance $\bar{\varrho}\,(1 - \bar{\varrho}) + v$; note that this aligns with what we found, plugging in $\delta = 1$, in (1).

Remark 3. When $\delta < 1$, the $\sqrt{N}$ in the definition of (2) needs to be replaced by $N^{\delta/2}$; it is readily checked that in the limiting stochastic differential equation (7) we then just have $g'(t)$ below the square-root sign. On the contrary, if $\delta > 1$ then the definition of (2) remains unchanged, but below the square-root sign in (7) we only have $h'(t)$.

2.4   Large Deviations Results Under Scaling

Where we above discussed the diffusion behavior of the process under study, we now consider rare events. We again focus on the scaling corresponding to $\delta = 1$, following the setup of [11]. Intuitively, the rare-event behavior is decomposed into the effect of the regime process, and that of the edge dynamics conditional on the regime process.

Let $\boldsymbol{g}(\cdot)$ be in U_T, defined as the set of non-negative d-dimensional functions such that the $g_i(s)$ sum to 1, for all $s \in [0, T]$. Then

$$\mathbb{J}_T(\boldsymbol{g}) := \int_0^T \sup_{\boldsymbol{u} \geq 0} \left(- \sum_{i=1}^d \frac{(Q\boldsymbol{u})_i}{u_i} g_i(s) \right) ds.$$

In addition,

$$\Lambda_{x,g}(\vartheta) := \sum_{i=1}^d g_i \left(x\mu_i(e^{-\vartheta} - 1) + (1 - x)\lambda_i(e^{\vartheta} - 1) \right).$$

Based on the findings in [11], one anticipates a sample-path LDP (of 'Mogulskii type'; cf. [4, Theorem 5.2]), with local rate function

$$I_{x,g}(y) := \sup_\vartheta (\vartheta y - \Lambda_{x,g}(\vartheta)).$$

This concretely means that, with $Y^\circ(t) := N^{-1}Y(t)$ and $t \in [0, T]$, and under mild regularity conditions on the set A,

$$\lim_{N \to \infty} \frac{1}{N} \log \mathbb{P}(Y^\circ(\cdot) \in A) = - \inf_{f \in A} \mathbb{I}_T(f),$$

with

$$\mathbb{I}_T(f) := \inf_{\boldsymbol{g}(\cdot) \in U_T} \left(\int_0^T I_{f(s),g(s)}(f'(s))ds + \mathbb{J}_T(\boldsymbol{g}) \right).$$

A formal derivation of this LDP is beyond the scope of this paper.

3   Erdős-Rényi Graphs with Resampling

An alternative dynamic Erdős-Rényi model (in discrete time) can be defined as follows; we refer to it as a Erdős-Rényi graph with resampling. Let the N edges alternate between two states: the edge has the value 0 when the corresponding edge is absent and 1 when it exists. In slot m, let the transition matrix of the presence of any of the N edges be given by

$$\begin{pmatrix} P_m & 1 - P_m \\ 1 - R_m & R_m \end{pmatrix},$$

where the sequence $(P_m, R_m)_{m \in \mathbb{N}}$ consists of i.i.d. vectors in $(0,1)^2$; we note that P_m and R_m (for a given time m, that is) are *not* necessarily assumed independent. It is stressed that the samples in slot m, i.e., P_m and R_m, hold for *any* of the edges—as a consequence, the individual edges (each of them alternating between absent and present) evolve dependently, as intended.

In this section we find the counterparts for the resampling model of all results that we derived for the regime switching model of Sect. 2. To make notation compact, let (P, R) denote a generic sample of (P_m, R_m).

3.1   Generating Function

Let us now analyze the object $\varphi_k(z) := \mathbb{E}\left(z^{Y_m} \mid Y_{m-1} = k\right)$. Realize that Y_m is the sum of (i) the edges that were present at time $m - 1$ and still are at m, and (ii) the edges that were not there at $m - 1$ but do appear at m. Both obey a binomial distribution (with appropriately chosen parameters). More precisely,

$$\varphi_k(z) = \mathbb{E}\left(\sum_{\ell=0}^{N-k} \binom{N-k}{\ell} (1 - P_m)^\ell P_m^{N-k-\ell} z^\ell \cdot \sum_{\ell=0}^{k} \binom{k}{\ell} R_m^\ell (1 - R_m)^{k-\ell} z^\ell \right),$$

which simplifies to

$$\mathbb{E}\left(\left((1 - P_m)z + P_m\right)^{N-k} \cdot \left(R_m z + 1 - R_m\right)^k \right).$$

Now consider the stationary random variable Y, through its z-transform $\varphi(z) := \mathbb{E}\, z^Y$. Based on the above computation, we have found the following fixed-point equation:

$$\varphi(z) = \mathbb{E}\left(\left((1 - P)z + P\right)^N \varphi\left(\frac{Rz + 1 - R}{(1 - P)z + P} \right) \right). \tag{8}$$

3.2   Moments

In this subsection, we compute the mean, variance and correlation in stationarity.

Mean. Let us first compute $\mathbb{E} Y$, by differentiating both sides to z and plugging in $z = 1$. To this end, we define

$$\psi_1(z) := \left((1 - P)z + P\right)^N, \quad \psi_2(z) := \varphi\left(\frac{Rz + 1 - R}{(1 - P)z + P} \right).$$

We first compute a number of quantities that we need in the sequel. It takes routine calculations to conclude that

$$\psi_1'(z) = (1-P)N((1-P)z+P)^{N-1},$$
$$\psi_1''(z) = (1-P)^2 N(N-1)((1-P)z+P)^{N-2},$$
$$\psi_2'(z) = \frac{P+R-1}{((1-P)z+P)^2}\varphi'\left(\frac{Rz+1-R}{(1-P)z+P}\right),$$

and

$$\psi_2''(z) = -2\frac{(P+R-1)(1-P)}{((1-P)z+P)^3}\varphi'\left(\frac{Rz+1-R}{(1-P)z+P}\right)$$
$$+ \frac{(P+R-1)^2}{((1-P)z+P)^4}\varphi''\left(\frac{Rz+1-R}{(1-P)z+P}\right).$$

As a consequence,

$$\psi_1'(1) = (1-P)N, \quad \psi_1''(1) = (1-P)^2 N(N-1), \quad \psi_2'(1) = (P+R-1)\varphi'(1),$$

and

$$\psi_2''(1) = -2(P+R-1)(1-P)\varphi'(1) + (P+R-1)^2\varphi''(1).$$

Regarding the first moment of Y, we obtain the equation $\alpha := \varphi'(1) = \mathbb{E}\,\psi_1'(1) + \mathbb{E}\,\psi_2'(1)$, or equivalently $\alpha = N(1-\mathbb{E}\,P) + \alpha(\mathbb{E}\,P + \mathbb{E}\,R - 1)$, and hence

$$\alpha = N\frac{1-\mathbb{E}\,P}{2-\mathbb{E}\,P-\mathbb{E}\,R}. \tag{9}$$

Variance. We now evaluate the quantity

$$\beta := \mathbb{E}\,Y(Y-1) = \varphi''(1) = \mathbb{E}\,\psi_1''(1) + 2\,\mathbb{E}\,\psi_1'(1)\psi_2'(1) + \mathbb{E}\,\psi_2''(1).$$

We thus obtain that β equals

$$N(N-1)\mathbb{E}\left((1-P)^2\right) + 2(N-1)\,\alpha\,\mathbb{E}\left((P+R-1)(1-P)\right) + \beta\,\mathbb{E}\left((P+R-1)^2\right),$$

and therefore

$$\beta = \frac{N(N-1)\mathbb{E}\left((1-P)^2\right) + 2(N-1)\,\alpha\,\mathbb{E}\left((P+R-1)(1-P)\right)}{1-\mathbb{E}\left((P+R-1)^2\right)}.$$

As a consequence, $\mathbb{V}\mathrm{ar}\,Y$ equals

$$\alpha - \alpha^2 + \frac{N(N-1)\mathbb{E}\left((1-P)^2\right) + 2(N-1)\,\alpha\,\mathbb{E}\left((P+R-1)(1-P)\right)}{1-\mathbb{E}\left((P+R-1)^2\right)}.$$

It takes an elementary but tedious computation to verify that if P and R equal (deterministically) p and r, respectively, then this variance reduces to $N\pi_0\pi_1$, as desired.

We also conclude that $\mathbb{V}\mathrm{ar}\, Y$ grows essentially quadratically in N. Indeed, it follows by standard computations that, with $\bar{P} := 1 - P$ and $\bar{R} := 1 - R$,

$$\mathbb{V}\mathrm{ar}\, Y = \gamma_1 N^2 + \gamma_2 N, \tag{10}$$

where

$$\gamma_1 = \frac{\mathbb{E}(\bar{R}^2)(\mathbb{E}\,\bar{P})^2 - 2\,\mathbb{E}(\overline{PR})\mathbb{E}\,\bar{P}\,\mathbb{E}\,\bar{R} + \mathbb{E}(\bar{P}^2)(\mathbb{E}\,\bar{R})^2}{\left(1 - \mathbb{E}\left((\bar{P} + \bar{R} - 1)^2\right)\right)\left(\mathbb{E}\,\bar{P} + \mathbb{E}\,\bar{R}\right)^2},$$

and

$$\gamma_2 = \frac{-\,\mathbb{E}(\bar{R}^2)\,\mathbb{E}\,\bar{P} + 2\,\mathbb{E}\,\bar{P}\,\mathbb{E}\,\bar{R} - \mathbb{E}(\bar{P}^2)\,\mathbb{E}\,\bar{R}}{\left(1 - \mathbb{E}\left((\bar{P} + \bar{R} - 1)^2\right)\right)\left(\mathbb{E}\,\bar{P} + \mathbb{E}\,\bar{R}\right)}.$$

Notice that γ_1 and γ_2 are symmetric in P and R, as desired, and observe that $\gamma_1 \geq 0$ (with equality only if P and R are deterministic). We conclude that no standard CLT applies (which would require that $\mathbb{V}\mathrm{ar}\, Y$ grows linearly in N) unless P and R are deterministic.

Correlation. We now focus on computing the limit of covariance $\mathbb{C}\mathrm{ov}(Y_m, Y_{m+1})$ as $m \to \infty$. Observe that

$$\lim_{m \to \infty} \mathbb{C}\mathrm{ov}(Y_m, Y_{m+1}) = \lim_{m \to \infty} \sum_{k=0}^{N} k\, \mathbb{E}(Y_{m+1} \mid Y_m = k)\, \mathbb{P}(Y_m = k) - (\mathbb{E}\, Y)^2,$$

which, in self-evident notation, reads

$$\sum_{k=0}^{N} k\, \mathbb{E}(\mathbb{B}\mathrm{in}(k, R))\, \mathbb{P}(Y = k) + \sum_{k=0}^{N} k\, \mathbb{E}(\mathbb{B}\mathrm{in}(N - k, 1 - P))\, \mathbb{P}(Y = k) - (\mathbb{E}\, Y)^2.$$

This reduces to

$$\mathbb{E}R \sum_{k=0}^{N} k^2\, \mathbb{P}(Y = k) + (1 - \mathbb{E}P) \sum_{k=0}^{N} k(N - k)\, \mathbb{P}(Y = k) - (\mathbb{E}\, Y)^2,$$

so that we obtain

$$\lim_{m \to \infty} \mathbb{C}\mathrm{ov}(Y_m, Y_{m+1}) = (\mathbb{E}P + \mathbb{E}R - 1)\mathbb{E}(Y^2) + (1 - \mathbb{E}P)N\,\mathbb{E}\, Y - (\mathbb{E}\, Y)^2,$$

which we can evaluate from the expressions for $\mathbb{E}\, Y$ and $\mathbb{V}\mathrm{ar}\, Y$.

3.3 Diffusion Results Under Scaling

We now consider the following scaling: for some $\delta > 0$ we put

$$P = 1 - \eta/N^\delta, \quad R = 1 - \zeta/N^\delta, \tag{11}$$

where η and ζ are non-negative random variables. The resulting model has some built-in 'inertia': for N large, the process has the inclination to stay in the same configuration. The mean number of vertices is $N\bar{\varrho}$, with

$$\bar{\varrho} := \frac{\mathbb{E}\,\eta}{\mathbb{E}\,\eta + \mathbb{E}\,\zeta},$$

irrespective of the value of δ. When analyzing the variance, however, the revealing issue is that the value of δ has crucial impact. More specifically, a minor computation tells us that $\mathbb{V}\mathrm{ar}\,Y$ essentially reads

$$N\,\bar{\varrho}\,(1-\bar{\varrho}) + N^{2-\delta}\frac{\mathbb{E}(\zeta^2)(\mathbb{E}\,\eta)^2 - 2\,\mathbb{E}(\eta\zeta)\mathbb{E}\,\eta\,\mathbb{E}\,\zeta + \mathbb{E}(\eta^2)(\mathbb{E}\,\zeta)^2}{2(\mathbb{E}\,\eta + \mathbb{E}\,\zeta)^3}.$$

Note that, due to the inertia that we incorporated, the variance is smaller than in the unscaled model, where the variance was effectively proportional to N^2. Observe from the above expression that there is a dichotomy that resembles the one we came across in Sect. 2, with some sort of transition at $\delta = 1$. For $\delta > 1$ the standard deviation scales as $\sqrt{N}$, whereas for $\delta < 1$ it scales as $N^{1-\delta/2}$. An intuitive explanation is that in the regime of relatively few transitions (i.e., $\delta > 1$) the system's inertia is so strong that its steady-state essentially behaves as an Erdős-Rényi graph with the probability that an edge exists being given by $\bar{\varrho}$. In the regime with relatively many transitions (i.e., $\delta < 1$), on the contrary, the (co-)variances play a role, in the sense that the increased variability caused by the resampling has impact; the limiting object is not of Erdős-Rényi-type.

Along the same lines, an elementary computation yields that the covariance between the numbers of edges at two subsequent epochs (in stationarity) behaves as

$$\mathbb{V}\mathrm{ar}\,Y\left(1 - \frac{\mathbb{E}\,\eta + \mathbb{E}\,\zeta}{N^\delta}\right);$$

this correlation coefficient essentially reads $1 - (\mathbb{E}\,\eta + \mathbb{E}\,\zeta)N^{-\delta}$ (for N large).

A Related Continuous-Time Model. In the remainder of this subsection we consider a specific explicit continuous-time model in which we can embed the discrete-time model discussed above, and in particular the scaling (11). To this end, we first describe the model without scaling, and then include the scaling.

Let, at time s, $M(s) \geqslant 0$ be the hazard rate of an existing vertex becoming inactive; likewise, $\Lambda(s) \geqslant 0$ is the hazard rate corresponding with a non-existing vertex becoming active. Here $M(s)$ and $\Lambda(s)$ are piecewise constant stochastic processes: for some $\Delta > 0$,

$$\Lambda(s) = \Lambda_i\,1_{\{(i-1)\Delta\leqslant s<i\Delta\}}, \qquad M(s) = M_i\,1_{\{(i-1)\Delta\leqslant s<i\Delta\}},$$

where $(M_i, \Lambda_i)_{i\in\mathbb{N}}$ is a sequence of i.i.d. bivariate random vectors such that both $\mathbb{V}\mathrm{ar}\,\Lambda$ and $\mathbb{V}\mathrm{ar}\,M$ are finite. Let $Y(t)$ be the number of vertices at time t, and Y its stationary counterpart. As it turns out, we can reuse quite a few results from the previous subsections, using the identification $Y(m\Delta) = Y_m$. In particular, it is seen that $\varphi(z) := \mathbb{E}\, z^Y$ satisfies (8), with

$$P := \frac{M}{\Lambda + M} + \frac{\Lambda}{\Lambda + M} e^{-(\Lambda+M)\Delta}, \quad R := \frac{\Lambda}{\Lambda + M} + \frac{M}{\Lambda + M} e^{-(\Lambda+M)\Delta}.$$

We thus obtain from (9)

$$\mathbb{E}\, Y = N \, \mathbb{E}\left(\frac{\Lambda}{\Lambda + M} \left(1 - e^{-(\Lambda+M)\Delta}\right) \right) \Big/ \mathbb{E}\left(1 - e^{-(\Lambda+M)\Delta} \right)$$

Similarly, we can compute the variance by (10).

Now we describe how to scale this model. The idea is to scale $\Delta \mapsto 1/N^\delta$, and to consider the regime in which we let N grow large, i.e., the transition rates are frequently resampled (and simultaneously the number of potential edges N grows). It is immediate that P and R fulfill (11) with $\eta = \Lambda$ and $\zeta = M$. We obtain that $\mathbb{E}\, Y$ tends to $\bar{\varrho} := \mathbb{E}\, \Lambda / \mathbb{E}\, \Gamma$, where $\Gamma := \Lambda + M$. In addition, $\mathrm{Var}\, Y$ satisfies the expansion $N\,\bar{\varrho}\,(1 - \bar{\varrho}) + N^{2-\delta}v + o(N^{\max\{1,2-\delta\}})$, where

$$v := \frac{1}{2\,\mathbb{E}\,\Gamma} \left(\bar{\varrho}^2 \,\mathrm{Var}\, M - 2\,\bar{\varrho}\,(1 - \bar{\varrho})\,\mathbb{C}\mathrm{ov}\,(\Lambda, M) + (1 - \bar{\varrho})^2 \,\mathrm{Var}\, \Lambda \right)$$

$$= \frac{1}{2\,\mathbb{E}\,\Gamma}\,\mathrm{Var}\,(\Lambda - \bar{\varrho}\,\Gamma).$$

The proof of a functional central limit theorem is very similar to the one for the regime switching model in Sect. 2; we therefore restrict ourselves to the key steps. With $P_1(\cdot)$ and $P_2(\cdot)$ as before,

$$Y(t) = P_1\left(\int_0^t \Lambda(s)(N - Y(s))\mathrm{d}s \right) - P_2\left(\int_0^t M(s)Y(s)\mathrm{d}s \right),$$

so that, for some martingale $K(t)$,

$$\mathrm{d}Y(t) = \Lambda(t)(N - Y(t))\mathrm{d}t - M(t)Y(t)\mathrm{d}t + \mathrm{d}K(t).$$

Then $\bar{Y}(t)$ is defined as in (3), with $\varrho(t) := \bar{\varrho} \cdot (1 - \exp(-t\,\mathbb{E}\,\Gamma))$. We define, with $\Gamma(s) = \Lambda(s) + M(s)$,

$$W(t) := e^{\Gamma_+(t)}\bar{Y}(t), \quad \text{with } \Gamma_+(t) := \int_0^t \Gamma(s)\mathrm{d}s.$$

After a few steps, this leads to the stochastic differential equation,

$$\mathrm{d}W(t) = e^{\Gamma_+(t)} \left(\sqrt{N}\left((\Lambda(t) - \mathbb{E}\,\Lambda) - \varrho(t)(\Gamma(t) - \mathbb{E}\,\Gamma) \right) \mathrm{d}t + \frac{\mathrm{d}K(t)}{\sqrt{N}} \right).$$

Consider the two terms in the previous display. For the first term, as $N \to \infty$,

$$\int_0^\cdot \sqrt{N} e^{\Gamma_+(s)} \left((\Lambda(s) - \mathbb{E}\,\Lambda) - \varrho(s)(\Gamma(s) - \mathbb{E}\,\Gamma) \right) \mathrm{d}s \to \int_0^\cdot e^{s\,\mathbb{E}\,\Gamma} \mathrm{d}G(s),$$

where $G(\cdot)$ satisfies

$$\langle G \rangle_t = g(t) := \int_0^t \mathbb{V}\mathrm{ar}\,(\Lambda - \varrho(s)\Gamma)\mathrm{d}s; \tag{12}$$

to see this note that, almost surely, uniformly on compacts, as $N \to \infty$,

$$e^{\Gamma_+(s)} = \exp\left(\frac{1}{N}\sum_{i=1}^{sN}(\Lambda_i + M_i)\right) \to \exp\left(s\,\mathbb{E}\,\Gamma\right),$$

and use this in combination with the (classical) functional central limit theorem for the random walk with i.i.d. increments [14, Theorem 4.3.5]. For the second term, as $N \to \infty$, due to the definition of the martingale $K(\cdot)$,

$$\int_0^{\cdot} \frac{1}{\sqrt{N}}e^{\Gamma_+(s)}\mathrm{d}K(s) \to \int_0^{\cdot} e^{\gamma^* s}\mathrm{d}H(s),$$

where $H(\cdot)$ is such that

$$\langle H \rangle_t = h(t) := \mathbb{E}\,\Lambda\int_0^t (1 - \varrho(s))\mathrm{d}s + \mathbb{E}\,M\int_0^t \varrho(s)\mathrm{d}s. \tag{13}$$

Combining the two terms studied above, it thus follows that, as $N \to \infty$, $W(\cdot)$ weakly converges to $W_\infty(\cdot)$, which is the solution to the stochastic differential equation (6), but now with the $g(\cdot)$ and $h(\cdot)$ given by (12) and (13), respectively. We obtain the following result.

Theorem 2. $\bar{Y}(\cdot)$ *converges weakly to* $\bar{Y}_\infty(\cdot)$, *which is the solution to the stochastic differential equation* (7), *with* $g(\cdot)$ *and* $h(\cdot)$ *given by* (12) *and* (13), *respectively.*

Remark 4. For large t ('in stationarity'), this stochastic differential equation essentially behaves as

$$\mathrm{d}\bar{Y}_\infty(t) = -\mathbb{E}\,\Gamma \cdot \bar{Y}_\infty(t)\,\mathrm{d}t + \sqrt{2\,\mathbb{E}\,\Gamma \cdot \bar{\varrho}(1-\bar{\varrho}) + 2\,\mathbb{E}\,\Gamma \cdot v}\,\mathrm{d}B(t),$$

corresponding with an OU process with mean 0 and variance $\bar{\varrho}\,(1 - \bar{\varrho}) + v$. Note that this is in line with what we found, plugging in $\delta = 1$, in the expansion $N\,\bar{\varrho}\,(1 - \bar{\varrho}) + N^{2-\delta}v + o(N^{\max\{1,2-\delta\}})$. Regarding the cases $\delta < 1$ and $\delta > 1$ a reasoning similar to that in Remark 3 applies.

3.4   Large Deviations Results Under Scaling

The above computations focused on the mean, variance, and correlation under the scaling proposed. We now consider rare events. Another straightforward calculation yields for the cumulant function, assuming Nx to be integer,

$$\log \mathbb{E} \exp\left(\vartheta(Y_m - Y_{m-1})\,|\,Y_{m-1} = Nx\right)$$
$$= \log \mathbb{E}\left(\left(e^{-\vartheta}(1 - R_m) + R_m\right)^{Nx}\left(e^{\vartheta}(1 - P_m) + P_m\right)^{N(1-x)}\right),$$

which, for $\delta = 1$, converges to

$$\Lambda_x(\vartheta) := \log \mathbb{E} \exp \left(x\zeta(e^{-\vartheta} - 1) + (1 - x)\eta(e^{\vartheta} - 1) \right)$$
$$= \log M \left(x(e^{-\vartheta} - 1), (1 - x)(e^{\vartheta} - 1) \right),$$

where $M(\cdot, \cdot)$ is the joint moment generating function of the random variables ζ and η (assuming that it exists). One thus finds a sample-path LDP where the local rate function is given by

$$I_x(y) := \sup_{\vartheta} \left(\vartheta y - \Lambda_x(\vartheta) \right).$$

More precisely, with $Y^\circ(t) := N^{-1} Y_{\lfloor Nt \rfloor}$ and $t \in [0, T]$, and under mild regularity conditions on the set A,

$$\lim_{N \to \infty} \frac{1}{N} \log \mathbb{P}(Y^\circ(\cdot) \in A) = -\inf_{f \in A} \mathbb{I}_T(f), \quad \text{with} \quad \mathbb{I}_T(f) := \int_0^T I_{f(s)}(f'(s)) \mathrm{d}s.$$

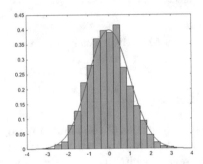 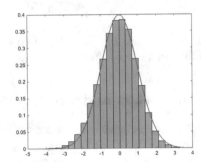

Fig. 1. Left panel: histogram of $\bar{Y}$ for situation (A). Right panel: histogram of $\bar{Y}$ for situation (B). In both cases we took $N = 45$.

4   Numerical Illustration

In this section we include a number of illustrative examples that assess the applicability of the diffusion limits. We consider two situations; in both cases we take $\delta = 1$. (A) In the first situation we consider the regime switching model of Sect. 2. The background process has two states, with $q_{12} = 2$ and $q_{21} = 3$; in addition $\lambda_1 = 0.3$, $\lambda_2 = 0.5$, $\mu_1 = 1$, and $\mu_2 = 0.1$. Using the formulae we derived in Sect. 2, we find $\mathbb{E} Y = 0.762 N$ and $\mathrm{Var}\, Y = 0.182 N$. (B) The second situation corresponds to the resampling model of Sect. 3. More, specifically, M has a uniform distribution on $[0, 3]$ and Λ a uniform distribution on $[0, 5]$. It is readily checked that $\mathbb{E} Y = 0.625 N$ and $\mathrm{Var}\, Y = 0.308 N$.

In Fig. 1 histograms are presented for the random variable

$$\bar{Y} := \frac{Y - \mathbb{E} Y}{\sqrt{\mathrm{Var}\, Y}}.$$

The number of experiments the estimates are based upon equals the number of this LNCS volume. Each simulation experiment starts with an empty system, and is then run for a sufficiently long time such that the process has reached equilibrium. The red curves in Fig. 1 correspond to the density of the standard Normal distribution. The figures confirm the convergence to the Normal distribution.

In Fig. 2 typical sample paths are depicted, illustrating the OU-like mean-reverting behavior. The red curves correspond to the mean of $Y(t)$.

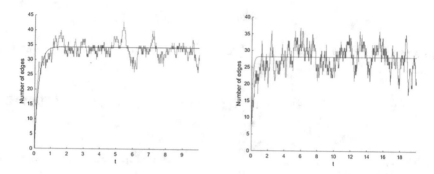

Fig. 2. Left panel: sample path of $Y(\cdot)$ for situation (A). Right panel: sample path of $Y(\cdot)$ for situation (B). In both cases we took $N = 45$.

5   Discussion and Concluding Remarks

In this paper we have discussed distributional properties of the number of edges in a dynamic Erdős-Rényi graph. We have considered two variants: one with the underlying mechanism being based on regime switching, and the other in which the transition probabilities are resampled at equidistant points in time. For both models we have succeeded in obtaining fairly explicit results for various transient and stationary quantities. Under a specific scaling a functional central limit theorem was established.

There is an interesting relation between the models considered in this paper and two-node closed queueing networks. In such closed networks a fixed number of jobs, say N, move between an active state ('in service') and an inactive state ('waiting'). Such models (but without regime switching or resampling) have been intensively studied in the literature in the context of so-called Engset models [5]; see e.g. [3] and references therein.

Topics for future research may relate to other graph metrics than the total number of edges. In the introduction, we mentioned that [13] considers the behavior of the Betti number, but one could also think of e.g. the evolution of the number of wedges or triangles in the random graph. In addition, one may wonder under what conditions the dynamic random graph in which the edges (independently) alternate between present and absent is almost surely connected; one would expect that if this alternating process is 'sufficiently fast' and the stationary up-probability is larger than $\log n/n$, this should be the case.

Acknowledgment. The authors thank Frank den Hollander (Leiden) for useful discussions.

Appendix

We now prove Lemma 1. We do so by establishing the claim for $k = 1$; plugging in $k\Gamma$ for Γ yields the stated. Write $F_\infty := (\gamma^\star)^{-1}\mathbf{1}\boldsymbol{\pi}^{\mathrm{T}}$ and abbreviate $F_N := F_{N,1}$.

As Q has a kernel of dimension 1, we can factorize Q as $Q = AB$, where $A \in \mathbb{R}^{d \times (d-1)}$ is of full column rank and $B \in \mathbb{R}^{(d-1) \times d}$ is of full row rank. It is not hard to show that BA is an invertible matrix. Moreover, every element in the right kernel of Q is a multiple of $\mathbf{1}$ and, likewise, every element in the left kernel of Q is a multiple of $\boldsymbol{\pi}^{\mathrm{T}}$.

Applying the Sherman-Morrison formula to $F_N = (\Gamma - NAB)^{-1}$, we find

$$F_N = \Gamma^{-1} + \Gamma^{-1}A\left(\frac{I_{d-1}}{N} - B\Gamma^{-1}A\right)^{-1}B\Gamma^{-1}. \tag{14}$$

Taking the limit for $N \to \infty$, we arrive at

$$F_\infty = \Gamma^{-1} - \Gamma^{-1}A(B\Gamma^{-1}A)^{-1}B\Gamma^{-1}, \tag{15}$$

where the invertibility of $B\Gamma^{-1}A$ is due to $\gamma^\star > 0$. One sees that $F_\infty A = 0$ and $BF_\infty = 0$. Hence F_∞ belongs to the left kernel of A and to the right kernel of B, so $F_\infty = c\,\mathbf{1}\boldsymbol{\pi}^{\mathrm{T}}$ for some $c \in \mathbb{R}$. One also has $F_\infty\Gamma\mathbf{1} = F_\infty\gamma = \mathbf{1}$, and hence $c = (\gamma^\star)^{-1}$, which gives the desired result for $\lim_{N\to\infty} F_N$.

We proceed by proving the expansion. Inserting

$$\left(\frac{I}{N} - B\Gamma^{-1}A\right)^{-1} = -(B\Gamma^{-1}A)^{-1} - \frac{1}{N}(B\Gamma^{-1}A)^{-2} + O(N^{-2})$$

into (14), one obtains

$$F_N = F_\infty - \frac{1}{N}\Gamma^{-1}A(B\Gamma^{-1}A)^{-2}B\Gamma^{-1} + O(N^{-2}).$$

Let A^+ (B^+, resp.) denote any left (right, resp.) inverse of A (B, resp.), so that $A^+A = BB^+ = I_{d-1}$. Then

$$\Gamma^{-1}A(B\Gamma^{-1}A)^{-2}B\Gamma^{-1} = \Gamma^{-1}A(B\Gamma^{-1}A)^{-1}BB^+A^+A(B\Gamma^{-1}A)^{-1}B\Gamma^{-1}.$$

Now, it follows from (15) that $\Gamma^{-1}A(B\Gamma^{-1}A)^{-1}B = I - F_\infty\Gamma$ and in addition $A(B\Gamma^{-1}A)^{-1}B\Gamma^{-1} = I - \Gamma F_\infty$. Hence,

$$F_N = F_\infty - \frac{1}{N}(I - F_\infty\Gamma)B^+A^+(I - \Gamma F_\infty) + O(N^{-2}). \tag{16}$$

We specialize to judicious choices of A^+ and B^+, namely

$$A^+ = \begin{pmatrix} I_{d-1} & 0 \end{pmatrix}A_1^{-1}, \quad B^+ = B_1^{-1}\begin{pmatrix} I_{d-1} \\ 0 \end{pmatrix}, \quad \text{where } A_1 := \begin{pmatrix} A & \mathbf{1} \end{pmatrix}, \; B_1 := \begin{pmatrix} B \\ -\boldsymbol{\pi}^{\mathrm{T}} \end{pmatrix},$$

and 0 stands here as well as below for a zero matrix or vector of appropriate dimensions. Both A_1 and B_1 are invertible, as an immediate consequence of the relation $A_1B_1 = Q - \mathbf{1}\boldsymbol{\pi}^{\mathrm{T}} = -(D + \mathbf{1}\boldsymbol{\pi}^{\mathrm{T}})^{-1}$. In addition,

$$B^+A^+ = B_1^{-1}\begin{pmatrix} I_{d-1} & 0 \\ 0 & 0 \end{pmatrix} A_1^{-1}, \quad B_1\mathbf{1} = -\begin{pmatrix} 0 \\ 1 \end{pmatrix}, \quad \boldsymbol{\pi}^{\mathrm{T}}A_1 = \begin{pmatrix} 0 & 1 \end{pmatrix}.$$

A straightforward computation gives with the above relations

$$B^+A^+ = B_1^{-1}A_1^{-1} - B_1^{-1}\begin{pmatrix} 1 \\ 0 \end{pmatrix}\begin{pmatrix} 1 & 0 \end{pmatrix}A_1^{-1} = -(D + \mathbf{1}\boldsymbol{\pi}^{\mathrm{T}}) + \mathbf{1}\boldsymbol{\pi}^{\mathrm{T}} = -D.$$

The result (for $k = 1$) now follows from (16). $\square$

References

1. Basu, P., Bar-Noy, A., Ramanathan, R., Johnson, M.: Modeling and analysis of time-varying graphs. arXiv:1012.0260 (2010)
2. Blom, J., de Turck, K., Mandjes, M.: Functional central limit theorems for Markov-modulated infinite-server systems. Math. Methods Oper. Res. **83**, 351–372 (2016)
3. Czachórski, T., Nycz, T., Nycz, M., Pekergin, F.: Traffic engineering: Erlang and Engset models revisited with diffusion approximation. In: Proceedings of 29th International Symposium on Computer and Information Sciences, Information Sciences and Systems 2014, pp. 249–256 (2014)
4. Dembo, A., Zeitouni, O.: Large Deviations Techniques and Applications, 2nd edn. Springer, Heidelberg (2010). https://doi.org/10.1007/978-3-642-03311-7
5. Engset, T.: Die Wahrscheinlichkeitsrechnung zur Bestimmung der Wählerzahl in automatischen Fernsprechämtern. Elektrotechnische Zeitschrift, Heft **31** (1918)
6. Erdős, P., Rényi, A.: On random graphs I. Publicationes Mathematicae Debrecen **6**, 290–297 (1959)
7. Gilbert, E.: Random graphs. Ann. Math. Stat. **30**, 1141–1144 (1959)
8. Holme, P., Saramäki, J.: Temporal networks. Phys. Rep. **519**, 97–125 (2012)
9. Holme, P.: Modern temporal network theory: a colloquium. Eur. Phys. J. B **88**, 1–30 (2015)
10. Huang, G., Jansen, H.M., Mandjes, M., Spreij, P., de Turck, K.: Markov-modulated Ornstein-Uhlenbeck processes. Adv. Appl. Probab. **48**, 235–254 (2016)
11. Huang, G., Mandjes, M., Spreij, P.: Large deviations for Markov-modulated diffusion processes with rapid switching. Stoch. Process. Appl. **126**, 1785–1818 (2016)
12. Mandjes, M., de Turck, K.: Markov-modulated infinite-server queues driven by a common background process. Stoch. Models **32**, 206–232 (2016)
13. Thoppe, G., Yogeshwaran, D., Adler, R.: On the evolution of topology in dynamic clique complexes. Adv. Appl. Probab. **48**, 989–1014 (2016)
14. Whitt, W.: Stochastic-Process Limits. Springer, New York (2002). https://doi.org/10.1007/b97479
15. Zhang, X., Moore, C., Newman, M.: Random graph models for dynamic networks. arXiv:1607.07570v1 (2016)

Wireless Network Algorithmics

Magnús M. Halldórsson[1(✉)] and Roger Wattenhofer[2]

[1] ICE-TCS, School of Computer Science, Reykjavik University,
Reykjavik, Iceland
mmh@ru.is
[2] ETH Zurich, Zürich, Switzerland
wattenhofer@ethz.ch

Abstract. The last decade has seen a large amount of algorithmic work analyzing wireless networks. In this paper we focus on some of the main lessons learned when studying the physical (SINR) wireless model, with a focus on link scheduling, without or with power control. We summarize the results in this domain, present simplified versions of some key results, and outline future directions along with major open questions.

1 Introduction

Wireless networks are ubiquitous. We use 802.11 Wi-Fi networks at home and in the office, and elsewhere our mobile devices connect to, e.g., GSM, LTE, Bluetooth. The bandwidth, latency, or error rates of wireless transmissions can be improved by carefully adjusting various parameters such as the modulation and coding scheme. However, apart from such *point-to-point* considerations, the *network* itself may also influence wireless communication.

In particular, in a network with more than two devices, concurrent transmissions may interfere. To prevent interference, one may (i) carefully *schedule* transmissions so that concurrent transmissions are separated in space or time. In addition, one may (ii) control the *transmission power* in order to reduce interference.

Increasing the transmission power of a sender will likely increase the probability that its packets are being received, but it also increases the interference for other concurrent transmissions. Similarly, scheduling a transmission at a different time may improve this transmission but generate interference for the now concurrent transmissions. Since scheduling and transmission power affect the whole network, they are difficult to understand.

There are several classic models and model variants to represent transmissions and interference in wireless networks. Here we just present two of the most common models; for a more comprehensive survey we recommend, e.g., [52]. A typical model to understand wireless networks is the so-called radio network model, e.g., [3].

This research was partially supported by Icelandic Research Fund grants 152679-051 and 174484-05.

B. Steffen and G. Woeginger (Eds.): Computing and Software Science, LNCS 10000, pp. 141–160, 2019.
https://doi.org/10.1007/978-3-319-91908-9_9

Definition 1 (Radio Network Model). *In the radio network model, the wireless network is modeled as a graph. The nodes of the graph are the wireless devices, either base stations or mobile nodes. There is an edge between two nodes if these nodes can communicate by wireless transmissions. In addition, edges also model interference. A node v can only receive a wireless transmission of a neighbor node $u \in N(v)$ if no other neighbor $w \in N(v)$ is transmitting concurrently.*

The radio network model was very influential to understand wireless networks, but it sometimes falls short because it is a *binary* model: either a node has interference or it has no interference. This is often too simplistic. In the real world, a node v may receive a packet of neighbor u despite interference of neighbor w if v is closer to u than w. This cannot be modeled by an unweighted graph. Also power control is difficult to represent with a radio network model. An improved model to understand wireless networks is the so-called disk model, e.g., [11].

Definition 2 (Disk Model). *In the geometric disk model, nodes are points in the Euclidean plane. A transmitting node u reaches all possible points within some radius r around u, where the radius may depend on the power that node u is using for the transmission. Again, a transmission will be successfully received if an intended receiver node v is inside the transmission disk of node u but not inside the transmission disk of another concurrent transmission.*

Setting the radii correctly, the disk model may be accurate enough to model some wireless phenomena, but it is still "too binary" to model reality well. Maybe a transmission can withstand a single concurrent interfering transmission if it is reasonably far away. But can it withstand multiple concurrent transmissions? Interference of electromagnetic waves is *additive*, and to truly understand wireless transmission and interference our model must be additive as well. Moreover, electromagnetic waves get weaker with distance – physics tells us that a signal drops at least *quadratically with distance*. If a receiver is closer to a sender, it may withstand more interference.

About a decade ago, researchers studying wireless network algorithms started dropping the radio network, the disk graph, and various other binary models in favor of a model that seemed to represent reality better: the so-called physical model, e.g., [47].

2   Physical Model

Definition 3 (Physical Model, Signal-to-Interference Ratio). *In the physical model, there is a gain between every pair of nodes u, v. The gain may be non-symmetric, i.e. the gain from u to v may be different from the gain from v to u. The gain describes how much the power of a transmission at u decreases on the way from u to v. If node u transmits with power p_u, node v will receive the signal with power $S = p_u \cdot g(u, v)$, where $g(u, v)$ is the gain from u to v. Interfering transmissions behave exactly the same, so a concurrent interfering*

transmission of node w will arrive at node v with interference power $p_w \cdot g(w, v)$.
Interference is additive, so all the interfering transmissions W accumulate to
$I = \sum_{w \in W} p_w \cdot g(w, v)$. *Whether or not node v can correctly receive u's trans-*
mission depends on the signal-to-interference ratio S/I. If this ratio is at least
some constant β, node v will receive the transmission correctly. The physical
model is also known as the signal-to-interference-ratio model.

The ratio β is hardware and coding dependent. For inexpensive hardware the
signal should be stronger than the interference, i.e., $\beta \geq 1$. However, reasonably
good hardware and/or coding may drive the value of β below 1.

Sometimes, we add a constant ambient noise term N to the interference of concurrent transmissions; the reception test then becomes a signal-to-
interference-plus-noise (SINR) test, i.e., we want $\frac{S}{I+N} \geq \beta$.

Definition 4 (Geometric and General Physical Model). *Sometimes, we*
add a geometric component to this physical model by assuming that the gain is
determined by the geometric distance, i.e. $g(u, v) = d(u, v)^{-\alpha}$, where $d(u, v)$ is
the Euclidean distance between u and v, and α is the so-called path-loss expo-
nent, typically $\alpha \geq 2$. We call this special case the geometric physical model. In
practice, wireless effects such as shadowing or reflection at walls may make the
gain non-geometric – if we have no restrictions on the gain function, the model
is simply known as general physical model.

Wireless networks offer a wide range of challenging algorithmic problems.
One family of problems stands out, however: the so-called *scheduling/capacity*
problem. Let us define this family of problems formally.

Definition 5 (Link). *A wireless communication link l is defined by a sending*
node s and a receiving node r, i.e., $l = (s, r)$. The length of l is the distance
$d(s, r)$ *from sender to receiver, which we shall overload with the notation l.*

Definition 6 (Feasible Link Set, Link Scheduling). *We use gain as intro-*
duced in Definition 3. A traffic demand is given by a set L of links. We want
to choose a subset $L' \subseteq L$ such that all links in L' are feasible, i.e., all links
can be scheduled concurrently. A subset L' is feasible if all links $l \in L'$ have a
signal-to-interference ratio of at least β. More formally, for any $l = (s, r) \in L'$,
we want $S_l/I_l \geq \beta$, where $S_l = p_s \cdot g(s, r)$ and $I_l = \sum_{l' \in L' \setminus \{l\}} p_{s'} \cdot g(s', r)$ with
$l' = (s', r')$ *being a link in $L' \setminus \{l\}$.*

The link scheduling problem has three main dimensions:

- Gain: Geometric or general gain as discussed in Definition 4.
- Power control: We will introduce power control in Definition 12.
- Objective: Finding the largest possible (weighted) subset L' is only one possible objective. Alternatively, we might want to partition all links L into as
  few as possible subsets $L_1, L_2, \ldots, L_k$, such that each subset is feasible, and
  then schedule the subsets sequentially. Finding a single subset L' is known as
  the *one-shot* problem, finding a partition is simply known as the *scheduling*
  problem.

The capacity problem is a close relative of the link scheduling problem, inheriting these three dimensions.

Definition 7 (Wireless Capacity). *The input to the wireless capacity problem is a set of nodes. On top of these nodes we need to specify a traffic pattern. We want to measure how much concurrent traffic is possible.*

On top of the link scheduling dimensions mentioned above, wireless capacity has additional parameters:

- Traffic Pattern: Typical traffic patterns include, e.g. every node must send a packet to every other node, or every node must send to a random node. Other classic traffic patterns form trees, e.g., all nodes must collect the average or median temperature at a specific node known as the sink.
- Node Distribution: Early capacity computations only worked if the nodes were distributed in some peculiar way, e.g. Poisson distributed nodes. Later, researchers studied best or worst case node distributions. Algorithmic analyses are able to handle arbitrary node distributions.
- Multi-Hop: Nodes may forward traffic for other nodes in a multi-hop fashion. Sometimes the routes are given, sometimes routing is part of the problem.

The scheduling/capacity problems measure how efficiently we can use a wireless network in the physical model. For wireless networks this is *the* core problem, as higher layers are generally not different from wireline networks.

Practically, link scheduling and wireless capacity will tell us how we should organize media access on the link layer, as it answers questions about optimal scheduling and power control. In wireless networks, link and network layers cannot be separated as nicely as in wireline networks as network issues will influence the link layer.

3   Link Scheduling Algorithms

We first explore algorithms for the *one-shot uniform-power geometric-gain link scheduling* problem, as introduced in Definition 6.

Short links are naturally preferable for maximizing the number of links: their signal is still relatively strong at the receiver, making them more tolerant to interference. We therefore start by sorting the input $L = \{l_1, l_2, \ldots, l_n\}$ into a non-decreasing order of length.

Greedy algorithms often work well for subset maximization. In our context, this leads to the natural approach of Algorithm 1.

Unfortunately, Algorithm 1 is too greedy. Suppose the second shortest link l_2 is just barely feasible when joined with the shortest link l_1, i.e. the signal-to-interference ratio of l_2 is exactly β. Then we cannot add *any* other link without violating the signal-to-interference ratio of l_2. In contrast, if the other links are well separated in space, the optimal set may contain all of them.

We should therefore be slightly less "greedy"! Before we present a greedy-like algorithm that works, we first introduce a convenient way of quantifying the impact of interference.

Algorithm 1. Too Naïve Greedy Algorithm for Link Scheduling

1: $R \leftarrow \emptyset$
2: **for** $i = 1$ to n **do**
3:     **if** $R \cup \{l_i\}$ is feasible **then**
4:         $R \leftarrow R \cup \{l_i\}$

Interference matters only in relation to the strength of the signal that is to be received. According to Definition 6, a transmission is received correctly if the strength of the interference is small enough *relative to* the strength of the signal. We ignore the effect of the ambient noise by setting $N = 0$. Noise can be included, but it complicates the treatment.

Definition 8 (Affectance). *Consider a link $l = (s, r)$ and an interfering link $l' = (s', r')$. The signal strength of l (as received at r) is $p/l^\alpha = p/d(s, r)^\alpha$, where p is the uniform power used by all senders. Similarly, the interference of l' is $p/d(s', r)^\alpha$. Then, the relative interference of l' on l is $\frac{1}{\beta} \cdot \frac{p/d(s', r)^\alpha}{p/d(s, r)^\alpha}$. For technical reasons, to define* affectance *we cap this relative interference of a single link at 1:*

$$\text{affectance } a_{l' \to l} := \min\left(\frac{1}{\beta} \cdot \frac{d(s', r)^{-\alpha}}{l^{-\alpha}}, 1 \right).$$

For convenience, let $a_{l \to l} = 0$.

The key feature of affectance is that it is cumulative. The affectance of a set S of links on a given link l is the sum of the individual affectances.

Definition 9 (Set Affectance). *Define*

$$a_{S \to l} = \sum_{s \in S} a_{s \to l} \text{ and } a_{l \to S} = \sum_{s \in S} a_{l \to s}.$$

Crucially, the question of whether a link l is feasible concurrently with set S of links is equivalent to the condition that $a_{S \to l} \leq 1$.

Definition 10 (Symmetric Affectance). *Let $a(x, y) = a_{x \to y} + a_{y \to x}$ be the symmetric version of affectance, and define $a(S, l) = \sum_{s \in S} a(s, l)$ as in Definition 9.*

Besides avoiding being too greedy, we could also allow infeasible intermediate solutions. Algorithm 2 from [29] combines these two approaches, using a stricter-than-absolutely-necessary criteria to add a link, yet allowing the already added links to accumulate more than affectance 1. A key feature is to bound not only the total affectance on the incoming link from the previous links, but also its total affectance on the previous links (by the same amount). Afterwards, we eliminate those that exceed their affectance budget.

We show here that the algorithm achieves a constant-factor approximation in the one-dimensional setting (when links are positioned on the line), utilizing some arguments of Kesselheim [41]. We first define some concepts.

Algorithm 2. Algorithm for Link Scheduling

1: $R \leftarrow \emptyset$
2: **for** $i = 1$ to n **do**
3:    **if** $a(R, l_i) < 1/2$ **then**
4:       $R \leftarrow R \cup \{l_i\}$
5: **return** $X := \{l \in R : a_{R \to l} \leq 1\}$

Definition 11 (Bi-feasible). *A set S of links is* bi-feasible *if it is feasible ($a_{S \to l} \leq 1$ for each $l \in S$), and if $a_{l \to S} \leq 2$, for each $l \in S$.*

Lemma 1. *Each feasible set S contains a bi-feasible subset of at least half the links.*

Proof. We use that $a_{S \to l} \leq 1$ for each $l \in S$. Hence,

$$|S| \geq \sum_{l \in S} a_{S \to l} = \sum_{l \in S} \sum_{l' \in S} a_{l' \to l} = \sum_{l \in S} a_{l \to S}.$$

In other words, the average "out-affectance" $a_{l \to S}$ of each link l is also at most 1. Since affectance is non-negative, less than half the links $l \in S$ can have affectance $a_{l \to S}$ more than twice the average.

Lemma 2. *With uniform power, two feasible links on a line cannot overlap if $\beta \geq 1$.*

Proof. Suppose there are links $l = (s, r)$ and $l' = (s', r')$ that overlap. There are two cases as to their configuration. In one case, sender s' is located inside the link l. But then, l' generates too much interference on l, and so with $\beta \geq 1$ we have $a_{l \to l'} = 1$. In the other case, the order of the nodes on the line is s, r', r, s'. Then, either s is closer to r' than s' is, or s' is closer to r than s is; either way, at least one of the links is infeasible.

Lemma 3. *Let m be a link and S be a bi-feasible set of links not smaller than m, with $m \notin S$. Then, $a(S, m) \leq 10$.*

Proof. Thanks to Lemma 2 we know that links in S do not overlap. Let l (r) be the link in S whose receiver is closest to m's receiver on the left (right), respectively. Let S_l (S_r) be the links of S to the left of l (right of r), respectively. Since l (r) is no smaller than m, and closer to each link in S_l (S_r), it receives more affectance from links in S_l (S_r) than m, respectively. Thus, $a_{S_l \to m} \leq a_{S_l \to l} \leq 1$ and $a_{S_r \to m} \leq a_{S_r \to r} \leq 1$. Since the affectance of single links is bounded by 1 (Definition 8), we get

$$a_{S \to m} = a_{l \to m} + a_{r \to m} + a_{S_l \to m} + a_{S_r \to m} \leq 4.$$

Similarly, we can bound $a_{m \to S} \leq 6$. Let x (y) be the link in S whose sender is closest to m's sender on the left (right), respectively. Let S_x (S_y) be the links of S to the left of x (right of y), respectively. Since x (y) is closer to each link in S_x (S_y), it creates more affectance on links in S_x (S_y) than m does, respectively. Thus, $a_{m \to S_x} \leq a_{x \to S_x} \leq 1$ and $a_{m \to S_y} \leq a_{y \to S_y} \leq 1$. Since the affectance on a single link is bounded by 1 and S being a bi-feasible set (Definition 11), we get

$$a_{m \to S} = a_{m \to x} + a_{m \to y} + a_{m \to S_x} + a_{m \to S_y} \leq 1 + 1 + 2 + 2 \leq 6.$$

Theorem 1. *Algorithm 2 is a constant approximation algorithm for one-dimensional one-shot uniform-power geometric-gain link scheduling problem, independent of α.*

Proof. Assume that all links are of different length, with symmetry broken arbitrarily. First, let us compare the sizes of the sets R and X found by Algorithm 2 on a given instance. The selection criterion in line 3 measures the affectance between the new link and all links in set R so far. At the end of the loop, each link $r \in R$ has been symmetrically affected exactly once by every other link $r' \in R$, i.e.

$$\sum_{r \in R} a(R, r) = \sum_{r \in R} \sum_{r' \in R} a(r', r) < \frac{1}{2}|R|.$$

Thus, on average the value of $a(R, r)$ is less than $1/2$. At least half the items in a non-negative set have a value within twice the average value. It follows that at least half the links $r \in R$ satisfy $a_{R \to r} \leq a(r, R) < 1$; i.e. $|X| \geq |R|/2$.

We now compare R with a maximum cardinality feasible set OPT. As we observed in Lemma 1, there is a bi-feasible subset O of OPT of size at least $|OPT|/2$. Split O into two parts: $O_1 = O \cap R$, and $O_2 = O \setminus R$. Since $O_1 \subseteq R$ we have $|O_1| \leq |R|$, but it remains to bound the size of O_2.

On each pair of links $r \in R$ and $o \in O_2$, define the weight function

$$w(r, o) = \begin{cases} a(r, o) & \text{if } o \text{ is longer than } r \\ 0 & \text{else} \end{cases}$$

The weight function w only considers the symmetric affectance between shorter links in r and longer links in O_2.

Let us consider the point in time when Algorithm 2 decided not to include link $o \in O_2$ to the set R in line 3; it did so because $a(R, o) \geq 1/2$. Since R contains then only links shorter than o, we have (i) $w(R, o) = a(R, o) \geq 1/2$. On the other hand, Lemma 3 implies that (ii) $w(O_2, r) \leq 10$, for every $r \in R$. With (i) and (ii) we get

$$\frac{1}{2}|O_2| \leq \sum_{o \in O_2} w(R, o) = \sum_{r \in R} \sum_{o \in O_2} w(r, o) = \sum_{r \in R} w(O_2, r) \leq 10|R|.$$

It follows that $|O_2| \leq 20|R|$. Since $|O_1| \leq |R|$, we get that $|OPT| \leq 2|O| = 2|O_1 + O_2| \leq 42|R| \leq 84|X|$.

Some observations are in order. Note that the approximation ratio is completely independent of α. This has not been observed before, but crucially needs the one-dimensional setting.

We also note that the performance analysis does not vitally utilize the definition of affectance, we only need a weak sense of monotonicity: $a_{x \to z} \leq a_{y \to z}$, if x is further away from z than y is. Thus, signal strength can be an arbitrary function of distance and the transmitter that is monotone in the distance.

Several heuristic variations are possible without affecting the performance ratio. The affectance threshold "1/2" can be any positive constant less than 1. Also, the greedy set can be formed more gradually, e.g., by eliminating the highest affectance links first.

Moreover, similar algorithms exist for different variants of the problem, multiple dimensions and also arbitrary power link scheduling can be solved similarly, using slightly more geometry in the proofs. We will summarize the most important results in Sect. 5.

The parameter β indicates how large the signal-to-interference-ratio must be for a signal to be decodable. This is a function of the technology used, both hardware (e.g. antenna design) and software (e.g. modulation, coding, error correction). One natural question is how much impact the value of β has on link scheduling and wireless capacity. Increasing β clearly makes decoding more challenging, but could there be some kind of threshold at which point the problem jumps from being very easy to very hard?

The answer is negative: Scaling β by a constant factor can only lengthen the schedule by a constant factor.

Theorem 2. *Let L be a set of links with affectance at most a, i.e., either $a_{L \to l} \leq a$ or $a(L, l) \leq a$ for $l \in L$. Then, for any $b > 0$, L can be partitioned into $\lceil 2a/b \rceil^2$ sets, each with affectance at most b.*

Proof. Let $\rho = \lceil 2a/b \rceil$. Process the links in L in an arbitrary order, assigning each link l to some set L_i, $i \in \{1, 2, \ldots, \rho\}$, where l's affectance from the previous links in L_i is at most $b/2$. Such a set must exist, since otherwise the affectance on the link l is larger than $\rho \cdot b/2 \geq a$.

Now process each set L_i in the opposite order, forming sets $L_{i,j}$, $j = 1, 2, \ldots, \rho$. The affectance on each link l is again at most $b/2$ from the earlier links, with the same argument. Since we processed the links in opposite order, the total affectance on link l is at most b in total.

A linear bound of $\lceil 2a/b \rceil$ was given in [6] using linear algebra. The implication to changing β applies when the noise term can be ignored. When noise is dominant because throughput can mostly be achieved by weak links, Theorem 2 still tells us that we can increase requirements for the spatial separations of links in a solution by paying only a constant factor.

4   Power Control

One of the most versatile tools for increasing throughput in wireless networks is the use of *power control*. Power control is a double-edged sword though:

Increasing the transmission power may make decoding easier at the intended receiver, but it also causes more *interference* for all other links.

Definition 12 (Power Assignment). *There are three types of power assignment:*

- Uniform *power does not depend on the length of the link.*
- Oblivious *power only depends on the length of the link. This includes* linear power l^α *and* mean power $l^{\alpha/2}$, *for links of length l.*
- Arbitrary *power can depend on all other links that are simultaneously transmitting.*

A tantalizing question is whether power control matters in a non-trivial way? How much gain is possible by using power control, as opposed to being limited to uniform power?

Theorem 3. *Power control matters. Mean power can be arbitrarily more efficient than uniform or linear power.*

Proof. Consider the following prototypical example, known as the *exponential chain*. Nodes are positioned on a line at locations $2^0, 2^1, \ldots, 2^n$ from left to right. There are bi-directional links between all adjacent nodes; i.e., for each $i = 1, \ldots, n$, there is a link $(2^{i-1}, 2^i)$ and the opposite link $(2^i, 2^{i-1})$. With uniform power, at most one node can transmit successfully to its left-hand neighbor: the left-most link will overpower any other transmission. Namely, if senders 2^i and 2^j transmit concurrently, where $i < j$, then the signal from 2^j at receiver 2^{j-1} is weaker than the signal from 2^i since $d(2^i, 2^{j-1}) < d(2^j, 2^{j-1})$.

Another popular and useful power assignment strategy is *linear power*, where links of length l transmit with power proportional to l^α. This strategy has the benefit of being frugal, in that the *received power* of each link is the same. Perhaps surprisingly, linear power fails equally badly on the exponential chain. Namely, at most one node can transmit successfully to its right-hand neighbor, and the right-most link will overpower any other transmission.

On the other hand, *mean power* $l^{\alpha/2}$ for links of length l works well here. The affectances from the other links form a geometric series, which converges to a constant. For instance, using that the power used on link i is $P_i = d(2^i, 2^{i-1})^{\alpha/2} = 2^{(i-1)\alpha/2}$, the affectances on link i by longer links is

$$\sum_{j=i+1}^{n} \frac{P_j/d(2^j, 2^{i-1})^\alpha}{P_i/d(2^i, 2^{i-1})^\alpha} <= \sum_{j=i+1}^{n} \frac{2^{(i-1)\alpha/2}}{2^{(j-1)\alpha/2}} == \sum_{k=1}^{n-i} \left(2^{-\alpha/2}\right)^k < \frac{1}{1 - 2^{-\alpha/2}}.$$

We leave the case of affectances by shorter links as an exercise.

Thus, by Theorem 2, the set can be scheduled in *constant* number of slots. Thus, we see here an example of *linear*-factor improvement in throughput, by using the right power assignment.

A natural question is whether oblivious power can be as powerful as arbitrary power. This has been answered negatively: For every oblivious power assignment, there is an instance with n links that is feasible under some power assignment, but only one link can be scheduled with oblivious power [18]. There is qualitative difference, though, in comparison to uniform power. In order to achieve these constructions, the lengths of the links must increase *doubly exponentially* [27,33], whereas our earlier construction of Theorem 3 only involved a singly-exponential chain. We compare the relative power of these power assignments in Table 1.

Table 1. Entry $f(\Delta)$ in row X and column Y represents that an optimal solution using power assignment X is at most an $f(\Delta)$ factor worse than the optimal solution using power assignment Y, where Δ is the link diversity, i.e., the ratio between longest and shortest link.

	Uniform	Mean	Arbitrary
Uniform	—	$\Theta(\log \Delta)$ [47]	$\Theta(\log \Delta)$
Mean	$O(1)$ [57]	—	$\Theta(\log \log \Delta)$ [18,27]

4.1 A Measure of Interference Under Power Control

The advent of power control means that we cannot use affectance directly when reasoning about links or instances, since it depends directly on the power assignment. We introduce here a stand-in replacement that avoids any reference to power, but still provides a measure of feasibility like affectance does in fixed-power settings.

First, some additional notation. We assume a total order $\prec$ on the links such that if l is shorter than l', then $l \prec l'$. To simplify notation we write $d_{ll'} = d(s, r')$, for links $l = (s, r), l' = (s', r')$. We generalize affectance to involve arbitrary power assignment $\mathcal{P}$, defining $a^{\mathcal{P}}_{l \to l'} = \min(1, \frac{P(l)/d^{\alpha}_{ll'}}{P(l')/(l')^{\alpha}})$. We also combine it with set notation as before, and define $a^{\mathcal{P}}(l, l') = a^{\mathcal{P}}_{l \to l'} + a^{\mathcal{P}}_{l' \to l}$. A set S of links is *bi-feasible* under power assignment $\mathcal{P}$ if it is feasible and $a^{\mathcal{P}}_{l \to S} \leq 2$ for each link $l \in S$.

Define the function W such that $W(l, l') = \min\left\{1, \frac{l^{\alpha}}{\min(d_{ll'}, d_{l'l})^{\alpha}}\right\}$ if $l \prec l'$, while $W(l, l') = 0$, otherwise. For set X and link l, define $W(X, l) = \sum_{l' \in X} W(l', l)$ and $W(l, X) = \sum_{l' \in X} W(l, l')$.

A key insight is that W lower bounds affectance under arbitrary power assignment. The term $l^{\alpha}/d^{\alpha}_{ll'}$ corresponds to the affectance of the shorter link l on the longer link l' using *linear power*, while $l^{\alpha}/d^{\alpha}_{l'l}$ matches the affectance of the longer link l' on l using *uniform power*. Both of these are minimal requirements for feasibility, modulo constant factors. We need the following bound that follows from the classic theorem of the geometric and arithmetic means.

Observation 4. *For any positive γ, x, y, it holds that $\gamma x + \frac{1}{\gamma} y \geq 2\sqrt{xy}$.*

Lemma 5. *For any links l and l' and power assignment $\mathcal{P}$, $W(l,l')+W(l',l) \leq 3^{\alpha/2}a^{\mathcal{P}}(l,l')$.*

Proof. Assume without loss of generality that $l \prec l'$. Then, $W(l',l) = 0$. Let $d_{\min} = \min(d_{ll'}, d_{l'l})$ and $d_{\max} = \max(d_{ll'}, d_{l'l})$. By the triangle inequality, $d_{\max} \leq d_{\min} + l + l' \leq 3 \cdot \max(l', d_{\min})$. Since $d_{ll'}d_{l'l} = d_{\min}d_{\max}$,

$$\frac{l \cdot l'}{d_{l'l}d_{ll'}} \geq \frac{l}{d_{\min}} \cdot \frac{l'}{3\max(l',d_{\min})} \geq \frac{1}{3}W(l,l')^{1/\alpha}\min(1, \frac{l}{d_{\min}}) = \frac{W(l,l')^{2/\alpha}}{3}.$$

Applying Observation 4 with $\gamma = P_{l'}/P_l$, $x = (l/d_{l'l})^{\alpha}$ and $y = (l'/d_{ll'})^{\alpha}$,

$$a^{\mathcal{P}}(l,l') = \frac{P_{l'}}{P_l}\left(\frac{l}{d_{l'l}}\right)^{\alpha} + \frac{P_l}{P_{l'}}\left(\frac{l'}{d_{ll'}}\right)^{\alpha} \geq \sqrt{\left(\frac{l}{d_{l'l}}\frac{l'}{d_{ll'}}\right)^{\alpha}} \geq \left(\frac{1}{3}\right)^{\alpha/2}W(l,l').$$

Close links cannot coexist in the same (highly) feasible set.

Lemma 6. *For links l,l' in a 3^{α}-feasible set, $d(l,l') \geq \frac{1}{2}\min(d_{ll'}, d_{l'l})$.*

Proof. Assume without loss of generality that $l \prec l'$. Suppose the claim is false. Let $d_{\min} = \min(d_{l,l'}, d_{l',l})$ and $d_{\max} = \max(d_{l,l'}, d_{l',l})$. By the triangle inequality and the supposition,

$$d_{\min} \leq l + d(l,l') < l + \frac{1}{2}d_{\min} \leq 2l. \tag{1}$$

By the strong feasibility, $3^{-2\alpha} \geq a^{\mathcal{P}}_{l \to l'} \cdot a^{\mathcal{P}}_{l' \to l} = \left(\frac{l \cdot l'}{d_l \cdot d_{l'}}\right)^{\alpha}$. Thus,

$$d_{\max} \cdot d_{\min} = d_{l,l'} \cdot d_{l',l} \geq 9ll'$$

Applying Inequality (1), we get that $d_{\max} > \frac{9}{2}l'$. But, by the triangle inequality, $d_{\max} \leq d(l,l') + l + l' \leq 3l + l' \leq 4l'$, which is a contradiction.

The following lemma is the counterpart of Lemma 3 for power control.

Lemma 7. *Let X be bi-feasible under some power assignment $\mathcal{P}$ and let l be a link (not necessarily in X). Then, $W(l,X) = O(1)$.*

Proof. We may assume without loss of generality that $l \prec l'$ for all links $l' \in T$, since $W(l,l') = 0$ otherwise. Apply Theorem 2 to partition T into $(2 \cdot 3^{\alpha})^2 = 4 \cdot 9^{\alpha}$ sets T_i, each of which is *strongly feasible* in the sense that $a^{\mathcal{P}}_{T_i \to v} \leq 3^{-\alpha}$, for each i and each link $l_v \in T_i$. We argue a bound for each T_i separately and add them up to obtain a bound on X.

Let $T = T_i$ be one of the strongly feasible subsets. Let $d(l_a, l_b)$ denote the shortest distance between a node on link l_a and a node on link l_b.

Let l_x be the link in T containing a node that is closest to a node on l, i.e. $d(l_x, l) = \min_{l' \in T} d(l', l)$. Let $l' \in T \setminus \{l_x\}$. By the triangle inequality, $d(l_x, l') \leq$

$d(l_x, l) + d(l, l') \leq 2d(l, l')$. Using this and Lemma 6, $\min(d_{l_x l'}, d_{l' l_x}) \leq 4d(l, l') \leq 4\min(d_{ll'}, d_{l'l})$. Thus,

$$W(l, l') = \min\left(1, \frac{l^\alpha}{\min(d_{ll'}, d_{l'l})^\alpha}\right) \leq \min\left(1, \frac{\min(l_x, l')^\alpha}{4^\alpha \min(d_{l_x l'}, d_{l' l_x})^\alpha}\right)$$
$$\leq 4^\alpha(W(l_x, l') + W(l', l_x)) \leq 3^{\alpha/2} 4^\alpha a^P(l_x, l'), \tag{2}$$

using the definition of W and Lemma 5. Summing over all l' in T' we have,

$$W(l, T) = W(l, l_x) + W(l, T \setminus \{l_x\}) \leq 1 + 4^\alpha \cdot 3^{\alpha/2} a^P(l_x, T).$$

Finally, summing over the subsets T_i of X yields

$$W(l, X) \leq 4 \cdot 9^\alpha + 4^\alpha 3^{\alpha/2} a^P(l_x, X) \leq 4 \cdot 9^\alpha + 4^\alpha \cdot 3^{\alpha/2+1},$$

using the bi-feasibility of X.

4.2   Power Control Algorithm

A constant-approximation algorithm for the *one-shot link scheduling* problem with arbitrary-power of Kesselheim [40] is given as Algorithm 3. The first part is equivalent to the first pass of Algorithm 2, but using the measure W instead of uniform-power affectance. The second pass assigns the links power in *decreasing* order of length, designed to assign each link just a little more power than is needed to overcome the interference from the longer links. Note that if the noise N is zero, the first (longest) link can be assigned arbitrary power.

Algorithm 3. One-Shot Link Scheduling with arbitrary power control

---
1: Given: A set L of links
2: Let $S = \emptyset$ and let $\tau = \frac{1}{2\beta(1+3^{\alpha+1})}$
3: **for** $l_w \in L$ in order of increasing length **do**
4:     **if** $W(S, l_w) \leq \tau$ **then**
5:         $S \leftarrow S \cup \{l_w\}$
6: **for** $l_v \in S$ in order of decreasing length **do**
7:     $P_v \leftarrow 2\beta l_v^\alpha (N + \sum_{l_w \in S, l_v \prec l_w} P_w / d_{wv}^\alpha)$

Theorem 4. *Let τ be as in Algorithm 3. If S is a set of links that satisfies, for each link $l \in S$, $W(S, l) \leq \tau$, then S is feasible. Moreover, the set S computed by Algorithm 3 is feasible with the power assignment computed.*

Proof. Let l_v be a link in S. The total interference received by l_v is $I_v^- + I_v^+$, where $I_v^- = \sum_{l_w \in S, l_w \prec l_v} P_w / d_{wv}^\alpha$ is the interference received by shorter links and $I_v^+ = N + \sum_{l_w \in S, l_v \prec l_w} P_w / d_{wv}^\alpha$ is the ambient noise plus interference received by longer links. Note that $I_v^+ = P_v / (2\beta l_v^\alpha)$, by the definition of P_v (in line 7). So, the focus is on bounding I_v^-, the interference from shorter links.

We first expand I_v^- using the assigned powers:

$$I_v^- = \sum_{\substack{l_w \in S \\ l_w \prec l_v}} \frac{P_w}{d_{wv}^\alpha} = 2\beta \sum_{\substack{l_w \in S \\ l_w \prec l_v}} \left(N l_w^\alpha \frac{1}{d_{wv}^\alpha} + \sum_{\substack{l_u \in S \\ l_w \prec l_u}} \frac{1}{d_{wv}^\alpha} \left(P_u \frac{l_w^\alpha}{d_{uw}^\alpha} \right) \right) . \tag{3}$$

The first term is bounded by $2\beta N\tau$, by the condition in line 4 of Algorithm 3 that defines S. Let $X_{uv} = \{l_w \in S : l_w \leq \min(l_v, l_u)\}$, for any link $l_u \in S$. By rearranging indices, we continue from (3) with

$$I_v^- \leq 2\beta N\tau + 2\beta \sum_{l_u \in S} \sum_{l_w \in X_{uv}} \frac{P_u l_w^\alpha}{d_{wv}^\alpha d_{uw}^\alpha}. \tag{4}$$

Let l_u be a link in S. Since $W(l_w, l_v) \leq W(X, l_v) \leq \tau < 1$, it holds that $l_w/d_{wv} < 1$, so $l_w \leq d_{wv}$ and $l_w^\alpha/d_{wv}^\alpha \leq W(l_w, l_v)$, for any link $l_w \in S$. Similarly, $l_w \leq d_{uw}$ and $l_w^\alpha/d_{uw}^\alpha \leq W(l_w, l_u)$.

We split the terms of the inner sum into two parts: $M_1 = \{l_w \in X_{uv} | d_{uv} \leq 3d_{uw}\}$ and $M_2 = X_{uv} \setminus M_1$. For each $l_w \in M_1$, using the definition of M_1 and the assumed bound on W,

$$\sum_{l_w \in M_1} \frac{l_w^\alpha}{d_{wv}^\alpha d_{uw}^\alpha} \leq \frac{3^\alpha}{d_{uv}^\alpha} \sum_{l_w \in M_1} \frac{l_w^\alpha}{d_{wv}^\alpha} \leq \frac{3^\alpha}{d_{uv}^\alpha} W(M_1, l_v) \leq \frac{3^\alpha}{d_{uv}^\alpha} \tau. \tag{5}$$

For each $l_w \in M_2$, we have by the triangle inequality that $d_{uv} \leq d_{uw} + l_w + d_{wv} \leq d_{uw} + 2d_{wv}$. By the definition of M_2, $d_{uv} > 3d_{uw}$, so $d_{uv} \leq \frac{1}{3}d_{uv} + 2d_{wv} \leq 3d_{wv}$. Hence, using the assumed bound on W,

$$\sum_{l_w \in M_2} \frac{l_w^\alpha}{d_{wv}^\alpha d_{uw}^\alpha} \leq \frac{3^\alpha}{d_{uv}^\alpha} \sum_{l_w \in M_2} \frac{l_w^\alpha}{d_{uw}^\alpha} \leq \frac{3^\alpha}{d_{uv}^\alpha} W(M_2, l_u) \leq \frac{3^\alpha}{d_{uv}^\alpha} \tau. \tag{6}$$

Applying Inequalities (5) and (6), along with the definition of P_v,

$$\sum_{\substack{l_u \in S, \, l_w \in X_{uv} \\ l_v \prec l_u}} \frac{P_u l_w^\alpha}{d_{wv}^\alpha d_{uw}^\alpha} \leq 2 \cdot 3^\alpha \tau \sum_{\substack{l_u \in S, \\ l_v \prec l_u}} \frac{P_u}{d_{uv}^\alpha} \leq 2 \cdot 3^\alpha \tau \frac{P_v}{2\beta l_v^\alpha}, \tag{7}$$

and, using also the definition of I_v^-,

$$\sum_{\substack{l_u \in S, \, l_w \in X_{uv} \\ l_u \prec l_v}} \frac{P_u l_w^\alpha}{d_{wv}^\alpha d_{uw}^\alpha} \leq 2 \cdot 3^\alpha \tau \sum_{\substack{l_u \in S, \\ l_u \prec l_v}} \frac{P_u}{d_{uv}^\alpha} = 4\beta \cdot 3^\alpha \cdot \tau \cdot I_v^-. \tag{8}$$

Plugging (7) and (8) into Eq. (3) gives,

$$I_v^- \leq 2\beta N\tau + 3^\alpha \tau \cdot P_v/l_v^\alpha + 4\beta 3^\alpha \tau \cdot I_v^-.$$

Solving for I_v^-, cancelling τ and using the bound $2\beta N \leq P_v/l_v^\alpha$,

$$I_v^- \leq \frac{2\beta N + 3^\alpha \cdot P_v/l_v^\alpha}{1/\tau - 4\beta 3^\alpha} \leq \frac{(1+3^\alpha)P_v/l_v^\alpha}{1/\tau - 4\beta 3^\alpha} = \frac{1}{2\beta} \cdot \frac{P_v}{l_v^\alpha}, \tag{9}$$

after plugging in the value of τ. Thus, the total interference on l_v is bounded by $I_v^- + I_v^- \leq \frac{1}{\beta} P_v / l_v^\alpha$, implying the required SINR for l_v, as desired.

Observe that the constant-approximation bound now follows from exactly the same arguments as in Theorem 1, just using W and Lemma 7 instead of a and Lemma 3.

Theorem 5. *Algorithm 3 is a constant approximation algorithm for one-shot arbitrary-power geometric-gain link scheduling problem.*

5   Bibliography

Gupta and Kumar [25] proposed the geometric version of the SINR model, where signal decays as a fixed polynomial of distance; it has since been the default model in analytic and simulations studies. They also initiated average-case analysis of network capacity, giving rise to a large body on "scaling law" results. Moscibroda and Wattenhofer [47] initiated the first algorithmic (worst-case) analysis in the SINR model.

The first algorithmic result on link scheduling for arbitrary link sets was by Moscibroda et al. [49]. This result was soon superseded by the first approximation results [8, 22]. These early approaches involved (directly or indirectly) partitioning links into length groups, which results in performance guarantees that are at least logarithmic in Δ, the link diversity [9, 16, 22, 27]. NP-hardness was established in [22]. Constant approximation for the One-shot Link Scheduling problem were given for uniform power [21], linear power [19, 58], fixed power assignments [29], and arbitrary power control [40]. This was extended to distributed learning [4, 16], admission control in cognitive radio [30], link rates [41], multiple channels [7, 59], spectrum auctions [35, 36], changing spectrum availability [13], jamming [14], and MIMO [61]. Numerous works on heuristics are known, as well as exponential time exact algorithms, e.g., [54].

Our treatment for uniform power is based on the algorithm of [29] and simplified arguments of [41]. Theorem 2 on signal-strengthening is due to [34]; an improved bound using linear algebra is given in [6]. Algorithm 3 for power control is due to [40, 41]; the proof given here holds for general metric space, but is significantly shorter than the one in [41].

A related problem is the scheduling problem where we want to partition the given set of links into fewest possible feasible sets. Early work on this problem includes [8, 12, 17]. Constant approximations for one-shot link scheduling immediately imply a $O(\log n)$-approximation for scheduling, where n is the number of links. Another approach is to solve links of similar lengths in groups, which results in a $O(\log \Delta)$-approximation [20, 22, 27]. NP-completeness results have been given for different variants [22, 38, 44], but as of yet no APX-hardness or stronger lower bounds are known. The weighted version of One-shot Link Scheduling – where the links have positive weights and the objective is to find a maximum weighted feasible set – behaves similar computationally as scheduling. Recently, a $O(\log^* \Delta)$-approximation algorithm was given for arbitrary-power scheduling and weighted One-shot Link Scheduling [32], by transforming the physical model into a conflict graph.

A problem of fundamental importance to sensor networks is *connectivity*: how efficiently can the nodes be connected into a strongly connected structure. This is an issue that affects the network as well as the link layer of the networking stack, as one must select the links in a spanning tree, choosing their power and scheduling them. The first analytic result in the SINR model showed that with the right power control, any set of nodes can be connected into a tree that can be scheduled in polylogarithmic, $O(\log^4 n)$, number of slots [47]. This was soon improved to $O(\log^2 n)$ [46,50] and later to $O(\log n)$ [31].

Other more complex problems studied include non-preemptive scheduling [20], joint power control, scheduling and routing [8], fixed-power multiflow [9], multi-path flow with general demand vectors [60], stochastic packet scheduling [42,56], and joint power control, routing and throughput scheduling in multiple channels [2], to name a few. Many of these rely on (weighted) One-shot Link Scheduling as a building block.

Beyond the computational aspects covered in this survey, there are challenging issues that arise when trying to achieve communication in a distributed setting. There is also some deep work on geometric characterizations of the regions in which specific transmissions can be decoded under the physical model, e.g., [37].

6 Beyond the Physical Model

6.1 Realistic Signal Propagation

The assumption of geometric gain is mathematically pleasing, but it can be quite far from reality, even in relatively simple environments [24,45,53,55]. On the other hand, the additivity of interference and the near-threshold nature of signal reception has been borne out in experiments [10,45,48,55,62].

Several proposals have been suggested for extending the standard physical model to capture the non-geometric aspects of signal propagation. The basic model allows the pathloss constant α to vary [25], giving a first-order approximation of the signal gain. Another more general approach is to view the variation as conforming the plane into a general metric space [18,29]. Much recent analytic work holds in arbitrary metric spaces [29,41], while some requires them to have a certain "bounded independence" property [32].

One practical alternative is to use facts-on-the-ground in the form of signal strength measurements, instead of the prescriptive distance-based formula [7,24]. This might suggest the general physical model (Definition 4), but that runs into the computational intractability monster, since such a formulation can encode highly-inapproximable problems like maximum independent set in graphs [21]. Instead, one can characterize the performance guarantee in terms of natural parameters of the gain matrix, such as its nearness to a metric [24]. Another such parameter is the weighted "inductive independence" [35], which has shown to be of wide general utility [28].

In the world of stochastic analysis, the default assumption is to model the variations in signal propagation by a probabilistic distribution [26]. Significant experimental literature exists that lends support for stochastic models [51], especially log-normal distributions [62]. There is a need to better understand the impact of such stochastic assumptions on effective algorithms.

The temporal aspect of signal variability is another dimension. The *dual graph model* [43] extends the radio network model to a pair of graphs, one of which contains the links that are unreliable, that may or may not transmit a message by adversarial control. Stochastic models usually assume independence across time. In such a setting Dams et al. [15] showed that temporal variations that follow as Rayleigh distribution do not significantly affect the performance of link scheduling algorithms, incurring only a $O(\log^* n)$-factor increase in performance.

6.2   Advances in Technology

In wireless communication, multiple-input and multiple-output (MIMO) is a method for expanding the capacity of a radio link using multiple transmission and receiving antennas [39]. MIMO is well established in practice, with several wireless standards supporting it. MIMO has also received a lot of attention from lower layer signal processing research and information theorists. Network wide MIMO applications are known as multi-user MIMO (MU-MIMO) or cooperative MIMO (CO-MIMO). These are still in research, and there are not many studies with an algorithmic flavor, but there are exceptions, e.g. [5].

Closely related to MIMO is beamforming using antenna arrays. Beamforming is a signal processing technique at either the transmission or the reception side. The idea is to carefully choose the phase of the signal of the various antenna in order to produce either constructive or destructive interference at different locations. Again this is an active research area in information theory, less so in algorithms.

Network coding [1] on the other hand only works in the presence of a network. While we assumed that concurrent wireless transmissions interfere, one may hope to make use of the additive nature of concurrent wireless signals. Consider three nodes u, v, w, with v sitting in the middle of u and w, and nodes u and w want to exchange a message. In the first time slot, let u and w transmit their own message concurrently. Node v may understand neither u's nor w's message because of interference, but v could just retransmit the received additive signal in the second time slot. Now both u and w receive the *additive* signal, and since they know their own original message, they can simply *subtract* their own message from the additive message, and consequentially get the missing message. All this requires just two time slots. Network coding has been analyzed from an algorithmic perspective, e.g. [23], but it is rarely used in the wild.

7   Open Questions

The last section discussed new directions that all need to be addressed better algorithmically. We list here some of the most significant open questions regarding the physical model:

1. Is there a constant-approximate algorithm for scheduling problem with uniform power? Only logarithmic factors are known, even in one dimension.
2. Are there small constant approximations of one-shot link scheduling, e.g. a 2-approximation? Can the possibility of an approximation scheme be disproved?
3. How much can the capacity of practical wireless networks be improved with good scheduling algorithms? How much of the gain is due to power control, and how much can be achieved already with uniform power?
4. What kind of infrastructure and/or assumptions are sufficient/necessary to achieve efficient distributed algorithms for link scheduling?
5. How can one capture the unreliability or time-variability seen in most actual wireless networks, to make such realistic but non-deterministic models algorithmically tractable?

Acknowledgement. We thank Tigran Tonoyan for helpful comments.

References

1. Ahlswede, R., Cai, N., Li, S.Y., Yeung, R.W.: Network information flow. IEEE Trans. Inf. Theory **46**(4), 1204–1216 (2006)
2. Al-Ayyoub, M., Gupta, H.: Joint routing, channel assignment, and throughput scheduling for throughput maximization in general interference models. IEEE Trans. Mob. Comput. **9**(4), 553–565 (2010)
3. Alon, N., Bar-Noy, A., Linial, N., Peleg, D.: A lower bound for radio broadcast. J. Comput. Syst. Sci. **43**(2), 290–298 (1991)
4. Ásgeirsson, E., Mitra, P.: On a game theoretic approach to capacity maximization in wireless networks. In: INFOCOM (2011)
5. Ásgeirsson, E.I., Halldórsson, M.M., Mitra, P.: Maximum MIMO flow in wireless networks under the SINR model. In: WiOpt, pp. 295–302 (2014)
6. Bang-Jensen, J., Halldórsson, M.M.: Vertex coloring edge-weighted digraphs. Inf. Process. Lett. **115**(10), 791–796 (2015)
7. Bodlaender, M.H.L., Halldórsson, M.M.: Beyond geometry: towards fully realistic wireless models. In Proceedings of 33rd ACM Symposium on Principles of Distributed Computing, PODC 2014, Paris, pp.347–356 (2014)
8. Chafekar, D., Kumar, V.S., Marathe, M., Parthasarathy, S., Srinivasan, A.: Cross-layer latency minimization for wireless networks using SINR constraints. In: Proceedings of 8th International Symposium on Mobile Ad Hoc Networking and Computing, MobiHoc, Montreal, pp. 110–119. ACM (2007)
9. Chafekar, D., Kumar, V.S.A., Marathe, M.V., Parthasarathy, S., Srinivasan, A.: Approximation algorithms for computing capacity of wireless networks with SINR constraints. In: INFOCOM, pp. 1166–1174 (2008)
10. Chen, Y., Terzis, A.: On the mechanisms and effects of calibrating RSSI measurements for 802.15.4 radios. In: Silva, J.S., Krishnamachari, B., Boavida, F. (eds.) EWSN 2010. LNCS, vol. 5970, pp. 256–271. Springer, Heidelberg (2010). https://doi.org/10.1007/978-3-642-11917-0_17
11. Clark, B.N., Colbourn, C.J., Johnson, D.S.: Unit disk graphs. Discret. Math. **86**(1–3), 165–177 (1990)
12. Cruz, R.L., Santhanam, A.: Optimal routing, link scheduling, and power control in multi-hop wireless networks. In: INFOCOM (2003)

13. Dams, J., Hoefer, M., Kesselheim, T.: Sleeping experts in wireless networks. In: Afek, Y. (ed.) DISC 2013. LNCS, vol. 8205, pp. 344–357. Springer, Heidelberg (2013). https://doi.org/10.1007/978-3-642-41527-2_24

14. Dams, J., Hoefer, M., Kesselheim, T.: Jamming-resistant learning in wireless networks. In: Esparza, J., Fraigniaud, P., Husfeldt, T., Koutsoupias, E. (eds.) ICALP 2014. LNCS, vol. 8573, pp. 447–458. Springer, Heidelberg (2014). https://doi.org/10.1007/978-3-662-43951-7_38

15. Dams, J., Hoefer, M., Kesselheim, T.: Scheduling in wireless networks with Rayleigh-fading interference. IEEE Trans. Mob. Comput. **14**(7), 1503–1514 (2015)

16. Dinitz, M.: Distributed algorithms for approximating wireless network capacity. In Proceedings of 29th International Conference on Computer Communications, INFOCOM, San Diego, CA, pp. 1–9. IEEE (2010)

17. ElBatt, T., Ephremides, A.: Joint scheduling and power control for wireless ad-hoc networks. In: INFOCOM (2002)

18. Fanghänel, A., Kesselheim, T., Räcke, H., Vöcking, B.: Oblivious interference scheduling. In: Proceedings of 28th Symposium on Principles of Distributed Computing, PODC, Calgary, pp. 220–229. ACM (2009)

19. Fanghänel, A., Keßelheim, T., Vöcking, B.: Improved algorithms for latency minimization in wireless networks. In: Albers, S., Marchetti-Spaccamela, A., Matias, Y., Nikoletseas, S., Thomas, W. (eds.) ICALP 2009. LNCS, vol. 5556, pp. 447–458. Springer, Heidelberg (2009). https://doi.org/10.1007/978-3-642-02930-1_37

20. Fu, L., Liew, S.C., Huang, J.: Power controlled scheduling with consecutive transmission constraints: complexity analysis and algorithm design. In: INFOCOM, pp. 1530–1538 (2009)

21. Goussevskaia, O., Halldórsson, M.M., Wattenhofer, R.: Algorithms for wireless capacity. IEEE/ACM Trans. Netw. (TON) **22**(3), 745–755 (2014)

22. Goussevskaia, O., Oswald, Y.A., Wattenhofer, R.: Complexity in geometric SINR. In: Proceedings of 8th International Symposium on Mobile Ad Hoc Networking and Computing, MobiHoc, Montreal, pp. 100–109. ACM (2007)

23. Goussevskaia, O., Wattenhofer, R.: Complexity of scheduling with analog network coding. In: Proceedings of 1st International Workshop on Foundations of Wireless Ad Hoc and Sensor Networking and Computing, FOWANC, Hong Kong, pp. 77–84. ACM (2008)

24. Gudmundsdottir, H., Ásgeirsson, E.I., Bodlaender, M., Foley, J.T., Halldórsson, M.M., Vigfusson, Y.: Measurement based interference models for wireless scheduling algorithms. In: MSWiM (2014). arXiv:1401.1723

25. Gupta, P., Kumar, P.R.: The capacity of wireless networks. IEEE Trans. Inf. Theory **46**(2), 388–404 (2000)

26. Haenggi, M., Andrews, J.G., Baccelli, F., Dousse, O., Franceschetti, M.: Stochastic geometry and random graphs for the analysis and design of wireless networks. IEEE J. Sel. Areas Commun. **27**(7), 1029–1046 (2009)

27. Halldórsson, M.M.: Wireless scheduling with power control. ACM Trans. Algorithms **9**(1), 7:1–7:20 (2012)

28. Halldórsson, M.M., Holzer, S., Mitra, P., Wattenhofer, R.: The power of non-uniform wireless power. In: Proceedings of 24th Symposium on Discrete Algorithms, SODA, New Orleans, LA, pp. 1595–1606. ACM-SIAM (2013)

29. Halldórsson, M.M., Mitra, P.: Wireless capacity with oblivious power in general metrics. In: Proceedings of 22nd Symposium on Discrete Algorithms, SODA, San Francisco, CA, pp. 1538–1548. ACM-SIAM (2011)

30. Halldórsson, M.M., Mitra, P.: Wireless capacity and admission control in cognitive radio. In: INFOCOM, pp. 855–863. IEEE (2012)

31. Halldórsson, M.M., Mitra, P.: Wireless connectivity and capacity. In: Proceedings of 23rd Symposium on Discrete Algorithms, SODA, Kyoto, pp. 516–526. ACM-SIAM (2012)

32. Halldórsson, M.M., Tonoyan, T.: How well can graphs represent wireless interference? In: Proceedings of 47th Annual ACM Symposium on Theory of Computing, STOC, pp. 635–644 (2015)

33. Halldórsson, M.M., Tonoyan, T.: The price of local power control in wireless scheduling. In: 35th IARCS Annual Conference on Foundations of Software Technology and Theoretical Computer Science, FSTTCS. Leibniz International Proceedings in Informatics (LIPIcs), vol. 45, pp. 529–542 (2015)

34. Halldórsson, M.M., Wattenhofer, R.: Wireless communication is in APX. In: Albers, S., Marchetti-Spaccamela, A., Matias, Y., Nikoletseas, S., Thomas, W. (eds.) ICALP 2009. LNCS, vol. 5555, pp. 525–536. Springer, Heidelberg (2009). https://doi.org/10.1007/978-3-642-02927-1_44

35. Hoefer, M., Kesselheim, T.: Secondary spectrum auctions for symmetric and submodular bidders. ACM Trans. Econ. Comput. 3(2), 9 (2015)

36. Hoefer, M., Kesselheim, T., Vöcking, B.: Approximation algorithms for secondary spectrum auctions. In: Proceedings of 23rd Symposium on Parallelism in Algorithms and Architectures, SPAA, San Jose, CA, pp. 177–186. ACM-SIAM (2011)

37. Kantor, E., Lotker, Z., Parter, M., Peleg, D.: The topology of wireless communication. In: Proceedings of 43rd Symposium on Theory of Computing, STOC, San Jose, CA, pp. 383–392. ACM (2011)

38. Katz, B., Volker, M., Wagner, D.: Energy efficient scheduling with power control for wireless networks. In: WiOpt, pp. 160–169. IEEE (2010)

39. Kaye, A., George, D.: Transmission of multiplexed pam signals over multiple channel and diversity systems. IEEE Trans. Commun. Technol. 18(5), 520–526 (1970)

40. Kesselheim, T.: A constant-factor approximation for wireless capacity maximization with power control in the SINR model. In: Proceedings of 22nd Symposium on Discrete Algorithms, SODA, San Francisco, CA, pp. 1549–1559. ACM-SIAM (2011)

41. Kesselheim, T.: Approximation algorithms for wireless link scheduling with flexible data rates. In: Epstein, L., Ferragina, P. (eds.) ESA 2012. LNCS, vol. 7501, pp. 659–670. Springer, Heidelberg (2012). https://doi.org/10.1007/978-3-642-33090-2_57

42. Kesselheim, T.: Dynamic packet scheduling in wireless networks. In: Proceedings of 31st Symposium on Principles of Distributed Computing, PODC 2012, Funchal, pp. 281–290. ACM (2012)

43. Kuhn, F., Lynch, N., Newport, C., Oshman, R., Richa, A.: Broadcasting in unreliable radio networks. In: PODC, pp. 336–345 (2010)

44. Lin, H., Schalekamp, F.: On the complexity of the minimum latency scheduling problem on the Euclidean plane. arXiv preprint arXiv:1203.2725 (2012)

45. Maheshwari, R., Jain, S., Das, S.R.: A measurement study of interference modeling and scheduling in low-power wireless networks. In: SenSys, pp. 141–154. ACM (2008)

46. Moscibroda, T.: The worst-case capacity of wireless sensor networks. In: Proceedings of 6th International Symposium on Information Processing in Sensor Networks, IPSN, Cambridge, MA, pp. 1–10. ACM (2007)

47. Moscibroda, T., Wattenhofer, R.: The complexity of connectivity in wireless networks. In: Proceedings of 25th International Conference on Computer Communications, INFOCOM 2006, Barcelona, pp. 1–13. IEEE (2006)

48. Moscibroda, T., Wattenhofer, R., Weber, Y.: Protocol design beyond graph-based models. In: Proceedings of 5th Workshop on Hot Topics in Networks, HotNets 2006, Irvine, CA, pp. 25–30. ACM (2006)

49. Moscibroda, T., Wattenhofer, R., Zollinger, A.: Topology control meets SINR: the scheduling complexity of arbitrary topologies. In: 7th ACM International Symposium on Mobile Ad Hoc Networking and Computing (MOBIHOC), Florence, Italy, May 2006

50. Moscibroda, T., Wattenhofer, R., Zollinger, A.: Topology control meets SINR: the scheduling complexity of arbitrary topologies. In: Proceedings of 7th International Symposium on Mobile Ad Hoc Networking and Computing, MobiHoc, Florence, pp. 310–321. ACM (2006)

51. Nikookar, H., Hashemi, H.: Statistical modeling of signal amplitude fading of indoor radio propagation channels. In: Proceedings of 2nd IEEE International Conference on Universal Personal Communications, vol. 1, pp. 84–88. IEEE (1993)

52. Schmid, S., Wattenhofer, R.: Algorithmic models for sensor networks. In: 14th International Workshop on Parallel and Distributed Real-Time Systems (WPDRTS), Island of Rhodes, Greece, April 2006

53. Sevani, V., Raman, B.: SIR based interference modeling for wireless mesh networks: a detailed measurement study. In: COMSNETS. IEEE (2012)

54. Shi, Y., Hou, Y.T., Kompella, S., Sherali, H.D.: Maximizing capacity in multihop cognitive radio networks under the SINR model. IEEE Trans. Mob. Comput. **10**(7), 954–967 (2011)

55. Son, D., Krishnamachari, B., Heidemann, J.: Experimental study of concurrent transmission in wireless sensor networks. In: SenSys, pp. 237–250. ACM (2006)

56. Tassiulas, L., Ephremides, A.: Stability properties of constrained queueing systems and scheduling policies for maximum throughput in multihop radio networks. IEEE Trans. Autom. Control **37**(12), 1936–1948 (1992)

57. Tonoyan, T.: On the capacity of oblivious powers. In: Erlebach, T., Nikoletseas, S., Orponen, P. (eds.) ALGOSENSORS 2011. LNCS, vol. 7111, pp. 225–237. Springer, Heidelberg (2012). https://doi.org/10.1007/978-3-642-28209-6_18

58. Tonoyan, T.: On some bounds on the optimum schedule length in the SINR model. In: Bar-Noy, A., Halldórsson, M.M. (eds.) ALGOSENSORS 2012. LNCS, vol. 7718, pp. 120–131. Springer, Heidelberg (2013). https://doi.org/10.1007/978-3-642-36092-3_14

59. Wan, P.-J.: Joint selection and transmission scheduling of point-to-point communication requests in multi-channel wireless networks. In: MobiHoc, pp. 231–240 (2016)

60. Wan, P.-J., Frieder, O., Jia, X., Yao, F., Xu, X., Tang, S.: Wireless link scheduling under physical interference model. In: INFOCOM, pp. 838–845. IEEE (2011)

61. Wan, P.-J., Xu, B., Frieder, O., Ji, S., Wang, B., Xu, X.: Capacity maximization in wireless MIMO networks with receiver-side interference suppression. In: MobiHoc, pp. 145–154 (2014)

62. Zamalloa, M.Z., Krishnamachari, B.: An analysis of unreliability and asymmetry in low-power wireless links. ACM Trans. Sens. Netw. (TOSN) **3**(2), 7 (2007)

Green Computing Algorithmics

Kirk Pruhs[(✉)]

University of Pittsburgh, Pittsburgh, PA 15260, USA
kirk@cs.pitt.edu
https://people.cs.pitt.edu/~kirk/

Abstract. We discuss what green computing algorithmics is, and what a theory of energy as a computational resource isn't. We then present some open problems in this area, with enough background from the literature to put the open problems in context. This background should also be a reasonably representative sample of the green computing algorithmics literature.

1 Introduction

Time arguably ascended over space as the dominant computational resource circa 1970, when semiconductor memory replaced magnetic core memory, and energy arguably ascended over time as the dominant computational resource circa 2000, when information technologies could no longer handle the exponentiality of Moore's law. Three examples illustrating the ascendancy of energy in the areas of computer chip design, data center management, and high performance computing are:

- In May 2004, Reuters reported that: **Intel Hits Thermal Wall:** "Intel Corp. said on Friday it has scrapped the development of two new computer chips (code-named Tejas and Jayhawk) for desktop/server systems in order to rush to the marketplace a more efficient chip technology more than a year ahead of schedule. Analysts said the move showed how eager the world's largest chip maker was to cut back on the heat its chips generate. Intel's method of cranking up chip speed was beginning to require expensive and noisy cooling systems for computers."
- In September 2002, the New York Times quoted then Google CEO Eric Schmidt as saying, "What matters most to the computer designers at Google is not speed, but power, low power, because data centers can consume as much electricity as a city."
- In 2010 the Advanced Scientific Computing Advisory Committee in their report *The Opportunities and Challenges of Exascale Computing* stated that one of the three main challenges is reducing power requirements. In particular, it said, "Based on current technology, scaling today's systems to an exaflop level would consume more than a gigawatt of power, roughly the output of Hoover Dam. Reducing the power requirement by a factor of at least 100 is a challenge for future hardware and software technologies."

© Springer Nature Switzerland AG 2019
B. Steffen and G. Woeginger (Eds.): Computing and Software Science, LNCS 10000, pp. 161–183, 2019.
https://doi.org/10.1007/978-3-319-91908-9_10

Thus we are about a decade into a green computing revolution in which a wide array of information technologies are being redesigned with energy as a first class design constraint [54]. Inevitably these new technologies have spawned new theoretical/algorithmic problems. The most obvious type of algorithmic problem arising from this green computing revolution involves directly managing power, energy or temperature as a computational resource. Additionally, these new, more green, technologies also often have different non-energy-related physical properties than previous technologies. For example, in many new memory technologies, writes are significantly more time consuming than reads. Thus the management of these new informational technologies, that will likely be adopted for reasons related to energy efficiency, often give rise to new algorithmic problems that do not directly involve managing energy. Green computing algorithmics is just the study of the algorithmic problems spawned by the green computing revolution.

When I (as one of the very few researchers working extensively on green computing algorithms) was asked to write this paper, I had first had to decide who my intended audience to be. I decided that my primary intended audience are researchers, particularly young researchers, who are potentially interested in initiating a research program in green computing algorithms. Another plausible audience for this paper are researchers who want to know what has happened in green computing algorithmics, and where the field is going.

Firstly we should discuss what research in green computing algorithms is like. Some of the problems spawned by the green computing revolution are algorithmically interesting, and many/most are not. For our purposes, let us say that a problem is algorithmically interesting if it is a problem for which a trained/expert algorithms researcher can obtain interesting results/insights that a generic application researcher likely wouldn't be able to attain. However, before algorithmic researchers can contribute, they have to become aware of these algorithmically interesting problems. From my experience, the bottleneck for algorithmic research community making a contribution to green computing is not a lack of researchers with the skills to make headway on algorithmically interesting problems, but a lack of researchers who make the effort to mine/identify algorithmically interesting management issues in new greener information technologies, formalize these problems, and then expose these problems to the algorithmic research community. And with all due respect to the experimental computer systems research communities, few researchers in those communities are able to identify algorithmically interesting problems, or are able to formalize the problems so that algorithmic research will provide maximum insight. There is a bit of an art to constructing a formal model/problem that accurately captures the complicated interactions and goals in the real computing technology, but that is still amenable to mathematical analysis that yields useful insight. Often the most obvious ways to formally model technological problems lead to uninteresting formal problems, for example because one gets a trivial impossibility result.

Thus much of green computing algorithmics research involves problem mining and problem formulation, not solving well-known formal problems. But as effective problem mining and formulation is usually difficult for researchers who are new to an application area, particularly if they are also junior researchers, I've decided structure this survey around a collection of formal algorithmic problems related to green computing algorithmics that I find interesting, instead of trying to do some sort of comprehensive survey, like the previous two surveys on green computing algorithmics [2,39]. The hope is these problems might provide a starting point for a researcher looking to initiate a research program on green computing algorithmics. This survey is certainly biased towards my own research. But still I think that these open problems, and the associated background that I give, should form a representative sample of the research in green computing algorithmics.

The outline for the rest of the survey is:

- Section 2 discusses why a theory of energy as a computational resource will look different than the established theory of time or space as computational resources.
- Section 3 discusses common modeling assumptions.
- Section 4 discusses online convex optimization problems that naturally arise from different data centers trying to handle a time-varying workload in the most energy efficient manner.
- Section 5 discusses energy efficient circuit routing in a network.
- Section 6 discusses near-threshold computing, and designing combinatorial circuits that optimally tradeoff energy efficiency and reliability.
- Section 7 discusses online scheduling on heterogeneous processors.
- Section 8 discusses the complexity of finding schedules that optimally tradeoff energy and performance.
- Section 9 provides a brief conclusion that compares the current state of the theory energy as a computational resource to the theories of time and space as computational resources.

2   The Theory of Energy as Computational Resource

At the start of this green computing revolution, there were several National Science Foundation sponsored visioning workshops, many of which I attended, and one of which, on the *The Science of Power Management*, I organized. A ubiquitous first demand of all manner of computing researchers at all of these visioning workshops was:

"We need a big Oh theory for energy!"

The universal demand for a such theory is a testament to the tremendous success of the current theory time (and space) as a computational resource within the broad computing community. Of course what they are talking about is only tangentially related to big Oh. They are referring to being able to label algorithms, and problems, with time and space complexities. So the algorithm MergeSort takes time $O(n \log n)$ and the problem of deciding whether two regular expressions requires exponential space. This is possible because of the time hierarchy and space hierarchy theorems, which are the bedrock of the theory of time and space as computational resources.

But the laws of physics make it difficult to assign algorithms, and thus problems, energy complexities. There are two natural possible approaches. The first approach is to assume that all standard computer operations use unit energy, analogous to the standard assumption that all operations take unit time. At first glance this assumption for energy seems not significantly more unreasonable than the assumption for time. But a consequence this assumption is that the energy used by an algorithm is equal to the time used by that algorithm. This is unsatisfying theoretically as it produces no new mathematical/theoretical questions, and is unsatisfying practically as the green computing revolution is being caused by the fact that optimizing for energy instead of time has lead to practitioners developing significantly different technologies/solutions.

The second natural approach would be to assume that different operations require different amounts of energy, where the amount of energy required by an operation would be the minimum energy allowed by the laws of physics. The most natural candidate for a physical law to lower bound the energy for computation is Landauer's principle, which is intuitively related to the second law of thermodynamics. Landauer's principle states that the amount of energy that must be expended each time a bit of information is lost is linear in the temperature. Thus irreversible operations, where information is lost, like overwriting a bit, or taking the AND of two bits, require energy. But Landauer's principle does not give a lower bound on energy for reversible operations, like swapping the contents of two memory locations. Thus Landauer's principle can give a lower bound on energy for a combinatorial circuit, or a particular implementation of an algorithm. But unfortunately for this approach, all computation can be made reversible. In the context of combinatorial circuits, there are reversible logically-complete gates, such as the controlled swap or Fredkin gate. In the context of Turing machine, all computation can be made reversible at a cost of a linear slowdown in time. Thus every algorithm can be implemented using only reversible operations. Thus its at best a bit tricky giving an algorithm an energy complexity as it depends on the implementation. And there is no way to give an energy complexity to a problem as every computable problem can be solved with arbitrarily little energy.

I know from experience that many researchers are reticent to accept that a theory of energy as a computational resource will not be based on complexity classes like $\mathrm{ENERGY}(n^2)$, that are analogous to the $\mathrm{TIME}(n^2)$ and $\mathrm{SPACE}(n^2)$ complexity classes that are the foundation of the current theory of time/space as a computational resource. But the lack of energy complexity classes seems to be dictated by physics, and their absence from the current theory of energy as a computational resource isn't an oversight.

But there should be ways in which a theory of energy as a computational resource will be similar to the established theory of time/space as computational resource. It should be based on simple models that balance the competing needs of accurately reflecting reality, and being mathematically tractable. It should serve engineers and computing researchers, when confronted with problems in which power/energy/temperature is the key scarce, as the current theory of time as a computational resources serves them when confronted with problems where time is the scarce resource. That is, it should give them appropriate simple models for commonly arising situations that will allow then to think heuristically about the preeminent issues.

For example, a common mechanism for achieving energy efficiency is building a system with heterogeneous devices, each with different energy and performance characteristics. For a given area and power budget, heterogeneous designs often give significantly better performance, for a given energy/hardware budget, for standard workloads than homogeneous designs [24,42,52,53]. One common scenario is that there might be some devices that are slow but energy efficient, and other devices that are fast but energy inefficient. The resulting management problem is how to choose the appropriate collection of devices for a workload to properly balance energy efficiency and performance. So a theory of energy as a computational resource should include appropriate models for such situations, and general algorithmic design and analysis techniques for dealing with such problems.

3   Common Modeling Assumptions

We quickly summarize common modeling assumptions. As much of the green computing algorithmic literature focuses on saving energy in processors, this discussion is biased toward models related to processors.

Energy is power integrated over time. Power has two components, dynamic power and static power. Dynamic power is the power used by the process of computing, and the static power is the energy used by the device just from being on. Thus the only real way to not spend energy on static power is to turn the device off. Before say the year 2000, the static power in common processors was generally negligible compared to the static power, but now the static power is often comparable to dynamic power. Generally there is a strictly convex relationship between speed and power. So faster processors have a higher ratio of power to speed than lower speed processors. Thus faster processors are less efficient than slower processors in terms of the energy that they expend per operation. Which seems to be a general consequence of the laws of physics, as for example, high performance cars invariably less energy efficient than lower performance cars. The most common model is that the dynamic power $P(s)$ is equal to s^α, where s is the speed and α is some constant that is strictly bigger than 1. For example, the well known cube-root rule for CMOS based devices states that the speed s is roughly proportional to the cube-root of the dynamic power P, or equivalently, the dynamic power is proportional to the speed cubed [25]. So the most common model for power in the literature is $P(s) = s^\alpha + \beta$, where β is constant representing the static power, and α is a constant that one thinks as being about 2 or 3. For more detail on modeling processor power see [26].

We now turn our attention to temperature. Cooling, and hence temperature, is a complex phenomenon that can not be modeled completely accurately by any simple model [60]. All the green computing literature that I have seen assumes that cooling is governed by Newton's law of cooling, and implicitly assumes that environmental temperature is constant (which is what a fan is in principle trying to achieve). Newton's law cooling states that the rate of cooling is proportional to the difference in temperature between the object and the environment. Without loss of generality one can scale temperature so that the environmental temperature is zero. A first order approximation for the rate of change T' of the temperature T is then $T' = aP - bT$, where P is the supplied power, and a and b are constants. The maximum temperature is within a factor of 4 of a times the maximum energy used over any interval of length $\frac{1}{b}$ [14]. This observation also shows that there is a relationship between total energy and maximum temperature optimization and simplifies the task of reasoning about temperature. If the cooling parameter b is 0 then maximum temperature minimization becomes equivalent (within a constant factor) to energy minimization. This also explains why some algorithms in the literature for energy management are poor for temperature management, that is, these algorithms critically use the fact that the parameter $b = 0$. If the cooling parameter b is ∞ then maximum temperature minimization becomes equivalent to minimizing the maximum power, or equivalently minimizing the maximum speed. [14] uses the term *cooling oblivious* to refer to an algorithm that doesn't rely on the particular values of a and b. Thus if a cooling oblivious algorithm performs well for the objective of minimizing the maximum temperature, it should perform reasonably well for the objective of minimizing the total energy and the objective of minimizing the maximum speed/power.

Moore's law states that the switch/transistor density in processors doubles about every other year. While at some point Moore's law has stop holding, it looks like it will continue to hold a bit longer. Up until around 2004, this also meant that processor speeds also doubled about every other year. But since 2004 the rate of improvement of processor performance (speed) lags the rate of transistor density. This is called Moore's gap. So let me now summarize some of the more energy efficient processor architecture designs that have arisen to cope with the exponentiality of Moore's law, and how they are generally modeled.

Speed Scalable Processors: A speed scalable processor has a collection of operational modes, each with a different speed and power. When performance is important the processor can be run at a high-speed (but with low energy efficiency) and when performance is less important, the processor can be run at a lower speed that has better energy efficiency. One gets a wide variety of models depending on whether the speed is assume to be discrete or continuous, whether there is an upper bound on speed, and the speed to power function.

Multiprocessor Chips: Another alternative design is multiprocessor chips. Roughly speaking, k speed s/k processors would use only about $1/k^2$ fraction of the power of a single speed s processor, but potentially would have the same processing capability. But the fact that such efficient parallelization of computation is not so easy to pull off in practice is one of the reasons for Moore's Gap. As best as I can tell there are three different visions of the future of multiprocessor chips:

- *Identical Processors:* The first is expressed by the following quote from Anant Agarwal, CEO of Tilera: "I would like to call it a corollary of Moore's Law that the number of cores will double every 18 months." [52].
- *Related Processors:* Others [24,42,43,52,53] predict that the future dominant multiprocessor architecture will be heterogeneous processors/cores. It is envisioned that these heterogeneous architectures will consist of a small number of high-performance processors (with low energy efficiency) for critical jobs, and a larger number of lower-performance (but more energy efficient) processors for less critical jobs (and presumably eventually processors of intermediate performance for jobs of intermediate importance). For a given area and power budget, heterogeneous designs can give significantly better performance for standard workloads [24,42,52,53]. Such technologies are probably best modeled by what is called "related" processors in the scheduling nomenclature: That is, each processor i has an associated speed s_i and power P_i.
- *Unrelated Processors:* Some architects claim that, again due to Moore's law, chip makers soon will hit another thermal wall in that the density of switches will become so great that it will be prohibitively expensive to cool the chip if all switches were active at the same time [29]. Thus it will be necessary that all times, some switches must be turned off. This commonly goes by the moniker "dark silicon". Thus it is envisioned that there will be processors specialized for particular types of jobs, and for jobs to be assigned to a processor best suited for that job; and the processors not best suited for the current jobs would be turned off. In such a setting the processors might naturally be modeled by what in scheduling parlance is called "unrelated machines", where the execution time of a job is dependent on the processor to which is it assigned (and there is no particular consistency between which processors are fastest between jobs). We should point out that even multiprocessors that were designed to be homogeneous, are increasingly likely to be heterogeneous at run time [24]: the dominant underlying cause is the increasing variability in the fabrication process as the feature size is scaled down.

4   Online Convex Optimization

The Definition of the Online Convex Optimization Problem (OCO): The input is an online sequence $F_1, F_2, \ldots, F_n$ of convex functions from $\mathbb{R}^k$ to $\mathbb{R}^+$. In response to the convex function F_t that arrives at time t, the online algorithm can move to any destination/point p_t in the metric space $\mathbb{R}^k$. The cost of such a feasible solution is $\sum_{t=1}^{n} (d(p_{t-1}, p_t) + F_t(p_t))$, where $d(p_{t-1}, p_t)$ is the distance between points p_{t-1} and p_t, that is, the distance traveled plus the value of the convex functions at the destination points. The objective is to minimize the cost.

The Motivating Data Center Application: The initial motivation for introducing and studying the OCO problem was due to its applications in rightsizing power-proportional data centers, see for example [4,46–49,51,65]. To explain this application, let us for simplicity initially assume that we have one data center consists of a homogeneous collection of servers/processors that are speed scalable and that may be powered down. The load on the data center varies with time, and at each time the data center operator has to determine the number of servers that will be operational. The standard assumption is that there is some fixed cost for powering a server on, or powering the server off. Most naturally this cost incorporates the energy used for powering up or down, but this cost may incorporate ancillary terms such as the cost of the additional wear and tear on the servers. In response to a load L_t at time t, the data center operator decides on a number of servers x_t to use to handle this load. In a data center, there are typically sufficiently many servers so that this discrete variable can be reasonably be modeled as a continuous one. The data center operator pays a convex cost of $|x_{t-1} - x_t|$ for either powering-up or powering-down servers, and a cost of $F_t(x_t) = x_t((L_t/x_t)^\alpha + \beta)$ for handling the load, which is the most energy efficient way to service the load L_t using x_t processors, assuming the standard model for processor power. So this corresponds to an instance of OCO on a line, that is, where $k = 1$.

A general instance of OCO would arise from a setting where there are k different types of servers, and where each type of server would generally have different power characteristics. Then $x_{i,t}$ would represent the number of servers of type i that are powered on, and $F_t(x_{1,t}, \ldots, x_{k,t})$ would represent the minimum cost way to handle the load L_t using the number of specified numbers of each type (which is convex for all standard models of power).

4.1   Looking Backward

Theoretical work on OCO deals primarily with the case that $k = 1$. [48] gave a 3-competitive deterministic full-history algorithm. [4] showed that there is an algorithm with sublinear regret, but that $O(1)$-competitiveness and sublinear regret cannot be simultaneously achieved. [13] gave a 2-competitive algorithm, that is most easily understood as a randomized algorithm that maintains a probability distribution p over destinations. [13] also observed that any randomized algorithm for OCO can be converted to a deterministic algorithm without any loss of approximation. [13] also give a simple 3-competitive memoryless algorithm, which in the context of OCO means that the algorithm determines p_t based solely on p_{t-1} and F_t, and showed that this competitiveness is optimal for deterministic memoryless algorithms. Finally [13] gave a general lower bound of 1.86 on the competitiveness of any algorithm, which shows that in some sense this problem is strictly harder than classic online ski rental problem [22].

The OCO problem is a special case of the classic *metrical task system* problem, where both the metric space and the cost functions can be arbitrary. The optimal deterministic competitive ratio for a general metrical task system is $2n - 1$, where n is the number of points in the metric [23], and the optimal randomized competitive ratio is $\Omega(\log n / \log \log n)$ [20,21], and $O(\log^2 n \log \log n)$ [30].

The Convex Body Chasing problem is a special case of OCO where the convex functions are restricted to be those that are zero within some convex region/body, and infinite outside that region. So in the Convex Body Chasing problem the algorithm sees a sequence of convex bodies, and must in response move to a destination within the last convex body. The objective is to minimize the total distance traveled. [31] observed that there is a lower bound of $\Omega(\sqrt{k})$ on the competitive ratio for Convex Body Chasing. Most of the upper bounds in the literature for Convex Body Chasing are for chasing certain special types of convex bodies. [31] gave a somewhat complicated algorithm and $O(1)$-competitiveness analysis for chasing lines in two dimensions, and observe that any $O(1)$-competitive line chasing algorithm for two dimensions can be extended to an $O(1)$-competitive line chasing algorithm for an arbitrary number of dimensions. [31] gave an even more complicated algorithm and $O(1)$-competitiveness analysis for chasing arbitrary convex bodies in two dimensions. [62] showed in a very complicated analysis that the work function algorithm is $O(1)$-competitive for chasing lines and line segments in any dimension. The (Generalized) Work Function Algorithm moves to the location p_t that minimizes a linear combination of $d(p_{t-1}, p_t)$ and $w_t(p_t)$, where $w_t(x)$ is is the cheapest cost to handle the first t requests and end in location x. [32] showed that the greedy algorithm is $O(1)$-competitive if $k = 2$ and the convex bodies are regular polygons with a constant number of sides.

[8] considered the relationship between OCO and Convex Body Chasing. [8] showed that an $O(1)$-competitive algorithm for Convex Body Chasing can be used to obtain an $O(1)$-competitive algorithm for OCO instances in which the convex functions have radial symmetry. This reduction is through an intermediate Lazy Convex Body Chasing problem, which is a special case of OCO in which the convex functions are zero within some convex region, and increase linearly as one moves away from this convex region. [8] also gave an online algorithm for Convex Body Chasing when the convex bodies are subspaces, in any dimension, and an $O(1)$-competitiveness analysis when $k = O(1)$. Finally [8] gave an online algorithm for chasing lines and line segments in any dimension, and show that it is $O(1)$-competitive. The underlying insight of this online algorithm is the same as in [31], to be greedy with occasional adjustments toward the area where the adversary might have cheaply handled recent requests. However, the algorithm and its analysis is cleaner/simpler than the algorithm in [31], as well as being essentially memoryless.

4.2   Open Problems

The two clear top open problems are:

Open Problem: Find an online algorithm for OCO that one can prove is $O(1)$-competitive when the number of dimensions is constant, which is a reasonable assumption in data center applications.

Open Problem: Find a provably $O(1)$-competitive algorithm for the special case of Convex Body Chasing. Convex Body Chasing is easier to think about, and one take away from our paper [8] is that probably OCO isn't too much harder than Convex Body Chasing.

Intuitively the main difficulty of obtaining a provably $O(1)$-competitive algorithm for Convex Body Chasing is balancing the competing needs of the algorithm remembering enough history to be able to be competitive, but keeping its consideration of history sufficiently simple to be analyzable. In some sense, most of the algorithms in the literature keep the consideration of history simple. These algorithms break the input into "phases", and then determine their new destination based only on the history within the current phase. And their analyses all have essentially the same form: after each "phase" in the input, either the location of the online algorithm has either moved closer to the adversary's location by an amount proportional to its cost in the phase, or the adversary is in some position where its costs are proportional to the online algorithm's costs. On the other one extreme is the Work Function algorithm, which uses all of the history in the most complete way imaginable. This makes it quite likely that the algorithm is $O(1)$-competitive, but also means that even for simple instances like line chasing, the analysis is quite involved, and we don't currently know how to analyze the Work Function algorithm for chasing more complex convex bodies.

To get some feel for the issues involved, let us consider two instances for halfspace chasing in three dimensions, which is the simplest setting where we don't know how to achieve $O(1)$-competitiveness. In the first instance, the halfspaces are rotating around a line L, say L is the z axis for the moment. So the halfspace arriving at time t (think of time as being continuous for the moment) would be $ax + by \geq 0$, where $a = \cos\ t$ and $b = \sin\ t$. Any $O(1)$-competitive algorithm would have to move quickly to the line L. From an algorithmic design viewpoint, this isn't a problem at all, as natural generalizations of the algorithms in the literature would move to L. But this instance is a bit of a problem from the standard algorithm analysis point of view. Observe that if the adversary's location is on the line L, but far from the online algorithm's location, then both the adversary's cost is low, and the algorithm isn't get closer to the adversary fast enough to offset its costs.

The second instance is a bit trickier. In this instance, as the halfspaces are again continuously rotating around the line L, but now the line L is simultaneously continuously spinning around the origin in such a way that the loci of points that L sweeps out is a cone. So L at time t could be the line where $0 = ax + by$ and $z^2 = x^2 + y^2$, where $a = \cos\ t$ and $b = \sin\ t$. Any $O(1)$-competitive algorithm would have to move quickly to the origin. But its a bit unclear how one could algorithmically recognize that the algorithm needs to move to the origin in a way that is both principled, and that uses the history in some sort of limited way.

5 Energy Efficient Routing

According to the US Department of Energy [1], data networks consume more than 50 billion kWH of energy per year, and a 40% reduction in wide-area network energy is plausibly achievable if network components were energy proportional.

5.1 Looking Back

Circuit routing, in which each connection is assigned a reserved route in the network with a guaranteed bandwidth, is used by several network protocols to achieve reliable communication [44]. [6] introduced the problem of routing circuits to minimize energy in a network of components that are speed scalable, and that may be shutdown when idle, using the standard models for circuit routing and component energy. The input consists of an undirected graph G, and a collection of source/sink vertex pairs. The output is a path, representing the circuit for a unit bandwidth demand, between each source/sink pair. The power used by an component with positive flow f is $\sigma + f^\alpha$, and the component is shutdown and consumes no power if it supports no flow. The objective is to minimize the aggregate power used over all the components. Primarily for reasons of mathematical tractability, the initial research assume that the speed scalable components are the edges.

The difficulty of these problems comes from the competing goals of minimizing static power, where it's best that flows are concentrated, and minimizing dynamic power, where it's best that the flows are spread out. A critical parameter is $q = \sigma^{1/\alpha}$. If the flow on an edge is at least q, then one knows that the dynamic power on that edge is at least the static power. [6] show that there is a limit to how well these competing demands can be balanced by showing that there is no polynomial-time algorithm with approximation ratio $o(\log^{1/4} n)$, under standard complexity theoretic assumptions. In contrast, [5] shows that these competing forces can be "poly-log-balanced" by giving a polynomial-time poly-log-approximation algorithm that uses several "big hammers" [27,40,59].

We have a line of papers [11,12,41] that significantly extend the results on this line of research. We started with [12], which considered the case of a common source vertex s for all request-pairs, that is all $s_i = s$. Applications for a common source vertex include data collection by base stations in a sensor network, and supporting a multicast communication using unicast routing. [12] gives a polynomial-time $O(1)$-approximation algorithm. The algorithm design and analysis is considerably easier than [5] because, after aggregation into groups, all the flow is going to the same place. [12] also gives an $O(\log^{2\alpha+1} k)$-competitive randomized online algorithm, by giving a procedure for forming the groups in an online fashion.

We then extended these ideas in [11], which contained two main results. The first main result was a polynomial-time $O(\log^\alpha k)$-approximation algorithm for the general problem. This algorithm consisted of 3 stages, each of which was essentially a combinatorial greedy algorithm:

Activating a Steiner Forest: The algorithm first activates a Steiner forest, to ensure minimal connectivity, using the standard $O(1)$-approximation algorithm for Steiner forest [66].

Activating the Hallucination Backbone: Then each request-pair, with probability $\Theta(\frac{\log k}{q})$ *hallucinates* that it wants to route q units of flow unsplittably on a path between its end points. This *hallucinated flow* is then routed using the natural greedy algorithm, all edges on which hallucinated flow is routed are then activated. (Note that no actual flow is routed here, this hallucinated flow is just used to determine which additional edges to activate).

Routing: The algorithm routes the flow on the activated edges using the natural greedy algorithm. The heart of the algorithm analysis is to appeal to the flow-cut gap for multicommodity flows [45,50] to show that there must be a low-congestion routing.

The second main result in [11] is a randomized $\tilde{O}(\log^{3\alpha+1} k)$-competitive online algorithm. The offline algorithm rather naturally extends to an online algorithm. The analysis however is considerably more involved than in the offline case. Since the edges are bought online, the analysis in [35] only shows that the dynamic power for the greedy algorithm is competitive against the power used in an optimal *"priority routing"*, where a request-pair can only route over edges bought by the online algorithm up until the arrival time of the request-pair. Thus to mimic the analysis in the offline case, we need to show that there is a low-congestion *priority* multicommodity flow on the bought edges. This is accomplished by characterizing the notion of *sparsest priority-cuts*, and then bounding the priority flow-cut gap for multicommodity flows.

Finally in [41] we made a start on extending the results in previous papers to the case that the speed scalable components of the graph are the vertices, and not the edges. The main difficulty in emulating the approaches in the previous (edge based) papers is that they all relied on the fact that it is possible to aggregate flows in a (Steiner) tree in such a way that there is low edge congestion, but we would need that there is low node congestion, which is not possible in some trees, e.g. a star. To surmount this difficultly we showed how to efficiently find a low-cost collection of nearly node-disjoint trees that span all terminals, which can then be used to obtain an aggregation of flows with low vertex congestion.

5.2   The Open Problems

Open Problem: Find a poly-log approximation algorithm, when the speed scalable components are the edges, where the polynomial doesn't depend on α.

All of the analysis of the energy used by circuit routing protocols in [5,6,11, 12,41] goes via congestion. To understand this consider the situation of randomly throwing n balls into n bins, where the resulting energy is the sum of the αth power of the bin sizes. An analysis in the spirit of the ones in [5,6,11,12,41] would argue that the resulting energy is within a $\tilde{O}(\log^\alpha n)$ factor of optimal because with high probability no bin has $\Omega(\log n)$ balls. As some bin likely has $\tilde{\Omega}(\log n)$ balls, this is the best bound one can obtain by only analyzing the fullest bin.

But in actuality, the energy used is $O(1)$ approximate to optimal because very few bins have loads near $\log n$. A competitive analysis of a poly-log competitive algorithm, where the polynomial doesn't depend on α, can not go via congestion, and would require reasoning about energy more directly. It is instructive to first see why the Hallucination algorithm won't work. The oversampling in the formation of the Hallucination backbone in [11] was required if the analysis was via congestion; otherwise there would likely be a cut without sufficient capacity to route all the flow across the cut with low congestion. But this oversampling meant that the hallucinated flow was a $\log n$ factor more than the actual flow, and thus increasing costs by a $\log^\alpha n$ factor. Thus one needs to be a bit more careful about how one oversamples. It seems that a new Hallucination algorithm, that is a modest tweak of the original Hallucination algorithm in [11] is a reasonable candidate algorithm. The hallucination backbone would be the union of $\log n$ sub-backbones. For each sub-backbone each source/sink hallucinates a flow of q with probability $\frac{1}{q}$, so there is no oversampling in a sub-backbone. Intuitively if the sub-backbones are (nearly) disjoint, then the static power would only be a $O(\log n)$ more than optimal, and there would still be sufficient capacity to route all flow with low dynamic power. The worry is that if all the sub-backbones had high overlap, then there would be insufficient capacity for a low energy routing. But for all the graphs that we can think of where the sub-backbones might overlap with some reasonable probability, it is the case that for these graphs oversampling is not required to obtain sufficient capacity for a low energy routing.

Open Problem: Find a poly-log competitive online algorithm when the speed scalable components are the vertices.

The obvious starting point is try to find a way to build online a low-cost collection of nearly node-disjoint trees that span all terminals.

6   Energy Efficient Circuit Design

The threshold voltage of a transistor is the minimum supply voltage at which the transistor starts to conduct current. However, if the designed supply voltage was exactly the ideal threshold voltage, some transistors would likely fail to operate as designed due to manufacturing and environmental variations. In the traditional approach to circuit design the supply voltages for each transistor/gate are set sufficiently high so that with sufficiently high probability no transistor fails, and thus the designed circuits need not be fault-tolerant. One potential method to attain more energy-efficient circuits is *Near-Threshold Computing*, which simply means that the supply voltages are designed to be closer to the threshold voltage. As the power used by a transistor/gate is roughly proportional to the square of the supply voltage [26], Near-Threshold Computing can potentially significantly decrease the energy used per gate. However, this energy savings comes at a cost of a greater probability of functional failure, which necessitates that the circuits must be more fault-tolerant, and thus contain more gates. As the total energy used by a circuit is approximately the energy used per gate times the number of gates, achieving energy savings with Near-Threshold Computing involves properly balancing the energy used per gate with the number of gates used.

6.1 Looking Back

In [10] we initiated the theoretical study of the design of energy-efficient circuits. We assumed that the design of the circuit specifies both the circuit layout as well as the supply voltages for the gates. We assume a failure-to-energy function $P(\epsilon)$ that specifies the power required to insure the probability that a gate fails is at most ϵ. For current CMOS technologies, it seems that the "right" model for failure-to-energy function is $P(\epsilon) = \Theta(\log^2(1/\epsilon))$ [28]. For simplicity we assume this failure-to-energy function, but the theoretical results are not particularly sensitive to the exact nature of this function. We subsequently had three follow-up papers [9, 18, 19] on theoretical issues related to near-threshold computing.

[10] showed how to use techniques from the literature on fault-tolerant circuits to obtain bounds on circuit energy. [10] show that $\Omega\left(s\log\left(s(1 - 2\sqrt{\delta})/\delta\right)\right)$ energy is required by any circuit that computes a relation with sensitivity s correctly with probability at least $(1 - \delta)$. [10] also showed, using techniques from [64] and [33, 55], that a relation h that is computable by a circuit of size c can, with probability at least $(1 - \delta)$, be computed by a circuit of faulty gates using $O(c\log(c/\delta))$ energy.

In [9] we considered the problem of: given a circuit C, an input I to C, and a desired circuit error bound δ, compute a supply voltage s that minimizes energy subject to the constraint that the error probability for the circuit is less than δ. The traditional approach/algorithm cranks up the supply voltage s until the error probability at each gate is δ/n, so that by the union bound the probability that the circuit is incorrect is at most δ. In [9] we observed that the traditional algorithm produces an $O(\log^2 n)$ approximation to the minimum energy. The main result in [9] is that is NP-hard to obtain an approximation ratio of $O(\log^{2-\epsilon} n)$. This shows that there are complexity theoretic barriers to systematically beating the traditional approach.

In [18] we showed that almost all Boolean functions require circuits that use exponential energy (foreshadowing slightly, this holds even if circuits can have heterogeneous supply voltages). This is not an immediate consequence of Shannon's classic result [61] that almost all functions require exponential sized circuits of faultless gates because (as we showed in [18]) the same circuit layout can compute many different functions, depending on the value of the supply voltage. The key step in the proof is to upper bound the number of different functions that one circuit layout can compute as the supply voltage changes.

While it may not currently be practical, in principle the supply voltages need not be homogeneous over all gates, that is, different gates could be supplied with different voltages. This naturally leads to the question of whether allowing heterogeneous supply voltages might yield lower-energy circuits than are possible if the supply voltages are required to be homogeneous. While each of [9,10,18] touched on this question, and [19] squarely addressed this question. Intuitively, heterogeneous voltages should benefit a circuit where certain parts of the computation are more sensitive to failure than others. For example, in order for a circuit to be highly reliable, gates near the output need to be highly reliable. However, it may be acceptable for gates that are far from the output to be less reliable if there is sufficient redundancy in the circuit.

We considered four variations on the question, depending on

- whether what one is trying to compute, $f : \{0,1\}^n \rightarrow \{0,1\}$, is a function, or an injective relation (meaning one doesn't care what the output is on some inputs), and
- whether one wants the circuit to be correct with a fixed/constant probability, or with high probability (so the error decreases inverse polynomially as the input size increases).

For each of these four variations, we wanted to determine whether $\omega(1)$ energy savings is possible for all, none, or some of the f. It is relatively straight-forward to observe that the maximum possible energy savings due to allowing heterogeneity is $O(\log^2 n)$ in all cases. Our answers to date can be found in Table 1.

Table 1. Possible energy savings from heterogeneous supply voltages

	Circuit error $\delta = \Theta(1)$	Circuit error $\delta = \Theta\left(\frac{1}{\text{poly}(n)}\right)$
Functions	$\Theta(1)$ for some	$\Theta(\log n)$ for all with linear size circuits
Injective relations	$\Theta(1)$ for some	$\Omega(\log^2 n)$ for some
		$\Omega(\log n)$ for all with linear sized circuits

So one can see from the table that we have a reasonable understanding of when heterogeneity can save energy when computing with high probability, as long as the functions and relations that have linear sized circuits. Functions/relations with (near) linear sized circuits presumably include those that one is most likely to want to implement in hardware. When computing with high probability, heterogeneous circuits can save a $\Theta(\log n)$ factor of energy for all functions with linear sized circuits, and an additional $\log n$ factor can be saved for some relations with linear sized circuits.

6.2 Open Problems

There are myriad open problems in this area, but if I had to pick one as the best open problem, it would be the following:

Open Problem: Does there exist a function (or injective relation) $f : \{0,1\}^n \rightarrow \{0,1\}$ where there is a heterogeneous circuit that computes f with constant error using an $o(1)$ factor less energy than any homogeneous circuit that computes f with constant error?

We know that heterogeneity can give at most constant energy savings for computing some functions with constant error. Not surprisingly one such function is the parity function as intuitively every part of any reasonable circuit for parity is equally highly sensitive to error. And there are examples of relations where heterogeneity helps the obvious circuit. In [10] we showed that the most obvious circuit, a tree of majority gates, to compute the super-majority relation can be made $o(1)$ more energy efficient by turning down the supply voltage near the input gates. But there is a less obvious circuit to compute super-majority [63], that seemingly can not be made more energy efficient with heterogeneous supply voltages.

This seems to be asking a fundamental question about computation. Is it true for it is always the case in the most energy efficient circuit to compute some function with constant error probability that essentially every part of the circuit is equally sensitive to error? (Recall that we know that this answer is no when computing with high probability.) If the answer is always yes for computing with constant probability then we known that heterogeneous circuits will not yield any energy savings for computing with constant error probability.

7   Online Scheduling of Power Heterogeneous Processors

The new architectural designs lead to a plethora of natural algorithmic scheduling problems related to balancing the competing demands of performance and energy efficiency. The natural resulting algorithmic management problems involve determining which task to run on each processor, and for speed scalable processors at what speed to run that task, so as to obtain a (near) optimal trade-off between the conflicting objectives of quality of service and energy efficiency.

There enough literature in this area to justify an independent survey. So in the interest of space, I will just discuss one result, which at least arguably is the culmination of this research line for the common processor models. We showed in [37] that there is a scalable algorithm, which we called SelfishMigrate, for scheduling unrelated machines to minimize a (user/application specified) linear combination of energy and weighted job delay (here some jobs are more important and contribute more to this total). The result holds even when each machine has an arbitrary convex speed-to-power function, and processors may be shutdown (and thus consume no energy). An algorithm is scalable if it guarantees that the objective value is within a constant factor of optimal for processors that run slightly slower at each power level. An algorithm is nonclairvoyant if does not know the size of a job. The algorithm does however need to know the suitability of each processor for each job, or more formally, the rate that each processor can process each job. Its easy to see that such knowledge is necessary to achieve any reasonable approximation. We had previously shown in [34] that the standard priority algorithms, like Highest Density First (HDF), that one finds in standard operating systems textbooks, can perform quite badly on heterogeneous processors when the quality of service objective is weighted delay [34]. So we knew we were not going to be able to obtain scalability with a known standard algorithm.

The SelfishMigrate algorithm can be best viewed in a game theoretic setting where jobs are selfish agents, and machines declare their scheduling policies in advance. Each machine maintains a virtual queue on the current set of jobs assigned to it; newly arriving jobs are appended to the tail of this queue. Each machine treats a migration of a job to it as an arrival, and a migration out of it as a departure. This means a job migrating to a machine is placed at the tail of the virtual queue. Each job j has a virtual utility function, which roughly corresponds to the inverse of the instantaneous weighted delay introduced by j to jobs ahead of it in its virtual queue, and their contribution to j's weighted delay. Using these virtual utilities, jobs perform sequential best response dynamics, migrating to machines (and get placed in the tail of their virtual queue) if doing so leads to larger virtual utility. Therefore, at each time instant, the job migration achieves a Nash equilibrium of the sequential best response dynamics on the virtual utilities. The analysis is via dual fitting, and involves showing that the Nash dynamics on virtual utilities directly corresponds to our setting of dual variables being feasible. In hindsight, we believe this framework is the right way to generalize the greedy dispatch rules and dual fitting analysis from previous works [3, 36].

This result suggests that perhaps that heterogeneous multiprocessors should be scheduled very differently than the way that uniprocessors and homogeneous multiprocessors have been scheduled.

7.1 Open Problem

Open Problem: Show that the standard priority scheduling algorithms are scalable for the objective of total flow time when scheduling on related processors.

The standard priority scheduling algorithms that one finds in introductory operating systems texts, e.g. Shortest Remaining Processing Time (SRPT), Shortest Job First (SJF), Shortest Elapsed Time First (SETF), Multi-Level Feedback (MLF), are all known to be scalable for the objective of total delay on one processor and on identical processors [38, 56, 57]. Given that it is often difficult to get new policies/protocols adopted, it would be good to know how bad things can get for these standard scheduling policies on heterogeneous processors. That is, are these algorithms scalable for total delay on related machines. Intuitively I see no reason to think that they are not scalable. The intuition why the standard algorithms are not scalable for weighted delay is that if one has multiprocessor with many slow processors and few fast processors then it can be difficult to harness the aggregate speed of the slow processors. Somehow it seems that, if jobs are of equal importance, this is not such an issue. The standard potential function and dual fitting approaches don't seem immediately applicable as there doesn't seem to be a simple algebraic expression for the contribution of a particular job towards the objective. So it seems that some innovation in algorithm analysis will be required.

8 Understanding Optimal Energy Tradeoff Schedules

8.1 Looking Back

Another line of my research related to speed scalable processors is to understand optimal energy-performance tradeoff schedules, primarily by finding efficient algorithms to compute them. We initiated this line of research in [58] by giving a polynomial time algorithm for scheduling jobs that have a common size with an objective of minimizing a linear combination of total delay and energy. In [15] we considered the problem of scheduling arbitrary sized jobs with the objective of minimizing a linear combination of fractional weighted delay and energy, and showed how to recognize an optimal schedule. In [7] we gave a polynomial time algorithm for scheduling arbitrary sized jobs with the objective of minimizing a linear combination of fractional weighted delay and energy. The algorithm in [7] can be viewed as a primal-dual algorithm that raises the dual variables in an organized way. In [16] we considered the setting of a sensor that consists of a speed-scalable processor, a battery, and a solar cell that harvests energy from its environment at a time-invariant recharge rate. The processor must process a collection of jobs of various sizes. Jobs arrive at different times and have different deadlines. The objective is to minimize the *recharge rate*, which is the rate at which the device has to harvest energy in order to feasibly schedule all jobs. The main result was a polynomial-time combinatorial algorithm for processors with a natural set of discrete speed/power pairs. The main takeaway form this paper was that it is much harder to reason about energy when it is supplied over time instead of all being initially available.

One can formulate many different optimization problems depending on how one models the processor (e.g., whether allowed speeds are discrete or continuous, and the nature of relationship between speed and power), the performance objective (e.g., whether jobs are of equal or unequal importance, and whether one is interested in minimizing waiting times of jobs or of work), and how one handles the dual objective (e.g., whether they are combined in a single objective, or whether one objective is transformed into a constraint). In [17] we finally bit the bullet, and determined the complexity of a reasonably full landscape of all the possible formulations.

One commonality of the algorithms that we developed in [7,16,58] is that they all can be viewed as continuous homotopic optimization algorithms. These homotopic algorithms trace the evolution of the optimal solution as either the objective function evolves from one, where it is simple to compute the optimal, to the desired objective, or the constraints evolve from ones, that are easy to satisfy, to the desired constraints. So one take away point from these results is that homotopic optimization can be a fruitful approach for computing and understanding optimal tradeoff schedules.

8.2   Open Problem

The clear top open problem in this area, which was left open in [17] is:

Open Problem: Determine the complexity of finding optimal schedule for the objective of total delay plus energy on a speed scalable processor.

In the optimal schedule it must be the case that at all times the job being processed is the one that has the least amount of work left to be processed. But this is of less help than it might first appear, as this doesn't help decide what speed the processor should run, and thus how much work should be left on this job at the next time step. The main difficulty of extending the algorithms in [7,58] is that the optimal total delay plus energy schedule for arbitrary work jobs is more fragile than if the jobs had unit size or the quality of service objective was fractional total delay. Still, many of the insights in [7,58] carry over. In particular, the power of a job should generally be proportional to the number of jobs that depend on that job. As a consequence of this, if one knew the ordering of the release times and completion times, obtaining an optimal schedule subject to such an ordering constraint is straightforward. So my intuition at this point says that this problem should be solvable in polynomial time. But I don't have any real idea how to touch this problem. I find it a bit surprising that even computing an optimal schedule when there are only 2 speeds seems hard. I think it would be fine to get an algorithm whose running time is polynomial in the number of jobs, but possibly exponential in the number of speeds, as usually the number of speeds is usually on the order of 5 to 10. However, it is certainly not inconceivable that there is no polynomial-time algorithm for this problem, say because the problem is NP-hard. There is no proof in the literature showing the hardness a speed scaling problem where the hardness somehow arose nontrivially from the speed scaling aspect of the problem. So a hardness proof would be interesting, as SRPT is optimal for a fixed speed processor, and its not clear where the hardness would come for a speed scalable processor.

9   Conclusion

Some characteristics of the theory of energy as a computational resource that has developed over the last decade are:

- Most problems arise at a lower layer of the information technology stack that is not aware of the exact nature of the computation taking place on the high layer.
- Most problems involve managing some mechanism/technology created/ installed to achieve greater energy efficiency.
- Most problems involve balancing dual objectives, one related to energy, and one related to performance. Often of these objectives is implicit as it has been turned into a constraint.

As a consequence, the current theory energy as a computational resource is less concentrated, and less distinct from other research areas, than the theory of time/space as a computational resource were in their first decade.

References

1. Vision and roadmap: routing telecom and data centers toward efficient energy use. In: Proceedings of Vision and Roadmap Workshop on Routing Telecom and Data Centers Toward Efficient Energy Use, May 2009
2. Albers, S.: Energy-efficient algorithms. Commun. ACM **53**(5), 86–96 (2010)
3. Anand, S., Garg, N., Kumar, A.: Resource augmentation for weighted flow-time explained by dual fitting. In: ACM-SIAM Symposium on Discrete Algorithms, pp. 1228–1241 (2012)
4. Andrew, L.L.H., Barman, S., Ligett, K., Lin, M., Meyerson, A., Roytman, A., Wierman, A.: A tale of two metrics: simultaneous bounds on competitiveness and regret. In: Conference on Learning Theory, pp. 741–763 (2013)
5. Andrews, M., Antonakopoulos, S., Zhang, L.: Minimum-cost network design with (dis)economies of scale. In: IEEE Symposium on Foundations of Computer Science, pp. 585–592 (2010)
6. Andrews, M., Fernández, A., Zhang, L., Zhao, W.: Routing for energy minimization in the speed scaling model. In: INFOCOM, pp. 2435–2443 (2010)
7. Antoniadis, A., Barcelo, N., Consuegra, M., Kling, P., Nugent, M., Pruhs, K., Scquizzato, M.: Efficient computation of optimal energy and fractional weighted flow trade-off schedules. In: Symposium on Theoretical Aspects of Computer Science (2014)
8. Antoniadis, A., Barcelo, N., Nugent, M., Pruhs, K., Schewior, K., Scquizzato, M.: Chasing convex bodies and functions. In: Kranakis, E., Navarro, G., Chávez, E. (eds.) LATIN 2016. LNCS, vol. 9644, pp. 68–81. Springer, Heidelberg (2016). https://doi.org/10.1007/978-3-662-49529-2_6
9. Antoniadis, A., Barcelo, N., Nugent, M., Pruhs, K., Scquizzato, M.: Complexity-theoretic obstacles to achieving energy savings with near-threshold computing. In: International Green Computing Conference, pp. 1–8 (2014)
10. Antoniadis, A., Barcelo, N., Nugent, M., Pruhs, K., Scquizzato, M.: Energy-efficient circuit design. In: Innovations in Theoretical Computer Science, pp. 303–312 (2014)
11. Antoniadis, A., Im, S., Krishnaswamy, R., Moseley, B., Nagarajan, V., Pruhs, K., Stein, C.: Energy efficient virtual circuit routing. In: ACM-SIAM Symposium on Discrete Algorithms (2014)
12. Bansal, N., Gupta, A., Krishnaswamy, R., Nagarajan, V., Pruhs, K., Stein, C.: Multicast routing for energy minimization using speed scaling. In: Even, G., Rawitz, D. (eds.) MedAlg 2012. LNCS, vol. 7659, pp. 37–51. Springer, Heidelberg (2012). https://doi.org/10.1007/978-3-642-34862-4_3
13. Bansal, N., Gupta, A., Krishnaswamy, R., Pruhs, K., Schewior, K., Stein, C.: A 2-competitive algorithm for online convex optimization with switching costs. In: Workshop on Approximation Algorithms for Combinatorial Optimization Problems, pp. 96–109 (2015)
14. Bansal, N., Kimbrel, T., Pruhs, K.: Speed scaling to manage energy and temperature. J. ACM **54**(1), 3 (2007)
15. Barcelo, N., Cole, D., Letsios, D., Nugent, M., Pruhs, K.: Optimal energy trade-off schedules. Sustain. Comput.: Inf. Syst. **3**, 207–217 (2013)
16. Barcelo, N., Kling, P., Nugent, M., Pruhs, K.: Optimal speed scaling with a solar cell. In: Chan, T.-H.H., Li, M., Wang, L. (eds.) COCOA 2016. LNCS, vol. 10043, pp. 521–535. Springer, Cham (2016). https://doi.org/10.1007/978-3-319-48749-6_38

17. Barcelo, N., Kling, P., Nugent, M., Pruhs, K., Scquizzato, M.: On the complexity of speed scaling. In: Italiano, G.F., Pighizzini, G., Sannella, D.T. (eds.) MFCS 2015. LNCS, vol. 9235, pp. 75–89. Springer, Heidelberg (2015). https://doi.org/10.1007/978-3-662-48054-0_7

18. Barcelo, N., Nugent, M., Pruhs, K., Scquizzato, M.: Almost all functions require exponential energy. In: Italiano, G.F., Pighizzini, G., Sannella, D.T. (eds.) MFCS 2015. LNCS, vol. 9235, pp. 90–101. Springer, Heidelberg (2015). https://doi.org/10.1007/978-3-662-48054-0_8

19. Barcelo, N., Nugent, M., Pruhs, K., Scquizzato, M.: The power of heterogeneity in near-threshold computing. In: International Green and Sustainable Computing Conference, pp. 1–4 (2015)

20. Bartal, Y., Bollobás, B., Mendel, M.: Ramsey-type theorems for metric spaces with applications to online problems. J. Comput. Syst. Sci. 72(5), 890–921 (2006)

21. Bartal, Y., Linial, N., Mendel, M., Naor, A.: On metric Ramsey-type phenomena. In: ACM Symposium on Theory of Computing, pp. 463–472 (2003)

22. Borodin, A., El-Yaniv, R.: Online Computation and Competitive Analysis. Cambridge University Press, Cambridge (1998)

23. Borodin, A., Linial, N., Saks, M.E.: An optimal on-line algorithm for metrical task system. J. ACM 39(4), 745–763 (1992)

24. Bower, F.A., Sorin, D.J., Cox, L.P.: The impact of dynamically heterogeneous multicore processors on thread scheduling. IEEE Micro 28(3), 17–25 (2008)

25. Brooks, D.M., Bose, P., Schuster, S.E., Jacobson, H., Kudva, P.N., Buyuktosunoglu, A., Wellman, J.-D., Zyuban, V., Gupta, M., Cook, P.W.: Power-aware microarchitecture: design and modeling challenges for next-generation microprocessors. IEEE Micro 20(6), 26–44 (2000)

26. Butts, J.A., Sohi, G.S.: A static power model for architects. In: ACM/IEEE International Symposium on Microarchitecture, pp. 191–201 (2000)

27. Chekuri, C., Khanna, S., Shepherd, F.B.: Multicommodity flow, well-linked terminals, and routing problems. In: ACM Symposium on Theory of Computing, pp. 183–192 (2005)

28. Dreslinski, R.G., Wieckowski, M., Blaauw, D., Sylvester, D., Mudge, T.N.: Near-threshold computing: reclaiming Moore's law through energy efficient integrated circuits. Proc. IEEE 98(2), 253–266 (2010)

29. Esmaeilzadeh, H., Blem, E.R., Amant, R.S., Sankaralingam, K., Burger, D.: Dark silicon and the end of multicore scaling. IEEE Micro 32(3), 122–134 (2012)

30. Fiat, A., Mendel, M.: Better algorithms for unfair metrical task systems and applications. SIAM J. Comput. 32(6), 1403–1422 (2003)

31. Friedman, J., Linial, N.: On convex body chasing. Discret. Comput. Geom. 9, 293–321 (1993)

32. Fujiwara, H., Iwama, K., Yonezawa, K.: Online chasing problems for regular polygons. Inf. Process. Lett. 108(3), 155–159 (2008)

33. Gács, P.: Reliable computation. In: Algorithms in Informatics, vol. 2. ELTE Eötvös Kiadó, Budapest (2005)

34. Gupta, A., Im, S., Krishnaswamy, R., Moseley, B., Pruhs, K.: Scheduling heterogeneous processors isn't as easy as you think. In: ACM-SIAM Symposium on Discrete Algorithms, pp. 1242–1253 (2012)

35. Gupta, A., Krishnaswamy, R., Pruhs, K.: Online primal-dual for non-linear optimization with applications to speed scaling. In: Erlebach, T., Persiano, G. (eds.) WAOA 2012. LNCS, vol. 7846, pp. 173–186. Springer, Heidelberg (2013). https://doi.org/10.1007/978-3-642-38016-7_15

36. Im, S., Kulkarni, J., Munagala, K.: Competitive algorithms from competitive equilibria: non-clairvoyant scheduling under polyhedral constraints. In: Symposium on Theory of Computing, pp. 313–322 (2014)
37. Im, S., Kulkarni, J., Munagala, K., Pruhs, K.: Selfishmigrate: a scalable algorithm for non-clairvoyantly scheduling heterogeneous processors. In: Symposium on Foundations of Computer Science, pp. 531–540 (2014)
38. Im, S., Moseley, B., Pruhs, K.: A tutorial on amortized local competitiveness in online scheduling. SIGACT News **42**(2), 83–97 (2011)
39. Irani, S., Pruhs, K.: Algorithmic problems in power management. SIGACT News **36**(2), 63–76 (2005)
40. Khandekar, R., Rao, S., Vazirani, U.V.: Graph partitioning using single commodity flows. J. ACM **56**(4), 19 (2009)
41. Krishnaswamy, R., Nagarajan, V., Pruhs, K., Stein, C.: Cluster before you hallucinate: approximating node-capacitated network design and energy efficient routing (2014)
42. Kumar, R., Tullsen, D.M., Jouppi, N.P.: Core architecture optimization for heterogeneous chip multiprocessors. In: International Conference on Parallel Architectures and Compilation Techniques, pp. 23–32. ACM (2006)
43. Kumar, R., Tullsen, D.M., Ranganathan, P., Jouppi, N.P., Farkas, K.I.: Single-ISA heterogeneous multi-core architectures for multithreaded workload performance. SIGARCH Comput. Archit. News **32**(2), 64 (2004)
44. Kurose, J.F., Ross, K.W.: Computer Networking: A Top-Down Approach. Addison-Wesley Publishing Company, Boston (2009)
45. Leighton, F.T., Rao, S.: Multicommodity max-flow min-cut theorems and their use in designing approximation algorithms. J. ACM **46**(6), 787–832 (1999)
46. Lin, M., Liu, Z., Wierman, A., Andrew, L.L.H.: Online algorithms for geographical load balancing. In: International Green Computing Conference, pp. 1–10 (2012)
47. Lin, M., Wierman, A., Andrew, L.L.H., Thereska, E.: Online dynamic capacity provisioning in data centers. In: Allerton Conference on Communication, Control, and Computing, pp. 1159–1163 (2011)
48. Lin, M., Wierman, A., Andrew, L.L.H., Thereska, E.: Dynamic right-sizing for power-proportional data centers. IEEE/ACM Trans. Netw. **21**(5), 1378–1391 (2013)
49. Lin, M., Wierman, A., Roytman, A., Meyerson, A., Andrew, L.L.H.: Online optimization with switching cost. SIGMETRICS Perform. Eval. Rev. **40**(3), 98–100 (2012)
50. Linial, N., London, E., Rabinovich, Y.: The geometry of graphs and some of its algorithmic applications. Combinatorica **15**(2), 215–245 (1995)
51. Liu, Z., Lin, M., Wierman, A., Low, S.H., Andrew, L.L.H.: Greening geographical load balancing. In: ACM SIGMETRICS International Conference on Measurement and Modeling of Computer Systems, pp. 233–244 (2011)
52. Merritt, R.: CPU designers debate multi-core future. EE Times, February 2008
53. Morad, T.Y., Weiser, U.C., Kolodny, A., Valero, M., Ayguade, E.: Performance, power efficiency and scalability of asymmetric cluster chip multiprocessors. IEEE Comput. Archit. Lett. **5**(1), 4 (2006)
54. Mudge, T.: Power: a first-class architectural design constraint. Computer **34**(4), 52–58 (2001)
55. Pippenger, N.: On networks of noisy gates. In: Symposium on Foundations of Computer Science, pp. 30–38 (1985)

56. Pruhs, K.: Competitive online scheduling for server systems. In: Special Issue of SIGMETRICS Performance Evaluation Review on New Perspectives in Scheduling, no. 4 (2007)

57. Pruhs, K., Sgall, J., Torng, E.: Online scheduling. In: Handbook of Scheduling: Algorithms, Models, and Performance Analysis (2004)

58. Pruhs, K., Uthaisombut, P., Woeginger, G.J.: Getting the best response for your erg. ACM Trans. Algorithms 4(3), 38:1–38:17 (2008)

59. Rao, S., Zhou, S.: Edge disjoint paths in moderately connected graphs. SIAM J. Comput. 39(5), 1856–1887 (2010)

60. Sergent, J.E., Krum, A.: Thermal Management Handbook. McGraw-Hill, New York (1998)

61. Shannon, C.E.: The synthesis of two-terminal switching circuits. Bell Syst. Tech. J. 28, 59–98 (1949)

62. Sitters, R.: The generalized work function algorithm is competitive for the generalized 2-server problem. SIAM J. Comput. 43(1), 96–125 (2014)

63. Valiant, L.G.: Short monotone formulae for the majority function. J. Algorithms 5(3), 363–366 (1984)

64. von Neumann, J.: Probabilistic logics and the synthesis of reliable organisms from unreliable components. In: Shannon, C.E., McCarthy, J. (eds.) Automata Studies, pp. 329–378. Princeton University Press, Princeton (1956)

65. Wang, K., Lin, M., Ciucu, F., Wierman, A., Lin, C.: Characterizing the impact of the workload on the value of dynamic resizing in data centers. In: IEEE INFOCOM, pp. 515–519 (2013)

66. Williamson, D.P., Shmoys, D.B.: The Design of Approximation Algorithms. Cambridge University Press, Cambridge (2011)

Brain Computation: A Computer Science Perspective

Wolfgang Maass[1]([✉]), Christos H. Papadimitriou[2], Santosh Vempala[3],
and Robert Legenstein[1]

[1] Institute for Theoretical Computer Science, Graz University of Technology,
Graz, Austria
{maass,robert.legenstein}@igi.tugraz.at
[2] Computer Science, Columbia University, New York, NY, USA
christos@columbia.edu
[3] Computer Science, Georgia Tech, Atlanta, GA, USA
vempala@gatech.edu

Abstract. The brain carries out tasks that are very demanding from
a computational perspective, apparently powered by a mere 20 W. This
fact has intrigued computer scientists for many decades, and is currently
drawing many of them to the quest of acquiring a computational understanding of the brain. Yet, at present there is no productive interaction of
computer scientists with neuroscientists in this quest. Research in computational neuroscience is advancing at a rapid pace, and the resulting
abundance of facts and models makes it increasingly difficult for scientists
from other fields to engage in brain research. The goal of this article is
to provide—along with a few words of caution—background, up-to-date
references on data and models in neuroscience, and open problems that
appear to provide good opportunities for theoretical computer scientists
to enter the fascinating field of brain computation.

1 Introduction

We have known since antiquity[1] that our brain gives rise to our perceptions,
memories, thoughts and actions, and yet precisely how these phenomena arise
remains the greatest scientific mystery and challenge of our time. This is despite
massive, brilliant and accelerating progress in our understanding of the brain,
its structure and molecular basis, its development and pathology, its neurons
and its synapses, as well as the complex ways in which they are modified by
experience[2].

---

[1] In the early 5th century BCE, Alcmaeon of Croton proclaimed the brain "the seat
of intelligence," conjectured that it is connected to sensory organs through channels, and discovered and dissected the optical nerve. Disappointingly, in his response
to Alcmaeon more than a century later, Aristotle argues instead that intelligence
springs from the heart...

[2] [1] is a standard graduate and [2] a standard undergraduate textbook in Neuroscience, while [3] is a mathematical treatment of the subject.

© Springer Nature Switzerland AG 2019
B. Steffen and G. Woeginger (Eds.): Computing and Software Science, LNCS 10000, pp. 184–199, 2019.
https://doi.org/10.1007/978-3-319-91908-9_11

How does the mind emerge from the brain? It seems very plausible, and has been strongly suggested over the decades [4–6], that the eventual answer to this question will be at least partly computational. We therefore believe that computer scientists, and theoreticians in particular, should work on this problem. And yet, despite important early connections between computer science and the study of the brain (see the brief historical account in Sect. 2), there is at present no community of computer theorists studying the brain[3]. Furthermore, there is no articulated suite of models, research questions, and early results in the interface between computer science and brain science, inviting computer scientists to participate in this grand quest[4]. This is significant, because such entry points have in the past marked the beginnings of successful interactions between computer science and other scientific disciplines, such as statistical physics [10], quantum physics [11,12] and economics [13,14].

This is the context and thrust of this paper. In Sect. 2 we give a brief historical overview of past interactions between computer science and the study of computational aspects of the brain, and we articulate David Marr's vision of computational research on the brain, *ca.* 1980. In Sect. 3 we discuss aspects of the methodology of the computational study of the brain, focusing on algorithms of the brain, abstract and simplified models of brain systems, and learning. In Sect. 4 we exemplify these principles by describing current work by our group on computational models for the formation, association, and binding of memories in the medial temporal lobe (MTL), a brain region believed to be involved with such activities. We conclude in Sect. 5 with an array of research questions and fronts.

2   History

The pioneers of computation were keenly interested in the brain. Turing saw the human brain as the archetype of computation [15], and later, famously, as an important challenge for computers [16]. Von Neumann in a posthumously published essay [17,18] compares the brain with the computers of his time. He observes that the brain is larger in number of elements (still is, but it is getting close), but slower (much more so now); he notes the analogue nature, but digital operation, of neurons and synapses, acknowledges the key role played by biology and genes, and ponders the brain's architecture (having himself pioneered the computer's). Remarkably, he hypothesized already that the brain is likely to carry out computations on a statistical level with algorithms that are *"characterized by less logical and arithmetical depth that we are normally used to"*. McCulloch and Pitts [19] and later Rosenblatt [20] proposed stylized neuron-like elements as a possible basis of brain-inspired computation, initiating a rich

---

[3] In contrast, there is a well developed theoretical field of investigation for the related field of Machine Learning, namely the COLT community.

[4] Valiant's work starting from the 1990s [7–9] is a notable exception discussed extensively later.

research tradition which eventually brought us deep learning (on which more later).

In 1980, computational neuroscience pioneer Marr proposed an influential three-level approach to understanding brain computation [21]:

- At the *computational or behavioural level* (today we would call it *specificational*) one identifies the input-output behavior of the system being studied; we refer to this as the first level.
- At the *software or algorithmic level*, one seeks to understand the organizations and dynamics of the particular processes and representations used by the system; we refer to this as the second level.
- Finally, the *biological implementation, or hardware, level* entails identifying the biophysical elements (e.g., neurons and synapses) and molecular mechanisms employed by the system to realize the algorithm; we refer to this as the third level.

We shall use Marr's taxonomy as the basic framework of our discussion of computational approaches to the brain.

3   On Methodology

Can we hope to use Marr's method to discover the overarching algorithmic principle underlying all of brain computation, the coveted *algorithm run by the brain?* In articulating his three-level proposal, we believe that Marr was expecting the various systems in the brain (probably hundreds of them) to have each its own function and specification, and its own algorithm and hardware. One should expect *large-scale algorithmic heterogeneity* in the brain—a plethora of principles, methods, procedures, and representations—and one has to be prepared for the long haul of understanding them one by one. (But see [22, 23] for a recent principled attempt at a compilation of a broad range of elementary computational tasks at Marr's level.)

There is a subtlety in Marr's level two, where we infer the algorithm used by the system: We know from the theory of computation that there are infinitely many algorithms for the same task, and furthermore classical universality results [24, 25] imply that neuron-like systems can in principle implement any process and algorithm whatsoever. Showing that one particular algorithm accomplishing the level-one task can be implemented in the hardware of level three, or that a class of algorithms can be so implemented (see for example [26]), constitutes no evidence whatsoever that this algorithm or class is actually used at level two. To solve the second level problem, one needs to rely on experimental results revealing properties of the hardware (level three), and use these to restrict the unlimited repertoire of possible algorithms.

In fact, one may speculate that the algorithmic second level may in many cases end up being simply the computational behavior of the hardware/third level: *The algorithm vanishes,* essentially because the hardware is well adapted to (probably has co-evolved with) the task, and the inputs (from sensors or other parts of the brain) as well as the parameters of the chemical environment are adequate for driving the hardware in an essentially "algorithm-free" way. In other cases, the algorithm may be disappointingly opaque and lacking in a meaningful explanation, perhaps because it is the result of a long evolutionary process of parameter setting though trial and error; recurrent neural networks often appear to be like this.

Computational work of the brain must get inspiration from, and be meticulously cognizant[5] of, the tremendously rich and informative current experimental work in neuroscience. In fact, one particular strand of this work seems especially well suited to enlighten the computational study of the brain: *Connectomics* [27,28], the ongoing herculean effort to create detailed large-scale maps of all actual neurons and synapses of animal brains. Would this project, once successful, facilitate—even obviate—the computational study of the brain? In pondering this question, it is useful to remember deep learning: We currently have at our disposal a wide variety of artificial neural network architectures solving sophisticated problems, and *we know to the last detail* the precise structure, connectivity, and vast array of numerical parameters of these networks. And yet we are lacking a meaningful explication of how each of these systems solves the problem at hand. Further, one should keep in mind that a static connectome of the brain does not exist, at least for higher vertebrates such as mice. Instead synaptic connections in the brain are known to rewire themselves on a time scale of hours to days [29–31]. Hence, any connectome can only be a momentary snapshot of a dynamically changing brain structure, and brain computation has to be understood in the context of this dynamics.

Models. The study of the brain often employs *models* of the brain (or, more commonly, of parts thereof). Models are important and useful, but must be created and used with care. *Abstract models* create mathematical abstractions— that is, generalizations—of the realities of the brain or a subsystem thereof. In employing an abstract model, one must remember that it is a generalization; this means that *some but not all* of its specializations will be reasonable models of the brain. In addition, an abstract model may not be sufficiently abstract, in the sense that models of biological neural networks that take into account experimentally verified and functionally relevant features of biological neurons or synapses may *not* be specializations of the abstract model. For example, we know that weights of synapses are subject to use-dependent short-term plasticity; apparently every biological synapse has an individual short-term plasticity, which implies that its effective weight for the second spike in a spike train is smaller or larger than for the first one, and assumes yet another value for the third spike, depending on the interspike intervals and the specific type of synapse (see Sect. 1 of [32] for references). This feature of biological synapses does appear to be functionally relevant, and provides clues about the types of algorithms that can be implemented by biological networks of neurons. On the other hand, it

---

[5] The use of "killer adjectives" such as *biologically plausible* is a poor substitute for computational models and results informed by experimental knowledge.

sets such networks apart from Boolean circuits and artificial neural networks, which require that the parameters of the units remain stable between steps.

Another genre of models are *simplified models*. Brain systems are often of tremendous complexity, and it is difficult and unwieldy to include all that is known from experiments in a single manageable model. In such cases, a *simplified model* can be invaluable for capturing the system's salient aspects, disregarding effects and interactions which seem largely inconsequential. However, in employing a simplified model one must remember what was thrown away, and in the end of the analysis go back to determine, for which kinds of predictions is the model suitable, and for which it is not. Simplified models are often further modified and implemented as *brain-inspired computational engines* for solving actual computational problems. This is of course valuable, but again one must remember that the success (or failure) of such engines may have little to teach us about the way brains work (deep learning comes again to mind).

Learning, Environments, and Language. One cannot engage in a computational study of the brain without considering how the brain is changed by the animal's experience—that is to say, how *learning*[6] happens in the brain. By "learning" one means changes occurring in the brain through interactions with other parts of the brain and, importantly, with the surrounding environment. Processes that implement learning are part of a large repertoire of plasticity processes that take place in the brain simultaneously at many different time scales, and whose function is only partially understood. Further, one cannot claim to understand the brain without also considering the brain's environment and its challenges. One subtlety here is that the environment is *affected* by the brain's activity—in the short term through motor action and animal interactions, in the longer term through design of the environment (dwellings, signs, etc.).

Language is itself an important environment (since utterances are the input to a specialized yet overarching brain activity in humans). This environment was designed from scratch, and, in evolutionary terms, *extremely* recently [34], at a time when the human brain had already been developed essentially to its present form. Human language is, so to speak, a last-minute adaptation. Furthermore, it has undergone its own vigorous evolutionary process over a window of very few thousands of generations. It seems natural to posit then that language has evolved to be well adapted to the human brain's strengths—for example, so it can be learned easily by babies. We believe that language is an especially important and opportune arena for the computational study of the brain and the mind.

4   Models of Memories and Cognitive Computation

Much current experimental work explores the nature and function of *memories:* the representation in the brain of distinct concepts, such as persons we know, places where we have been, or words we use. It is estimated that many tens

---

[6] In fact, Poggio [33] proposes that learning is so fundamental for brain computation so as to constitute an extra top level of Marr's hierarchy.

of thousands of such memories are represented in the human brain, along with *associations* between them. We believe that memories, because of their discrete and symbolic nature, and their close relationship with language, are an interesting place for theoretical computer scientists to start thinking about the brain. In this section we focus on recent work by our group on memory creation, association, and binding; a reader more interested in a birds eye view of the subject may want to go directly to the next section on open questions.

Valiant's Model. Leslie G. Valiant's *neuroidal model* was proposed in 1994 as a possible basis of a computational theory of the brain, and ultimately of cognition. He posits a random directed graph of neuroids (model neurons with discrete internal states) as nodes, and synapses as directed edges. Parameters of the neuroids and the synapses (e.g., internal state, threshold, strength, etc.) are modified in clocked discrete steps in a distributed, automaton-like manner. Valiant used this model to develop his theory of memory based on *items*. An item is a set of neurons whose simultaneous firing is coterminous with the subject thinking one particular thought (such as "apple"); items may or may not overlap, yielding two different models. Valiant defines Boolean-style operations on items: JOIN (e.g., "apple" may be joined with "green" to form a new item which will fire every time the two constituent items fire together) and LINK (e.g., "apple" linked to the item representing the class "fruit"). The operations of JOIN and LINK can be implemented within the neuroidal model by deterministic algorithms that switch between states of neurons and synapses, including synaptic weights and thresholds—the algorithms must switch rather arbitrarily between states in order to achieve the desired functionality— and by exploiting the random nature of the underlying directed graph to recruit and manipulate new neurons.[7]

Valiant's model was a brave and inspiring early attempt to make computational sense of the brain. In the two decades since the publication of [7], experimental neuroscience has provided much insight into various details of computation and plasticity (learning) of networks of neurons in the brain; some of these findings align well with the premises and predictions of Valiant's model, but others do not. Even though the complete rules for synaptic plasticity (the ways in which synaptic weights change in response to neural activity, effecting learning) are still not known, we now understand that Hebbian plasticity (changes in synaptic weights resulting from the near-simultaneous firing of neurons) can increase synaptic weights by some limited amount within a given time window, say, by 100% within a day; see e.g. [37], and furthermore there is a lot of variability in this respect among different synapses, and within the same synapse over time. Hence it cannot be assumed that synaptic weights can be set to an arbitrary and precise value during learning.

---

[7] Recently, Valiant's theory was extended by the introduction of the *predictive join*, or PJOIN [35], a more algorithmically apt version of JOIN, which however is subject to the same criticism. It is an interesting question as to whether the conceptual primitives of JOIN, LINK, PJOIN, which enable rich computation [36], can be implemented in more realistic models.

Similarly, as we discuss below, neural recordings both from the animal and the human brain [38] suggest that salient concepts are indeed encoded in the brain through distributed "assemblies" of neurons, so that a fair portion of the neurons in an assembly will fire whenever the corresponding concept is invoked. However, these assemblies are not static entities, since the concrete set of firing neurons varies substantially from trial to trial, presumably in dependence on the context, and, as we discuss below, the underlying set can be changed by experience. Also, even though, as we shall see, there is now evidence that associations somewhat akin to the ones predicted by Valiant's JOIN do happen in the human brain, such associations appear to be of a different nature and form than JOIN: Associations seem to be recorded by the assemblies "bleeding" into each other, as opposed to collaborating to create an altogether new assembly[8].

The Ison et al. Experiment. In a recent experiment [40], the formation of associations between memories in the human medial temporal lobe (MTL, a brain region long thought to be crucial to the representation of memories) has been documented. They recorded from a few neurons[9] in the MTL of a human subject to whom many (over a hundred) pictures of known people and places were shown in a precise protocol. They found a particular neuron that fired every time the Eiffel tower was shown, but not when other familiar images, such as Barack Obama's, were shown[10]. Then a combined image of the two was presented, and the neuron duly fired (as it always did when the Eiffel tower was in sight). Remarkably, when a picture of Obama was presented next, the neuron also fired: the subject had learned the connection, or *association*, between Obama and the Eiffel tower! And the recorded neuron was a part of the representation of this association. The principle that associations between memory items are accompanied by overlaps in the corresponding assemblies was confirmed more recently also for long-term representations of associations [41].

Neural Network Models of Memory. Memories and their associations, especially in view of the experimental results just described, constitute a very concrete description at the first (specificational) level of Marr's framework, begging important questions about the third and second levels: How are memories represented in the animal MTL, how are these representations created, and how are they altered to record associations between memories?

We start by proposing an answer to the third-level problem: There are by now ample reasons to believe that *assemblies of neurons* play an important role in answering these questions. A *neuronal assembly* is a set of neurons that are likely to fire together, or at proximal times. It has not been established that the neurons in an assembly are interconnected by strong synaptic connections, but

---

[8] Earlier experiments with rodents and monkeys did however find neurons that only responded to a specific combination of stimulus features but not to any of these features in isolation, see e.g. [39], supporting in this case Valiant's version.

[9] There were many human subjects, and a total of hundreds of recorded neurons, see [40] for details, but in this exposition we focus on one subject and one neuron.

[10] Illustrating example.

this is a reasonable hypothesis (in Valiant's model, intra-item connections do not matter). Assemblies were conjectured by Hebb [42] already in 1949 (who depicted them as Hamilton paths of strong synaptic connections). Since researchers have discovered in human subjects neurons responding to the Eiffel tower or Jennifer Aniston [40, 43] by recording from only a few hundreds of randomly chosen neurons in MTL, and presenting a few hundreds of familiar stimuli, it is plausible that many more neurons (in the tens of thousands at least) respond consistently to this same stimulus. Further, it is tempting to assume that the reason these groups of neurons fire together after the image presentation is because they form an assembly. Neural computation in the rodent brain has also been found to be dominated by activations of assemblies of neurons, and in fact transiently active assemblies of neurons seem to have replaced attractors as the putative tokens of neural network activity, providing a link between single neurons and entities on the cognitive level [38]. However, a theory of neural computation with assemblies is still missing at this point.

How exactly does an assembly, corresponding to a particular memory, materialize in the MTL? And how are associations between two assemblies formed, in a way that explains the experiment in [40] (Obama causing the Eiffel neuron to fire)? Ongoing simulations [44], demonstrate that a model neuronal system, with parameters for synaptic connectivity and plasticity of synaptic weights that are compatible with what we know about the MTL exhibits similar behavior:

- when presented with particular input patterns for long enough, neurons tend to form groups that fire consistently when the same pattern appears later; and
- when presented simultaneously with two such previously encountered patterns, some of the neurons in the two corresponding groups subsequently respond to both patterns.

Hence the formation of assemblies and the creation of associations between them can be reproduced in silico.

Theoretical Model. It is difficult to model synaptic plasticity in a neural network so that the model (a) is consistent with experimental findings and (b) remains theoretically tractable. One approach used in the past is to analyze equilibrium points of the dynamics of synaptic weights in a network, see [45]. In [46] we propose a simplified *linearized* model of neurons and plasticity, in which the synaptic input is interpreted as a measure of the probability that the neuron fires, along with a novel variant of random graphs. Equilibrium analysis of the linearized model predicts that a stable assembly emerges which includes certain neurons with high synaptic projection from the stimulus, but also neurons with high synaptic projection from (recursively) other assembly neurons; interestingly, such behavior had been recently observed [47] in the formation of *olfactory* memories in the piriform cortex.

We also analyze a simplified *nonlinear* discrete-time model of this system, where we assume that the K (a fixed number) neurons with the highest synaptic input fire at each step; this assumption is an attempt to capture implicitly the effect of a population of inhibitory neurons interacting with the excitatory ones under consideration. Importantly, we assume that the population of excitatory neurons is randomly and sparsely connected, a reasonable model in view of experimental data [48]. In particular, our model of synaptic connectivity (between pyramidal/excitatory cells) is a $G_{n,p}$ [49] directed graph with an added bias for "pattern completions" [50] (such a model had been proposed for different purposes in [35]): Conditioned on the existence of edges (a, b) and (b, c), edges (b, a) or (a, c) are many times more likely to exist than predicted by chance and the baseline parameter p. We show in [46] that this simplified model predicts the formation of a stable assembly in response to the presentation of a stimulus, and the association of two assemblies—two assemblies shifting slightly their support to increase their intersection—in response to the concurrent presentation of two previously established stimuli.

Binding. A fundamental capability of the brain, especially the human brain, is to form and apply abstract rules. Such a rule could specify how to behave in a particular social context, how to pick up an object, or how to form a syntactically correct sentence. Applying such rules requires to bind temporarily a variable in an abstract rule to a concrete context. For example, a simple sentence may consist of a subject, a patient, and a verb, and these must be bound to specific words during sentence formation. Recently, evidence has been emerging from fMRI imaging of the human brain [51] about the processes that occur during this binding process. Binding is related to Valiant's LINK operation. However, that operation connects coequal memories, whereas binding involves an abstract concept (such as "verb," possibly represented not by an assembly but by a whole brain area as suggested by the results in [51]) bound to an ordinary memory.

We propose that assemblies also play a prominent role during the binding of a variable to a context. Recent simulations [52] suggest that such binding operation can be implemented in a realistic neural model through so-called *assembly pointers*. Such pointer would connect an assembly representing "go" to a newly formed assembly within the intended brain area that represents the concept "verb", in a process similar to the assembly formation discussed above (with the "go" assembly now playing the role of the input stimulus).

Association Graphs. Occasionally, computational research on the brain will yield an interesting theoretical problem worthy of scrutiny through the methodology of theoretical computer science; we next describe briefly one such instance. As more and more memories and associations will be formed through life, an intricate network will be created [41], with intersections that are initially larger and then appear to shrink, and it would be of some interest to develop a theory of this aspect of cognition. It appears safe to assume that synaptic connections between the neurons of two assemblies A and B get strengthened when an association between the corresponding concepts is learned; this provides a plausible explanation for the previously described finding that both assemblies extend so that their intersection becomes larger (estimates range between a 4% and 40% of the size of a single assembly [41]). In an abstract model one can focus solely on these overlaps between associated assemblies, and ignore synaptic weights altogether. Such a network can be represented as an edge-weighted undirected graph (V, E, w) such that each vertex v is a memory, each edge $[u, v]$ is an association between memories u and v, and its weight w_{uv} represents the strength of this association, say the proportion of the neurons in the two assemblies that also lie in their intersection. We call such graphs *association graphs*.

One immediate question is, are all weighted graphs association graphs? The answer is trivially "yes" if no further assumptions are made, which can be shown through a straightforward modification of the Erdős construction of intersection graphs [53]. However, this construction may require that the size (number of neurons) of the assemblies/vertices differ considerably and that intersections are very small. What if we also insist that the assembly sizes are kept the same, or approximately so? This gives rise to an interesting theoretical problem. The requirement that the association graph be realized by intersecting assemblies by approximately equal size can be expressed as a linear program, whose variables are real numbers x_S representing the (normalized) number of neurons belonging to precisely all the assemblies in the set $S \subseteq V$. The constraints correspond to the vertices and the edges of the graph. One seeks to minimize the maximum relative difference between sizes of nodes. Interestingly, a related but more general problem had been addressed during the 1990s by philosophers [54].

It turns out that solving this linear program through the dual ellipsoid method is related to the *cut norm* [55], a well known challenge in combinatorics. In collaboration with Nima Anari and Amin Saberi we have shown that the problem is in fact NP-hard, even to approximate within some n^α factor, but can be approximated in certain interesting special cases. Another interesting variant is the one in which only the unweighted graph is given, with edges representing intersections of size above a threshold, while non-edges stand for intersections of size below a lower threshold; in this model again not all graphs can be represented, but a large class of graphs can.

There are many more questions and directions in connection to the graph-theoretic modeling of associations that seem worth exploring.

5   Open Questions

The purpose of the previous section was to describe ongoing work in just one possible direction—an important and opportune one, in our view—where familiar methods from theoretical computer science can support modeling, analyzing, and ultimately understanding brain function. The intended message of this article is that there are several such opportunities, not just in connection with memories but also with many other important questions and directions of research on brain computation; below is an assortment of such opportunities, starting with the ones closest to the described work.

- Neurons tend to have surprisingly different levels of activity (measured for example through their long-term average firing rate); this is true even for neurons of the same general type, e.g. pyramidal cells. Furthermore a few neurons are connected by really strong synapses while most are not [56]. These differences show up in statistical analyses as heavy-tailed distributions (often approximated by a log normal) of measurements such as long-term firing rates, synaptic weights, see e.g. [57,58][11]. The question arises: what do these differences between neurons imply for the organization of neural computation? Do they point to an implicit hierarchical organization of neurons even within a single brain area, where more frequently firing neurons remember, process and transmit information in a coarser way—possibly even initialized through the genetic code—while less frequently firing neurons contribute refinements in a more flexible and experience-based manner?

- Another surprising invariant of neural activity in the awake brain is the scale-free (power law) distribution of avalanches of neural activity, i.e., of continuous episodes of neural activity within a patch of a brain area, or within larger brain areas, see e.g. [59,60]. Scale-free distributed activity is commonly interpreted as a sign that the brain computes in a critical or near-critical regime [61]. Criticality of network dynamics could be an important clue for the large-scale organization of neural computations in the brain. However, several pieces of the puzzle are missing. Criticality is typically studied in deterministic dynamical system, while the brain is best modeled as a stochastic one; and we are not aware of a rigorous, computational understanding of criticality in dynamical systems. See [62,63], and also [32], for references to first steps in this direction.

- A further surprising feature of brain activity is that it is not input driven: the brain is almost as active when there is (seemingly) nothing to compute. For example, the neurons in the primary visual cortex (area V1) are almost as active as during visual processing as they are in complete darkness [64]. Since brain activity consumes a fair portion of the energy budget of an organism, it is unlikely that this spontaneously ongoing brain activity is just an accident, and highlights a clear organizational difference between computers and brains. A challenge for theoretical work is to understand the role of spontaneous activity in brain computation and learning.

- Another ubiquitous and mysterious feature of neural network activity in the brain is the prominence of stereotypical spatio-temporal firing patterns of neurons that occur both during active processing of sensory stimuli and spontaneously, see e.g. [65–67]. These experimental data undermine theoretical models that are based on an orderly bottom-up organization of encoding and computational transformation, where individual neurons report through their firing the presence of a specific feature of a sensory stimulus, or a specific value of an analog feature (for example in so-called population codes). These puzzles are nicely described in [68] for the case of area V1, which is one of the brain areas where neural coding has been studied the most. The presence of stereotypical spatio-temporal firing patterns of neurons points to a more

---

[11] In fact, such lognormal distribution of synaptic weights can be predicted theoretically from a simplified model of plasticity.

implicit coding and computing mechanisms, and better computing paradigms and computational models are needed.

- As we have already discussed briefly, *language* appears to be a most attractive research arena for the computational study of the brain. One particular intriguing – and well studied from the theoretical point of view – aspect of language is *syntax*, the way our brain appears to form larger linguistic units such as phrases and sentences from smaller units such as words. Can we define a biologically plausible *small set of primitives* for syntactic processing during language generation and parsing? We believe that the mechanisms for assembly creation, association, and binding described in the previous section may be of relevance to this quest.

- *Visual invariants* are one of the mysteries of vision: How is it possible that a plethora of very different images and sensations (an object such as a person's face, and its various translations, rotations, zoom-ins and -outs, occlusions, etc., not to mention the person's last name, or voice) are mapped instantaneously and unambiguously to the same "memory"? We suspect that the processes of assembly formation and association may provide some insight to this problem, see [69,70] for experimental data and related theories.

- Randomness, its nature and utility, is one of the beloved research themes of Theoretical Computer Science. Valiant proposes that random synaptic connections are an essential ingredient of the brain's power and versatility. A further hypothesis, begging for algorithmic verification, is that *pattern completion* deviations from the randomness of $G_{n,p}$ graphs (see the brief discussion in the previous section) play an important role. Randomness is also ubiquitous everywhere in neural activity, resulting in a wide range of trial-to-trial variation in almost any brain experiment. We refer to Sects. 3 and 4 of [32] for references to related experimental data. It is essential to incorporate randomness in computational models of brain systems, and to understand its origins and function in the brain. Examples of algorithms that exploit the randomness of neural firing are given in [71,72].

- The foundational understanding of the apparent power of deep learning is an important current challenge for Theoretical Computer Science. How does this quest relate to the brain? We refer to [73] for a discussion of related literature. Deep learning of some sort does happen in the brain (consider the visual cortex and the hierarchical processing through its areas, from V1 to V2 and V4 all the way to MT and beyond). But there are differences, and perhaps the most fundamental among them is the existence of *lateral and backward connections* between brain areas. What is their function, and how do they enhance learning?

- A complementary question is, *what replaces backpropagation in brain circuits?* The famous backpropagation algorithm that is used to efficiently optimize deep neural networks is incompatible with our understanding of brain connectivity, as it requires reciprocal connections with weight updates that are maintained to levels identical to those of the forward connections. An intriguing recent finding in this regard is the surprising learning capability of (rather shallow) neural networks in which, instead of backpropagation, feedback is carried out with *fixed random weights* [74].

6 Summary

We sketched the history, current status, and prospects of research interaction between computer scientists and neuroscientists in the quest of unraveling the organization of brain computation. We then focused on the specific question, how are memories and a web of associations between memories implemented in networks of neurons in the brain. This question appears to be especially well suited for contributions by theoretical computer scientists, since (a) a theory that is consistent with recent recordings from the human brain is missing; and (b) scaling and asymptotic analysis of model data structures and algorithms seem essential for understanding how the human brain can create and maintain an association web of tens of thousands of concepts. We concluded with a sprinkling of open questions, each accompanied by references to some of the most recent research articles and review papers in neuroscience. Since for most domains one cannot extract from the literature a single model or set of assumptions, familiarity with a diversity of models and experimental results is a prerequisite for any lasting contribution to our understanding of brain computation. Ultimately, an informed and fruitful dialogue and collaboration between computer scientists and neuroscientists may be the brightest hope we have for finally unraveling the mysteries of brain computation.

Acknowledgments. Written under partial support by the Human Brain Project of the European Union #604102 and #720270, and NSF grants CCF-1408635, CCF-1563838 and CCF-1717349.

References

1. Kandel, E.R., Schwartz, J.H., Jessell, T.M., Siegelbaum, S.A., Hudspeth, A.J.: Principles of Neural Science, vol. 5th. McGraw-Hill, New York (2013)
2. Purves, D., Augustine, G.J., Fitzpatrick, D., Hall, W.C., LaMantia, A.S., White, L.E.: Neuroscience, 5th edn. Sinauer Associates, Inc., Sunderland (2011)
3. Dayan, P., Abbott, L.F.: Theoretical Neuroscience, vol. 10. MIT Press, Cambridge (2001)
4. Marr, D.: Vision: A Computational Investigation into the Human Representation and Processing of Visual Information. Henry Holt and Co. Inc., New York (1982)
5. Valiant, L.G.: A theory of the learnable. Commun. ACM **27**(11), 1134–1142 (1984)
6. Hawkins, J., Blakeslee, S.: On intelligence. Times Books, New York (2004)
7. Valiant, L.G.: Circuits of the Mind. Oxford University Press, Oxford (1994)
8. Valiant, L.G.: A neuroidal architecture for cognitive computation. J. ACM **47**(5), 854–882 (2000)
9. Valiant, L.G.: Memorization and association on a realistic neural model. Neural Comput. **17**(3), 527–555 (2005)
10. Jerrum, M., Sinclair, A.: Polynomial-time approximation algorithms for the Ising model. SIAM J. Comput. **22**(5), 1087–1116 (1993)

11. Yao, A.C.C.: Quantum circuit complexity. In: 1993 Proceedings of 34th Annual Symposium on Foundations of Computer Science, pp. 352–361. IEEE (1993)

12. Bernstein, E., Vazirani, U.: Quantum complexity theory. SIAM J. Comput. **26**(5), 1411–1473 (1997)

13. Papadimitriou, C.: Algorithms, games, and the internet. In: Proceedings of the Thirty-Third Annual ACM Symposium on Theory of Computing, pp. 749–753. ACM (2001)

14. Nisan, N., Ronen, A.: Algorithmic mechanism design. In: Proceedings of the Thirty-First Annual ACM Symposium on Theory of Computing, pp. 129–140. ACM (1999)

15. Turing, A.M.: On computable numbers, with an application to the Entscheidungsproblem. Proc. Lond. Math. Soc. **2**(1), 230–265 (1937)

16. Turing, A.M.: Computing machinery and intelligence. Mind **59**(236), 433–460 (1950)

17. Von Neumann, J.: The Computer and the Brain. Yale University Press, New Haven (1958)

18. Von Neumann, J., Burks, A.W.: Theory of Self-reproducing Automata. University of Illinois Press, London (1966)

19. McCulloch, W.S., Pitts, W.: A logical calculus of the ideas immanent in nervous activity. Bull. Math. Biophys. **5**(4), 115–133 (1943)

20. Rosenblatt, F.: The perceptron: a probabilistic model for information storage and organization in the brain. Psychol. Rev. **65**(6), 386 (1958)

21. Marr, D.C., Poggio, T.: From understanding computation to understanding neural circuits. Technical report AI-M-357, Massachusetts Institute of Technology, Cambridge, MA, US (1976)

22. Marcus, G.F.: The Algebraic Mind: Integrating Connectionism and Cognitive Science. MIT Press, Cambridge (2003)

23. Marcus, G.F., Marblestone, A., Dean, T.: The atoms of neural computation. Science **346**(6209), 551–552 (2014)

24. Hornik, K., Stinchcombe, M., White, H.: Multilayer feedforward networks are universal approximators. Neural Netw. **2**(5), 359–366 (1989)

25. Barron, A.R.: Universal approximation bounds for superpositions of a sigmoidal function. IEEE Trans. Inf. Theory **39**(3), 930–945 (1993)

26. Eliasmith, C., Anderson, C.H.: Neural Engineering: Computation, Representation, and Dynamics in Neurobiological Systems. MIT Press, Cambridge (2004)

27. Seung, H.S.: Neuroscience: towards functional connectomics. Nature **471**(7337), 170–172 (2011)

28. Lichtman, J.W., Livet, J., Sanes, J.R.: A technicolour approach to the connectome. Nat. Rev. Neurosci. **9**(6), 417–422 (2008)

29. Holtmaat, A., Svoboda, K.: Experience-dependent structural synaptic plasticity in the mammalian brain. Nat. Rev. Neurosci. **10**(9), 647–658 (2009)

30. Minerbi, A., Kahana, R., Goldfeld, L., Kaufman, M., Marom, S., Ziv, N.E.: Long-term relationships between synaptic tenacity, synaptic remodeling, and network activity. PLoS Biol. **7**(6), e1000136 (2009)

31. Kasai, H., Fukuda, M., Watanabe, S., Hayashi-Takagi, A., Noguchi, J.: Structural dynamics of dendritic spines in memory and cognition. Trends Neurosci. **33**(3), 121–129 (2010)

32. Maass, W.: Searching for principles of brain computation. Curr. Opin. Behav. Sci. (Spec. Issue Comput. Model.) **11**, 81–92 (2016)

33. Riesenhuber, M., Poggio, T.: Hierarchical models of object recognition in cortex. Nat. Neurosci. **2**(11), 1019–1025 (1999)

34. Berwick, R.C., Chomsky, N.: Why Only Us: Language and Evolution. MIT Press, Cambridge (2016)
35. Papadimitriou, C.H., Vempala, S.S.: Cortical learning via prediction. In: Proceedings of COLT (2015)
36. Papadimitriou, C.H., Petti, S., Vempala, S.: Cortical computation via iterative constructions. In: Proceedings of the 29th Conference on Learning Theory, COLT 2016, 23–26 June 2016, New York, USA, pp. 1357–1375 (2016)
37. Froemke, R.C., Debanne, D., Bi, G.Q.: Temporal modulation of spike-timing-dependent plasticity. Front. Synaptic Neurosci. (2010). https://doi.org/10.3389/fnsyn.2010.00019
38. Buzsaki, G.: Neural syntax: cell assemblies, synapsembles, and readers. Neuron **68**(3), 362–385 (2010)
39. Komorowski, R.W., Manns, J.R., Eichenbaum, H.: Robust conjunctive item-place coding by hippocampal neurons parallels learning what happens where. J. Neurosci. **29**(31), 9918–9929 (2009)
40. Ison, M.J., Quiroga, R.Q., Fried, I.: Rapid encoding of new memories by individual neurons in the human brain. Neuron **87**(1), 220–230 (2015)
41. De Falco, E., Ison, M.J., Fried, I., Quiroga, R.Q.: Long-term coding of personal and universal associations underlying the memory web in the human brain. Nat. Commun. **7**, 13408 (2016)
42. Hebb, D.O.: The Organization of Behavior: A Neuropsychological Theory. Wiley, New York (1949)
43. Quiroga, R.Q., Reddy, L., Kreiman, G., Koch, C., Fried, I.: Invariant visual representation by single neurons in the human brain. Nature **435**(7045), 1102–1107 (2005)
44. Pokorny, C., Ison, M.J., Rao, A., Legenstein, R., Papadimitriou, C., Maass, W.: Associations between memory traces emerge in a generic neural circuit model through STDP. bioRxiv:188938 (2017)
45. Nessler, B., Pfeiffer, M., Buesing, L., Maass, W.: Bayesian computation emerges in generic cortical microcircuits through spike-timing-dependent plasticity. PLOS Comput. Biol. **9**(4), e1003037 (2013)
46. Legenstein, R., Maass, W., Papadimitriou, C.H., Vempala, S.S.: Long-term memory and the densest k-subgraph problem. In: Proceedings of 9th Innovations in Theoretical Computer Science (ITCS) Conference, 11–14 January 2018, Cambridge, USA (2018)
47. Franks, K.M., Russo, M.J., Sosulski, D.L., Mulligan, A.A., Siegelbaum, S.A., Axel, R.: Recurrent circuitry dynamically shapes the activation of piriform cortex. Neuron **72**(1), 49–56 (2011)
48. Wang, X.J., Kennedy, H.: Brain structure and dynamics across scales: in search of rules. Curr. Opin. Neurobiol. **37**, 92–98 (2016)
49. Erdős, P., Renyi, A.: On the evolution of random graphs. Publ. Math. Inst. Hungary Acad. Sci. **5**, 17–61 (1960)
50. Guzman, S.J., Schlögl, A., Frotscher, M., Jonas, P.: Synaptic mechanisms of pattern completion in the hippocampal CA3 network. Science **353**(6304), 1117–1123 (2016)
51. Frankland, S.M., Greene, J.D.: An architecture for encoding sentence meaning in left mid-superior temporal cortex. Proc. Natl. Acad. Sci. **112**(37), 11732–11737 (2015)
52. Legenstein, R., Papadimitriou, C.H., Vempala, S., Maass, W.: Assembly pointers for variable binding in networks of spiking neurons. arXiv preprint arXiv:1611.03698 (2016)

53. Erdős, P., Goodman, A., Posa, L.: The representation of graphs by set intersections. Can. J. Math. **18**, 106–112 (1966)
54. Pitowsky, I.: Correlation polytopes: their geometry and complexity. Math. Program. **50**(1), 395–414 (1991)
55. Alon, N., Naor, A.: Approximating the cut-norm via Grothendieck's inequality. SIAM J. Comput. **35**(4), 787–803 (2006)
56. Song, S., Sjöström, P.J., Reigl, M., Nelson, S., Chklovskii, D.B.: Highly nonrandom features of synaptic connectivity in local cortical circuits. PLoS Biol. **3**(3), e68 (2005)
57. Buzsaki, G., Mizuseki, K.: The log-dynamic brain: how skewed distributions affect network operations. Nat. Rev. Neurosci. **15**(4), 264–278 (2014)
58. Grosmark, A.D., Buzsaki, G.: Diversity in neural firing dynamics supports both rigid and learned hippocampal sequences. Science **351**(6280), 1440–1443 (2016)
59. Beggs, J.M., Plenz, D.: Neuronal avalanches in neocortical circuits. J. Neurosci. **23**(35), 11167–11177 (2003)
60. Bellay, T., Klaus, A., Seshadriand, S., Plenz, D.: Irregular spiking of pyramidal neurons organizes as scale-invariant neuronal avalanches in the awake state. eLife **4**, e07224 (2015)
61. Priesemann, V., Wibral, M., Valderrama, M., Pröpper, R., Le Van Quyen, M., Geisel, T., Triesch, J., Nikolic, D., Munk, M.H.: Spike avalanches in vivo suggest a driven, slightly subcritical brain state. Front. Syst. Neurosci. **8**, 108 (2014)
62. Legenstein, R., Maass, W.: Edge of chaos and prediction of computational performance for neural circuit models. Neural Netw. **20**(3), 323–334 (2007)
63. Legenstein, R., Maass, W.: What makes a dynamical system computationally powerful. In: New Directions in Statistical Signal Processing: From Systems to Brain, pp. 127–154 (2007)
64. Fiser, J., Chiu, C., Weliky, M.: Small modulation of ongoing cortical dynamics by sensory input during natural vision. Nature **431**, 573–583 (2004)
65. Luczak, A., Barthó, P., Harris, K.D.: Spontaneous events outline the realm of possible sensory responses in neocortical populations. Neuron **62**(3), 413–425 (2009)
66. Bathellier, B., Ushakova, L., Rumpel, S.: Discrete neocortical dynamics predict behavioral categorization of sounds. Neuron **76**(2), 435–449 (2012)
67. Miller, J.e.K., Ayzenshtat, I., Carrillo-Reid, L., Yuste, R.: Visual stimuli recruit intrinsically generated cortical ensembles. Proc. Natl. Acad. Sci. **111**(38), E4053–E4061 (2014)
68. Olshausen, B.A., Field, D.J.: How close are we to understanding V1? Neural Comput. **17**(8), 1665–1699 (2005)
69. DiCarlo, J.J., Cox, D.D.: Untangling invariant object recognition. Trends Cogn. Sci. **11**(8), 333–341 (2007)
70. Cox, D.D.: Do we understand high-level vision? Curr. Opin. Neurobiol. **25**, 187–193 (2014)
71. Maass, W.: Noise as a resource for computation and learning in networks of spiking neurons. Spec. Issue Proc. IEEE "Eng. Intell. Electron. Syst. Based Comput. Neurosci." **102**(5), 860–880 (2014)
72. Lynch, N., Musco, C., Parter, M.: Spiking neural networks: an algorithmic perspective (2017). https://groups.csail.mit.edu/tds/papers/Musco/neuralBda.pdf
73. Marblestone, A.H., Wayne, G., Kording, K.P.: Toward an integration of deep learning and neuroscience. Front. Comput. Neurosci. **10** (2016)
74. Lillicrap, T.P., Cownden, D., Tweed, D.B., Akerman, C.J.: Random feedback weights support learning in deep neural networks. arXiv preprint arXiv:1411.0247 (2014)

Rating Computer Science via Chess
In Memoriam Daniel Kopec and Hans Berliner

Kenneth W. Regan[✉]

Department of CSE, University at Buffalo, Amherst, NY 14260, USA
regan@buffalo.edu

Abstract. Computer chess was originally purposed for insight into the human mind. It became a quest to get the most power out of computer hardware and software. The goal was specialized but the advances spanned multiple areas, from heuristic search to massive parallelism. Success was measured not by standard software or hardware benchmarks, nor theoretical aims like improving the exponents of algorithms, but by victory over the best human players. To gear up for limited human challenge opportunities, designers of chess machines needed to forecast their skill on the human rating scale. Our thesis is that this challenge led to ways of rating computers *on the whole* and also rating the effectiveness of our field at solving *hard problems*. We describe rating systems, the workings of chess programs, advances from computer science, the history of some prominent machines and programs, and ways of rating them.

1 Ratings

Computer chess was already recognized as a field when LNCS began in 1971. Its early history, from seminal papers by Shannon [1] and Turing [2], after earlier work by Zuse and Wiener, has been told in [3–5] among other sources. Its later history, climaxing with humanity's dethronement in the victory by IBM's DEEP BLUE over Garry Kasparov and further dominance even by programs on smartphones, will be subordinated to telling how *rating* the effectiveness of hardware and software components indicates the progress of computing. Whereas computer chess was first viewed as an AI problem, we will note contributions from diverse software and hardware areas that have also graced the volumes of LNCS.

In 1971, David Levy was feeling good about his bet made in 1968 with Alan Newell that no computer would defeat him in a match by 1978 [6]. That year also saw the adoption by the World Chess Federation (FIDE) of the Elo Rating System [7], which had been designed earlier for the United States Chess Federation (USCF). Levy's FIDE rating of 2380, representative of his International Master (IM) title from FIDE, set a level of proficiency that any computer needed to achieve in order to challenge him on equal terms.

The Elo system has aged well. It is employed for physical sports as well as games and has recently been embraced by the statistical website *FiveThirtyEight* [8] for betting-style projections. At its heart is a simple idea:

© Springer Nature Switzerland AG 2019
B. Steffen and G. Woeginger (Eds.): Computing and Software Science, LNCS 10000, pp. 200–216, 2019.
https://doi.org/10.1007/978-3-319-91908-9_12

A difference of x rating points to one's opponent corresponds to an expectation of scoring a p_x portion of the points in a series of games.

This lone axiom already tells much. When $x = 0$, p_x must be 0.5 because the two players are interchangeable. The curve likewise has the symmetry $p_{-x} = 1 - p_x$. When x is large, the value p_x approaches 1 but its rate of change must slow. This makes p_x a sigmoid (that is, roughly S-shaped) curve. Two eminent choices are the cumulant of the normal distribution and the simple logistic curve

$$p_x = \frac{1}{1 + e^{-Bx}}, \tag{1}$$

where B is a scaling factor. Originally the USCF used the former with factors to make $p_{200} = 0.75$, but they switched to the latter with $B = (\ln 10)/400$, which puts the expectation of a 200-points higher-rated player a tad under 76%.

If your rating is R and you use your opponents' ratings to add up your p_x for each of N games, that sum is your expected score s. If your actual score S is higher then you gain rating points, else your new rating R' stays even or goes down. Your *performance rating* over that set of games could be defined as the value R_p whose expectation s_p equals S; in practice other formulas with patches to handle the cases $S = N$ or $S = 0$ are employed. The last issue is how far to move R in the direction of R_p to give R'. The amount of change is governed by a factor called K whose value is elective: FIDE makes K four times as large for young or beginning players as for those who have ever reached a rating of 2400.

Despite issues of rating uncertainty whose skew causes actual scores by 200-points higher rated players to come in *under* 75% (see [9]), unproven suspicions of "rating inflation," proven drift between FIDE ratings and those of the USCF and other national bodies, and alternative systems claiming superiority in *Kaggle* competitions [10], the Elo system is self-stabilizing and reasonably reliable for projections. Hence it is safe to express benchmarks on the FIDE rating scale, whose upper reaches are spoken of as follows:

- 2200 is the colloquial threshold to call a player a "master";
- 2400 is required for granting the IM title, 2500 for grandmaster (GM);
- 2600 and above colloquially distinguishes "Strong GMs";
- 2800+ has been achieved by 11 players; Bobby Fischer's top was 2785.

Kasparov was the first player to pass 2800; current world champion Magnus Carlsen topped Kasparov's peak of 2851 and reached 2882 in May 2014. Computer chess players, however, today range far over 3000. How did they progress through these ranks to get there? Many walks of computer science besides AI contributed to confront a *hard problem*. Just how hard in raw complexity terms, we discuss next.

2   Complexity and Endgame Tables

Chess players see all pertinent information. There are no hidden cards as in bridge or poker and no element of chance as in backgammon. Every chess position is well-defined as W, D, or L—that is, winning, drawing, or losing for the player to move. There is a near-universal belief that the starting position is D, as was proved for checkers on an 8×8 board [11]. So how can chess players lose? The answer is that chess is *complex*.

Here is a remarkable fact. Take any program P that runs within n units of memory. We can set up a position P' on an $N \times N$ board—where N and the number of extra pieces are "moderately" bigger than n—such that P' is W if and only if P terminates with a desired answer. Moreover, finding the winning strategy in P' quickly reveals a solution to the problem for which P was coded.

Most remarkably, even if P runs for 2^n steps, such as for solving the Towers of Hanoi puzzle with n rings, individual plays of the game from P' will take far less time. The "Fifty Move Rule" in standard chess allows either side to claim a draw if 50 moves have been played with no capture or pawn advance. Various reasonable ways to extend it to $N \times N$ boards will limit plays to time proportional to N^2 or N^3. The exponential time taken by P is sublimated into the branching of the strategy from P' within these time bounds. For the tower puzzle, the first move frames the middle step of transferring the bottom ring, then play branches into similar but separate combinations for the 'before' and 'after' stages of moving the other $n - 1$ rings.

If we allow P on size-n cases z of the problem to use 2^n memory as well as time, then we must lift the time limit on plays from P', but the size of the board and the time to calculate P' from P and z remain moderate—that is, bounded by a polynomial in n. In terms of computational complexity as represented by Allender's contribution [12], $N \times N$ chess is *complete in polynomial space* with a generalized fifty-move rule [13], and *complete in exponential time* without it [14]. This "double-rail" completeness also hints that the decision problem for chess is relatively hard to parallelize. Checkers, Go, Othello, and similar strategy games extended to $N \times N$ boards enjoy at least one rail of hardness [15–18].

These results as N grows do not dictate high complexity for $N = 8$ but their strong hint manifests quickly in chess. The *Lomonosov tables* [19] give perfect strategies for all positions of up to 7 pieces. They reside only in Moscow and their web-accessible format takes up 140 terabytes. This huge message springs from a small seed because the rules of chess fit on a postcard, yet is *computationally deep* insofar as the effort required to generate it is extreme. The digits of π are as easy as pie by comparison [20]. These tables may be the deepest message we have ever computed.

Even with just 4 pieces, the first item in our history after 1971 shows how computers tapped complexity unsuspected by human players. When defending with king and rook versus king and queen, it was axiomatic that the rook needed to stay in guarding range of the king to avoid getting picked off by a fork from the queen. Such huddling made life easier for the attacker. Computers showed that the rook could often dance away with impunity and harass from the sides to delay up to 31 moves before falling to capture—out of the 50 allotted for the attacker to *convert* by reducing (or changing) the material. Ken Thompson tabulated this endgame for his program BELLE and in 1978 challenged GM Walter Browne to execute the win. Browne failed in his first try, and after extensive study before a second try, squeaked through by capturing the rook on move 50.

Thompson generated perfect tables for 5 pieces with positions tiered by distance-to-conversion (DTC)—that is, the maximum number of moves the defender could delay conversion. In distance-to-mate (DTM), the king and queen versus king and rook endgame can last 35 moves. The 5-piece tables in Eugene Nalimov's popular DTM format occupy 7.1 GB uncompressed. Distance-to-zero (DTZ) is the minimum number of moves to force a capture or pawn move while retaining a W value; if the DTZ is over 50 then its "Z50" flavor flips the position value from W to D in strict accordance with the 50-move draw rule.

Thompson also generated tables for all 6-piece positions without pawns. He found positions requiring up to 243 moves to convert and 262 moves to mate. In many more, the winning strategy is so subtle and painstaking as to be thought beyond human capability to execute. The Lomonosov tables, which are DTM-based, have upped the record to 545 moves to mate—more precisely, 1,088 ply with the loser moving first. Some work on 8-piece tablebases is underway but no estimate of when they may finish seems possible. This goes to indicate that positions with full armies are intractably complex, so that navigating them becomes a heuristic activity. What ingredients allow programs to cope?

3   The Machines: Software to Hardware to Software

Computer chess players began largely as hardware entities but have evolved into software, with enough convergence in basic architecture and interchangeability under APIs that they are now called *engines*. Three main components are identifiable:

1. *Position representation*—by which the rules of chess are encoded and legal moves are generated;
2. *Position evaluation*—by which "knowledge" is converted into numbers; and
3. *Search heuristics*—whose ingenuity marches on through the present.

Generating legal moves is cumbersome especially for the *sliding pieces* bishop, rook, and queen. A software strategy used early on was to maintain and update their limits in each of the compass directions. Limit squares can be off the board, and the trick of situating the board inside a larger array pays a second dividend of disambiguating differences in square indices. For example, the "0x88" layout uses cells 0–7 then 16–23 and so on up to 112–119. Cell pairs with differences in the range $[-7,7]$ must then belong to the same rank (that is, row). The 0x88 layout aligns differences a multiple of 15 southeast-northwest, 16 south-north, and 17 southwest-northeast. Off-board squares are distinguished by having nonzero bitwise-AND with 10001000, which is 0x88 in hexadecimal.

Such tricks go only yea-far, and it became incumbent to implement board operations directly in hardware. As noted by Lucci and Kopec [21], the best computer players from BELLE through DEEP BLUE went this route in the 1980s and 1990s. They avoided the "von Neumann bottleneck" via multiprocessing of both data support and calculation. Chess programs realize less than full benefits of extra processing cores [22], an echo of the parallel hardness mentioned above.

The advent of 64-bit processing decisively favored an alternate representation that had been discussed since the late 1950s: *bitboards*. Instead of storing the position in one 8×8 array, each piece has its own 8×8 binary array—or several—coded as one 64-bit unsigned integer. A rook on the square b2 might be represented by the number 2^9 and its potential moves along the second rank by $r_m = 2^8$ plus the sum of 2^{10} through 2^{15}. If a same-colored piece arrives on a square to its right, coded by $s = 2^i$, then its mobility can be updated by

$$r_m := r_m \ \& \ (s - 1),$$

in just two machine cycles. A similar subtraction trick finds the least bit set to 1 in any position code. Similar operations for files and diagonals, perhaps virtually rotated [23] into horizontal position to avail tricks like this, enable fast move generation and updates. Newer generic hardware instructions, such as population-count (POPCNT) which gives the number of bits set to 1, also speed many operations. All this has lessened the advantage of specialized hardware, exemplified by Robert Hyatt's evolution of CRAY BLITZ into the open-source program CRAFTY.

Evaluation assigns to each position p a numerical value $e_0(p)$. The values are commonly output in discrete units of 0.01 called *centipawns* (cp), figuratively $1/100$ the base value of a pawn. The knight and bishop usually have base values between 300 and 350 cp, the rook around 500 cp, and the queen somewhere between 850 and 1,000 cp. The values are adjusted for positional factors, such as pawns becoming stronger when further advanced and "passed" but weaker when "doubled" or isolated. Greater mobility and attacks on forward and central squares bring higher values. King safety is a third important category, judged by the structure of the king's pawn shield and the proximity of attackers and defenders. The fourth factor emphasized by DEEP BLUE [24] is "tempo," meaning ability to generate threats and moves that enhance the position score. Additional factors face a tradeoff against the need for speedy evaluation, but this is helped by computing them in parallel pipes and by keeping the formula linear. Much human ingenuity goes into choosing and formulating the *factors*, but of late their *weights* have been determined by massive empirical testing (see [25]).

3.1   Search and Soundness

Search has a natural recursive structure. We can replace $e_0(p)$ by the maximum—from the player to move's point of view—of $e_0(p')$ over the set F_1 of positions p' reachable by one legal move, calling this $e_1(p)$. From the other player's point of view those positions have value $e_0'(p') = -e_0(p')$. Now let F_2 be the set of positions p'' reachable by a move from some p' and define $e_1'(p')$ to be the maximum of $e_0'(p'')$ over all p'' reached from p'. From the first player's view this becomes a minimizing update $e_1(p')$; then re-doing the maximization at the root p over these values yields $e_2(p)$. This so-called the *negamax* form of minimax search is often coded as a recursion exactly so. The sequence p', p'' such that $e_2(p) = e_1(p') = e_0(p'')$ (breaking any ties in the order nodes were considered) traces out the *principal variation* (PV) of the search, and the move m_1 leading to p' is the engine's *best-move* (or *first-move*).

Continuing for $d \geq 3$, we define F_d to comprise all positions r reached by one move from a position $q \in F_{d-1}$. Multiple lines of play may go from p to r through different q. Such *transpositions* may also have different lengths so that F_d overlaps F_i for some $i < d$ of the same parity. Given initial evaluations $e_0(r)$ for all $r \in F_d$, minimax well-defines $e_d(p)$ and a PV to a node $r \in F_d$ so that all nodes in the PV have value $e_d(p) = e(r)$. In case of overlap at a node u in F_i the value with higher *generation* subscript—namely j in $e_j(u)$—is preferred. The *simple depth-d search* has $e(r) = e_0(r)$ for all $r \in F_d$, but we may get other values $e(r)$ by *search extension* beyond the *base depth* d, possibly counting them as having higher generation and extending the PV.

The 50-move rule ensures that $e_d(p)$ converges to the true value $+M$, 0, or $-M$ of p, where a big number M is used as the *mate value*. Convergence is aided by the rule that the side bringing the third occurrence of any position in a game can claim a draw. Engines avoid cycles in search by the sharper policy of giving any node q repeating a position earlier in the line of search (or game) a fixed value $e(q) = 0$ of highest generation. The goal of search is to visit a subset E of nodes within a feasible time budget so that minimax from values $e_0(r)$ over sufficiently many "floor nodes" r in E well-defines a value $v_d(p)$ so that for $c \leq d \leq D$ with d and D as high as possible:

– E includes enough of F_c that no value $e_0(q)$ for an unvisited node $q \in F_c \setminus E$ affects $v_d(p)$ by minimax;
– most of the time this is true for F_d in place of F_c; and
– $v_d(p)$ approximates $e_D(p)$.

The first clause is solidly defined and says that the search is *sound for depth* c. The second clause aspires to soundness for a stipulated depth d and motivates our first considering search strategies that alone cannot violate such soundness. The third clause is about trying to *extend* the search to depths $D > d$ without reference to soundness.

Nearly all chess programs use a structure of *iterative deepening* in successive *rounds* $d = 1, 2, 3, \ldots$ of search. The sizes of the sets $E = E_d$ of nodes visited in round d nearly always follow a geometric series so that the *effective branching factor* (*ebf*) of the search—variously reckoned as $|E_d|/|E_{d-1}|$ or as $|E_d|^{1/d}$ for high enough d—is bounded by a constant. This constant should be significantly less than the "basic" branching factor $|F_d|/|F_{d-1}|$. Similar remarks apply for the overall time T_d to produce $v_d(p)$ and the number N_d of node visits (counting multiple visits to the same node) in place of $|E_d|$.

3.2   Alpha-Beta

The first search strategy involves guessing α and β such that our ultimate $v_d = v_d(p)$ will belong to a *window* (α, β) with $\beta - \alpha$ as small as we dare. One motive for iterative deepening is to compute v_{d-1} on which to center the window for round d. Values outside the window are reckoned as "$\geq\beta$" or "$\leq\alpha$" and these endpoint-values work fine in minimax—if $e_d(p)$ crosses one of them then we *fail high* or *fail low*, respectively. After a fail-low we can double the lower window width by taking $\alpha' = 2\alpha - v_{d-1}$ and try again, doing similar for a fail-high, and possibly winding back to an earlier round $d' < d$. Using endpoints relieves the burden of being precise about values away from v_d. This translates into search savings via *cutoffs* described next.

Suppose we enter node p as shown in Fig. 1 with window $(1,6)$ and the first child p' yields value 3 along the current PV. This lets us search the next child q' with the narrower window $(3,6)$. Now suppose this fails because its first child q'' gives value 2. It returns the value "≤ 2" for q' without needing to consider any more of its children, so search is *cut off* there and we pop back up to p to consider its next child, r'. Next suppose r' yields value 7. This breaks β for p and all further children of p are considered *beta-cutoffs*. If p is the root then this fail-high re-starts the search until we find a bound β' that holds up when $v_d(p)$ is returned. If not—say if the $\beta = 6$ value came from a sibling n of p as shown in the figure—then p gets the value "≥ 6" and pops up to its parent. A value $v_{d-1}(r') = 4$, however, would move the PV to go through r' and keep the search going with exact values in telescoping windows between α and β.

One further note is that if we had advance confidence that the adversary's first reply at q' would show its inferiority to going to p', then we could call search at q' with the *null window* $(3,3)$ there instead, propagating it downward as needed. If we were wrong then we'd have to undo any ersatz cutoffs from $\beta'' = 3$ along the way, but if we're right then we've pocketed their time savings.

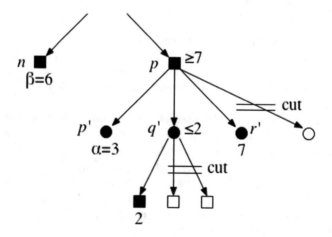

Fig. 1. Alpha-beta search example

Returning to the beta-cutoff from $v(r') = 7$, consider what happened along the new PV in nodes below r'. Every defensive move m' at r' needed to be tried in order to show that none kept the lid under $\beta = 6$; there were no *alpha-cutoffs* on these moves. This situation propagates downward so we've searched all children of half the nodes on the PV. If there are always ℓ such children then we've done about $\ell^{d/2} = (\sqrt{\ell})^d$ work. This is the general best-case for alpha-beta search when soundness is kept at depth d, and it is often approachable. A further move-ordering idea that helps is to try "killer moves" that achieved cutoffs in sibling positions first, even recalling them from searches at previous moves in the game. But with ℓ between 30 and 40 in typical chess positions, optimizing cutoffs alone brings the *ebf* down only to about 6.

Further savings come from storing values $e_j(q)$ at hashed locations $h(q)$ in the *transposition table*. The most common scheme assigns a "random"-but-fixed 64-bit code to each combination of 12 kinds of piece and square. This makes $12 \times 64 = 768$ codes, plus one for the side to move, four for White and Black castling rights, and eight for the files of possible *en-passant* captures. The *primary key* $H(q)$ is the bitwise-XOR of the basic codes that apply to q. Then the *secondary key* $h(q)$ can be defined by $H(q)$ modulo the size N of the hash table, or when $N = 2^k$ for some k, by taking k bits off one end of $H(q)$. Getting $H(r)$ for the next or previous position r merely requires XOR-ing the codes for the destination and source squares of the piece moved, any piece captured, the side-to-move code, and any other applicable codes. Besides storing $e_j(q)$ we store $H(q)$ and j (and/or other "age" information), the former to confirm sameness with the position probed and the latter to tell whether $e_j(q)$ went as deep as we need. If so, we save searching an entire subtree of the current parent of q. We may ignore the possibility of primary-key collisions $H(q) = H(r)$ for distinct positions q, r in the same search. Collisions of secondary keys $h(q) = h(r)$ are frequent but errors from them are often "minimaxed away" (see also [26]).

3.3   Extensions and Heuristics

We can get more mileage by extending D beyond d. Shannon [1] already noted that many depth-d floor nodes come after a capture or check or flight from check and have moves that continue in that vein. Those may be further expanded until a position identified as *quiescent* is reached. Human players tend to calculate such forced sequences as a unit. Thus the game-logical floor for round d may be deeper along important branches than the nominal depth-d floor.

Furthermore, the PV may accrue many nodes q whose value hangs strongly on one move m to a position q', so that a large change to $e_i(q')$ would change $e_{i+1}(q)$ by the same amount. The move m is called *singular* and warrants a better fix on its value by expanding it deeper. Such *singular extensions* could be reserved for cases of delaying moves by a defender on the ropes or moves known to affect positions already seen in the search, or liberalized to consider groups of two or more move options as "singular" [27, 28].

Other extensions have been tried. Search depths are commonly noted as "d/D" where d is the nominal depth and D is the maximum extended depth. Their values $e(r)$ for $r \in F_d$ may differ widely from $e_0(r)$ but this does not violate our notion of depth-d soundness which takes those values $e(r)$ as given.

We have added more nodes beyond F_d but not saved any more inside it than we had from cutoffs. Further progress needs compromise on soundness.

From numerous heuristics we mention two credited with much of the software side of performance gain. The idea of *late move reductions* (LMR) is simply to do only the first yea-many moves from the previous round's rank order to nominal depth d, the rest to lower depths c. If $d/c = 2$, say, this can prevent a subtle mate-in-n-ply from being seen until the search has reached round $2n$. Even $c = d - 4$ or $d - 3$ can make terms in $(\sqrt{\ell})^c$ minor enough to replace $(\sqrt{\ell})^d$ by $(\sqrt{a})^d$ for $a < 4$, which is enough to bring the *ebf* under 2.

The second idea compresses search "vertically" rather than "horizontally" in situations where we are trying to prove a cutoff value v after a "killer" but might not know how to order our subsequent moves to cut off lower down too. If the defender is really bad off then allowing two moves in a row might not improve the score beyond v or much at all. Inserting *null moves* for our turns can cement the search-depth halving on our side and also branch on fewer defensive sequences than using two alternating levels of search would bring. To be sure, there are so-called *Zugzwang* situations where letting the opponent move twice gives *us* an unfair advantage—propagating the illusion of "killer moves" when there really are none. However, these situations tend to occur in endgames where they are recognizable in advance and errors especially for nodes away from the PV may be stopped by minimax from propagating to the root.

 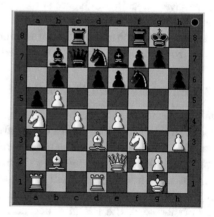

Fig. 2. Left: Position illustrating search phenomena. Right: Bratko-Kopec test position 22.

The position at left in Fig. 2 illustrates many of the above concepts. The Lomonosov 7-piece tables show it a draw with best play. Evaluation gives White a 100–200 cp edge on material with bishop and knight versus rook, but engines may differ on other factors such as which king is more exposed. After 1. Qd4+ Kc2 2. Qc5+, Black's king cannot return to d1 because of the fork 3. Nc3+, so Black steps out with 2...Kb3. Then White has the option 3. Qb6+ Kc2 4. Qxb1+

Kxb1 5. Nc3+ Kc2 6. Nxe2. Since Black is not in check and has no captures, this position may be deemed *quiescent* and given a +600 to +700 value or even higher since the extra bishop plus knight is generally a winning advantage. However, Black has the quiet 6...Kd3 which forks the bishop and knight and wins one of them, leaving a completely drawn game. What makes this harder to see is that White can delay the reckoning over longer *horizons* by giving more checks: 4. Qc7+ Kb3 5. Qb8+ Kc2 6. Qc8+ Kb3 7. Qb7+ Kc2 8. Qc6+ Kb3. White has not repeated any position and now has three further moves 9. Qc3+ Ka2 (if Black rejects ...Ka4) 10. Qa5+ Kb3 11. Qb4+ Kc2 before needing to decide whether to take the plunge with 12.Qxb1+. Pushing things even further is that White can preface this with 1. Ke7 threatening 2. Nb4 with Black's queen unable to give check. Black must answer by 1...Rb7+ and after 2. Kd6 must meekly return by 2...Rb1. Especially in the position after 1. Ke7 Rb7+, values can differ widely between engines and between depths for the same engine and be isolated to changes in the size of the hash table. Evidently the high degree of singularity raises the chance of a rogue $e(r)$ value propagating to the root.

How often is the quality of play compromised? It is one thing to try these heuristics against human players, but surely a "sounder" engine is best equipped to punish any lapses. Silver [29] reports an experiment where a current engine running on a smartphone trounced one from ten years ago that was given hardware fifty times faster. Although asking for depth d really gives a *mélange* of c and D with envelope E lopsidedly bunched along the PV, it all works.

We have glossed over many variants and ideas, including Hans Berliner's B^* search [30] which uses endpoints exclusively. Many have been studied and debated in the journal and symposia of the International Computer Chess Association, now evolved into the International Computer *Games* Association (ICGA), including LNCS conference proceedings. We argue that their sum achievement is most neatly expressed by plotting the engines' position values v against the portion p_v of points that human players of a given rating went on to score from positions of value v with either side to move. Figure 3 plots this from all standard-time games recorded in [31] between players rated within 10 points of a "milepost" 2600, 2625, 2650, or 2675, and likewise for levels in the 1600s range. Both sets give a near-perfect fit to a two-parameter logistic curve:

$$p_v = A + \frac{1 - 2A}{1 + e^{-Bv}}. \tag{2}$$

Here A represents the frequency of losing or drawing a "completely won" game and is small enough that we can focus on B. The one parameter B does double-duty: it is the scaling conversion from engine values to expectation and also scales with the skill of the players. The y-axis and B are the same as in our Eq. (1) for expectation based on rating difference. This suggests that skill is largely the sharpness of perceptions of value. If a chess program were to value a queen at 15 rather than 9 and so on for other terms in its evaluation function, we would have to scale B down by 3/5 to preserve the correspondence to scoring frequency. The figures have about the same ratio of B, which suggests that values are 60% more vivid to 2600s-rated players than to 1600s-rated players.

Their simplicity gives such curves the force of natural law. Amir Ban, co-creator of the (DEEP) JUNIOR chess program, argued [32] that the logistic relationship optimizes both the predictive accuracy and playing skill of the programs. In a skin-deep way this is *false*: the programs can post-process their values in any way that preserves the rank order of moves without affecting their play. In order to rule out this possibility, we have used the *open-source* STOCKFISH program (official version 7 release) to analyze the human games for the plots. That the evaluation terms, search heuristics, and minimax dynamics conform to the logistic relationship shows their *natural* acuity.

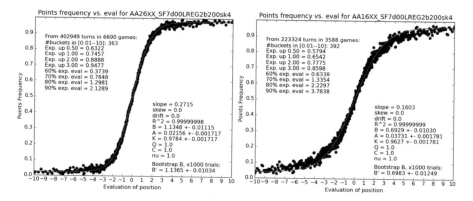

Fig. 3. Points expectation for 2600s-rated and 1600s-rated players from STOCKFISH 7 values.

4 Benchmarking Progress

All the notable human-computer matchups under standard tournament conditions over the past 40 years total in the low hundreds of games. A dozen such games at most are available for major iterations of any one machine or program. Games in computer-computer play do not connect into the human rating system. With ratings based only on a few bits of information—the outcomes of games and opponents' ratings—the sample size is too small to get a fix. Ratings based on 25 or fewer games are labeled "provisional" by the USCF. However much we feel the lack in retrospect, it applied all the more years ago looking forward.

Various internal ways were used to project skill. Programs could be played against themselves with different depth or time limits of search. The scoring rate of the stronger over the weaker translates into an Elo difference by the curve (1). Thompson [33] carried this out with BELLE at single-digit search depths, finding a steady gain of about 200 Elo per extra ply, but a followup experiment joined by Condon [34] found *diminishing returns* beyond depth 7.

The two prior versions of CHESS 4.7 triumphed in amateur and regional tournaments before its match with Levy, but the first provisional ratings above 2200 were earned by CRAY BLITZ and BELLE in the early 1980s. Berliner integrated his B^* search and high-tech parallel hardware to make his HITECH machine the first recognized as surpassing 2400 in 1988. Feng-hsiung Hsu, Thomas Anantharaman, and Murray Campbell, working apart from Berliner at Carnegie Mellon, developed CHIPTEST. Mike Browne and Andreas Nowatzyk joined them for DEEP THOUGHT, which was the first to beat a GM (Bent Larsen) in regulation play and gain a GM-level rating (2552). A flurry of activity followed in 1989 but with no clear forecast of further progress. Berliner et al. [35] conducted extensive self-play experiments and were led to state in their abstract:

> Projections of potential gain have time and again been found to overestimate the actual gain. [Our work] suggests that once a certain knowledge gap has been opened up, it cannot be overcome by small increments in searching depth. The conclusion ... is that extending the depth of search without increasing the present level of knowledge will not in any foreseeable time lead to World Championship level chess.

Hsu et al. [36] reached the opposite conclusion regarding DEEP THOUGHT, projecting that a 14 or 15-ply basic search with extensions beyond 30 ply would achieve a 3400 rating. The Thoresen engine competition site today shows no rating above 3230 [37]. One can say that its evolution into DEEP BLUE landed between the two projections. A chart from 1998 by Moravec [38] seems to justify the extrapolation to 3400 by its notably linear plot of ascribed engine ratings up to DEEP THOUGHT II near 2700 and 11 ply in 1991 and 1994, but it plots DEEP BLUE well under the line at 13 ply and only a 2700–2750 rating.

Already in the late 1970s, Bratko and Kopec conceived that an *external* test applicable to both human and computer players and less taxing than fully staged games could provide a reliable metric. The published form [39, 40] was a suite of twenty-four positions, twelve on tactics and twelve emphasizing strategy of pawn structure in particular. The former are instantly solved by today's computers but the latter retain their challenge, especially position 22 pictured in Fig. 2 which they deemed "hardest." The official STOCKFISH 8 version with 256 MB hash on one core thread in its "Single-PV" playing mode takes until depth 26 to settle on the key move—yet this happens within 20 s on an eight-year-old PC. Writing in 1990, Marsland [41] opined:

> Although one may disagree with the choice of test set, question its adequacy and completeness, and so on, the fact remains that the designers of computer chess programs still do not have an acceptable means of estimating the performance of chess programs, without resorting to time-consuming and expensive "matches" against other subjects. Clearly there is considerable scope for such test sets, as successes in related areas like pattern recognition attest.

What further distinguished the Bratko-Kopec work were tests on human subjects rated below-1600, 1600–1799, 1800–1999, 2000–2199, 2200–2399, and 2400+. The results filled the whole range from only two correct out of 24 to

21-of-24, showing a clear correspondence to rating. The Elo rating chart in [40] assigned 2150 to BELLE, 2050 to CHESS 4.9, and ratings 1900 and under to DUCHESS and other tested programs. Their results were broadly in accord with those ratings. But all these results were from small data.

Haworth [42] proposed using endgame tables to benchmark humans—and computers not equipped with them. The DTM, DTC, and/or DTZ metrics furnish numerical scores that are indisputable and objective, and the 6- and later 7-piece tables expand the range of realistic test positions. Humans of a given rating class could be benchmarked from games in actual competition that entered these endgames.

Matej Guid led Bratko back into benchmarking with a scheme using depth 12 of CRAFTY as authority to judge all moves (after the first twelve turns) in all games from world championship matches by intrinsic quality [43]. This was repeated with other engines as judges [44] including then-champion RYBKA 3 to reported depth 10, which arguably compares best to depth 13 or 14 on other engines since RYBKA treats its bottom four search levels as a unit [45]. Coming back to Haworth and company joined by this writer, two innovations of [46,47] were doing un-pruned full-depth analysis of multiple move options besides the best and played moves, and judging prior likelihoods of those moves by *fallible agents* modeling player skill profiles in a Bayesian setting. This led in [48] to using RYBKA 3 to analyze essentially all legal moves to reported depth 13, training a frequentist model on thousands of games over all rating classes from 1600 to 2700, and conditioning noise from the observed greater magnitude of errors in positions where one side has a non-negligible advantage. The model supplies not only metrics and projections but also error bars for various statistical tests of concordance with the judging engine(s) and an "Intrinsic Performance Rating" (IPR) based only on analysis of one's moves rather than results of games.

For continuity with this past work—and because an expanded model with versions of KOMODO and STOCKFISH as judges is not fully trained and calibrated at press time—we apply the scheme of [48] to rate the most prominent human-computer matches as well as some ICCA/ICGA World Computer Chess Championships (WCCC). This comes with cupfuls of caveats: RYBKA 3 to reported depth 13 is far stronger than CRAFTY to depth 12 but needs the defense [49] of the latter to justify IPR values over 2900 and probably loses resolution before 3100. The IPR currently measures *accuracy* more than *challenge* put to the opponent and is really measuring similarity to RYBKA 3. Although moves from turn 9 onward (skipping repeating sequences and positions with one side ahead over 300 cp) give larger sample sizes than games, the wide two-sigma error bars reflect the overall paucity of data and provisional nature of this work.

5   A "Moore's Law of Games" and Future Prospects

Figure 4 lays out IPRs over 37 years of top events in computer chess. Despite individual jumps in results, their wide error bars, and loss of resolution beyond 3000, some coherent points emerge from the long view:

Year	Engine	Score	IPR	moves	Event/Opponent(s)	Opp. IPR	moves
1978	CHESS 4.7	1.5/6	2120 +- 490	159	IM David Levy	2280 +- 415	159
1983	BELLE	5.5/10	2180 +- 300	279	US Open oppts.	2175 +- 320	280
1983	BELLE	3/5	2070 +- 415	126	WCCC oppts.	2130 +- 420	131
1983	CRAY BLITZ	4.5/5	2265 +- 350	144	WCCC oppts.	2065 +- 405	152
1986	CRAY BLITZ	4/5	2605 +- 315	153	WCCC oppts.	2135 +- 395	155
1986	HITECH	4/5	1975 +- 625	111	WCCC oppts.	1805 +- 660	115
1988	HITECH	5/7	2495 +- 270	188	avail. Open oppts.	2165 +- 385	194
1989	HITECH	3.5/4	3085 +- 275	97	GM A. Denker	2100 +- 555	98
1989	HITECH	3.5/5	2445 +- 325	146	WCCC oppts.	2485 +- 245	149
1989	BEBE	4/5	2415 +- 420	141	WCCC oppts.	1910 +- 505	144
1989	CRAY BLITZ	3.5/5	2470 +- 375	195	WCCC oppts.	2255 +- 360	196
1989	CHIPTEST	2/5	2540 +- 285	185	The Hague oppts.	2545 +- 250	181
1989	DEEP THOUGHT	5/5	2600 +- 255	126	WCCC oppts.	1890 +- 445	132
1988	DEEP THOUGHT	5.5/7	2780 +- 230	269	Long Beach oppts.	2400 +- 265	270
1989	DEEP THOUGHT	4/4	2885 +- 325	74	Levy	1820 +- 560	79
1989	DEEP THOUGHT	2/4	2325 +- 400	85	GM R. Byrne	2215 +- 690	83
1989	DEEP THOUGHT	2/5	2955 +- 245	131	Miles/Renet/Valvo	2585 +- 275	131
1989	DEEP THOUGHT	3.5/4	2830 +- 290	130	Amer. Open oppts.	1990 +- 440	133
1989	DEEP THOUGHT	0/2	2265 +- 815	53	Kasparov	2445 +- 340	51
1991	DEEP THOUGHT	2.5/7	2205 +- 430	213	Hannover oppts.	2400 +- 265	214
1993	DEEP BLUE	1.5/4	2820 +- 215	173	GM Bent Larsen	2800 +- 210	172
1993	DEEP BLUE	4.5/9	2720 +- 210	249	Copenhagen oppts.	2340 +- 295	246
1995	DEEP BLUE	3/3	3080 +- 220	100	ACM oppts.	2550 +- 420	103
1995	DEEP BLUE	3.5/5	2695 +- 430	119	WCCC oppts.	2420 +- 475	120
1996	DEEP BLUE	2/6	2915 +- 200	222	Kasparov	2610 +- 235	220
1997	DEEP BLUE	3.5/6	2850 +- 190	205	Kasparov	2585 +- 260	205
1999	REBEL 10	0.5/2	2915 +- 590	58	GM V. Anand	2660 +- 605	58
2000	DEEP JUNIOR	4.5/9	2845 +- 165	300	Dortmund oppts.	2605 +- 220	298
2002	DEEP FRITZ	4/8	3055 +- 140	221	GM V. Kramnik	2885 +- 155	221
2003	DEEP JUNIOR	3/6	2855 +- 275	148	Kasparov	2750 +- 305	148
2003	FRITZ X3D	2/4	2955 +- 175	107	Kasparov	2475 +- 395	108
2004	FRITZ	3.5/4	2945 +- 255	134	Bilbao HC oppts.	2530 +- 305	136
2004	HYDRA	3.5/4	3045 +- 230	176	Bilbao HC oppts.	2510 +- 275	176
2004	DEEP JUNIOR	1.5/4	2835 +- 290	124	Bilbao HC oppts.	2910 +- 155	121
2005	FRITZ	2/4	2705 +- 350	170	Bilbao HC oppts.	2740 +- 280	170
2005	HYDRA	3/4	3080 +- 190	99	Bilbao HC oppts.	2600 +- 340	101
2005	JUNIOR	3/4	3085 +- 100	251	Bilbao HC oppts.	2935 +- 115	251
2005	SHREDDER	9.5/10	2990 +- 165	239	Lopez ITT oppts.	2265 +- 275	243
2005	HYDRA	5.5/6	3160 +- 115	210	GM M. Adams	2825 +- 175	208
2006	DEEP FRITZ	4/6	2985 +- 160	208	Kramnik	2740 +- 265	208
2009	POCKET FRITZ	9.5/10	2905 +- 165	290	Mercosur oppts.	2250 +- 265	292
2011	JUNIOR	6/8	3065 +- 120	311	next 4 in WCCC	3035 +- 65	1,418
2013	JUNIOR	7.5/10	2995 +- 120	446	next 4 in WCCC	3095 +- 55	1,615
2015	JONNY	7/8	2970 +- 110	432	next 4 in WCCC	3035 +- 50	1,668

Fig. 4. IPRs from major human-computer events and some computer championships.

– There has been steady progress.
– Early estimated ratings of computers were basically right.
– Computers had GM level in sight before DEEP THOUGHT's breakthrough.
– Not long after the retirement of DEEP BLUE, championship quality became accessible to off-the-shelf hardware and software.
– A few years later smartphones had it, e.g. HIARCS 13 as "Pocket Fritz."
– Progress as measured by Elo gain flattens out over time.

The last point bears comparison with Moore's Law and arguments over its slowing or cessation. Those arguments pivot on whether the law narrowly addresses chip density or clock speed or speaks more general measure of productivity. With games we have a fixed measure—results backed by ratings—but a free-for-all on how this productivity is gained.

We may need to use Elo's transportability to other games to meter future progress. The argument that Elo sets a hard ceiling in chess goes as follows: We can imagine that today's strong engines E could hold a non-negligible portion d of draws against *any* strategy. This may need randomly selecting slightly inferior moves to avoid strategies with foresight of deterministic weaknesses. If E has rating R, then no opponent can ever be rated higher than $R + x$ by playing E, where with reference to (1), $p_{-x} = 0.5d$. The ceiling $R + x$ may be near at hand for chess but higher for Go—despite its recent conquest by Google DeepMind's ALPHAGO [50]. Games of Go last over a hundred moves for each player and have hair-trigger difference between win and loss.

A greater potential benefit comes from how large-scale data from deep engine analysis of human games may reveal new regularities of the human mind, especially in decision-making under pressure. Why and when do we stop thinking and take action, and what causes us to err? For instance, this may enable transforming the analysis of blunders in [51] into a smooth treatment of error in perception. Although computer chess left the envisaged mind and knowledge-based trajectory, its power-play success may boost the original AI aims.

References

1. Shannon, C.: Programming a computer for playing chess. Philos. Mag. **41**, 256–275 (1950)
2. Turing, A.: Computing machinery and intelligence. Mind **59**, 633–660 (1950)
3. Marsland, T.A.: A short history of computer chess. In: Marsland, T.A., Schaeffer, J. (eds.) Computers, Chess, and Cognition, pp. 3–7. Springer, New York (1990). https://doi.org/10.1007/978-1-4613-9080-0_1
4. Campbell, M., Feigenbaum, E., Levy, D., McCarthy, J., Newborn, M.: The History of Computer Chess: An AI Perspective (2005). http://www.computerhistory.org/collections/catalog/102651382. Video, The Computer History Museum
5. Larson, E.: A brief history of computer chess. Best Sch. Mag. (2015)
6. Levy, D.: Computer chess-past, present and future. Chess Life Rev. **28**, 723–726 (1973)
7. Elo, A.: The Rating of Chessplayers, Past and Present. Arco Pub., New York (1978)

8. Silver, N.: Introducing Elo Ratings (2014). https://fivethirtyeight.com/datalab/introducing-nfl-elo-ratings/

9. Glickman, M.E.: Parameter estimation in large dynamic paired comparison experiments. Appl. Stat. **48**, 377–394 (1999)

10. Sonas, J., Kaggle.com: Chess ratings: Elo versus the Rest of the World (2011). http://www.kaggle.com/c/chess

11. Schaeffer, J., Burch, N., Björnsson, Y., Kishimoto, A., Müller, M., Lake, R., Lu, P., Sutphen, S.: Checkers is solved. Science **317**, 1518–1522 (2007)

12. Allender, E.: The complexity of complexity. In: Day, A., Fellows, M., Greenberg, N., Khoussainov, B., Melnikov, A., Rosamond, F. (eds.) Computability and Complexity. LNCS, vol. 10010, pp. 79–94. Springer, Cham (2017). https://doi.org/10.1007/978-3-319-50062-1_6

13. Storer, J.: On the complexity of chess. J. Comput. Syst. Sci. **27**, 77–100 (1983)

14. Fraenkel, A., Lichtenstein, D.: Computing a perfect strategy for n x n chess requires time exponential in n. J. Comb. Theory **31**, 199–214 (1981)

15. Lichtenstein, D., Sipser, M.: Go is polynomial-space hard. J. ACM **27**, 393–401 (1980)

16. Robson, J.: The complexity of Go. In: Proceedings of the IFIP Congress, pp. 413–417 (1983)

17. Robson, J.: N by N checkers is Exptime complete. SIAM J. Comput. **3**, 252–267 (1984)

18. Iwata, S., Kasai, T.: The Othello game on an n*n board is PSPACE-complete. Theoret. Comput. Sci. **123**, 329–340 (1994)

19. Zakharov, V., Makhnychev, V.: Creating tables of chess 7-piece endgames on the Lomonosov supercomputer. Superkomp'yutery **15** (2013)

20. Bailey, D., Borwein, P., Plouffe, S.: On the rapid computation of various polylogarithmic constants. Math. Comput. **66**, 903–913 (1997)

21. Lucci, S., Kopec, D.: Artificial Intelligence in the 21st Century. Mercury Learning, Dulles (2013)

22. Chess Programming Wiki: Parallel Search. chessprogramming.wikispaces.com/Parallel+Search. Accessed 2017

23. Hyatt, R.: Rotated bitmaps, a new twist on an old idea. ICCA J. **22**, 213–222 (1999)

24. IBM Research: How Deep Blue works (1997). https://www.research.ibm.com/deepblue/meet/html/d.3.2.html

25. Chess Programming Wiki: Automated Tuning. https://chessprogramming.wikispaces.com/Automated+Tuning. Accessed 2017

26. Hyatt, R., Cozzie, A.: The effect of hash signature collisions in a computer chess program. ICGA J. **28**, 131–139 (2005)

27. Anantharaman, T., Campbell, M., Hsu, F.: Singular extensions: adding selectivity to brute-force searching. Artif. Intell. **43**, 99–110 (1990)

28. Hsu, F.H.: Behind Deep Blue: Building the Computer that Defeated the World Chess Champion. Princeton University Press, Princeton (2002)

29. Silver, A.: Komodo 8: the smartphone vs desktop challenge (2014). https://en.chessbase.com/post/komodo-8-the-smartphone-vs-desktop-challenge

30. Berliner, H.: The B* tree search algorithm: a best-first proof procedure. Artif. Intell. **12**, 23–40 (1979)

31. ChessBase: Big 2017 Chess Database (2017)

32. Ban, A.: Automatic learning of evaluation, with applications to computer chess. Technical Report Discussion Paper 613, Center for the Study of Rationality, Hebrew University (2012)

33. Thompson, K.: Computer chess strength. In: Advances in Computer Chess, vol. 3, pp. 55–56. Pergamon Press (1982)

34. Condon, J., Thompson, K.: Belle. In: Frey, P. (ed.) Chess Skill in Man and Machine, pp. 201–210. Springer, Heidelberg (1982). https://www.springer.com/us/book/9780387908151

35. Berliner, H., Geotsch, G., Campbell, M., Ebeling, C.: Measuring the performance potential of chess programs. Artif. Intell. **43**(1), 7–20 (1990)

36. Hsu, F.H., Anantharaman, T., Campbell, M., Nowatzyk, A.: A grandmaster chess machine. Sci. Am. **263**, 44–50 (1990)

37. Top Chess Engine Championship: Ratings after Season 9 - Superfinal. http://tcec.chessdom.com/archive.php. Accessed 2017

38. Moravec, H.: When will computer hardware match the human brain? J. Evol. Technol. **1** (1998)

39. Bratko, I., Kopec, D.: A test for comparison of human and computer performance in chess. In: Advances in Computer Chess, vol. 3, pp. 31–56. Elsevier (1982)

40. Kopec, D., Bratko, I.: The Bratko-Kopec experiment: a comparison of human and computer performance in chess. In: Advances in Computer Chess, vol. 3, pp. 57–72. Elsevier (1982)

41. Marsland, T.: The Bratko-Kopec test revisited. ICCA J. **13**, 15–19 (1990)

42. Haworth, G.: Reference fallible endgame play. ICGA J. **26**, 81–91 (2003)

43. Guid, M., Bratko, I.: Computer analysis of world chess champions. ICGA J. **29**, 65–73 (2006)

44. Guid, M., Bratko, I.: Using heuristic-search based engines for estimating human skill at chess. ICGA J. **34**, 71–81 (2011)

45. Rajlich, V., Kaufman, L.: Rybka 3 chess engine (2008). www.rybkachess.com

46. DiFatta, G., Haworth, G., Regan, K.: Skill rating by Bayesian inference. In: Proceedings of 2009 IEEE Symposium on Computational Intelligence and Data Mining (CIDM 2009), Nashville, TN, pp. 89–94 (2009)

47. Haworth, G., Regan, K., Di Fatta, G.: Performance and prediction: Bayesian modelling of fallible choice in chess. In: van den Herik, H.J., Spronck, P. (eds.) ACG 2009. LNCS, vol. 6048, pp. 99–110. Springer, Heidelberg (2010). https://doi.org/10.1007/978-3-642-12993-3_10

48. Regan, K., Haworth, G.: Intrinsic chess ratings. In: Proceedings of AAAI 2011, San Francisco, pp. 834–839 (2011)

49. Guid, M., Pérez, A., Bratko, I.: How trustworthy is Crafty's analysis of world chess champions? ICGA J. **31**, 131–144 (2008)

50. Silver, D., et al.: Mastering the game of Go with deep neural networks and tree search. Nature **529**, 484–489 (2016)

51. Chabris, C., Hearst, E.: Visualization, pattern recognition, and forward search: effects of playing speed and sight of the position on grandmaster chess errors. Cogn. Sci. **27**, 637–648 (2003)

Knowledge Harvesting: Achievements and Challenges

Gerhard Weikum[1](✉), Johannes Hoffart[2], and Fabian Suchanek[3]

[1] Max Planck Institute for Informatics, Saarbrücken, Germany
weikum@mpi-inf.mpg.de
[2] Ambiverse GmbH, Saarbrücken, Germany
johannes@ambiverse.com
[3] Telecom ParisTech University, Paris, France
fabian@suchanek.name

Abstract. This article gives an overview on knowledge harvesting: automatically constructing large high-quality knowledge bases from Internet sources. The first part reviews key principles and best-practice methods. The second part points out open challenges for future research.

1 Introduction

Enhancing computers with "machine knowledge" that can power intelligent applications is a long-standing goal of computer science [34]. Major advances on *knowledge harvesting* – methods for turning noisy Internet content into crisp knowledge structures on entities and relations – have made this formerly elusive vision practically viable today.

A prominent use case where *knowledge bases (KB's)* have become a key asset is search engines. When we send a query like "jobs biography" to Bing or Google, we obtain information on the life of Steve Jobs. So the search engine automatically detects that we are interested in facts about an individual entity. On the other hand, for a query like "jobs in bay area", the search engine locates the spatial entity Bay Area and properly interprets the query as a request for local job ads. Finally, for the query "jobs at apple", the system returns a mix of two different interpretations. All this is feasible because the search engine has a huge knowledge base on its back-end servers, aiding in the discovery of entities in user requests (and their contexts) and in finding concise answers.

The KB's in this setting are centered on individual entities, containing:

- entities like people, places, organizations, products, events (e.g., `SteveJobs`, the `GoldenGateBridge`, the `Pixar` company, the `iPhone7`, the `Woodstock Concert`),
- the semantic classes to which entities belong (e.g., `SteveJobs type entrepreneur`, `SteveJobs type computerPioneer`, `SteveJobs type ZenBuddhist`),

ⓒ Springer Nature Switzerland AG 2019
B. Steffen and G. Woeginger (Eds.): Computing and Software Science, LNCS 10000, pp. 217–235, 2019.
https://doi.org/10.1007/978-3-319-91908-9_13

- relationships between entities (e.g., `SteveJobs founded AppleInc`,
  `SteveJobs invented iPhone`, `SteveJobs diedOf PancreaticCancer`), as well as
- their validity times (e.g., `SteveJobs wasCEOof Pixar [1986,2006]`).

This concept of a comprehensive KB goes back to pioneering work in Artificial Intelligence on universal knowledge bases in the 1980s and 1990s, most notably, the *Cyc* project at MCC in Austin [35] and the *WordNet* project at Princeton [19]. However, these knowledge collections have been hand-crafted and manually curated. Thus, knowledge acquisition was inherently limited in scope and scale. Starting this millenium with the Semantic Web vision, domain-specific *ontologies* [59] have been developed, but these are also manually created. In the last decade, *automatic knowledge harvesting* from Web and text sources has become a major research avenue, and has made substantial practical impact. Knowledge harvesting is the core methodology for the automatic construction of large knowledge bases, going beyond manually compiled knowledge collections like Cyc or WordNet.

These achievements are rooted in academic research and community projects. Salient projects that started ten to fifteen years ago are DBpedia [2], Freebase [5], KnowItAll [18], WebOfConcepts [11], WikiTaxonomy [50] and Yago [60]. More recent projects with publicly available data include BabelNet [44], ConceptNet [58], DeepDive [57], EntityCube (aka. Renlifang) [46], KnowledgeVault [15], NELL [7] Probase [73], Wikidata [68], XLore [70].

The largest general-purpose KB's with publicly accessible contents are Babel-Net (babelnet.org), DBpedia (dbpedia.org), Wikidata (wikidata.org) and Yago (yago-knowledge.org). They contain millions of entities, organized in hundreds to hundred thousands of semantic classes, and hundred millions to billions of relational facts on entities. These and other knowledge resources are interlinked at the entity level, forming the Web of Linked Open Data [24].

Our own endeavor on knowledge harvesting was motivated by research on semantic search. Later it became the Yago-Naga project, with the first release of the Yago KB (yago-knowledge.org) in February 2007. The strength of Yago is its rich type system with hundred thousands of classes. When IBM Watson won the Jeopardy quiz show, it leveraged Yago's knowledge of fine-grained entity types for semantic type checking [28]. More recent Yago releases incorporated temporal and spatial knowledge [25] and multilingual properties [53]. Yago is maintained as a joint project of the Max Planck Institute for Informatics and the Télécom ParisTech University.

Over the last five years, knowledge harvesting has been adopted at big industrial stakeholders, and large KB's have become a key asset in a variety of commercial applications, including semantic search (see, e.g., [4]), analytics (e.g., aggregating by entities), recommendations and data integration (i.e., to combine heterogeneous datasets in and across enterprises). Examples are the Google Knowledge Graph (with Freebase as a catalyst), the use of KB's in IBM Watson, Amazon's Evi, the Baidu Knowledge Graph, Facebook's Graph Search, Microsoft Satori, Wolfram Alpha as well as domain-specific knowledge bases in business, finance, life sciences, and more (e.g., at Bloomberg, Mayo Clinic, Siemens, Walmart, etc.). In addition, KB's have found wide use as a distant supervision source for a variety of tasks in natural language processing, such as entity linking.

This article gives an overview of knowledge harvesting. Section 2 reviews research achievements and the state of the art, identifying key principles and best-practice methods. Section 3 presents open challenges that provide opportunities for future research.

2   Achievements

2.1   Knowledge Base Model

Knowledge representation has received great attention in AI research, leading to sophisticated forms of epistemic logics and, with the advent of the Semantic Web, description logics for ontologies [59]. However, none of these powerful models ever led to sizable collections of knowledge. The main reason then was the lack of data to populate knowledge models with interesting instances.

Entities, Classes and Relations: The former limitation of sparse data on instances was eventually overcome by the advent of knowledge-sharing communities like Wikipedia and the increasing availability of public datasets. This enabled the extraction of entities and their properties from high-quality Internet sources to populate a KB. Most of today's KB's use a simple relational representation where all knowledge is cast into grounded formulas of n-ary predicates (i.e., relation symbols). Constants (i.e., 0-ary predicates) denote *entities* or *literal values* (e.g., coordinates, dates and other numbers), unary predicates correspond to *classes* of same-type entities, and higher-arity predicates are used to capture entity *attributes* or *relationships* with other entities.

SPO Triples: The widely used RDF data model even restricts n-ary relations to be binary and casts the unary predicates for class membership into the binary form ⟨*entity*⟩ type ⟨*class*⟩ – in infix notation, with type being the predicate. The elementary formulas in an RDF-compliant KB are also called *subject-predicate-object* triples, or *SPO triples* for short. S is required to be an entity, whereas O can be either an entity (e.g., someone's spouse) or a literal (e.g., someone's birthdate). The following shows examples for such triples (in conceptual form, disregarding the specifics of the RDF syntax):

`SteveJobs type computerPioneer`	`SteveJobs type entrepreneur`
`entrepreneur subclassOf businessperson`	`businessperson subclassOf person`
`SteveJobs hasDaughter LisaBrennan`	`AppleLisa namedAfter LisaBrennan`
`SteveJobs diedOf PancreaticCancer`	`SteveJobs diedOn 5-Oct-2011`

The two triples in the first line above are about class membership. In standard logics these would be written as unary-predicate formulas: *computerPioneer (SteveJobs)* and *entrepreneur (SteveJobs)*. This form of knowledge about *instances of classes* forms the backbone of a KB. The two triples in the second line above organize classes in a subsumption hierarchy of subtypes and supertypes. To avoid that this `subclassOf` predicate takes second-order form, the class predicates are cast into binary form with the `type` predicate. All triples for the `type` and `subclassOf` predicate constitute the *taxonomic knowledge* of a KB. Prior work on ontologies mostly focused on intensional knowledge centered on the `subclassOf` predicate, and hardly captured any instances for the `type` predicate.

Many KB's require that the subject arguments of `type` be *individual entities* (aka. named entities) that can be uniquely identified in the real world, this way disregarding abstract entities (aka. general concepts) which are prone to subjective interpretation. For example, concepts such as universe, love or quantum physics are intentionally excluded to stay clear of potential pitfalls. This way, it has become feasible to construct huge KB's with millions of entities for many thousands of classes with negligible error rate and very high agreement on what is correct knowledge.

Taxonomic knowledge is already a huge asset for applications like search and analytics. For example, a query such as "Which singers have won the Nobel prize?" can be easily answered from the following triples (by intersecting instances of different classes):

| `BobDylan type singer` | `BobDylan type NobelPrizeLaureates` |

Likewise, an analytic task that compares frequencies of queries, clicks or references for musicians vs. politicians, is made easy by a KB that provides the class memberships of entities along with subclass knowledge such as:

| `singer subclassOf musician` | `stateSecretary subclassOf politician` |

SPO triples with predicates other than `type` or `subclassOf` are referred to as *facts*. The largest KB's contain billions of facts for several thousand different predicates. The predicates of interest (e.g., `bornIn`, `hasDaughter`, `namedAfter` etc.) are often pre-specified. We will reconsider this point in Sect. 2.2.5.

Beyond SPO Triples: KB's with this focus on binary relational facts are often called *knowledge graphs (KG's)*, as they correspond to labeled graphs with nodes denoting entities and predicate-labeled edges for the facts. However, the restriction to binary predicates is an oversimplification. There are many cases where ternary and higher-arity relations are needed to represent real-world situations. One important case is *temporal knowledge*: extending facts with their validity times, a timepoint or a timespan. For example, capturing when Steve Jobs (co-)founded Apple or from when until when he was CEO of his various companies calls for ternary predicates with an additional time argument:

| `SteveJobs founded AppleInc 1-April-1976` |
| `SteveJobs wasCEOof AppleInc [9-July-1997, 24-Aug-2011]` |

Generally, events often require three or more arguments to fully capture them: several entities involved in various roles, time, place, etc. As an example, consider the football match where Germany won 7:1 against Brazil on 8-July-2014 in Belo Horizonte. Such a composite fact cannot be broken down into binary facts without losing information. The RDF data model then usually escapes to so-called reification: assigning an entity id to the entire event, and adding multiple triples for the event's different aspects with the entity id as their common subject argument. However, this technique makes querying and reasoning with knowledge more tedious. Higher-arity predicates, on the other hand, are a natural representation.

Canonicalization: An important point in capturing crisp knowledge is the uniqueness of representing entities and facts. Many (but not all) KB's strive to *canonicalize* all arguments in their SPO triples and other facts. For classes, this implies that differently named classes have (potentially) different instances (e.g., singer vs. songwriter vs. musician); conversely, differently named classes that would always agree on their instances should be unified (e.g., humans vs. people). For entities, the same principle applies: an entity can have different names, but should be captured only once with a unique id. For example, knowledge about the company Apple should not be registered twice or spread across different names like "Apple", "Apple Inc.", "Apple company". Instead, we need to map all relevant facts to the same entity, canonically denoted, for example, as AppleInc, and keep its diverse surface names as *labels* (aka. alias names). This issue calls for *named entity disambiguation* (aka. entity linking) (see, e.g., [38,56]). For populating a KB, this step can be integrated into a knowledge harvesting method or dealt with by specialized methods and tools.

The canonicalization principle carries over to entire facts. For example, a high-quality KB should represent the gist of the sentences *"Jobs was born in San Francisco."* and *"Apple's charismatic Steve is from the City by the Bay"* in a single fact SteveJobs bornIn SanFrancisco. Without this unique representation, querying a KB and using it for inference would be awkward.

Lessons Learned: A key point in enabling knowledge harvesting at large scale has been to use a simple SPO-style representation as a backbone. This is sufficient for a *core KB* to capture taxonomic classes and basic facts about millions of individual entities. We emphasize, however, that this does not rule out additional knowledge using higher-arity predicates and more sophisticated representations. In particular, a rich KB should also comprise intensional assertions about the world: constraints that couple different predicates or rules for deducing additional facts. For example, specifying that a person can have only one birthplace and that the birthplace must be an entity of type location, is a vital piece of knowledge. Obviously, this calls for more expressive predicate logics. We will come back to this in Sect. 2.2.4.

2.2 Knowledge Gathering and Cleaning

For a KB model as outlined above, the core task of knowledge harvesting is to (i) identify appropriate data sources as input, (ii) extract entities, classes and relational facts, and (iii) organize them into a clean KB. This builds on techniques from the area of *information extraction (IE)*, based on patterns in

Web pages and text documents (see [9,55] for surveys). However, IE copes with one source as fixed input (e.g., one Web site), whereas knowledge harvesting has freedom in choosing its sources and can exploit redundancy and statistics across many sources. Important knowledge is often expressed in many sources in complementary ways. We can pick low-hanging fruit by choosing the best suitable sources and treat sources with different degrees of noise in very different ways.

This principle suggests a layered approach where we first tap sources with limited noise in content and structure, using robust extraction methods for high-quality output. This is why many KB's intensively build on harvesting semi-structured elements of Wikipedia: category names, infoboxes, lists, headings, etc. For specific domains (e.g., health), there are often specific sources that should be prioritized (e.g., repositories such as Medscape, DrugBank, FAERS, etc.).

As a second stage, additional knowledge can then be harvested from riskier sources. We will see below that the previously compiled high-quality knowledge is beneficial in filtering noise and cleaning candidate facts. In other words, once we have a strong core KB, it is an asset in acquiring more knowledge, deeper knowledge and better knowledge – without degrading in quality.

2.2.1   Harvesting Entities and Classes

The first goal of knowledge harvesting is to compile a comprehensive set of semantic classes (e.g., guitarists, electric guitarists, left-handed guitarists, etc.) and their instances (i.e., individual entities such as Bob Dylan, Jimmy Page, Jimi Hendrix, etc.). In addition, we want to capture subsumptions among classes. We could address this task *ab initio*, starting with raw Internet contents, but it would be unwise to ignore pre-existing high-quality resources. First, classic work on linguistics and cognition led to *WordNet* [19], a large repository of words and word senses with lexical relations like synonymy, antonymy, hypernymy (i.e., subsumption), etc. This can be seen as a source of more than 100,000 semantically classes, carefully organized into a subclass/superclass taxonomy. Second, knowledge-centric communities like *Wikipedia* organize articles in category systems. While these were noisy in the early years of Wikipedia (with improper or misleading categories), the editorial guidelines and manual curation of Wikipedia have eventually led to a very rich and reasonably accurate system of about half a million categories. Given these prior assets, one line of successful research has derived taxonomic knowledge for high-quality KB's from WordNet and Wikipedia [44,50,60]. The Yago KB, for example, has carefully unified Word-Net classes and Wikipedia categories and constructed a high-quality taxonomy with more than 300,000 fine-grained classes.

Once we settle on a class taxonomy, the next step is to populate the classes with individual entities (where one entity can belong to several classes). Here, Wikipedia is by far the largest and best asset to tap into, as it already organizes articles about entities within its category system. Most of the large KB's have seized this opportunity. It is straightforward when the taxonomy is based on Wikipedia categories. For connecting to WordNet classes, though, clever alignment and pruning techniques are needed [60]. The philosophy of "picking low-hanging fruit first" also carries over beyond Wikipedia. For example, Yago has integrated GeoNames (geonames.org) for spatial entities [25]. For health entities like diseases, symptoms, drugs, etc., manually curated sources like UMLS, MeSH, DrugBank, etc. can be used very effectively (see, e.g., [17]). Generally, entities of specific types (e.g., books, songs, medical drugs, etc.) can often be harvested from dedicated sources or specific identifier systems [62]. As a caveat, we note that this does not completely cover the world of *emerging entities* like new events or people who suddenly become notable (e.g., a new singer). This aspect of knowledge dynamics will be discussed in Sect. 2.3.

A major alternative to relying on Wikipedia-style sources is to tap all kinds of Internet sources at large scale. A classic approach for this line of *taxonomy induction* research is to use so-called Hearst patterns like *X such as Y* or *X, Y and other Z* and match them against Web and text contents to extract class-entity or subclass-superclass pairs [23]. Using advanced data-mining and machine-learning techniques, this idea can be greatly generalized, to tap into additional patterns, http links and HTML tables (where a column name and cell value may indicate a class-entity pair), or into query-and-click logs of big search engines (see, e.g., [10,31,47,67,69,73]). These are powerful methods; however, they require large-scale machinery and access to big data like complete Web crawls or search engine logs.

2.2.2   Gathering Facts from Wikipedia

The most straightforward way of gathering binary facts is to harvest infoboxes in Wikipedia. These provide attributes and relationships of the entity featured in an article, in semi-structured form. Here is an example in the wiki markup language:

```
{{ Infobox person
    | name        = Steve Jobs
    | birth_date  = Birth date|1955|2|24|mf=y
    | birth_place = [[San Francisco]], California, U.S.
    | death_cause = [[Pancreatic cancer]] and [[respiratory arrest]]   }}
```

Naturally, these P and O components for SPO triples can be extracted by regular expressions (i.e., finite state automata). These expressions may even be automatically learned from samples with manual markup. Unfortunately, even Wikipedia infoboxes exhibit noise and terminological diversity. For example, birthplaces could be stated differently in different articles: birth_place = ..., born_in = ..., born_in_city = ..., etc.; and the values may be encoded in different ways (e.g., with or without the state in a country). To cope with this heterogeneity, *type-checking* the outputs of a regex matcher is a boost in quality [25,60]. Here, having rich taxonomic knowledge – entities and their fine-grained types – is a huge benefit. The result is clean facts in canonicalized form.

There are other opportunities to extract facts from semi-structured elements (i.e., headings, tables, etc.) in Wikipedia or similar high-quality sources. As the diversity of how facts are expressed increases, this calls for stochastic variants of automata, like Conditional Random Fields (CRF's). Facts from infoboxes can be used to train CRF-based extractors (e.g., [72]).

2.2.3 Gathering Fact Candidates from Text

For high recall (i.e., gathering as many facts as possible), we eventually need to tap into natural language text as input, facing even higher degrees of noise and variability. In this setting, *pattern-based harvesting* has been the method of choice. For example, birthplaces of people are often expressed by phrases such as "his birthplace is", "her hometown", "is from", etc. Of course, it would be daunting to manually specify such patterns for hundreds or thousands of predicates. Instead, a distantly supervised approach has become prevalent, centered on the principle of *pattern-fact duality* [1,6,18,40]. For each relation of interest, a small set of *seed facts* is needed, for example, the correct birthplaces of a few prominent people (which could be obtained from semi-structured high-quality sources). These facts can be matched against a corpus (or the entire Internet) by searching for sentences that contain the subject entity and the object entity. The key idea then is that facts frequently co-occur with connecting phrases (e.g., verbal phrases) that can be distilled into patterns. The patterns in turn co-occur with other, newly seen facts. This procedure – alternating between facts and patterns – can be iterated, and eventually yields a large number of new fact candidates. Patterns can be surface phrases, but can also cover generalizations such as lifting the words "his" and "her" into personal pronouns, capture non-adjacent words, or use dependency parsing to consider the syntactic structure of sentences. Also, HTML tables in Web pages can be tapped for fact harvesting in a similar vein; this has been successfully pursued, for example, by the NELL [41] and Knowledge Vault [15] projects.

Of course, this gathering process needs to be comlemented by computing statistical measures of confidence and support. Otherwise, spurious patterns may easily lead to drifting targets. For example, starting with Steve Job's birthplace San Francisco among the seed facts, the method could pick up the pattern "his favorite place" after a few iterations. By judicious thresholding, one can obtain a good set of assertions for facts. This approach typically results in an accuracy around 80% – that is, there are still 20% of the assertions incorrect, due to noise in the patterns.

2.2.4 Cleaning Fact Candidates

The high recall of the outlined gathering methods comes at the expense of potentially degrading in precision: introducing many false candidates for facts. For example, we may obtain the following assertions for the `birthplace` relation:

SteveJobs birthplace SanFrancisco	SteveJobs birthplace USA
SteveJobs birthplace Kyoto	SteveJobs birthplace AppleInc

These fact candidates may be derived from diverse patterns for the `birthplace` predicate, such as "his hometown", "citizen of", "his favorite place" or "mostly at". The resulting triples have to be cleaned: removing spurious assertions, and also mapping patterns of good triples – "his hometown" in the above case – onto canonicalized predicates. Next, we discuss methods for this purpose.

Consistency Constraints: A key idea is to mimic human skepticism: use plausibility considerations to rule out dubious assertions. In technical terms, we can impose *consistency constraints* on the candidate space, to discard assertions that violate certain conditions. The simplest idea is to enforce *type constraints*, and this actually provides enormous mileage towards building a high-quality KB. For the above example, the relation about where people are born should be specified with a type signature `birthplace`: *person* × *location*, or more specifically `birthplace`: *person* × *city*. This constitutes a logical constraint:

$$\forall x, y \, (birthplace(x, y) \Rightarrow (type(x, person) \wedge type(y, city)))$$

The constraint is violated by 2 of the 4 candidate facts above, leaving only San Francisco and Kyoto as possible cities where Steve Jobs was born.

This logics-based approach is far more general than mere type checking. There are other kinds of constraints to be harnessed, most notably, *functional constraints* – many relations are actually functions – and *inclusion constraints* between different relations. For example, each person can have only one birthplace, and birthplaces are usually among the cities where a person has lived:

$$\forall x, y, z \, ((birthplace(x, y) \wedge birthplace(x, z)) \Rightarrow y = z)$$
$$\forall x, y \, (birthplace(x, y) \Rightarrow livedIn(x, y))$$

These constraints have to be manually specified by a knowledge engineer. However, this is a fairly easy modeling task, and not a bottleneck at all. There are also techniques for automatically learning constraints from data (see, e.g., [7,41]), but this comes at a higher risk. In general, constraints can be hard or soft: absolutely excluding any violation or tolerating a certain degree of exceptions. For example, the above formula that couples `birthplace` and `livedIn` is soft. In such cases, the constraints may be weighted. Fact candidates are weighted as well, typically by some notion of confidence based on statistics from the gathering stage. This opens the way to deciding between San Francisco and Kyoto for the birthplace of Steve Jobs.

Consistency Reasoning: Fact candidates should not solely be checked against each constraint in isolation. Instead, it is beneficial to perform *joint inference* over a set of assertions and a set of constraints. Consider, for example, the following noisy candidates and soft constraints, with the last two constraints stating that someone can either be a scientist or a musician, but never both:

BobDylan hasWon Grammy
BobDylan hasWon LiteratureNobelPrize
BobDylan hasWon PhysicsNobelprize
$\forall x \, (hasWon(x, Grammy) \Rightarrow type(x, musician))$
$\forall x \, (hasWon(x, PhysicsNobelPrize) \Rightarrow type(x, scientist))$
$\forall x \, (type(x, scientist) \Rightarrow \neg type(x, musician))$
$\forall x \, (type(x, musician) \Rightarrow \neg type(x, scientist))$

There is no way to keep all three fact candidates while enforcing all constraints. There are two different combinations of prizes, though, that are consistent. By viewing the data as a set of logical formulas, this becomes a test for *satisfiability*. By grounding the constraints with the constants from the candidate fact pool, the problem is reduced to an instance of the *MaxSat problem*. Moreover, since each individual formula has a weight (see above), the task is to compute a *Weighted MaxSat* solution. Although this is a classical NP-hard problem, there are good approximation techniques and there are ways of customizing them to this specific task of knowledge cleaning [43,61]. In the example, assume that the weight for the Grammy fact is much higher than the weight for the Physics Nobel Prize and the weights for the three constraints are identical. Then, the best solution is to accept the facts about the Grammy and Literature Nobel Prize while dropping the assertion about the Physics Nobel Prize.

Probabilistic Graphical Models: The above line of thought has been very fruitful for knowledge cleaning and comes in a variety of ways: MaxSat reasoning is one approach, integer linear programming another one, and there are also powerful probabilistic inference methods along these lines. The latter include especially probabilistic graphical models, where random variables for accepting or refuting fact candidates are coupled through logical constraints [14,30]. In this setting, the MAP inference (MAP = maximum a posteriori) is equivalent to solving a weighted MaxSat problem. Approximation algorithms include SAT solvers, Monte Carlo sampling, variational calculus and more. Applications to knowledge harvesting have been developed, among others, by [7,52,57,61,74,75]. Constraints have also been leveraged for estimating the confidence in specific extractions and for training fact extraction methods (see, e.g., [41]).

Beyond Triples: Methods of this kind can be further extended to go beyond binary relations. An important use case is *temporal knowledge* where facts need to be annotated with timepoints or timespans when they are valid [37,63,71]. For example, properly interpreting a fact such as BobDylan spouseOf SaraDylan requires the corresponding time scope [Nov-1965, June-1977]. So strictly speaking, we are looking at a ternary relation here: spouseOf: *person × person × time*. This is a special case of *higher-arity relations*, often but not only in combination with entities of type *event*. Knowledge harvesting methods, as outlined above, can be further extended to this end (see, e.g., [32]).

2.2.5   Other Approaches

A potential concern about the above methods is their limitation to pre-specified predicates. For example, we can harvest composers of songs or artists who covered songs only after a human curator provides the relevant predicates with type signatures: composedMusic: *musician × song* and coveredMusic: *musician × song*. On the other hand, facts on song lyrics being about specific people cannot be harvested unless we explicitly model such a predicate. Therefore, we refer to the presented methods as *model-driven knowledge harvesting*.

Open IE: The paradigm of *Open Information Extraction (Open IE)* [3,12,39] offers unsupervised harvesting of fact triples in an open-ended manner, without any modeling effort. Using linguistic patterns, Open IE collects all kinds of triples where S, P and O are meaningful phrases, typically noun phrases for S and O and verbal phrases for P. These are not canonicalized; so outputs could be:

"Dylan's Hurricane"	"covers the story of"	"the black boxer Carter"
"Hurricane"	"is a protest song about"	"racist victim Carter"
"Sara"	"is a love song about"	"Dylan's wife"
"the love song Sara"	"is about"	"his ex-wife Sara Dylan"

Such output requires disambiguating the S and O arguments of the phrase-level triples, which is typically an entity-linking task [56] against an existing KB of entities. Canonicalizing the P components, on the other hand, is an open challenge as the space of possible predicates is unknown in this open-ended setting. Research along these lines, based on clustering techniques, includes [20].

Deep Learning: With recent breakthroughs in deep learning [33], an intriguing thought could be to bypass the explicit construction of a KB, and rather use end-to-end learning on a per-task basis (e.g., question answering or describing videos). However, this raises caveats. First, it would require huge amounts of labeled training data which are often unavailable. Second, this expensive training would have to be repeated for every new task. Third, machine learning outputs (i.e., predictions, recommendations, answers or even decisions) are not easily explainable to human users. Explicit KB's, on the other hand, are a reusable asset for many tasks, they can inform and constrain the learning of models, and they support user-comprehensible explanations.

2.3 Knowledge Evolution and Quality

Change is the only constant in knowledge. Attribute values of entities (e.g., city populations) and relationships between entities (e.g., the CEO of a company or a person's spouse) change over time. Moreover, new entities of interest are created all the time and need to be added to the KB (e.g., new songs, sports matches, babies of celebrities). Also, existing entities may be irrelevant for a KB at some point, but become prominent at a later point. Typical examples are when a "garage band" or "garage company" becomes succesful. If Wikipedia had already existed in 1976, it would probably have dismissed Apple for insufficient notability.

Temporal Knowledge: So KB's must be continuously updated. This requires keeping *versions of facts*, along with their *temporal validity* scopes. We already discussed methods for harvesting temporal knowledge in Sect. 2.2.4. Some of the major KB's have rigorously followed this principle (e.g., [25]).

Active Knowledge: For some kinds of highly dynamic and specialized knowledge, explicitly capturing fact versions is not practically feasible. For example, the chart positions of a song and the box office counts of a movie change so rapidly that it is hardly meaningful to materialize such facts in the KB. Instead, a preferable way is to keep links to specialized databases and to Web services that return up-to-date values on demand [51].

Emerging Entities: A specific aspect of dynamic knowledge is to cope with newly emerging entities. When discovering entity names in input sources (text, Web tables, etc.), we first aim to disambiguate them onto the already known entities in the KB. However, even if there is a good match in the KB, it is not necessarily the proper interpretation. For example, when the documentary movie "Amy" was first mentioned a few years ago, it would have been tempting to link the name to the soul singer Amy Winehouse. However, although the movie is about the singer's life, the two entities must not be confused. To rectify this situation, each observed name should always be potentially associated with an additional virtual candidate: *none* of the known entities [26]. When the evidence for the name denoting an *out-of-KB entity* is stronger than for a known entity, we capture the name as a new entity, along with its context. After a while, we will thus obtain a repository of recently emerging entity names. Then, clustering techniques can be used to group the names, and knowledge curators can be asked to confirm these canoncialized groups. Finally, the confirmed entities can be registered in the KB. To keep the effort for the curation step as low as possible, new entity candidates should be presented with informative context [27].

On-the-fly Knowledge Bases: A specific case for out-of-KB entities is constructing ad-hoc KB's on the fly. Suppose a new corpus of documents becomes available, for example, the Panama Papers or a batch of articles on a hot political or health topic, such as the UK Brexit or Zika infections. Then we should be able to automatically build a domain- and corpus-specific KB overnight, to support journalists and analysts in exploring the topic and analyzing particularly interesting issues.

Knowledge Curation: As a KB is continuously updated and keeps growing, it is virtually inevitable that errors sneak in and degrade the KB quality. Versioning of facts helps to control the maintenance process, but may also lead to conflicting versions. For example, when a new name for the CEO for a company is detected by harvesting fresh online sources, should this be added as a new fact or is it, perhaps, evidence that the previous fact in the KB was incorrect? One case leads to a new version, the other should result in overwriting the prior version. Even worse, an error may be detected only post-hoc, days or weeks after a new version was added and became interlinked with other facts.

Thus, *quality assurance* requires a fundamental solution. Fact cleaning, as discussed in Sect. 2.2.4 is an important element, and so is versioning. However, more is needed for a comprehensive approach. Today, very large KB's resort to *manual curation*, by having human volunteers (e.g., in an online community like Wikidata) or paid workers (in a commercial KB) checking newly added or altered facts. Such a *crowdsourcing* solution can be orchestrated in various ways, with the goal of optimizing the benefit/cost ratio (e.g., [29]).

Fact Checking: An alternative or complement to human curators is to harness the sources of evidence for doubtful facts in a more principled manner. This may entail actively searching for evidence or counter-evidence about facts, as a continuous background process. A typical approach is to consider a small number of alternative O values for given S and P of a fact, such as birthplaces for Steve Jobs: San Francisco vs. Cupertino vs. Kyoto. Then statistics derived from Internet sources (i.e., databases, Web sites, news, etc.) can guide the analysis and assessment of candidates towards finding the truth (see [36] for a survey).

This form of *knowledge corroboration* or *knowledge fusion* aggregates the observation confidence from different sources, where sources are weighted by their *trustworthiness*. Therefore, reasoning on truth (of statements) and trust (of sources) are often intertwined. Not surprisingly, joint inference methods, based on probabilistic models, have been pursued to this end (e.g., [16,42,48,49]).

3   Challenges

Notwithstanding the great advances of knowledge harvesting over the last decade, there are major challenges left open – raising the bar for what computers should know. In the following, we discuss a few strategic challenges, pointing out opportunities for future research.

3.1   Knowledge Base Coverage

No matter how large a KB can grow, it will never be fully complete. The gaps, relative to an ideal KB, take different forms as discussed next.

Locally Incomplete Knowledge: This form of incompleteness can be formally characterized by referring to SPO triples that are in the KB and triples that should ideally be included but are missing. The most obvious case is when some O values are absent for a given S and P value – for example, when the KB contains some movies of a director but not all of them. Another case is when for a given P value, we have O values for some S but not all of them – for example, knowing spouses of some people but not knowing any spouses for other married people. The challenge here is not just to fill these gaps, but to realize when and where gaps exist. Reasoning over locally closed worlds is one recent approach [22]. More research is needed to equip KB's with self-reflection abilities to automatically detect their own gaps.

Long-tail Entities and Classes: There are many lesser known musicians, regional politicians and good but not exactly famous scientists. How can we identify these long-tail entities in the Internet, and harvest facts about them? Long-tail classes pose a similar problem: even with hundred thousands of classes in some KB's, one could always add more interesting ones. For example, what if we want to capture classes like `YogaPractitioners` or `BobDylanFans` (both of which would have Steve Jobs as a member)? Where in the class taxonomy should these classes be placed, and how can we find their instances?

Missing Facts: KB's have largely been constructed in an opportunistic manner, tapping into Wikipedia and its semi-structured data elements. If something is not explicitly said in Wikipedia or stated only in sophisticated form in the article's text, most KB's will miss it. This has resulted in high coverage of elementary facts like birthdates, marriages, albums of musicians, etc., but has neglected a diversity of salient facts that stand out to a human but are not easily captured by a machine. For example, what is notable about Bob Dylan's album Blonde on Blonde? KB's offer the release date, the list of songs, etc. To a human, however, salient properties are, for example, that this was one of the first albums on which Dylan "went electric" (using electric instruments – irritating many of his folk music fans), and that its song "Sad Eyed Lady of the Lowlands" is about Dylan's wife Sara. The song was later covered by Joan Baez, who had a romantic relationship with Bob Dylan in the early 1960s and with Steve Jobs in the early 1980s. Her song "Diamonds and Rust" is about Bob Dylan. None of this is captured by any KB; most do not even have the proper predicates like `romanceWith` or `songIsAbout`.

3.2   Commonsense, Rules and Socio-Cultural Knowledge

Automatically constructed KB's have mostly focused on harvesting encyclopedic fact knowledge. However, for semantic search and other intelligent applications (e.g., conversational bots in social media), machines need a broader understanding of the world: properties of everyday objects, human activities, plausibility invariants and more. This overriding goal calls for various research directions.

Commonsense: One objective is to distill commonsense from Internet sources. This is about properties of objects like size, color, shape, parts or substance of which an object is made of, etc., and knowledge on which objects are used for which activities as well as when and where certain activities typically happen. For example, a rock concert involves musicians, instruments – almost always including drums and guitars, speakers, a microphone for the singer; the typical location is a stage, and so on. This background knowledge is beneficial for the interpretation of user questions, and also for retrieving images and videos when queries refer to abstractions or emotions that cannot be directly matched by captions, tags or other text. Today's search engines perform poorly on queries such as "exhausted band at hippie concert" (where users may want to find footage of concerts by the Grateful Dead or the Doors). Recent work on acquiring commonsense includes ConceptNet [58] and WebChild [64]; research with the specific focus of organizing knowledge on human activities includes [65]. There is, however, still a long way to go for computers to learn what every child knows.

Visual Knowledge: Commonsense knowledge is often more expressed in visual form than in textual sources; for example, think of colors, shapes and sizes of objects. This observation entails the dual goals of (i) tapping visual contents like images and videos for acquiring knowledge and (ii) constructing a KB *about* visual properties. Along the latter lines, ImageNet [13] is the most notable endeavor, which has populated a large fraction of WordNet classes with images.

The NEIL project [8] has a gone a step further by extracting visual relationships between objects. WebChild has acquired different kinds of part-whole knowledge, at large scale, from combining textual and visual cues [66]. This is an instantiation of the general challenge of jointly distilling knowledge from vision and language (e.g., from movie scenes and their narratives [54]).

Rules: Another key element for advancing the intelligent behavior of machines is to capture invariants over certain kinds of facts, in the form of logical rules. For example, a rule about scientists and their advisors could state that the advisor be on the faculty of the scientist's alma mater – as of the time when the scientist graduated. Similarly to the role of constraints in fact cleaning (see Sect. 2.2.4), rules can have exceptions. But regardless of their soft nature, rules can be a great asset to answer more queries and to infer additional facts for *KB completion*. For example, a person who has or had a position on the government of a certain country, is most likely a citizen of that country. To acquire this kind of intensional knowledge, rule mining methods have been applied to large KB's [21]. However, the state of the art has major limitations: rules are restricted in their logical form to Horn clauses or at least clauses. This disallows rules with existential quantifiers or with disjunctions in the rule head; for example, expressing that every human person has a mother and that every human is male or female, would be beyond the current scope. An alternative approach to KB completion, which bypasses logical representations, is to start with a tensor of SPO triples and use matrix or tensor factorization methods to predict additional triples (similarly to recommender systems) [45]. However, the derivation of new facts is not easily explainable with such methods.

Commonsense rules were already in the focus of the seminal Cyc project [35], but Cyc relied on human experts to manually specify logical axioms. A major challenge with automatic rule mining arises from the *open world assumption* that underlies KB's and the *bias in observations* from Internet sources. For example, if a KB does not contain any person who has won two different Nobel prizes, this should not imply a functionality constraint or cardinality constraint. In fact, Marie Curie is a counterexample anyway, but some KB's may have only a partial list of her awards. Likewise, a KB may have a restricted view on the wealth of entrepreneurs: for example, all founders of IT companies have become billionaires. This can be caused by the bias in the KB construction (e.g., by harvesting only successful entrepreneurs from Wikipedia), and should not entail a rule in the open world.

Socio-Cultural Knowledge: Another dimension where today's KB's have a huge gap is the socio-cultural context of facts or rules. Consider statements on people making discoveries and inventions. On first glance, one would expect that these are objective and universally agreed upon. On second thought, however, it becomes clear that it depends on the background and viewpoint of users. For example, most people in the US would say that the computer was invented by Eckert and Mauchley, whereas a German would give the credit to Konrad Zuse and a British may point out Alan Turing (or perhaps Charles Babbage). This depends not just on geographical context; for example, teenagers may widely think of Steve Jobs as the (re-) inventor of the (mobile) computer. For common-sense knowledge, it is even more critical to capture socio-cultural contexts. For example, shaking hands when people meet is the usual way of welcoming some-one only in parts of the world. In other regions, people often hug or kiss each other (e.g., in France), or make gestures with both hands (e.g., in Thailand).

4   Conclusion

Knowledge harvesting has made great impact in enabling the automatic con-struction of large knowledge bases, sometimes called knowledge graphs. These have become essential assets in search and analytics over Internet contents and enterprise data. In addition to reviewing the underlying methodological achieve-ments, this article has pointed out open challenges towards the next level of machine knowledge.

The success of deep learning, to enable smart computer behavior by training on raw data, may open up new perspectives on knowledge harvesting as well. Do computers need this kind of explicit knowledge representation at all, or is task-specific end-to-end learning in a sub-symbolic manner sufficient? We believe that machine knowledge and machine learning are complementary assets: the more you know the better you learn, and better learning enables acquiring more and deeper knowledge. A final challenge and research opportunity is to explore this potential synergy.

References

1. Agichtein, E., Gravano, L.: Snowball: extracting relations from large plain-text collections. In: ACM DL (2000)
2. Auer, S., Bizer, C., Kobilarov, G., Lehmann, J., Cyganiak, R., Ives, Z.: DBpedia: a nucleus for a web of open data. In: Aberer, K., et al. (eds.) ASWC/ISWC - 2007. LNCS, vol. 4825, pp. 722–735. Springer, Heidelberg (2007). https://doi.org/10.1007/978-3-540-76298-0_52
3. Banko, M., et al.: Open information extraction from the web. In: IJCAI (2007)
4. Bast, H., Buchhold, B., Haussmann, E.: Semantic search on text and knowledge bases. Found. Trends Inf. Retrieval 10(2–3) (2016)
5. Bollacker, K., et al.: Freebase: a collaboratively created graph database for struc-turing human knowledge. In: SIGMOD (2008)
6. Brin, S.: Extracting patterns and relations from the world wide web. In: Atzeni, P., Mendelzon, A., Mecca, G. (eds.) WebDB 1998. LNCS, vol. 1590, pp. 172–183. Springer, Heidelberg (1999). https://doi.org/10.1007/10704656_11
7. Carlson, A.J., et al.: Toward an architecture for never-ending language learning. In: AAAI (2010)
8. Chen, X., Shrivastava, A., Gupta, A.: NEIL: extracting visual knowledge from web data. In: ICCV (2013)
9. Chiticariu, L., Li, Y., Reiss, F.: Transparent machine learning for information extraction: state-of-the-art and the future. In: EMNLP (Tutorial) (2015)
10. Craven, M., et al.: Learning to construct knowledge bases from the world wide web. Art. Intell. 118(1) (2000)

11. Dalvi, N., et al.: A web of concepts. In: PODS (2009)
12. Del Corro, L., Gemulla, R.: ClausIE: clause-based open information extraction. In: WWW 2013 (2013)
13. Deng, J., et al.: ImageNet: a large-scale hierarchical image database. In: CVPR (2009)
14. Domingos, P., Lowd, D.: Markov Logic: An Interface Layer for Artificial Intelligence. Morgan & Claypool, San Rafael (2009)
15. Dong, X.L., et al.: Knowledge vault: a web-scale approach to probabilistic knowledge fusion. In: KDD (2014)
16. Dong, X.L., et al.: Knowledge-based trust: estimating the trustworthiness of web sources. PVLDB **8**(9) (2015)
17. Ernst, P., et al.: KnowLife: a versatile approach for constructing a large knowledge graph for biomedical sciences. BMC Bioinform. **16**(157) (2015)
18. Etzioni, O., et al.: Unsupervised named-entity extraction from the web: an experimental study. Art. Intell. **165**(1) (2005)
19. Fellbaum, C., Miller, G.: WordNet: An Electronic Lexical Database. MIT Press, Cambridge (1998)
20. Galarraga, L., et al.: Canonicalizing open knowledge bases. In: CIKM (2014)
21. Galarraga, L., et al.: Fast rule mining in ontological knowledge bases with AMIE+. VLDB J. **24**(6) (2015)
22. Galarraga, L., et al.: Predicting completeness in knowledge bases. In: WSDM (2017)
23. Hearst, M.: Automatic acquisition of hyponyms from large text corpora. In: COLING (1992)
24. Heath, T., Bizer, C.: Linked Data: Evolving the Web into a Global Data Space. Morgan & Claypool, San Rafael (2011)
25. Hoffart, J., et al.: YAGO2: a spatially and temporally enhanced knowledge base from wikipedia. Art. Intell. **194** (2013)
26. Hoffart, J., Altun, Y., Weikum, G.: Discovering emerging entities with ambiguous names. In: WWW 2014 (2014)
27. Hoffart, J., et al.: The knowledge awakens: keeping knowledge bases fresh with emerging entities. In: WWW 2016 (2016)
28. Ferrucci, D.A.: "This is Watson". IBM J. Res. Dev. **56**(3/4) (2012). Special Issue
29. Kobren, A., et al.: Getting more for less: optimized crowdsourcing with dynamic tasks and goals. In: WWW 2015 (2015)
30. Koller, D., Friedman, N.: Probabilistic Graphical Models. MIT Press, Cambridge (2009)
31. Kozareva, Z., Hovy, E.H.: Learning arguments and supertypes of semantic relations using recursive patterns. In: ACL (2010)
32. Krause, S., Li, H., Uszkoreit, H., Xu, F.: Large-scale learning of relation-extraction rules with distant supervision from the web. In: Cudré-Mauroux, P., et al. (eds.) ISWC 2012. LNCS, vol. 7649, pp. 263–278. Springer, Heidelberg (2012). https://doi.org/10.1007/978-3-642-35176-1_17
33. LeCun, Y., Bengio, Y., Hinton, G.: Deep learning. Nature **521** (2015)
34. Lenat, D., Feigenbaum, E.: On the thresholds of knowledge. Art. Intell. **47**(1) (1991)
35. Lenat, D.: CYC: a large-scale investment in knowledge infrastructure. Commun. ACM **38**(11) (1995)
36. Li, Y., et al.: A survey on truth discovery. SIGKDD Explor. **17**(2) (2015)
37. Ling, X., Weld, D.: Temporal information extraction. In: AAAI (2010)

38. Ling, X., Singh, S., Weld, D.: Design challenges for entity linking. TACL **3** (2015)
39. Mausam, et al.: Open language learning for information extraction. In: EMNLP-CoNLL (2012)
40. Mintz, M., et al.: Distant supervision for relation extraction without labeled data. In: ACL/IJCNLP (2009)
41. Mitchell, T., et al.: Never-ending learning. In: AAAI (2015)
42. Mukherjee, S., Weikum, G., Danescu-Niculescu-Mizil, C.: People on drugs: credibility of user statements in health communities. In: KDD (2014)
43. Nakashole, N., Theobald, M., Weikum, G.: Scalable knowledge harvesting with high precision and high recall. In: WSDM (2011)
44. Navigli, R., Ponzetto, S.: BabelNet: the automatic construction, evaluation and application of a wide-coverage multilingual semantic network. Art. Intell. **193** (2012)
45. Nickel, M., et al.: A review of relational machine learning for knowledge graphs. Proc. IEEE **104**(1) (2016)
46. Nie, Z., Wen, J.-R., Ma, W.-Y.: Statistical entity extraction from the web. Proc. IEEE **100**(9) (2012)
47. Pasca, M.: Open-domain fine-grained class extraction from web search queries. In: EMNLP (2013)
48. Pasternack, J., Roth, D.: Latent credibility analysis. In: WWW 2013 (2013)
49. Popat, K., et al.: Where the truth lies: explaining the credibility of emerging claims on the web and social media. In: WWW 2017 (2017)
50. Ponzetto, S., Strube, M.: Deriving a large-scale taxonomy from wikipedia. In: AAAI (2007)
51. Preda, N., et al.: Active knowledge: dynamically enriching RDF knowledge bases by web services. In: SIGMOD (2010)
52. Pujara, J., Miao, H., Getoor, L., Cohen, W.: Knowledge graph identification. In: Alani, H., Kagal, L., Fokoue, A., Groth, P., Biemann, C., Parreira, J.X., Aroyo, L., Noy, N., Welty, C., Janowicz, K. (eds.) ISWC 2013. LNCS, vol. 8218, pp. 542–557. Springer, Heidelberg (2013). https://doi.org/10.1007/978-3-642-41335-3_34
53. Rebele, T., Suchanek, F., Hoffart, J., Biega, J., Kuzey, E., Weikum, G.: YAGO: a multilingual knowledge base from wikipedia, wordnet, and geonames. In: Groth, P., et al. (eds.) ISWC 2016. LNCS, vol. 9982, pp. 177–185. Springer, Cham (2016). https://doi.org/10.1007/978-3-319-46547-0_19
54. Rohrbach, A., et al.: A dataset for movie description. In: CVPR (2015)
55. Sarawagi, S.: Information extraction. Found. Trends Databases **1**(3) (2008)
56. Shen, W., Wang, J., Han, J.: Entity linking with a knowledge base: issues, techniques, and solutions. IEEE Trans. Knowl. Data Eng. **27**(2) (2015)
57. Shin, J., et al.: Incremental knowledge base construction using deepdive. PVLDB **8**(11) (2015)
58. Speer, R., Havasi, C.: Representing general relational knowledge in ConceptNet 5. In: LREC (2012)
59. Staab, S., Studer, R.: Handbook on Ontologies. Springer, Heidelberg (2009)
60. Suchanek, F., Kasneci, G., Weikum, G.: YAGO: a core of semantic knowledge. In: WWW 2007 (2007)
61. Suchanek, F., Sozio, M., Weikum, G.: SOFIE: a self-organizing framework for information extraction. In: WWW 2009 (2009)
62. Talaika, A., et al.: IBEX: harvesting entities from the web using unique identifiers. In: WebDB 2015 (2015)
63. Talukdar, P., Wijaya, D., Mitchell, T.: Coupled temporal scoping of relational facts. In: WSDM 2012 (2012)

64. Tandon, N., et al.: WebChild: harvesting and organizing commonsense knowledge from the web. In: WSDM (2014)
65. Tandon, N., et al.: Knowlywood: mining activity knowledge from hollywood narratives. In: CIKM (2015)
66. Tandon, N., et al.: Commonsense in parts: mining part-whole relations from the web and image tags. In: AAAI 2016 (2016)
67. Venetis, P., et al.: Recovering semantics of tables on the web. PVLDB 4(9) (2011)
68. Vrandecic, D., Krötzsch, M.: Wikidata: a free collaborative knowledgebase. Commun. ACM 57(10) (2014)
69. Wang, R., Cohen, W.: Iterative set expansion of named entities using the web. In: ICDM (2008)
70. Wang, Z., et al.: XLore: a large-scale English-Chinese bilingual knowledge graph. In: ISWC (2013)
71. Wang, Y., et al.: Coupling label propagation and constraints for temporal fact extraction. In: ACL (2012)
72. Wu, F., Hoffmann, R., Weld, D.: Information extraction from wikipedia: moving down the long tail. In: KDD (2008)
73. Wu, W., et al.: Probase: a probabilistic taxonomy for text understanding. In: SIGMOD (2012)
74. Yao, L., et al.: Structured relation discovery using generative models. In: EMNLP (2011)
75. Zhu, J., et al.: StatSnowball: a statistical approach to extracting entity relationships. In: WWW 2009 (2009)

Methods, Languages and Tools for Future System Development

Methods, Languages and Tools for Future System Development

Bernhard Steffen[✉]

Chair for Programming Systems, TU Dortmund University, Dortmund, Germany
steffen@cs.tu-dortmund.de

Abstract. Language design for simplifying programming, analysis/verification methods and tools for guaranteeing, for example, security and real-time constraints, and validation environments for increasing automation during quality assurance can all be regarded as means to factor out and generically solve specific concerns of the software development process and then reuse the corresponding solutions. In this sense, reuse, a guiding engineering principle, appears as a unifying theme in software science, and it is not surprising that the corresponding research is continuously converging. The following summary of the contributions of the second topical part of the celebration volume LNCS 10,000 aims at establishing a common perspective and indicating the state and progress of this convergence.

Keywords: Programming languages and paradigms
Integrated Development Environments · Domain-Specific Languages
Modeling · Simulation · Cyber-Physical Systems · Bootstraping
Deductive verification · Static analysis · Proactive/reactive security
Software architecture · Model checking · Markov decision processes
Continuous time models · Strategy/controller synthesis
Statistical model checking · Rare Events · Runtime verification
Fuzzing · Test generation · (Dynamic) symbolic execution
Monitoring · Specification mining · Automata learning
Register automata

1 Introduction

Technical progress does not necessarily mean conceptual improvement, as summarized by Dijkstra [9]: "*as long as there were no machines, programming was no problem at all; when we had a few weak computers, programming became a mild problem, and now we have gigantic computers,[1] programming has become an equally gigantic problem*". This quote from 1972, which expresses Dijkstra's frustration in having to deal with increasingly powerful, but also increasingly

---

[1] This perspective underlines the "miracle" of the last few decades. Nobody would have predicted the recent 'digital revolution' in 1972, neither in its technical, let alone in its social dimension.

© Springer Nature Switzerland AG 2019
B. Steffen and G. Woeginger (Eds.): Computing and Software Science, LNCS 10000, pp. 239–249, 2019.
https://doi.org/10.1007/978-3-319-91908-9_14

difficult-to-handle machinery, embodies an important message to software scientists, the quest for *simplicity*[2], a message even more important today.

Of course, there is no general agreement on what to consider simple, but people understand that things become simpler for them when their task is reduced, for example, they only have to take care of the functionality of a program, but not the user interface, the underlying security mechanism, or the performance. In this sense, the change in software development from a 'one-man show' to a coordinated collaborative enterprise involving different kinds of stakeholders responsible for different aspects, like required functionality, security, real-time guarantees, quality assurance, platform specifics, etc., is clearly a simplicity improvement. On the other hand, this change imposes a challenge: how to reliably manage or coordinate this collaborative effort.

This is a good example of trade-offs, which are omnipresent in computer science. Typical are the three dimensions time vs. space, precision vs. performance, and generality vs. ease. Another dimension of trade-off, language abstraction vs. complexity of compilation, illustrates an important paradigm of software science, reuse: the complexity of writing a compiler typically pays off because of its high amount of reuse. In fact, there are interesting (re)use-oriented ways of solving trade-off dilemmas. For example, in the 1990s, Microsoft became 'famous' for treating the quality vs. time-to-market lemma by exploiting its millions of users as testers, an approach also responsible for the often surprisingly high quality of open source software. The *"release early and release often"* slogan of the *perpetual beta* paradigm[3] underlying many of Google's applications seems, indeed, to be adequate for many of today's fast-moving applications. In fact, the power of this approach to quality assurance is a direct consequence of the high amount of (re)use, be it the (re)use of Microsoft Office to, for example, write texts, of Google Maps or the (re)use of (generic) modules of an open source library: the higher the amount of (re)use, the more intense the testing, and the better the quality.

The quest for reuse is in fact one of the driving forces of software science: how to solve certain tasks once and for all? In particular, when combined with the popular divide-and-conquer approach this allows one to factor out and then solve repetitive tasks. Ideally, in the long run, this leads to libraries of generalized solutions whose quality increases with the frequency of (re)use.

Fifty years back, when the term *software engineering* was coined [25][4] nobody would have imagined that the then anticipated *software crisis* would largely be tamed by a sociological change: today's library-based software development is

---

[2] In [24] simplicity is emphasized as an important indicator of maturity.

[3] Cf., Sect. 4 *"End of the Software Release Cycle."* of [26].

[4] It is interesting to read today that during the preparation of the famous NATO Software Engineering Conference in 1968 in Garmisch-Partenkirchen *"The phrase 'software engineering' was deliberately chosen as being provocative, in implying the need for software manufacture to be based on the types of theoretical foundations and practical disciplines, that are traditional in the established branches of engineering."*

a community effort which does not only increase the development performance but also the software quality.

The concept of reuse inherent in software science comprises, however, much more than the reuse of, for example, components provided by a software library: effort spent on the development of powerful programming or modeling languages and their corresponding Integrated Development Environments (IDEs) or on validation and verification tools has a much bigger but often underestimated reuse potential. Programmers are often not aware of the wealth of formal methods technologies they are relying on. Today's complex IDEs comprise many such technologies in order to provide, for example, syntax-based guidance, type-checking, model checking, and sophisticated validation and debugging support. In fact, using runtime verification technology this support also continues after deployment. It is this general kind of reuse we rely on today when building systems of a complexity far beyond what the participants of the software engineering conference in Garmisch-Partenkirchen in 1968 could have imagined.

The following three sections discuss the contributions of this topical part of the volume according to which concept of reuse they support. In this discussion, automation is considered a particularly powerful means of reuse.

2 Languages

The evolution of programming and modeling languages and their corresponding IDEs has an enormous impact on the productivity of software developers. For example, depending on the chosen language paradigm[5], solutions to certain programming tasks may differ drastically. It is therefore not surprising that new language proposals try to embed the essential parts of all paradigms in one comprehensive language in order to allow programmers to elegantly and efficiently solve conceptually different tasks without switching context. Leveraging the enormous power of such 'super' languages, however, is not easy. It requires 'super' developers who not only need to master all the individual paradigms involved, but who must also understand how these different paradigms may interfere.

A complementary line of programming language research aims at a dedicated system development targeting specific domains. Resulting (often called domain-specific) languages typically provide a much stronger development support where applicable, but at the price of an often strongly reduced area of application. The three chapters sketched in the following three paragraphs (1) discuss what makes a programming language successful, (2) present a dedicated domain-specific environment for modeling and simulating cyber-physical systems based on Julia, a programming language designed to support numerical computation, and (3) propose a style of (software) system development which is based on the systematic design of domain-specific (modeling) languages.

---

[5] Classically imperative (which today comprises object-oriented), functional and declarative programming were distinguished.

The Next 7000 Programming Languages [6] can be regarded as a retrospective view on Peter Landin's seminal paper "The next 700 programming languages" of 1966 [22] under the Darwinistic perspective of the 'survival of the fittest'. Considering the features (genes) of these languages and how they fared in the past it discusses the divergence between the languages empirically used in 2017 and the language features one might have expected if the languages of the 1960s had evolved optimally to fill programming niches. In particular it characterizes three divergences, or 'elephants in the room', where actual current language use, or feature provision, differs from that which evolution might suggest: the immortality of C, the renaissance of dynamically typed languages, and the chaotic treatment of parallelism. Thus rather than predicting the convergence towards a universal programming language corresponding to Landin's ISWIM, the authors foresee an increased productivity of software development due to fast evolution of (niche-specific) language-supporting tooling.

While the next paragraph talks about such a concrete domain/niche-specific, tool-supported language, the last paragraph of this section sketches a new system engineering approach based on the systematic construction of domain-specific development environments.

Multi-mode DAE Models – Challenges, Theory and Implementation [3] considers the domain of modeling and simulation of Cyber-Physical Systems (CPS) such as robots, vehicles, and power plants. Characteristic here is that CPS models are *multi-mode* in the sense that their structure may change during simulation due to the desired operation, due to failure situations or due to changes in physical conditions. The approach presented in the chapter focuses on multi-mode Differential Algebraic Equations (DAEs), and, in particular, on the problem of how to switch from one mode to another when the number of equations may change and variables may exhibit impulsive behavior. The new methods presented to solve this problem are evaluated with both the experimental modeling and simulation system Modia, a domain specific language extension of the programming language Julia, and SunDAE, a novel structural analysis library for multi-mode DAE systems.

The following quote taken from [10] indicates that languages like Modia are still exceptions, and that domain-specific support is still rare in general: "*Programming language research is short of its ultimate goal – provide software developers tools for formulating solutions in the languages of problem domains*". The ambitions of the chapter sketched below go even beyond this goal.

Language-Driven Engineering: From General Purpose to Purpose-Specific Languages [30] presents a paradigm characterized by its unique support for division of labor based on stakeholder-specific Domain-Specific Languages (DSLs). Language-Driven Engineering (LDE) allows the involved stakeholders, including the application experts, to participate in the system development and evolution process using DSLs supporting their domain-specific mindset. In the considered proof-of-concept, the interplay between the involved DSLs is technically realized in a service-oriented fashion which eases system evolution through introduction and exchange of entire DSLs. The authors argue for the potential of this approach by pointing at the widely available, typically graphical DSLs used in the various fields of application that can be enriched to satisfy the LDE requirements. For an economic technical realization they refer to the bootstrapping[6] effect, a recursive form of reuse, when considering the construction of corresponding development environments as the domain of interest.

The power and practicality of a programming/modeling language strongly depend on the power of the corresponding IDE. The following two sections provide an impression of powerful methods and tools that may be integrated in future IDEs to enhance the software development process.

3   Verification Methods and Tools

The mathematical roots of computer science are nicely reflected in the very early attempts to formally prove the correctness of programs [11,16]. Here, the inductive assertion method, and Hoare's syntax-driven proof organization can be regarded as means to reduce the manual effort in a reuse fashion. Today's deductive program verification reflects 50 years of research in this direction. The chapter sketched in the next paragraph provides a comprehensive overview of the recent corresponding development, whereas the subsequent paragraphs essentially exploit the abstract interpretation paradigm [8] to reduce the considered problem scenarios to decidable ones. This move toward decidable scenarios can be regarded as a transition from *weaker* formal methods to *stronger* formal methods in the sense of Wolper [32].

Deductive Verification: From Pen-and-Paper Proofs to Industrial Tools [15] provides a retrospective view on the development of deductive software verification, the discipline aiming at formally verifying that all possible behaviors of a given program satisfy formally defined, possibly complex properties, where the verification process is based on logical inference. Following the trajectory of the field from its inception in the late 1960s via its current state to its promises for the future, from pen-and-paper proofs for programs written in small, idealized languages to highly automated proofs of complex library or system code written in mainstream languages, the chapter establishes the state-of-the-art and provides a list of the most important challenges for the further development of the field. Of practical importance are, in particular, the integration of methods and tools in existing software production environments in order to support easy (re)use and exchange.

Deductive verification is known to be extremely labor intensive which led to the rule of thumb: "A verified program equals a PhD thesis". In contrast, static analysis, the topic of the next paragraph, originally aimed at compiler optimization and therefore had to be highly efficient.

Static Analysis for Proactive Security [18] reflects on current problems and practices in system security, distinguishing between *reactive* security – which

---

[6] An impressive illustration of the power of bootstrapping is Futamura's partial evaluation-based approach [12,20].

deals with vulnerabilities as they are being exploited – and *proactive* security – which aims to make vulnerabilities un-exploitable by removing them from a system entirely. It is argued that static analysis is well positioned to support approaches to proactive security, since it is sufficiently expressive to represent many vulnerabilities yet sufficiently efficient to detect vulnerabilities prior to system deployment, and it interacts well with both confidentiality and integrity aspects. In particular, static analysis can be used to provide proactive security concerning some models, such as those for access control. This indicates a high reuse potential for static analyzers tuned for certain security models. Interestingly, the chapter also hints at bootstrapping-based reuse: the static analysis of the static analyzer. That verifiers/analyzers should themselves be verified is an inevitable future requirement.

There is a strong link between static analysis and model checking which can even be exploited to automatically generate efficient static analysis algorithms via partial evaluation of a model checker for the specifying temporal formula [28]. This emphasizes the high reuse potential for model checkers. On the other hand, the wide range of application scenarios led to a wealth of model-checking methods and tools, all with their specific application profile.

In 1995, the year when LNCS celebrated its 1000th issue, a layered architecture to help manage the plurality of model checking methods was proposed [29]. This architecture was elaborated in [31] to even synthesize, for example, specialized model checkers from a temporal specification on the basis of a component library. The chapter sketched in the next paragraph presents a three-tier architecture particularly emphasizing the integration of multiple input languages and back-end analyzers.

Software Architecture of Modern Model-Checkers [21] summarizes the recent trends in the design and architecture of model checking tools and proposes a concrete architecture specifically designed to support many input languages (front-end) and many verification strategies (back-end). In this architecture, a common intermediate layer – either in the form of an intermediate language or a common API – is used to mediate between the many, often domain-specific input languages for both systems and properties, and the corresponding variants of model checking tools implementing different verification technologies. (Re)using this intermediate layer allows one to easily add further languages and tools just by hooking onto this layer. The impact of this approach is impressively illustrated with application examples for LTSmin, and the difference between the language and API variant of the intermediate layer is discussed according to their practical implications. Altogether the chapter contributes to the alignment of and leverages synergies between model checking methods and tools.

The following two paragraphs sketch chapters that focus on more domain-specific verification scenarios: Markov decision processes and continuous-time models. The presented methods provide dedicated support for their respective fields of application, but are constrained in their range of reuse.

The 10,000 Facets of MDP Model Checking [2] presents how probabilistic model checking can be applied to Markov Decision Processes (MDP), which have a wide range of application areas ranging from stochastic and dynamic optimization problems to robotics. Given an MDP and a property ϕ written in some probabilistic logic, MDP model checking fully automatically determines all states of the MDP that satisfy property ϕ. If successful, MDP model checking additionally provides optimal policies as a by-product of verification. For robotics, this by-product can be exploited to synthesize optimal strategies for tasks in uncertain environments that are specified in terms of a probabilistic logic. This nicely illustrates the close relationship between checking-based approaches that control whether certain properties are guaranteed or can be satisfied, and methods for property enforcement that aim at synthesizing property conforming solutions.

Continuous-time Models for System Design and Analysis [1] illustrates the ingredients of the state-of-the-art of the model-based approach for the formal design and verification of cyber-physical systems. To capture the interaction between a discrete controller and its continuously evolving environment, formal models of timed and hybrid automata are used. The approach is illustrated via step-wise modeling and verification using the tools Uppaal and SpaceEx with a case study based on a dual-chamber implantable pacemaker monitoring a human heart. In particular, it is shown how to design a model as a composition of components, how to construct models at varying levels of detail, how to establish that one model is an abstraction of another, how to specify correctness requirements using temporal logic, and how to verify that a model satisfies a logical requirement. The chapter closes with a discussion of directions for future research and specific challenges, like the combination with probabilistic methods such as those addressed in the previous paragraph.

A common hurdle for the application of model checking based technologies is the state explosion problem: the models to be considered grow exponentially with the number of their variables and parallel components. Bounded model checking has been proposed as a heuristic to overcome this problem [7]. An alternative heuristic is addressed in the chapter sketched in the next paragraph which treats the state explosion in a statistical, some people would say in a Monte Carlo-like, fashion.

Statistical Model Checking [23] is a verification technology for quantitative models of computer systems like the MDP discussed above. In contrast to classical verification, which provides yes/no-answers as a response to a verification task, statistical model checking answers probabilistically, indicating how well the considered system satisfies the property in question. An important challenge here is the treatment of *Rare Events*: What happens when the probability that S satisfies a certain property is extremely small? The proposed techniques to address this problem, *Importance Sampling* and *Importance Splitting*, are then also employed for optimal planning, and later further refined to obtain optimal control. The technical development of the corresponding synthesis algorithms is evaluated using the problem of changing a flock of birds from an initial random configuration into a V-formation. Finally, introducing the notion of *V-formation games*, it is shown how to ward off cyber-physical attacks.

Similar to testing, statistical model checking does not suffer the state explosion problem. However, looking at the technique from the verification perspective, we note that the guarantees achieved are only statistically valid, and the value of this validity very much depends on assumptions about adequate probability distributions. Seen from the testing perspective, however, statistical model checking establishes, where applicable, a frequency-sensitive quality measure, different to the usual coverage metrics traditionally used in testing which typically treat all statements alike.

The three chapters sketched in the next section elaborate on formal methods-based, dynamic (testing-oriented) technologies in a different fashion.

4   Validation: Testing and Beyond

In general, testing cannot be done exhaustively. Thus one has to find adequate ways for test selection [13]. Whereas the first of the chapters sketched in the following three paragraphs directly addresses how to automate the test selection process, the other two focus on how to maximize the information produced when running a system and how to automatically infer behavioral models from test runs, respectively.

Automated Software Test Generation: Some Challenges, Solutions, and Recent Advances [5] discusses automated test generation from a practical perspective. After explaining random testing and input fuzzing, the chapter turns to test generation via dynamic symbolic execution, whose precision improves over 'traditional', for example, coverage-heuristics-based test generation approaches. In order to explain inherent trade-offs of the new approach, the chapter describes the operation of a symbolic execution engine with a worklist-style algorithm, before it addresses individual challenges like good search heuristics for loops, summaries and state merging, efficient constraint solving, and parallelization. Subsequently, it presents the white-box fuzzing system SAGE and the selective symbolic execution system SSE, Microsoft's prime tools for revealing security vulnerabilities in, for example, Microsoft Windows. Whether or not other application domains justify the use of the quite heavy machinery presented in this chapter depends on the concrete situation.

Runtime verification borrows ideas from deductive verification to analyze and possibly control a system while it is running, or to analyze a system execution post-mortem. This overcomes typical decidability or performance problems of (deductive) verification, however at the price that errors may be detected too late: what should be done if an automatic pilot reaches a property violation? Handing over to a human pilot may not always be sufficient. The chapter sketched in the following paragraph provides insights into this multi-faceted research field.

Runtime Verification – Past Experiences and Future Projections [14] provides an overview of the work performed by the authors since the year 2000 in the field of *runtime verification*. Runtime verification is the discipline of analyzing program/system executions using rigorous methods. The discipline covers topics such as (1) specification-based monitoring, where single executions are checked against formal specifications; (2) predictive runtime analysis, where properties about a system are predicted/inferred from single (good) executions; (3) fault protection, where monitors actively protect a running system against errors; (4) specification mining from execution traces; (5) visualization of execution traces; and to be fully general (6) computation of any interesting information from execution traces. The chapter attempts to draw lessons learned from this work, and to project expectations for the future of the field.

The final chapter discusses automata learning, which, from a practical perspective, can be regarded as a form of test-based modeling [27]. Whereas its strong links to testing are also discussed in [4], its applicability to runtime verification was demonstrated in [19].

Combining Black-Box and White-Box Techniques for Learning Register Automata [17] presents model learning, a black-box technique for constructing state machine models of software and hardware components, which has been successfully used in areas such as telecommunication, network protocols, and control software. The underlying theoretical framework (active automata learning) was first introduced by Dana Angluin for finite state machines. In practice, scalability to larger models of increased expressivity is important. Recently, techniques have been developed for learning models which combine control flow with guards and assignments. Inferring the required guards and assignments just from observations of the test output is extremely costly. The chapter discusses how black-box model learning can be enhanced using often available white-box information, with the aim to maintain the benefits of dynamic black-box methods while making effective use of information that can be obtained through, for example, static analysis and symbolic execution.

5   Conclusions

We have summarized the chapters of the topical part 'Languages, Methods and Tools for Future System Development' under the unifying perspective of reuse. It appears that the individual contributions can be regarded as different answers to trade-offs such as (1) generic vs. domain-specific, (2) manual vs. automatic, (3) static vs. dynamic, (4) post mortem vs. by construction, (5) statistical vs. absolute, etc. The continuum of the solution space for responding to these trade-offs constitutes, at the same time, the space for the convergence of the described methods. We are convinced that this space will be investigated much more systematically in the future, leading to tailored solutions exploiting the characteristics of given circumstances, in a way similar to the methods for combining black-box and white-box knowledge presented in the last chapter of this celebration volume.

References

1. Alur, R., Giacobbe, M., Henzinger, T., Larsen, K., Mikučionis, M.: Continuous-time models for system design and analysis. In: Steffen, B., Woeginger, G. (eds.) Computing and Software Science. LNCS, vol. 10000, pp. 452–477. Springer, Heidelberg (2018)
2. Baier, C., Hermanns, H., Katoen, J.P.: The 10,000 facets of MDP model checking. In: Steffen, B., Woeginger, G. (eds.) Computing and Software Science. LNCS, vol. 10000, pp. 420–451. Springer, Heidelberg (2018)
3. Benveniste, A., Caillaud, B., Elmqvist, H., Ghorbal, K., Otter, M., Pouzet, M.: Multi-Mode DAE models - challenges, theory and implementation. In: Steffen, B., Woeginger, G. (eds.) Computing and Software Science. LNCS, vol. 10000, pp. 283–310. Springer, Heidelberg (2018)
4. Berg, T., Grinchtein, O., Jonsson, B., Leucker, M., Raffelt, H., Steffen, B.: On the correspondence between conformance testing and regular inference. In: Cerioli, M. (ed.) FASE 2005. LNCS, vol. 3442, pp. 175–189. Springer, Heidelberg (2005). https://doi.org/10.1007/978-3-540-31984-9_14
5. Candea, G., Godefroid, P.: Automated software test generation: some challenges, solutions, and recent advances. In: Steffen, B., Woeginger, G. (eds.) Computing and Software Science. LNCS, vol. 10000, pp. 505–531. Springer, Heidelberg (2018)
6. Chatley, R., Donaldson, A., Mycroft, A.: The next 7000 programming languages. In: Steffen, B., Woeginger, G. (eds.) Computing and Software Science. LNCS, vol. 10000, pp. 250–282. Springer, Heidelberg (2018)
7. Clarke, E.M., Klieber, W., Nováček, M., Zuliani, P.: Model checking and the state explosion problem. In: Meyer, B., Nordio, M. (eds.) LASER 2011. LNCS, vol. 7682, pp. 1–30. Springer, Heidelberg (2012). https://doi.org/10.1007/978-3-642-35746-6_1
8. Cousot, P., Cousot, R.: Abstract interpretation: a unified model for static analysis of programs by construction or approximation of fixpoints. In: Proceedings of 4th ACM Symposium on Principles of Programming Languages, pp. 238–252 (1977)
9. Dijkstra, E.W.: The humble programmer. Commun. ACM **15**(10), 859–866 (1972)
10. Felleisen, M., Findler, R.B., Flatt, M., Krishnamurthi, S., Barzilay, E., McCarthy, J., Tobin-Hochstadt, S.: A programmable programming language. Commun. ACM **61**(3), 62–71 (2018)
11. Floyd, R.W.: Assigning meaning to programs. In: Proceedings of Symposium on Applied Mathematics. Mathematical Aspects of Computer Science, vol. 19, pp. 19–32. American Mathematical Society (1967)
12. Futamura, Y.: Partial evaluation of computation process - an approach to a compiler-compiler. Syst. Comput. Controls **2**(5), 45–50 (1971)
13. Goodenough, J.B., Gerhart, S.L.: Toward a theory of test data selection. IEEE Trans. Softw. Eng. **SE-1**(2) (1975)
14. Havelund, K., Rosu, G., Reger, G.: Runtime verification - past experiences and future projections. In: Steffen, B., Woeginger, G. (eds.) Computing and Software Science. LNCS, vol. 10000, pp. 532–562. Springer, Heidelberg (2018)
15. Hähnle, R., Huisman, M.: Deductive software verification: from pen-and-paper proofs to industrial tools. In: Steffen, B., Woeginger, G. (eds.) Computing and Software Science. LNCS, vol. 10000, pp. 345–373. Springer, Heidelberg (2018)
16. Hoare, C.A.R.: An axiomatic basis for computer programming. Commun. ACM **12**(10), 576–580 (1969)

17. Howar, F., Jonsson, B., Vaandrager, F.: Combining black-box and white-box techniques for learning register automata. In: Steffen, B., Woeginger, G. (eds.) Computing and Software Science. LNCS, vol. 10000, pp. 563–588. Springer, Heidelberg (2018)

18. Huth, M., Nielson, F.: Static analysis for proactive security. In: Steffen, B., Woeginger, G. (eds.) Computing and Software Science. LNCS, vol. 10000, pp. 374–392. Springer, Heidelberg (2018)

19. Isberner, M., Howar, F., Steffen, B.: The TTT algorithm: a redundancy-free approach to active automata learning. In: Bonakdarpour, B., Smolka, S.A. (eds.) RV 2014. LNCS, vol. 8734, pp. 307–322. Springer, Cham (2014). https://doi.org/10.1007/978-3-319-11164-3_26

20. Jones, N.D., Sestoft, P., Søndergaard, H.: Mix: a self-applicable partial evaluator for experiments in compiler generation. LISP Symbolic Comput. 2(1), 9–50 (1989)

21. Kordon, F., Leuschel, M., van de Pol, J., Thierry-Mieg, Y.: Software architecture of modern model-checkers. In: Steffen, B., Woeginger, G. (eds.) Computing and Software Science. LNCS, vol. 10000, pp. 393–419. Springer, Heidelberg (2018)

22. Landin, P.J.: The next 700 programming languages. Commun. ACM 9(3), 157–166 (1966)

23. Legay, A., Lukina, A., Traonouez, L.M., Yang, J., Smolka, S., Grosu, R.: Statistical model checking. In: Steffen, B., Woeginger, G. (eds.) Computing and Software Science. LNCS, vol. 10000, pp. 478–504. Springer, Heidelberg (2018)

24. Margaria, T., Steffen, B.: Simplicity as a driver for agile innovation. Computer 43(6), 90–92 (2010)

25. Naur, P., Randell, B. (eds.): Software Engineering: Report of a Conference Sponsored by the NATO Science Committee, Garmisch, Germany, 7–11 October 1968. Scientific Affairs Division, NATO, Brussels 39 Belgium (1969)

26. O'Reilly, T.: What is Web 2.0. Design Patterns and Business Models for the Next Generation of Software, September 2005. http://www.oreilly.com/pub/a/web2/archive/what-is-web-20.html. Accessed 03 Apr 2018

27. Raffelt, H., Merten, M., Steffen, B., Margaria, T.: Dynamic testing via automata learning. Int. J. Softw. Tools Technol. Transf. (STTT) 11(4), 307–324 (2009)

28. Steffen, B.: Generating data flow analysis algorithms from modal specifications. Selected Papers of the Conference on Theoretical Aspects of Computer Software, pp. 115–139. Elsevier Science Publishers B. V., Sendai (1993). http://portal.acm.org/citation.cfm?id=172313

29. Steffen, B., Claßen, A., Klein, M., Knoop, J., Margaria, T.: The fixpoint-analysis machine. In: Lee, I., Smolka, S.A. (eds.) CONCUR 1995. LNCS, vol. 962, pp. 72–87. Springer, Heidelberg (1995). https://doi.org/10.1007/3-540-60218-6_6

30. Steffen, B., Gossen, F., Naujokat, S., Margaria, T.: Language-driven engineering: from general-purpose to purpose-specific languages. In: Steffen, B., Woeginger, G. (eds.) Computing and Software Science. LNCS, vol. 10000, pp. 311–344. Springer, Heidelberg (2018)

31. Steffen, B., Margaria, T., Braun, V.: The electronic tool integration platform: concepts and design. Int. J. Softw. Tools Technol. Transf. (STTT) 1(1–2), 9–30 (1997)

32. Wolper, P.: The meaning of "formal": from weak to strong formal methods. Int. J. Softw. Tools Technol. Transf. (STTT) 1(1), 6–8 (1997)

The Next 7000 Programming Languages

Robert Chatley[1], Alastair Donaldson[1], and Alan Mycroft[2(✉)]

[1] Department of Computing, Imperial College, London, UK
{robert.chatley,alastair.donaldson}@imperial.ac.uk
[2] Computer Laboratory, University of Cambridge, Cambridge, UK
alan.mycroft@cl.cam.ac.uk

Abstract. Landin's seminal paper "The next 700 programming languages" considered programming languages prior to 1966 and speculated on the next 700. Half-a-century on, we cast programming languages in a Darwinian 'tree of life' and explore languages, their features (genes) and language evolution from the viewpoint of 'survival of the fittest'.

We investigate this thesis by exploring how various languages fared in the past, and then consider the divergence between the languages *empirically used in 2017* and the language features one might have expected if the languages of the 1960s had evolved optimally to fill programming niches.

This leads us to characterise three divergences, or 'elephants in the room', where actual current language use, or feature provision, differs from that which evolution might suggest. We conclude by speculating on future language evolution.

1 Why Are Programming Languages the Way They Are? and Where Are They Going?

In 1966 the ACM published Peter Landin's landmark paper "The next 700 programming languages" [22]. Seven years later, Springer's "Lecture Notes in Computer Science" (LNCS) was born with Wilfred Brauer as editor of the first volume [5]. Impressively, the contributed chapters of this first volume covered almost every topic of what we now see as core computer science—from computer hardware and operating systems to natural-language processing, and from complexity to programming languages. Fifty years later, on the occasion of LNCS volume 10000, it seems fitting to reflect on where we are and make some predictions—and this essay focuses on *programming languages and their evolution*.

It is worth considering the epigraph of Landin's article, a quote from the July 1965 American Mathematical Association Prospectus: "... today ... 1,700 special programming languages used to 'communicate' in over 700 application areas". Getting an equivalent figure nowadays might be much harder—our title of 'next 7000 languages' is merely rhetorical.

© Springer Nature Switzerland AG 2019
B. Steffen and G. Woeginger (Eds.): Computing and Software Science, LNCS 10000, pp. 250–282, 2019.
https://doi.org/10.1007/978-3-319-91908-9_15

On one hand, Conway and White's 2010 survey[1] (the inspiration behind RedMonk's ongoing surveys) found only 56 languages used in *GitHub* projects or appearing as *StackOverflow* tags. This provides an estimate of the number of languages "in active use", but notably excludes those in large corporate projects (not on GitHub) particularly where there is good local support or other disincentives to raising programming problems in public. One the other hand, programming languages continue to appear at a prodigious rate; if we count every proposed language, perhaps including configuration languages and research-paper calculi, the number of languages must now be in six digits.

The main thrust of Landin's paper was arguing that the next 700 languages after 1966 ought to be based around a language family which he named ISWIM and characterised by: (*i*) nesting by indentation (perhaps to counter the Fortran-based "all statements begin in column 7" tendency of the day), (*ii*) flexible scoping mechanisms based on λ-calculus with the ability to treat functions as first-class values and (*iii*) imperative features including assignment and control-flow operators. Implicit was an expectation that there should be a well-defined understanding of when two program phrases were semantically equivalent and that compound types such as tuples should be available.

While the lightweight lexical scope '{ . . . }' is now often used for nesting instead of adopting point (*i*),[2] it is entertaining to note that scoping and control (*ii*) and (*iii*) have recently been drivers for enhancements in Java 8 and 9 (e.g. lambdas, streams, `CompletableFutures` and reactive programming).

Landin argued that ISWIM should be a family of languages, parameterised by its 'primitives' (presumably to enable it to be used in multiple application-specific domains). Nowadays, domain-specific use tends to be achieved by introducing abstractions or importing libraries rather than via adjustments to the core language itself. Indeed there seems to be a strong correlation between the number and availability of libraries for a language and its popularity.

The aim of this article is threefold: to explore trends in language design (both past, present and future), to argue that Darwinian evolution by fitness holds for languages as well as life-forms (including reasons why some less-fit languages can persist for extended periods of time) and to identify some environmental pressures (and perhaps even under-occupied niches) that language evolution could, and we argue should, explore.

Our study of programming-language niches discourages us from postulating a universal core language corresponding to Landin's ISWIM.

1.1 Darwinian Evolution and Programming Languages

We start by drawing an analogy between the evolution of programming languages and that of plants colonising an ecosystem. Here species of plants correspond to

---

[1] http://www.dataists.com/2010/12/ranking-the-popularity-of-programming-langauges/ [sic].

[2] Mainstream languages using indentation include Python and Haskell.

programming languages, and a given area of land corresponds to a family of related programming tasks (the word 'nearby' is convenient in both cases).

This analogy enables us to think more deeply about language evolution. In the steady-state (think of your favourite bit of land—be it countryside, scrub, or desert) there is little annual change in inhabitation. This is in spite of the various plants, or adherents of programming languages, spreading seeds—either literally, or seeds of dissent—and attempting to colonise nearby niches.

However, things usually are not truly steady state, and invasive species of plants may be more fitted to an ecological niche and supplant current inhabitants. In the programming language context, invasive languages can arise from universities, which turn out graduates who quietly adopt staid programming practices in existing projects until they are senior enough to start a new project— or refactor[3] an old one—using their education. Invasive languages can also come from industry—how many academics would have predicted that, by 2016 according to RedMonk, JavaScript would be the most popular language on GitHub and also be most tagged in StackOverflow? A recent empirical study shows that measuring popularity via volume of code in public GitHub repositories can be misleading due to code duplication, and that JavaScript code exhibits a high rate of duplication [24]. Nevertheless, it remains evident that JavaScript is one of the most widely used languages today.

It is useful here to distinguish between the success of a species of plant (or a programming language) and that of a gene (or programming language concept). For example, while pure functional languages such as Haskell have been successful in certain programming niches the idea (gene) of passing side-effect-free functions to *map*, *reduce*, and similar operators for data processing, has recently been acquired by many mainstream programming languages and systems; we later ascribe this partly to the emergence of multi-core processors.

This last example highlights perhaps the most pervasive form of competition for niches (and for languages, or plants, to evolve in response): climate change. Ecologically, an area becoming warmer or drier might enable previously non-competitive species to get a foothold. Similarly, even though a given programming task has not changed, we can see changes in available hardware and infrastructure as a form of climate change—what might be a great language for solving a programming problem on a single-core processor may be much less suitable for multi-core processors or data-centre solutions.

Amusingly, other factors which encourage language adoption (e.g. libraries, tools, etc.) have a plant analogy as symbiotes—porting (or creating) a wide variety of libraries for a language enhances its prospects.

The academic literature broadly lumps programming languages together into *paradigms*, such as *imperative*, *object-oriented* and *declarative*; we can extend our analogy to view paradigms as being analogous to major characteristics of plants, with languages of particular paradigms being particularly well-adapted to certain niches; for example xerophytes are well-adapted for deserts, and functional

---

[3] Imagine the discussions which took place at Facebook on how to post-fit types to its one million lines of PHP, and hence to the Hack programming language.

languages are well-suited to processing of inductively defined data structures. Interestingly, the idea of *convergent evolution* appears on both sides of the analogy, in our example this would be where two species had evolved to become xerophytes, despite their most recent common ancestor not being a xerophyte. Similarly language evolution can enable languages to acquire aspects of multiple paradigms (Ada, for example, is principally an imperative language despite having object-oriented capabilities, and C# had a level of functional capabilities from the off, amplified by the more-recent LINQ library for data querying).

Incidentally, the idea of a programming-language ecosystem with many niches provides post-hoc academic justification for why past attempts to create a 'universal programming language' (starting back as far as PL/I) have often proved fruitless: a language capable of expressing multiple programming paradigms risks becoming inherently complex, and thus difficult to learn and to use effectively. A central cause of this complexity is the difficulty of reasoning about *feature interaction*. A modern language that has carefully combined multiple paradigms since its inception is Scala. However, due to the resulting flexibility, there can be many different stylistic approaches to solving a particular programming problem in Scala, using different elements of the language. The language designer, Martin Odersky, describes Scala as "... a bit of a chameleon. ... depending at [sic] what piece of code you look at, Scala might look very simple or very complex."[4]

Finally, there is the issue of *software system* evolution. Just as languages evolve, a given software system (solution to a programming problem) is more likely to survive if it evolves to exploit more powerful concepts offered by later versions of a language. It is noteworthy that tool support often helps here, and we observe the growing importance of tools in supporting working with, adding to and transforming large programs in a given language.

We discuss some of these ideas more concretely in Sect. 3 but to summarise, the main external (climate-change) pressures on language evolution as we currently see them are:

- the change from single-core to multi-core and cloud-like computing;
- support for large programs with components that change over time;
- error resilience, helping programmers to produce reliable software;
- new industrial trends or research developments.

Conceptual Framework. In our setting the principal actors are *programming tasks* which are implemented to produce *software systems* using *programming languages*; the underlying available range of *language concepts* and *hardware and systems models* continue to change, and together with fashion (programmer-perceived and industrial views of fitness) drive the mutual evolution of programming languages and software systems.

We see evolution as 'selection of the fittest' following mutation (introduction of new genes etc.). While the mechanism for mutation (human design in programming languages vs. random mutation in organisms) differs this does not affect

---

[4] http://www.scala-lang.org/old/node/8610.

the selection aspect. While all living things undergo evolution, we centre on plant analogies as these help us focus on colonies rather than worrying about individual animal conflicts. 'Fitness' extends naturally: it captures the probability that adopting a given programming language in a project will cause programmers to report favourably upon it later—just as botanical fitness includes the probability a seed falling in a niche will germinate and mature to produce viable seeds itself. We discuss aspects of fitness later (e.g. ease of programming).

1.2   Paper Structure

We start by taking a more detailed look at history (Sect. 2), discuss the factors that drive programming language evolution (Sect. 3), and review the most popular programming languages at time of writing, according to the RedMonk, IEEE Spectrum and TIOBE rankings (Sect. 4). Our analysis identifies three 'elephants in the room'—language trends that rather conflict with a 'survival of the fittest' viewpoint—which we discuss in some detail (Sect. 5). We conclude by speculating on future language evolution (Sect. 6).

2   What's New Since 1966?

By 1966, much of the modern gene-pool of programming language concepts was well-established. We had Fortran, Algol 60 and Lisp capturing familiar concepts, e.g. stack-allocated local variables, heap-allocated records, if-then-else and iteration, named procedures and functions (including recursion), both static and dynamic typing, and a peek around the corner to 1967 and 1968 gave us references to structured data with named components (Algol 68) and object-orientation and subtyping (Simula 67).[5] The historic importance of COBOL should not be understated: from 1959 it provided a way to describe, read, print and manipulate fixed-format text and binary records—which fed both into language design (records) and databases.

Some early divergences remain: compare programming paradigms (functional, relational, object-oriented etc.) with the four major groups of plants (flowering plants, conifers, mosses and ferns). Another programming-language example is between static and dynamic typing. Modern fashion in real-world programming appears once again to be embracing dynamic typing for practical programming (witness the use of JavaScript, Python, Ruby and the like), often acting as glue languages to connect libraries written in statically typed languages.

We now briefly outline what we see as some of the main developments in programming languages, and drivers of programming language evolution, since these early days.

---

[5] Landin emphasised the λ-calculus as a theoretical base for programming languages, and did not mention the richer notion of scoping which object-orientation adds.

What We Do not Cover. Space precludes us from covering all such languages and drivers. Our selection is guided by those languages currently most used for mainstream software development, and their ancestors. As a result, there are certain important categories of language that we do not cover, e.g. logic and probabilistic programming languages.

2.1 Tasks, Tools and Teams

In the early days of computing, computers were mainly used for business processing or for scientific endeavour. Over the years, the range of problems that programming is applied to has exploded, along with the power and cost-effectiveness of computing hardware. As programming languages have evolved to inhabit these niches, the range of people who use them and the situations that they use them in has expanded, and conversely the widening set of applications has encouraged language evolution: there has been an increasing need for languages to provide features that help programmers to manage complexity, and to take better advantage of computing resources.

Another decision point in choosing a language is "get it working" versus "get it right" versus "get it fast/efficient". In different situations, each might be appropriate, and the software-system context, or niche, determines the fitness of individual languages and hence guides the language choice. A quick script to do some data-processing is obviously quite different from an I/O driver, or the control system of a safety-critical device.

Software was initially developed by one person at one computer. Now it is developed by distributed teams, often spanning across continents or organisations. The size of software systems has also increased massively. From systems running on one machine, distributed systems can now execute across hundreds or thousands of machines in data-centres around the world, and comprise tens of millions of lines of code. Language implementations have evolved to help humans manage this complexity, e.g. by providing sophisticated support for packages and modules, including dynamic loading and versioning. Some languages (or runtimes) provide these as core functionality, for example Java and C# provide the ability to dynamically load classes from jar files or assemblies. For other languages, accompanying tools have been developed that help to manage and compose dependencies, e.g. 'npm' (Node Package Manager) for Node.js. Such language features and tools can help to avoid so-called "dependency hell" ("DLL hell" in Windows applications), whereby an application depends on a given shared library that, due to poorly planned sets of inter-component dependencies, in turn depends on an intricate mixture of specific versions of additional library components, some of which conflict with one another, and many of which are in essence irrelevant to the application under construction.

The way that teams work to develop software has also changed. Single-person approaches were succeeded by waterfall-style development processes for managing multi-person software projects, which in turn have been largely superseded (for all but the most safety-critical systems) by more *agile* approaches such as eXtreme Programming [4]. Agile methods require analysis, testing and transformation tools to support frequent and reliable change, and to provide the rapid feedback essential for developer productivity. Languages where these are well supported have a natural advantage in the ecosystem.

Finally, one of the biggest changes since 1967 has been in the tools we use to support programming—enabled, of course, by the vast increase in computing power over this time. While classical editors, compilers and (static) linkers are still present there has been an explosion in new forms of tool support and their use: integrated development environments (IDEs) including support for code analysis and refactoring, version control systems, test generators, along with tools for dynamically linking to code and data outwith the project. These evolve much more quickly and largely independently of the huge code bases in software systems; the latter in general only evolve incrementally to capture software-feature change (and even more slowly in reflecting their underlying programming-language evolution). We claim that appropriate tool support is a strong factor in programming-language fitness, and hence for language choice in a given software project.

2.2   Systems Programming and the Rise of C

The success of the C programming language and that of Unix are inseparably intertwined. Ritchie [35] writes: "C came into being in the years 1969–1973, in parallel with the early development of the Unix operating system; the most creative period occurred during 1972." In ecosystem terms, C is significant as it successfully out-competed rival languages to become almost the only widely used systems programming language. Gabriel remarks that "Unix and C are the ultimate computer viruses" [11], arguing that their "worse-is-better" design, where implementation simplicity is favoured over other features such as full correctness and interface simplicity, makes Unix and C so easy to port that they virally infected practically all systems. Alluding to natural selection, Gabriel writes: "worse-is-better, even in its straw-man form, has better survival characteristics than the-right-thing".

Designed for relatively low-level systems programming, C provides mechanisms for fine-grained and efficient management of memory—needed to build operating systems and device drivers, or for programming resource-constrained environments such as embedded systems. C is usually the first higher-than-assembly-level language supported on a new architecture. Regarded for a long time (and still to a large degree) as an inevitable price for its high performance, C is an *unsafe* language: run-time errors, such as buffer overflows, are not typically caught by language implementations, so a program may continue to execute after an erroneous operation. This provides wide scope for attacks, e.g. control-flow hijacking and reading supposedly confidential data. A botanical analogy might be the prevalence of cacti in deserts, when some would prefer orchids as prettier and lacking spines; we have to either adjust the niche—requiring beauty (or security), contribute more to fitness by human intervention, or produce a new plant species (or language) that better fits the existing niche while having the desired characteristics.

Certainly C has been one of the most influential programming languages, influencing the syntax, and to some degree semantics, of C++, Java and C#, and forming the basis of parallel programming languages such as CUDA (NVIDIA's proprietary language for graphics-processing unit (GPU) programming) and OpenCL (an industry-standard alternative). Moreover, C continues to be very widely used; arguably much more so than it should be given its unsafe nature. We return to this point in Sect. 5.1.

2.3   Object-Orientation and the Rise of Java

The object-oriented paradigm, where domain entities are represented as objects that communicate by sending messages, became the dominant style of commercial software development in the 1990s. Building on Kay's original ideas, embodied in Smalltalk, came a number of very influential languages, including Delphi, Eiffel, Oberon, Self, and Simula 67. These impacted the design of what are now the most widely used object-oriented languages—Java, C++ and C#—which continue to thrive while many of these earlier languages are now extinct or restricted to communities of enthusiasts. (We acknowledge that some purists question whether languages such as Java, C++ and C# are truly object-oriented—e.g. they fail the so-called "Ingalls Test"[6] [30, Sect. 11.6.4]—but they are widely regarded as belonging to the object-oriented paradigm.)

We also see influence in the growth of tooling, with the modern day Eclipse IDE having its roots in IBM's VisualAge for Java, which in turn evolved from VisualAge for Smalltalk. A significant driver of Java's early spread was its "write once, run anywhere" philosophy, whereby a Java compiler generates code that can run on any conformant implementation of the *Java Virtual Machine* (JVM). Support for the JVM by web browsers, and the popularity of 'applets' embedded in web-pages drove the adoption of Java. Its clean design and safe execution made it a popular teaching language in universities.

Other features also drove adoption: Java, C++ and C# provided support for exceptions—meeting a practical need for mainstream languages to capture this idiom. Java and C# embraced ideas originating in languages such as Lisp and Smalltalk—automatic memory-management (garbage collection) and the idea of *managed run-time environment* abstracting away from the underlying operating system (or browser!). There remains a tension between C/C++, with manual allocation and the associated lack of safety, and Java and C# which, while safe, can be problematic in a resource-constrained or real-time environment.

Note that there are two separate genes, representing class-based inheritance (originating in Simula) and prototype-based inheritance (originating in Self, initially a dialect of Smalltalk) for object-oriented languages. There are arguments in favour of each: the former allows static typing and is used by more main-

---

[6] https://www.youtube.com/watch?v=Ao9W93OxQ7U, 26 min in.

stream languages; the latter is used in JavaScript, and therefore in some sense more successful!

2.4 Web Programming, the Re-emergence of Dynamic Typing, and the Rise of JavaScript

Although some early programming languages were *dynamically* typed—notably Lisp—the focus of much research into programming languages in the 70s, 80s and 90s was on statically typed languages with stronger and richer type systems. In industry, relatively strongly, statically typed, languages also became increasingly popular, with dynamically typed languages largely restricted to scripting and introductory programming.

The massive change since then has been the importance of programming for the web, through languages such as JavaScript and PHP, which are dynamically typed. Web programming is so pervasive that JavaScript is now one of the most widely used programming languages. From a language-design perspective this is somewhat ironic. Although a lot of high-end research into dynamically typed programming languages had been conducted (e.g. notably working with systems like CLOS [13], and building on those with languages like Self [47]), in fact Brendan Eich designed and implemented JavaScript (then named Mocha) in 10 days, seemingly with no recourse to these research endeavours [42].

Other dynamically typed languages have developed a strong following including Python and Ruby. Both are general-purpose languages, but Python has become particularly popular among scientists [33], and a major driver of Ruby adoption was the *Rails* framework of Heinemeier Hansson [36] designed to facilitate server-side web-application programming and easy database integration. We reflect further on the popularity of dynamically typed languages in Sect. 5.2.

2.5 Functional Programming Languages

Functional languages, where function abstraction and application are the main structuring regime, originated in Lisp. For many years, functional programming languages lived in an "enthusiasts' ghetto", attracting strong supporters for specific programming areas, but their discouraging of mutating existing values was a step too far for many mainstream programmers. Recently however, their ideas appear to be becoming mainstream. Two of the most influential functional languages, Haskell and ML, are currently among the most widely used functional languages (with the OCaml dialect enjoying the most use in the case of ML), and both languages being used in quantitative (equity) trading applications in banks, who argue that these languages allow their *quant* analysts to code more quickly and correctly.[7] One justification for this resurgence is that concurrency and mutation appear hard for programmers to use together in large systems, needing error-prone locks or hard-to-document whole-program assumptions of when and how data structures can be modified.

---

[7] https://adtmag.com/Ramel0911.

Functional languages have also inspired so-called "multi-paradigm" languages, principally F# and Scala, both of which feature first-class functional concepts; these in turn have been incorporated into mainstream object-oriented languages, most notably the LINQ extensions to C#, and lambdas in Java 8 and C++11.

Even aspects (genes) of functional languages which previously seemed abstruse to the mainstream have been incorporated into modern general-purpose languages. For example Java 8's streams incorporate the ideas of lazy evaluation, deforestation and the functional idiom of transforming one infinite stream into another.

2.6 Flexible Type Systems

At the time of Landin's article, and indeed for most of the decade following it, there was a split between, on one hand, dynamically typed languages such as Lisp, which checked types at run time at the cost of reduced execution efficiency and unexpected errors and, on the other hand, statically typed languages giving increased efficiency and the possibility of eliminating type errors at compile time (even if this had holes, such as in C and Algol 60). However, such static type systems were often inexpressive; a running joke at the time of one author's PhD was that, e.g. in Pascal one had to write functions only differing in types for finding the lengths of integer lists and string lists so that the compiler could generate duplicated code. The late 1970's saw parameterised types, and polymorphically typed (or 'generic') functions for operating over them. The language ML (originally part of the Edinburgh LCF theorem-proving system) was hugely instrumental here. In a sense ML was almost exactly "ISWIM with types", albeit without syntax-by-indentation. Types have continued to grow in expressiveness, with type systems in Java and C# including three forms of polymorphism (generics, overloading and (bounded) sub-type polymorphism) all in the same language.

More heavyweight type disciplines, such as dependently typed languages (e.g. Agda, Coq) remain firmly away from the mainstream, in spite of the high precision that they offer and their potential link to program verification (see Sect. 6.2). There is an argument that very precise types can end up revealing details about a system's internals, and that the desire for a particular type structure can have a more direct influence on program structure than might really be desirable; these have been dubbed the "Visible Plumbing Program" and the "Intersection Problem", respectively [9].

2.7 Parallelism and the Rise of Multi-core

The appearance of multi-core x86 processors from 2005 was, in retrospect, hugely disruptive to programming languages. While parallel processing was not new (e.g. High Performance Fortran offered relatively sophisticated language support for parallel programming [20]), multi-core (and later GPU) technology caused everyday programmers to want their language to support it. This world feels a little like Landin's in 1966—there are many language features and libraries offering support for various aspects of parallelism. Dedicated languages and libraries include Cilk Plus, Threading Building Blocks and OpenMP for multi-core CPUs, and OpenCL, CUDA, Vulkan, Metal and RenderScript for targeting GPUs. Within a single language there can be many mechanisms by which to exploit parallelism: in Java one can use parallel streams, an executor service, create one's own thread objects; in Haskell there are also multiple approaches [27]. More than a decade on, language support for parallelism remains patchy and has converged less than we might have hoped, a point to which we return in Sect. 5.3.

2.8   Domain-Oriented Programming Languages

Just as in Landin's day, many languages have been created for solving problems in particular domains. While Turing completeness means that we should be able to apply any general purpose language to any programming task, domain-specific languages often offer more convenient syntax and library support than would be possible in a mainstream language, with examples including spreadsheets, SQL, MATLAB and R, along with scripting languages for computer-game and graphics-rendering engines.

3   Observed Programming Language Evolution

We now re-cast the changes of the previous section as language evolution pressures, discussing: the factors that keep programming languages alive (Sect. 3.1), the forces that lead to language evolution (Sect. 3.2), and cases where languages have become practically extinct due to not having evolved (Sect. 3.3).

3.1   Factors that Keep Programming Languages Alive

Although the landscape of programming languages evolves, many languages take root and stick around. We observe several forces that keep languages alive. In the evolutionary model, these 'forces' sum to contribute to the overall fitness of a language in a given niche.

Legacy Software. The amount of software in the world increases day by day. New systems (and modules within systems) are created at a much faster rate than they are deleted. Existing code that performs valuable business functions needs to be updated and upgraded to provide additional functionality or to integrate with other systems. Replacing a system wholesale is a major decision, and costly for large systems. The need to tend to existing successful systems, using whatever language they were originally written in, is a strong force in keeping languages alive. Even though COBOL is often perceived as a dead language, as recently as 2009, it was estimated to have billions of lines of code in active use[8] and some of these surely remain, even if they are not widely advertised.

---

[8] http://skeptics.stackexchange.com/questions/5114/did-cobol-have-250-billion-lines-of-code-and-1-million-programmers-as-late-as-2 [sic].

Community. Enthusiasm and support for a particular programming language is often fostered if there is an active and encouraging community around it. This can be helpful in encouraging beginners, or in supporting programmers in their daily tasks, by providing advice on technical problems as they come up. Language communities, like any social group, tend to reflect the design parameters of the language they discuss; some are seen as formal and academic and others more down-to-earth.. For example, there is a saying in the Ruby community, which has a reputation for being supportive and helpful: "Matz [the language creator] is nice and so we are nice".[9] In contrast, the community that has grown up around Scala is perceived to be much more academically focused, biased towards more mathematical thinking and language, and sometimes perceived as less welcoming to people from a "general developer" background. In his (somewhat polemical) ScalaDays 2013 keynote[10], Rod Johnson gives his impressions of the Scala community as being somewhere where "there do seem to be quite a few people who aren't highly focused on solving real world problems" and where some members appear to have the opinion that "ignorance should be punished".

Ease of Getting Started. In order for a new language to take hold, it helps if it is easy for new programmers (either novices, or just newcomers to the language in question) to get started quickly. The speed with which a new programmer can write and run their first program depends on many things: the simplicity of language design, clarity of tutorials, the amount one needs to learn before getting started, and the support of tooling (including helpful error messages, a subject taken to heart by languages like Elm). This in turn can affect the longevity of a language—as this depends on a continued influx of new programmers.

Habitability. In his book *Patterns of Software* [12], Gabriel describes the characteristic of *habitability*: "Habitability makes a place livable, like home. And this is what we want in software—that developers feel at home, can place their hands on any item without having to think deeply about where it is." If a language has widely adopted idioms, and projects developed in that language are habitually laid out according to familiar structure then it easy for programmers to feel at home. Languages that promote "one way to do things" may help to engender this consistency. Habitability may also come from having a common tool-ecosystem[11]. For example, if we download a Java project and find that it is structured as a Maven[12] project, then it is easy to locate the source, tests, dependencies, build configuration, etc., if we are familiar with other Maven projects. Similarly in modern Ruby projects we might expect a certain structure and the

---

[9] https://en.wiktionary.org/wiki/MINASWAN .

[10] https://www.youtube.com/watch?v=DBu6zmrZ_50 particularly from 21 min in.

[11] Note that other uses of 'ecosystem' in this paper refer to the ecosystem of languages competing for a programming niche, but the 'tool-ecosystem' refers to the toolset available to support programming in a given language—we earlier noted that this improved the fitness of a given language by behaving as a symbiote.

[12] https://maven.apache.org/.

use of Bundler[13] to perform a similar role. These sort of tools are often only de-facto standards, as a result of wide adoption, but consistent project layout, build process, etc., provided by standard tools, reduces cognitive load for the developer, and in turn may make a programmer feel more at home working in a given language, especially when coming to work on a new project [14].

Libraries. The availability of libraries of reusable code adds to the ease of getting things done in a particular language. Whether we want to read a file, invoke a web service over HTTP, or even recognise car licence plates in a photograph, if we can easily find a library to do so in a particular language, that language is appealing for getting the job done in the short term. Some languages come with rich standard libraries as part of their distribution. In other cases the proliferation of community-contributed libraries on sites like GitHub leads to a plethora of options. When there are a large number of libraries available, it often becomes part of the culture in the community centred around a particular language to contribute. The plentiful supply of libraries begets the plentiful supply of libraries. We note, however, that recent trends to rely on third-party libraries for even the simplest of routines can lead to problems. For example, the removal of the widely used 'left-pad' library from the 'npm' JavaScript package manager caused a great deal of chaos.[14]

Tools. Although language designers may hope or believe that their new language allows programming tasks to be solved in new, perhaps more elegant ways, it is not the language alone that determines the productivity of a programmer at work. A programmer needs to write and change code, navigate existing code bases, debug, compile, build and test, deploy their code, and often integrate existing components and libraries, in order to get their work done and to deliver working features into the hands of their users. A programming language therefore exists within a tool-ecosystem.

Java, for example, is a very popular language that is highly productive for many development teams. This is not only down to the design of the language itself—some might argue that it is in fact in spite of this, as Java is often seen as relatively unsophisticated in terms of language features. It is also—indeed, perhaps largely—due to the supply of good tools and libraries that are available to Java developers. Anecdotally we have heard stories from many commercial developers who have actively chosen to work in Java rather than working with a more sophisticated language, due to the availability of powerful Java-focused tools such as IntelliJ's IDEA,[15] with their rich support for automated refactoring and program transformation, contrasted with the comparative lack of tool support for richer languages. This gap in tool support can even inhibit the uptake of JVM-targeted languages such as Scala, something addressed with the recent IntelliJ IDEA support for Scala and Java 9.

---

[13] http://bundler.io/.

[14] http://www.theregister.co.uk/2016/03/23/npm_left_pad_chaos.

[15] https://www.jetbrains.com/idea/.

To some degree, tools can compensate for perceived deficiencies in a language, and generally evolve faster than the language itself, because a change to a tool does not have the same impact on existing software as a change to a language specification does.

Support of Change. One might think that agile methods would favour dynamically typed languages, and indeed part of their popularity is the sense that they allow a developer to get something done without having to worry about a lot of the "boiler-plate" associated with stricter and more verbose languages. But there is a counter-pressure for statically typed languages when working on large systems. Agile methods promote embracing change, with code bases evolving through a continuous sequence of updates and refactorings [10]. These activities of transforming a code base are more easily done when supported by tools, and refactoring tools work better when type information is available [40]. However, this is not a one-way street. The increased complexity of Scala's type system over Java makes it harder to create effective automated refactoring tools. Also the additional sophistication of the compiler means that compared to Java the compilation and build times are relatively long. This can lead to frustration when developers want to make frequent small changes.

A workflow that involves making frequent small changes to a working system requires a harness that developers can rely on to mitigate risk and to allow sustainable progress. A practice commonly used by agile teams is test-driven development (TDD) [3]. It is misleading to say that particular languages explicitly support TDD, but in a language like Java or C# with good tooling, we can get a lot done working in a TDD fashion because the tools can *generate* a lot of our implementation code for us based on tests and types—although this is really just a mechanisation of mundane manual work, there is no real intelligent synthesis at play.[16] In dynamic languages we need tests even more, because we have less assurance about the safety and correctness of our program from the type system. Fortunately, some flavours of test—for example tests using mock objects [25]—may be more convenient to write in dynamic languages as we do not have to introduce abstractions to 'convince' the type system that a particular *test double*[17] can be used in a type-compatible manner as a substitute for a real dependency, given the late binding that is characteristic of such languages.

Supply of Talent. When building a new system, the choice of language is not just a technical decision, but also an economic one. Do we have the developers needed to build this system? If we need to hire more, or one day need to replace a current staff member, how much would it cost to hire someone with the relevant skills? Knowledge of some languages is easy to find, whilst others are specialist niches. At the time of writing there is a good supply of programmers in the

---

[16] This is in contrast to methods such as property-based testing, that synthesise tests in a smart manner by exploiting type-system guarantees and programmer-defined property specifications [7].

[17] https://martinfowler.com/bliki/TestDouble.html.

job market who know Java, C#, JavaScript etc. There are comparatively few Haskell, Rust or Erlang developers. This scarcity of supply relative to demand naturally leads to high prices.

High Performance. Some languages (C and C++ in particular) are not going to die in the immediate future because they are so performant. We return to the longevity of C in Sect. 5.1 and speculate on the future of C and C++ in Sect. 6.1. A design goal of the relatively new Rust language is to achieve C-like performance without sacrificing memory safety, through type system innovations. In order to achieve high performance, Rust in particular aims to provide *static* guarantees of memory safety, to avoid the overhead of run-time checks.

An Important Niche. Some languages just solve an important class of problem particularly well. Ada is barely used if we look globally, but it is very much alive (particularly the SPARK subset of Ada) for building high-assurance software [28]. The same is true for Fortran, but with respect to scientific computing. Both languages have reasonably recent standards (Ada 2012 and Fortran 2008).

3.2   Incentives for Evolution

Technological Advances. Advances in technology make new applications possible in principle, and languages adapt to make them possible—and feasible to build— in practice. An early aim of Java was to be the language of the web, and the mass adoption of the web as a platform for applications has led to sustenance and growth of languages such as JavaScript and PHP. The fact that JavaScript is the only programming language commonly supported by all web browsers has made it a de-facto standard for front-end web developers. The rise of the iPhone and its native apps saw a surge in Objective-C development as programmers created apps, with Apple later creating the Swift language to provide a better developer experience on iOS. Multi-core processor technology has led to parallelism being supported, albeit in a fragmented manner, in many more languages than would otherwise be the case.

Reliability and Security. As discussed in Sect. 2.3, many languages are now *managed*, so that basic correctness properties are checked at run time, and such that the programmer can be less concerned with memory allocation and deallocation. This eliminates large classes of security vulnerabilities associated with invalid memory access. It is common for language syntax and semantics to evolve in support of program reasoning: through keywords for programmer-specified assertions and contracts (particularly notable in the evolution of Ada, thanks to its SPARK subset [28][18]); via more advanced type systems, such as generics (to avoid unsafe casts), types to control memory ownership (in Rust, for example), and dependent types to encode richer properties (increasingly available in

---

[18] Our point here is that some languages have *evolved* to provide support for contracts. Contracts have also enjoyed first-class support from the *inception* of some languages, e.g. Eiffel.

functional languages); by updating language specifications with more rigorous semantics for operations that were previously only informally specified;[19] and by adding facilities for programmers to specify software engineering intent (an example being the option to annotate an overriding method with @Override in Java, or with the override specifier in C++, to fault misspelt overrides statically). As well as language evolution leading to improved reliability and security, there is also the notion of language *subsets* that promote more disciplined programming, or that provide more leverage for analysis tools, including a proposed safe subset of C++[20], the ECMAScript "strict" mode for JavaScript, and, again, the SPARK subset of Ada.

In addition to the above points, which centre on enabling programmers to avoid *their own* errors, it is also important to manage situations where external failures occur: power loss, network loss, hardware failure and the like. Classically this was achieved by checkpointing and rollback recovery. But as systems grow, especially in concurrency and distribution, there is increasing trend for more-locally managed failure. The Erlang *fail fast* design style seems to work effectively: tasks can be linked together, so that if one fails (for example an unanticipated programming situation leading to an uncaught exception, but particularly useful for external failures) then all its linked tasks are killed, and the creator can either re-start the tasks if the error is transitory, or clean up gracefully. Another inspiration is the functional-style absence of side effects, exploited for example by Google MapReduce [8]. If a processor doing one part of the 'map' fails, then another processor can just repeat the work. This would be far more complicated with side-effects and distributed rollback. An interesting project along these lines was the Murray et al. [31] CIEL cloud-execution engine (and associated scripting language Skywriting) where computational idempotence was a core design principle.

Competition Between Languages. Some languages evolve via competition. For example, many features of C# were influenced by Java; in turn, support for lambdas in Java 8 seems to have been influenced by similar capabilities in C#, and C++ was augmented with higher-order function support at roughly the same time. In the multi-core world there is clear competition between CUDA and OpenCL, with CUDA leading on advanced features that NVIDIA GPUs can support, and OpenCL gradually adopting the successful features that can also be implemented across GPU vendors. Competition-driven evolution demonstrates the value to users of having multiple languages occupying the same niche.

Company and Community Needs. Several languages have been born, or evolved, to meet company needs. Usually this occurs in scenarios where the companies in question are large enough to benefit from the new or evolved language even if it is only used internally, though many languages have found large external

---

[19] One example is C++11 adding concurrency semantics for weak memory models; the difficulty of this was illustrated by its unwanted "out of thin air" (OOTA) behaviour.

[20] http://www.stroustrup.com/resource-model.pdf.

communities. Notable examples include Microsoft's extensions to C and C++, the design of Go, Rust and Swift by Google, Mozilla and Apple, respectively, and Hack as an extension of PHP by Facebook.[21] Open source communities have also produced influential language extensions—perhaps most notably the various GNU extensions to C and C++.

3.3   Extinction due to Non-evolution

Languages become extinct when they are no longer used, but we must separate "no longer used for new projects" (e.g. COBOL) from "(probably) no systems using them left in existence" (e.g. Algol 60). (Of course community support for historic languages and systems means that even these definitions are suspect.) What interests us is the question of why a previously influential language might become used less and less? There seem to be two overlapping reasons for this: (*i*) *revolutionary replacement:* the concepts of the language were innovative, but its use in the wider ecosystem was less attractive—other languages which incorporated its features have now supplanted it; and (*ii*) *loss of fitness:* the language was well-used in many large projects, but doubts about its continuing ecological fitness arose. Algol 60 and arguably Smalltalk fits the first of these criteria well, while Fortran, Lisp, C and arguably COBOL fit the second.

Languages in the latter category can avoid extinction by evolving. This is most notably the case for Fortran, but C also fit this scheme, as does C++: new features have been added to the languages in successive versions. Similarly Lisp has evolved with Common Lisp, Racket and Clojure being modern forms. The key issue here is backwards compatibility: old programs must continue to work in newer versions of the language with at most minor textual changes. A popular technique for removing old features felt to be harmful for future versions of the language is to *deprecate* them—marking them for future deletion and allowing tool-chains to warn on their use. This technique is used in the ISO standards for C and Fortran (most recent standards in 2011 and 2008 respectively); Lisp dialects have evolved more disparately, but are still largely backwards compatible.

It is worth noting here that Fortran's evolution fits the plant-ecosystem model quite well. However, the *revolutionary replacement* model is more akin to 'artificial life' or 'genetically modified organisms' in the way the existing genetic features are combined into a new plant or programming language.

In closing this section, we note that Fortran (first standardised in 1958, most recent standard in 2008, and Fortran 2015 [sic] actively in standardisation) seems practically immortal for large-scale numeric code, such as weather forecasting and planetary modelling. Anecdotally, it largely fights off C++ because of the power that C++ provides for writing code that others cannot easily understand or that contains subtle bugs. One example of this is that Fortran largely forbids aliasing, which limits the flexibility of the language for general-purpose programming, but reduces the scope for aliasing-related programmer errors, and aids

---

[21] http://hacklang.org/.

compilers in generating efficient code. By contrast Algol, in spite of being perhaps the most influential language of all time, has effectively become extinct—the attempt to move from Algol 60 to Algol 68 did not prove effective in holding on to its territory. It's hard to pin down the exact reason: other languages developed while the Algol standard was effectively frozen awaiting Algol 68, the lack of support for (or even community-belief in) separate compilation, the default of call-by-name meaning that any sensible upgrade would fail to be backward-compatible, etc.

There's an interesting comparison here: "would you prefer to be immortal or to be posthumously praised for spreading your genes around the world?" A quote from Joe Armstrong also seems relevant here [41]:

> People keep asking me "What will happen to Erlang? Will it be a popular language?" I don't know. I think it's already been very influential. It might end up like Smalltalk. I think Smalltalk's very, very influential and loved by an enthusiastic band of people but never really very widely adopted.

4   Range of Important Languages in 2017

Posing the question "What are the important languages of 2017?" gives a range of answers from "well it's obviously X, Y and Z" to "what do you mean by important?". While there are important legacy languages with millions lines of existing code (Fortran, and perhaps COBOL and arguably even C), here we pragmatically explore various recent programming language popularity rankings: the RedMonk Programming Language Rankings (June 2016),[22] the 2015 Top 10 Programming Languages according to IEEE Spectrum (July 2015),[23] and the TIOBE Index (February 2017).[24]

These are of course just a subset of available rankings; the rankings differ as to how language importance is measured; data for the amount of code written is hard to come by when much deployed code is not publicly available at the source level (Wired reported in 2015 that "Google is 2 billion lines of code—and it's all in one place"[25]); and it unlikely that code duplication is accounted for when judging how much code is associated with a particular language—a recent study by Lopes et al. shows that accounting for duplication is challenging [24]. We note that these rankings assess language importance based on volume of code, rather than by assessing how influential a language is in terms of ideas (genes) it contains, or introduces, that are used in later languages.

Nevertheless, we believe the data these rankings offer provides a reasonable snapshot capturing at least the core set of languages broadly agreed to be in wide use today. They are summarised in Table 1, with the IEEE Spectrum ranking stopping at 10 and the other rankings at 20 (modulo a 20th-place tie).

---

[22] http://redmonk.com/sogrady/category/programming-languages/.

[23] http://spectrum.ieee.org/computing/software/the-2015-top-ten-programming-languages.

[24] http://www.tiobe.com/tiobe-index/.

[25] https://www.wired.com/2015/09/google-2-billion-lines-codeand-one-place/.

Table 1. Popular languages according to three sources (mid-2015–early 2017)

Position	RedMonk (2016)	IEEE Spectrum (2015)	TIOBE (2017)
1	JavaScript	Java	Java
2	Java	C	C
3	PHP	C++	C++
4	Python	Python	C#
5	(5=) C#	C#	Python
6	(5=) C++	R	PHP
7	(5=) Ruby	PHP	JavaScript
8	CSS	JavaScript	Visual Basic
9	C	Ruby	Delphi/Object Pascal
10	Objective-C	MATLAB	Perl
11	Shell		Ruby
12	R		Swift
13	Perl		Assembly language
14	Scala		Go
15	Go		R
16	Haskell		Visual Basic
17	Swift		MATLAB
18	MATLAB		PL/SQL
19	Visual Basic		Objective-C
20	(20=) Clojure		Scratch
21	(20=) Groovy		

We broadly partition the languages in these rankings into five categories:

- *Mainstream*: languages whose presence and approximate position in the rankings comes as no surprise, and that we expect to be around for the foreseeable future.
- *Rising*: languages that we perceive to have rapidly growing user communities, with an associated buzz of excitement. The popularity of *rising* language is likely to be recent, and expected to increase either directly, or indirectly through influence on mainstream languages.
- *Declining*: languages that are still in active use, including for new projects, but which we perceive to be on the decline, e.g. because they are less widely used than mainstream languages, yet lack the buzz of excitement surrounding rising languages.
- *Legacy*: languages that are largely used in order to maintain legacy systems, and in which we expect very little new code is developed.
- *Domain-oriented*: languages that are key to important application domains, but that one would not normally use to develop general-purpose software.

This partitioning into categories between them is skewed by our personal biases, perspectives and experience; no doubt our allocations to *rising* and *declining* will be controversial.

Mainstream. Firmly in the top ten of all three rankings, it is widely agreed that the major imperative and object-oriented languages—C, C++, C# and Java— are mainstream. These include the languages used to implement most systems infrastructure (C/C++), a large body of enterprise applications (Java/C#), the majority of desktop computer games (C++), and most Android apps (Java). These languages are all statically typed. We also regard JavaScript, Python and Ruby—all dynamically typed—as mainstream. JavaScript tops the RedMonk ranking, Python is in the top 5 in all rankings, and Ruby is top-ten in all but the TIOBE ranking, where it sits at 11th place.

Rising. We sense a great deal of excitement surrounding functional programming languages, and languages with first class functional-programming features, thus we regard Haskell, Clojure and Scala as rising. These three languages feature in the lower half of the RedMonk chart, but do not appear on the TIOBE list. One of the authors recalls being taught Haskell as an undergraduate student in 2000, at which point there seemed to be little general expectation that the language, though clearly important and influential, would become close to mainstream; the situation is very different 17 years later. We also see the influence of Haskell and functional programming in up-and-coming languages like Elm. Elm is written in Haskell and has a Haskell-like syntax but compiles to HTML, CSS and JavaScript for the browser, making it a candidate for a wide range of web-programming tasks.

Swift is evidently rising as the language of choice for iOS development, in part as a replacement for Objective-C. Swift's syntax is clearly influenced by languages like Ruby, although Swift is statically typed. As Swift has now been open-sourced, we are seeing the community around it growing, and helping to improve its tool-ecosystem.

With the exception of Swift, which enjoys good support in Apple's Xcode, when one compares the tool support for these rising languages to that for the languages we class as mainstream, the contrast is stark. If these languages continue to rise, we expect and hope that better tooling will evolve around them.

Some languages that do not make these rankings, but which we regard as rising, include: Rust, which has certainly generated a lot of academic excitement in relation to its type system; F# (well-supported by Visual Studio), which like Scala is multi-paradigm with strong functional programming support; and Kotlin, which by being built together with its IDE might avoid the tools-shortage risk of a new language. Another language with a syntax influenced by Ruby is Elixir, which targets the Erlang virtual machine and promotes an actor model of concurrency.

Declining. It seems that niches occupied by Objective-C, PHP and Perl are gradually being dominated by Swift, JavaScript, and Python/Ruby, thus we view these languages as declining. Similarly our impression is that Visual Basic is a declining language, its niches perhaps being taken over by C#.

Legacy. We attribute the presence of Object Pascal (and its Delphi dialect) in the top ten of the TIOBE ranking to the significant amount of such code being maintained in legacy software, and speculate that this language is rarely used for new projects.

Domain-Oriented. It is encouraging to see Scratch, an educational language, mentioned in the TIOBE list; we class this as domain-oriented since the goal of Scratch is to teach programming rather than for production development. Among the languages used by people who often do not regard themselves as programmers, R and MATLAB are probably the most widely used, with applications including data science and machine learning. We also class the query language dialect PL/SQL as domain-oriented.

We do not have a feeling for whether Go—ranked top 20 by both RedMonk and TIOBE—is rising or declining. Our impression is that it plays a useful role in implementing server software, a niche that it may continue to capably occupy without becoming mainstream. The same might be said of several languages not ranked in Table 1: Erlang, which occupies an important distributed systems niche for which it is widely respected; Fortran, often the language of choice for scientists; VHDL and Verilog in processor design; and OpenCL and CUDA in the parallel programming world, for example.

Of the remaining languages listed in Table 1, CSS is not a full-blown programming language, and "Shell" and "Assembly language" span a multitude of shell scripting and assembly languages for different platforms, which we do not attempt to categorise. (As an aside, we are doubtful regarding the high rank of "Assembly language" in the TIOBE ranking.)

5   The Elephants in the Room

Given the rich array of programming languages that have evolved over the past half century, and in general the successful manner in which languages have emerged or evolved to cope with technological change, we note three strange facts: that C remains an extremely popular language despite its shortcomings (Sect. 5.1), that dynamically typed languages are among the most popular programming languages despite decades of advances in static type systems (Sect. 5.2), and that despite the rise of multi-core processing, support for parallelism is patchwork across today's languages (Sect. 5.3).

At first sight these conflict with our 'selection of the fittest' thesis, and indeed perhaps we are even slightly embarrassed as computer scientists as to the state of the real world. We return this issue in Sect. 6 where we discuss the role of time, and inertia, in evolution.

5.1   The Popularity of C

Legacy aside, our view is that C has two main strengths as a language: its core features are simple, and it offers high performance. The price for performance is that virtually no reliability or security guarantees are provided. An erroneous C program can behave in unpredictable ways, and can be vulnerable to attack. Some of the most famous software vulnerabilities of recent years, including the Heartbleed bug,[26] arise from basic errors in C programs, and a great deal of effort still goes into writing and deploying "sanitiser" tools to find defects in C code, such as AddressSanitizer and MemorySanitizer from Google.[27] Further, despite having a simple core, the semantics of C are far from simple when one considers the host of undefined and implementation-defined behaviours described in the language specification. Indeed, decades since the language's inception, top programming language conferences are still accepting papers that attempt to rigorously define the semantics of C [15, 29], and recent programming models for multi-core and graphics processors, such as OpenCL and Metal, have based their accelerator programming languages on C.

Given that the majority of code written today does not need to perform optimally, and given the advances in techniques such as just-in-time compilation that in many cases allow managed languages to achieve performance comparable to that of C, we ask: why does C remain so popular, and will this trend continue?

A major reason for C's longevity is that it is used to develop all major operating systems and many supporting tools. It is also typically the language of choice for embedded programming, partly due to the language's small memory footprint, and also because C is usually the first language for which a compiler targeting a new instruction set becomes available (the latter motivated by the fact that such a compiler is required to compile an operating system for the new target platform). Beyond compilers, the language is also well supported by tools, such as debuggers, linkers, profilers and sanitisers, which can influence a language's selection for use.

Kell points out various fundamental merits to systems programming that C brings, beyond it simply being a de-facto standard [18]. He argues that "the very 'unsafety' of C is based on an unfortunate conflation of the language itself with how it is implemented", and makes a compelling case that a safe implementation of C, with sufficiently high performance for the needs of systems programming, is possible. He also argues that a key property of C that many higher-level languages sacrifice is its ability to facilitate communication with 'alien' system components (including both hardware devices and code from other programming languages). This flexibility in communication owes to the ability to linking together object files that respect the same application binary interface, in C's use of memory as a uniform abstraction for communication. Kell concludes: "C is far from sacred, and I look forward to its replacements—but they must not forget the importance of communicating with aliens."

---

[26] http://heartbleed.com/.
[27] https://github.com/google/sanitizers.

In short, no other current language approaches the fitness of C (when measured along with its symbiotic tool-ecosystem) for the systems-programming niche.

5.2 The Rise of Dynamically Typed Languages

Static type systems have the ability to weed out large classes of programmer-induced defects ahead of time. In addition, as discussed in Sect. 3.1, static types facilitate automated refactoring—key to agile development processes—and enable advanced compiler optimisations that can improve performance. Yet many of today's most popular languages, including JavaScript, PHP, Ruby and Python, do not feature static types, or make static types optional (and unusual in practice).

In the case of JavaScript, we argue that its prevalence is driven by the web as a programming platform, and web browsers as a dominant execution environment. As the only language supported by all browsers, in a sense, JavaScript is to browsers what C is to Unix. JavaScript has also seen broad uptake in server-side development of recent times, with the Node.js platform. A major driver for this is developer mindshare. Many developers already know JavaScript because of previous work in the browser, so having a server environment where they can code in the language they already know lets them transfer many of their existing skills without having to learn Python, Ruby or PHP. In evolutionary terms, while no language per se is favoured in the server-side world, the additional fitness of JavaScript with its symbiote "programmer experience" has enabled it to colonise this niche.

One reason for the popularity of dynamic languages in general is that they tend to come with excellent library support, providing just the right methods to offer a desired service. Representing structured data without a schema in statically typed languages is generally more challenging (e.g. what types to use), but recent work by Petricek et al. on inferring shapes for F# type providers is promising [34].

A more fundamental reason may be "beginner-friendliness". It is easy to get some code up and running to power a web page using JavaScript; writing a simple utility in Python is usually more straightforward than would be the case in C (where one would need to battle with string manipulation), or in Java (where one would need to decide which classes to create).

The importance of beginner-friendliness should not be underestimated. Many people writing software these days are not trained computer scientists or software engineers. As coding becomes a skill required for a large number of different jobs, we have more and more programmers, but they may not have the time or inclination to learn the intricacies of a complex languages—they just want to get something done. Currently Python (supported by technologies like iPython Notebooks) is popular with scientists and others just wanting to get going quickly on some fairly simple computational task. This category of programmers seems likely only to grow in the future, and as such the world will accumulate growing amounts of fairly simple software, in languages that are comparatively easy for non-specialists to work with.

The danger, historically exemplified by Facebook's use of PHP, is that a system that starts as a simple program in a dynamically typed language may grow beyond practical maintainability. We question the extent to which dynamically typed languages are suitable for building large-scale infrastructure that needs to be maintained and refactored over many years by a changing team. Facebook's Hack language, which extends PHP with types in a manner that permits an untyped code base to be *incrementally* typed, is one example where a valuable code base without static types is being migrated to a typed form to enable faster defect detection and better readability and maintenance.[28] We also see similar trends in the JavaScript world, for example in the TypeScript[29] and Flow[30] initiatives from Microsoft and Facebook respectively.

We can summarise that various features of dynamic languages—rapid prototyping, beginner-friendliness, avoidance of intellectually sound but challenging type systems—adds to the fitness of such languages in niches that appreciate these properties over others.

5.3   The Patchwork Support for Parallelism

As discussed in Sect. 2.7 under "Parallelism and the rise of multi-core", the last decade has seen a wealth of research papers and industrial programming models to aid in writing parallel code, itself building on a long history of focused work by the (previously niche) parallel programming community. Yet it seems that, from a general purpose programmer's perspective, progress has been limited. There are a wide range of language features to support parallelism at different levels of abstraction (see Sect. 2.7 for examples), but even a single abstraction level there are many competing choices, both between and within languages. But despite, and perhaps *because of* all this choice, it is far from clear to a programmer without parallelism expertise, which language and mechanism to choose when wishing to accelerate a particular application.

A seemingly reasonable programmer strategy might be to invoke parallel versions of operations wherever it is safe to do so, e.g. defaulting to a `ParallelStream` over a `Stream` in Java unless the parallel version is unsafe, and leave it to the run-time system to decide when to actually employ parallelism.[31] This strategy is analogous to other strategies that are often followed during software development, such as favouring the most general type for a function argument, making data immutable when possible, and limiting the visibility

---

[28] https://code.facebook.com/posts/264544830379293/hack-a-new-programming-language-for-hhvm/.

[29] https://github.com/Microsoft/TypeScript.

[30] https://github.com/facebook/flow.

[31] Determining whether parallel execution is safe might be left to the programmer, as in the case of parallel streams in Java, or might be facilitated by tool support or guaranteed by language semantics (e.g. due to language purity).

of module internals unless higher visibility is required. However, this "use parallelism wherever it would be safe" approach is, at present, naïve, and usually leads to *reduced* performance for reasons of task granularity and memory hierarchy effects when running multiple small threads. This demonstrates that we have a long way to go before parallel programming becomes truly mainstream.

Currently it often seems that the many language concurrency primitives are each fittest for a given niche, with no unifying model.

6   The Next 7000 Programming Languages

Is the Evolutionary Theory Wrong? The previous section observed three situations where languages have counter-fitness aspects (genes). We observe that this is not unexpected; time and inertia are also important in translating evolutionary fitness to niche occupancy. Even if a species, or language, becomes less fit than a competitor, its present dominance may still cause it to produce more seeds in total than the fitter, but less dominant, competitor—even if these seeds individually are less likely to thrive. Thus changes in fitness (e.g. an upgrading of the important of security affecting our perceived fitness of C) are likely only to change the second derivative of percentage niche-occupancy. Incidentally, recent evidence seems to suggest that dinosaurs were in relative decline to mammals for around 50 million years before the Chicxulub asteroid impact which completed the task [39]. We simultaneously argue that Sect. 5 *does* correctly reflect niche occupancy today, and at the same time, in this section propose predictions of future niche occupancy based on current notions of fitness.

Emboldened by Landin's success, we now make some predictions—starting with the 'elephants in the room' of the previous section.

6.1   A Replacement for C/C++?

The short answer to "What will replace C/C++ in the light of its unsafe features?" appears to be "Nothing in the short term". One explanation for this is that the C family of languages is so intimately bound to all major operating systems that its replacement is unthinkable in the short term. One pragmatic reason beyond simple inertia is that much of the system software tool chain (compilers, debuggers, linkers, etc.) either directly targets C or is designed to be most easily used in conjunction with a C software stack. The investment required to re-target this tool chain is so vast that there is a strong economic argument to continue using C.

Taking the idea of evolutionary inertia above, the nearest botanical analogue is perhaps "How long would it take for giant redwoods (sequoia) to be supplanted by a locally fitter competitor species?", answered by "rather longer than it takes moss to colonise a damp lawn".

That having been said, there are innovations quietly chipping away at the current "we'll just have to put up with the insecurities of C/C++".

One direction is languages such as Rust, that offer better safety guarantees through types, as well the safe subset of C++ mentioned in Sect. 3.2.

Another direction is the concept of Unikernel (or 'library OS') exemplified by MirageOS.[32] MirageOS is coded in the managed functional-style language OCaml and exploits its powerful module system. Experiments show that the additional cost of a managed language (5–10% for low-level drivers) is mitigated by the reduced need for context-switching to protect against pointer-arithmetic in unsafe languages [26]. Could the Linux kernel be similarly re-coded? Can the immediate performance penalty be compensated by more flexible and high-level structuring mechanisms?

A second thrust is "let's make C secure". At first this seems impossible because of pointer arithmetic. But using additional storage to represent pointer metadata (e.g. base, limit and offset) at run time can give a pointer-safe C implementation; this can be achieved via *fat pointers*, which change the pointer representation itself and thus break compatibility with code that does not use fat pointers [19,44],[33] or via compile-time instrumentation methods that do not change the representation of pointers and thus facilitate integration with un-instrumented code [16,32,37]. Either way, dynamic bounds checking reduces the attack surface in that buffer overflows and the like can no longer be exploited to enable arbitrary code execution—in short the result is no worse (but no better than) `NullPointerException` in Java. Recent work abstracts fat pointers to *capabilities* and does this checking in hardware: the Cheri project, e.g. [6], has a whole C tool-chain replacement (from FPGA-based hardware to compilers and debuggers) for a hardware-agnostic capability extension instantiated in a MIPS-like instruction set. The run-time cost of this appears in the order of 1%. Intel's MPX[34] (Memory Protection Extensions) has a similar aim, but relative performance data for whole operating systems on MPX is not yet available. As discussed in Sect. 5.1, Kell also makes a compelling argument that a safe and relatively performant implementation of C may be feasible [18].

6.2 From Dynamic to Static Types, to Verified Software

We envisage that *gradual typing* [1,43,46] will become increasingly prominent in future languages, whereby static types can be incrementally added to an otherwise dynamically typed program, so that full static typing is enabled once enough types are present, with type inference algorithms still allowing types to be omitted to some degree. This captures the "beginner-friendliness" and flexibility of dynamic types, but facilitates a gradual transition towards the guarantees that static types provide. Ideas along these lines are explored by Facebook's Hack language, as discussed in Sect. 5.2. Takikawa et al. recently studied the performance

---

[32] https://github.com/mirage.

[33] A subtlety is that the C standard currently requires pointers to occupy no more space than the integer type `intptr_t`. So often fat pointers need to use indirection or bit-level packing techniques which are both expensive in software.

[34] https://en.wikipedia.org/wiki/Intel_MPX.

of gradual typing in the context of Racket, with current results suggesting that work is needed to reduce the overhead of crossing a typed/untyped boundary at run time, and that performance tended to dip as static types were introduced to programs, unless they were introduced everywhere [45]. Still, it seems that such performance issues can be solved via a combination of advanced type inference and different implementation choices, and furthermore types confer many advantages besides performance, especially in relation to refactoring.

A gradual-typing spectrum provides increased benefits as developers invest in writing more type annotations. As developers devote more time to writing richer specifications they reap the benefits of stronger static and dynamic analysis and verification. We can see this approach as part of a bigger picture of confidence of correctness, given the many pressures to create more reliable software. Types are merely one example of techniques to perform checks on correctness. In addition to such static analysis, we see the rise of dynamic checks and executable specifications, from the automated tests that support test-driven development and agile methods to formally verified software.

We see a unified whole, where types, tests and specifications are complementary, and can be developed before, during or after the software system (a form of 'gradual verification'). As the system evolves, the degree of correctness checking demanded can evolve too, and we foresee developments that make transitioning along this spectrum a natural progression over the life of a system. A documented example of formal correctness requirements being added to a system post-hoc is the Pentium 4 floating-point multiplier [17] (40,000 lines of HDL); co-development of software and specifications are visible in the CompCert [23] and CakeML [21] verified compiler projects.

6.3   Increased Fragmentation of Parallelism Support

We would like to optimistically predict that revolutions in programming language, compiler and run-time system technology will resolve the situation of patchwork support for parallelism discussed in Sect. 5.3. However, we fear that this is wishful thinking, and that balkanisation may actually increase.

If a programmer is working in a very limited domain and does not require flexibility for their application to evolve, they may benefit from a domain-oriented language, such as MATLAB or Julia, for which there is good potential for automatic parallelism—exploiting domain properties and the lack of hard-to-parallelise language features—even if this has not been achieved yet. So by using programming at higher levels of abstraction, thereby trading against language flexibility, good and predictable parallel performance is possible. But if a programmer *does* require the flexibility offered by more general languages then the situation becomes more difficult and other trade-offs emerge. A functional language may eliminate the problems of aliasing that make imperative and object-oriented languages hard to parallelise, but performance is at the mercy of decisions made by the compiler and run-time system, which can be hard to control in a declarative setting and yet may need to be controlled to avoid brittle performance changes as software evolves. A high-level object-oriented language like Java provides features unrelated to parallelism for high-productivity programming, and various libraries catering for parallelism at a relatively high level of abstraction. But it can still be difficult to achieve high and predictable performance without breaking this abstraction layer, or resorting to otherwise poor software engineering practices that sacrifice modularity and compositionality. Of course, there are lower-level languages such as OpenCL that enable fine-grained performance tuning, but lead to software that is hard to maintain and evolve.

Our prediction is that in domains where exploiting parallelism is essential— e.g. machine learning, computer vision, graph processing— communities will settle on de-facto standard domain-specific languages and libraries that are a good fit for the task at hand. These approaches will in turn be implemented on top of lower-level languages and libraries providing access to underlying hardware and implemented in languages such as OpenCL. We see the greatest potential for parallelism support in higher-level general-purpose languages to be for distributed processing, where work can be partitioned at a sufficiently coarse level of granularity to allow run-time systems to make decisions on parallel deployment dynamically, without sacrificing parallel speedup in the process.

6.4 Error Resilience

As systems grow, and become more distributed, then structured approaches to error resilience (coping with transient and permanent errors) will become more important. Section 3.2 explored the Erlang fail-fast model (fail on unexpected situations and expect your owner to fix things up) along with the suggestion that functional-style idempotence is more likely to be fruitful in highly distributed systems than classical imperative-style checkpoint and rollback.

6.5 Supporting Better Software Engineering Practices

We foresee a closer integration between languages and the tools that support them. Rather than being developed separately, languages and tools will be developed as one in symbiosis. At the time of writing we are beginning to see a move (back) towards tools being created together with languages. With languages like Kotlin, we see an example of the requirement to provide excellent tool support for working with a language being a primary driver for decisions in the design of the language itself.

Programs and software systems will continue to grow in size, and with this we foresee a change in how developers work with programs, a move away from treating programs as text to be edited, and towards graphs to be transformed. We may no longer edit individual lines of code, but encode and apply transformations, either in the form of refactorings (building on those currently supported by sophisticated IDEs for Java and C#) or by writing code that writes (or edits) code, such as those being developed by Atomist.[35] This brings to mind the possibility of code being synthesised from a specification using AI techniques, which we discuss further in Sect. 6.6.

---

[35] https://www.atomist.com/.

Software systems will continue to grow and so we foresee more explicit language features for describing modular structures and componentisation. Java 9's *module system* is a good start in this direction, but it does not yet address the issues of versioned, and independently developed, software components. Modularity helps humans—whose brains sadly have not increased in computational power at the same rate as the machines that we manufacture—to comprehend, manage and change these large systems by thinking at appropriate levels of abstraction. Alternatively, instead of enriching languages with more powerful features, we can imagine a state where more developers get their work done with simple languages supported by good tools. Although a code base written in a more sophisticated language may be smaller, it may also be more difficult to work with if the developer tools are less powerful. We foresee the speed of evolution of tooling exceeding that of the languages they support, with the result that developers may well be able to get more done because they have better tools, rather than because they have better building blocks.

6.6 Program Synthesis and AI

We predict strong potential for advances in artificial intelligence methods to reduce the human effort associated with programming. In the near future one can imagine routine learning being regularly deployed to provide smart auto-completion and refactoring, learning from data on programmer habits collected from users of a particular IDE. This might go further: automating those laborious program overhauls that often take hours or days to complete, but during which one can feel to be in auto-pilot mode. Nevertheless, making such semantics-aware transformations would appear to go well beyond the pattern-recognition tasks at which machine learning has been shown to excel. It seems apparent that there is scope for effective program synthesis in suitably restricted domains, such as the development of standard device drivers [38]. The prospect of synthesising a correct implementation of a non-trivial class, given a precise definition of its interfaces and a set of unit tests that it should pass, seems within reach in the foreseeable future: recent work on synthesising programs from input-output examples shows promise [2] and has gained widespread media attention.[36] However, we regard software development in general as a creative process that stretches human ingenuity to its limits, and thus do not predict general breakthroughs here unless human-level AI is achieved.

6.7 A Non-prediction

In discussing the three elephants in the room of Sect. 5 we might hope for, although we do not explicitly predict it, general purpose languages with a unified concurrency model, which are type-safe, offer a flexible balance between static and dynamic typing, along with suitability for low-level programming. Indeed

---

[36] https://www.newscientist.com/article/mg23331144-500-ai-learns-to-write-its-own-code-by-stealing-from-other-programs/.

we might hope for a single universal language which is suitable for all niches, as has been a recurring hope since Landin's time.

However, the evolutionary model does not predict this. It does predict that *if* a language is fitter for multiple niches then it will eventually colonise both. It says nothing about the existence of such a language, and past attempts to create universal languages do not add encouragement.

Some Final Words

While we hope to have provided some updated discussion and predictions following Landin's work half a century ago, these can only reflect the present structure of languages and evolution is ongoing. We wonder what a follow-up article in another 50 years would say.

Acknowledgements. We are grateful to Sophia Drossopoulou, Stephen Kell, Tom Stuart, Joost-Pieter Katoen, Flemming Nielson and Bernhard Steffen for their useful feedback on an earlier draft of this work.

Alastair Donaldson was supported by an EPSRC Early Career Fellowship (EP/N026314/1).

References

1. Anderson, C., Drossopoulou, S.: BabyJ: from object based to class based programming via types. Electr. Notes Theor. Comput. Sci. **82**(7), 53–81 (2003). https://doi.org/10.1016/S1571-0661(04)80802-8
2. Balog, M., Gaunt, A.L., Brockschmidt, M., Nowozin, S., Tarlow, D.: DeepCoder: Learning to write programs. CoRR abs/1611.01989 (2016). http://arxiv.org/abs/1611.01989
3. Beck, K.: Test Driven Development: By Example. Addison-Wesley Longman Publishing Co., Inc., Boston (2002)
4. Beck, K., Andres, C.: Extreme Programming Explained: Embrace Change, 2nd edn. Addison-Wesley Professional, Boston (2004)
5. Brauer, W. (ed.): Gesellschaft für Informatik e.V. LNCS, vol. 1. Springer, Heidelberg (1973). https://doi.org/10.1007/978-3-642-80732-9. 3 Jahrestagung, Hamburg, Deutschland, 8–10 Oktober 1973
6. Chisnall, D., Rothwell, C., Watson, R.N., Woodruff, J., Vadera, M., Moore, S.W., Roe, M., Davis, B., Neumann, P.G.: Beyond the PDP-11: architectural support for a memory-safe C abstract machine. SIGARCH Comput. Archit. News **43**(1), 117–130 (2015). https://doi.org/10.1145/2786763.2694367
7. Claessen, K., Hughes, J.: QuickCheck: a lightweight tool for random testing of Haskell programs. In: Odersky, M., Wadler, P. (eds.) Proceedings of the Fifth ACM SIGPLAN International Conference on Functional Programming (ICFP 2000), 18–21 September 2000, Montreal, Canada, pp. 268–279. ACM (2000). https://doi.org/10.1145/351240.351266
8. Dean, J., Ghemawat, S.: MapReduce: a flexible data processing tool. Commun. ACM **53**(1), 72–77 (2010). https://doi.org/10.1145/1629175.1629198
9. Foster, N., Greenberg, M., Pierce, B.C.: Types considered harmful. Invited talk at Mathematical Foundations of Programming Semantics (MFPS) (2008). http://www.cis.upenn.edu/~bcpierce/papers/harmful-mfps.pdf

10. Fowler, M., Beck, K.: Refactoring: Improving the Design of Existing Code. Object Technology Series. Addison-Wesley Longman Publishing Co., Inc., Boston (1999)
11. Gabriel, R.P.: Lisp: good news, bad news, how to win big (1991). https://www.dreamsongs.com/WIB.html
12. Gabriel, R.P.: Patterns of Software: Tales from the Software Community. Oxford University Press Inc., New York (1996)
13. Gabriel, R.P., White, J.L., Bobrow, D.G.: CLOS: integrating object-oriented and functional programming. Commun. ACM **34**(9), 29–38 (1991). https://doi.org/10.1145/114669.114671
14. Garner, S.: Reducing the cognitive load on novice programmers. In: Barker, P., Rebelsky, S. (eds.) Proceedings of EdMedia: World Conference on Educational Media and Technology, pp. 578–583. ERIC (2002)
15. Hathhorn, C., Ellison, C., Rosu, G.: Defining the undefinedness of C. In: Grove, D., Blackburn, S. (eds.) Proceedings of the 36th ACM SIGPLAN Conference on Programming Language Design and Implementation, 15–17 June 2015, Portland, OR, USA, pp. 336–345. ACM (2015). https://doi.org/10.1145/2737924.2737979
16. Jones, R.W.M., Kelly, P.H.J.: Backwards-compatible bounds checking for arrays and pointers in C programs. In: AADEBUG, pp. 13–26 (1997). http://www.ep.liu.se/ecp/article.asp?issue=001&article=002
17. Kaivola, R., Narasimhan, N.: Formal verification of the pentium®4 floating-point multiplier. In: Proceedings of the Conference on Design, Automation and Test in Europe, DATE 2002, pp. 20–27. IEEE Computer Society, Washington, DC (2002). http://dl.acm.org/citation.cfm?id=882452.874523
18. Kell, S.: Some were meant for C: the endurance of an unmanageable language. In: Torlak, E., van der Storm, T., Biddle, R. (eds.) Proceedings of the 2017 ACM SIGPLAN International Symposium on New Ideas, New Paradigms, and Reflections on Programming and Software, Onward! 2017, 23–27 October 2017, Vancouver, BC, Canada, pp. 229–245. ACM (2017). https://doi.org/10.1145/3133850.3133867
19. Kendall, A.S.C.: Bcc: runtime checking for C programs. In: USENIX Summer Conference, pp. 5–16. USENIX (1983)
20. Kennedy, K., Koelbel, C., Zima, H.P.: The rise and fall of High Performance Fortran: an historical object lesson. In: Ryder, B.G., Hailpern, B. (eds.) Proceedings of the Third ACM SIGPLAN History of Programming Languages Conference (HOPL-III), 9–10 June 2007, San Diego, California, USA, pp. 1–22. ACM (2007). https://doi.org/10.1145/1238844.1238851
21. Kumar, R., Myreen, M.O., Norrish, M., Owens, S.: CakeML: a verified implementation of ML. In: Jagannathan, S., Sewell, P. (eds.) The 41st Annual ACM SIGPLAN-SIGACT Symposium on Principles of Programming Languages, POPL 2014, 20–21 January 2014, San Diego, CA, USA, pp. 179–192. ACM (2014). https://doi.org/10.1145/2535838.2535841
22. Landin, P.J.: The next 700 programming languages. Commun. ACM **9**(3), 157–166 (1966). https://doi.org/10.1145/365230.365257
23. Leroy, X.: Formal verification of a realistic compiler. Commun. ACM **52**(7), 107–115 (2009). https://doi.org/10.1145/1538788.1538814
24. Lopes, C.V., Maj, P., Martins, P., Saini, V., Yang, D., Zitny, J., Sajnani, H., Vitek, J.: Déjàvu: a map of code duplicates on github. In: PACMPL, vol. 1, no. OOPSLA, pp. 84:1–84:28 (2017). https://doi.org/10.1145/3133908
25. Mackinnon, T., Freeman, S., Craig, P.: Endo-testing: unit testing with mock objects. In: Succi, G., Marchesi, M. (eds.) Extreme Programming Examined, pp. 287–301. Addison-Wesley Longman Publishing Co., Inc., Boston (2001). http://dl.acm.org/citation.cfm?id=377517.377534

26. Madhavapeddy, A., Mortier, R., Rotsos, C., Scott, D., Singh, B., Gazagnaire, T., Smith, S., Hand, S., Crowcroft, J.: Unikernels: library operating systems for the cloud. In: Proceedings of the Eighteenth International Conference on Architectural Support for Programming Languages and Operating Systems, ASPLOS 2013, pp. 461–472. ACM, New York(2013). https://doi.org/10.1145/2451116.2451167

27. Marlow, S.: Parallel and Concurrent Programming in Haskell. O'Reilly, Sebastopol (2013)

28. McCormick, J.W., Chapin, P.C.: Building High Integrity Applications with SPARK. Cambridge University Press, Cambridge (2015)

29. Memarian, K., Matthiesen, J., Lingard, J., Nienhuis, K., Chisnall, D., Watson, R.N.M., Sewell, P.: Into the depths of C: elaborating the de facto standards. In: Krintz, C., Berger, E. (eds.) Proceedings of the 37th ACM SIGPLAN Conference on Programming Language Design and Implementation, PLDI 2016, 13–17 June 2016, Santa Barbara, CA, USA, pp. 1–15. ACM (2016). https://doi.org/10.1145/2908080.2908081

30. Mitchell, J.C.: Concepts in Programming Languages. Cambridge University Press, Cambridge, October 2002

31. Murray, D.G., Schwarzkopf, M., Smowton, C., Smith, S., Madhavapeddy, A., Hand, S.: CIEL: a universal execution engine for distributed data-flow computing. In: Proceedings of the 8th USENIX Conference on Networked Systems Design and Implementation, NSDI 2011, pp. 113–126. USENIX Association, Berkeley (2011). http://dl.acm.org/citation.cfm?id=1972457.1972470

32. Nagarakatte, S., Zhao, J., Martin, M.M.K., Zdancewic, S.: SoftBound: highly compatible and complete spatial memory safety for C. In: Hind, M., Diwan, A. (eds.) Proceedings of the 2009 ACM SIGPLAN Conference on Programming Language Design and Implementation, PLDI 2009, 15–21 June 2009, Dublin, Ireland, pp. 245–258. ACM (2009). https://doi.org/10.1145/1542476.1542504

33. Perez, F., Granger, B.E., Hunter, J.D.: Python: an ecosystem for scientific computing. Comput. Sci. Eng. 13(2), 13–21 (2011). https://doi.org/10.1109/MCSE.2010.119

34. Petricek, T., Guerra, G., Syme, D.: Types from data: making structured data first-class citizens in F#. In: Proceedings of the 37th ACM SIGPLAN Conference on Programming Language Design and Implementation, PLDI 2016, pp. 477–490. ACM, New York (2016). https://doi.org/10.1145/2908080.2908115

35. Ritchie, D.: The development of the C language. In: Lee, J.A.N., Sammet, J.E. (eds.) History of Programming Languages Conference (HOPL-II), Preprints, 20–23 April 1993, Cambridge, Massachusetts, USA, pp. 201–208. ACM (1993). https://doi.org/10.1145/154766.155580

36. Ruby, S., Copeland, D.B., Thomas, D.: Agile Web Development with Rails 5.1. Pragmatic Bookshelf, Raleigh (2017)

37. Ruwase, O., Lam, M.S.: A practical dynamic buffer overflow detector. In: Proceedings of the Network and Distributed System Security Symposium, NDSS 2004, San Diego, California, USA. The Internet Society (2004). http://www.isoc.org/isoc/conferences/ndss/04/proceedings/Papers/Ruwase.pdf

38. Ryzhyk, L., Walker, A., Keys, J., Legg, A., Raghunath, A., Stumm, M., Vij, M.: User-guided device driver synthesis. In: Flinn, J., Levy, H. (eds.) 11th USENIX Symposium on Operating Systems Design and Implementation, OSDI 2014, 6–8 October 2014, Broomfield, CO, USA, pp. 661–676. USENIX Association (2014). https://www.usenix.org/conference/osdi14/technical-sessions/presentation/ryzhyk

39. Sakamoto, M., Benton, M., Venditti, C.: Dinosaurs in decline tens of millions of years before their final extinction. Proc. Natl. Acad. Sci. 113(18), 5036–5040 (2016)

40. Schäfer, M.: Refactoring tools for dynamic languages. In: Proceedings of the Fifth Workshop on Refactoring Tools, WRT 2012, pp. 59–62. ACM, New York (2012). https://doi.org/10.1145/2328876.2328885
41. Seibel, P.: Coders at Work, 1st edn. Apress, Berkeley (2009)
42. Severance, C.: Javascript: designing a language in 10 days. Computer **45**, 7–8 (2012)
43. Siek, J.G., Taha, W.: Gradual typing for functional languages. In: Proceedings of the Scheme and Functional Programming Workshop, pp. 81–92 (2006)
44. Steffen, J.L.: Adding run-time checking to the portable C compiler. Softw. Pract. Exp. **22**(4), 305–348 (1992). https://doi.org/10.1002/spe.4380220403
45. Takikawa, A., Feltey, D., Greenman, B., New, M.S., Vitek, J., Felleisen, M.: Is sound gradual typing dead? In: Bodík, R., Majumdar, R. (eds.) Proceedings of the 43rd Annual ACM SIGPLAN-SIGACT Symposium on Principles of Programming Languages, 20–22 January 2016, POPL 2016, St. Petersburg, FL, USA, pp. 456–468. ACM (2016). https://doi.org/10.1145/2837614.2837630
46. Tobin-Hochstadt, S., Felleisen, M.: Interlanguage migration: from scripts to programs. In: Tarr, P.L., Cook, W.R. (eds.) Companion to the 21th Annual ACM SIGPLAN Conference on Object-Oriented Programming, Systems, Languages, and Applications, OOPSLA 2006, 22–26 October 2006, Portland, Oregon, USA, pp. 964–974. ACM (2006). https://doi.org/10.1145/1176617.1176755
47. Ungar, D., Chambers, C., Chang, B.W., Hölzle, U.: Organizing programs without classes. Lisp Symb. Comput. **4**(3), 223–242 (1991). https://doi.org/10.1007/BF01806107

Multi-Mode DAE Models - Challenges, Theory and Implementation

Albert Benveniste[1], Benoît Caillaud[1], Hilding Elmqvist[2], Khalil Ghorbal[1(✉)],
Martin Otter[3(✉)], and Marc Pouzet[4]

[1] Inria, Rennes, France
{albert.benveniste,benoit.caillaud,khalil.ghorbal}@inria.fr
[2] Mogram AB, Lund, Sweden
hilding.elmqvist@mogram.net
[3] DLR-SR, Oberpfaffenhofen, Germany
martin.otter@dlr.de
[4] ENS, Paris, France
marc.pouzet@ens.fr

Abstract. Our objective is to model and simulate Cyber-Physical Systems (CPS) such as robots, vehicles, and power plants. The structure of CPS models may change during simulation due to the desired operation, due to failure situations or due to changes in physical conditions. Corresponding models are called multi-mode. We are interested in multidomain, component-oriented modeling as performed, for example, with the modeling language Modelica that leads naturally to Differential Algebraic Equations (DAEs). This paper is thus about multi-mode DAE systems. In particular, new methods are discussed to overcome one key problem that was only solved for specific subclasses of systems before: How to switch from one mode to another one when the number of equations may change and variables may exhibit impulsive behavior? An evaluation is performed both with the experimental modeling and simulation system Modia, a domain specific language extension of the programming language Julia, and with SunDAE, a novel structural analysis library for multi-mode DAE systems.

Keywords: Multi-Mode systems · Cyber-Physical Systems · CPS
Modia · Modelica · Differential algebraic equations · DAE
Differential index · Structural analysis · Operational semantics
Constructive semantics · Nonstandard analysis

1 Introduction

Modeling with block diagrams described with Ordinary Differential Equations in state space form (ODE) has become a key pillar in the development of Cyber-Physical Systems (CPS). Block diagrams, however, suffer from a lack of modularity and reuse that is best illustrated in Fig. 1. This figure shows two

© Springer Nature Switzerland AG 2019
B. Steffen and G. Woeginger (Eds.): Computing and Software Science, LNCS 10000, pp. 283–310, 2019.
https://doi.org/10.1007/978-3-319-91908-9_16

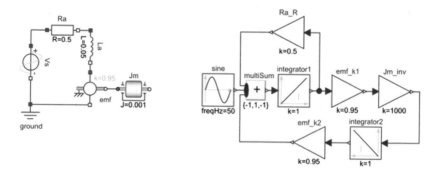

Fig. 1. DAE (left) vs. ODE (right) based modeling.

models of the same system consisting of a simple model of an electrical motor and of the rotational inertia of the motor. On the left hand side a (Modelica) schematic/component diagram of the system is shown that connects physical components through non-directed interactions resulting from the first principles of physics. On the right hand side the same model is shown as a block diagram in which input/output oriented blocks are connected with a directed wiring manually specified by the designer. Adding one more physical component is straightforward in the schematic, whereas it may need a complete redesign in the block diagram.

This should not come as a surprise, as the first principles of physics naturally lead to considering acausal models such as the one in Fig. 1-left. Consider, for example, the case of electric circuits. So-called *circuit laws* such as Kirchhoff laws, are naturally expressed as balance equations: the algebraic sum of currents in a network of conductors meeting at a point is zero; or, the sum of all the voltages around a loop is equal to zero. Similarly, some components (such as, e.g., resistors or capacitors) come with no input/output prespecified orientation. A same circuit can be assigned different input/output status for its variables, depending on which ones are declared as sources. The same situation arises in mechanics or in thermodynamics. Engineers interested in multi-physics modeling have identified this fact since the 70's by proposing *bond graphs* [17,31], in which electric circuits, mechanical systems, and thermodynamical systems, are abstracted to a common framework manipulating *efforts, flows,* and *junctions.* To summarize, for systems made of a large number of interconnected components, getting the usual input/output state space model (such as in Simulink block diagrams) becomes intractable, whereas it remains manageable if acausal models are supported.

In addition to being naturally described by an acausal model, a system may have different modes for different reasons. One reason is the physics: mechanical impacts where the bodies may remain in contact after a collision or an active grasping/docking, idealized electrical or hydraulic switching elements, are examples of situations requiring different sets of equations for their modeling. Another reason is the control of complex scenarios like repairing a satellite with robots, changing operations of a system like a power plant with start-up, normal operation and shut down. Finally, safety needs may lead to so-called degraded modes in which the system dynamics may become very different (some components, sensors or actuators getting down for example). Models of this kind are called *multi-mode* models.

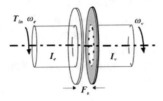

Fig. 2. A simple clutch with two shafts.

Acausal multi-mode models present, however, subtle difficulties at mode changes. Consider for instance the case of an idealized clutch model, illustrated in Fig. 2. The clutch possesses two modes: released (the two shafts rotate freely) and engaged (the two shafts are in contact). Deriving acausal models from the first principles is simple and rather elegant for each single mode alone. The intuition tells us that, when the clutch gets engaged, the different velocities of the two shafts will, in zero time, merge to a unique identical angular velocity under impulsive torques. One also expects that the resulting common velocity is entirely determined and depends only on the individual inertia and velocity of each shaft, prior to engagement. Determining manually the restart conditions is required if one resorts to using oriented block-diagrams like in Simulink. We argue that such task is difficult for this simple example and becomes even impossible for real-life models. Those restart conditions should rather be synthesized automatically by the compiler and made available at run time to simulate the model. This work advocates therefore the use of acausal modelling languages since they

1. make the specification of large (single mode) Cyber Physical Systems more modular, more elegant, and with better reuse;
2. are indispensable to synthesize proper restart conditions at mode changes, for models where this cannot be done manually—the idealized clutch model being a simple example.

It should also be clear that classical state space input/output formalisms (such as Simulink block diagrams) do not address the above challenges. Neither does the formalism of *hybrid automata* [1] used as the model of hybrid systems by several verification tools such as Flow* or SpaceEx.

Causal input/output state space models are based on Ordinary Differential Equations (ODE), of the form $\dot{x} = f(x, u)$ where x is the state and u the input, whereas acausal models à la Modelica are based on Differential Algebraic Equations (DAE) of the form $f(\dot{x}, x, v) = 0$ where x is a state and v an algebraic variable, for which no input or output status can be a priori specified.

In this paper we propose a theory to support the compilation of multi-mode DAE based models in a systematic and mathematically sound way. We want to reject some models that are in some sense spurious. And we want to synthesize (whenever needed, not in all cases) the computation of the restart conditions at mode changes. All of this will be performed at compile time, through a special static analysis called the *structural analysis,* which is an important topic of this paper. This structural analysis is an essential preprocessing step prior to generating simulation code. We will illustrate our purpose by an example from electro-mechanics that includes a clutch as one of its subsystems. The specification, analysis, compilation, and simulation of this model will be illustrated using the recently proposed experimental modeling language called Modia.

2   State-of-the-Art and Related Work

There exists an extensive body of work related to the numerical solution of *single-mode DAEs,* especially [9], as well as to the modeling and simulation of *single-mode multi-domain* models leading to DAEs[1].

Mechanical systems featuring impulses are known since the 18th century. A large literature about multi-body systems with contacts and impulses exists, for example [25, 26]. The current research focuses on simulating contacts between many bodies using time stepping methods. Contact equations are usually described approximately on velocity or acceleration level (if contact occurs, the relative velocity or acceleration between the relevant bodies is constrained to be zero). Since the constraints on position level are not explicitly taken into account, typically a drift occurs that is usually not relevant for systems with many contacting bodies but is not acceptable for general multi-mode DAEs. An exception is [29], where constraints on position level are enforced. It is not obvious how the specialized multi-mode methods for multi-body systems can be generalized to any type of multi-mode DAE.

Also for electrical circuits with idealized switches, like ideal diodes, impulses can occur. Again a large literature is available concentrating mostly on specialized electrical circuits such as piecewise-linear networks with idealized switches [2, 16, 32]. Again, it is not obvious how to generalize methods in this specialized area to general multi-mode DAEs.

The paper of Mehrmann et al. [20] contains interesting results regarding numerical techniques to detect chattering between modes. It, however, assumes that consistent reset values are explicitly given for each mode. Such an assumption does not hold in general, especially for a compositional framework where one wants to assemble pre-defined physical components.

In the PhD-thesis of Zimmer [33] variable-structure multi-domain DAEs are defined with a special modeling language and a run-time interpreter is used that processes the DAE equations at run-time, when the structure and/or the index is changing. Limitations of this work are that impulsive behavior is not supported

---

[1] See the extensive literature available in https://www.modelica.org/publications.

and that the user has to define the transfer of variable values from one mode to the next mode explicitly, which is not practical for large models.

Describing variable structure systems with *causal* state machines is discussed by Pepper et al. [24].

Elmqvist et al. [13,19] propose a high level description of multi-mode models as an extension to the synchronous Modelica 3.3 state machines by using continuous-time state machines having continuous-time models as "states". Besides ODEs as used in hybrid automata, also *acausal DAE models with physical connectors* can be a "state" of a state machine. Such a state machine is mapped into a form so that the resulting equations can be processed by standard symbolic algorithms supported by Modelica tools. The major restrictions of this approach are that mode changes with impulsive behavior are not supported and that not all types of multi-mode systems can be handled due to the static code generation.

Benveniste et al. [3,5] tackle the problem of variable structure, varying index DAEs from a fundamental point of view by using a low level description of DAEs with a few language elements only and a precise mathematical description of the semantics based on non-standard analysis. A proof-of-concept mockup, SunDAE, was developed implementing this approach.

3   The Modia Language

Modelica [21] is a state-of-the-art modeling language for multi-domain modeling. Recently, an experimental language which is similar to Modelica and called Modia [11,12] has been designed and implemented. Modia is a domain specific language extension of Julia [8] by means of structured macros, that is, the Julia parser is used to parse Modia models. The Modia language elements will be introduced through a small set of examples.

Elementary Modia Constructs. A model of a rotating inertia can be defined as follows (# start a comment until end of the line):

```
@model Inertia begin
  J = 1
  w0 = 0.0
  w = Float(start = w0)
  flange = Flange()
  @equations begin
    w = flange.w
    J*der(w) = flange.tau
  end
end
```

The @model macro has one section for declarations and one section for equations and connections. The construct J = 1 defines the parameter J with default value of 1. A variable w with a start value of w0 is introduced by w = Float(start = w0). The construct flange = Flange() calls the constructor for Flange which is defined as follows:

```
@model Flange begin
    w = Float()                    # Angular velocity
    tau = Float(flow=true)         # Torque
end
```

This model consists just of two variable declarations with type Float modeling the interaction when the Inertia is mechanically coupled via a shaft to other mechanical components. The attribute flow = true tells that if several shafts are connected to flange, the internal and external torques are all summed to zero.

The equation J*der(w) = flange.tau is Euler's equation for the rotational motion of the inertia. The operator der() denotes time derivative.

A model with two rigidly connected inertias can be defined as shown below:

```
@model TwoInertias begin
    inertia1 = Inertia(J=0.1)
    inertia2 = Inertia(J=0.4, w0=10.0)
    @equations begin
        connect(inertia1.flange, inertia2.flange)
    end
end
```

Note that parameters are changed in the Inertia constructor call. The connect() primitive models a physical coupling. In this case the semantics is:

```
inertia1.flange.w = inertia2.flange.w
inertia1.flange.tau + inertia2.flange.tau = 0
```

Note, that inertia2 has initial angular velocity of 10 rad/s, whereas inertia1 has the default of 0. The result of simulation shows a constant angular velocity for both inertias of 8 rad/s. Since the initial angular velocities are different there will be a Dirac impulse in the torque to make them equal. The resulting joint angular velocity is according to theory weighted as $w = (J1*w1+J2*w2)/(J1+J2) = 8$.

Advanced Modia Constructs. Modia has many other features, such as inheritance, size and type inference, type declarations, component redeclarations, time events, state event, and nested simulations. More information can be found in [11,12]. It is possible to declare variables with specific SI units. As an example, an electric Pin connector can be defined as shown below using predefined variable constructors Voltage() and Current() with associated SI units (Volt and Ampere):

```
@model Pin begin
    v = Voltage()
    i = Current(flow=true)
end
```

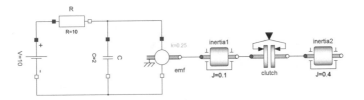

Fig. 3. Schematics of MotorAndLoad model.

Modia Multi-mode Modeling: Running Example. We model in Modia a multi-mode DAE system containing the idealized clutch introduced informally in Sect. 1. The model has an electric motor, two load inertia and a clutch, see Fig. 3. The electric motor model is based on a model of the electro-mechanical force (emf). It has two Pin connectors (p and v) and one Flange connector. The specific equations for an emf are:

```
k*flange.w = p.v - n.v
flange.tau = -k*p.i
```

Note that a Capacitor is connected across the emf.

A simple Clutch model is used which is either engaged or not engaged. It is modeled as two different set of equations:

```
@model Clutch begin
    flange1 = Flange()
    flange2 = Flange()
    engaged = Boolean()
@equations begin
    if engaged
        flange1.ẇ = flange2.w
        flange1.tau + flange2.tau = 0
    else
        flange1.tau = 0
        flange2.tau = 0
    end
  end
end
```

When the clutch is engaged, the angular velocities of the two flanges are the same and the torques sum to zero. When not engaged, the torques are zero and there are no constraints on the angular velocities. The definition of the input engaged is made in the surrounding environment of the clutch:

```
clutch.engaged = time < 100 || time >= 300
```

The DAE index is changing depending on the state of the clutch. Furthermore, Dirac impulses occur initially and when the mode changes to engaged. The techniques needed to analyze and simulate such models are described in subsequent sections.

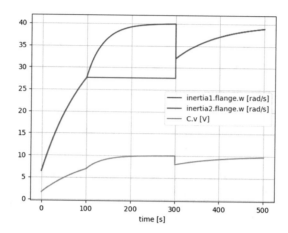

Fig. 4. Simulation results of the MotorAndLoad model.

The results of a simulation are shown in Fig. 4. The initial angular velocity of inertia1 is 0 rad/s and 10 rad/s for inertia2. The capacitor is initially uncharged. The upper two partly overlapping curves are the angular velocities of inertia1 and inertia2. When the clutch is disengaged, the angular velocity of inertia2 is constant. The lower curve shows the voltage over the capacitor. Since the clutch is engaged at initialization, Dirac impulses occur at time $= 0$ s. As a result, after initialization the angular velocities of the two inertia are identical. The common angular velocity at time $= 0$ s is not 8 rad/s as in the example TwoInertias, but 6.4 rad/s. The reason is that the capacitor acts in the same way as an additional moment of inertia to inertia1. The effective inertia is $J1' = J1 + k^2 * C = 0.1 + 0.25^2 * 2 = 0.225$. Thus, the angular velocity at time=0 s becomes $w = (J1' * w1 + J2 * w2)/(J1' + J2) = (0.225 * 0 + 0.4 * 10)/(0.225 + 0.4) = 6.4$ rad/s. There are no Dirac impulses at time $= 100$ s when the clutch disengages, but again Dirac impulses at time $= 300$ s when the clutch engages again.

4   Simulating a Restricted Class of Multi-Mode DAEs

In this section, we propose a method to simulate a restricted class of multi-mode DAE systems, encompassing in particular our example of Fig. 3 and its simulation result in Fig. 4.

Throughout this paper, we use the classical notations $\dot{x}$ and $\ddot{x}$ to denote the first and second time-derivatives of a function of continuous time $x : \mathbb{R} \mapsto \mathbb{R}$. When such a notation is not appropriate for readability reasons, we sometimes write instead x' and x''. The notation for higher order derivatives is indicated when needed. We write vectors and matrices in boldface. The transpose of a matrix $\boldsymbol{G}$ is written $\boldsymbol{G}^T$.

4.1   Problem Setting

The goal is to simulate the following class of multi-mode DAE systems:

$$
\begin{aligned}
&\textbf{if } \gamma_1(\dot{\boldsymbol{x}}_\gamma^-, \boldsymbol{x}_\gamma^-, t) \textbf{ then } \boldsymbol{f}_1(\dot{\boldsymbol{x}}_1, \boldsymbol{x}_1, t) = \mathbf{0} \\
&\textbf{elseif } \gamma_2(\dot{\boldsymbol{x}}_\gamma^-, \boldsymbol{x}_\gamma^-, t) \textbf{ then } \boldsymbol{f}_2(\dot{\boldsymbol{x}}_2, \boldsymbol{x}_2, t) = \mathbf{0} \\
&\qquad\qquad\qquad\vdots \\
&\textbf{else } \boldsymbol{f}_m(\dot{\boldsymbol{x}}_m, \boldsymbol{x}_m, t) = \mathbf{0}
\end{aligned}
\tag{1}
$$

where

- vector $\boldsymbol{x}_\gamma$ of length n_γ collects variables that are present in all modes and in the predicates $\gamma_i(\dots)$,
- vector $\boldsymbol{x}_i$ of length n_i collects all variables that are used in mode i ($\boldsymbol{x}_\gamma$ is a subset of $\boldsymbol{x}_i$), and
- $\gamma_i \in \mathbb{R}^{n_\gamma} \times \mathbb{R}^{n_\gamma} \times \mathbb{R} \to$ Boolean, $\quad \boldsymbol{f}_i \in \mathbb{R}^{n_i} \times \mathbb{R}^{n_i} \times \mathbb{R} \to \mathbb{R}^{n_i}$.

Hence the considered system switches between different modes, each described by a DAE having n_i equations and n_i unknowns. The switching conditions are predicates denoted by γ_i and depend on time and/or on the left limit of the DAE variables assuming they exist and are finite, that is

$$
\boldsymbol{x}_\gamma^-(t) =_{\text{def}} \lim_{\varepsilon \searrow 0} \boldsymbol{x}_\gamma(t - \varepsilon) \text{ and } \dot{\boldsymbol{x}}_\gamma^-(t) =_{\text{def}} \lim_{\varepsilon \searrow 0} \dot{\boldsymbol{x}}_\gamma(t - \varepsilon).
$$

When changing from mode i to mode j it is assumed that the initial conditions $\boldsymbol{x}_\gamma^-$ are known from the previous mode. A concrete example will be given in Sect. 4.3. we also refer to [13] for a more generic treatment. When changing from one mode to another the set of equations that govern the dynamics of the system may change. Thus, some variables may experience discontinuities or even impulses. Throughout this section we assume that the system spends a strictly positive duration in each mode in such a way that instants of mode changes are cleanly isolated.

Note that the class (1) of multi-mode systems is not compositional as the predicates $\boldsymbol{x}_\gamma$ are global. We restricted ourselves to this class in order to simplify the exposure below. This restriction is relaxed in the actual implementation in Modia. For instance, @model Clutch in Sect. 3 has a *local* definition of the predicate to engage or disengage the clutch and there is *no global* if-clause. In Sect. 5, where an alternative approach is discussed, such restrictions are not present.

4.2   Handling Mode Changes

In a mode i, an initial value problem $\boldsymbol{f}_i(\dot{\boldsymbol{x}}_i, \boldsymbol{x}_i, t) = \mathbf{0}$ has to be solved. It is well-known that only special classes of DAEs can be directly numerically integrated [9]. For this reason, general DAEs might be first transformed in to a DAE class where reliable integration methods exist. For nonlinear systems such a transformation means that equations of the DAE might need to be (analytically) differentiated. The best integration methods exist for ODEs $\dot{x} = \bar{f}(x, t)$. However, transforming a DAE to this form requires in general to solve nonlinear algebraic equation systems at every model evaluation and therefore the benefit of ODE integration methods might get lost. For this reason, another approach is used in this section where the transformation to a numerically solvable form is performed *without* solving algebraic equation systems. In Assumption 1 we define the target DAE class for this transformation:

Assumption 1. *For each mode i of System (1), the DAE $\boldsymbol{f}_i(\dot{\boldsymbol{x}}_i, \boldsymbol{x}_i, t) = \boldsymbol{0}$ has the following form (we omit the index i for better readability)*

$$\begin{aligned} \boldsymbol{f}_d(\dot{\boldsymbol{x}}, \boldsymbol{x}, t) &= \boldsymbol{0} \\ \boldsymbol{f}_c(\boldsymbol{x}, t) &= \boldsymbol{0} \end{aligned} \tag{2}$$

$$where \; \boldsymbol{J} = \begin{bmatrix} \dfrac{\partial \boldsymbol{f}_d}{\partial \dot{\boldsymbol{x}}} \\ \dfrac{\partial \boldsymbol{f}_c}{\partial \boldsymbol{x}} \end{bmatrix} \quad is \; regular \; (that \; is, \; invertible). \tag{3}$$

In (2), subscripts "$_d$" and "$_c$" are reminiscent of "dynamics" and "constraint", respectively. Condition (3) means that System (2) has differentiation index one.[2]

Transforming General DAEs to System (2, 3). If the model equations in a given mode are *not* in the form (2, 3), they are transformed to it. This transformation is non-trivial and it is beyond the scope of this paper to explain the details. Only a short overview is given here: Typically, the Pantelides algorithm [23], or a variant like [27], is used to determine which equations of the original DAE must be differentiated in order that the highest derivative variables can be uniquely determined from the highest derivative equations. By differentiating the corresponding equations analytically it is then possible to transform to ODE form. Hereby, algebraic equation systems might need to be solved. In [22] a new algorithm is proposed to transform every DAE that can be treated with the Pantelides algorithm to the form of Assumption 1 *without solving algebraic equation systems*. This algorithm is a generalization of [15] that was developed for single-mode multi-body systems. In Sect. 4.3 it is applied to multi-mode multi-body systems.

Simulating System (2, 3). A number of methods exist for solving system (2, 3) numerically. In particular, fixed or variable step-size BDF (Backward Differentiation Formula) methods can be used [9]. In all cases, consistent initial conditions have to be provided that fulfill (2) and the so-called *latent equations*

$$\frac{\partial \boldsymbol{f}_c}{\partial \boldsymbol{x}}(\boldsymbol{x}, t) \, \dot{\boldsymbol{x}} + \frac{\partial \boldsymbol{f}_c}{\partial t}(\boldsymbol{x}, t) = \boldsymbol{0} \tag{4}$$

---

[2] A DAE $\boldsymbol{f}(\dot{\boldsymbol{x}}, \boldsymbol{x}, t) = \boldsymbol{0}$ has *differentiation index* n if one or more equations must be differentiated n-times until the equations can be algebraically transformed to an ODE form $\dot{\boldsymbol{x}} = \bar{f}(\boldsymbol{x}, t)$, see for example [30].

obtained by differentiating the constraint $\boldsymbol{f}_c(\boldsymbol{x}, t) = \boldsymbol{0}$, see [9,23]. Integration methods, including BDF, assume that $\boldsymbol{x}$ is smooth. Therefore, standard integration methods cannot be applied if $\boldsymbol{x}$ is discontinuous at a mode change.

Computing Restart Values. We now propose a scheme for computing restart conditions. More precisely, let t_{ev} be an instant of mode change of System (1), meaning that one of the guards γ_i changes its value. The objective is to compute consistent restart values

$$\boldsymbol{x}^+ = \boldsymbol{x}(t_{ev}^+) =_{\text{def}} \lim_{s \searrow t_{ev}} \boldsymbol{x}(s) \text{ and } \dot{\boldsymbol{x}}^+ = \dot{\boldsymbol{x}}(t_{ev}^+) =_{\text{def}} \lim_{s \searrow t_{ev}} \dot{\boldsymbol{x}}(s) \tag{5}$$

for the index one system (2, 3), given values

$$\boldsymbol{x}^- = \boldsymbol{x}(t_{ev}^-) =_{\text{def}} \lim_{s \nearrow t_{ev}} \boldsymbol{x}(s) \tag{6}$$

just prior to entering the new mode. Note that, since $\boldsymbol{x}^-$ are variable values in the previous mode, they will not, in general, be *consistent* for the new mode, that is the second equation of System (2) might not be satisfied by $\boldsymbol{x}^-$. Still, these equations must be satisfied by the (yet unknown) $\boldsymbol{x}^+$. Since $\boldsymbol{x}(t)$ may be discontinuous at t_{ev}, the derivative of $\boldsymbol{x}(t)$ may be a Dirac impulse.

To derive our method for computing the restart values, we first restrict the class of systems with the following additional assumption. We then discuss the general case.

Assumption 2. *Assume DAE System* (2) *has the following special structure:*

$$\begin{aligned} 0 &= \boldsymbol{A}(\boldsymbol{x}_s, t)\dot{\boldsymbol{x}} + \boldsymbol{b}(\boldsymbol{x}, t) \quad (= \boldsymbol{f}_d(\dot{\boldsymbol{x}}, \boldsymbol{x}, t)) \\ 0 &= \boldsymbol{f}_c(\boldsymbol{x}, t) \end{aligned} \tag{7}$$

where $\boldsymbol{x}_s$ collects the smooth elements of $\boldsymbol{x}$, that is those being continuous and of bounded variation around the mode change.[3] Other elements of $\boldsymbol{x}$ might be discontinuous. Furthermore, we assume that $\boldsymbol{x}, \boldsymbol{A}(\ldots), \boldsymbol{b}(\ldots)$ are continuous functions of their arguments and remain bounded around the instant of mode change.

Note that Assumption 2 does not forbid that the triple defining the dynamics (7) actually varies with the mode i, that is has the form $(\boldsymbol{A}_i, \boldsymbol{b}_i, \boldsymbol{f}_{c,i})$. Since elements of $\boldsymbol{x}$ may be discontinuous, $\dot{\boldsymbol{x}}$ may have Dirac impulses. In (7) it is therefore assumed that $\dot{\boldsymbol{x}}$ having potentially Dirac impulses appear linearly and the linear factors are continuous functions without discontinuities.

Under Assumption 2, the mathematical solution of the restart problem can be determined as follows: In a first step, since $\boldsymbol{x}_s$ is smooth at the instant t_{ev} of mode change, the matrix $\boldsymbol{A}(\boldsymbol{x}_s, t_{ev})$ is immediately known once a change has been detected at t_{ev}. To evaluate all the elements of $\boldsymbol{x}$ right after t_{ev} we

---

[3] A function $f : \mathbb{R} \mapsto \mathbb{R}$ is said to have bounded variation if it is the primitive of a Lebesgue integrable function [10]. As a consequence, $\int_t^{t+h} \dot{f}(s)ds \to 0$ when $h \to 0$.

proceed by integrating (7) over $[t_{ev} - \varepsilon, t_{ev} + \varepsilon]$ using the well known properties of Lebesgue integrals and Dirac measure. To this end, we decompose

$$\boldsymbol{x} = \begin{bmatrix} \boldsymbol{x}_s \\ \boldsymbol{x}_{ns} \end{bmatrix} \text{ and } \boldsymbol{A} = \begin{bmatrix} \boldsymbol{A}_s \ \boldsymbol{A}_{ns} \end{bmatrix}$$

where $\boldsymbol{x}_{ns}$ collects the nonsmooth entries of $\boldsymbol{x}$ that may experience discontinuities at the instant of mode change and $\boldsymbol{A}$ is decomposed accordingly. The following approximations hold, where the integrals $\int_{t_{ev}-\varepsilon}^{t_{ev}+\varepsilon}$ mean $\int_{[t_{ev}-\varepsilon, t_{ev}+\varepsilon]}$:

$$\int_{t_{ev}-\varepsilon}^{t_{ev}+\varepsilon} \boldsymbol{f}_d(\dot{\boldsymbol{x}}, \boldsymbol{x}, t) dt = \underbrace{\int_{t_{ev}-\varepsilon}^{t_{ev}+\varepsilon} \left(\boldsymbol{A}_s(\boldsymbol{x}_s, t)\dot{\boldsymbol{x}}_s + \boldsymbol{b}(\boldsymbol{x}, t) \right) dt}_{\approx 0 \text{ by footnote 3}} + \underbrace{\int_{t_{ev}-\varepsilon}^{t_{ev}+\varepsilon} \boldsymbol{A}_{ns}(\boldsymbol{x}_s, t)\dot{\boldsymbol{x}}_{ns} dt}_{\dot{\boldsymbol{x}}_{ns} dt \text{ is a Dirac at } t_{ev}}$$

$$\approx \boldsymbol{A}_{ns}(\boldsymbol{x}_s, t_{ev}) \left(\boldsymbol{x}_{ns}(t_{ev} + \varepsilon) - \boldsymbol{x}_{ns}(t_{ev} - \varepsilon) \right)$$

$$\approx \boldsymbol{A}(\boldsymbol{x}_s, t_{ev}) \left(\boldsymbol{x}(t_{ev} + \varepsilon) - \boldsymbol{x}(t_{ev} - \varepsilon) \right)$$

In the above two approximations, the first one follows from the property of the Dirac measure and the fact that $t \mapsto \boldsymbol{A}_{ns}(\boldsymbol{x}_s(t), t)$ is continuous, and the second one follows from the fact that $\boldsymbol{A}_s(\boldsymbol{x}_s, t_{ev}) \left(\boldsymbol{x}_s(t_{ev} + \varepsilon) - \boldsymbol{x}_s(t_{ev} - \varepsilon) \right) \approx 0$.

   This leads to proposing the following scheme for computing the restart values $\boldsymbol{x}^+$ from $\boldsymbol{x}^-$ at the instant t_{ev} of mode change, cf. Eqs. (5) and (6):

$$\begin{aligned} 0 &= \boldsymbol{A}(\boldsymbol{x}_s, t_{ev})(\boldsymbol{x}^+ - \boldsymbol{x}^-) \\ 0 &= \boldsymbol{f}_c(\boldsymbol{x}^+, t_{ev}) \end{aligned} \tag{8}$$

Since (7) may not hold at t_{ev}^-, and $\boldsymbol{x}^+ - \boldsymbol{x}^-$ need not to be small, the Implicit Function Theorem cannot be invoked to argue about the existence and uniqueness of a solution around $\boldsymbol{x}^-$. Since the Jacobian $\frac{\partial f}{\partial \boldsymbol{x}^+}$ of (8) is regular due to (3) and Assumption 2, (8) can be numerically solved with a Newton-type method. Fortunately, in many practical cases (such as a mechanical impact) the nonlinear part of $\boldsymbol{f}_c(\boldsymbol{x}, t)$ is often satisfied by $\boldsymbol{x}^-$ and then only a linear equation system needs to be solved for $\boldsymbol{x}^+$, in which case a unique solution exists, see also Sect. 4.3. The physical interpretation of (8) is that we look for restart values that are consistent for the new mode (second equation) and meet the integral of $\boldsymbol{f}_d(\ldots)$ across the mode change (first equation).

   In a modeling language such as Modelica or Modia, the model code has the form (2), not the special form (7). It is therefore desirable to compute restart values only with the form (2), without being forced to generate special code that reveals the details of the equations as in (7). On the basis of Assumption 1, we can nevertheless consider the following two systems of equations, where $\boldsymbol{x}^+$ are the unknowns and $h > 0$ is small:

mixed explicit/implicit Euler	implicit Euler	
$0 = h\boldsymbol{f}_d\left(\dfrac{\boldsymbol{x}^+ - \boldsymbol{x}^-}{h}, \boldsymbol{x}^-, t_{ev}\right)$	$0 = h\boldsymbol{f}_d\left(\dfrac{\boldsymbol{x}^+ - \boldsymbol{x}^-}{h}, \boldsymbol{x}^+, t_{ev} + h\right)$	(9)
$0 = \boldsymbol{f}_c(\boldsymbol{x}^+, t_{ev} + h)$	$0 = \boldsymbol{f}_c(\boldsymbol{x}^+, t_{ev} + h)$	

Schemes (9) only require Assumption 1. Under Assumption 2, Schemes (9) take the form

mixed explicit/implicit Euler	implicit Euler	
$0 = \boldsymbol{A}(\boldsymbol{x}_s, t_{ev})(\boldsymbol{x}^+ - \boldsymbol{x}^-)$ $+ h \cdot \boldsymbol{b}(\boldsymbol{x}^-, t_{ev})$ $0 = \boldsymbol{f}_c(\boldsymbol{x}^+, t_{ev} + h)$	$0 = \boldsymbol{A}(\boldsymbol{x}_s, t_{ev} + h)(\boldsymbol{x}^+ - \boldsymbol{x}^-)$ $+ h \cdot \boldsymbol{b}(\boldsymbol{x}^+, t_{ev} + h)$ $0 = \boldsymbol{f}_c(\boldsymbol{x}^+, t_{ev} + h)$	(10)

where we have used the fact that $\boldsymbol{x}_s^- \approx \boldsymbol{x}_s^+$ since $\boldsymbol{x}_s$ is smooth. These schemes reduce to (8) for $h \approx 0$.

Thus, if Assumption 2 holds, the form (2) for the system model at mode i can be used to numerically compute restart values for this mode: At the instant of the mode change integrate (2) with either mixed explicit/implicit Euler or implicit Euler schemes, from $\boldsymbol{x}^-$ over a small step-size h, thereby scaling the dynamic part of the model, $\boldsymbol{f}_d(..)$, with h. The solution of the nonlinear equation system (9) converges to the solution of the system (8).

Discussing the General Case. Schemes (9) can be applied to any index one system. Such a brute force use without Assumption 2, however, raises questions that we review now:

- Relaxing the continuity assumption on $\boldsymbol{A}(\dots)$, so that $\boldsymbol{A}(\boldsymbol{x}, t)$ might have discontinuous elements: As a result the first contribution in the decomposition of the integral $\int_{t_{ev}}^{t_{ev} + \varepsilon} \boldsymbol{f}_d(\dot{\boldsymbol{x}}, \boldsymbol{x}, t) dt$ is no longer negligible and it is unclear, from the literature, whether a well-defined meaning to this term exists.
- Removing the linearity assumption on $\dot{\boldsymbol{x}}$: The solution is no longer a Dirac and it is again unclear whether a well-defined solution exists. It is not even clear that h is the proper scaling factor for $\boldsymbol{f}_d$. Note that the linearity assumption quite often holds for physical system models, since balance equations in physics are linear in their derivatives.

To summarize, there is some evidence that precautions must be taken when relaxing Assumption 2.

Completing Consistent Restart. After the consistent restart values $\boldsymbol{x}^+$ have been computed, the corresponding consistent restart values of $\dot{\boldsymbol{x}}^+$ can be determined with (4) and the first equation of (2), by solving the following non-linear equation system in the unknowns $\dot{\boldsymbol{x}}^+$ (in case Assumption 2 holds, this is a linear equation system with a regular Jacobian, so a unique solution exists):

$$\boldsymbol{f}_d(\dot{\boldsymbol{x}}^+, \boldsymbol{x}^+, t_{ev}) = 0$$
$$\frac{\partial \boldsymbol{f}_c}{\partial \boldsymbol{x}}(\boldsymbol{x}^+, t_{ev}) \dot{\boldsymbol{x}}^+ + \frac{\partial \boldsymbol{f}_c}{\partial t}(\boldsymbol{x}^+, t_{ev}) = 0 \qquad (11)$$

Addressing Initialization. Note that the combined use of (9) and (11) provides a method for consistent initialization: The initial mode i and guesses for $\boldsymbol{x}_{i,\text{init}}^-$ must be provided by the modeler. Afterwards, consistent values $(\dot{\boldsymbol{x}}_{i,\text{init}}^+, \boldsymbol{x}_{i,\text{init}}^+)$ for the initialization are computed with (9, 11).

4.3   A Class of Multi-mode Multi-body Systems Satisfying Assumptions 1 and 2

In this section we exhibit a practically useful class of systems satisfying Assumptions 1 and 2. We consider a multi-body system whose model at each mode i has the following structure:

$$
\begin{aligned}
\dot{q} &= v & (m_1) \\
M(q,t)\dot{v} + G_i^T(q,t)\lambda_i &= h(q,v,t) & (m_2) \\
0 &= g_i(q,t) & (m_3)
\end{aligned}
\tag{12}
$$

where $M = M^T$ is positive definite, and $G_i = \dfrac{\partial g_i}{\partial q}$ has full row rank. (13)

Equation (12) describes a multi-body system with generalized position coordinates q, generalized velocity coordinates v and generalized constraint forces λ_i due to the constraints (m_3) of the ith mode. Both the constraints (m_3) and the constraint forces $G_i^T(q,t)\lambda_i$ can vary with the mode i. In particular the constraints can also be completely removed. M, however, remains invariant through the different modes. Whenever a set of constraints is changing at a new mode, impulses might occur. In case an impulse is due to an impact, it is assumed that the impact is completely inelastic. We now show that Eq. (12) can be put to a form satisfying Assumptions 1 and 2.

Equation (12) is first transformed to an index *two* DAE with the method of Gear et al. [15]:

$$
\begin{aligned}
\dot{q} &= v - G_i^T(q,t)\mu_i & (m_1^a) \\
M(q,t)\dot{v} + G_i^T(q,t)\lambda_i &= h(q,v,t) & (m_2) \\
0 &= g_i(q,t) & (m_3) \\
0 &= G_i(q,t)v + g_i^{(1)}(q,t) & (\dot{m}_3)
\end{aligned}
\tag{14}
$$

$$
\text{with } g_i^{(1)}(q,t) = \frac{\partial g_i}{\partial t}.
\tag{15}
$$

In Eq. (14) the constraint equation (m_3) is differentiated once and new auxiliary variables μ_i are introduced so that the number of equations and unknowns remain the same. (14) has the same solution as (12) because $\mu_i = 0$ holds as we explain now: Inserting (m_1^a) in $(\dot{m}_3)$ yields:

$$
0 = G_i(\dot{q} - G_i^T\mu_i) + G_i^{(1)}
\tag{16}
$$

Subtracting the derivative of (m_3) from (16) results in equation $0 = G_iG_i^T\mu_i$. Since G_i has full row rank according to assumption (13), $G_iG_i^T$ is regular and therefore $\mu_i = 0$.

As proposed by Gear [14], by using the substitutions ($\lambda_{int,i}$ is the integral of λ_i and $\mu_{int,i}$ is the integral of μ_i):

$$
\dot{\lambda}_{int,i} = \lambda_i, \quad \dot{\mu}_{int,i} = \mu_i
\tag{17}
$$

the DAE (14) which is index 2 in the variables $\boldsymbol{q}, \boldsymbol{v}, \boldsymbol{\lambda}_i, \boldsymbol{\mu}_i$ is transformed to the following DAE which is index 1 in the variables $\boldsymbol{q}, \boldsymbol{v}, \boldsymbol{\lambda}_{int,i}, \boldsymbol{\mu}_{int,i}$:

$$
\begin{aligned}
\dot{\boldsymbol{q}} &= \boldsymbol{v} - \boldsymbol{G}_i^T(\boldsymbol{q}, t)\dot{\boldsymbol{\mu}}_{int,i} && (m_1^b)\\
\boldsymbol{M}(\boldsymbol{q}, t)\dot{\boldsymbol{v}} + \boldsymbol{G}_i^T(\boldsymbol{q}, t)\dot{\boldsymbol{\lambda}}_{int,i} &= \boldsymbol{h}(\boldsymbol{q}, \boldsymbol{v}, t) && (m_2^b)\\
0 &= \boldsymbol{g}_i(\boldsymbol{q}, t) && (m_3)\\
0 &= \boldsymbol{G}_i(\boldsymbol{q}, t)\boldsymbol{v} + \boldsymbol{g}_i^{(1)}(\boldsymbol{q}, t) && (\dot{m}_3)
\end{aligned}
\tag{18}
$$

(18) has equation structure (7), with

$$
\boldsymbol{x} = \begin{bmatrix} \boldsymbol{q} \\ \boldsymbol{v} \\ \boldsymbol{\lambda}_{int,i} \\ \boldsymbol{\mu}_{int,i} \end{bmatrix} \quad \boldsymbol{A} = \begin{bmatrix} \boldsymbol{I} & 0 & 0 & \boldsymbol{G}_i^T(\boldsymbol{q}, t) \\ 0 & \boldsymbol{M}(\boldsymbol{q}, t) & \boldsymbol{G}_i^T(\boldsymbol{q}, t) & 0 \end{bmatrix}
\tag{19}
$$

$$
\boldsymbol{b} = \begin{bmatrix} -\boldsymbol{v} \\ -\boldsymbol{h}(\boldsymbol{q}, \boldsymbol{v}, t) \end{bmatrix} \quad \boldsymbol{f}_c = \begin{bmatrix} \boldsymbol{g}_i(\boldsymbol{q}, t) \\ \boldsymbol{G}_i(\boldsymbol{q}, t)\boldsymbol{v} + \boldsymbol{g}_i^{(1)}(\boldsymbol{q}, t) \end{bmatrix}.
$$

The Jacobian (3) of (18) is ($\boldsymbol{P}$ is a permutation matrix to exchange (m_3) and $(\dot{m}_3)$ in order that the regularity of the Jacobian is at once visible):

$$
\boldsymbol{J} = \begin{bmatrix} \dfrac{\partial \boldsymbol{f}_d}{\partial \dot{\boldsymbol{x}}} \\[2mm] \dfrac{\partial \boldsymbol{f}_c}{\partial \boldsymbol{x}} \end{bmatrix} = \boldsymbol{P} \begin{bmatrix} \boldsymbol{I} & 0 & 0 & \boldsymbol{G}_i^T \\ 0 & \boldsymbol{M} & \boldsymbol{G}_i^T & 0 \\ 0 & \boldsymbol{G}_i & 0 & 0 \\ \boldsymbol{G}_i & 0 & 0 & 0 \end{bmatrix}
\tag{20}
$$

As required by Assumption 1, this Jacobian is regular because $\boldsymbol{M}$ is positive definite and $\boldsymbol{G}_i$ has full row rank. With reference to Assumption 2, it remains to show that it is legitimate to take $\boldsymbol{x}_s = \boldsymbol{q}$, which amounts to requiring that $\boldsymbol{q}$ is continuous and has bounded variation around the instant of mode change. Before an impact occurs, the normal distance d_j to a constraint surface j is defined as $d_j = g_j(\boldsymbol{q}, t)$ and $d_j > 0$ when the multi-body system is not in contact with the constraint surface. Contact occurs when $d_j = 0$ and therefore the constraint $g_j(\boldsymbol{q}, t) = 0$ at the time instant of the impact and $\boldsymbol{q}$ is continuous. In the fully inelastic impact case, $\boldsymbol{q}$ has bounded variation because the multi-body system remains in contact with the contact surface after the impact and it is assumed that $g_j(\boldsymbol{q}, t)$ is smooth. The scheme above can be easily extended to elastic impacts. In such a case, $\boldsymbol{q}$ has bounded variation provided instants of mode changes do not form a Zeno sequence.

4.4 Example: Ideal Clutch with Motor

We will show in this section how the example of Fig. 3 can be simulated with the method developed in the previous sections. The modular description with Modia is mapped to a set of about 25 equations that are first pre-processed (such as performing alias elimination). To avoid overloading the development with unnecessary details, we only show the results after this pre-processing is performed (these equations can also be easily derived manually from the circuit). In the following model, C, k, J, R are constants; $u_0(t), \gamma(t)$ are given time functions; $\gamma = \text{T}$ if the clutch is released and F if it is engaged:

$$
\begin{aligned}
R(i_1 + i_2) + u &= u_0 && \text{(sum of voltages in left loop)} \\
C\dot{u} &= i_1 && \text{(capacitor)} \\
k\omega_1 &= u && \text{(emf)} \\
\tau_1 &= ki_2 && \text{(emf)} \\
J_1\dot{\omega}_1 &= \tau_1 - \tau_2 && \text{(inertia1)} \\
J_2\dot{\omega}_2 &= \tau_2 && \text{(inertia2)} \\
\textbf{if } \gamma \textbf{ then } \tau_2 \textbf{ else } \omega_1 - \omega_2 &= 0 && \text{(idealized clutch)}
\end{aligned}
\tag{21}
$$

All the following analysis could be performed with (21). To concentrate on the essential details, the equations are further simplified by using the following relationships from (21), as well as the substitution $\dot{\tau}_{int,2} = \tau_2$

$$
\begin{aligned}
\tau_1 &:= J_1\dot{\omega}_1 + \tau_2 \\
i_2 &:= \tau_1/k = (J_1\dot{\omega}_1 + \dot{\tau}_{int,2})/k \\
i_1 &:= C\dot{u}
\end{aligned}
\tag{22}
$$

and the equation system (21) can be simplified to the following four equations:

$$
\begin{aligned}
J_1\dot{\omega}_1 + \dot{\tau}_{int,2} + kC\dot{u} - k(u_0 - u)/R &= 0 \\
J_2\dot{\omega}_2 - \dot{\tau}_{int,2} &= 0 \\
\textbf{if } \gamma \textbf{ then } \dot{\tau}_{int,2} \textbf{ else } \omega_1 - \omega_2 &= 0 \\
k\omega_1 - u &= 0
\end{aligned}
\tag{23}
$$

With $\boldsymbol{x} = [u \,;\, \omega_1 \,;\, \omega_2 \,;\, \tau_{int,2}]^T$, (23) is in both modes an index one DAE of the form (7):

$\gamma = \text{T}$ (mode 1) :

$$
\boldsymbol{A}_1 = \begin{bmatrix} kC & J_1 & 0 & +1 \\ 0 & 0 & J_2 & -1 \\ 0 & 0 & 0 & +1 \end{bmatrix} \quad \boldsymbol{b}_1 = \begin{bmatrix} -k(u_0 - u)/R \\ 0 \\ 0 \end{bmatrix} \quad \boldsymbol{f}_{c,1} = k\omega_1 - u
\tag{24}
$$

$\gamma = \text{F}$ (mode 2) :

$$
\boldsymbol{A}_2 = \begin{bmatrix} kC & J_1 & 0 & +1 \\ 0 & 0 & J_2 & -1 \end{bmatrix} \quad \boldsymbol{b}_2 = \begin{bmatrix} -k(u_0 - u)/R \\ 0 \end{bmatrix} \quad \boldsymbol{f}_{c,2} = \begin{bmatrix} k\omega_1 - u \\ \omega_1 - \omega_2 \end{bmatrix}
$$

With (8), or alternatively with (9) and $h \approx 0$, restart values can be computed:

$\gamma = \text{F} \to \text{T}$ (assuming $\boldsymbol{x}^-$ satisfies mode 2 with $\boldsymbol{A}_2, \boldsymbol{b}_2, \boldsymbol{f}_{c,2}$) :
$$
\omega_1^+ = \omega_1^-, \quad \omega_2^+ = \omega_2^-, \quad u^+ = u^-
$$

$\gamma = \text{T} \to \text{F}$ (assuming $\boldsymbol{x}^-$ satisfies mode 1 with $\boldsymbol{A}_1, \boldsymbol{b}_1, \boldsymbol{f}_{c,1}$) :
$$
\omega_1^+ = \frac{J_1\omega_1^- + J_2\omega_2^- + kCu^-}{J_1 + J_2 + k^2 C}, \quad \omega_2^+ = \omega_1^+, \quad u^+ = k\omega_1^+
$$

$$\tag{25}$$

When the clutch is disengaging, the variables are continuous at the mode change. When the clutch is engaging, the variables are discontinuous at the mode change and Dirac impulses occur.

4.5   Implementation of Multi-mode Features in Modia

The implementation of Modia is described in [12]. An extension of Modia to support a restricted class of multi-mode DAE systems along the lines developed in this section is currently under development. Since completely different sets of equations can be present in different modes, the implementation is based on just-in-time symbolic transformations and code generation of residue functions. A dictionary from a Boolean vector of mode flags to functions is used as a cache to avoid symbolic transformations and code generation in case the same modes have been active before and a corresponding function is already available to calculate the residues.

The final values of all variables from one simulation is extracted when a mode change event happens. These are inputs to one very short implicit Euler step with the residue function for the newly enabled modes in order to correctly simulate possible impulses. The new values of the state vector is used to start a new simulation until the next mode change.

5   Structural Analysis of Multi-Mode DAE Systems

In Sect. 4 we proposed an approach to analyze and simulate multi-mode DAE systems based on a generalization of DAE theory.

In this section we propose an alternative approach, more computer science oriented and detailed in [3] (as well as its companion technical report [5]), which works for general multi-mode systems and uses a small number of principles. The key ideas are as follows.

1. Mode changes may result in discontinuous jumps and, therefore, resets must be performed in discrete computation steps. Hence, we first map the original system to discrete time by using a first order Euler scheme. This brings to discrete time both the reset actions and the dynamics within each mode, hence the principles of index analysis uniformly apply, albeit *in discrete time*. Also, a new principle of *mode causality* is invoked.

2. Mapping the dynamics to discrete time results in approximations. No approximation, however, results if we interpret the Euler scheme via *nonstandard analysis* [18, 28] by using an *infinitesimal* time step. The analysis is then performed over the nonstandard reals. A final *standardization* step is applied to recover an effective numerical scheme.

To keep the exposure simple, we develop this on the example of ideal clutch with motor, see Sect. 4.4. More precisely, we consider again (23) where, for simplicity, we substitute $\dot{\tau}_{int,2}$ by τ:

$$J_1\dot{\omega}_1 + \tau + kC\dot{u} - k(u_0 - u)/R = 0$$
$$J_2\dot{\omega}_2 - \tau = 0$$
$$k\omega_1 - u = 0 \qquad (26)$$
$$\textbf{if } \gamma \textbf{ then } \tau \textbf{ else } \omega_1 - \omega_2 = 0$$

We first analyze separately the model for each mode of the clutch.

5.1   Separate Analysis of Each Mode, in Discrete Time

We begin by providing the model for each mode. We highlight in blue the equations that are unique to the considered mode. Other equations are shared. In the "released" mode, the two shafts are independent. In the "engaged" mode, the velocities of the two shafts are algebraically related.

Following key idea 1, we replace derivatives by their first order explicit Euler scheme, in discrete time with constant step size $\delta > 0$. Let

$$w^\bullet(t) =_{\text{def}} w(t + \delta) \tag{27}$$

be the forward time shift operator by an amount of δ. System (26) expands as:

$$\left.\begin{aligned}
(e_1): \ & 0 = J_1(w_1^\bullet - w_1) + kC(u^\bullet - u) \\
& \quad - \delta.(\tau - k(u_0 - u)/R) \\
(e_2): \ & 0 = J_2(w_2^\bullet - w_2) - \delta.\tau \\
(e_3): \ & 0 = kw_1 - u \\
(e_4): \ & 0 = \tau
\end{aligned}\right\} \text{ and } \left\{\begin{aligned}
(e_1): \ & 0 = J_1(w_1^\bullet - w_1) + kC(u^\bullet - u) \\
& \quad - \delta.(\tau - k(u_0 - u)/R) \\
(e_2): \ & 0 = J_2(w_2^\bullet - w_2) - \delta.\tau \\
(e_3): \ & 0 = kw_1 - u \\
(e_5): \ & 0 = w_1 - w_2
\end{aligned}\right. \tag{28}$$

$$\underbrace{\qquad\qquad\qquad}_{\text{System (26)-released}} \qquad\qquad \underbrace{\qquad\qquad\qquad}_{\text{System (26)-engaged}}$$

Let us first focus on System (26)-released. The state variables are u, w_1, w_2 and their respective values are known initially. The current step must determine the values of the leading variables $\tau, u^\bullet, w_1^\bullet, w_2^\bullet$.

Towards this, we first form the incidence graph $\mathcal{G}$ of each system, which is a nondirected bipartite graph having as vertices: the four leading variables, plus the two systems of equations $\{(e_1), (e_2), (e_3), (e_4)\}$ and $\{(e_1), (e_2), (e_3), (e_5)\}$. An edge from an equation to a leading variable exists if and only if this variable is involved in that equation. Incidence graphs for models (26-released) and (26-engaged) are:

$$\left.\begin{aligned}
e_1 &\text{ ———— } w_1^\bullet, u^\bullet, \tau \\
e_2 &\text{ ———— } w_2^\bullet, \tau \\
e_3 &\text{ ———— } \\
e_4 &\text{ ———— } \tau
\end{aligned}\right\} \text{ and } \left\{\begin{aligned}
e_1 &\text{ ———— } w_1^\bullet, u^\bullet, \tau \\
e_2 &\text{ ———— } w_2^\bullet, \tau \\
e_3 &\text{ ———— } \\
e_5 &\text{ ———— }
\end{aligned}\right.$$

$$\underbrace{\qquad\qquad\qquad}_{\text{System (26)-released}} \qquad \underbrace{\qquad\qquad\qquad}_{\text{System (26)-engaged}}$$

Observe that, for both models, equation (e_3) involves no leading variable: it is a *consistency* equation, i.e., a constraint that must be satisfied as a result of the execution of previous time steps. Once initialization is performed, (e_3) is indeed satisfied and can thus be seen as a fact for both modes. The same holds for (e_5) in the engaged mode. In turn these equations cannot be used, when determining the leading variables from the state variables. In this case, for the two systems (26), we have 4 variables but only 3 and 2 equations, respectively: one cannot determine the leading variables as functions of the state variables by using System (26). Since the considered models are time-invariant, every solution has also satisfy the equations obtained by shifting forward any equation of the model. Shifting forward equations that do not bring variables that are shifted more than originally present in the system, yields so-called *latent equations*. For our two models, we add the latent equations, highlighted in blue:

$$
\left.
\begin{aligned}
(e_1) &: 0 = J_1(\omega_1^\bullet - \omega_1) + kC(u^\bullet - u) \\
&\quad - \delta.(\tau - k(u_0 - u)/R) \\
(e_2) &: 0 = J_2(\omega_2^\bullet - \omega_2) - \delta.\tau \\
(e_3) &: 0 = k\omega_1 - u \\
(e_3^\bullet) &: 0 = k\omega_1^\bullet - u^\bullet \\
(e_4) &: 0 = \tau
\end{aligned}
\right\}
\quad \text{and} \quad
\left\{
\begin{aligned}
(e_1) &: 0 = J_1(\omega_1^\bullet - \omega_1) + kC(u^\bullet - u) \\
&\quad - \delta.(\tau - k(u_0 - u)/R) \\
(e_2) &: 0 = J_2(\omega_2^\bullet - \omega_2) - \delta.\tau \\
(e_3) &: 0 = k\omega_1 - u \\
(e_3^\bullet) &: 0 = k\omega_1^\bullet - u^\bullet \\
(e_5) &: 0 = \omega_1 - \omega_2 \\
(e_5^\bullet) &: 0 = \omega_1^\bullet - \omega_2^\bullet
\end{aligned}
\right.
\qquad (29)
$$

$$\underbrace{\hspace{5cm}}_{\text{Eq. (29)-released}} \qquad \underbrace{\hspace{5cm}}_{\text{Eq. (29)-engaged}}$$

The associated incidence graphs are augmented accordingly and we remove the consistency equations:

$$
\left.
\begin{aligned}
e_1 &\relbar \omega_1^\bullet, u^\bullet, \tau \\
e_2 &\relbar \omega_2^\bullet, \tau \\
e_3^\bullet &\relbar \omega_1^\bullet, u^\bullet \\
e_4 &\relbar \tau
\end{aligned}
\right\}
\quad \text{and} \quad
\left\{
\begin{aligned}
e_1 &\relbar \omega_1^\bullet, u^\bullet, \tau \\
e_2 &\relbar \omega_2^\bullet, \tau \\
e_3^\bullet &\relbar \omega_1^\bullet, u^\bullet \\
e_5^\bullet &\relbar \omega_1^\bullet, \omega_2^\bullet
\end{aligned}
\right.
\qquad (30)
$$

$$\underbrace{\hspace{5cm}}_{\text{Eq. (29)-released}} \qquad \underbrace{\hspace{5cm}}_{\text{Eq. (29)-engaged}}$$

In the two incidence graphs of (30), we show in red a *pairing function* $\mathbf{e}$, i.e., a bijection, from the set of variables, to the set of equations, such that $(\mathbf{e}(x), x)$ is a edge of $\mathcal{G}$ for every leading variables $\boldsymbol{x}$. This pairing function defines an orientation for $\mathcal{G}$ as follows: for each edge $(\mathbf{e}(x), x) \in \mathcal{G}$, we set $\mathbf{e}(x) \to x$ and $y \to \mathbf{e}(x)$ for every $y \neq x$ such that $(\mathbf{e}(x), y)$ is a edge of $\mathcal{G}$. The minimal cycles of the resulting directed graph form blocks of equations to be solved for their assigned variables. The blocks are partially ordered by the directed graph. According to [23], if a pairing function exists for its incidence graph, the system of equations possesses, in a generic sense, a unique solution for its leading variables, assuming consistent values for the state variables. "Generic" here means that the statement holds outside some exceptional numerical values when the non-zero coefficients of the Jacobian of this system of equations vary in a neighborhood.

The above reasoning applies in continuous time where the forward shift is substituted back using differentiation. As far as structural analysis is concerned, we can freely exchange continuous and discrete time using the correspondence $\dot{\omega} \leftrightarrow \frac{\omega^\bullet - \omega}{\delta}$.

5.2 Global Discrete-Time Analysis

In this section, we handle each of the two modes as well as the mode changes in a uniform way. Let's consider now the discretized version of our two modes System (26):

$$(e_1): \qquad 0 = J_1(\omega_1^\bullet - \omega_1) + kC(u^\bullet - u) - \delta.(\tau - k(u_0 - u)/R)$$
$$(e_2): \qquad 0 = J_2(\omega_2^\bullet - \omega_2) - \delta.\tau$$
$$(e_3): \qquad 0 = k\omega_1 - u \qquad\qquad (31)$$
$$(e_4): \quad \text{if } \gamma \text{ do } 0 = \tau$$
$$(e_5): \text{if not } \gamma \text{ do } 0 = \omega_1 - \omega_2$$

Notice how model (31) encompasses both the released and engaged modes, as well as the mode changes, in the same uniform setting of discrete time systems. This calls for using similar reasoning to determine the new values of the leading variables regardless of whether the system is evolving in continuous mode or is at an event of mode change. We now detail the how and when the different involved equations are used.

1. *Using* $(e_1), \ldots, (e_3)$ Those three equations are active in all modes. Equation (e_3) is useless, so we are left with 2 equations and 4 leading variables and no subset of them can be evaluated using the 3 available equations only. We thus have to evaluate the guard γ in order to know which equation among (e_4) or (e_5) is active. We successively analyze the two cases below.

2-released. Case $\gamma = \text{T}$ Equation (e_4) is enabled and equation (e_5) is disabled. The reasoning proceeds exactly as for getting the model (29-released). The difference is that we take the consistency equation (e_3) as an assumption, since its satisfaction results from the execution of the previous time step. The resulting model is thus:

$$\text{assuming} : (e_3): \ 0 = k\omega_1 - u$$
$$\text{if } \gamma = \text{T do (29-released} \setminus \{(e_3)\}) \qquad\qquad (32)$$

where (29-released $\setminus \{(e_3)\}$) means that equation (e_3) is removed from system 29-released. Note that model (29-released) applies both within the "released" mode and at the instant of mode change $\gamma : \text{F} \to \text{T}$.

2-engaged. Case $\gamma = \text{F}$ Equation (e_4) is disabled and equation (e_5) is enabled. With reference to system (29-engaged), an important difference occurs: assuming that the consistency equation (e_5) results from having executed the previous time step is not always valid (equation (e_5) is guarded and can thus be disabled). Consequently the following two sub-cases need to be considered:

Case $\omega_1 = \omega_2$ *follows from previous time step.* This corresponds to the case in which the system was already in mode "engaged" at the previous time step. The separate analysis developed for the "engaged" mode in Sect. 5.1 applies with no change. The model, as augmented with the two latent equations $(e_3^\bullet, e_5^\bullet)$ is (29-engaged), in which (e_3, e_5) are taken as assumptions:

$$\text{assuming} : \begin{cases} (e_3): \ 0 = k\omega_1 - u \\ (e_5): \ 0 = \omega_1 - \omega_2 \end{cases}$$
$$\text{if } \gamma = \text{F do (29-engaged} \setminus \{(e_3), (e_5)\}) \qquad\qquad (33)$$

Case $\omega_1 = \omega_2$ *does not follow from previous time step.* This arises if the system is engaged at the current instant t, but was released at the immediate previous time step, $t - \delta$, i.e., t is an instant of mode change $\gamma : \mathrm{T} \to \mathrm{F}$. This yields a new situation, not seen in Sect. 5.1. The engaged mode requires the consistency equation $\omega_1 = \omega_2$, whereas $\omega_1(t)$ and $\omega_2(t)$ were both evaluated at the previous time step $t - \delta$, at which $\omega_1^\bullet(t - \delta) = \omega_2^\bullet(t - \delta)$ was *not* enforced. As a consequence, equation (e_5) of System (31) is enabled. Unfortunately, (e_5) possesses no dependent variable and the values of the state variables ω_1 and ω_2 were set at previous time step $t - \delta$, with no guarantee that $\omega_1(t) = \omega_2(t)$ would result. System (31) is thus overdetermined at time t. A first idea would be to reject this kind of model. This would be unfortunate as our original model (26) was natural for our electromechanical system. To overcome this issue, we invoke the following

Principle 1 (Mode Causality Principle). *A guard must be evaluated before the equation it controls.*

This principle leads to *shifting forward* equation (e_5) in model (29-engaged). We expect this modification to be very mild since it consists in delaying the satisfaction of the constraint by a small amount of time. Performing this yields:

$$\begin{aligned} \text{assuming} &: (e_3): \; 0 = k\omega_1 - u \\ \text{if } \gamma = \mathrm{F} \text{ do } & (\text{29-engaged} \setminus \{(e_3), (e_5)\}) \end{aligned} \qquad (34)$$

Systems (33) and (34) possess identical right hand sides but were obtained by different reasoning—the fact that identical right hand sides were obtained is incidental to this example. System (32, 33, 34) replaces the original System (31).

As a final remark, observe that the same analysis would work without changes if the guard γ was a predicate in the state variables u, ω_1, ω_2.

The corresponding complete execution scheme is shown in Fig. 5. In this figure, boxes are the *states* of the execution scheme and their content specifies the configuration of guard, variables, and equations. For the guard and the variables: v (resp. $\overline{v}$) means $v = \mathrm{T}$ (resp. $v = \mathrm{F}$). For equations, e (resp. $\overline{e}$) means that e is active (resp. disabled) and $\sharp e$ means that the body of e is assumed from previous time step. Not mentioning a variable or an equation in a box means that this variable is not evaluated yet and this equation is not solved yet; for shifted equations added by the algorithm, however, we mention them <u>underlined</u>. The *transitions* of the state machine indicate the actions performed when moving to the next state. FS(e) indicates that e is shifted. PR(e) indicates that e is known to be satisfied. LE($e^\bullet$) indicates that we add $e^\bullet$ as a latent equation. Blue (resp. black) transitions belong to a continuous-time (resp. discrete-time) dynamics. The red transition is impulsive. A semicolon is the sequential composition of computations, and the $+$ sign denotes enabled blocks of equations, ready to be solved. The following comments are in order.

1. Observe first the parallel between the models sitting in the boxes of the diagram of Fig. 5 on the one hand, and the mixed explicit/implicit scheme (9) on the other hand. For this comparison, variables with superscript "+" in (9) correspond to shifted variables in Fig. 5 and variables with superscript "−" in (9) correspond to non shifted variables in Fig. 5.

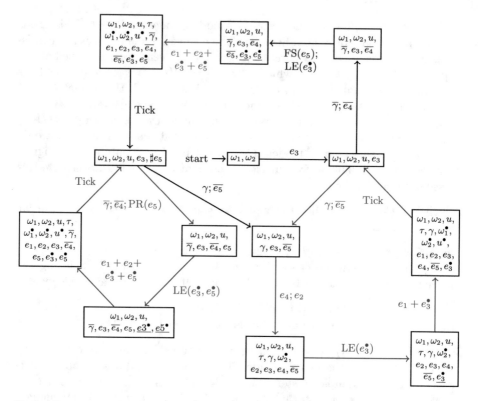

Fig. 5. Structural analysis of System (31): state machine describing the execution scheme of one time step of System (31).

2. Our development relies on a small set of principles:
   - We map the continuous time multi-mode System (26) to discrete time System (31) by mapping derivatives $\dot{x}$ to their explicit Euler scheme $\frac{x^\bullet - x}{\delta}$.
   - Our massaging of the equations only depends on the values taken by the guards, and the assumption regarding the satisfaction/violation of the consistency equations (here (e_3), and (e_5) for the engaged mode). Otherwise, we make no distinction between instants of mode changes and other instants: our treatment is uniform.
   - Our massaging of the equations has two objectives: finding latent equations if needed, and shifting forward equations when required by the principle of mode causality (Principle 1).

This set of principles is small, clean, and powerful enough to encompass general systems with a structural analysis alike the one we developed here for the clutch example. See [3] for a presentation of this approach for general multi-mode DAE systems.

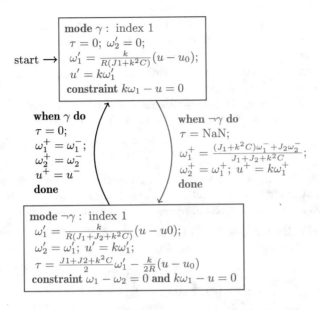

Fig. 6. Actual simulation code for the clutch.

5.3 Effective Simulation Code

So far the execution scheme of Fig. 5 is not satisfactory, as it uses an explicit first order Euler scheme. From the execution scheme of Fig. 5, however, the actual simulation code shown on Fig. 6 is derived. Observe that it consists of

- a DAE model of index zero or one for each mode, and
- code for resetting the state variables at mode changes.

The model for each mode can be simulated, e.g., using a BDF method as proposed in Sect. 4.2. Regarding the resets at mode changes, ω_i^- is the previous value of state variable ω_i, which is the left limit of ω_i when exiting a mode. Similarly, ω_i^+ is the reset value for state variable ω_i when entering the new mode. Continuous-time dynamics are colored blue; non-impulsive (resp. impulsive) resets are colored black (resp. red). The dynamics in each mode are defined by an over-determined index-1 DAE system consisting of an ODE system coupled to an algebraic constraint. In the transition from mode $\bar{\gamma}$ to mode γ, variable τ is impulsive, and its value is not computed—it is set to NaN (Not a Number). Let us explain how the code of Fig. 6 is deduced from the execution scheme of Fig. 5.

Nonstandard Analysis. First, we select the step size δ to be infinitesimal in the sense of nonstandard analysis [18, 28], of which we informally recall the background we need.

In nonstandard analysis, the set $\mathbb{R}$ of real numbers is extended with infinite numbers, which are larger than any real number, and infinitesimal numbers, which are smaller (in absolute value) than any nonzero real number. The resulting set $^*\mathbb{R}$ is an extension of $\mathbb{R}$ that keeps its basic properties. In particular, it is an ordered field. We will be writing $x \approx y$ if $x - y$ is an infinitesimal. Any finite element $z \in {}^*\mathbb{R}$ has a standard part, defined as the unique real number $st(z)$ such that $z \approx st(z)$. Any element of $\mathbb{R}$ is called standard.

If $\boldsymbol{x}(t)$ is a standard differentiable function of time, its derivative $\dot{\boldsymbol{x}}(t)$ satisfies the property that, for any infinitesimal nonzero time step δ,

$$\dot{\boldsymbol{x}}(t) \approx \frac{\boldsymbol{x}(t+\delta) - \boldsymbol{x}(t)}{\delta}. \tag{35}$$

That is, taking an explicit first order Euler scheme with infinitesimal step size yields an exact match for an ODE, up to an infinitesimal error. Formally, one says that this Euler scheme *standardizes* as the solution of the ODE.

DAE Model for Each Mode. Each (blue) mode in Fig. 6 corresponds to a blue cycle in Fig. 5. For instance, the equation

$$(e_2): \quad 0 = J_2(\omega_2^\bullet - \omega_2) - \delta.\tau$$
$$\text{becomes } (e_2): \quad 0 = J_2 \frac{\omega_2^\bullet - \omega_2}{\delta} - \tau,$$

which, by Eq. (35), standardizes as the ODE $(e_2): 0 = J_2\dot{\omega}_2 - \tau$. The reader is referred to [3] for details about standardization.

Computing the Reset Values. As in the development of Sect. 4, one key contribution of our approach is the reset code for the mode transitions. Let us now explain how this part of Fig. 6 is derived from Fig. 5. Here the reasoning is different since we do not target a continuous time dynamics, but rather a finite sequence of discrete time steps implementing the reset actions.

Let's focus on the transition $\gamma : \mathrm{T} \to \mathrm{F}$ shown in red in Fig. 6, which originates from the path sitting at the top, from the right- to the left blue cycle in Fig. 5. The corresponding dynamics is (34) and we target a discrete time dynamics involving the forward shift $^\bullet$ and no differentiation. Hence, in Eq. (34), equations $(e_3^\bullet), (e_5^\bullet)$ have the convenient form. In turn, one can no longer interpret (e_1) or (e_2) as differential equations. We must rather regard them as difference equations. Since they involve the infinitesimal parameter δ, standardization must be performed with care. Indeed, due to the equation $(e_5^\bullet)$ of (34) and since (e_5) is not assumed, the velocities ω_i experience a discrete jump. By (e_1) and (e_2) and since δ is infinitesimal, we infer that τ must be impulsive. This propagates throughout the different equations of the system. For impulses, the *rescaling*

$$\tau' =_{\text{def}} \delta.\tau$$

of the system variables is applied, guided by the equations and the incidence graph (30-right) of the system, see the *impulse analysis* developed in [3]. Using this rescaling, the block of equations of (34) becomes

$$\begin{aligned}
(e_1) &: \ 0 = J_1(\omega_1^\bullet - \omega_1) + kC(u^\bullet - u) - \tau' + \delta.k(u_0 - u)/R \\
(e_2) &: \ 0 = J_2(\omega_2^\bullet - \omega_2) - \tau' \\
(e_3^\bullet) &: \ 0 = k\omega_1^\bullet - u^\bullet \\
(e_5^\bullet) &: \ 0 = \omega_1^\bullet - \omega_2^\bullet
\end{aligned} \tag{36}$$

The term shown in blue involves state variables and is multiplied by the infinitesimal δ. Zeroing this blue term in System (36) leaves us with a *structurally regular* system that we can solve for its dependent variables $\tau', u^\bullet, \omega_1^\bullet, \omega_2^\bullet$. Solving (36) yields in particular the reset values for the state variables $u^+ =_{\text{def}} u^\bullet$, and $\omega_i^+ =_{\text{def}} \omega_1^\bullet = \omega_2^\bullet$. We recover in particular the formulas (25) from Sect. 4.4.

5.4 Constructive Semantics

The essential step in getting the final code of Fig. 6 was the construction of the state machine of Fig. 5. This state machine is called the *Constructive Semantics* of the original System (31). The notion of constructive semantics was first introduced in the context of reactive synchronous programming languages [4,6,7], where it played an important role in grounding compilation on solid mathematical foundations. Essentially, a constructive semantics for a discrete time dynamical system consists of:

1. A specification of the set of *atomic actions*, which are effective, non interruptible, state transformation operations. Executing an atomic action is often referred to as performing a *micro-step*;
2. A specification of the correct scheduling of the set of micro-steps constituting a *reaction*, by which discrete time progresses, from the current instant to the next one.

The effect of atomic actions is to propagate knowledge regarding the statuses (*not evaluated, evaluated*) and values of variables. The computation of the constructive semantics of a synchronous program may succeed, and then the execution code is generated. Or it may fail, and then the program is rejected. The decision success/failure is formally sound, see [4,6,7].

For synchronous languages, atomic actions are restricted to either (*i*) the evaluation of a single expression, or (*ii*) control flow operations.

In contrast, the class of atomic actions for multi-mode difference algebraic equations systems comprises: (*i*) Evaluating a guard; (*ii*) Solving a block of numerical equations; (*iii*) Equation management operations, such as shifting an equation, adding a latent equation, or changing the status involved/not involved of an equation at a given mode.

In [3] we develop in detail the constructive semantics for multi-mode DAE systems. This allows us to formally define which model can be compiled and then simulated, and which cannot. Models that are under- or overdetermined are rejected. In addition, models which are not handled by the Principle 1 of mode causality, are rejected as well. This approach is implemented in the SunDAE proof of concept tool.

The standardization of the constructive semantics remains open in part although its main principles have been clarified. The Standardization, however, requires symbolic processing related to computer algebra.

6   Challenges in DAE Based Modeling Languages

DAE based modeling languages are essential to the design of CPS. The development of such languages raise a number of challenges.

The correct simulation of mode changes and the need for resetting state variables is a first—mostly open—difficulty, particularly when impulses occur. In this paper, we proposed two different approaches for addressing this issue. The first approach relies on a transformation of the system model to a special index one form, followed by the application of a new formula for resetting the state variables. Arguments supporting this formula were given under additional assumptions on the model. The second approach builds on the use of nonstandard analysis, combined with the heritage of synchronous languages in computer science, particularly on the concept of constructive semantics. The classes of accepted/rejected models are well defined and simulation code is always produced for accepted models. In turn, the physical interpretation is understood only for restricted classes of models.

A particular difficulty of DAE based modeling languages is the need for sophisticated symbolic preprocessing of the model, called structural analysis. The Pantelides algorithm for computing the latent equations of a (single-mode) DAE model gave birth to a large body of literature since 1988. Our paper shows that structural analyses are also essential to handle mode changes.

Structural analyses play also a central role in scaling-up to huge models involving millions of equations. The community of High Performance Computing has provided important related contributions, for single-mode DAE systems. Yet, modularity in compilation and simulation remains open.

Overall, we see as a grand challenge the development of a DAE based modeling language and tool with the following features: DAE models with a very large number of modes are supported; accepted/rejected models are formally characterized; huge models are supported and can be handled in a modular way. We see the new language Modia and the SunDAE library as good starting points for tackling such challenges.

Acknowledgements. The authors want to thank Toivo Henningsson, Lund, Sweden for the collaboration regarding Julia and the design of Modia, as well as the implementation of instantiation and flattening.

References

1. Alur, R., Courcoubetis, C., Henzinger, T.A., Ho, P.-H.: Hybrid automata: an algorithmic approach to the specification and verification of hybrid systems. In: Grossman, R.L., Nerode, A., Ravn, A.P., Rischel, H. (eds.) HS 1991-1992. LNCS, vol. 736, pp. 209–229. Springer, Heidelberg (1993). https://doi.org/10.1007/3-540-57318-6_30
2. Barela, M.: A complementarity approach to modeling dynamic electric circuits. Ph.D. thesis, University of Iowa (2016)

3. Benveniste, A., Caillaud, B., Elmqvist, H., Ghorbal, K., Otter, M., Pouzet, M.: Structural analysis of multi-mode DAE systems. In: HSCC, pp. 253–263. ACM (2017)
4. Benveniste, A., Caillaud, B., Guernic, P.L.: Compositionality in dataflow synchronous languages: specification and distributed code generation. Inf. Comput. **163**(1), 125–171 (2000)
5. Benveniste,A., Caillaud, B., Pouzet, M., Elmqvist, H., Otter, M.: Structural analysis of multi-mode DAE systems. Research report RR-8933, Inria, July 2016
6. Benveniste, A., Caspi, P., Edwards, S.A., Halbwachs, N., Guernic, P.L., de Simone, R.: The synchronous languages 12 years later. Proc. IEEE **91**(1), 64–83 (2003)
7. Berry, G.: Constructive semantics of Esterel: from theory to practice (abstract). In: Wirsing, M., Nivat, M. (eds.) AMAST 1996. LNCS, vol. 1101, p. 225. Springer, Heidelberg (1996). https://doi.org/10.1007/BFb0014318
8. Bezanson, J., Edelman, A., Karpinski, S., Shah, V.B.: Julia: a fresh approach to numerical computing. SIAM Rev. **59**(1), 65–98 (2017)
9. Brenan, K.E., Campbell, S.L., Petzold, L.R.: Numerical Solution of Initial Value Problems in Differential-Algebraic Equations. SIAM (1996)
10. Dunford, N., Schwartz, J.: Linear Operators, Part I, General Theory. Wiley-Interscience (1958)
11. Elmqvist, H., Henningsson, T., Otter, M.: Systems modeling and programming in a unified environment based on Julia. In: Margaria, T., Steffen, B. (eds.) ISoLA 2016. LNCS, vol. 9953, pp. 198–217. Springer, Cham (2016). https://doi.org/10.1007/978-3-319-47169-3_15
12. Elmqvist, H., Henningsson, T., Otter, M.: Innovations for future Modelica. In: Jiri Kofranek, F.C. (ed.) Proceedings of the 12th International Modelica Conference, May 2017. http://www.ep.liu.se/ecp/132/076/ecp17132693.pdf
13. Elmqvist, H., Mattsson, S.-E., Otter, M.: Modelica extensions for multi-mode DAE systems. In: Tummescheit, H., Arzèn, K.-E. (eds.) Proceedings of the 10th International Modelica Conference, Lund, Sweden. Modelica Association, September 2014. http://www.ep.liu.se/ecp/096/019/ecp14096019.pdf
14. Gear, C.W.: Differential-algebraic equation index transformations. SIAM J. Sci. Stat. Comput. **9**(1), 39–47 (1988)
15. Gear, C.W., Leimkuhler, B., Gupta, G.K.: Automatic integration of euler-lagrange equations with constraints. J. Comput. Appl. Math. **12**, 77–90 (1985)
16. Heemels, W.P.M.H., Camlibel, M.K., Schumacher, J.M.: On the dynamic analysis of piecewise-linear networks. IEEE Trans. Circ. Syst. I: Fundam. Theory Appl. **49**(3), 315–327 (2002)
17. Karnopp, D., Margolis, D., Rosenberg, R.: System Dynamics: A Unified Approach. Wiley, Hoboken (1990)
18. Lindstrøm, T.: An invitation to nonstandard analysis. In: Cutland, N. (ed.) Nonstandard Analysis and its Applications, pp. 1–105. Cambridge University Press, Cambridge (1988)
19. Mattsson, S.-E., Otter, M., Elmqvist, H.: Multi-mode DAE systems with varying index. In: Elmqvist, H., Fritzson, P. (eds.) Proceedings of the 11th International Modelica Conference, Versailles, France. Modelica Association, September 2015. http://www.ep.liu.se/ecp/118/009/ecp1511889.pdf
20. Mehrmann, V., Wunderlich, L.: Hybrid systems of differential-algebraic equations - analysis and numerical solution. J. Process Control **19**(8), 1218–1228 (2009). Special Section on Hybrid Systems: Modeling, Simulation and Optimization

21. Modelica: A unified object-oriented language for systems modeling. Language Specification, Version 3.4. Technical report, Modelica Association, April 2017. https://www.modelica.org/documents/ModelicaSpec34.pdf

22. Otter, M., Elmqvist, H.: Transformation of differential algebraic array equations to index one form. In: Kofranek, J., Casella, F. (eds.) Proceedings of the 12th International Modelica Conference, May 2017. http://www.ep.liu.se/ecp/132/064/ecp17132565.pdf

23. Pantelides, C.: The consistent initialization of differential-algebraic systems. SIAM J. Sci. Stat. Comput. **9**(2), 213–231 (1988)

24. Pepper, P., Mehlhase, A., Höger, C., Scholz, L.: A compositional semantics for Modelica-style variable-structure modeling. In: 4th International Workshop on Equation-Based Object-Oriented Modeling Languages and Tools (2011). http://www.ep.liu.se/ecp/056/006/ecp1105606.pdf

25. Pfeiffer, F.: On non-smooth multibody dynamics. Proc. Inst. Mech. Eng. Part K: J. Multi-body Dyn. **226**(2), 147–177 (2012). http://journals.sagepub.com/doi/pdf/10.1177/1464419312438487

26. Pfeiffer, F., Glocker, C.: Multibody Dynamics with Unilateral Contacts. Wiley, Hoboken (2008)

27. Pryce, J.D.: A simple structural analysis method for DAEs. BIT **41**(2), 364–394 (2001)

28. Robinson, A.: Nonstandard Analysis. Princeton Landmarks in Mathematics (1996). ISBN 0-691-04490-2

29. Schoeder, S., Ulbrich, H., Schindler, T.: Discussion of the Gear-Gupta-Leimkuhler method for impacting mechanical systems. Multibody Sys. Dyn. **31**, 477–495 (2013)

30. Campbell, S.L., Gear, C.W.: The index of general nonlinear DAEs. Numer. Math. **72**, 173–196 (1995)

31. Thoma, J.: Introduction to Bond Graphs and Their Applications. Pergamon International Library of Science, Technology, Engineering and Social Studies. Pergamon Press (1975)

32. Trenn, S.: Distributional differential algebraic equations. Ph.D. thesis, Technischen Universität Ilmenau (2009). https://www.db-thueringen.de/servlets/MCRFileNodeServlet/dbt_derivate_00018071/ilm1-2009000207.pdf

33. Zimmer, D.: Equation-based modeling of variable-structure systems. Ph.D. thesis, ETH Zürich, no. 18924 (2010). http://www.inf.ethz.ch/personal/fcellier/PhD/zimmer_phd.pdf

Language-Driven Engineering: From General-Purpose to Purpose-Specific Languages

Bernhard Steffen[1(✉)], Frederik Gossen[1,2], Stefan Naujokat[1],
and Tiziana Margaria[2]

[1] Chair for Programming Systems, TU Dortmund University, Dortmund, Germany
{steffen,stefan.naujokat}@cs.tu-dortmund.de
[2] Lero - The Irish Software Research Centre, University of Limerick, Limerick, Ireland
{frederik.gossen,tiziana.margaria}@lero.ie

Abstract. In this paper, we present the paradigm of Language-Driven Engineering (LDE), which is characterized by its unique support for division of labour on the basis of Domain-Specific Languages (DSLs) targeting different stakeholders. LDE allows the involved stakeholders, including the application experts, to participate in the system development and evolution process using dedicated DSLs, while at the same time establishing new levels of reuse that are enabled by powerful model transformations and code generation. Technically, the interplay between the involved DSLs is realized in a service-oriented fashion. This eases a product line approach and system evolution by allowing to introduce and exchange entire DSLs within corresponding Mindset-Supporting Integrated Development Environments (mIDEs). The impact of this approach is illustrated along the development and evolution of a profile-based email distribution system. Here we do not want to emphasize the precise choice of DSLs, but rather the flexible DSL-based modularization of the development process, which allows one to freely introduce and exchange DSLs as needed to optimally capture the mindsets of the involved stakeholders.

Keywords: Service orientation · Domain-specific languages
Mindset · DSLs as a service · Software development environments
Software evolution · Product lines · Code generation
Decision diagrams

1 Introduction

"Programming language research is short of its ultimate goal–provide software developers tools for formulating solutions in the languages of problem domains.":
This quote appeared in CACM [31] shortly before our final version deadline. It ideally paves the way for establishing our vision and approach. We therefore decided to use the *Language-Oriented Programming* (LOP) approach of the

© Springer Nature Switzerland AG 2019
B. Steffen and G. Woeginger (Eds.): Computing and Software Science, LNCS 10000, pp. 311–344, 2019.
https://doi.org/10.1007/978-3-319-91908-9_17

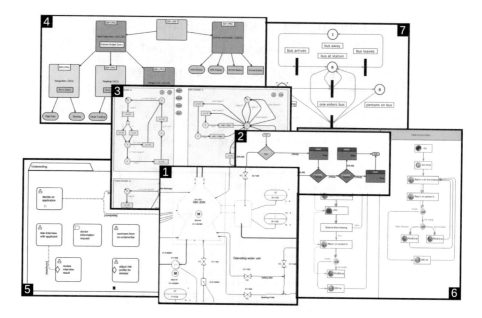

Fig. 1. (1) Piping & instrumentation diagram [107] (2) flow graph [107] (3) probabilistic timed automata [81] (4) hierarchical scheduling systems [26] (5) OMG's case management CMMN [105] (6) EasyDelta pick and place DSL [21] (7) place/transition net [79]

Racket team presented there as a means to highlight some essential features of our *Language-Driven Engineering* (LDE) approach.

It is surprising how different these approaches are despite their similar naming and guiding vision: While our LDE approach aims at enriching typically graphical domain languages[1] like the ones shown in Fig. 1 in order to define an external DSL for which full code can be generated, LOP aims at capturing domain-specific features by establishing tailored internal domain-specific languages (there called *embedded DSLs* or *eDSLs*) on top of LISP/Racket (see, e.g., Fig. 2).[2]

As a consequence, in the LOP approach the addressed software developers are clearly programmers,[3] while it is the goal of LDE to provide tailored (graphical) languages that allow application experts without programming knowledge to act themselves as software developers.

In order to set the scene for our LDE development, we structure the introduction in four parts: a sketch of the vision, followed by a description of the

---

[1] Which are very popular in practice, as *"pictures are (often) worth a thousand words"*.

[2] The difference between internal and external DSLs can be sketched as follows: an internal DSL is added (e.g. via API functionality) to a host language, which is usually a general-purpose programming language, while an external DSL comes with an own syntax that is completely independent of already existing languages.

[3] Cf. Fig. 2 (reprinted from [16]) for an exemplary Racket eDSL, accompanied by a simple graphical representation for communication with the reader.

```
01 #lang video
02
03 (image "splash.png" #:length 100)
04
05 (fade-transition #:length 50)
06
07 (multitrack (blank #f)
08             (composite-transition 0 0 1/4 1/4)
09             slides
10             (composite-transition 1/4 0 3/4 1)
11             presentation
12             (composite-transition 0 1/4 1/4 3/4)
13             (image "logo.png" #:length (producer-length talk)))
14
15 ; where
16 (define slides
17   (clip "slides05.MTS" #:start 2900 #:end 80000))
18
19 (define presentation
20   (playlist (clip "vid01.mp4")
21            (clip "vid02.mp4")
22            #:start 3900 #:end 36850))
23
24 (fade-transition #:length 50)
25
26 (image "splash.png" #:length 100)
```

Fig. 2. A script in the Racket-based *Video language* (reprinted from [16]).

background, the discussed application scenario, and a summary of the contributions of this paper.

1.1 Vision and Approach

We envisage a development paradigm for bridging the *(semantic) gap* [82] of software (system) engineering by allowing all stakeholders[4] to solve their respective tasks using *domain/purpose-specific* languages (DSLs) supporting their established *mindsets*.[5] Technically this requires Mindset-Supporting Integrated Development Environments (mIDEs) that orchestrate the individual stakeholder-specific artifacts and aggregate them to a whole from which entire software systems are automatically generated.

The different mindsets of the involved stakeholders are the main reason for the semantic gap. Making these mindsets precise and allowing orchestration and aggregation of mindset-specific artifacts is a major challenge. Key to the

---

[4] The various application experts involved, domain modelers, platform and GUI experts, software architects, programmers, etc.

[5] In the following, we assume the established notion of *domain-specific* languages to also comprise the even more specific flavor of *purpose-specific* languages.

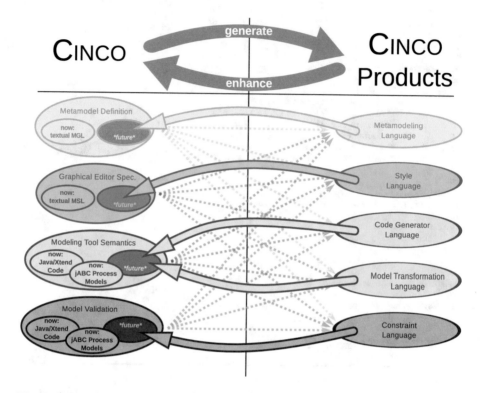

Fig. 3. Enhancing the CINCO framework with CINCO-developed graphical languages in a bootstrapping fashion (reprinted from [80]).

proposed Language-Driven Engineering (LDE) approach is therefore a new class of stakeholders whose task is to generate and maintain the required mIDEs. This task comprises language and code generator design as well as the aggregation of all aspects required to obtain mIDEs that support full code generation.

That multi-DSL design is very promising is also emphasized in [31] where the authors state: *"Large projects often employ a tower involving a few dozen languages, all helping manage the daunting complexity in modern software systems."* In fact, we believe that the number of graphical DSLs used in the various fields of application easily outnumbers their textual counterparts, and that it is possible to enrich many of these DSLs to satisfy the LDE requirements (cf. Fig. 1). Moreover, we envisage that bootstrapping (cf. [36,50]) will help overcoming the major hurdle for LDE currently perceived: the construction of the required mIDEs. Considering mIDE development as the domain of interest and using dedicated mIDEs for developing and refining mIDEs imposes a natural continuous improvement cycle. Figure 3 sketches this cycle for CINCO, our mIDE for generating mIDEs [80]: the meta-level family of DSLs used to develop the essential aspects of mIDEs are used to create new DSLs for DSL development,

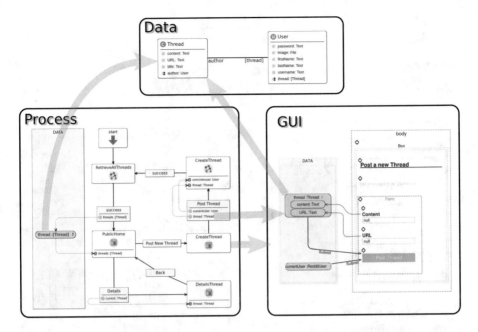

Fig. 4. Horizontal composition of specialized modeling languages for data, processes and GUI as provided by the DIME framework (reprinted from [79]).

which in turn can be fed back into the overall ecosystem of languages in a boot-strapping fashion. Our experience with CINCO [79] is very encouraging.

The semantic requirements for allowing the orchestration and aggregation of the artifacts written in stakeholder-specific languages are in general very complex. This paper therefore concentrates on a *service-oriented* version of orchestration and aggregation of language artifacts as well as, at the meta-level, of entire DSLs.

1.2   Background

There is consensus that modular system development should ideally support *horizontal composition*, so that for example the composition of modules/procedures should not depend on implementation details of the promised functionality, as well as *vertical refinement*, so that for example refinement should be possible without considering the global usage scenario, and also that *evolution* should be decomposed into steps of local impact. The underlying motivation is a general design principle: the more one can rely on things that do not change – called *Archimedean points* in [102] – the better one can control in a separation of concerns manner the change a development or evolution step imposes. In practice, service-oriented development proved practical to support this goal [73,74]: it does not even require a common implementation language.

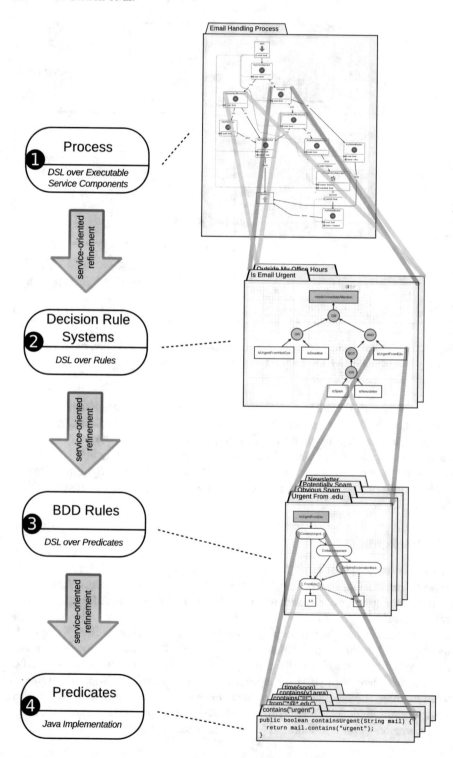

Fig. 5. Vertical DSL-based refinement

The Language-Driven Engineering (LDE) approach presented in this paper hinges on the observation that a similar picture is found also at the meta level, when developing mIDEs, for example using language workbenches [32]:

In a language engineering setting, *horizontal composition* refers to the development of complementary modeling languages, e.g., for processes, data, and GUI. As common practice for the implementation of different (same-level) procedures of a program, the DSLs and mIDEs for modeling data or processes should only be required to support the required meta-level interface, like for example the create, read, update and delete operations that define the interplay between data and process models. For instance, Fig. 4 illustrates how DIME [22,23], our mIDE for graphical modeling of Web applications, uses in each model type dedicated model elements that *represent* entities (in this case the thread entity) of other (horizontal) same-level models, this way guaranteeing the type-correct relation between models of the different languages.

Vertical refinement, on the other hand, addresses cascading domain-specific languages that become increasingly more specific and therefore more powerful and safer/easier to use for the corresponding stakeholder. This is illustrated in Fig. 5, where for example the language for decision rule systems is used for service-oriented refinement of the process language.

Finally, the *evolution* of mIDEs should – like in modular system design – follow the locality principle. The consideration of DSLs as units of evolution and exchange establishes a level of locality that is new and characteristic for LDE. For example, in Sect. 4.2 a BDD-based DSL for modeling binary decisions is (simply) replaced by variants of DSLs for fuzzy logic.

1.3   LDE Application Example

The essence and impact of the proposed *service-oriented* form of DSL composition, refinement, and evolution will be illustrated along the stepwise development and evolution of a profile-based email distribution system (Sect. 2). Service-oriented means here that DSLs are treated themselves as units of evolution and exchange during a hierarchical mIDE development, i.e., DSLs are treated as services themselves. For vertical refinement and evolution, the focus of this paper, the situation is as follows:

– Vertical DSL refinement is illustrated in Fig. 5: the decision nodes of the process model are refined in three hierarchical steps:
  1. the decision nodes of the process model are refined using a DSL for Decision Rule Systems: a decision is expressed as rules in this DSL,
  2. the leaf nodes of a Decision Rule System are refined by decision diagrams: the domain concepts are expressed as a BDD over primitive concepts that are domain-specific predicates, and
  3. the internal nodes of the decision diagrams are refined by native calls implementing the required predicates: a predicate is "evaluated" by executing native Java code.

– Evolution is illustrated in Fig. 9 (cf. Sect. 4): it shows the extensive reuse when changing the DSL for decision rules from Binary Decision Diagrams (BDDs) to Algebraic Decision Diagrams (ADDs) [18] for fuzzy logic and to n-ary decisions.

The setup is chosen to illustrate the role of the diverse DSLs addressing different concerns, ranging from ease of use for the involved stakeholders to efficiency. In fact, graphical process modeling languages have proved to be successful in involving non-programmers, the graphical syntax diagram notation is convenient for specifying logical combinations of arbitrary predicates, and decision diagrams are a de facto standard for the efficient treatment of Boolean functions.

These quite diverse DSLs address a wide range of intents and mindsets of professionals. E.g., (business) process experts are meant to directly 'draw' their intended 'workflows', and rule designers should be able to combine elementary decision rules to more complex ones without worrying about implementation details or efficiency. Moreover, decision diagrams are an intuitive representation for small predicates/rules, and also a scalable means to generate highly efficient code via their underlying well-known minimization technology (cf. [1,90,91]).

Our goal is to provide all stakeholders with a means to express their desires in terms of what they want to achieve (WHAT/Requirement level), without worrying about possible ways of realization (HOW/Implementation level). It should be clear that the WHAT level of one stakeholder may well be a HOW level for another stakeholder. E.g., BDDs are certainly at the HOW level for process and rule experts, while they are at the WHAT level for someone who is responsible for efficient rule implementation. Likewise, Java may well be the HOW level for the rule implementors, whereas it is typically WHAT level for someone who is responsible for code generation.

The case study focuses on vertical refinement and DSL-based system evolution during the development of a basic email distribution system and highlights the role of the service-oriented interplay between the various DSLs thus illustrating DSL-based refinement. Along Fig. 5, the provided dedicated DSLs address

1. process experts, here through a simple flow chart language to model under which circumstances which email handling criteria should be applied (see Sect. 3.1),
2. rule engineers, here through a simple predicate logic for modeling the required email distribution criteria according to a given email profile (see Sects. 3.2 and 3.3),
3. algorithmic experts, for guaranteeing performance on the basis of BDD/ADD technology,
4. programmers, to realize the profile extraction from incoming mails, e.g. in Java (see Sect. 3.4), and also
5. meta-modeling experts, for providing the required mIDEs including their required code generators, e.g. using the CINCO framework [79,80].

Subsequently, Sect. 4 illustrates the DSL-driven evolution process which is designed to clearly separate concerns and to control potential feature interaction in a two-dimensional fashion: At the meta level to generate the required new mIDEs and at the object level to use these mIDEs for modeling the new functionality (cf. Fig. 9).

1.4   Contribution

The LDE paradigm proposed in this paper supports division of labour among different stakeholders on the basis of stakeholder-specific languages. Key to this approach is to accompany system development with the development of dedicated mIDEs: the conceptual decompositions typical for system development are coherently matched by the provision of adequate mIDEs for the stakeholders, so that they can contribute to the actual system development in their mindset. The required parallel maintenance of DSLs and system models is particularly elegant as long as a *service-oriented* style of DSL composition, refinement, and evolution is adopted.

LDE allows all the involved stakeholders, including the application experts, to directly contribute to the system development and evolution using dedicated DSLs for their level of expertise. This approach establishes three levels of reuse, each supporting a specific kind of LDE stakeholder:

- mIDE-based development provides an intrinsic simplification that manifests itself as a powerful form of IDE support that goes beyond the usual IDE support for generic programming. Being domain-specific, it can exploit domain knowledge like "this has to run on a certain platform" to generate the entire running system from a purely functional description developed with a (stakeholder-specific) DSL. The task "get it to run on the platform" is materialized as an mIDE artifact using another, dedicated DSL, and thus can be simply stored and factored out for future reuse.
- DSLs are considered as units of reuse during mIDE construction. For example, a DSL for GUI design may be reused independently of the platform (e.g., Web, mobile phone, etc.) where the actual user application runs.
- mIDE development environments can be reused for the construction of DSLs and further mIDEs. For example, our meta tooling suite CINCO [79] can be (re)used to generate graphical domain-specific development tools, or even entire mIDE. In particular, the DSL for DSL specification underlying CINCO and its corresponding code generator have been reused over and over again. This kind of reuse is particularly interesting for its bootstrapping effect: an mIDE for code generation generated with CINCO may well become part of CINCO itself, as described in [80] and illustrated in Fig. 3.

LDE is based on a very general notion of service: a service is a means to bridge the various HOW/WHAT gaps in system development, and it stands simply for any form of aggregation of technical detail to a new (behavioral) unit that serves a specific (user-defined) purpose or concern at the higher level. Typical examples of such services are the decision functions of the email process, which are implemented using DSLs for rule composition and predicate definition (cf. Sect. 3).

Such services allow for a more abstract level of system composition, where certain lower level concerns are already taken care of inside the service components.[6]

LDE goes a step further by considering DSLs as services themselves, namely as meta-level services that can simply be used for mIDE design in order to provide stakeholders with their mindset-specific mIDE. This way, the interplay between different mindsets during system development and evolution can be supported in a *DSL as a Service* fashion as illustrated in Sect. 4. The essence of the corresponding system refinement and evolution happens indeed at the meta level. For example, the change of mindset required when moving from Boolean to fuzzy logic is entirely taken care of by a corresponding (service-oriented) exchange of DSLs of the corresponding mIDE (cf. Sect. 4.2).

Whereas the elegance of achieving user-intended solutions is a consequence of the purpose-specific WHAT perspective, efficiency hinges on additional HOW knowledge expressed in a language whose purpose is to support efficient implementation. BDDs and ADDs are good examples for such efficiency-oriented DSLs with high potential to be frequently reused as a service.

Language-Driven Engineering (LDE) aims at enabling a new level of cooperative system development whose support does not end with the deployment but continues throughout the systems' life cycle by continuously providing all the involved stakeholders with languages tailored to their own task and its corresponding mindset. The goal is a consequent separation of concerns that allows developers to focus on required functionality, while trusting that the remaining issues, like performance, security, or platform-specific anomalies, are already taken care of or delegated to dedicated experts. As discussed in [79,107], providing dedicated DSLs allows the involved stakeholders, including the application experts, to directly participate in the development process. For example, in the project described in [107], experts in industrial fluid processing could be involved thanks to a specialized DSL resembling piping and instrumentation diagrams, and electrical engineers thanks to another specialized DSL expressing connectivity on the basis of cabinet layouts familiar to them.

All the mIDEs of all DSLs used in our example are generated with the CINCO meta-modeling framework [79], which is open source and available on GitLab[7]. Also the ADD-Lib framework for dealing with decision diagrams is open source, so readers may replicate entirely the development described in this paper[8].

In the remainder of the paper, Sect. 2 sketches LDE along the above introduced application scenario that we will use to illustrate the pragmatics and impact of LDE, before Sect. 3 presents the pragmatics of system development via DSL-based decomposition and Sect. 4 discusses the potential of system evolution via DSL introduction and exchange. The paper closes after a discussion

---

[6] This notion of service is more general than the very constrained notion proposed by the Web service community, which is typically directly linked to the use of certain specialized technologies and protocols, nor is it necessarily linked to the component view of today's popular service-oriented architectures.

[7] https://gitlab.com/scce/cinco

[8] Please see the LDE case study at [2].

of related work and potential application fields in Sect. 5 with our conclusions and future perspectives in Sect. 6.

2 Example-Based Sketch of LDE

We will show, how a simple service for the automatic extraction of urgent emails from a stream of incoming emails using binary logic can be evolved in an LDE-fashion towards an efficient distribution service based on fuzzy logic. Here, vertical DSL-based decomposition will be used to improve the scalability and performance of the basic email distribution system (cf. Sect. 3), and DSL-based evolution will be useful for treating different variants of fuzzy rules (cf. Sect. 4). Figure 5 summarizes the vertical decomposition using four DSLs:

1. At the top level, processes allow for a user-level definition of the business logic. Such process descriptions are comparable to languages like BPMN [86] and UML's activity diagrams [85], but additionally provide full code generation. We use here a specialized variant of the process language from the DIME framework [22] which provides fully model-based development of all aspects of a multi-user single-page web application[9]. As the DIME processes are the technological successors of the *Service Logic Graphs* (SLGs) of the jABC framework [84,100], they comprise building blocks for the inclusion of executable services, and these building blocks are connected according to their flow of control. Included services provide functionality for, e.g., putting emails into (named) baskets and email forwarding, as well as profile-based decision services – the starting points for the vertical decomposition described next.
2. Decision services are components 'simply used' within the process layer. Of course they could be directly implemented in code, however we aim for a user-level definition of the decisions and introduce a domain-specific language that allows to define *Decision Rule Systems* as compositions of *Decision Rules*. These rules are again provided in a service-oriented fashion: Without needing to know how exactly such rules are realized/implemented, users can combine them with simple logic operators in a graphical language.
3. Binary decision diagrams [30] (BDDs), the level 3 components of Fig. 5, are a common graphical language for decision modeling. They are intuitively defined and understood, and form a research field on their own. Thus, algorithms for optimization, minimization, etc. are widely available.
4. Rules (and their compositions) are based on a *profile* of the processed email, which comprises various predicates resulting from the analysis of the email's body, header, and other metadata. We decide to break the chain of graphical user-level languages at this point, and allow for the inclusion of arbitrary predicate implementations given in Java: 'general-purpose programming' seems to be now an adequate 'domain'. Of course, we could have also included further DSLs, e.g. using regular expressions to model text matching.

---

[9] The full DIME framework comprises various languages for the web domain, all spanning the horizontal dimension of our LDE approach (cf. Fig. 4).

In addition to this vertical dimension, each level may as well have its own dimension of in-language hierarchy. For example, an executable service component in a process can be a process itself; a rule in a rule system can be itself a composite rule system; a predicate/variable decision in a BDD can be another BDD, and the implemented Java method has access to the full language potential of structuring the program: method calls, classes, libraries, etc.

The second dimension, the DSL-based evolution, is characterized by a generalization of BDDs to Algebraic Decision Diagrams (ADDs) in order to adequately treat fuzzy rules. This generalization can easily be extended to also comprise multi-basket capability. Our corresponding two-step definition of decision functions defined as composite rules made of BDDs (cf. Sect. 3.2), which might look a bit artificial in isolation, is ideal to illustrate the DSL-based WHAT/HOW interplay outlined above:

- It establishes a logical layer for hierarchical WHAT-level reuse in a service-oriented way: whatever library of domain-specific rules are available, this layer supports their combination with the typical logical operators. In the refined settings arising during the system evolution (cf. Sect. 4), this layer will comprise more general algebraic operators.
- It establishes a HOW-level for performance optimization: logical combinations of BDDs can be 'partially evaluated' to obtain a redundancy-free representation in terms of BDDs that guarantees that every embodied predicate is evaluated at most once at runtime. The impact of this optimization is particularly striking for the refined setting where 'fuzzy' domain-specific predicates (cf. Sect. 4.1) are represented as ADDs.

We will see that the service-oriented interplay between these two layers eases the system evolution process by keeping the changes at the different modeling layers and at the code generators to a minimum.

3   Vertical DSL-Based Decomposition

The pragmatics of vertical DSL-based decomposition concern in particular the support of the service-oriented interplay between the involved DSLs in order to establish a clear separation of concerns and of the cooperative development using stakeholder-specific mIDEs. We discuss the 4 level stepwise refinement from the top-level perspective of the global (distribution) process, via two DSL-supported layers for decision rule definition to a programming layer for implementing so-called *native services*. Besides easing the involvement of stakeholders with different backgrounds, these four layers are meant to decouple/modularize the system in such a way that the impact of later evolution steps is localized, an effect discussed in Sect. 4.

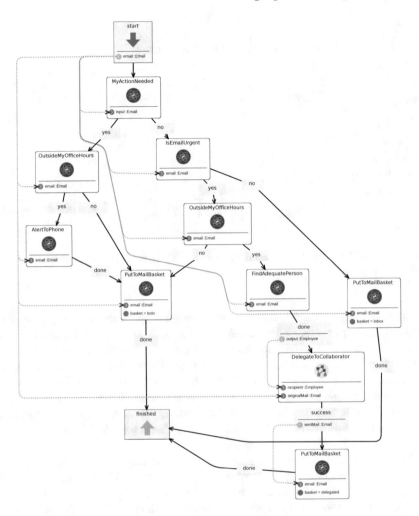

Fig. 6. Email handling process in DIME

3.1   The Global Email Distribution Process

The global process layer is conceived to allow the customers of the envisioned email distribution system to describe their desires at a WHAT level: the language refers to notions from the user perspective and, in particular, it does not require any programming knowledge. Process descriptions must also be precise enough to enable full code generation once the service-oriented refinement at the other three layers is complete. Figure 6 shows the DIME process model of the email handling process. This model is self-explaining, and it can be even constructed by non-programmers using DIME's easy-to-use component libraries with little training.

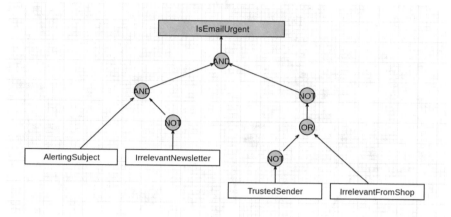

Fig. 7. IsEmailUrgent: a composed rule in the DSL for the composition of Binary Decision Diagrams.

Customers are usually presented with palettes of ready building blocks and use them in their process definition. A customer may also customize or extend the DSL by 'inventing' new components, name them to reflect their domain-related intention and perhaps add some documentation. Such atomic building blocks can be directly used in a process model, and be refined and implemented later on. In practice, process modelers start with the available palette of building blocks and propose new building blocks only at need, a typical case during system evolution. Such top-down/bottom-up interplay is characteristic for service-oriented refinement and it occurs at all DSL layers.

Service-oriented refinement substitutes the building blocks definition with one or more corresponding implementations, the key enabling mechanism of full code generation. The following three subsections illustrate this refinement for the decision services, in particular the building block that decides whether an email is urgent. This refinement is organized in three levels of DSLs:

- Syntax diagrams for the (propositional) logical combination of elementary decision rules,
- BDDs for the definition of elementary decision rules on the basis of elementary predicates, and
- Java for the implementation of elementary predicates.

We will show how this service-oriented decomposition enables cooperative development, supports reuse, and eases evolution.

3.2   A DSL for Rule-Based Composition of Decision Services

The decision services occurring in the process model are defined by the corresponding stakeholder as logical compositions of decision rules[10] that are already available or to be implemented later. Figure 7 shows the inner structure of the "IsEmailUrgent" decision service as a logical composition of five decision rules.[11] The syntax tree-like look of the DSL is easy to handle and to read, even for hierarchical decision service definitions. In the corresponding propositional logic-based mIDE, users specify their intents simply by drag and drop from component libraries. If a new rule is needed, users may introduce a placeholder and directly use them. Such placeholders are requests for new rules, to be handled by the responsible experts who turn the 'partial' specification into a complete specification for which full code can be generated.[12]

Using this mIDE to compose rules is quite easy after a short introduction. Understanding the logical impact of the rule compositions on the other hand is by no means trivial and requires expertise, or an adequate mindset. Our mIDE helps building up this mindset by easing experimentation and providing immediate feedback for the specifier, to check whether the intents were met. The decision services can be simulated and logical inconsistencies can be automatically detected. In particular, the consistency check is a great help, as inconsistencies in decision service definitions can be just flaws, but may also point to a major misconceptions.

DSLs and their corresponding mIDEs are powerful means to factor out tasks for a specific domain and provide support to solve them once and for all. This support can be the stronger the more specific the DSL. E.g., while for a generic programming language it is difficult to characterize inconsistency, for appropriately defined DSLs, like the BDDs introduced in the next subsection for rule definitions, this is very easy.

3.3   A Language for Efficient Decision Rule Implementation

Intuitively, decision rules are 'if-then' specifications[13] that describe under which circumstances which action/decision has to be taken. In the binary case decision rules are formally Boolean predicates. In the evolution steps we will use more

---

[10] In this basic setting, the decision rules are (predefined) predicates and the logical combination considered in this section is just a simple means for a hierarchical specification of more complex predicates. Why we chose to call these predicates rules will become clearer at the lower level and in view of evolution, in Sect. 4.

[11] The composition model is obviously not minimal. Instead, it reflects the individual user's mindset. It will be optimized automatically during code generation.

[12] In a pure top-down development from scratch, no library components are available: They must be introduced as part of the specification and subsequently refined. In practice, after some time most of the required components can be drawn from libraries and only a few need to be introduced.

[13] Popular representatives of decision rules are Event Condition Action Rules [14,29] or weighted rules [37].

general rules: Fuzzy rules, tailored to deal with uncertainty, and n-ary rules supporting decisions with more than two outcomes.

In our example, we use as DSLs for rules definition Binary Decision Diagrams (BDDs, [24])[14] and corresponding generalizations. BDDs represent decision trees as minimal directed acyclic graphs (DAGs) whose nodes are associated with Boolean variables or predicates, whose two outgoing edges encode the outcome of the predicate evaluation, and whose leaves are the Boolean constants TRUE and FALSE, denoted by 1 and 0, respectively. Given a fixed order of the variables resp. predicates, BDDs are canonical normal forms. Formal definitions and details are available in [30].

While huge BDDs have been used for decades as boolean encodings for hardware verification, SAT solving, and similar machine-managed representation domains, small BDDs as those shown in Fig. 8 are well suited to establish domain-specific libraries of (elementary) rules at the WHAT level: the meaning of these BDDs is intuitively clear also for unexperienced users.[15] Once the implementation code for the involved elementary predicates is available, the BDDs shown in Fig. 8 are sufficient to generate fully executable code for the composition of Fig. 7.

In the seminal paper [24], BDDs were established as an efficient data structure for Boolean functions $\mathbb{B}^n \to \mathbb{B}$, with efficient logical operators to evaluate a complex formula to a single result BDD. The formula corresponding to the syntax tree of Fig. 7 evaluates to the BDD shown in Fig. 11(a) using the BDD definitions of the single predicates shown in Fig. 8. This evaluation technology allows one to generate code whose performance can be hardly achieved via manual coding. The canonical nature of the BDDs eases many frequent analyses: e.g., checking functional equivalence of expanded BDDs reduces to rooted DAG isomorphy, and inconsistent formulas are reduced to the one-node BDD FALSE, a particularly handy property when dealing with large rule compositions.

3.4 Implementation of Elementary Predicates

Elementary predicates like those extracting certain characteristics from incoming emails, may well be implemented in Java, here considered the 'generic DSL' for everything where there is no specific DSL support. An important feature of service-oriented refinement is in fact that it allows one to link to programming languages at any point during the refinement process without harm. In facts, refinements typically end with implementations of elementary services in a generic programming language. The level at which one decides to turn to generic programming may change in the course of a larger project. For example, one could later decide to introduce regular expressions for text matching as a new DSL layer. Service-oriented refinement is ideal to support this form of evolution.

---

[14] BDDs earned their fame more on the HOW level, where they support amazing optimizations, at a small scale they are quite intuitive even for unexperienced users.

[15] We adopt the de facto standard graphical representation for BDDs where a solid edge represents a node's then-successor, and a dashed edge its else-successor.

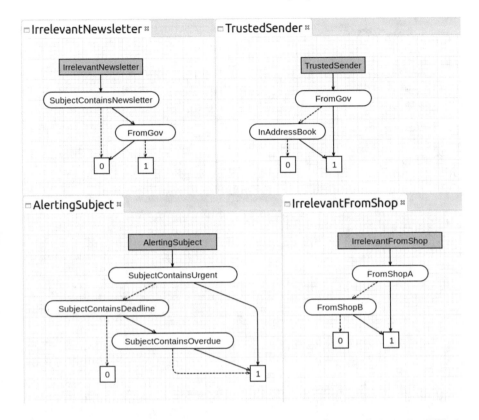

Fig. 8. Elementary classification services for urgent emails specified in the DSL for Binary Decision Diagrams as BDD rules

4   DSL-Based Evolution

We already saw one DSL-based evolution step: the evolution to optimized BDDs sketched in the transformation indicated by Fig. 9(a) illustrates that the HOW-knowledge about the BDD-based decision rule realization can be used for optimization purposes, by partially evaluating the expression that defines the logical composition of the decision rules. The realization of this optimization is almost for free: the rule partial evaluation step needs to be implemented as a new code generator[16], but the entire grey part remains unchanged, constituting an Archimedean point.

---

[16] This is quite simple, using available open source libraries [1,90,91].

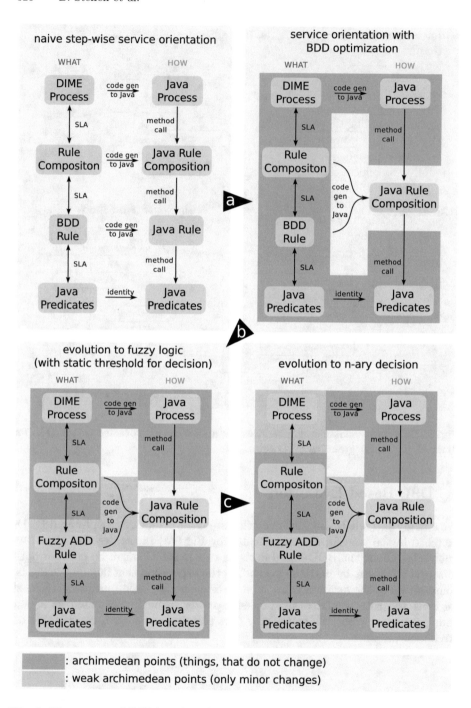

Fig. 9. Three steps of DSL-based evolution: from the initial implementation to optimized and fuzzy n-ary decisions. In this figure, SLA refers to a meta-level variant of service-level agreement.

Two restrictions of the modeling with propositional logic (and BDDs) that can be quite severe in practice are addressable with evolution to new DSL specializations:

- Decision rules for our example are often not strict: criteria like keywords, subjects, or origin are typically only indicators for urgency, and the more of such indications apply, the stronger becomes the indication and the corresponding decision support. Fuzzy rules are an adequate technique to address this issue, and ADDs provide an efficient realization technology (HOW level) that only requires very local changes (cf. Fig. 9(b)).
- Many applications mandate to decide between more than two alternatives. In our example, to distinguish more levels of urgency of incoming email requests requires generalization, for which ADDs turn out to provide the technology of choice. In contrast to the previous two evolution steps, this generalization also requires a change at the process level, as the decision service has now more than two outgoing edges that need to be adequately connected in the process graph (cf. Fig. 9(c)).

We will now sketch how ADDs generalize BDDs and then describe the two evolution steps displayed in Fig. 9(b) and (c). They illustrate the principle of service-oriented refinement with its corresponding high potential for reuse, inter stakeholder cooperation, and Archimedean point-oriented evolution [102].

4.1 ADDs for Dealing with Uncertainty

BDDs are compact representations of decision structures based on Boolean algebra:
$$\mathcal{A}_{bool} := (\mathbb{B}, \{\wedge, \vee\}, \{\neg\})$$
yielding optimized evaluation structures for expressions over a set $\mathbb{B}$ that use the binary operators $\wedge, \vee$ and the unary operator $\neg$.

It is straightforward to lift this pattern of evaluation structure to any algebraic structure consisting of a set S together with a carrier set of binary operators $\mathcal{O}_b$ and a set of unary operators $\mathcal{O}_u$, resulting in the Algebraic Decision Diagrams (ADDs). The CUDD package [90,91] is a prominent C library that includes ADD support. ADDs are mainly used for arithmetics, i.e., for algebraic structures supporting integer computation $(\mathbb{Z}, \{+, *\}, \{-\})$ or floating point computation $(\mathbb{Q}, \{+, *\}, \{-\})$.

In contrast, our evolution steps use two simple fuzzy logics given by the following two algebras: a min - max algebra

$$\mathcal{A}_{fuzzy} := ([0, 1], \{\wedge_f, \vee_f\}, \{\neg_f\}) \tag{1}$$
$$\text{with} \quad a \wedge_f b := \min(a, b) \tag{2}$$
$$a \vee_f b := \max(a, b) \tag{3}$$
$$\neg_f a := 1 - a \tag{4}$$

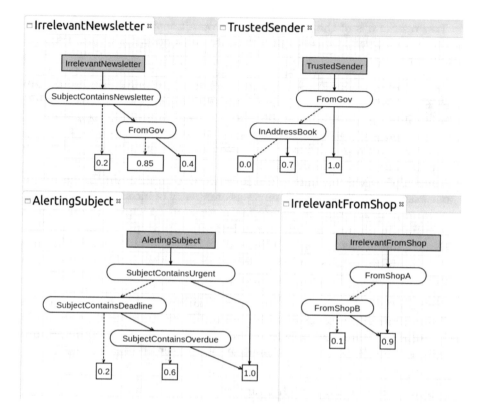

Fig. 10. Classification services for urgent emails specified in a Fuzzy purpose-specific language for Algebraic Decision Diagrams

and an algebra with a probabilistic interpretation of $\wedge$, $\vee$, and $\neg$

$$\mathcal{A}_{prob} := ([0, 1], \{\wedge_p, \vee_p\}, \{\neg_p\}) \tag{5}$$

$$\text{with} \quad a \wedge_p b := ab \tag{6}$$

$$a \vee_p b := 1 - (1 - a)(1 - b) \tag{7}$$

$$\neg_p a := 1 - a. \tag{8}$$

Several other variants can deal with uncertainty, all with their specific strength and weaknesses, and we do not claim this choice to be optimal. Instead, we want to show that service-oriented refinement is an ideal means to switch between such options depending on which variant is most adequate. Such a switch is not just a matter of easing the development: each choice comes with a specific mindset, and it is the role of DSLs to provide mindset-specific support.

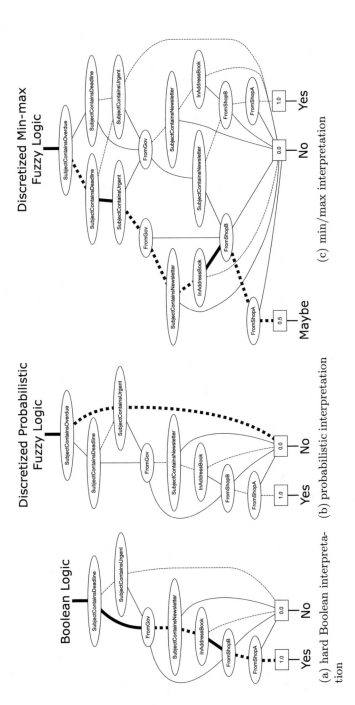

Fig. 11. Generated Algebraic Decision Diagrams for an email classification service as composed by the model in Fig. 7. From the left to the right: Standard Boolean Logic, Probabilistic Fuzzy Logic (Thresholded at $\frac{1}{2}$), and min/max Fuzzy Logic (Thresholded at $\frac{1}{3}$ and $\frac{2}{3}$) with thresholded min/max logic compared to standard Boolean logic. The highlighted path defines the decision made for an email that was sent from a sender in the address book and that mentions "deadline" but not "overdue".

4.2 Dealing with Uncertainty

Rules for decision support typically provide recommendations rather than strict knowledge: certain senders or subjects of an email are often only indications for, e.g., urgency. By allowing fuzzy rules as in Fig. 10, the values at the leaves indicate the level of certainty. The corresponding evolution of our email handling process is described in Fig. 9(c) and requires only little effort:

- the DSL for the rules is generalized to allow for more than two leaf nodes and floating point values in $[0, 1]$. This is an easy task using CINCO.
- we do not intend to touch the structure for rule composition, so only the semantics of the operators needs to be adapted to reflect the chosen variant of fuzzy logic. In our current implementation this is done in Java, consistent with our decision to end the DSL refinement at this level. However, we intend to also provide a corresponding DSL as part of the ADD-Lib [1], our framework for ADD-based modeling.
- the partial evaluation of the composition structure connecting the individual rules is implemented using the ADD-Lib [1] based on the CUDD library. After discretization into two, respectively three categories it results in the three kinds of ADDs shown in Fig. 11: (a) for the hard Boolean interpretation discussed earlier, (b) for the probabilistic interpretation, and (c) for the min/max interpretation. The only required change to the code generator is the threshold-based discretization of the ADDs, in order to allow n-ary branching in the process models.
- the decision to place the threshold-based interpretation of the leaf values in the code generator requires a change of the process model only in case the discretization distinguishes more than two categories.

Actually, we did not just evolve the email handling system, but also its corresponding mIDEs: the described changes, which concern the rule DSL and the threshold-based interpretation only, are, in fact, at the meta level. Using CINCO, we are able to fully automatically generate the two new mIDEs for the min/max and the probabilistic interpretation after slight variations of the meta model for BDDs.

The Gain of Threshold-Based Decision. To illustrate the nature of explicit uncertainty modeling for both the min/max and the probabilistic interpretation we consider two scenarios: binary decisions with a threshold of $1/2$ and a ternary decision with thresholds $1/3$ and $2/3$ which models a separate treatment of unclear cases. Figure 11 illustrates the impact for our example:

- The min/max interpretation does not add anything new to the binary case. In fact, its aggregated decision diagram coincides with the BDD shown in Fig. 11(a). In contrast, the probabilistic interpretation shows a difference (cf. Fig. 11(b)), as, e.g., small uncertainties are amplified in conjunctions.
- The min/max interpretation makes a difference in the ternary case as shown in Fig. 11(c). In fact, in the ternary case, our example path distinguishes all

three interpretations, as the probabilistic interpretation would also result in 0.0 in this case.

Adequacy and mindset of these interpretations are quite different, and none is universally superior to the others. Thus easing the context-specific choice is important.

5   The LDE Landscape

Considering the history and context of the LDE approach, we sketch the roots of LDE (Sect. 5.1), then discuss its related work (Sect. 5.2) and its connections to the work presented in the other contributions of this volume (Sect. 5.3).

5.1   LDE: The Roots

The first direct experience with the power of DSL-based mindsets came with the attempt to prove the optimality of an algorithm for partial redundancy elimination [77]. Thinking in terms of temporal logic and thereby directly in terms of the desired (temporal) properties rather than in terms of fixpoint computations as it was common at that time, radically changed the mindset. It led to a drastically shortened proofs and later allowed us to elegantly solve two important open related problems: the optimal reduction of register pressure [56–58,87],[17] and an algorithm for eliminating all partial redundancies [94]. Essentially, this was due to the compositionality of temporal logic specifications, in particular concerning conjunction.

This context also bore the idea of introducing corresponding code generators [89,92,93]. Similar to our choice to use the well established CUDD tool for the accompanying example of this paper, that code generator was based on a pre-existing model checker. In fact, full code generation became a central objective throughout all the further developments.

The idea of using components, called Service-Independent Building Blocks (SIBs) by the ITU-T Standard [46,47], which can easily be recombined due to the simplicity of their interfaces, was motived by the fast growing library of special commands for the Concurrency Workbench [28]. SIBs, semantically characterized using simple taxonomies for classification could profitably be used to automatically synthesize tailored command sequences from small temporal logic specifications [68,99], a technique later also used for automatic mediator synthesis [67].

The SIB concept combined with taxonomic classification and model checking also became the heart of a very successful industrial cooperation resulting in the Siemens Nixdorf INXpress Service Definition Environment for Intelligent Network value added services [97,98]. Their evaluation of our technology revealed

---

[17] This algorithm, which can be generated from a four line CTL specification, is now a standard for optimizing compilers, as it is both more efficient and more powerful than its competitors.

a time to market reduction of the services of a factor 5! This success drove us to transform our corresponding development environment, the METAFrame tool [96], stepwise into a more general IDE for application development called Application Building Center (ABC) and later jABC [100] when we moved from the C++ implementation to Java.

The easy service-oriented definition and exchange of functionality turned out to be a good way of communicating between the stakeholders [74]: with all the stakeholders working on the same artifact (the *One Thing* as we called it [70, 101]) but at their dedicated level of abstraction defined by the underlying service hierarchy[18]. jABC's full code generation philosophy, which avoids typical round-trip problems, maintained controllability during the entire life-cycle of a system at the modeling level [62,71]. jABC's model checking and model synthesis facility, in addition, provided dedicated support for logically controlling evolution and establishing product lines via their behavioural (temporal) properties [52,63].

The final enabling step for LDE was the move from DSLs defined via taxonomically organized service libraries to CINCO, our framework for meta-model-based generation of graphical mIDEs [78,79]. CINCO allows one to generate entire mIDEs on the basis of enriched modeling languages used, e.g., in industry. Figure 1 already sketched a few of such languages we have adopted and supported in the past. The resulting mIDEs may be combined to form more complex mIDEs supporting the cooperative development of all stakeholders involved using the One Thing Approach.

5.2   Related Work

Two properties are characteristic for LDE and its corresponding mIDEs:

- It aims at enabling all the stakeholders (in particular the application experts) to co-develop software without programming.
- It explicitly supports the multi-DSL-based cooperation of the individual stakeholders.

To our knowledge, the related work can be partitioned into approaches that address the first or the second characteristic.

Languages for Non-Programmers. Fowler, who coined the popular term *Language Workbenches* [32], characterizes in [33, p. 34] the role of, in his case textual, DSLs: "it's not that domain experts will write the DSLs themselves; but they can read them and thus understand what the system thinks it's doing". On the other hand, several graphical languages became very successful in dedicated application domains, like MatLab/Simulink [75], ladder diagrams [49], and Modelica [20,34]. The understanding that one should address application experts with graphical notations is also shared by the developers of the KIELER framework [35]. They provide means to automatically generate domain-specific

---

[18] The most recent version of the jABC supported even higher-order services [83,84].

graphical views for textual DSLs realized in the Eclipse modeling context.[19] We therefore concentrate on graphical DSLs in this subsection.

Prominent frameworks for the development of graphical modeling languages are MetaEdit+ [9,55], GME [12,64,65], Pounamu/Marama [8,39,108] or DeVIL [54,88]. These powerful frameworks are designed for generating graphical IDEs, including corresponding code generators, for a specified graphical DSL. The aspect of coordinating stakeholders with different mindsets in a cooperative fashion is not addressed. The same also applies to the Eclipse modeling ecosystem [38] with the Rich Client Platform (RCP) [76] and the Eclipse Modeling Framework (EMF) [103]. However, while there is good support for textual DSLs in Eclipse (e.g. using the Xtext [13] framework), building graphical DSLs with GMF [6], Graphiti [7], or even the Epsilon [4,5,59,60] project is very tedious.

In general, applying LDE is independent of any frameworks for the development of domain-specific languages. However, as designing the LDE languages and mIDEs required for a project is already a difficult task, CINCO explicitly aims at maximum for a higher simplicity for their technical realization.

Language-Driven Development. The *Language-Oriented Programming* approach (LOP) of the Racket team [31] is very similar to LDE concerning the second property. In fact, *Language-Oriented Programming*:

- advocates multiple cooperating languages for a project,
- has a feature called FFI (foreign-function interface) similar to our notion of native services, and
- uses a meta language 'syntax parse' to define languages

However, there are clear conceptual differences which limit the cooperation with non-programmers: LOP is based on internal DSLs (called embedded DSLs, eDSLs) based on a single base language (Racket [10], one of the successors to Lisp [106]). In [16], the exemplary DSL code is accompanied with some simple graphical notation for readability (cf. Fig. 2), which suggests that also the members of the Racket teams do not consider their DSLs as a vehicle for communication with non-programmers.

Another approach to language-driven development is projectional editing [104] as most prominently provided by JetBrains' Meta Programming Systems (MPS) [48]. However, also this approach clearly addresses programmers, or even super-programmers, capable of mastering various (programming) languages.

---

[19] While the KIELER framework is indeed mature and powerful – so that it is by now generalized as the Eclipse incubation project *Eclipse Layout Kernel* (ELK) [3] – its primary goal is to provide views to better communicate with non-programmers, while the actual (textual) models still require programmers or highly technical experienced domain experts.

5.3   Volume-Related Interrelations

LDE has the potential to enter many disciplines. In this section, we briefly sketch the interrelationship between LDE and the topics addressed in the other papers of the *Methods, Languages and Tools for Future System Development* part of this volume.

[20] is a good example for an approach based on its own elaborate DSL, Modelica, and [27] clearly indicates that one language is not enough, even for generic programming. The architecture presented in [61] which specifically addresses the need for dealing with multiple (domain-specific) languages is quite close in spirit to the LDE approach. It could profit from LDE-based language organization presented in [81] as well as from dedicated languages for orchestrating different analysis methods or abstractions along the lines presented in [69,95].

Also the approaches presented in the remaining papers could profit from DSLs, e.g., as follows: [41] for specifying certain assertions or contracts, [43] for specifying data flow analyses[20], [25] for specifying test models, [42] for defining learning alphabets or representing the learning result, [40] for modularly specifying the required code instrumentation, e.g. in an aspect-oriented fashion, and [15,19,66] for conveniently specifying their enriched system structures. Corresponding mIDEs (could) then guide the development by exploiting the DSL's specifics, e.g., the interpretation of assertions, security predicates, time, or probabilities. The corresponding code generators would transform the domain-specific specification directly into input for the target tool or platform.

On the other hand, LDE could also profit from the approaches presented in the other papers. In particular, all the involved analysis, verification and validation methods of [15,19,25,40–43,61,66] are good candidates for inclusion in mIDEs in order to improve the development support and/or to control nonfunctional constraints. Finally, [27] provides a wealth of observations and techniques with potential to impact the future mIDE development.

6   Conclusions and Perspectives

We have presented Language-Driven Engineering (LDE) as a paradigm for supporting division of labour on the basis of stakeholder-specific domain-specific languages. LDE is unique in allowing all the involved stakeholders, including the application experts, to directly participate in the system development and evolution process, while at the same time establishing new levels of reuse enabled via powerful transformations and code generation. We have illustrated how the service-oriented interplay between the involved DSLs eases product lining and system evolution through the introduction and exchange of entire DSLs together with their corresponding mIDEs.

Conceptually, LDE follows the One Thing Approach [70,101] which is reminiscent of the model-view-control pattern in that it

---

[20] In [92,93] this has profitably been done in temporal logic, cf. also Sect. 5.1.

- provides stakeholders with simplicity-oriented [72] individual views that are expressive enough to
- control their part of responsibility and aggregates all these views to a
- global, consistent model from which full code can be generated.

The striking new aspect of LDE is that the DSLs become first class citizens of the system development, which establishes a new level for reuse, refinement and evolution by evolving the underling mIDEs in order to resemble the domain and purpose-specific structure currently of interest. As the mIDEs for all DSLs are specifically generated, each stakeholder can get maximum support for his tasks, while (accidental) misuse is reduced to a minimum. In a sense, the mIDE functions here both as tool for maximum purpose-specific support, and as sandbox that prohibits damage. In particular, purpose-specific support can be easily enhanced by, e.g., integrating corresponding analysis and verification tools in a service-oriented fashion. Figure 1 summarizes some of the graphical DSLs from our recent industrial cooperations and student projects.

The practicality of this approach depends on the ease of DSL and mIDE development guaranteed in our context by the CINCO framework which also exploits itself service-oriented refinement. This allows, e.g., to exchange the variants of fuzzy logic simply by adapting the algebraic structure of the representing ADDs. Everything else can remain unchanged as it is captured by ADD-Lib, our ADD framework [1] which, in fact, has also been developed using the CINCO framework. The major remaining hurdle is the development of the code generators for the various mIDEs. We are currently developing a dedicated CINCO tool (an mIDE) for this purpose, which generalizes the approach presented in [51,53].

We are convinced that LDE with its growing tool stack has the potential to radically change the way software will be written in the future, as it enables the involved stakeholders to directly participate in the development process using dedicated tools matching their mindset, and it also increases the mere development performance due to its generative nature. Recommending dedicated DSL development even for individual projects sounds unintuitive at first, but we experienced an enormous leverage due to the bootstrapping effect, which steadily improves the mIDE development performance: the meta-level libraries of reusable components grow, and the CINCO-based mIDEs for e.g. program/DSL analysis and code generation become directly part of the meta-level support. This in turn increases the performance of CINCO-based mIDE and system development. Even in cases where developing the first running version takes a little bit longer with the LDE approach, this price has been paid off very early along the system's life-cycle.

With its new dimension of system development and evolution, LDE is an exciting research area with yet to be explored potential and enormous practical impact. It comprises and harmonizes many fields, like program and analysis and verification, constraint-based synthesis, meta-modeling, code generation, test- and learning-based validation, software product lines, system evolution, etc. In fact, the holistic nature of LDE radically changed our own way of system development, as it supports and motivates us to take the medicine we propose to others. Essentially, the development of all our projects and tools, even the code generation framework, follows the LDE paradigm. We invite everybody to share this exciting experience with us in an open source platform [11].

As a new and encompassing modeling paradigm, LDE requires its own pragmatics and expertise, e.g., to avoid a drift to excessive, ad hoc DSL generation. We envisage instead new DSLs to resemble, instrument, and refine modeling languages already used in established fields of application, leveraging their own established mindsets. Examples are BNF for syntax definition [17], SQL for data querying [45], or piping and instrumentation diagrams for e.g., modeling the flow within fluid-processing machinery [44]. New DSLs are foreseen too, but they should be developed with care, with a clear vision of their potential impact in mind. As part of the continuous improvement cycle, we envision taxonomically classified libraries of DSLs ready to be reused for the construction of new mIDEs. The DSLs for decision diagrams presented in this paper are good candidates for such a library.

Acknowledgments. This work was supported, in part, by Science Foundation Ireland grant 13/RC/2094 and co-funded under the European Regional Development Fund through the Southern & Eastern Regional Operational Programme to Lero - the Irish Software Research Centre (www.lero.ie).

References

1. ADD-Lib. http://add-lib.scce.info
2. ADD-Lib LDE Case Study. http://add-lib.scce.info/language-driven-engineering-case-study
3. Eclipse Layout Kernel. http://www.eclipse.org/elk/. Accessed 23 Mar 2018
4. Epsilon. http://www.eclipse.org/epsilon/. Accessed 10 Apr 2018
5. Epsilon EuGENia. http://www.eclipse.org/epsilon/doc/eugenia/. Accessed 10 Apr 2018
6. Graphical Modeling Framework (GMF) Tooling. http://eclipse.org/gmf-tooling/. Accessed 10 Apr 2018
7. Graphiti - A Graphical Tooling Infrastructure. http://www.eclipse.org/graphiti/. Accessed 10 Apr 2018
8. Marama. https://wiki.auckland.ac.nz/display/csidst/Welcome. Accessed 10 Apr 2018
9. MetaCase - Domain-Specific Modeling with MetaEdit+. http://www.metacase.com. Accessed 10 Apr 2018
10. Racket. https://racket-lang.org/. Accessed 23 Mar 2018
11. SCCE - Service Centered Continuous Engineering. http://scce.info
12. WebGME. https://webgme.org/. Accessed 10 Apr 2018
13. Xtext - Language Engineering Made Easy! http://www.eclipse.org/Xtext/. Accessed 10 Apr 2018
14. Almeida, E.E., Luntz, J.E., Tilbury, D.M.: Event-condition-action systems for reconfigurable logic control. IEEE Trans. Autom. Sci. Eng. 4(2), 167–181 (2007)
15. Alur, R., Giacobbe, M., Henzinger, T., Larsen, K., Mikučionis, M.: Continuous-time models for system design and analysis. In: Steffen, B., Woeginger, G. (eds.) Computing and Software Science. LNCS, vol. 10000, pp. 452–477. Springer, Cham (2018)

16. Andersen, L., Chang, S., Felleisen, M.: Super 8 languages for making movies (functional pearl). In: Proceedings of the ACM on Programming Languages 1 (ICFP) (2017)

17. Backus, J.W.: The syntax and semantics of the proposed international algebraic language of the Zurich ACM-GAMM conference. In: IFIP Congress, pp. 125–131 (1959)

18. Bahar, R., Frohm, E., Gaona, C., Hachtel, G., Macii, E., Pardo, A., Somenzi, F.: Algebric decision diagrams and their applications. Formal Methods Syst. Des. **10**(2), 171–206 (1997). https://doi.org/10.1023/A:1008699807402

19. Baier, C., Hermanns, H., Katoen, J.P.: The 10,000 facets of MDP model checking. In: Steffen, B., Woeginger, G. (eds.) Computing and Software Science. LNCS, vol. 10000, pp. 420–451. Springer, Cham (2018)

20. Benveniste, A., Caillaud, B., Elmqvist, H., Ghorbal, K., Otter, M., Pouzet, M.: Multi-mode DAE models - challenges, theory and implementation. In: Steffen, B., Woeginger, G. (eds.) Computing and Software Science. LNCS, vol. 10000, pp. 283–310. Springer, Cham (2018)

21. Berg, A., Donfack, C.P., Gaedecke, J., Ogkler, E., Plate, S., Schamber, K., Schmidt, D., Sönmez, Y., Treinat, F., Weckwerth, J., Wolf, P., Zweihoff, P.: PG 582 - industrial programming by example. Technical report, TU Dortmund (2015). http://hdl.handle.net/2003/34106

22. Boßelmann, S., et al.: DIME: a programming-less modeling environment for web applications. In: Margaria, T., Steffen, B. (eds.) ISoLA 2016. LNCS, vol. 9953, pp. 809–832. Springer, Cham (2016). https://doi.org/10.1007/978-3-319-47169-3_60

23. Boßelmann, S., Neubauer, J., Naujokat, S., Steffen, B.: Model-driven design of secure high assurance systems: an introduction to the open platform from the user perspective. In: Margaria, T., Solo, M.G.A. (eds.) The 2016 International Conference on Security and Management (SAM 2016). Special Track "End-to-end Security and Cybersecurity: from the Hardware to Application", pp. 145–151. CREA Press (2016)

24. Bryant, R.E.: Graph-based algorithms for boolean function manipulation. IEEE Trans. Comput. **35**(8), 677–691 (1986)

25. Candea, G., Godefroid, P.: Automated software test generation: some challenges, solutions, and recent advances. In: Steffen, B., Woeginger, G. (eds.) Computing and Software Science. LNCS, vol. 10000, pp. 505–531. Springer, Cham (2018)

26. Chadli, M., Kim, J.H., Larsen, K.G., Legay, A., Naujokat, S., Steffen, B., Traonouez, L.M.: High-level frameworks for the specification and verification of scheduling problems. Softw. Tools Technol. Transf. (2017)

27. Chatley, R., Donaldson, A., Mycroft, A.: The next 7000 programming languages. In: Steffen, B., Woeginger, G. (eds.) Computing and Software Science. LNCS, vol. 10000, pp. 250–282. Springer, Cham (2018)

28. Cleaveland, R., Parrow, J., Steffen, B.: The concurrency workbench: a semantics-based tool for the verification of concurrent systems. ACM Trans. Program. Lang. Syst. **15**(1), 36–72 (1993). https://doi.org/10.1145/151646.151648

29. Dittrich, K.R., Gatziu, S., Geppert, A.: The active database management system manifesto: a rulebase of ADBMS features. In: Sellis, T. (ed.) RIDS 1995. LNCS, vol. 985, pp. 1–17. Springer, Heidelberg (1995). https://doi.org/10.1007/3-540-60365-4_116

30. Drechsler, R., Sieling, D.: Binary decision diagrams in theory and practice. Softw. Tools Technol. Transf. (STTT) **3**(2), 112–136 (2001)

31. Felleisen, M., Findler, R.B., Flatt, M., Krishnamurthi, S., Barzilay, E., McCarthy, J., Tobin-Hochstadt, S.: A programmable programming language. Commun. ACM **61**(3), 62–71 (2018)

32. Fowler, M.: Language Workbenches: The Killer-App for Domain Specific Languages? June 2005. http://martinfowler.com/articles/languageWorkbench.html. Accessed 10 Apr 2018

33. Fowler, M., Parsons, R.: Domain-Specific Languages. Addison-Wesley/ACM Press (2011). http://books.google.de/books?id=ri1muolw_YwC

34. Fritzson, P.: Principles of Object-Oriented Modeling and Simulation with Modelica 2.1. Wiley, Hoboken (2004)

35. Fuhrmann, H., von Hanxleden, R.: Taming graphical modeling. In: Petriu, D.C., Rouquette, N., Haugen, Ø. (eds.) MODELS 2010. LNCS, vol. 6394, pp. 196–210. Springer, Heidelberg (2010). https://doi.org/10.1007/978-3-642-16145-2_14

36. Futamura, Y.: Partial evaluation of computation process - an approach to a compiler-compiler. Syst. Comput. Controls **2**(5), 45–50 (1971)

37. Gossen, F., Margaria, T.: Generating optimal decision functions from rule specifications. Electron. Commun. EASST (to appear)

38. Gronback, R.C.: Eclipse Modeling Project: A Domain-Specific Language (DSL) Toolkit. Addison-Wesley, Boston (2008)

39. Grundy, J., Hosking, J., Li, K.N., Ali, N.M., Huh, J., Li, R.L.: Generating domain-specific visual language tools from abstract visual specifications. IEEE Trans. Softw. Eng. **39**(4), 487–515 (2013)

40. Havelund, K., Rosu, G., Reger, G.: Runtime verification - past experiences and future projections. In: Steffen, B., Woeginger, G. (eds.) Computing and Software Science. LNCS, vol. 10000, pp. 532–562. Springer, Cham (2018)

41. Hähnle, R., Huisman, M.: Deductive software verification: from pen-and-paper proofs to industrial tools. In: Steffen, B., Woeginger, G. (eds.) Computing and Software Science. LNCS, vol. 10000, pp. 345–373. Springer, Cham (2018)

42. Howar, F., Jonsson, B., Vaandrager, F.: Combining black-box and white-box techniques for learning register automata. In: Steffen, B., Woeginger, G. (eds.) Computing and Software Science. LNCS, vol. 10000, pp. 563–588. Springer, Cham (2018)

43. Huth, M., Nielson, F.: Static analysis for proactive security. In: Steffen, B., Woeginger, G. (eds.) Computing and Software Science. LNCS, vol. 10000, pp. 374–392. Springer, Cham (2018)

44. International Organization for Standardization: Diagrams for the chemical and petrochemical industry - Part 1: Specification of diagrams. ISO 10628-1:2014, September 2014. https://www.iso.org/standard/51840.html

45. International Organization for Standardization: Information technology - Database languages - SQL - Part 1: Framework (SQL/Framework). ISO 9075-1:2016, December 2016. https://www.iso.org/standard/63555.html

46. International Telecommunication Union: CCITT Recommendation I.312 / Q.1201 - Principles of Intelligent Network Architecture, October 1992. https://www.itu.int/rec/T-REC-I.312-199210-I/en

47. International Telecommunication Union: ITU-T Recommendation Q.1211 - Introduction to Intelligent Network Capability Set 1, March 1993. https://www.itu.int/rec/T-REC-Q.1211-199303-I/en

48. JetBrains: Meta Programming System. https://www.jetbrains.com/mps/. Accessed 10 Apr 2018

49. John, K.H., Tiegelkamp, M.: IEC 61131–3: Programming Industrial Automation Systems: Concepts and Programming Languages, Requirements for Programming

Systems, Decision-Making Aids, 2nd edn. Springer, Heidelberg (2010). https:// doi.org/10.1007/978-3-642-12015-2

50. Jones, N.D., Sestoft, P., Søndergaard, H.: Mix: a self-applicable partial evaluator for experiments in compiler generation. LISP Symb. Comput. **2**(1), 9–50 (1989)

51. Jörges, S.: Construction and Evolution of Code Generators - A Model-Driven and Service-Oriented Approach. LNCS, vol. 7747. Springer, Heidelberg (2013). https://doi.org/10.1007/978-3-642-36127-2

52. Jörges, S., Lamprecht, A.L., Margaria, T., Schaefer, I., Steffen, B.: A constraint-based variability modeling framework. Int. J. Softw. Tools Technol. Transf. (STTT) **14**(5), 511–530 (2012)

53. Jörges, S., Margaria, T., Steffen, B.: Genesys: service-oriented construction of property conform code generators. Innov. Syst. Softw. Eng. **4**(4), 361–384 (2008)

54. Kastens, U., Pfahler, P., Jung, M.: The Eli system. In: Koskimies, K. (ed.) CC 1998. LNCS, vol. 1383, pp. 294–297. Springer, Heidelberg (1998). https://doi.org/10.1007/BFb0026439

55. Kelly, S., Lyytinen, K., Rossi, M.: MetaEdit+ a fully configurable multi-user and multi-tool CASE and CAME environment. In: Constantopoulos, P., Mylopoulos, J., Vassiliou, Y. (eds.) CAiSE 1996. LNCS, vol. 1080, pp. 1–21. Springer, Heidelberg (1996). https://doi.org/10.1007/3-540-61292-0_1

56. Knoop, J., Rüthing, O., Steffen, B.: Lazy code motion. In: Proceedings of the ACM SIGPLAN 1992 Conference on Programming Language Design and Implementation (PLDI), pp. 224–234. ACM (1992)

57. Knoop, J., Rüthing, O., Steffen, B.: Lazy strength reduction. J. Program. Lang. **1**, 71–91 (1993)

58. Knoop, J., Rüthing, O., Steffen, B.: Optimal code motion: theory and practice. ACM Trans. Program. Lang. Syst. **16**(4), 1117–1155 (1994)

59. Kolovos, D.S., Rose, L.M., Abid, S.B., Paige, R.F., Polack, F.A.C., Botterweck, G.: Taming EMF and GMF using model transformation. In: Petriu, D.C., Rouquette, N., Haugen, Ø. (eds.) MODELS 2010. LNCS, vol. 6394, pp. 211–225. Springer, Heidelberg (2010). https://doi.org/10.1007/978-3-642-16145-2_15

60. Kolovos, D., Rose, L., García-Domínguez, A., Paige, R.: The Epsilon Book (2015). http://eclipse.org/epsilon/doc/book/. Accessed 4 Feb 2015

61. Kordon, F., Leuschel, M., van de Pol, J., Thierry-Mieg, Y.: Software architecture of modern model-checkers. In: Steffen, B., Woeginger, G. (eds.) Computing and Software Science. LNCS, vol. 10000, pp. 393–419. Springer, Cham (2018)

62. Kubczak, C., Jörges, S., Margaria, T., Steffen, B.: eXtreme model-driven design with jABC. In: CTIT Proceedings of the Tools and Consultancy Track of the Fifth European Conference on Model-Driven Architecture Foundations and Applications (ECMDA-FA), vol. WP09-12, pp. 78–99 (2009)

63. Lamprecht, A.L., Naujokat, S., Schaefer, I.: Variability management beyond feature models. IEEE Comput. **46**(11), 48–54 (2013)

64. Lédeczi, A., Maróti, M., Völgyesi, P.: The generic modeling environment. Technical report, Institute for Software Integrated Systems, Vanderbilt University, Nashville (2003). http://www.isis.vanderbilt.edu/sites/default/files/ GMEReport.pdf

65. Ledeczi, A., Maroti, M., Bakay, A., Karsai, G., Garrett, J., Thomasson, C., Nordstrom, G., Sprinkle, J., Volgyesi, P.: The generic modeling environment. In: Workshop on Intelligent Signal Processing (WISP 2001) (2001)

66. Legay, A., Lukina, A., Traonouez, L.M., Yang, J., Smolka, S., Grosu, R.: Statistical model checking. In: Steffen, B., Woeginger, G. (eds.) Computing and Software Science. LNCS, vol. 10000, pp. 478–504. Springer, Cham (2018)

67. Margaria, T., Bakera, M., Kubczak, C., Naujokat, S., Steffen, B.: Automatic generation of the SWS-challenge mediator with jABC/ABC. In: Petrie, C., Margaria, T., Zaremba, M., Lausen, H. (eds.) Semantic Web Services Challenge, pp. 119–138. Springer, Boston (2008). https://doi.org/10.1007/978-0-387-72496-6_7

68. Margaria, T., Meyer, D., Kubczak, C., Isberner, M., Steffen, B.: Synthesizing semantic web service compositions with jMosel and Golog. In: Bernstein, A., Karger, D.R., Heath, T., Feigenbaum, L., Maynard, D., Motta, E., Thirunarayan, K. (eds.) ISWC 2009. LNCS, vol. 5823, pp. 392–407. Springer, Heidelberg (2009). https://doi.org/10.1007/978-3-642-04930-9_25

69. Margaria, T., Nagel, R., Steffen, B.: jETI: a tool for remote tool integration. In: Halbwachs, N., Zuck, L.D. (eds.) TACAS 2005. LNCS, vol. 3440, pp. 557–562. Springer, Heidelberg (2005). https://doi.org/10.1007/978-3-540-31980-1_38. http://www.springerlink.com/content/h9x6m1x21g5lknkx

70. Margaria, T., Steffen, B.: Business process modelling in the jABC: the one-thing-approach. In: Cardoso, J., van der Aalst, W. (eds.) Handbook of Research on Business Process Modeling. IGI Global (2009)

71. Margaria, T., Steffen, B.: Continuous model-driven engineering. IEEE Comput. **42**(10), 106–109 (2009)

72. Margaria, T., Steffen, B.: Simplicity as a driver for agile innovation. Computer **43**(6), 90–92 (2010)

73. Margaria, T., Steffen, B.: Service-orientation: conquering complexity with XMDD. In: Hinchey, M., Coyle, L. (eds.) Conquering Complexity, pp. 217–236. Springer, London (2012). https://doi.org/10.1007/978-1-4471-2297-5_10

74. Margaria, T., Steffen, B., Reitenspieß, M.: Service-oriented design: the roots. In: Benatallah, B., Casati, F., Traverso, P. (eds.) ICSOC 2005. LNCS, vol. 3826, pp. 450–464. Springer, Heidelberg (2005). https://doi.org/10.1007/11596141_34

75. MathWorks: Simulink. http://www.mathworks.com/products/simulink. Accessed 3 Apr 2018

76. McAffer, J., Lemieux, J.M., Aniszczyk, C.: Eclipse Rich Client Platform, 2nd edn. Addison-Wesley Professional, Boston (2010)

77. Morel, E., Renvoise, C.: Global optimization by suppression of partial redundancies. Commun. ACM **22**(2), 96–103 (1979)

78. Naujokat, S.: Heavy Meta. Model-Driven Domain-Specific Generation of Generative Domain-Specific Modeling Tools. Dissertation, TU Dortmund, Dortmund, August 2017. http://hdl.handle.net/2003/36060

79. Naujokat, S., Lybecait, M., Kopetzki, D., Steffen, B.: CINCO: a simplicity-driven approach to full generation of domain-specific graphical modeling tools. Softw. Tools Technol. Transf. (2017)

80. Naujokat, S., Neubauer, J., Margaria, T., Steffen, B.: Meta-level reuse for mastering domain specialization. In: Margaria, T., Steffen, B. (eds.) ISoLA 2016. LNCS, vol. 9953, pp. 218–237. Springer, Cham (2016). https://doi.org/10.1007/978-3-319-47169-3_16

81. Naujokat, S., Traonouez, L.-M., Isberner, M., Steffen, B., Legay, A.: Domain-specific code generator modeling: a case study for multi-faceted concurrent systems. In: Margaria, T., Steffen, B. (eds.) ISoLA 2014. LNCS, vol. 8802, pp. 481–498. Springer, Heidelberg (2014). https://doi.org/10.1007/978-3-662-45234-9_33

82. Naur, P., Randell, B. (eds.): Software Engineering: Report of a Conference Sponsored by the NATO Science Committee, Garmisch, Germany, 7–11 October 1968. Scientific Affairs Division, NATO, Brussels 39 Belgium (1969)

83. Neubauer, J., Steffen, B.: Plug-and-play higher-order process integration. IEEE Comput. **46**(11), 56–62 (2013)

84. Neubauer, J., Steffen, B., Margaria, T.: Higher-order process modeling: product-lining, variability modeling and beyond. Electron. Proc. Theor. Comput. Sci. **129**, 259–283 (2013)
85. Object Management Group: Unified Modeling Language. http://www.uml.org/. Accessed 14 Mar 2018
86. Object Management Group (OMG): Documents Associated with BPMN Version 2.0.1, September 2013. http://www.omg.org/spec/BPMN/2.0.1/. Accessed 10 Apr 2018
87. Rüthing, O., Knoop, J., Steffen, B.: Sparse code motion. In: Proceedings of the 27th ACM SIGPLAN-SIGACT Symposium on Principles of Programming Languages (POPL 2000), pp. 170–183. ACM (2000)
88. Schmidt, C., Cramer, B., Kastens, U.: Generating visual structure editors from high-level specifications. Technical report, University of Paderborn, Germany (2008)
89. Schmidt, D., Steffen, B.: Program analysis *as* model checking of abstract interpretations. In: Levi, G. (ed.) SAS 1998. LNCS, vol. 1503, pp. 351–380. Springer, Heidelberg (1998). https://doi.org/10.1007/3-540-49727-7_22. http://portal.acm.org/citation.cfm?coll=GUIDE&dl=GUIDE&id=760066
90. Somenzi, F.: Efficient manipulation of decision diagrams. Int. J. Softw. Tools Technol. Transf. **3**(2), 171–181 (2001). https://doi.org/10.1007/s100090100042
91. Somenzi, F.: CUDD: CU Decision Diagram Package Release 3.0.0. University of Colorado at Boulder, December 2015
92. Steffen, B.: Data flow analysis as model checking. In: Ito, T., Meyer, A.R. (eds.) TACS 1991. LNCS, vol. 526, pp. 346–364. Springer, Heidelberg (1991). https://doi.org/10.1007/3-540-54415-1_54. http://www.springerlink.com/content/y5p607674g6q1482/
93. Steffen, B.: Generating data flow analysis algorithms from modal specifications. Sci. Comput. Program. **21**(2), 115–139 (1993)
94. Steffen, B.: Property-oriented expansion. In: Cousot, R., Schmidt, D.A. (eds.) SAS 1996. LNCS, vol. 1145, pp. 22–41. Springer, Heidelberg (1996). https://doi.org/10.1007/3-540-61739-6_31
95. Steffen, B., Margaria, T., Braun, V.: The electronic tool integration platform: concepts and design. Int. J. Softw. Tools Technol. Transf. (STTT) **1**(1–2), 9–30 (1997)
96. Steffen, B., Margaria, T., Claßen, A., Braun, V.: The METAFrame'95 environment. In: Alur, R., Henzinger, T.A. (eds.) CAV 1996. LNCS, vol. 1102, pp. 450–453. Springer, Heidelberg (1996). https://doi.org/10.1007/3-540-61474-5_100
97. Steffen, B., Margaria, T., Claßen, A., Braun, V., Reitenspieß, M.: An environment for the creation of intelligent network services. In: Intelligent Networks: IN/AIN Technologies, Operations, Services and Applications - A Comprehensive Report, pp. 287–300. IEC: International Engineering Consortium (1996)
98. Steffen, B., Margaria, T., Claßen, A., Braun, V., Nisius, R., Reitenspieß, M.: A constraint-oriented service creation environment. In: Margaria, T., Steffen, B. (eds.) TACAS 1996. LNCS, vol. 1055, pp. 418–421. Springer, Heidelberg (1996). https://doi.org/10.1007/3-540-61042-1_63
99. Steffen, B., Margaria, T., Freitag, B.: Module configuration by minimal model construction. Technical report, Fakultät für Mathematik und Informatik, Universität Passau (1993)

100. Steffen, B., Margaria, T., Nagel, R., Jörges, S., Kubczak, C.: Model-driven development with the jABC. In: Bin, E., Ziv, A., Ur, S. (eds.) HVC 2006. LNCS, vol. 4383, pp. 92–108. Springer, Heidelberg (2007). https://doi.org/10.1007/978-3-540-70889-6_7

101. Steffen, B., Narayan, P.: Full life-cycle support for end-to-end processes. IEEE Comput. **40**(11), 64–73 (2007)

102. Steffen, B., Naujokat, S.: Archimedean points: the essence for mastering change. In: Steffen, B. (ed.) Transactions on Foundations for Mastering Change I. LNCS, vol. 9960, pp. 22–46. Springer, Cham (2016). https://doi.org/10.1007/978-3-319-46508-1_3

103. Steinberg, D., Budinsky, F., Paternostro, M., Merks, E.: EMF: Eclipse Modeling Framework, 2nd edn. Addison-Wesley, Boston (2008)

104. Voelter, M., Siegmund, J., Berger, T., Kolb, B.: Towards user-friendly projectional editors. In: Combemale, B., Pearce, D.J., Barais, O., Vinju, J.J. (eds.) SLE 2014. LNCS, vol. 8706, pp. 41–61. Springer, Cham (2014). https://doi.org/10.1007/978-3-319-11245-9_3

105. Weckwerth, J.: Cinco Evaluation: CMMN-Modellierung und -Ausführung in der Praxis. Master's thesis, TU Dortmund (2016)

106. Weissman, C.: LISP 1.5 Primer. Dickenson Publishing Company Inc., Belmont (1967)

107. Wortmann, N., Michel, M., Naujokat, S.: A fully model-based approach to software development for industrial centrifuges. In: Margaria, T., Steffen, B. (eds.) ISoLA 2016. LNCS, vol. 9953, pp. 774–783. Springer, Cham (2016). https://doi.org/10.1007/978-3-319-47169-3_58

108. Zhu, N., Grundy, J., Hosking, J.: Pounamu: a meta-tool for multi-view visual language environment construction. In: 2004 IEEE Symposium on Visual Languages and Human Centric Computing (2004)

Deductive Software Verification: From Pen-and-Paper Proofs to Industrial Tools

Reiner Hähnle[1(✉)] and Marieke Huisman[2]

[1] Department of Computer Science, Technische Universität Darmstadt,
64295 Darmstadt, Germany
haehnle@cs.tu-darmstadt.de
[2] Faculty EEMCS, Formal Methods and Tools, University of Twente,
7500 AE Enschede, The Netherlands
M.Huisman@utwente.nl

Abstract. Deductive software verification aims at formally verifying that all possible behaviors of a given program satisfy formally defined, possibly complex properties, where the verification process is based on logical inference. We follow the trajectory of the field from its inception in the late 1960s via its current state to its promises for the future, from pen-and-paper proofs for programs written in small, idealized languages to highly automated proofs of complex library or system code written in mainstream languages. We take stock of the state-of-art and give a list of the most important challenges for the further development of the field of deductive software verification.

1 Introduction

Deductive software verification aims at formally verifying that all possible behaviors of a given program satisfy formally defined, possibly complex properties, where the verification process is based on some form of logical inference, i.e., "deduction". In this article we follow the trajectory of the field of deductive software verification from its inception in the late 1960s via its current state to its promises for the future. It was a long way from pen-and-paper proofs for programs in small, idealized languages to highly automated proofs of complex library or system code written in mainstream programming languages. We argue that the field has reached a stage of maturity that permits to use deductive verification technology in an industrial setting. However, this does not mean that all problems are solved. On the contrary, formidable challenges remain, and not the smallest among them is how to bring about the transfer into practical software development. Hence, the second contribution of this article is to present an overview of what we consider the most important challenges in the area of deductive software verification.

To render this article feasible in length (and to avoid overlap with other contributions in this volume) we focus on *contract-based, deductive verification of*

© Springer Nature Switzerland AG 2019
B. Steffen and G. Woeginger (Eds.): Computing and Software Science, LNCS 10000, pp. 345–373, 2019.
https://doi.org/10.1007/978-3-319-91908-9_18

imperative and object-oriented programs. Hence, we do not discuss model checking, SMT solvers, general proof assistants, program synthesis, correctness-by-construction, runtime verification, or abstract interpretation. Instead, we refer to the articles *Runtime Verification: Past Experiences and Future Projections, Software Architecture of Modern Model-Checkers, Statistical Model Checking,* as well as *The 10,000 Facets of MDP Model Checking* in this issue. We also do not cover fully automated verification tools for generic safety properties (see the article *Static Analysis for Proactive Security* in this issue for some aspects on these). This is not at all to say that these methods or tools are unimportant or irrelevant. On the contrary, their integration with deductive verification appears to be highly promising, as we point out in Sect. 5.2 below.

This paper is organized as follows: in the next section we walk through a non-trivial example for contract-based verification to clarify the scope and illustrate some of the important issues. In Sect. 3 we sketch the main developments in the field ca. up to the year 2000. In Sect. 4 we sketch the current state-of-art and we discuss the two main approaches to deductive verification: symbolic execution and verification condition generation. The core of the paper is Sects. 5 and 6, where we discuss the main achievements and the remaining challenges of the field, divided into technical and non-technical aspects. We conclude in Sect. 7.

2 An Example

Properties to be proven by deductive verification are expressed in a formal specification language. Ada was the first language that supported expressing formal specification annotations directly as structured comments next to the program elements they relate to [97]. As this proved to be natural and easy to use, this was followed for other programming languages. Eiffel [99] propagated a *contract-based* paradigm, where the prerequisites and obligations of each method[1] are laid down in a contract. This has the very important advantage that methods, as the central abstraction concept to structure a program, have a direct counterpart in formal specifications. Hence, specifications and programs follow the same structure. For most major imperative/object-oriented programming languages there exist dedicated contract-based annotation languages (see Sect. 5.1).

We give an example of contract-based formal specification and verification of a Java program with the Java Modeling Language (JML) and provide informal explanations of JML specification elements; more details are in [66,85]. Consider the Java method `search()` in Fig. 1 which implements binary search in a sorted integer array. Its code is completely specified, so it can be compiled and run from a suitable `main()` method.

The method contract (lines 1–7) specifies the intended behavior, whenever `search()` terminates normally. The contract's only requirement (line 2) is that the input array is sorted (in JML all reference types are assumed to be non-null by default, so this does not need to be spelled out). Sortedness is specified with the help of a *model method* `isSorted()` that is not shown. The contract

---

[1] We use Java terminology for what is also called procedure, function, subroutine, etc.

```
1  /*@ public normal_behavior
2  @    requires isSorted(a);
3  @    ensures ((\exists int x; 0 <= x && x < a.length; a[x] == v) ?
4  @                    \result >= 0 && \result < a.length && a[\result] == v :
5  @                    \result == -1);
6  @    assignable \strictly_nothing;
7  @*/
8  public static /*@ pure @*/ int search(int[] a, int v) {
9    int l = 0;
10   int r = a.length - 1;
11
12   if      (a.length == 0) { return -1; }
13   else if (a.length == 1) { return a[0] == v ? 0 : -1; }
14   /*@ loop_invariant 0 <= l && l < r && r < a.length
15   @            && (\forall int x; 0 <= x && x < l;        a[x] < v)
16   @            && (\forall int x; r < x && x < a.length; v < a[x]);
17   @ assignable \strictly_nothing;
18   @ decreases r - l;
19   @*/
20   while(r > l + 1) {
21     int mid = l + (r - l) / 2;
22     if      (a[mid] == v) { return mid; }
23     else if (a[mid] > v)  { r = mid; }
24     else                  { l = mid; }
25   }
26   if(a[l] == v) return l;
27   if(a[r] == v) return r;
28   return -1;
29 }
```

Fig. 1. Formal JML specification of a Java binary search method

says that whenever `search()` is called with a sorted, non-null array then the call terminates and in the final state the property given in the ensures clause (lines 3–5) is satisfied. In addition, the assignable clause (line 6) says that the execution has strictly no side effects, not even creation of new objects. The contract is valid for *any* input of unbounded size that satisfies the requirements.

We take a closer look at the ensures clause: line 3 is the guard of a conditional term saying that the value v occurs as an entry of a. If true, an array index where v is found is returned as the result, and -1 otherwise. We do not specify whether the result is the smallest index, but make sure that is in a valid range.

The loop invariant (lines 14–16) specifies the valid range of the pivots and says that v can never occur below index l or above r. To ensure termination of `search()` it is sufficient to ensure termination of the loop. This is achieved by the decreases clause (line 18), an expression over a well-ordered type that becomes strictly smaller in each iteration.

A central advantage of contract-based verification is compositionality and scalability: after showing that a method satisfies its contract, each call to that method can be replaced with its contract, instead of inlining the code. Specifically, if the callee's requires clause is satisfied at the call point, then its ensures clause can be assumed and the values of all memory locations of the caller, except the assignable ones, are preserved. We illustrate the idea with a simple client method, see Fig. 2.

```
1  //@ public invariant next >= 0;
2  private /*@ spec_public @*/ int[] indices;
3  private /*@ spec_public @*/ int next;
4
5  /*@ public normal_behavior
6  @ requires isSorted(a) && a != indices && next < indices.length;
7  @ ensures (\exists int i; i >= 0 && i < a.length; a[i] == v) ?
8  @           indices[\old(next)] == \result :
9  @           (next == \old(next) && indices[next] == \old(indices[next]));
10 @ ensures (\exists int i; i >= 0 && i < a.length; a[i] == v) ?
11 @           a[\result] == v  : \result == -1;
12 @ assignable indices[next], next;
13 @ also
14 @ public exceptional_behavior
15 @ requires isSorted(a);
16 @ requires (\exists int i; i >= 0 && i < a.length; a[i] == v);
17 @ requires next >= indices.length;
18 @ signals (ArrayIndexOutOfBoundsException) true;
19 @ assignable \nothing;
20 @*/
21 public int addIndex(int[] a, int v) {
22   int idx = search(a,v);
23   if (idx >= 0) {
24     indices[next] = idx;
25     next++;
26   }
27   return idx;
28 }
```

Fig. 2. Formal JML specification of a Java client method

Method addIndex() searches for value v in a. If the entry was found at index idx, then it is appended to the array contained in the field indices and returned. The specification is surprisingly complex. First of all, as specified in the exceptional termination case (lines 14–19), an ArrayIndexOutOfBoundsException is thrown if the array indices is full and the given value is found (line 16): in this case the array has to be extended (line 17). The assignable clause (line 19) is not strict, because a new exception object is created. Sortedness of parameter a is necessary to ensure that the contract of search() can go into effect.

The specification case for normally terminating behavior (lines 5–12) of addIndex() is similar to that of search(): in addition we require (line 6) that a and indices are different arrays (Java arrays can be aliased) and that there is still space for a new entry (next < indices.length). The latter could be weakened by disjoining the condition that the value is found. The second ensures clause (lines 10–11) is almost identical to the one of search() (we left out the bounds on the result). The first ensures clause (lines 7–9) says that, if the value is found then its index is appended to indices; otherwise, indices and next are unchanged. We use the keyword \old to refer to a value in the prestate. This is necessary, because next was updated in the method.

Typically, one also specifies class invariants that, for example, capture consistency properties of the instance fields that all methods must maintain. In JML any existing class invariants are implicitly added to all requires and ensures clauses which helps to keep them concise. In the example, we maintain the invariant that next is non-negative (line 1). Class invariants must be established by all constructors (not shown here).

Discussion. Even our small example shows that precise contracts, even of seemingly innocent methods, can become bulky. The specification of addIndex() is about twice as long as its implementation. And, as pointed out, that specification could be made even more precise. But without further information about the call context it is hard to decide whether that is useful. A subtle question is whether the annotation \result >= 0 && \result < a.length in line 4 of Fig. 1 is needed at all: if it doesn't hold then the expression a[\result] is not well-defined in Java anyway. But most verifiers will not be able to deduce this by themselves, because they treat such an expression as *underspecified*. The semantics of most tools, including the JML standard, is not always unambiguous.

It is very easy to forget parts of specifications: in most cases, the first attempt will not be verifiable. While developing the example we forgot a != indices in line 6 of Fig. 2, a typical omission. Good feedback from the verification tool is very important here. Vice versa, some of the specification annotations should be automatically derivable, for example, the bounds. Note that reuse of specification elements is essential to obtain concise and readable annotations.

It took about one hour (for an expert) to specify and verify the example reproduced here. After finding the correct specifications, formal verification with the system KeY [3] is fully automatic and takes about 6 s on a state-of-the-art desktop, including the constructor and model methods not displayed. The most complex method, search(), led to a proof tree with ca. 4,000 nodes and 27 branches. Interestingly, when we loaded the verified example in OpenJML [37], we only had to rename some KeY-specific keywords such as \strictly_nothing (replaced by \nothing , and then most of the example could be verified directly. The only specification that could not be verified was the exceptional behavior specification of method addIndex, as OpenJML adds extra proof obligations to every array access instruction, capturing that the index should be between the bounds of the array, to ensure the absence of runtime errors.

3   History Until LNCS 1750 (aka Y2000)

The Roots of Deductive Verification. The history of deductive software verification dates back to the 1960s and 70s. Seminal work in this area is Floyd-Hoare logic [48,61], Dijkstra's weakest preconditions [42], and Burstall's intermittent assertions [31].

Floyd and Hoare introduced the notion of pre- and postcondition to describe the behaviour of a program: a Hoare triple $\{P\}S\{Q\}$ is used to express that if program S is executed in an initial state σ, such that the precondition P holds for σ, then if execution of S terminates in a state σ', the postcondition Q holds for the final state σ'. This relation is also called *partial correctness* (partial, because termination is not enforced). Any pair of states (σ, σ') for which the Hoare triple holds, must be contained in the big-step semantics [110] of S. Floyd and Hoare proposed a set of syntactic proof rules to prove the correctness of an algorithm. One classical example of such a proof rule is the rule for statement composition:

$$\frac{\{P\}S_1\{R\} \qquad \{R\}S_2\{Q\}}{\{P\}S_1; S_2\{Q\}}$$

This rule expresses that to prove that if $S_1; S_2$ is executed in a state satisfying precondition P, if it terminates in a state satisfying Q, it is sufficient to find an intermediate assertion R, such that R can be established as a postcondition for the first statement S_1, and is a sufficient precondition for S_2 to establish postcondition Q. Rules like this break up the correctness problem of a complete algorithm into a correctness problem of the individual instructions.

Dijkstra observed that it is possible to compute the minimal precondition that is necessary to guarantee that a program will establish a given postcondition. This simplifies verification, because in this way, one does not have to "invent" the intermediate predicate that describes the state between two statements, but this can be computed. In particular, the weakest precondition wp for a statement $S_1; S_2$ can be computed using the following rule:

$$\mathsf{wp}(S_1; S_2, Q) = \mathsf{wp}(S_1, \mathsf{wp}(S_2, Q))$$

For other instructions, similar rules exist. A *Verification Condition Generator* (VCG) is a deductive verification tool that produces proof obligations expressing that the specified precondition is stronger than the weakest precondition as computed by the wp rules. For this approach to work, we require the presence of loop invariants and method contracts for all methods called in the verified code, which give rise to additional proof obligations.

VCGs in essence apply wp transformation rules backwards through the target program, starting with the postcondition to be proven. However, it is also possible to verify a program in the forward direction of its control flow. Burstall [31] proposed to combine symbolic execution with induction to show that a program implies its postcondition (see also Sect. 4).

First Deductive Verification Tools. The early program verification techniques were, to a large extent, a pen-and-paper activity. However, the limitations of doing such proofs with pen-and-paper were immediately obvious, and several groups started to develop tools to support formal verification. These efforts were all isolated, and usually still required extensive user interaction. Nevertheless, the correct application of the proof rules was checked by the system, and many obvious errors were avoided this way. It is not possible to give a complete overview of early verification systems, but we mention some representative tools and their main characteristics.

Tatzelwurm [41] was a VCG for a subset of UCSD Pascal. It accepted specification annotations in sorted first-order logic and used a tableau-based theorem prover with a decision procedure for linear integer expressions to discharge verification conditions.

Higher-order logic theorem provers were frequently used to construct a verified program verifier. The soundness of the verification technique was proven inside the theorem prover, and the program to be verified was encoded in the logic of the theorem prover, after which the verified rules could be applied. This approach was used for example in the Loop project, where Hoare logic rules were formalized in PVS (later also Isabelle) to reason about Java programs [65,67], the Sunrise project, which used a verification condition generator verified in HOL for a standard while-language [64], by Von Oheimb who formalized a Hoare logic for Java in Isabelle/HOL [126], and by Norrish, who formalized a Hoare logic for C in HOL [105].

SPARK [112] and ESC [90] were among the first tools to directly implement the weakest precondition calculus. Development of SPARK started in an academic setting, was further extended and refined in an industrial setting, and is now maintained and marketed by AdaCore and Altran. SPARK realizes a VCG for (a safety-critical subset of) Ada and is still actively developed [60]. The ESC (Extended Static Checker) tool originally targeted Modula-3, but was then adapted to Java [88]. ESC was designed with automation in mind: it traded off correctness and completeness with the capability to quickly identify possible problems in a program, thus providing the programmer with useful feedback.

Another early implementation of the weakest precondition calculus was provided in the B Toolkit [113] that realized tool support for the B Method [1]. The B Method is based on successive refinement of a sequence of abstract state machines—weakest precondition reasoning is used to establish invariants, preconditions, and intermediate assertions for a state machine. The B Method is one of the industrially most successful formal methods (see [93] for an overview), however, it is not a deductive software verification approach and, for this reason, not discussed further.

The KIV system [51] was the first[2] interactive program verifier based on dynamic logic, an expressive program logic that can be viewed as the syntactic closure of the language of Hoare triples with respect to first-order connectives

---

[2] The first verification system based on dynamic logic is reported in [95], but it was based on an axiomatic calculus and had no further impact.

and quantifiers [54]. It formalizes Burstall's [31] approach as a dynamic logic calculus whose rules mimic a symbolic interpreter [55]. Induction rule schemata permit complete symbolic execution of loops. KIV is still actively being developed, and much effort has been put into automation, and an expressive specification language, using higher-order algebraic specifications [45]. It has been used for verification of smart card applications and the Flashix file system.

ACL2 (A Computational Logic for Applicative Common Lisp) is a program verification tool for Lisp [78]. As other members of the Boyer-Moore family of provers, it has a small trusted core, and all other proof rules are built on top of this trusted core and cannot introduce inconsistencies. Its main proof strategies are based on induction and rewriting. The ACL2 prover is actively developed. It has been used to verify properties of, for example, models of microprocessors, microcode, the Sun Java Virtual Machine, and operating system kernels.

STeP, the Stanford Temporal Prover, used a combination of deductive and algorithmic techniques to verify temporal logic properties of reactive and real-time systems. It features a set of verification rules which reduce temporal properties of systems to first-order verification conditions and implements several techniques for automated invariant generation [19].

4   From LNCS 1750 to LNCS 10000

A Deductive Verification Community. After the year 2000, we see a gradual change from tools developed in isolation to a community of deductive software verification tool developers and users. Within this community, there is active exchange and discussion of ideas and knowledge. Effort has been put into standardizing specification languages, notably JML, now used by most contemporary tools aiming at verification of Java. Further, the VS-Comp and VerifyThis[3] program verification competitions have been established, where the developers and users of various deductive verification tools are challenged to solve program verification competition problems within a limited time frame [68]. After the competition, participants present their solutions to each other, which leads to substantial cross-fertilization.

Deductive Verification Architectures. As mentioned above, there are two main approaches for the construction of deductive verification tools: VCG and symbolic execution. Tools based on VCG use transformation rules to reduce an annotated program to a set of verification conditions whose correctness entails correctness of the annotated program. Tools that use symbolic execution collect constraints on the program execution by executing the program with symbolic variables. If the collected constraints can be fulfilled and imply the annotations at each symbolic state, then the annotated program is correct. Both approaches can be formalized within suitable program logics.

Kassios et al. [77] report that symbolic execution tends to be faster than VCG, but the former is sometimes less complete and occasionally suffers from

---

[3] http://www.verifythis.org/.

path explosion. However, the completeness issue seems to derive from the specific architecture of the symbolic execution tool that was used in their study, which relies on an inherently incomplete separation of heap reasoning and arithmetic SMT solving. Path explosion, however, is clearly an issue for symbolic execution of complex target code [39]. It was recently shown that it can be mitigated with symbolic state merging techniques [117].

Long-Running Deductive Verification Projects. Several tools whose development started around the year 2000 still exist currently, or evolved into new tools. We sketch the development of some of these tools.

Work on the KeY tool [3] started in 1998 [53] and it has been actively developed ever since. Like KIV, KeY is based on symbolic execution formalized in dynamic logic, but it extends the KIV approach to contract-based verification of Java programs and uses loop invariants as a specific form of induction that is more amenable to automation. KeY is not merely focused on functional verification, but complements it with debugging and visualization [3, Chap. 11] or test generation [3, Chap. 12]. It covers the complete JavaCard language [102] and was used to identify a bug in the Timsort algorithm [39], the standard sorting algorithm provided in the Oracle JDK, Python, Android, and other frameworks.

The development of ESC/Java [88] was taken over by David Cok and Joe Kiniry, resulting in ESC/Java2 [38]. Initially, their goal was to bring ESC/Java up-to-date, as well as to provide support for a larger part of JML and more Java features. ESC/Java2 is not actively developed as a separate tool anymore, however, it formed the foundation for the static verification support in the OpenJML framework [37]. Over the years, the proving capabilities of the static verification support in OpenJML have been strengthened. Like ESC/Java, it still prioritizes a high degree of automation, but soundness is not traded off anymore. OpenJML offers not merely support for static verification, but also for runtime verification.

The original ESC/Java development team around Rustan Leino moved into a different direction. In 2004, they presented Spec#, a deductive verification tool for C# [11], which reused much of the philosophy of ESC/Java. In parallel to the development of Spec#, the team also designed Boogie, as an intermediate language for static verification [10]. Boogie is a very simple programming language, for which it is straightforward to build correct verification tools. To provide support for more advanced programming languages, it is sufficient to define an encoding into Boogie. Boogie is used as the intermediate verification language for various programming languages, including Java (in OpenJML), Java bytecode [86], and C# (in Spec#). After the work on Spec# and Boogie, Leino took a slightly different approach: instead of developing a verification tool for an existing programming language, he designed Dafny, which is a programming language with built-in support for specification and verification [89], and in particular supporting dynamic frames [76].

Another widely used intermediate language is Why3 [24] which nowadays is used as a backend for SPARK 2014, the current version of SPARK/Ada [81], and Frama-C, a tool for the verification of C programs [80], specified with the JML-like language ACSL. Its original version (Why [47]) has been used as a backend for Krakatoa [98] (for Java programs) and Jessie (for C programs). Frama-C provides more than mere deductive verification: it also supports runtime verification, and it contains analysis tools such as a slicer and a tool for dependency analysis. Much attention is given to the combination and interaction between these tools, for example how testing can be used automatically to understand why a proof fails [109]. Intermediate languages in the context of model checking are discussed in the article *Software Architecture of Modern Model-Checkers* in this issue.

A final example is the Infer tool [32], which supports fully automated deductive verification techniques to reason about memory safety properties of C programs. Infer uses separation logic, an extension of classical Hoare logic, which is especially suited to reason about pointer programs. The development of separation logic resulted in the creation of a series of research prototype tools (Smallfoot, Space Invader, Abductor) as a way to automatically analyze memory safety of programs. As the focus of Infer is on a restricted set of properties, specifications are not required (but it is possible to obtain the specs that infer derives from the analysis). Infer is integrated in the Facebook code inspection chain, and is used as one of the standard checks before code changes are committed.

All tools mentioned above have their specific strengths and weaknesses. However, they share that they target the verification of realistic programming languages, and have made substantial progress in this direction. Several of the tools mentioned above are used in undergraduate teaching (both at Bachelor and Master level). Importantly, this does not happen only at the universities of the tools' own developers, but also at other universities where lecturers find it important to teach their students state-of-the-art techniques that can help to improve software reliability.

There exist many verification case studies, where unmodified (library) code was annotated and verified, and often bugs were discovered, see e.g. [39,79, 102,111,116]. Despite those success stories, there is a growing realization that post-hoc verification and, in particular, specification, remains difficult and challenging, and that there always is a trade-off between the verification effort and the level of reliability that is required for an application. A result of this realization is that we see a shift of emphasis from proving correctness of an application to bug-finding and program understanding.

5   Achievements and Challenges: Technical

5.1   Specification Languages

Deductive verification starts with specifying *what* should be verified, i.e., what behaviour we expect from the implementation. This is where the specification language comes into play.

In essence, expected program behaviour is described in the form of a method contract: a precondition specifies the assumptions under which a method may be called; a postcondition specifies what is achieved by its implementation, e.g., the computed result, or its effect on the global state. Eiffel was the first mainstream programming language that featured such method specifications [100].[4]

Achievements. For the deductive software verification community, the design of JML, the Java Modeling Language [66,84], has been a major achievement. Figures 1 and 2 in Sect. 2 illustrate typical JML specifications. JML features method contracts, similar to Eiffel, but in addition provides support for more high-level specification constructs for object-oriented programming languages, such as class invariants, model elements, and history constraints [94]. One of the important design principles of JML is that its notation is similar to Java. Properties in JML are basically Java expressions with Boolean types, and only a few specific specification-only constructs such as quantification, and implication have been added. As a result, JML specifications have a familiar look and feel, and can easily be understood. JML is also used as a specification language for other formal validation techniques, such as test case generation, and runtime assertion checking, which further increases its usability in the software development process.

JML is a rich specification language; complex specifications can be expressed in it. It provides extensive support for abstraction in the form of a fully-fledged theory of model specification elements, based on the idea of data abstraction as introduced by Hoare [62]. The principles behind this are old, but JML turns it into a technique that can be used in practice. Abstraction allows a clear separation of concerns between specification language and implementation [33], and increases portability of specifications.

The design of JML has been influential in the design of other specification languages for deductive verification, such as the ANSI/ISO C Specification Langage (ACSL), which is used in the Frama-C project [80], and the Spec# specification language for C# [11] and its spin-off Code Contracts [96].

Challenges. A central problem of deductive verification is that specifications cannot be as declarative and abstract as one would like them, in order for verification proofs to succeed. Specifications become polluted with intermediate assertions and implementation properties that are necessary as hints for the verification engine. This becomes problematic in the verification of large code bases and is exacerbated by usage of off-the-shelf libraries. To improve the situation, we believe attention should be given to address the following two challenges:

S.1 Provide specifications for widely-used APIs. At the very least, these should describe under which circumstances methods will (not) produce exceptions. For specific APIs, such as the standard Java collection library, also functional specifications describing their intended behaviour are required. This task is work-intensive and has little (direct) scientific reward. It is, therefore, difficult to find funding to conduct the required work, see also challenge F.1.

---

[4] However, Eiffel contracts were intended for runtime (rather than static) verification.

S.2 Develop techniques to infer specifications from code in a (semi-)automated manner. Many specification details that have to be spelled out explicitly, actually can be inferred from the code (as illustrated in the example of Sect. 2). There is work on specification generation [63,101], but it is not integrated into deductive verification frameworks (see challenge I.9).

5.2   Integration

Integration aspects of formal verification appear on at least three levels. On the most elementary level, there is the software engineering aspect of tool integration and reuse. Then there is the aspect of integrating different methods and analyses to combine their complementary strengths. Finally, there is the challenge to integrate formal verification technology into an existing production environment such that added value is perceived by its users. We discuss each aspect in turn in the following subsections.

Tool Integration and Reuse. Software reuse is still considered to be a challenging technology in Software Engineering[5] in general. Therefore, it is not surprising that this is the case for formal verification in particular. The situation is exacerbated there, due to the complexity of interfaces and data structures.

Achievements. One success story of tool reuse in deductive verification is centered around Boogie [10] (see also Sect. 4), an intermediate specification and verification language and VCG tool chain, most often complemented by the SMT solver Z3 [40] as its backend. Boogie is a minimalist language, optimized for formal verification. It is used as a backend in several verification tool chains, including Chalice [87], Dafny [89], Spec# [11], and VCC [36]. More recently, also the intermediate verification language Silver [104], which has built-in support for permission-based reasoning, reuses Boogie as one its backends. In addition, it also comes with its own verification backend, an SE-based tool called Silicon. Interestingly, Silver in turn, is used as a backend in the VerCors platform [8] for reasoning about concurrent Java and OpenCL programs. Similarly, but with less extensive reuse, the WhyML intermediate verification language is used in the verification systems Frama-C [80] and Krakatoa [47]. Recently, a translation from Boogie to WhyML was presented [5] that links both strands. The state-of-art on tool integration in the model checking domain is discussed in the article *Software Architecture of Modern Model-Checkers* in this issue.

Challenges. Intermediate verification languages are good reuse candidates, because they are small and have a clear semantics. In addition, compilation is a well-understood, mainstream technology with excellent tool support. This makes it relatively easy to implement new frontends. On the other hand, tool reuse at the "user level", for example, for JML/Java or ACSL/C is much harder to achieve and we are not aware of any significant case.

---

[5] There is a whole conference series devoted to this topic, see https://en.wikipedia.org/wiki/International_Conference_on_Software_Reuse.

I.1 Equip frontend (JML, Java, ACSL, C, ...) as well as backend (Boogie, Silver, Why, ...) languages with precise, preferably formal, semantics. In the case of complex frontend languages this involves identifying a "core" that must then be supported by all tools.

I.2 Equip formal verification tools with a clear, modular structure and offer their functionality in well-documented APIs. This is a work-intensive task with few scientific rewards and, therefore, closely related to Challenge F.1.

I.3 Establish and maintain a tool integration community, to foster work on reuse and increase its appreciation as a valuable contribution.[6]

Method Integration. Arguably, one of the largest, self-imposed stumbling blocks of formal methods has been the propagation of monolithic approaches. At least in deductive verification, it became very clear within the last decade that software development, formal specification, formal verification, runtime verification, test case generation, and debugging are not separate activities, but they have to be done in concert. At the same time, formal specifications have to be incrementally developed and debugged just as the pieces of code whose behavior they describe. This is now commonly accepted in the community, even if the infrastructure is not there yet; however, there are encouraging efforts.

Achievements. It is impossible to list exhaustively the flurry of papers that recently combined formal verification with, for instance, abstract interpretation [117], debugging [58], invariant generation [82], software IDEs [92], testing [109], to give only a few examples.

Most deductive verification tools (as well as proof assistants) provide an interface to SMT solvers via the SMT-LIB [12] standard. There is growing interest in formal verification from the first-order theorem proving community where tools can be integrated via the TPTP standard [119]. There is also work towards the exchange of correctness witnesses among verifiers [17].

An interesting recent trend is that specialized verification and static analysis tools are being equipped with more general techniques. For example, the termination analysis tool AProVE [50] as well as the safety verification tool CPAchecker [18] both implement a symbolic execution engine to improve their precision. We observe that boundaries between different verification subcommunities that used to be demarcated by different methods and tools are dissolving.

Challenges. In addition to the tool integration challenges mentioned above, on the methodological level, questions of semantics and usability arise. To mention just one example, there is a plethora of approaches to loop invariant generation, see e.g., [46,63,114]. All of them come with certain limitations. They tend to be

---

[6] Relating to formal methods-based software tools in general, the journal *Software Tools for Technology Transfer (STTT)*, as well as the conference *Tools and Algorithms for the Construction and Analysis of Systems (TACAS)*, were established as dedicated venues to foster tool integration and maturation. The article [118] discusses the history and the challenges of this endeavor, see also I.7.

driven by the technology they employ, not by applications and they are designed as stand-alone tools. This makes their effective usage very difficult.

Another area from whose integration deductive verification could benefit is machine learning, specifically, automata learning (see also the article *Combining Black-Box and White-Box Techniques for Learning Register Automata* in this issue).

I.4 Calls to auxiliary tools must return certificates, which must be re-interpreted in the caller's correctness framework. This is necessary to ensure correctness arguments without gaps.

I.5 The semantic assumptions on which different analysis methods are based must be spelled out, so that it is possible to combine different approaches in a sound manner. Some work in this direction has been done for the .NET static analyzer Clousot [35], but such investigations should be done on a much larger scale.

I.6 There is a plethora of possible combinations of tools and methods. So far, method and tool integration is very much *ad hoc*. There should be a systematic investigation about which combinations make methodological sense, what there expected impact is, and what effort their realization would require.

I.7 A research community working on method integration should be established.

Integration with the Software Production Environment. It is very difficult to integrate software verification technology into a production environment. Some of the reasons are of a non-technical nature and concern, for example, usability or the production context. These are explored in Sect. 6 below. Another issue might be the lack of coverage, see Sect. 5.3. In the following, we concentrate on processes and work flows.

Achievements. Our guiding question is: How can formal software verification be usefully integrated into a software development process? The emerging integration of verification, test generation, and debugging aspects into single tool chains, as described above, is an encouraging development. We begin to see deductive verification tools that are intentionally presented as enhanced software development environments, for example, the Symbolic Execution Debugger (SED) [56] based on Eclipse or the Dafny IDE [91] based on MS Visual Studio.

Several verification tools support users in keeping track of open proof obligations [59,80,91] after changes to the code or specification. This is essential to support incremental software development, but not sufficient. To realize versioning and team-based development of *verified* software, it is necessary to generalize code repositories into proof repositories [30]: a commit computes not merely changes, but a minimal set of new proof obligations that arise as a consequence of what was changed.

Another issue is that most verification attempts fail at first. It requires often many tries to render a complex verification target provable [39]. It is crucial to provide feedback to the user about the possible cause behind a failed proof.

Systems, such as KeY [3], can provide symbolic counter examples, and SED [56] computes symbolic backward slices from failure nodes in symbolic evaluation trees. The system StaDy [109] goes beyond this and uses dynamic verification to analyze failed proofs. The StaRVOOrS framework [34] generates optimized runtime assertion monitors for the unprovable parts of a specification.

In the context of commercial software production one can question whether functional verification is a worthwhile and realistic goal in the first place. Arguably, for safety- and security-critical code, as well as for software libraries used by millions, it is, but probably not for any kind of software. However, this does not mean that formal verification technology is restricted to the niches mentioned above, because there are many relevant formal verification scenarios, in addition to functional verification, notably: bug finding (discussed in Sect. 4) [15], information flow [44], and symbolic fault injection [83].

Challenges. The nature of software development is mostly incremental and evolutionary, and this must be accounted for by formal verification technology when used in commercial production. This is not the case at the moment.

Perhaps the biggest obstacle in functional verification is the lack of detailed enough specification annotations in the form of contracts and loop invariants. Without contracts, in particular for library methods, deductive verification does not scale. For some verification scenarios less precise annotations will do, but in general this is a huge bottleneck [13].

I.8 Implement proof repositories that support incremental and evolutionary verification and integrate them with verification tools.
I.9 Integrate automated specification generation techniques into the verification process.

5.3 Coverage

To make sure that deductive verification tools are practically usable, they need to support verification of a substantial part of the programming language. This means that for every construct of the programming language, verification techniques need to be developed (or at least, clear boundaries have to be provided, detailing what is covered, and what is not). Moreover, once the verification techniques are there, all variations of the programming language construct need to have tool support. Developing suitable verification techniques is typically a scientific challenge, but ensuring that a tool supports all variations of a language construct is mainly an engineering issue. If a language construct is not supported, preferably the tool design is such that it gracefully ignores the non-understood construct, and warns the user about this.

Achievements. State-of-the-art tools for deductive verification currently cover a very large part of the sequential fragment of industrially-used languages. To mention a few: OpenJML [37], KeY [3] and KIV [45] for Java, Frama-C [80], VeriFast [72] and Infer [32] for C, AutoProof [120] for Eiffel, and SPARK [60] for Ada. These tools are mature enough to verify non-trivial software applications, and to identify real bugs in them, as discussed in Sect. 4. However, for more advanced language features such as reflection, and recent features such as lambdas in Java, verification technology still has to be developed (and thus, is currently not supported by these tools).

To provide tool support for a realistic programming language entails verification techniques such as reasoning about integer types (including overflow) [16], reference types, and exceptions [70]. Some of these, for example, support to reason about exceptions, became mainstream and are built into all modern deductive verification tools. In contrast, precise reasoning about integers, including overflow, often clutters up specifications and renders verification much harder. Therefore, many deductive verification tools abstract away from it, or provide it as an optional feature.

There is active research to investigate how to extend support for deductive verification to concurrent software. This opens up a whole new range of problems, because one has to consider all possible interleavings of the different program threads. Pen-and-paper verification techniques existed already for a long time [75,107], however, tool support for them remained a challenge.

The advent of concurrent separation logic [28,106] gave an important boost, as it enabled modular verification of individual threads in a (relatively) simple way. This has given rise to a plethora of new program logics to reason about both coarse-grained and fine-grained concurrency, see [29] for an overview. Also variations of separation logic for relaxed memory models have been proposed [121,124]. However, most of these logics still lack tool support.

In parallel to the theoretical developments, the basic ideas of concurrent separation logic, extended with permissions [25,26] started to find their way into deductive verification tools. Existing tools such as VeriFast [72], VerCors [9,20] and VCC [36] support verification of data race-freedom for different programming languages, using both re-entrant locks [6] and atomic operations as synchronisation primitives [7,71]. Current investigations focus on the verification of functional properties of concurrent software by means of abstraction [23]. In addition to Java and C, the VerCors tool set also supports reasoning about OpenCL kernels, which is using a different concurrency paradigm [22]. Also the KeY verifier provides some support to reason interactively about data race freedom of concurrent applications [103]. This approach can be used in addition to VeriFast and VerCors, and is in particular suitable to trace the source of a failing verification.

There also exist alternative verification techniques for concurrent software that use a restricted setup to achieve their goals. In particular, Cave [123] automatically proves memory safety and linearizability using an automated inference algorithm for RGSep, a combination of rely-guarantee reasoning and separation logic [125]. Just as the Infer tool mentioned above, it achieves automation by restricting the class of properties that can be verified. Another alternative line of work is to investigate more restricted concurrency models that allow near-sequential verification techniques. This is the approach advocated in ABS [74] which supports cooperative multitasking with explicit scheduling points [43].

Challenges. The main challenges with respect to coverage go into two different directions: one is to cover more aspects of the programming languages already supported; the other is to cover new classes of programming languages.

C.1 Precise verification of floating point numbers is essential for many algorithms, in particular in domains such as avionics. There is preliminary work [108], but a full-fledged implementation of floating point numbers in deductive verification systems is not yet available. A promising recent breakthrough is an automatable formal semantics for floating points numbers [27] which found its way also into the SMT-LIB and the SMT competition.

C.2 Tool support for verification of concurrent software is still in its infancy. We need further developments in two directions: (1) automated support of functional properties of fine-grained concurrency, which does not require an overwhelming amount of complex annotations, and can be used by non-experts in formal verification, and (2) verification techniques for relaxed memory models that resemble realistic hardware-supported concurrent execution models.

C.3 Reasoning techniques for programs that use reflection are necessary for application scenarios such as the analysis of obfuscated malware, or of dynamic software updates.

C.4 The rapid evolution of industrial programming languages (e.g., substantial new features are added to Java every 2–3 years) is a challenge for tools that are maintained with the limited manpower of academic research groups. Translation to intermediate languages is one way out, but makes it harder to provide feedback at the source level. Ulbrich [122] suggested a systematic framework for combining deductive verification at the intermediate language level with user interaction at the source level, but it has yet to be integrated into a major tool.

C.5 Deductive verification technology is not merely applicable to software, but also to cyber-physical systems, as they exhibit similar properties [52]. Computational engineers are mainly working with partial differential equations to describe their systems, and they implement these in C, MATLAB, etc. There are some results and tools for deductive verification of hybrid systems [49]. Hybrid systems have been traditionally modeled with differential equations (see the article *Multi-Mode DAE Models: Challenges, Theory and Implementation* in this issue) and automata-based techniques (article *Continuous-time Models for System Design and Analysis* in this issue). It is an open problem to find out how these different methodological approaches relate to and could benefit from each other.

6 Achievements and Challenges: Non-technical

6.1 Usability

Research in formal verification is method- and tool-driven. As a consequence, the effectiveness of a novel method or a new tool is usually simply claimed without justification or, at best, underpinned by citing execution statistics. The latter are often micro benchmarks carried out on small language fragments. The best case are industrial case studies which may or may not be representative and in nearly all publications these are performed by the researchers and tool builders themselves, not by the intended users.

To convince industrial stakeholders of the usefulness of a formal verification approach, it is not only necessary to demonstrate that it can fit into the existing development environment (see Sect. 5.2), but also to argue that one can solve tasks more effectively or faster than with a conventional solution. This is only possible with the help of experimental user and usability studies.

Achievements. There are very few usability studies around formal verification tools. We know of an evaluation of KeY and Isabelle based on focus groups [14], while the papers [21,57,69] contain user studies or analyses on API usage, prover interfaces, and proof critics, respectively. There are a few papers that attempt to construct user models or elicit user expectations, but [57] seems to be the *only* experimental user study so far that investigated the impact of design decisions taken in a verification system on user performance.

Challenges. To guide research about formal verification so that it has impact on industrial practice, it is essential to back up claims on increased effectiveness or productivity with controlled user experiments. This has been proven to be beneficial in the fields of Software Engineering and Computer Security.

U.1 Claims about increased effectiveness or productivity attributed to new methods or tools should be backed up by experimental user studies.
U.2 Establish the paper category *Experimental User Study* as an acceptable kind of submission in formal verification conferences and journals.

6.2 Funding

To support formal verification of industrial languages in real applications requires a sustained effort over many years. As detailed in the previous sections, to specify and to reason about programs means that the semantics of the language they are written in must be fully and deeply understood, solutions for inference and its automation must be found, suitable specification abstractions must be discovered. To formulate appropriate theoretical and methodological underpinnings took decades and the process is still not complete for complex aspects such as floating point types and weak memory models (Sect. 5.3).

The road from the first axiomatic descriptions of program logics (Sect. 3) to the verification of software written in major programming language that is actually in use was long, and we are by far not at its end. It takes a long view, much patience, and careful documentation to avoid "re-invention of the wheel" or even regression. Tool building is particularly expensive and can take decades. To protect these large investments and to ensure measurable progress, long-term projects turned out to be most suitable.

Achievements. There are several long-term projects in deductive software verification that have sufficiently matured to enable industrial applicability (see also Sect. 4). We mention ACL2[7], Boogie[8], KeY[9], KIV[10], OpenJML[11], SparkPro[12], and Why/Krakatoa[13].

Challenges. Some of the long-term projects mentioned above are supported by research labs with strong industrial ties (Altran, INRIA, MSR). Unfortunately, neither the trend to embedded industrial research nor the current climate of academic funding are very well suited for this kind of enterprise. The challenge for ambitious projects, such as DeepSpec[14], is their continuation after the initial funding runs out. It is worrying that all existing long-term academic projects on deductive software verification were started before 2000. Further detrimental factors to long-time engineering-heavy projects are the publication requirements for tenured positions in Computer Science as well as the unrealistic expectations on short-term impact demanded from many funding agencies. Successful long-term research is not "disruptive" in its nature, but slowly and systematically builds on previous results. On the other hand, usability aspects of formal verification are hardly ever evaluated.

F.1 The academic reward system should give incentives for practical achievements and for long-term success (see [4] for some concrete suggestions how this could be achieved).

F.2 Large parts of Computer Science should be classified and treated as an Engineering or Experimental Science with an according funding model. Specifically, there needs to be funding for auxiliary personnel (professional software developers) and for software maintenance: complex software systems should be viewed like expensive equipment, such as particle colliders. The base level of funding should be that of an engineering or experimental science, not a mathematical science.

F.3 Grant proposals should foresee and include funding to carry out systematic experimental studies, also involving users. For example, money to reward the participants of user studies must be allocated.

6.3   Industrial and Societal Context

The best prospects for industrial take-up of deductive verification technology is in application areas that are characterized by high demands on software quality.

---

[7] http://www.cs.utexas.edu/~moore/acl2/.

[8] https://github.com/boogie-org/boogie.

[9] http://www.key-project.org/.

[10] http://www.isse.uni-augsburg.de/en/software/kiv/.

[11] http://www.openjml.org/.

[12] http://www.adacore.com/sparkpro/.

[13] http://krakatoa.lri.fr/.

[14] https://deepspec.org/.

This is clearly the case for safety- and security-critical domains that are regulated by formal standards overseen by certification authorities.

In many other application domains, however, timely delivery or new features are considered to be more important than quality. A contributing factor are certainly the relatively weak legal regulations about software liability. With the ongoing global trend in digitalization, however, we might experience a surge in software that can be deemed as safety- or security-critical, in particular, in the embedded market (e.g., self-driving cars [2], IoT). On the other hand, that market is partially characterized by a strong vendor lock-in in the form of modeling tools such as MATLAB/Simulink, which have no formal foundations. An interesting side effect of digitalization is the arrival of companies on the software market that so far had no major stake in software. Here is an opportunity for formal methods and formal verification, in particular, since software verification tools are as well applicable to cyber-physical systems [52,73] (see Challenge C.5).

Formal specification and deductive verification methods are expressed relative to a target programming language. New features of languages such as C/C++ or Java are not introduced with an eye on verifiability, making formal verification and coverage unnecessarily difficult.

Achievements. The latest version of the DO-178C standard [115], which is the basis for certification for avionics products, contains the *Formal Methods Supplement* DO-333 that permits formal methods to complement testing. This makes it, in principle, possible to argue that formal verification can speed up or decrease the cost of certification.

The development of the concurrent modeling language ABS [74] demonstrated that it is possible to design a complex programming language with many advanced features that has an associated verification tool box with high coverage [127], provided that analyzability and verifiability are taken into account during language design.

Challenges. In order to ensure substantial impact of deductive software verification in society and industry, a coordinated effort is necessary to influence standardization and certification activities.

ISC.1 Researchers from the formal verification area should become involved in language standardization. In general, research in the fields of programming languages and formal verification must be better coordinated.
ISC.2 Researchers from the formal verification area should become actively involved in the standardization efforts of certification authorities.
ISC.3 Specific quality assurance measures for verification tools such as test coverage, incremental testing, external validation, etc. should be developed and applied. If deductive software verification should become usable in certification activities, the software quality of the verification tools themselves is a critical issue.

7   Summary

We described the progress made in the area of deductive software verification. Starting as a pen-and-paper activity in the late 1960s, deductive verification nowadays is a mature technique and it can substantially increase the reliability of software in actual production. Advanced tool support is available to reason about the behaviour of complex programs and library code, written in mainstream programming languages. Industrial applicability of deductive verification is witnessed by several success stories.

However, there are many challenges that need to be addressed to make the transfer from an academic technique to a technique that is a *routine* part of *commercial* software development processes. We divided these challenges into two categories: technical and non-technical. Technical challenges relate to what properties can be verified, what programs can we reason about, how we can make verification largely automatic, and how we provide feedback when verification fails. Non-technical challenges relate to how we can fund all necessary engineering efforts, how we can ensure that tool developers get sufficient scientific credits, and how to convince industrial management that the extra effort needed for verification will actually be beneficial. We hope that these challenges can serve as an incentive for future research directions in deductive software verification.

Acknowledgements. We are grateful to Alastair Donaldson, Michael Leuschel, Peter H. Schmitt and Bernhard Steffen, for carefully reading our paper and for their very useful feedback. Many thanks to Richard Bubel for help with the preparation of the example in Sect. 2.

References

1. Abrial, J.-R.: The B Book: Assigning Programs to Meanings. Cambridge University Press, Cambridge (1996)
2. Ackerman, E.: Hail, robo-taxi!. IEEE Spectr. **54**(1), 26–29 (2017)
3. Ahrendt, W., Beckert, B., Bubel, R., Hähnle, R., Schmitt, P., Ulbrich, M. (eds.): Deductive Software Verification-The KeY Book: From Theory to Practice. LNCS, vol. 10001. Springer, Heidelberg (2016). https://doi.org/10.1007/978-3-319-49812-6
4. Alglave, J., Donaldson, A.F., Kroening, D., Tautschnig, M.: Making software verification tools really work. In: Bultan, T., Hsiung, P.-A. (eds.) ATVA 2011. LNCS, vol. 6996, pp. 28–42. Springer, Heidelberg (2011). https://doi.org/10.1007/978-3-642-24372-1_3
5. Ameri, M., Furia, C.A.: Why just boogie? Translating between intermediate verification languages. In: Ábrahám, E., Huisman, M. (eds.) IFM 2016. LNCS, vol. 9681, pp. 79–95. Springer, Cham (2016). https://doi.org/10.1007/978-3-319-33693-0_6
6. Amighi, A., Blom, S., Darabi, S., Huisman, M., Mostowski, W., Zaharieva-Stojanovski, M.: Verification of concurrent systems with VerCors. In: Bernardo, M., Damiani, F., Hähnle, R., Johnsen, E.B., Schaefer, I. (eds.) SFM 2014. LNCS, vol. 8483, pp. 172–216. Springer, Cham (2014). https://doi.org/10.1007/978-3-319-07317-0_5

7. Amighi, A., Blom, S., Huisman, M.: Resource protection using atomics. In: Garrigue, J. (ed.) APLAS 2014. LNCS, vol. 8858, pp. 255–274. Springer, Cham (2014). https://doi.org/10.1007/978-3-319-12736-1_14
8. Amighi, A., Blom, S., Huisman, M.: VerCors: a layered approach to practical verification of concurrent software. In: 24th Euromicro International Conference on Parallel, Distributed, and Network-Based Processing, PDP, Heraklion, Crete, Greece, pp. 495–503. IEEE Computer Society (2016)
9. Amighi, A., Haack, C., Huisman, M., Hurlin, C.: Permission-based separation logic for multithreaded Java programs. Logical Methods Comput. Sci. 11(1) (2015)
10. Barnett, M., Chang, B.-Y.E., DeLine, R., Jacobs, B., Leino, K.R.M.: Boogie: a modular reusable verifier for object-oriented programs. In: de Boer, F.S., Bonsangue, M.M., Graf, S., de Roever, W.-P. (eds.) FMCO 2005. LNCS, vol. 4111, pp. 364–387. Springer, Heidelberg (2006). https://doi.org/10.1007/11804192_17
11. Barnett, M., Leino, K.R.M., Schulte, W.: The spec# programming system: an overview. In: Barthe, G., Burdy, L., Huisman, M., Lanet, J.-L., Muntean, T. (eds.) CASSIS 2004. LNCS, vol. 3362, pp. 49–69. Springer, Heidelberg (2005). https://doi.org/10.1007/978-3-540-30569-9_3
12. Barrett, C., Stump, A., Tinelli, C.: The SMT-LIB standard: version 2.0. In: Gupta, A., Kroening, D. (eds.) Proceedings of the 8th International Workshop on Satisfiability Modulo Theories, Edinburgh, UK (2010)
13. Baumann, C., Beckert, B., Blasum, H., Bormer, T.: Lessons learned from microkernel verification - specification is the new bottleneck. In: Cassez, F., Huuck, R., Klein, G., Schlich, B. (eds.) Proceedings of the 7th Conference on Systems Software Verification. EPTCS, vol. 102, pp. 18–32 (2012)
14. Beckert, B., Grebing, S., Böhl, F.: A usability evaluation of interactive theorem provers using focus groups. In: Canal, C., Idani, A. (eds.) SEFM 2014. LNCS, vol. 8938, pp. 3–19. Springer, Cham (2015). https://doi.org/10.1007/978-3-319-15201-1_1
15. Beckert, B., Klebanov, V., Ulbrich, M.: Regression verification for Java using a secure information flow calculus. In: Monahan, R. (ed.) Proceedings of the 17th Workshop on Formal Techniques for Java-Like Programs, FTfJP, Prague, Czech Republic, pp. 6:1–6:6. ACM (2015)
16. Beckert, B., Schlager, S.: Software verification with integrated data type refinement for integer arithmetic. In: Boiten, E.A., Derrick, J., Smith, G. (eds.) IFM 2004. LNCS, vol. 2999, pp. 207–226. Springer, Heidelberg (2004). https://doi.org/10.1007/978-3-540-24756-2_12
17. Beyer, D., Dangl, M., Dietsch, D., Heizmann, M.: Correctness witnesses: exchanging verification results between verifiers. In: Zimmermann, T., Cleland-Huang, J., Su, Z. (eds.) Proceedings of the 24th ACM SIGSOFT International Symposium on Foundations of Software Engineering, FSE, Seattle, WA, USA, pp. 326–337. ACM (2016)
18. Beyer, D., Lemberger, T.: Symbolic execution with CEGAR. In: Margaria, T., Steffen, B. (eds.) ISoLA 2016. LNCS, vol. 9952, pp. 195–211. Springer, Cham (2016). https://doi.org/10.1007/978-3-319-47166-2_14
19. Bjørner, N., Browne, A., Colón, M., Finkbeiner, B., Manna, Z., Sipma, H., Uribe, T.E.: Verifying temporal properties of reactive systems: a step tutorial. Formal Methods Syst. Des. 16(3), 227–270 (2000)
20. Blom, S., Huisman, M.: The VerCors tool for verification of concurrent programs. In: Jones, C., Pihlajasaari, P., Sun, J. (eds.) FM 2014. LNCS, vol. 8442, pp. 127–131. Springer, Cham (2014). https://doi.org/10.1007/978-3-319-06410-9_9

21. Blom, S., Huisman, M., Kiniry, J.: How do developers use APIs? A case study in concurrency. In: International Conference on Engineering of Complex Computer Systems (ICECCS), Singapore, pp. 212–221. IEEE Computer Society (2013)

22. Blom, S., Huisman, M., Mihelčić, M.: Specification and verification of GPGPU programs. Sci. Comput. Program. **95**, 376–388 (2014)

23. Blom, S., Huisman, M., Zaharieva-Stojanovski, M.: History-based verification of functional behaviour of concurrent programs. In: Calinescu, R., Rumpe, B. (eds.) SEFM 2015. LNCS, vol. 9276, pp. 84–98. Springer, Cham (2015). https://doi.org/10.1007/978-3-319-22969-0_6

24. Bobot, F., Filliâtre, J.-C., Marché, C., Paskevich, A.: Why3: shepherd your herd of provers. In: Boogie 2011: First International Workshop on Intermediate Verification Languages (2011)

25. Bornat, R., Calcagno, C., O'Hearn, P., Parkinson, M.: Permission accounting in separation logic. In: Palsberg, J., Abadi, M. (eds.) Proceedings of the 32nd ACM SIGPLAN-SIGACT Symposium on Principles of Programming Languages, POPL, Long Beach, California, USA, pp. 259–270. ACM (2005)

26. Boyland, J.: Checking interference with fractional permissions. In: Cousot, R. (ed.) SAS 2003. LNCS, vol. 2694, pp. 55–72. Springer, Heidelberg (2003). https://doi.org/10.1007/3-540-44898-5_4

27. Brain, M., Tinelli, C., Rümmer, P., Wahl, T.: An automatable formal semantics for IEEE-754 floating-point arithmetic. In: 22nd IEEE Symposium on Computer Arithmetic, ARITH 2015, Lyon, France, pp. 160–167. IEEE (2015)

28. Brookes, S.: A semantics for concurrent separation logic. Theoret. Comput. Sci. **375**(1–3), 227–270 (2007)

29. Brookes, S., O'Hearn, P.: Concurrent separation logic. ACM SIGLOG News **3**(3), 47–65 (2016)

30. Bubel, R., Damiani, F., Hähnle, R., Johnsen, E.B., Owe, O., Schaefer, I., Yu, I.C.: Proof repositories for compositional verification of evolving software systems. In: Steffen, B. (ed.) Transactions on Foundations for Mastering Change I. LNCS, vol. 9960, pp. 130–156. Springer, Cham (2016). https://doi.org/10.1007/978-3-319-46508-1_8

31. Burstall, R.M.: Program proving as hand simulation with a little induction. In: Information Processing 1974, pp. 308–312. Elsevier/North-Holland, Amsterdam (1974)

32. Calcagno, C., Distefano, D.: Infer: an automatic program verifier for memory safety of C programs. In: Bobaru, M., Havelund, K., Holzmann, G.J., Joshi, R. (eds.) NFM 2011. LNCS, vol. 6617, pp. 459–465. Springer, Heidelberg (2011). https://doi.org/10.1007/978-3-642-20398-5_33

33. Cheon, Y., Leavens, G., Sitaraman, M., Edwards, S.: Model variables: cleanly supporting abstraction in design by contract. Softw. Pract. Exp. **35**, 583–599 (2005)

34. Chimento, J.M., Ahrendt, W., Pace, G.J., Schneider, G.: StaRVOOrS: a tool for combined static and runtime verification of Java. In: Bartocci, E., Majumdar, R. (eds.) RV 2015. LNCS, vol. 9333, pp. 297–305. Springer, Cham (2015). https://doi.org/10.1007/978-3-319-23820-3_21

35. Christakis, M., Müller, P., Wüstholz, V.: An experimental evaluation of deliberate unsoundness in a static program analyzer. In: D'Souza, D., Lal, A., Larsen, K.G. (eds.) VMCAI 2015. LNCS, vol. 8931, pp. 336–354. Springer, Heidelberg (2015). https://doi.org/10.1007/978-3-662-46081-8_19

36. Cohen, E., Dahlweid, M., Hillebrand, M., Leinenbach, D., Moskal, M., Santen, T., Schulte, W., Tobies, S.: VCC: a practical system for verifying concurrent C. In: Berghofer, S., Nipkow, T., Urban, C., Wenzel, M. (eds.) TPHOLs 2009. LNCS, vol. 5674, pp. 23–42. Springer, Heidelberg (2009). https://doi.org/10.1007/978-3-642-03359-9_2

37. Cok, D.: OpenJML: software verification for Java 7 using JML, OpenJDK, and Eclipse. In: Dubois, C., Giannakopoulou, D., Méry, D. (eds.) 1st Workshop on Formal Integrated Development Environment, (F-IDE). EPTCS, vol. 149, pp. 79–92 (2014)

38. Cok, D.R., Kiniry, J.R.: ESC/Java2: uniting ESC/Java and JML. In: Barthe, G., Burdy, L., Huisman, M., Lanet, J.-L., Muntean, T. (eds.) CASSIS 2004. LNCS, vol. 3362, pp. 108–128. Springer, Heidelberg (2005). https://doi.org/10.1007/978-3-540-30569-9_6

39. de Gouw, S., Rot, J., de Boer, F.S., Bubel, R., Hähnle, R.: OpenJDK's Java.utils.Collection.sort() is broken: the good, the bad and the worst case. In: Kroening, D., Păsăreanu, C.S. (eds.) CAV 2015. LNCS, vol. 9206, pp. 273–289. Springer, Cham (2015). https://doi.org/10.1007/978-3-319-21690-4_16

40. de Moura, L., Bjørner, N.: Z3: an efficient SMT solver. In: Ramakrishnan, C.R., Rehof, J. (eds.) TACAS 2008. LNCS, vol. 4963, pp. 337–340. Springer, Heidelberg (2008). https://doi.org/10.1007/978-3-540-78800-3_24

41. Deussen, P., Hansmann, A., Käufl, T., Klingenbeck, S.: The verification system *Tatzelwurm*. In: Broy, M., Jähnichen, S. (eds.) KORSO: Methods, Languages, and Tools for the Construction of Correct Software. LNCS, vol. 1009, pp. 285–298. Springer, Heidelberg (1995). https://doi.org/10.1007/BFb0015468

42. Dijkstra, E.: A Discipline of Programming. Prentice-Hall, Upper Saddle River (1976)

43. Din, C.C., Bubel, R., Hähnle, R.: KeY-ABS: a deductive verification tool for the concurrent modelling language ABS. In: Felty, A.P., Middeldorp, A. (eds.) CADE 2015. LNCS (LNAI), vol. 9195, pp. 517–526. Springer, Cham (2015). https://doi.org/10.1007/978-3-319-21401-6_35

44. Do, Q.H., Bubel, R., Hähnle, R.: Exploit generation for information flow leaks in object-oriented programs. In: Federrath, H., Gollmann, D. (eds.) SEC 2015. IAICT, vol. 455, pp. 401–415. Springer, Cham (2015). https://doi.org/10.1007/978-3-319-18467-8_27

45. Ernst, G., Pfähler, J., Schellhorn, G., Haneberg, D., Reif, W.: KIV: overview and verifythis competition. STTT **17**(6), 677–694 (2015)

46. Ernst, M.D., Perkins, J.H., Guo, P.J., McCamant, S., Pacheco, C., Tschantz, M.S., Xiao, C.: The Daikon system for dynamic detection of likely invariants. Sci. Comput. Program. **69**(1–3), 35–45 (2007)

47. Filliâtre, J.-C., Marché, C.: The Why/Krakatoa/Caduceus platform for deductive program verification. In: Damm, W., Hermanns, H. (eds.) CAV 2007. LNCS, vol. 4590, pp. 173–177. Springer, Heidelberg (2007). https://doi.org/10.1007/978-3-540-73368-3_21

48. Floyd, R.W.: Assigning meanings to programs. Proc. Symp. Appl. Math **19**, 19–31 (1967)

49. Fulton, N., Mitsch, S., Quesel, J.-D., Völp, M., Platzer, A.: KeYmaera X: an axiomatic tactical theorem prover for hybrid systems. In: Felty, A.P., Middeldorp, A. (eds.) CADE 2015. LNCS (LNAI), vol. 9195, pp. 527–538. Springer, Cham (2015). https://doi.org/10.1007/978-3-319-21401-6_36

50. Giesl, J., et al.: Proving termination of programs automatically with AProVE. In: Demri, S., Kapur, D., Weidenbach, C. (eds.) IJCAR 2014. LNCS (LNAI), vol. 8562, pp. 184–191. Springer, Cham (2014). https://doi.org/10.1007/978-3-319-08587-6_13

51. Hähnle, R., Heisel, M., Reif, W., Stephan, W.: An interactive verification system based on dynamic logic. In: Siekmann, J.H. (ed.) CADE 1986. LNCS, vol. 230, pp. 306–315. Springer, Heidelberg (1986). https://doi.org/10.1007/3-540-16780-3_99

52. Kamburjan, E., Hähnle, R.: Uniform modeling of railway operations. In: Artho, C., Ölveczky, P.C. (eds.) FTSCS 2016. CCIS, vol. 694, pp. 55–71. Springer, Cham (2017). https://doi.org/10.1007/978-3-319-53946-1_4

53. Hähnle, R., Menzel, W., Schmitt, P.: Integrierter deduktiver Software-Entwurf. Künstliche Intelligenz, pp. 40–41, December 1998

54. Harel, D., Kozen, D., Tiuryn, J.: Dynamic Logic. Foundations of Computing. MIT Press, Cambridge (2000)

55. Heisel, M., Reif, W., Stephan, W.: Program verification by symbolic execution and induction. In: Morik, K. (ed.) GWAI-87 11th German Workshop on Artifical Intelligence. Informatik-Fachberichte, vol. 152, pp. 201–210. Springer, Heidelberg (1987). https://doi.org/10.1007/978-3-642-73005-4_22

56. Hentschel, M., Bubel, R., Hähnle, R.: Symbolic execution debugger (SED). In: Bonakdarpour, B., Smolka, S.A. (eds.) RV 2014. LNCS, vol. 8734, pp. 255–262. Springer, Cham (2014). https://doi.org/10.1007/978-3-319-11164-3_21

57. Hentschel, M., Hähnle, R., Bubel, R.: An empirical evaluation of two user interfaces of an interactive program verifier. In: Lo, D., Apel, S., Khurshid, S. (eds.) Proceedings of the 31st IEEE/ACM International Conference on Automated Software Engineering (ASE), Singapore, pp. 403–413. ACM Press, September 2016

58. Hentschel, M., Hähnle, R., Bubel, R.: The interactive verification debugger: effective understanding of interactive proof attempts. In: Lo, D., Apel, S., Khurshid, S. (eds.) Proceedings of the 31st IEEE/ACM International Conference on Automated Software Engineering (ASE), Singapore, pp. 846–851. ACM Press, September 2016

59. Hentschel, M., Käsdorf, S., Hähnle, R., Bubel, R.: An interactive verification tool meets an IDE. In: Albert, E., Sekerinski, E. (eds.) IFM 2014. LNCS, vol. 8739, pp. 55–70. Springer, Cham (2014). https://doi.org/10.1007/978-3-319-10181-1_4

60. Hoang, D., Moy, Y., Wallenburg, A., Chapman, R.: SPARK 2014 and GNATprove: a competition report from builders of an industrial-strength verifying compiler. STTT **17**(6), 695–707 (2015)

61. Hoare, C.A.R.: An axiomatic basis for computer programming. Commun. ACM **12**(10), 576–580, 583 (1969)

62. Hoare, C.A.R.: Proof of correctness of data representations. Acta Informatica **1**, 271–281 (1972)

63. Hoder, K., Kovács, L., Voronkov, A.: Invariant generation in vampire. In: Abdulla, P.A., Leino, K.R.M. (eds.) TACAS 2011. LNCS, vol. 6605, pp. 60–64. Springer, Heidelberg (2011). https://doi.org/10.1007/978-3-642-19835-9_7

64. Homeier, P.V., Martin, D.F.: A mechanically verified verification condition generator. Comput. J. **38**(2), 131–141 (1995)

65. Huisman, M.: Reasoning about Java programs in higher order logic with PVS and Isabelle. Ph.D. thesis, University of Nijmegen (2001)

66. Huisman, M., Ahrendt, W., Grahl, D., Hentschel, M.: Formal specification with the Java modeling language. In: Ahrendt, W., Beckert, B., Bubel, R., Hähnle, R.,

Schmitt, P., Ulbrich, M. (eds.) Deductive Software Verification - The KeY Book. LNCS, vol. 10001, pp. 193–241. Springer, Cham (2016)

67. Huisman, M., Jacobs, B.: Java program verification via a Hoare logic with abrupt termination. In: Maibaum, T. (ed.) FASE 2000. LNCS, vol. 1783, pp. 284–303. Springer, Heidelberg (2000). https://doi.org/10.1007/3-540-46428-X_20

68. Huisman, M., Monahan, R., Müller, P., Poll, E.: VerifyThis 2016: a program verification competition. Technical report TR-CTIT-16-07, Centre for Telematics and Information Technology, University of Twente, Enschede (2016)

69. Ireland, A., Jackson, M., Reid, G.: Interactive proof critics. Formal Asp. Comput. **11**(3), 302–325 (1999)

70. Jacobs, B.: A formalisation of Java's exception mechanism. In: Sands, D. (ed.) ESOP 2001. LNCS, vol. 2028, pp. 284–301. Springer, Heidelberg (2001). https://doi.org/10.1007/3-540-45309-1_19

71. Jacobs, B., Piessens, F.: Expressive modular fine-grained concurrency specification. In: Ball, T., Sagiv, M. (eds.) Proceedings of the 38th ACM SIGPLAN-SIGACT Symposium on Principles of Programming Languages, POPL, Austin, TX, USA, pp. 271–282. ACM (2011)

72. Jacobs, B., Smans, J., Philippaerts, P., Vogels, F., Penninckx, W., Piessens, F.: VeriFast: a powerful, sound, predictable, fast verifier for C and Java. In: Bobaru, M., Havelund, K., Holzmann, G.J., Joshi, R. (eds.) NFM 2011. LNCS, vol. 6617, pp. 41–55. Springer, Heidelberg (2011). https://doi.org/10.1007/978-3-642-20398-5_4

73. Jeannin, J., Ghorbal, K., Kouskoulas, Y., Gardner, R., Schmidt, A., Zawadzki, E., Platzer, A.: Formal verification of ACAS X, an industrial airborne collision avoidance system. In: Girault, A., Guan, N. (eds.) International Conference on Embedded Software, EMSOFT, Amsterdam, Netherlands, pp. 127–136. IEEE (2015)

74. Johnsen, E.B., Hähnle, R., Schäfer, J., Schlatte, R., Steffen, M.: ABS: a core language for abstract behavioral specification. In: Aichernig, B.K., de Boer, F.S., Bonsangue, M.M. (eds.) FMCO 2010. LNCS, vol. 6957, pp. 142–164. Springer, Heidelberg (2011). https://doi.org/10.1007/978-3-642-25271-6_8

75. Jones, C.: Tentative steps toward a development method for interfering programs. ACM Trans. Program. Lang. Syst. **5**(4), 596–619 (1983)

76. Kassios, I.T.: The dynamic frames theory. Formal Asp. Comput. **23**(3), 267–288 (2011)

77. Kassios, I.T., Müller, P., Schwerhoff, M.: Comparing verification condition generation with symbolic execution: an experience report. In: Joshi, R., Müller, P., Podelski, A. (eds.) VSTTE 2012. LNCS, vol. 7152, pp. 196–208. Springer, Heidelberg (2012). https://doi.org/10.1007/978-3-642-27705-4_16

78. Kaufmann, M., Moore, J.S.: Design goals for ACL2. In: Third International School and Symposium on Formal Techniques in Real Time and Fault Tolerant Systems, pp. 92–117 (1994)

79. Kiniry, J.R., Morkan, A.E., Cochran, D., Fairmichael, F., Chalin, P., Oostdijk, M., Hubbers, E.: The KOA remote voting system: a summary of work to date. In: Montanari, U., Sannella, D., Bruni, R. (eds.) TGC 2006. LNCS, vol. 4661, pp. 244–262. Springer, Heidelberg (2007). https://doi.org/10.1007/978-3-540-75336-0_16

80. Kirchner, F., Kosmatov, N., Prevosto, V., Signoles, J., Yakobowski, B.: Frama-C: a software analysis perspective. Formal Asp. Comput. **27**(3), 573–609 (2015)

81. Kosmatov, N., Marché, C., Moy, Y., Signoles, J.: Static versus dynamic verification in Why3, Frama-C and SPARK 2014. In: Margaria, T., Steffen, B. (eds.) ISoLA 2016. LNCS, vol. 9952, pp. 461–478. Springer, Cham (2016). https://doi.org/10.1007/978-3-319-47166-2_32

82. Kovács, L.: Symbolic computation and automated reasoning for program analysis. In: Ábrahám, E., Huisman, M. (eds.) IFM 2016. LNCS, vol. 9681, pp. 20–27. Springer, Cham (2016). https://doi.org/10.1007/978-3-319-33693-0_2

83. Larsson, D., Hähnle, R.: Symbolic fault injection. In: Beckert, B. (ed.) Proceedings of the 4th International Verification Workshop (Verify) in Connection with CADE-21 Bremen, Germany, vol. 259, pp. 85–103. CEUR Workshop Proceedings (2007)

84. Leavens, G.T., Baker, A.L., Ruby, C.: Preliminary design of JML: a behavioral interface specification language for Java. Technical report 98-06y, Iowa State University, Department of Computer Science (2003). Revised June 2004

85. Leavens, G.T., Poll, E., Clifton, C., Cheon, Y., Ruby, C., Cok, D., Müller, P., Kiniry, J., Chalin, P., Zimmerman, D.M., Dietl, W.: JML Reference Manual, May 2013. Draft revision 2344

86. Lehner, H., Müller, P.: Formal translation of bytecode into BoogiePL. Electr. Notes Theor. Comput. Sci. $190(1)$, 35–50 (2007)

87. Leino, K.R.M., Müller, P., Smans, J.: Verification of concurrent programs with Chalice. In: Aldini, A., Barthe, G., Gorrieri, R. (eds.) FOSAD 2007-2009. LNCS, vol. 5705, pp. 195–222. Springer, Heidelberg (2009). https://doi.org/10.1007/978-3-642-03829-7_7

88. Leino, K., Nelson, G., Saxe, J.: ESC/Java user's manual. Technical report SRC 2000-002, Compaq System Research Center (2000)

89. Leino, K.R.M.: Dafny: an automatic program verifier for functional correctness. In: Clarke, E.M., Voronkov, A. (eds.) LPAR 2010. LNCS (LNAI), vol. 6355, pp. 348–370. Springer, Heidelberg (2010). https://doi.org/10.1007/978-3-642-17511-4_20

90. Leino, K.R.M., Nelson, G.: An extended static checker for Modula-3. In: Koskimies, K. (ed.) CC 1998. LNCS, vol. 1383, pp. 302–305. Springer, Heidelberg (1998). https://doi.org/10.1007/BFb0026441

91. Leino, K.R.M., Wüstholz, V.: The Dafny integrated development environment. In: Dubois, C., Giannakopoulou, D., Méry, D. (eds.) Proceedings of the 1st Workshop on Formal Integrated Development Environment, F-IDE, Grenoble, France. EPTCS, vol. 149, pp. 3–15 (2014)

92. Leino, K.R.M., Wüstholz, V.: Fine-grained caching of verification results. In: Kroening, D., Păsăreanu, C.S. (eds.) CAV 2015. LNCS, vol. 9206, pp. 380–397. Springer, Cham (2015). https://doi.org/10.1007/978-3-319-21690-4_22

93. Leuschel, M., Falampin, J., Fritz, F., Plagge, D.: Automated property verification for large scale B models with ProB. Formal Asp. Comput. $23(6)$, 683–709 (2011)

94. Liskov, B., Wing, J.: A behavioral notion of subtyping. ACM Trans. Program. Lang. Syst. $16(1)$, 1811–1841 (1994)

95. Litvintchouk, S.D., Pratt, V.R.: A proof-checker for dynamic logic. In: Reddy, R. (ed.) Proceedings of the 5th International Joint Conference on Artificial Intelligence, pp. 552–558. William Kaufmann, Cambridge (1977)

96. Logozzo, F.: Practical verification for the working programmer with CodeContracts and abstract interpretation. In: Jhala, R., Schmidt, D. (eds.) VMCAI 2011. LNCS, vol. 6538, pp. 19–22. Springer, Heidelberg (2011). https://doi.org/10.1007/978-3-642-18275-4_3

97. Luckham, D.C., von Henke, F.W.: An overview of Anna, a specification language for Ada. IEEE Softw. **2**(2), 9–22 (1985)
98. Marché, C., Paulin-Mohring, C., Urbain, X.: The KRAKATOA tool for certificationof JAVA/JAVACARD programs annotated in JML. J. Log. Algebr. Program. **58**(1–2), 89–106 (2004)
99. Meyer, B.: Applying "design by contract". IEEE Comput. **25**(10), 40–51 (1992)
100. Meyer, B.: Object-Oriented Software Construction, 2nd edn. Prentice-Hall, Englewood Cliffs (1997)
101. Mohsen, M., Jacobs, B.: One step towards automatic inference of formal specifications using automated VeriFast. In: ter Beek, M.H., Gnesi, S., Knapp, A. (eds.) FMICS/AVoCS -2016. LNCS, vol. 9933, pp. 56–64. Springer, Cham (2016). https://doi.org/10.1007/978-3-319-45943-1_4
102. Mostowski, W.: Fully verified Java Card API reference implementation. In: Beckert, B. (ed.) Proceedings of the 4th Interenational Verification Workshop in connection with CADE-21, Bremen, Germany. CEUR Workshop Proceedings, vol. 259. CEUR-WS.org (2007)
103. Mostowski, W.: Dynamic frames based verification method for concurrent Java programs. In: Gurfinkel, A., Seshia, S.A. (eds.) VSTTE 2015. LNCS, vol. 9593, pp. 124–141. Springer, Cham (2016). https://doi.org/10.1007/978-3-319-29613-5_8
104. Müller, P., Schwerhoff, M., Summers, A.J.: Viper: a verification infrastructure for permission-based reasoning. In: Jobstmann, B., Leino, K.R.M. (eds.) VMCAI 2016. LNCS, vol. 9583, pp. 41–62. Springer, Heidelberg (2016). https://doi.org/10.1007/978-3-662-49122-5_2
105. Norrish, M.: C formalised in HOL. Ph.D. thesis, University of Cambridge (1998)
106. O'Hearn, P.W.: Resources, concurrency and local reasoning. Theoret. Comput. Sci. **375**(1–3), 271–307 (2007)
107. Owicki, S., Gries, D.: An axiomatic proof technique for parallel programs. Acta Informatica J. **6**, 319–340 (1975)
108. Paganelli, G., Ahrendt, W.: Verifying (in-)stability in floating-point programs by increasing precision, using SMT solving. In: Bjørner, N., Negru, V., Ida, T., Jebelean, T., Petcu, D., Watt, S.M., Zaharie, D. (eds.) 15th International Symposium on Symbolic and Numeric Algorithms for Scientific Computing, SYNASC 2013, Timisoara, Romania, 23–26 September 2013, pp. 209–216. IEEE Computer Society (2013)
109. Petiot, G., Kosmatov, N., Botella, B., Giorgetti, A., Julliand, J.: Your proof fails? Testing helps to find the reason. In: Aichernig, B.K.K., Furia, C.A.A. (eds.) TAP 2016. LNCS, vol. 9762, pp. 130–150. Springer, Cham (2016). https://doi.org/10.1007/978-3-319-41135-4_8
110. Plotkin, G.D.: A structural approach to operational semantics. J. Log. Algebr. Program. **60–61**, 17–139 (2004)
111. Polikarpova, N., Tschannen, J., Furia, C.A.: A fully verified container library. In: Bjørner, N., de Boer, F. (eds.) FM 2015. LNCS, vol. 9109, pp. 414–434. Springer, Cham (2015). https://doi.org/10.1007/978-3-319-19249-9_26
112. Praxis Critical Systems. SPARK–The SPADE Ada Kernel, 3.2 edition (1996)
113. Robinson, K.: The B method and the B toolkit. In: Johnson, M. (ed.) AMAST 1997. LNCS, vol. 1349, pp. 576–580. Springer, Heidelberg (1997). https://doi.org/10.1007/BFb0000503
114. Rodríguez-Carbonell, E., Kapur, D.: Automatic generation of polynomial invariants of bounded degree using abstract interpretation. Sci. Comput. Program. **64**(1), 54–75 (2007)

115. RTCA. DO-178C, Software Considerations in Airborne Systems and Equipment Certification, January 2012

116. Schellhorn, G., Ernst, G., Pfähler, J., Haneberg, D., Reif, W.: Development of a verified flash file system. In: Ameur, Y.A., Schewe, K. (eds.) Abstract State Machines, Alloy, B, TLA, VDM, and Z. LNCS, vol. 8477, pp. 9–24. Springer, Heidelberg (2014). https://doi.org/10.1007/978-3-662-43652-3_2

117. Scheurer, D., Hähnle, R., Bubel, R.: A general lattice model for merging symbolic execution branches. In: Ogata, K., Lawford, M., Liu, S. (eds.) ICFEM 2016. LNCS, vol. 10009, pp. 57–73. Springer, Cham (2016). https://doi.org/10.1007/978-3-319-47846-3_5

118. Steffen, B.: The physics of software tools: SWOT analysis and vision. Softw. Tools Technol. Transf. (STTT) **19**(1), 1–7 (2017)

119. Sutcliffe, G.: The TPTP problem library and associated infrastructure. J. Autom. Reason. **43**(4), 337–362 (2009)

120. Tschannen, J., Furia, C.A., Nordio, M., Polikarpova, N.: AutoProof: auto-active functional verification of object-oriented programs. In: Baier, C., Tinelli, C. (eds.) TACAS 2015. LNCS, vol. 9035, pp. 566–580. Springer, Heidelberg (2015). https://doi.org/10.1007/978-3-662-46681-0_53

121. Turon, A., Vafeiadis, V., Dreyer, D.: GPS: navigating weak memory with ghosts, protocols, and separation. In: Black, A.P., Millstein, T.D. (eds.) Proceedings of the ACM International Conference on Object Oriented Programming Systems Languages & Applications, OOPSLA, Portland, OR, USA, pp. 691–707. ACM (2014)

122. Ulbrich, M.: Dynamic logic for an intermediate language: verification, interaction and refinement. Ph.D. thesis, Karlsruhe Institute of Technology (2013)

123. Vafeiadis, V.: Automatically proving linearizability. In: Touili, T., Cook, B., Jackson, P. (eds.) CAV 2010. LNCS, vol. 6174, pp. 450–464. Springer, Heidelberg (2010). https://doi.org/10.1007/978-3-642-14295-6_40

124. Vafeiadis, V., Narayan, C.: Relaxed separation logic: a program logic for C11 concurrency. In: OOPSLA 2013. ACM (2013)

125. Vafeiadis, V., Parkinson, M.: A marriage of rely/guarantee and separation logic. In: Caires, L., Vasconcelos, V.T. (eds.) CONCUR 2007. LNCS, vol. 4703, pp. 256–271. Springer, Heidelberg (2007). https://doi.org/10.1007/978-3-540-74407-8_18

126. von Oheimb, D.: Hoare logic for Java in Isabelle/HOL. Concur. Comput.: Pract. Exp. **13**(13), 1173–1214 (2001)

127. Wong, P.Y.H., Albert, E., Muschevici, R., Proença, J., Schäfer, J., Schlatte, R.: The ABS tool suite: modelling, executing and analysing distributed adaptable object-oriented systems. STTT **14**(5), 567–588 (2012)

Static Analysis for Proactive Security

Michael Huth[1][(✉)] and Flemming Nielson[2]

[1] Department of Computing, Imperial College London, London SW7 2AZ, UK
m.huth@imperial.ac.uk
[2] Department of Mathematics and Computer Science,
Technical University of Denmark, 2800 Kongens Lyngby, Denmark
fnie@dtu.dk

Abstract. We reflect on current problems and practices in system security, distinguishing between *reactive* security – which deals with vulnerabilities as they are being exploited – and *proactive* security – which means to make vulnerabilities un-exploitable by removing them from a system entirely. Then we argue that static analysis is well poised to support approaches to proactive security, since it is sufficiently expressive to represent many vulnerabilities yet sufficiently efficient to detect vulnerabilities prior to system deployment. We further show that static analysis interacts well with both confidentiality and integrity aspects and discuss what security assurances it can attain. Next we argue that security models such as those for access control can also be statically analyzed to support proactive security of such models. Finally, we identify research problems in static analysis whose solutions would stand to improve the effectiveness and adoption of static analysis for proactive security in the practice of designing, implementing, and assuring future ICT systems.

1 Introduction

In the past 10–15 years, we witnessed a very substantial and increasingly accelerated transformation of Information and Communications Technology (ICT), the advent of smart phones and of digital social networks with global reach being two prominent examples. In addition, the emergent so called Internet of Things (IoT) and Cyber Physical Systems (CPS) are a recent but major development which could be highly disruptive in sectors not traditionally associated with ICT.

All of these systems or systems of systems contain software as crucial ingredients. The reliability of such software is traditionally assured through systematic testing as a best industrial practice. The limitations of this approach have been widely recognized, and its effectiveness has been somewhat improved through its combination with more formal techniques to validate critical software such as device drivers, and complemented with a range of other techniques such as manual code review. In fact, important formal methods such as type theories and static analyses are mature technologies that are routinely integrated in compilers and thus markedly improve the reliability of software – although programmers and IT project managers may be oblivious to that fact.

© Springer Nature Switzerland AG 2019
B. Steffen and G. Woeginger (Eds.): Computing and Software Science, LNCS 10000, pp. 374–392, 2019.
https://doi.org/10.1007/978-3-319-91908-9_19

Traditionally, commercial ICT software is deployed under a *Caveat Emptor* regime: producers of software tend not to accept any liability should the execution of their software cause any damage, even when run as intended. This regime was adopted for proprietary software but this ownership model was challenged by the open-source and freeware movements, which see software production and validation as a transparent, community-driven effort; the Linux operating system being a prominent and most impactful outcome of such efforts. Caveat Emptor is also not appropriate for software written for embedded systems, where software bugs may cause physical harm or loss of life.

But all software can contain errors, which may represent security vulnerabilities that could realize privileged access to systems, services or information. One may see such conceived wisdom as justification for the current liability regime and software validation practice. Yet, this is being challenged by the next wave of digitization that the IoT and CPS will bring about. For example, smart cars will become increasingly autonomous, so critical software components will have to meet very high correctness standards to ensure safety of passengers and those within the car's environment, and security vulnerabilities may be exploited to corrupt safety mechanisms. Therefore, security – to name Confidentiality, Integrity, and Availability – will no longer be an isolated concern but one that impinges on safety, reliability, and other concerns of future IoT/CPS systems. And liability models may shift: German law makers, e.g., are presently considering to make car manufacturers or even programmers liable for accidents caused by future, fully autonomous cars [7].

Standard engineering practice is tensioned by the increased blurring of system security and system safety aspects. To illustrate, we may not be able to apply redundancy and physical separation principles familiar from the aircraft industry in the domain of smart cars, where consumers expect to interface with their familiar devices such as smart phones and where cost and competitive pressure constrain engineering and validation. But we may realize *logical* separation, say, through security policies. The well known Jeep Cherokee hack [26], e.g., exploited a vulnerability in the car's entertainment system and the fact that the cellular provider did not restrict communication with that system to the car's internal systems, giving remote attackers' access to safety-critical components such as brakes. A security policy or modified default configuration that an attacker could not circumvent would have addressed this issue. These concerns extend to critical infrastructure such as electricity grids (e.g. the cyberattack on the Ukrainian power grid in 2015) and vital IT systems (e.g. the AnnaCry ransomware attack that severely disrupted some hospital services in the UK in 2017) – turning software reliability and resiliency into national security issues.

Security. The traditional understanding of security is that it is comprised of three components. *Confidentiality* is intended to protect the disclosure of data to third parties; it is intimately related to ensuring the *privacy* of citizens, and the protection of intellectual property. *Integrity* is intended to ensure the trustworthiness of data; it is intimately connected to ensuring the *authentication* of those who modify data and the control state of IT systems. *Availability* is intended to ensure that systems remain operational even in the presence of an active adversary, e.g. in a denial of service attack. Much of the research in security focuses on achieving confidentiality and integrity while availability is substantially harder to attain due to the physical components that form part of the IT systems.

A security management in which software gets patched routinely, as in the so called *Patch Tuesday*, means owners of software are responsible for installing updates regularly. Such practices led to a *reactive* approach to security: a security problem in software gets discovered, a fix for the vulnerability is identified (if possible), and that fix is shipped as a software update to all systems that run that software. Moreover, this reactive approach is also used by the attacking ecosystems, where vulnerabilities are discovered and sold in a layered market of increasing capabilities: from a potential memory leak applicable to some systems to Ransom as a Service with complete attack capabilities, financial accounts, and so forth. This reactive approach is hardly satisfactory for security engineering, and will not do in future IoT and CPSs for reasons already alluded to.

Proactive Security. In contrast, *proactive security* is an approach to system security that uses a set of techniques to construct ICT systems or systems of systems that have almost no vulnerabilities (and thereby dramatically reduce the need for reactive security measures) and that incorporate exploit prevention or at least exploit mitigation into all phases of system construction – including design, implementation, and assurance activities.

Proactive security has been prominently advocated by Schell [50] in 2012. The need for it seems even more pressing now than when its first notable developments in system security were made. The initial efforts of developing proactive security facilitated the construction of IT systems living up to the demands of the famous "Orange Book", developed in the US with Schell as a leading contributor. This formed the basis for the current *Common Criteria* [1] standard that provides a systematic approach to the design and implementation of a variety of IT systems offering different levels of security guarantees. Schell laments that the use of proactive techniques seems to have given way to the use of more reactive techniques; in other words, that our current approach to system security takes a passive rather than an active, proactive approach.

There are several explanations for the current predominance of reactive security. Business pressures, such as time-to-market considerations, often demand the rapid construction and validation of products based on common product families or user feedback as seen in code production for social networks [13]. The construction of systems that meet the Common Criteria may be neither feasible nor appropriate in such use contexts. Another factor is perhaps that security engineering is rarely taught in the ICT and Computer Science curricula and that there is a global skills gap in cybersecurity professionals.

Formal Methods. The Common Criteria standard offers a range of *Evaluation Assurance Levels* that describe the amount of rigour exercised in the security validation. To meet the higher Evaluation Assurance Levels, it is not expected to formally validate the entire IT system in question, but it is emphasized that its critical components must be validated through the rigorous use of formal methods. We can see this as a form of *risk management*: only higher such levels demand use of rigorous methods, and even for those higher levels is it too costly or presently not feasible to formally validate full functional and non-functional behaviour of complex IT systems – e.g. a code base of a few million lines of code.

But it is feasible to do such formal validation for critical components or code units – e.g. a discrete controller for a safety-critical component. Another good example of targeting a critical component with rigorous formal methods is the validation of the micro-kernel seL4 [31], which was fully formally verified; and one could then leverage the reliability and resiliency of that component to more complex systems that critically rely on it, e.g. a drone [27]. And formal methods are not confined to executable code: in [36], it is proposed to use generics and functional programming to get more trustworthy implementation types from UML models.

The Common Criteria don't endorse particular formal methods. This, too, is consistent with a risk-management approach to system assurance, which would seek to use a combination of techniques that best meets the requirements and constraints at hand. The formal methods used may range from validation carried out by semi-automatic proof assistants such as Isabelle (used to verify the micro-kernel seL4) and Coq (used in the verification/validation of a compiler [34]), to validation carried out by fully automatic model checkers and SMT solvers, and to validation using fully automatic and often very efficient static analysers.

Even if formal certification for Common Criteria is not sought, there is a strategic advantage in using proactive system security: in case a system built still contains exploits, the fact that is was built with that approach will enable a much better understanding of where those exploits may occur and what capabilities they may have, including what system components they may impact. In fact, we may see the emergence of new certification standards that reflect specific assurance needs of cyber physical systems and their application domains [5].

Static Analysis. Formal methods will continue to play an important role in future certification schemes. Here we focus on the many methods from *Static Analysis* or *Program Analysis* [43]. These techniques may use data-flow equations, constraint systems, abstract interpretation, type systems, and type and effect systems to mention just the most widely used ones here. A principal advantage that Static Analysis offers, above and beyond what other approaches in Formal Methods provide, is that its techniques typically realize analysis capabilities that come with low computational complexity – usually polynomial time, sometimes even linear time, rather than exponential time or worse. This makes them an attractive choice for proactive security engineering, certainly as a "first line of defence" that rules out certain security vulnerabilities at low computational cost and at almost no development or production cost.

Static analyses gain this advantage by making abstractions of the systems they analyze. This is typically an over-approximation of some precise analysis result – whose full precision is typically non-computable. Such abstraction and the compositional reasoning that this can support make Static Analysis a tool set for ensuring the security of entire systems or systems of systems – which may span ICT, IoT, and CPS systems. Whilst it is a unique opportunity to explore the potential of Static Analysis in the next generation of digital systems, the challenge will be to engineer static analyses that make judicious trade-offs between their effectiveness (that the over-approximation still provides useful insights at the right level of abstraction, and with sufficient security assurances) and their cost (that the computation of results has sufficiently low complexity in terms of the scale of the system under analysis). Effectiveness here includes that analysis findings are reported in a manner that is useful for those who need to act on such results: ordinary programmers, modellers, and so forth. There is little research on this aspect, which is argued in [13] to be critical for transfer and adoption of static analysis in practice.

Overview. To meet this challenge, the development of security mechanisms for system engineering (e.g. security policies), the development of effective yet easily usable Formal Methods (in particular of static analyses) need to go hand in hand. In this paper, we will outline some key approaches, challenges, and further considerations that mean to provoke thinking and future research in this important area of security engineering for future digital systems. Admittedly, our exposition reflects a certain scientific bias, as it is not our intent to be encyclopedic in our treatment of static analysis and (proactive) security. Our express aim is, as already stated, to provoke thinking and to encourage new research in this important space whose future systems stand to profoundly impact us all.

2   The Security Landscape: Setting the Scene

As stated above, Static Analysis (or Program Analysis) [43] is mainly concerned with giving a sound over-approximation of the behaviour that a program may exhibit upon execution. If the sound over-approximation does not exhibit any malicious behaviour, this ensures that no malicious behaviour can arise during program execution. Security is largely concerned with ensuring that programs do not violate the confidentiality and integrity policies that are in place. Many of the key considerations of security have a strong analogy to questions studied in static analysis while some go a bit beyond. In this section, we will illustrate this close relationship because it is the basis for *why* static analysis forms a good foundation for ensuring proactive security – both for actual code and for the models that arise during software development.

Let us begin by explaining one of the fundamental static analyses traditionally used in compilers. *Definition-use* chaining aims at linking each definition of a variable (or assignment to a variable) to those uses of the variable where the value will be the one set at the definition (or assignment) point [43]. Soundness of definition-use chaining requires that we do not miss any uses; precision requires that we do not wildly over-approximate the set of uses.

To guard against errors in the formulation of the definition-use analysis one should prove that the analysis always soundly over-approximates. The first problem to be addressed is the informality of such a formulation, one needs to be precise also for intricate features such as aliasing (where different variables are names for the same entity in storage). Many approaches can be explored to gain formality. Often, a good balance is found by using a so-called *instrumented semantics* [30], which explains actual code behaviour and keeps track of additional information, for example at which program point a variable was last defined. Then soundness of the definition-use analysis merely amounts to over-approximating the observations that can be made using the *instrumented semantics*.

For security, both confidentiality and integrity are guaranteed by assuring that information in ICT systems or socio-technical systems flows only in the intended and secure way. Control-flow integrity, e.g., ensures a program does not deviate from its normal control flow in order to initiate a privilege escalation attack. And the human decision of whether or not to open a certain web page should protect the confidentiality of personal information.

A key approach to security is through the study of information flow in programs as pioneered by [17]. Whenever we have an assignment, $x := \cdots y \cdots$, the value of y flows into x. We call this an *explicit flow* because the value of y is part of what is stored into x; we also call it a direct flow because it happens as the result of a single assignment. The analogy to definition-use chaining is immediate. Whenever we have an assignment $x := \cdots y \cdots$ at some program point, definition-use chaining would be able to tell us which of the program points defining y might influence the current definition of x.

Frequently, assignments are performed in bodies of conditionals, which thereby influence the decision to perform an assignment. As an example, for boolean variables x and y, there is hardly any difference to the behaviour of the program if y then $x :=$ true else $x :=$ false with respect to that of the program $x := y$. But the former has no explicit flow while the latter has.

The consideration of implicit flows takes care of this anomaly: there is an *implicit flow* from y to x whenever an assignment to x occurs inside the scope of a conditional that uses the variable y [17].

Apart from explicit and implicit flows, there are other and more suble forms of *covert flows* (paraphrasing the notion of covert channels). They may arise due to termination issues, timing issues, and dependencies between non-deterministic or parallel computations. However, we shall concentrate on the direct flows comprised of explicit and implicit flows as illustrated, and on the transitive closure of the direct flows – the latter traditionally referred to as *indirect flows*.

In our discussion of security concepts in Sect. 1, Confidentiality was explained as preventing disclosure of data to third parties; this amounts to ensuring the absence of indirect flow from the data to a use belonging to a non-trusted party. Similarly, Integrity was explained as ensuring the trustworthiness of data; this amounts to ensuring the absence of indirect flow to the data from a definition belonging to a non-trusted party. In summary, simple considerations of explicit and implicit indirect flows – which use modest generalisations of definition-use chains – suffice for ensuring Confidentiality and Integrity.

We are confident that approaches rooted in static analysis will continue to be useful when security policies grow in complexity as demonstrated in later sections. The main research challenge of static analysis is to ensure that the sound over-approximation is sufficiently informative (in excluding behaviour that cannot arise) while keeping the computational complexity at a manageable level (preferably close to linear).

The composition of systems considered to be secure (in isolation) does, too often, not result in a secure system. Running cryptographic security protocols "on top of each other" is a case in point. It remains a research challenge to facilitate the *compositional* construction of secure systems. While progress is being made, it is still beyond the state of the art to do so in general – let alone for IoT systems in which security, safety, and other concerns are co-dependent.

In the light of the lack of compositionality in security engineering, the low computational complexity of many static analyses may come to the rescue: It makes it feasible to perform whole-program analyses rather than attempting to achieve compositionality.

3   Static Analysis of Security Models

Static analysis is also applicable to models of IT Systems, not only source code or binaries. UML diagrams and access-control models are important examples thereof. Access-control models specify which subjects have access to what resources, and under which circumstances. Prominent examples are Role-Based Access Control (RBAC) [49], XACML (see e.g. [4]), and OAuth [2].

In RBAC, users are associated with one or more roles, and roles are associated with access permissions: a user gets a permission if she has a role with such a permission. This de-coupling facilitates scalability of specifications and change management of permissions. The core RBAC model has also been extended in numerous ways, for example with administrators who have permissions to make role-user assignments. XACML is a policy language in which one can specify the circumstances for granting access, based on attributes and their fine-grained combination. OAuth, on the other hand, is a protocol that is widely used on the web as it can give third-party applications limited access to an HTTP service, for example by giving the third party an access token as in the User Managed Access architecture of the Kantara initiative.

Instances of such access-control models specify the allowed and disallowed access within a system. Therefore, we need to validate that such instances capture intended access restrictions and permissions. Static analysis, and its close cousin *model checking* [9,42,51,53], can proactively validate such intent for instances of such access-control models. Extensions of RBAC, such as ARBAC that also provides support for administration, can be statically analyzed to determine whether models meet specified security requirements – for example that certain users or roles never gain certain access permissions (see e.g. [18,48]). The algorithms used may explore the state space exhaustively (provided sets of users, roles, and resources are finite) but are often too complex. While such techniques may be seen to be static analyses, the static analysis tool box may be more fruitfully applied by devising provably sound abstractions of access-control models: for example, it may be possible to simulate role hierarchies through a temporal sequence of administrative actions, and so a security analysis may then be performed on a less complex simulation – an ARBAC system without role hierarchies and lower computational complexity.

The XACML models contain policies that consist of access-control rules as crucial ingredient. Validating an XACML model therefore benefits from statically proving that policies meet certain specifications. This is particularly important since languages such as XACML support access control in distributed, and potentially open systems. Therefore, we need security guarantees on the composition of policies and where a composition algebra may support a range of operators, e.g., logical ones such as Conjunction, and control structures such as Conditional Delegation. A prominent validation problem is to determine whether a policy has anything to say on an access request of interest; if not, this under-specification may be a potential vulnerability. Another validation problem is that the composition of policies may provide conflicting evidence for granting or denying an access. We also want support for reliable change management: if one policy is modified to another one, is the modified one a refinement of the original one in that it preserves important grant and deny decisions?

The work on PBel [11], was motivated by such questions and designed a rule-based policy-composition language in which basic rules where composed with operators expressible in Belnap's 4-valued logic (see e.g. [21]) and where these operators are functionally complete for that logic. Validation problems such as the ones discussed above, were then shown to be transformable into satisfiability problems over the predicates used in rules within policies. The approach made use of the 4-valued Belnap logic to capture not only grant and deny decisions, but also conflicts and under-specifications. That paper took an atomic view of predicates that build rules of PBel. But the semantics of PBel and its validation analyses would also work for richer predicates, for example those expressed in quantifier-free first-order logic. A nice example and application of how to interpret richer predicates for policy analysis in XACML is given in [47,55].

PBel was designed for studying the aforementioned problems, not for being used in practice. However, there is an opportunity in influencing the design of real-world access-control languages such that they support a formal and statically analyzable core, the full language is mere syntactic sugar of that PBel core, and the full language is user-facing. Such an approach is familiar from programming language design [52] and its benefits are clear: practical relevance since the full language is what users (here policy writers and administrator) want, support for proactive security through an analyzable core, and transfer of analysis from a core representation to a semantically equivalent full-language policy.

In fact, a core language may even be extended or equipped with interfaces to obtain a user-facing language that hides the concrete syntactic nature and semantics of the core. This may be particularly useful if such details are irrelevant or incomprehensible to those who specify and manage access control. To illustrate, BelLog [54] is a datalog-like language for physical access control – extended to Belnap logic: in a building with a fixed topology of rooms and hallways, where each door has a digital lock, we seek simple policies for each lock that – in their entirety – enforce building-wide security policies such as "This room can only be accessed through previous entry into the lobby." In [54], it is shown how synthesis techniques for temporal logic can be adjusted to BelLog so that a solution to the synthesis problem realizes all specified security problems, and also maps this solution to local solutions for each digital lock. Moreover, local solutions are simple formulas of first-order logic that are easy to implement and enforce locally. One could imagine to extend this with synthesis techniques rooted in satisfiability of the temporal logic CTL, so that it becomes possible to specify and enforce security policies during the physical-layout design.

One challenge that we would then face, and that is often overlooked in academic research in static analysis, is that analysis results would have to be rendered in a form that is intelligible and actionable to the stakeholders of the application domain, in this example architects and physical security experts. As [13] pointed out, there is already need for more work on this when stakeholders are source code developers.

The case study in [28], e.g., considers this problem for a trust-aggregation language in which rules represent "trust signals" that are interpreted as real numbers. Such numbers are aggregated with composition operators, such as maximum or weighted average, to reflect how an overall computed score of all observed signals should support decision making. For example, whether or not to rent out a car to a client at a certain rate may be informed by a weighting of years of accident-free driving, the type of car, and so forth [29]. We then need to validate the manner in which such scores are aggregated, e.g., to rule out that this always supports the same decision. The tool developed in [28] reduced such validation analyses to satisfiability problems that an SMT solver could solve. But the reduction makes the evidence computed with such an automated theorem prover not meaningful to those who wrote the aggregation policy. Fortunately, it is possible to devise a static analysis over the semantics of the trust-aggregation language that renders an over-approximated but sound version of this evidence – and meaningful in terms of the aggregation semantics [28].

A good question in that context is what academics and practitioners can do to encourage a better alignment of foundational work and practical R&D in security engineering. One problem is that the value systems of academia and industry are not well aligned. For example, research on user-facing analysis reporting may find it hard to get into a top academic research conference. For another example, excellent foundational work may only be adopted in industry if funnelled through or integrated within industrial standards or if produced in-house.

4   Security Assurances: Information Leakage

Formal methods traditionally have promised to provide *absolute* guarantees of correctness – to the extent of providing a mathematical and flawless proof. However, it is easier to motivate the use of formal methods in software development if it is presented as a way of enhancing the quality of software against errors and attacks. "Continuing the metaphor, we have found that software engineers more readily grasp the concept and practical value [...] if we dub it *exhaustively testable pseudo-code*." [41, p. 71] Moreover, it has been argued that methods which seek mathematical proof of program correctness can deliver such guarantees only for mathematical abstractions and not for programs as causal models within operational environments [16, 19, 40]. While this may suggest principal limitations of the reach of formal methods, the past decades have seen tremendous advances in foundations and applications of formal methods for software verification.

Clearly, formal methods operate on an *abstraction* of the real world system and it is a key lesson of security that abstractions pave the way for security holes. "Abstraction is an important concept we cannot do without when designing and understanding complex systems. [...] However, software security problems arise when intuitive properties of an abstraction do not match its concrete implementation." [23, p. 179] Indeed, even the hardware upon which software is executed is an abstraction. As an example, it is generally believed that computer memories will retain their values until explicitly changed or until power is cut off. However, cosmic radiation or even heat may make this abstraction invalid [25].

In the next three paragraphs we consider three key approaches to providing assurances of the correct use of static analysis for ensuring the security of systems. One of these takes its origin in traditional ways of ensuring the correctness of static analyses [43]. Another one goes back to techniques for establishing non-interference results that show the absence of information flow [56]; for example that no sensitive information is reaching unintended parties. The third approach replaces the qualitative view with a quantitative one by characterising the information leakage with respect to entropy [14]; this may support decisions of whether the computed leakage is acceptable or not.

Instrumented Semantics. Whenever we employ a static analysis we should establish its correctness – especially when safety, security, and their interplay is at stake. For some static analyses the notion of correctness is rather immediate, such as when we are analysing the values of some variables or perhaps the combinations of values of all variables. Assuming that we deal correctly with the bit strings that programs operate on – such as taking into account that integers have a maximal value and that the multiplication of two positive 32-bit integers is not necessarily positive – it is fairly obvious how to formalise correctness.

For other static analyses the notion of correctness is less immediate – this is typical of situations in which we analyse the past or future behaviour of programs. As a simple example, consider definition-use chaining where each definition (or assignment) of a variable is linked to all the potential uses of the value given to the variable at that point [43]. One way to formulate correctness is to consider potentially infinite execution traces. A more amenable way is to formulate an *instrumented semantics* that keeps track of certain elements of the manner in which computations are performed as well as the results they are intended to give. This suffices for proving the correctness of definition-use chaining as was discussed in Sect. 2.

More importantly, this set of techniques immediately generalises to handling the correctness of *explicit* information flows – both for confidentiality and integrity. These techniques can be augmented with considerations of the *implicit* information flows that occur due to conditional branching [44] as discussed in Sect. 2.

One advantage of the instrumented semantics approach is that the notion of correctness, once formalised, usually has a rather direct intuition (with respect to the overall security goals of the system), thereby reducing the risk for security holes due to abstraction. Also, it is feasible to extend the instrumented semantics approach with some of the more advanced security considerations such as declassification and endorsement where the security policy is deliberately violated at selected points [37].

An obvious disadvantage of the instrumented semantics approach is the possibility of basing correctness on an inadequate (read incorrect) instrumented semantics. Especially when dealing with non-determinism and parallelism it may be hard to correctly model the covert flows that arise.

Non-interference. The use of instrumented semantics is a qualitative approach requiring inspection of the way in which computations are performed and results produced. Another qualitative approach is that of non-interference, which only inspects results produced. Specifically, suppose an attacker may want to learn the values of some sensitive inputs to a program. The program satisfies non-interference if any variation in the input values of sensitive variables would not result in any observable difference in program outputs.

There are many different approaches to the formalisation of *non-interference* and we cannot touch upon all of them. In [22], it was required that observations on traces should be invariant under certain permutations of the actions in the traces. In [56], a simulation based approach was taken but only for deterministic and terminating programs. In [38], it was required that certain projections of traces should be equal; while there are clearly differences in the formal definitions, there also is a substantial amount of similarity, e.g. the trace based development of [38] reuses the proofs of the simulation based development of [56] (see [38, p. 15]). In [57], it is required that two executions should produce comparable sets of outcomes (thereby taking account of non-determinism) where non-termination is made observable (so as to avoid masking covert channels due to non-termination).

The main advantage of the non-interference approach is that we mitigate the risk of basing correctness on an inadequate instrumented semantics. A disadvantage of the non-interference approach is that it is still open to security holes due to abstraction since non-interference is usually established for models that are more abstract than a traditional instrumented semantics. More importantly, it is argued in [44, Sect. 8] that many formulations of non-interference fail to maintain a distinction between *confidentiality* and *integrity*, which constitute two of the key dimensions of the security landscape, and hence they fall short of convincing the security engineer of their relevance. (In short, non-interference is good at characterising the semantic influences but not whether they arise due to confidentiality or integrity breaches.) Yet another disadvantage is that it may prove futile to establish a non-interference result for what would seem to be an acceptable security policy; this may arise because non-interference often is "asking for too much", and so in particular non-interference finds it hard to adequately incorporate cryptography as a way to achieve secure systems.

Regarding our discussion of the lack of compositionality in Sect. 2, it is fair to say that non-interference often just deals with the program in isolation whereas more complex considerations (such as non-deducibility on computation [33]) are required to regain some compositionality.

Entropy. For a more precise account of information leakage, one may consider quantitative approaches based on entropy. The basic assumption is that we have joint probability distributions available to characterise how sets of variables take their values. Given such data we can then define the amount of information that is derivable from an observation by its *entropy*. The assumption is that a program variable x is now a random variable taking values in a finite set V. *Shannon's Entropy* $H(x)$ is the expected value of information contained in each observation of x. This is an information-theoretic measure that is non-negative, additive for independent random variables, and monotone. Such intuitive properties characterize function H up to a constant. An important derived concept is that of *conditional entropy*: $H(x \mid y)$ denotes the portion of the entropy of variable x that is independent from another random variable y.

There are two extreme cases of the conditional entropy $H(x \mid y)$. One extreme case is where x, y are aliases for the same entity. Then, we will always make the same value observations for x and y: we obtain $H(x \mid y) = 0$ which indicates that we learn nothing further if we learn the value of x, given that we already know the value of y – the value of y determines the value of x. The other extreme case is where x and y are truly independent; then, we get $H(x \mid y) = H(x)$ – indicating that our previous knowledge of y tells us nothing of x.

The advantage of this quantitative approach to information flow is its ability to precisely quantify the amount of information $H(x) - H(x \mid y)$ that might be leaked due to information flow. This amount "should" be 0 if we have been able to prove a non-interference result, and if it is even slightly larger than 0 it "should" be impossible to establish a non-interference result. This suggests to accept a system as secure if the conditional entropy is sufficiently close to 0. A current disadvantage of this approach is that we have less tool support for analysing the security of systems according to information-theoretic, quantitative measures.

Perspective. In our view, non-interference is both demanding too much (in not permitting minute flows) and discriminating too little (in not distinguishing between confidentiality and integrity) to be useful for validating the use of static analysis in ensuring the security of systems. On the other hand, approaches based on instrumented semantics should interact well with state of the art in static analysis tools while methods based on entropy should be investigated as they offer to provide stronger assurances, and they can lead to metrics for the support of decision making in security engineering.

5   Discussion

A static analysis is subject to potentially conflicting aims. It needs to be *abstract* since many concrete properties of interest to it are undecidable for general programs and programming languages. Given that need for abstraction, it also needs to be *precise* enough, so that it will often enough arrive at findings that are digestible and useful to the analysts. But the static analysis should also be *sound*. By this we mean that the analysis models all possible executions of the program. This is important for security considerations: if some real executions are missed by the analysis (e.g. because the meaning of a language construct may depend on the implementation environment), these executions may be security vulnerabilities that an attacker might exploit. Finally, the static analysis should *scale* so that we can run it on large programs or code bases effectively.

The discussion around soundness superficially seems similar to a discourse documented partly in [16,19]: the question of whether formal verification can prove the correctness of an executing program with mathematical certainty. This was posed at a time when it was very difficult to promote use of formal methods into R&D and to get credibility for devising such methods. It is fair to say that we have come a long way! Major ICT companies such as Amazon, Facebook, and Microsoft are using a range of formal methods in tactical and strategic ways, and this was made possible by persistent research and tool building of formal-methods researchers in the past decades.

Formal methods such as static analysis are very useful for security engineering. First, if a static analysis fails to formally verify a property – such as the absence of memory leaks – at a higher level of abstraction, then this can also be a validation concern within the actual execution environment and so may require code modifications.

Second, static analysis tools may help us understand the scope of unsoundness that may occur when transferring reasoning that is sound at one abstraction layer to another one. For example, the work in [24,46] provides static analyses with which we may understand the differences and input sensitivities of programs between an idealized execution with mathematical real numbers and a finite-precision implementation of real numbers.

Third, code development operates at several abstraction layers and static analyses can certainly validate higher such layers in isolation. For example, the use of generics at the level of UML specifications [36] minimizes the risk of type incompatibilities in implementations; the use of static analysis to validate information flow of process models [6] is validating security properties of the process design itself; and the use of automated theorem proving in examining specified language standards such as those for Javascript [10] can flag up issues of interest to the standardization committees.

Fourth, there may be a compelling business case for formally verifying specific system components. For example, one may build an operating system in such a way that only its small micro kernel ever runs in supervisor mode – meaning that it runs at the most privileged level of the supporting hardware. There is then an incentive in formally verifying such a micro kernel if it is planned to be used in a variety of security- or safety-critical systems. As already discussed, this has been done for the micro kernel seL4 [31]. A lot of the verification effort here went into assuring that the kernel will interact correctly with its environment, for example that the access control is correctly enforced, and that binaries of the kernel correctly implement the C semantics of its source code. Change management is a challenge for such efforts, and the authors discuss in [31] the degree of severity with which different types of kernel code changes impact the overall verification effort. The DARPA initiative [27] demonstrated that use of such a formally verified micro kernel can significantly harden the security and resiliency of systems that rely on it, for example a drone that white-hack teams can no longer compromise.

The ability to deal with change is one of the main selling points of any security validation method for software and executing systems in practice. The paradigm shift from single to multi-core CPUs, and even the advent of GPU and FPGA development environments provide exiting research opportunities for language design, compiler technology, and static analysis as tools for producing secure software on heterogenous or bespoke hardware. But they also challenge conceived ideals and models of computation, such as memory consistency and thread schedulings and force us to rethink the use of static analyses in this setting. Technological innovations in isolation technology, such as Intel's SGX [15], also mean that static analyses for proactive security may have to be adjusted to reflect such innovations and their isolation architectures.

Another important trend we see is the recognition that verification tools and static analyzers should be the object of verification themselves. While this invites an infinite logical regress, it makes perfect sense from an engineering perspective. For example, Cadar and Donaldson predict in [12] that, by 2025, the analysis of static analyzers and entire compilers will be common place. There are already efforts at producing compilers that are provably correct within the abstraction level of such reasoning; let us mention the CompCert project [34] that offers a mathematical proof that the compiler introduces no bug in the convertion from source code to binary, and the CakeML project which work on verifying system implementations of substantial parts of Standard ML (see e.g. [32]). And there is already some work on certifying the results of model checkers [39]. These efforts are related to the need to better understand how static analyzes can be adapted to best support code development within professional development environments. We refer to [35] for a discussion of such needs.

We think that static analysis and its practical use can be furthered by use of big data and data analytics. Static analysis and formal verification of a software system will no doubt make that system more secure. But reactive security mechanisms may be needed to improve the resiliency of that system at run-time; for example, to prevent RowHammer attacks that aim to compromise security by breaking an abstraction [8]. It then makes sense to base such a reaction on available data for security vulnerabilities, the probability of them turning into active security threats, and the system impact that exploits – which realize such threats – may have. In fact, one may use formal techniques such as solvers or optimizers to reason about how best to devise such reactive security postures and their evolution [20,45].

A static analysis tool may also use data and quantitative analytics to determine a "scheduling" of which bugs to report and why. For example, this may inform the ordering or prioritizing of such reporting. Past exploit data, the potential impact path of a program point or stochastic assumptions about program input may inform which bugs to report. Put in another way, if a security engineer has time to look at 4 bugs, which ones should the static analysis present to her? Such rankings may even include prioritizations based on risk appetite or specific attack models. Indeed, we see such work already happening in the realm of security operations centres (SOCs) and the use of data mining and artificial intelligence in enterprise platforms (see e.g. [3]), where one concern is to understand human behaviour and where "bugs" are now potentially suspicious human behaviours that may be worth reporting: which ones to report may well depend on a particular concern an analyst has.

6   Conclusion

For a long time, IT systems have been central to our society but they are becoming increasingly complex, pervasive, and autonomous. This development offers many benefits to society but also creates risks related to the safety and security of societies relying on the correct functioning of their IT systems. Furthermore, globalisation and the Internet of Everything mean that software is becoming a commodity for which a system integrator may have little insight in the way its code has been developed nor how it performs in corner cases that trade off soundness and completeness of a static analysis.

Computer Science not only offers the software and algorithms making this development of today's IT systems possible – it also provides key methods and techniques for ensuring the correct behaviour of complex and inhomogeneous IT systems. Compositionality lies at the heart of a component-based approach to the construction of IT systems. Formal methods may be used to harden critical components. But too frequently the composition of secure components does not result in a secure system (as was discussed for cryptographic protocols). Also, compositional security seems an even harder goal when it comes to the IoT systems of systems that will shape our future in the Internet of Everything.

Static analysis is noteworthy among the formal methods approaches in offering a variety of analyses of low computational complexity that therefore are likely to scale to systems built out of many components. We have argued that a number of security considerations related to confidentiality, privacy, integrity and authenticity can be addressed using techniques from static analysis. These techniques apply equally well to existing code, to access control policies, and to designs (or models) of systems under development. Further advances in static analysis are likely to go beyond the mere optimization of software in order to fully tackle the challenge of proactively ensuring the security of complex IT/IoT systems.

Acknowledgements. We expressly thank Marieke Huisman, Alan Mycroft, and David Schmidt for their very useful comments on drafts of this paper. The first author was supported in part by the UK EPSRC, through the grants EP/N023242/1, EP/N02334X/1, and EP/N020030/1, and by funding from Intel Corporation. The second author was supported in part by the IDEA4CPS Research Centre studying the Foundations for Cyber Physical Systems funded by the Danish Research Foundation for Basic Research (DNRF86-10).

References

1. Common criteria for information technology security evaluation. http://www.commoncriteriaportal.org
2. OAuth 2.0. IETF OAuth WG. https://oauth.net/2/
3. Status today: Artificial intelligence that understands human behavior. https://www.statustoday.com/
4. eXtensible Access Control Markup Language (XACML) Version 3.0. OASIS Standard, 22 January 2013. http://docs.oasis-open.org/xacml/3.0/xacml-3.0-core-spec-os-en.html
5. Framework for cyber-physical systems. Release 1.0, May 2016. US NIST, Cyber Physical Systems Public Working Group
6. Accorsi, R., Wonnemann, C.: Static information flow analysis of workflow models. In: INFORMATIK 2010 - Business Process and Service Science - Proceedings of ISSS and BPSC, 27 September–1 October 2010 in Leipzig, Germany, pp. 194–205 (2010)
7. Adee, S.: Germany to create world's first high-way code for driverless cars. Online title, 21 September 2016. New Scientist
8. Aweke, Z.B., Yitbarek, S.F., Qiao, R., Das, R., Hicks, M., Oren, Y., Austin, T.M.: ANVIL: software-based protection against next-generation rowhammer attacks. In: Proceedings of the Twenty-First International Conference on Architectural Support for Programming Languages and Operating Systems, ASPLOS 2016, Atlanta, GA, USA, 2–6 April 2016, pp. 743–755 (2016)
9. Baier, C., Katoen, J.-P.: Principles of Model Checking. MIT Press, Cambridge (2008)
10. Bodin, M., Charguéraud, A., Filaretti, D., Gardner, P., Maffeis, S., Naudziuniene, D., Schmitt, A., Smith, G.: A trusted mechanised JavaSript specification. In: The 41st Annual ACM SIGPLAN-SIGACT Symposium on Principles of Programming Languages, POPL 2014, San Diego, CA, USA, 20–21 January 2014, pp. 87–100 (2014)
11. Bruns, G., Huth, M.: Access control via Belnap logic: intuitive, expressive, and analyzable policy composition. ACM Trans. Inf. Syst. Secur. **14**(1), 9:1–9:27 (2011)
12. Cadar, C., Donaldson, A.F.: Analysing the program analyser. In: Proceedings of the 38th International Conference on Software Engineering, ICSE 2016, Austin, TX, USA, 14–22 May 2016 - Companion Volume, pp. 765–768 (2016)
13. Calcagno, C., et al.: Moving fast with software verification. In: Havelund, K., Holzmann, G., Joshi, R. (eds.) NFM 2015. LNCS, vol. 9058, pp. 3–11. Springer, Cham (2015). https://doi.org/10.1007/978-3-319-17524-9_1
14. Clark, D., Hunt, S., Malacaria, P.: A static analysis for quantifying information flow in a simple imperative language. J. Comput. Secur. **15**(3), 321–371 (2007)
15. Costan, V., Devadas, S.: Intel SGX explained. IACR Cryptology ePrint Archive 2016:86 (2016)

16. DeMillo, R.A., Lipton, R.J., Perlis, A.J.: Social processes and proofs of theorems and programs. Commun. ACM **22**(5), 271–280 (1979)
17. Denning, D.E., Denning, P.J.: Certification of programs for secure information flow. Commun. ACM **20**(7), 504–513 (1977)
18. Ferrara, A.L., Madhusudan, P., Nguyen, T.L., Parlato, G.: VAC - verifier of administrative role-based access control policies. In: Biere, A., Bloem, R. (eds.) CAV 2014. LNCS, vol. 8559, pp. 184–191. Springer, Cham (2014). https://doi.org/10.1007/978-3-319-08867-9_12
19. Fetzer, J.H.: Program verification: the very idea. Commun. ACM **31**(9), 1048–1063 (1988)
20. Fielder, A., Panaousis, E.A., Malacaria, P., Hankin, C., Smeraldi, F.: Decision support approaches for cyber security investment. Decis. Support Syst. **86**, 13–23 (2016)
21. Fitting, M.: Bilattices and the theory of truth. J. Philos. Logic **18**(3), 225–256 (1989)
22. Goguen, J.A., Meseguer, J.: Security policies and security models. In: 1982 IEEE Symposium on Security and Privacy, Oakland, CA, USA, 26–28 April 1982, pp. 11–20 (1982)
23. Gollmann, D.: Computer Security, 3rd edn. Wiley, Hoboken (2011)
24. Goubault, E., Putot, S.: Static analysis of finite precision computations. In: Jhala, R., Schmidt, D. (eds.) VMCAI 2011. LNCS, vol. 6538, pp. 232–247. Springer, Heidelberg (2011). https://doi.org/10.1007/978-3-642-18275-4_17
25. Govindavajhala, S., Appel, A.W.: Using memory errors to attack a virtual machine. In: 2003 IEEE Symposium on Security and Privacy (S&P 2003), Berkeley, CA, USA, 11–14 May 2003, pp. 154–165 (2003)
26. Greenberg, A.: The Jeep Hackers are Back to Prove Car Hacking Can Get Much Worse, 8 January 2018
27. Hartnett, K.: Computer Scientists Close In on Perfect, Hack-proof Code, 23 September 2016
28. Huth, M., Kuo, J.: Quantitative threat analysis via a logical service. Technical report 2014/10, ISSN 1469–4174, Department of Computing, Imperial College London (2014)
29. Huth, M., Kuo, J.H.-P.: On designing usable policy languages for declarative trust aggregation. In: Tryfonas, T., Askoxylakis, I. (eds.) HAS 2014. LNCS, vol. 8533, pp. 45–56. Springer, Cham (2014). https://doi.org/10.1007/978-3-319-07620-1_5
30. Jones, N.D., Nielson, F.: Abstract interpretation: a semantics-based tool for program analysis. In: Handbook of Logic in Computer Science, vol. 4, pp. 527–636. Oxford University Press (1995)
31. Klein, G., Andronick, J., Elphinstone, K., Murray, T.C., Sewell, T., Kolanski, R., Heiser, G.: Comprehensive formal verification of an OS microkernel. ACM Trans. Comput. Syst. **32**(1), 2:1–2:70 (2014)
32. Kumar, R., Myreen, M.O., Norrish, M., Owens, S.: CakeML: a verified implementation of ML. In: The 41st Annual ACM SIGPLAN-SIGACT Symposium on Principles of Programming Languages, POPL 2014, San Diego, CA, USA, 20–21 January 2014, pp. 179–192 (2014)
33. Lanotte, R., Maggiolo-Schettini, A., Troina, A.: Time and probability-based information flow analysis. IEEE Trans. Softw. Eng. **36**(5), 719–734 (2010)
34. Leroy, X.: Formal verification of a realistic compiler. Commun. ACM **52**(7), 107–115 (2009)

35. Livshits, B., Sridharan, M., Smaragdakis, Y., Lhoták, O., Amaral, J.N., Chang, B.-Y.E., Guyer, S.Z., Khedker, U.P., Møller, A., Vardoulakis, D.: In defense of soundiness: a manifesto. Commun. ACM **58**(2), 44–46 (2015)
36. Murphy, R.: Increasing assurance levels through early verification with type safety. J. Cyber Secur. Inf. Syst. **3**(2) (2015). https://www.csiac.org/journal-article/increasing-assurance-levels-through-early-verification-with-type-safety/
37. Myers, A.C., Liskov, B.: A decentralized model for information flow control. In: Proceedings of the Sixteenth ACM Symposium on Operating System Principles, SOSP 1997, St. Malo, France, 5–8 October 1997, pp. 129–142 (1997)
38. Myers, A.C., Sabelfeld, A., Zdancewic, S.: Enforcing robust declassification and qualified robustness. J. Comput. Secur. **14**(2), 157–196 (2006)
39. Namjoshi, K.S.: Certifying model checkers. In: Berry, G., Comon, H., Finkel, A. (eds.) CAV 2001. LNCS, vol. 2102, pp. 2–13. Springer, Heidelberg (2001). https://doi.org/10.1007/3-540-44585-4_2
40. Nelson, D.A.: Deductive program verification (a practitioner's commentary). Mind. Mach. **2**(3), 283–307 (1992)
41. Newcombe, C., Rath, T., Zhang, F., Munteanu, B., Brooker, M., Deardeuff, M.: How amazon web services uses formal methods. Commun. ACM **58**(4), 66–73 (2015)
42. Nielson, F., Nielson, H.R.: Model checking *Is* static analysis of modal logic. In: Ong, L. (ed.) FoSSaCS 2010. LNCS, vol. 6014, pp. 191–205. Springer, Heidelberg (2010). https://doi.org/10.1007/978-3-642-12032-9_14
43. Nielson, F., Nielson, H.R., Hankin, C.: Principles of Program Analysis. Springer, Heidelberg (1999). https://doi.org/10.1007/978-3-662-03811-6
44. Nielson, H.R., Nielson, F.: Content dependent information flow control. J. Logical Algebraic Methods Program. (2016, in press)
45. Livshits, B., Katz, O.: Toward an evidence-based design for reactive security policies and mechanisms. Technical report, November 2016
46. Putot, S.: Analyse statique de programmes et systèmes numériques. Tech. Sci. Inform. **33**(1–2), 159–162 (2014)
47. Kencana Ramli, C.D.P., Nielson, H.R., Nielson, F.: The logic of XACML. In: Arbab, F., Ölveczky, P.C. (eds.) FACS 2011. LNCS, vol. 7253, pp. 205–222. Springer, Heidelberg (2012). https://doi.org/10.1007/978-3-642-35743-5_13
48. Ranise, S., Truong, A., Armando, A.: Boosting model checking to analyse large ARBAC policies. In: Jøsang, A., Samarati, P., Petrocchi, M. (eds.) STM 2012. LNCS, vol. 7783, pp. 273–288. Springer, Heidelberg (2013). https://doi.org/10.1007/978-3-642-38004-4_18
49. Samarati, P., de Vimercati, S.C.: Access control: policies, models, and mechanisms. In: Focardi, R., Gorrieri, R. (eds.) FOSAD 2000. LNCS, vol. 2171, pp. 137–196. Springer, Heidelberg (2001). https://doi.org/10.1007/3-540-45608-2_3
50. Schell, R.R.: Current cybersecurity best practices - a clear and present danger to privacy. Keynote, ERCIM News 90 (2012). http://ercim-news.ercim.eu/en90/keynote
51. Schmidt, D., Steffen, B.: Program analysis *as* model checking of abstract interpretations. In: Levi, G. (ed.) SAS 1998. LNCS, vol. 1503, pp. 351–380. Springer, Heidelberg (1998). https://doi.org/10.1007/3-540-49727-7_22
52. Schmidt, D.A.: The Structure of Typed Programming Languages. Foundations of Computing Series. MIT Press, Cambridge (1994)
53. Steffen, B.: Data flow analysis as model checking. In: Ito, T., Meyer, A.R. (eds.) TACS 1991. LNCS, vol. 526, pp. 346–364. Springer, Heidelberg (1991). https://doi.org/10.1007/3-540-54415-1_54

54. Tsankov, P.: Access control with formal security guarantees. Ph.D. thesis, Computer Science, ETH Zurich (2016)
55. Turkmen, F., den Hartog, J., Ranise, S., Zannone, N.: Analysis of XACML policies with SMT. In: Focardi, R., Myers, A. (eds.) POST 2015. LNCS, vol. 9036, pp. 115–134. Springer, Heidelberg (2015). https://doi.org/10.1007/978-3-662-46666-7_7
56. Volpano, D.M., Irvine, C.E., Smith, G.: A sound type system for secure flow analysis. J. Comput. Secur. 4(2/3), 167–188 (1996)
57. Zdancewic, S., Myers, A.C.: Observational determinism for concurrent program security. In: 16th IEEE Computer Security Foundations Workshop (CSFW-16 2003), Pacific Grove, CA, USA, 30 June–2 July 2003, p. 29 (2003)

Software Architecture of Modern Model Checkers

Fabrice Kordon[1]([✉]), Michael Leuschel[2], Jaco van de Pol[3],
and Yann Thierry-Mieg[1]

[1] Sorbonne Université, CNRS UMR 7606 LIP6, 75005 Paris, France
{Fabrice.Kordon,Yann.Thierry-Mieg}@lip6.fr
[2] Institut für Informatik, Univ. Düsseldorf, Universitätsstr. 1, Düsseldorf, Germany
leuschel@cs.uni-duesseldorf.de
[3] Department of Computer Science,
University of Twente, Enschede, The Netherlands
J.C.vandePol@utwente.nl

Abstract. Automated formal verification using model checking is a mature field with many tools available. We summarize the recent trends in the design and architecture of model checking tools. An important design goal of modern model checkers is to support many input languages (front-end) and many verification strategies (back-end), and to allow arbitrary combinations of them. This widens the applicability of new verification algorithms, avoids duplicate implementation of the analysis techniques, improves quality of the tools, and eases use of verification for a newly introduced high-level specification, such as a domain specific language.

1 Introduction

The evolution of model-based engineering and domain specific languages (DSL [73]) in industrial practice has led to a proliferation of small executable languages dedicated to a specific purpose. Model checking is a mature field [20] with many technological solutions and tools that can guarantee behavioral correctness of such specifications.

However, due to the complexity of the problem in general, different model checking tools are better at tackling different classes of systems, and it is difficult for an end-user to know beforehand which technique would be most effective for his or her specific model. It is thus highly desirable to embed such expert knowledge in a tool that integrates several solution engines (*e.g.* partial order reduction, decision-diagram based encoding, SAT/SMT techniques, etc.) behind a unified front-end.

Ideally a modern model checker should be adaptive, able to transparently select for a given model instance and a given property the best verification strategy. This design goal forces the software architecture of model checkers to evolve from tightly integrated or *monolithic* approaches to more open architectures that rely on *pivot representations* to support both many languages and many verification strategies.

© Springer Nature Switzerland AG 2019
B. Steffen and G. Woeginger (Eds.): Computing and Software Science, LNCS 10000, pp. 393–419, 2019.
https://doi.org/10.1007/978-3-319-91908-9_20

The objective of this paper is to summarize the current situation of modern model checking tools in terms of architecture and usage to solve typical industrial-like problems, where specifications may not be written in a traditional verification language such as PROMELA [39], CSP [38], Petri nets [33], B [1] or TLA$^+$ [49].

Recent work also considers software verification (*i.e.* analyzing programs directly at the code level). Program verification mainly relies on strong abstractions of programs to cope with the combinatorial explosion caused by analysis at the instruction level, thus generating abstract models from software. This abstraction process for software verification is not considered directly in this paper; we focus on verification engines for model checking.

Another approach worth mentioning is the Electronic Tool Integration (ETI) platform [69]. This platform focuses on integration of tools (rather than algorithms) by providing a distributed coordination mechanism, enabling verification tasks that would not be possible in a single tool. Its successor, jETI [56] uses webservices technology and Eclipse support for seamless tool integration and graphical user interfaces. While ETI focuses on integration and coordination of existing tools, this paper focuses on integrating verification algorithms within a single, modular tool.

Section 2 presents the current trends in architectures for model checkers; Sect. 3 shows a first approach involving ProB and existing languages (*e.g.* Prolog, Java) while Sects. 4 and 5 are presenting updated visions (language based and library based) of such an architecture when analyzing high-level languages. Finally, Sect. 6 details two typical examples before a conclusion.

2   Trends on the Architecture for Model Checking

Model checkers exist now for more than three decades and have proven their usefulness to understand and debug complex systems. However, their software architecture is evolving, following a similar evolution as compilers, which were once monolithic but are now structured for a better reuse of code.

Figure 1 depicts such an evolution. On the left (Fig. 1a) is the "traditional" architecture, where a model checker is associated with a dedicated formalism

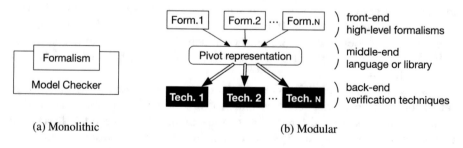

(a) Monolithic   (b) Modular

Fig. 1. Evolution of model checking tool's architecture.

and proposes its verification algorithm, possibly with numerous variants and enhancements to perform its task efficiently. The most emblematic example is Spin [39].

Unfortunately, such an architecture has several drawbacks. First, the single entry point of the tool is the formalism it processes. Second, adapting the verification engine is also quite difficult since all the features of the input language are exploited and become naturally twisted with the algorithms themselves.

Progressively, several attempts have tried to separate the verification engine from the input formalism. Then, the notion of "pivot representation" naturally arises as the interface to an "upper level" dealing with the input specification. Below this "pivot representation", is a set of "verification engines" being able to process this pivot representation. Languages such as AltaRica [5], NUPN [31], or FIACRE [11], as well as a tool like the model checking Kit [64], could be seen as early attempts of this approach. Fixed-point equations have also been proposed as pivot representation to generalize multiple model checking questions [68]. In a similar fashion, the introduction of SMT-LIB [8] as a standard format for automated reasoning over data theories can be viewed as the successful introduction of a pivot representation.

Such an architecture (Fig. 1b) is similar to the font-end + middle-end + back-end architecture of current compilers. It has two main advantages. First, it decouples the high-level specification language from its verification. Then, the specification language designer may work independently from the verification mechanics as long as they provide a sound and formal semantics to their notation. This is of particular interest when input languages are numerous, because it does not hinder the access to efficient verification engines via the pivot representation. The bridging of AADL with FIACRE for verification purposes is a typical example of this interest [21].

The second important advantage is the emphasis on the fundamentals of the semantics (expressed in the pivot representation) required to perform efficient model checking, thus providing a better access to various verification technologies (e.g. algorithms based on different approaches such as partial order reduction, the use of decision diagrams, the use of SAT/SMT solvers, etc.).

Moreover, it avoids, when dealing with the analysis of high-level specification, to choose between selecting (a priori) one verification technology, or performing as many translations as the number of selected verification engines.

The modular architecture of Fig. 1b can be interpreted in several ways (see Fig. 2):

– components may be linked together as object files and libraries, (see Fig. 2a), as this is the case for LTSmin [42] or SPOT [26],
– components may collaborate via an intermediate language (see Fig. 2b), as this is the case for ITS-Tools [71] (originally relying on enhanced decision diagrams) or Boogie [6] (originally relying on SMT solvers).

In the library based vision of the modular architecture of model checking tools, the pivot representation is materialized as an API. The role of such an

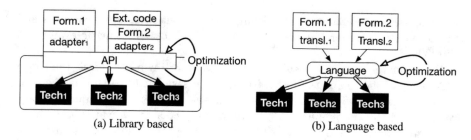

Fig. 2. The two interpretations of the modular architecture of model checkers

interface is to expose the internal structure of the pivot representation, so that, efficient algorithms can be built on the one hand, while it remains easy to connect a higher formalism module on the other hand. Basically, formalisms are connected through adapters implementing the main semantic characteristics of the input formalism like the definition of a state or the successor function.

The main advantages of the library vision are: *(i)* it isolates the algorithms from the input pivot notation, allowing only access to relevant data structures, and *(ii)* it easily allows to embed executable code in the input formalism (with the necessary precautions to preserve the soundness of the input formalism semantics) that can be executed during model checking. Insertion of such code (e.g. data computation) is performed by the adapter.

Its main drawback is that one must cope with the existing data-structures when adding a new verification technology. This may hinder the addition of some new technology for which the existing data structures are not adapted (like connecting SAT/SMT based algorithms alongside existing automata-based ones).

In the language based vision of the modular architecture of model checking tools, the pivot representation is a language itself. Such a language offers a semantic support that is "agnostic" in the sense it can support various execution models. Connection with high-level languages is done thanks to a transformation into the pivot language, thus acting as an "assembly language" dedicated to verification.

The main advantages of this vision are: *(i)* it provides a strict barrier between high-level formalisms and the implemented verification modules that can use various relevant data structures suitable for the corresponding verification technology, and *(ii)* it enables possible optimization at the pivot language level so that the underlying selected verification algorithm features can be fully exploited. So, it is easier to plug new verification engines based on very different theory since adapted data structure can be then developed for this module only.

Unfortunately, it is quite complex to link executable code to a high-level formalism (under the necessary precautions to preserve the soundness of the input formalism semantics) without a heavy and complex support included in the pivot language itself. Such a feature is used in tools like Spin [39] (monolithic approach) or LTSmin [42] (modular/library based approach).

Obviously, the two interpretations of the modular architecture can be combined, thus exposing either a pivot language based on an API, or an API using a pivot language to connect to some underlying verification technology. The next section introduces some high-level logic based formalisms and investigates how they can be mapped to an efficient model checking engine.

3   High-Level Logic-Based Input Languages

High-level logic-based languages, i.e., specification languages which are not necessarily executable [36], can provide a convenient way to translate a wide variety of domain specific formalisms. Logic and set theory pervade large areas of computer science, and are used to express many formalisms, properties and concepts. On the one hand this explains the popularity of SAT and SMT solvers: many properties from wide areas of computer science can be expressed or compiled to logic. Similarly, the dynamic behaviour of a wide variety of languages and formalisms can be easily expressed in terms of a state-based formal method using logic and set theory.

Several formal methods have a common foundation in predicate logic, set theory and arithmetic: B [1], Event-B [2], TLA$^+$ [49], VDM and Z [66] are the most commonly used ones. Their high abstraction level make them a target for conveniently modelling a large class of systems to be validated. Indeed, the high abstraction level helps avoiding errors in the modelling process and can lead to a considerable reduction in modelling time [63]. These methods are also convenient for expressing the semantics of domain specific formalisms and develop model checking tools for them. E.g., the following tools use a translation to B to obtain a model checking tool for the source formalism: UML-B [65], SAP choreography [67], SafeCap [41], Coda [18].

One drawback of such a high-level input language is performance: determining the successor states of a given state may require constraint solving of logical predicates with quantification over higher-order data structures. As a simple example, we present the B encoding of derivation steps for a formal (possibly context-sensitive) grammar with productions P over an alphabet A. It is maybe not the most typical model checking example, but shows how easy one can translate a mathematical definition such as a formal grammar derivation step [40] into a high-level language like B. The B/Event-B model would just have a single event with four parameters L, R, a, b defined as

$$\textbf{event } rewrite(L, R, a, b) =$$

$$\textbf{when } (L \mapsto R) \in P \wedge a \in seq(A) \wedge b \in seq(A) \wedge cur = a \;\hat{}\; L \;\hat{}\; b$$

$$\textbf{then } cur := a \;\hat{}\; R \;\hat{}\; b \textbf{ end}$$

This is very close to the mathematical definition in theoretical computer science books such as [40]. The main difference is the use of $\hat{}$ for concatenating sequences and $seq(A)$ for finite sequences over the set A. Executing this event within a model checker, however, requires a limited form of constraint solving: to compute the next state for a given value of cur, one needs to determine the possible decompositions of cur into three substrings a, L, b such that L is a left-hand side of a grammar production in P. E.g., given $P = \{N \mapsto [y, N, z]\}$ and $cur = [x, N, N, x]$, there are two ways to execute the event, leading to two possible successor states with $cur = [x, y, N, z, N, x]$ and $cur = [x, N, y, N, z, x]$.

In this section we will focus on B [1] and TLA$^+$ [49], illustrated by the model checkers PROB [50] and TLC [76].

3.1   Monolithic Approach: Directly Encoding the Semantics

One approach for model checking a high-level specification language is exhibited by the TLC model checker. It directly encodes the operational semantics expressed in Java in the model checker; i.e., it follows the classical monolithic approach.

This leads to a quite efficient explicit state model checker (albeit slower than e.g. Spin) where library functions can be directly written in Java. TLC can be parallelised, and can run in the cloud.

The disadvantage is that the model checker is really intertwined with the TLA$^+$ implementation and language and cannot be easily used for other languages, unless these are translated to TLA$^+$. TLC also cannot perform constraint solving, meaning that the above rewrite specification cannot be handled. Such specifications have to be re-written manually, so that left-to-right evaluation leads to finite and reasonably efficient enumeration.

3.2   Prolog as an Intermediate Verification Language

From its conception, the animator and model checker PROB was designed to target multiple specification languages and to use Prolog as a pivot language, or more precisely as an intermediate verification language (cf. Sect. 4.1) for specifying language semantics. As such, the B semantics (or rather a superset thereof, denoted by B+ in Fig. 3, which is a pivot language in itself) is expressed using a Prolog interpreter, which specifies the set of initial states, the successor relation and the state properties.

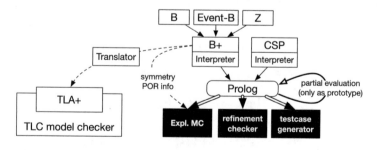

Fig. 3. The TLC and PROB model checkers

This approach has a few advantages. It is easy to use the tool for other languages by providing an interpreter (or compiler). This is helped by the fact that Prolog, aka logic programming, is quite convenient to express the semantics of various programming and specification languages, in particular due to its support for non-determinism. E.g., the operational semantics rules of CSP [61] can be translated into Prolog clauses [51]. Furthermore, within Prolog one can make use of constraint logic programming for dealing with complex specifications, such as the grammar rewriting specification above. Finally, it is relatively straightforward to combine or integrate several formalisms, as was done for CSP ∥ B [17].

On the negative side, a Prolog interpreter will be slower (but easier to write) than a C or Java interpreter or even a compiler. Also, complex Prolog code such as the B interpreter of PROB, is not suited for analyses required for model checking optimisations, e.g., dependence information for partial order reduction or symmetry information. Within PROB such information is provided in an ad-hoc manner per supported language. Better solutions to this will be shown later, either by better pivot languages Sect. 4 or by the greybox approach Sect. 5.

Quite a few other tools also use Prolog as an intermediate input language. E.g, the XMC model checker [60] provides an explicit-state CTL model checker, targeting languages such as CCS via an interpreter or via translation. Techniques such as partial evaluation [52] and unfold-fold transformations [29] can be used for optimization, but also for a form of infinite state model checking. Finally, constraint programming techniques can be used for various validation tasks [23, 24]. Similarly, in Horn-Clause Verification, SMT solvers are applied to Prolog or Datalog like specifications [12,58].

3.3 Other High-Level Languages

There are many other high-level modelling languages. The languages VDM and ASM are very similar in style to B and TLA$^+$, and some translators between these languages exist. The process algebra CSP [61] also features sets and sequences as data types, but its operational semantics is quite different. The successful FDR tool [62] is to some extent a monolithic model checker (or more precisely refinement checker), even though it also performs an internal linearisation. CSP has also been a popular target for domain specific formalisms such as Casper [54] for security protocols or Circus [74]. For the latter there is also a recent translation to CSP∥B [75], and Circus itself is sometimes the target for other formalisms such as UML [16].

The toolset around mCRL, a process algebra with abstract datatypes, is based on an internal linearisation technique [34]. In the mCRL toolset, linear processes are viewed as an intermediate verification language (in the sense of Sect. 4.1). Due to their flattened form, they can be subjected to further optimization, and they are well-suited for adaptation to an on-the-fly API (in the sense of Sect. 5).

We would also like to mention the PAT model checker [53,77]. Its conception is similar to PROB but using C-Sharp instead of Prolog as an intermediate language.

Finally, instead of validating high-level specifications, it is also quite common to work directly with programming languages such as Java or C. The Java Pathfinder [35] tool translates a Java program to Promela for modelling with the Spin model checker [39]. Here, only certain aspects of the programming language are modelled (such as concurrency), abstracting away from other aspects. Another successful tool is CBMC [45] for bounded model checking, which provides bit-precise modelling for C and checking specific properties such as buffer overflows and exceptions. An alternative to model checking is abstract interpretation, such as used by the ASTRÉE analyzer [22] which has been successfully used for verification of C programs.

3.4   Summary

In summary, high-level logic-based languages are very popular for modelling and for expressing domain specific formalisms. We have shown how an intermediate pivot language like Prolog provides a good way to integrate formalisms, and allows a model checker to target a variety of dialects and related formalisms. The downside is performance: efficient model checking is very difficult to achieve in Prolog, and some information like symmetry and dependence for partial order reduction is difficult to extract from more involved Prolog representations. The approaches in the following sections will provide solutions to this. Section 4 provides other internal representations, while Sect. 5 presents a greybox API approach, which enables to connect a low-level model checking engine written in C with interpreters for higher-level languages. In Sect. 6.1 we will actually show how this has led to the latest generation model checking technique for B, by combining PROB's Prolog interpreter with LTSmin's model checking C engine.

4   Using an Intermediate Language as a Pivot

As discussed in Sect. 2, the role of an intermediate representation is to allow separate evolution of input languages with respect to model checking and verification algorithms. This section focuses on approaches reifying this pivot representation using an intermediate verification language (IVL). Section 4.1 presents the general approach, while Sect. 4.2 details a specific instance of an IVL called Guarded Action Language.

4.1   Intermediate Verification Language

An IVL is a language specifically designed to fit the role of pivot: rather than a language particularly comfortable for end users, it is designed as a general purpose input for a verification engine. The focus when designing an IVL is on providing a small set of semantic bricks while preserving good expressivity. The end-user manipulates a user-friendly domain specific language (DSL) [73] that is translated into the IVL prior to the actual model checking or verification.

Historically, most model checkers were built in monolithic fashion, with a single supported input language and a single solution engine. This prevented a lot of reuse of actual code between model checkers, similar algorithms being reimplemented for each language. In this setting, to use a particular solver, you need to translate manually or automatically your specification to the solver's language.

For instance Promela the language of Spin [39] has often been used as a target for translation [15]. However it is a complex language with many semantic idiosyncrasies such as the support for embedded C code or the behavior attached to the *atomic* keyword. It also offers a wide variety of syntactic constructs, that make direct modeling in Promela comfortable for end-users. These features make life hard for a provider of a new algorithm or verification strategy. Because the language is complex, the development cost of supporting Promela in a tool is high. Many third-party tools for Promela analysis [42,71] only support a limited subset of Promela (typically excluding C code, and/or dynamic task creation).

IVL in the Literature. Hence while Promela has been used as an IVL it is not particularly well suited for that purpose, since it was not a design goal of the language. However many recent verification efforts include the definition of an intermediate languages, explicitly designed to be an intermediate verification language (e.g. [5,6,11,71]).

The SMV language [19] was designed to support symbolic verification (using either BDD or SAT based solvers) and serves as language based front-end to these technologies. The semantics is synchronous and thus well adapted to modeling of hardware components, but makes expression of asynchronous behaviors cumbersome.

In Sect. 3.2 we have already discussed the use of Prolog as a pivot language, and its limitations, e.g., related to partial order reduction or symmetry detection.

For program verification, the Boogie language (Microsoft) [6] is expressly designed as an intermediate language, helping to bridge the gap from programs to SMT based verification engines. Initially designed to support Spec#, i.e. annotated .Net bytecode, it has been extended to cover a host of programming languages using this intermediate language approach. All of these input languages thus benefit from improvements made to the verification engine (development of interpolants, new verification conditions,...).

The standard format SMT-lib [7] for SMT problems is itself a pivot intermediate language sharing many design goals with an IVL, but with a broader scope than the pivot languages considered in this paper.

Focusing more on concurrent semantics and finite state systems, the Guarded Action Language (GAL) [71] is an IVL that is supported by a decision diagram based symbolic verification engine. It helps bridge the gap between asynchronous and concurrent systems expressed in a variety of formalisms (Promela, Petri nets, timed automata,...) and a symbolic expression of their transition relation.

Section 4.2 presents the design choices we made when defining this language and the architecture of the ITS-tools model checker built around it.

Domain Specific Languages and Verification. This intermediate language approach integrates well with current model-based industrial practice. It helps solve two large stumbling blocks that prevent more widespread adoption of model checking. Firstly, due to automated translations, the end-user is isolated from ever needing to know about the specifics of how the verification is performed. This reduces adoption cost since training software engineers to build formal models is a difficult task, and helps achieve the "push-button" promise of automated verification. Secondly, the DSL models are developed with several purposes in mind, that typically include code generation or simulation. This means the models developed have precise behavioral semantics necessary for analysis, and also reduces the gap between what you prove correct (the formal model) and the running system. Provided the translations are correct and consistent with one another, the running system and the formal model both conform to the semantics of the DSL. Verification of the more abstract DSL is however usually easier than analyzing models extracted from actual implementations of the design.

Language Engineering. Language engineering using metamodeling technology has evolved rapidly over the last two decades, pushed by the OMG consortium and the development of the UML standard. Because UML is a particularly complex language, with a very broad scope, new technologies for model definition and manipulations were defined based on the concept of metamodel. These tools are now mature with industry strength quality (e.g. EMF [70]), and can be applied to a variety of models and languages that bear no relationship with UML.

In a model-centric approach, a metamodel is defined to describe a language, where models are instances of this metamodel. Because the metamodel is itself an instance of a metametamodel, common to all language definitions, powerful tools can be engineered that take a language (a metamodel) as input.

Tools such as XText [28] make development of new languages easier, with a full-blown modern end user experience (code completion, on the fly error detection...) available at a very low development cost.

Using model transformations to build formal models expressed in an IVL can thus be done using several alternative technological paths [27], and is well-understood by modern software engineers. This facilitates third-party adoption.

Technology Agnostic. The underlying verification engine is weakly constrained by an intermediate language approach. Model checking can use structural analysis, SAT technology, decision diagrams, explicit state... with solvers implemented in any programming language.

Because an IVL offers a complete view of the semantics to the analysis tools (in the absence of black-box behavior such as embedded code) it is still possible to write property specific abstractions such as slicing and simplifications such as constant removal. Such abstractions can usually be expressed as a transformation to a simpler model expressed in the same language. Hence all analysis tools benefit from their existence. Section 5.3 will present how some of these issues can be addressed using a *greybox* API (e.g. to provide partial order reduction), but the abstractions that can be offered using an IVL are more powerful in general.

Modular Decomposition. Support for modular definition of a specification in the IVL is highly desirable. It helps support modular verification scenarios where only part of the system is analyzed to prove system-wide properties. This requires some weak hypothesis on how a component interacts with its environment to make compositional reasoning possible. The Mocha environment [4] uses such compositional reasoning, thanks to founding the semantics with reactive modules [3]. Other examples based on I/O automata [55], assume/guarantee contracts for components [59], or asynchronous composition such as in CADP [32] try to exploit compositional reasoning to provide simpler proofs.

4.2   GAL Within ITS-Tools

ITS-tools offers model checking (CTL, LTL) of large concurrent specifications expressed in a variety of formalisms: communicating process (Promela, DVE), timed specifications (Uppaal timed automata, time Petri nets) and high-level Petri nets. The tool is focused on verification of (large) globally asynchronous locally synchronous specifications. Its architectures is presented in Fig. 4.

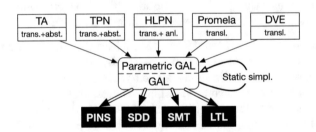

Fig. 4. Instantiation of the modular architecture for ITS-tools

It leverages model transformation technology to support model checking of domain specific languages (DSL). Models are transformed to the Guarded Action Language (GAL), a simple yet expressive language with finite Kripke structure semantics.

Guarded Action Language. GAL is a pivot language that essentially describes a generator for a labeled finite Kripke structure using a C like syntax. This simple yet expressive language makes no assumptions on the existence of high-level concepts such as processes or channels. While direct modeling in GAL is possible (and a rich eclipse based editor is provided), the language is mainly intended to be the target of a model transformation from a (high-level) language closer to the end-users.

A **GAL** model contains a set of integer variables and fixed size integer arrays defining its state, and a set of guarded transitions bearing a label chosen from a finite set. We use C 32 bit signed integer semantics, with overflow effects; this ensures all variables have a finite (if large 2^{32}) domain. GAL offers a rich signature consisting of all C operators for manipulation of the int and boolean data type and of arrays (including nested array expressions). There is no explicit support for pointers, though they can be simulated with an array *heap* and indexes into it. In any state (i.e. an assignment of values to the variables and array cells of the GAL) a transition whose boolean guard predicate is true can fire executing the statements of its body in a single atomic step. The body of the transition is a sequence of statements, assigning new values to variables using an arithmetic expression on current variable values. A special *call*(λ) statement allows to execute the body of any transition bearing label λ, modeling non-determinism as a label based synchronization of behaviors.

Parametric GAL. specifications may contain parameters, that are defined over a finite range. These parameters can be used in transition definitions, compactly representing similar alternatives. They can also be used to define finite iterations (for loop), and as symbolic constants where appropriate. Parameters do not increase expressive power, the verification engine does not know about them, as specifications are instantiated before model checking. The tool applies rewriting strategies on parametric transitions before instantiation, in many cases avoiding the polynomial blowup in size resulting from a naive parameter instantiation. Rewriting rules that perform static simplifications (constant identification, slicing, abstraction...) of a GAL benefit all input formalisms.

Model to Model Transformations. Model-driven engineering (MDE) proposes to define domain specific languages (DSL), which contain a limited set of domain concepts [73]. This input is then transformed using model transformation technology to produce executable artifacts, tests, documentation or to perform specific validations. In this context GAL is designed as a convenient target formally expressing model semantics. We thus provide an EMF [70] compliant meta-model of GAL that can be used to leverage standard meta-modeling tools to write model to model transformations. This reduces the adoption cost of using formal validation as a step of the software engineering process.

Third-Party Support. We have implemented translations to GAL for several popular formalisms used by third party tools. We rely on XText for several of these: with this tool we define the grammar and meta-model of an existing formalisms, and it generates a rich code editor (context sensitive code completion, on the fly error detection,...) for the target language. For instance, we applied this approach to the Promela language of Spin [39] and the Timed Automata of Uppaal [9].

For Promela, channels are modeled as arrays, processes give rise to control variables that reflect the state they are in. A first analysis of Promela code is necessary to build the underlying control flow graph (giving an automaton for each process). There is currently no support for functions and the C fragment of Promela. The support for TA and TPN uses discrete time assumptions, and will be detailed in Sect. 6.2.

Solution Engines. The main solution engine offered by ITS-tools is a symbolic model checker relying on state of the art decision diagram (DD) technology. A more recent addition is an SMT based encoding of GAL semantics, that enables a bounded model checking/induction decision procedure for safety properties. This SMT encoding also enables many static analysis tests such as computing interference between events that enable precise partial order reductions. A bridge from GAL to the PINS API (see Sect. 5) enables the many solution engines offered by LTSmin.

GAL thus successfully plays the pivot role of an intermediate verification language, allowing to separately choose the input language and the solution engine for verification. This approach is, however, not always applicable, e.g., when embedded code is associated with a model or when executing the high-level source language requires constraint solving not present in the intermediate language (cf., Sect. 3.2). The API approach presented in the next section is one solution for this problem.

5   The API Approach to Reusing Verification Engines

The focus in this section is on generic programming interfaces (API) between formal specification languages and model checking algorithms. The underlying wish is to reuse software implementations of model checking algorithms for specifications in different formal languages.

Semantically, the operational semantics of a specification language gives rise to a transition system, with labels on states or transitions, or both. Model checking algorithms can be viewed as graph algorithms over these transition systems. Many model checking algorithms operate *on-the-fly*, intertwining state space generation with analysis. In many cases, in particular when hunting for counter examples, only a fraction of the complete state space is visited. To facilitate this, the state space graph is often exposed to the algorithm through an API, providing the functionality to compute the desired part of the graph.

Black-Box API. Clearly, a black-box view on states and transitions would provide maximal genericity. Here states are opaque objects for the model checker and it just needs a function to retrieve the initial state, and another one to compute the next states of any given state. All information on the internal structure of states and transitions are nicely encapsulated in language modules specific to a formal language.

A prominent example of this approach is the OPEN/CAESAR interface [30], which allows the CADP toolset to operate on input models in various process algebra-oriented languages, like Lotos, LNT, EXP and FSP. This facilitates the reuse of backend algorithms in CADP for model checking, bisimulation checking and reduction, test generation, simulation and visualisation. The OPEN/CAESAR architecture also allowed to link external toolsets, for instance μCRL and LTSmin.

Greybox API, PINS. The disadvantage of a black-box API is that it prohibits many methods for mitigating the state space explosion. For instance, state space compression techniques, symbolic model checking and partial-order reduction require information on the structure of states and transitions. For this reason, the toolset LTSmin [14,42] introduced a *greybox API*, called PINS, the Partitioned Interface to the Next-State function, cf. Fig. 5. Here states are partitioned in vectors of N chunks, and the transition relation is partitioned into M subtransitions that operate on a *part* of the state vector. Depending on the specification language and the intended granularity, chunks can represent state variables, program counters, or subprocesses. Transitions could represent lines or blocks of code, or synchronized communication actions. Finally, the language frontend provides a static Dependency Matrix (DM) that declares which chunks in the state vector are affected by a certain transition group. Thus, locality of transitions is exposed to the model checking algorithms. See Table 1 for further details.

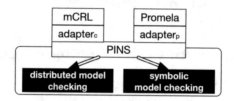

Fig. 5. Original instantiation of the modular architecture in LTSmin

Table 1. Parameters and functions of the PINS greybox API

N	Fixed length of the state vector
M	Number of disjunctive transition groups
init()	Function that returns the initial state vector
next(s, i, f)	Function that calls back f on any successor of s in transition group i
DM[M][N]	Dependency Matrix of Booleans: DM[i][j] means transition group i depends on variable j

In the sequel, we demonstrate how gradually exposing more structure enables more and more model checking techniques to be applied, basically following the historical development of the LTSmin toolset.

5.1   Distributed and Multi-core Model Checking

In distributed model checking, it must be frequently tested whether a locally generated successor state already exists globally. This is usually solved by sending (batches of) states over the network to the machine that "owns" them.

Ultimately, the network bandwidth forms the performance bottleneck of this approach. In this section, we show how partitioning the state vector enables state space compression and leads to a reusable solution.

A distributed database and compression scheme was proposed for the μCRL toolset [13], which reduced the bandwidth to roughly two integers per state. That compression approach depends on (recursively) indexing the first and second half of a state vector, thus forming a binary tree of databases. The leaves of this tree consist of an index of algebraic data terms of μCRL. A piggy-backing scheme ensured global consistency of all databases.

The original motivation of the LTSmin toolset [14] was to offer this approach to multiple model checkers with their own specification languages, in particular to Promela models in SPIN. There were three considerations to combine these languages for distributed model checking: First, the interface had to support the action-based process algebra μCRL, as well as the state-based Promela models of SPIN. Also, besides the algebraic data-types of μCRL, it had to support the direct machine integer-representation of SPIN models. Finally, the database compression technique required access to various parts of a single state. These considerations led to the greybox PINS interface (Table 1), supporting both state and edge labels, and assuming and exposing a fixed-length state vector.

The separation provided by PINS turned out to be quite versatile for further experimentation: Initially, we conceived to link the MPI/C code of the distributed model checker directly to SPIN generated code, but this was deemed to be too fragile. The PINS interface allowed to switch freely to NIPS-VM, a virtual machine to interpret Promela models, and to SpinJa, a compiler for SPIN models. Actually, these experiments can be viewed as instances of combining a fixed API to various intermediate language representations in the spirit of Sect. 4.

Currently, LTSmin supports an arbitrary number of edge and state labels, allowing to handle for instance Mealy machines (input/output), probabilistic automata (actions/probabilities) and games (actions/players). By now, several more language modules have been constructed, enabling to reuse the same model checking algorithms for DVE (DiViNE), PetriNets (PNML), mCRL2, Timed Automata (Uppaal, cf. Sect. 6.2), B models (PROB, cf. Sect. 6.1), etc.

Finally, when we developed new multi-core algorithms, based on concurrent hash tables in shared memory and concurrent tree compression [48], the PINS interface allowed to effortlessly and directly carry out scalability experiments on benchmark models from this large variety of specification languages.

5.2 Symbolic BDD-Based Model Checking

The effectiveness of state compression can be explained from the locality of transitions, leading to the relative independence of the system components (e.g. processes). Binary Decision Diagrams (BDD) provide even more opportunities to compress sets of state vectors, by sharing common prefixes and suffixes. Can we gain more than just a concise representation? Here we want to emphasize that by exposing transition locality explicitly, we can also achieve computations on sets of states. That is, we obtain the benefits of traditional symbolic model checking for models that are only provided through an on-the-fly API, without requiring a symbolic specification of the transition relation.

The main idea is that the static dependency matrix DM provided by PINS allows to deduce much information from one next-state call, in particular when the dependency-matrix is sparse (i.e., there is a lot of locality). Consider a state vector $x_0, \ldots, x_n$ in which a transition group t_k is enabled, that only affects $x_0, \ldots, x_i$, according to the DM. Then we can deduce the following two facts:

- All successors are of the form $x'_0, \ldots, x'_i, x_{i+1}, \ldots, x_n$
- All states of the form $x_0, \ldots, x_i, y_{i+1}, \ldots, y_n$ have successors from transition group t_k of the form $x'_0, \ldots, x'_i, y_{i+1}, \ldots, y_n$.

The short pair $x_0, \ldots, x_i \mapsto x'_0, \ldots, x'_i$ can be stored in a local BDD R_k and reused in relational product computations during further state space generation.

So, the PINS interface allows full-fledged symbolic model checking for explicit-state specification languages (Promela, mCRL2, DVE, PROB, etc.) without the need for manual symbolic encodings or automated model translations. The price to pay is that every language module should define transition groups at some level of granularity, and perform some kind of static analysis to identify the dependencies on state variables. Rough overapproximations of the dependency matrix are still correct, but more precise analyses expose more locality. This effort has to be performed for every specification language only once, and a precise analysis is rewarded by a more efficient model checker for that language.

Again, the PINS architecture proved to be very flexible, allowing experiments with among others Multiway Decision Diagrams, List Decision Diagrams, and also scalable multi-core implementations of decision diagrams [25] on a wide variety of benchmark models in many specification languages.

Another lesson learnt was that exposing more information leads to more efficient model checking. This seems obvious, but the sweet spot is not clear. In [57] we experimented with splitting transition groups in *guards* and *updates*, refining the Dependency Matrix to distinguish *read-* from *write*-dependencies. This led to considerable performance gains in symbolic model checking.

Note that existing language modules wouldn't profit from this refinement, but at least they don't break. Implementing the refined analysis for some specification language is incentivized by a more efficient model checking procedure.

5.3   Other Extensions as Pins2Pins Wrappers

So far we showed that the PINS-API allows combining multiple model checking algorithms with multiple specification languages, increasing the efficiency for the whole research community. We can take this one step further: a single state space optimization technique could be reused for *any* model checking algorithm and *any* specification language. This is supported by rewiring, using so-called PINS2PINS-wrappers, as in Fig. 6, which remotely resemble Unix-pipes: The original model is available on-the-fly to the PINS2PINS wrapper, which in

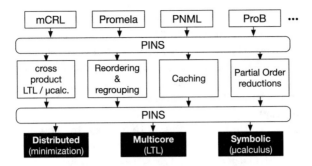

Fig. 6. On-the-fly state space transformers provided as PINS2PINS-wrappers in LTSmin

turns provides the reduced state space in an on-the-fly manner to the actual model checker. In reality, this involves a quite complicated rewiring of the call-back mechanism.

We will discuss a couple of instances. A simple instance is transition-caching: For highly expressive specification languages the next-state calculation will be slow. In case of high locality (sparse Dependency Matrix), it could pay off to have an intermediate caching layer that stores the results of all next-state calls for future reuse. This cache has to be implemented once, and can be reused for all models in all supported specification languages and for all model checking algorithms. (Note that this is not helpful for the symbolic model checker, since it already stores these transitions in the local BDDs R_k.)

A second example is reordering state variables and regrouping similar transition groups. It is well-known that the variable order greatly influences the efficiency of symbolic model checking. We investigated if the information from the read-write Dependency Matrix is sufficient to compute a good static variable order. The PINS interface with its DM allowed to apply many bandwidth reduction algorithms on matrices out-of-the box, and enabled us to compare them experimentally across multiple specification languages and multiple decision diagram types [25]. At the same time, we noticed that having too many transition groups leads to a considerable overhead. So the regrouping layer also recombines several transition groups that indicate the same (or similar) dependencies.

A third example is the computation of cross-products. For LTL model checking, the cross-product with a Büchi automaton is conveniently provided as a PINS2PINS-wrapper. For μ-calculus model checking, another PINS2PINS-wrapper computes the product of an LTS and a Boolean Equation System, resulting in a Parity Game (using the fact that LTSmin supports multiple edge labels to encode players and priorities). A more generic product automata wrapper, that could support compositional model checking, is under construction.

Finally, we shortly discuss some experiments with partial-order reduction. We investigated if the DM contains sufficient information to implement state space reduction based on the stubborn-set approach to POR [72]. The bad news is that the achieved reductions would be suboptimal: from the DM it can only be deduced that two subtransitions are independent (e.g. t_k doesn't modify variables that t_ℓ reads or writes). However, to achieve the full effectiveness of POR we had to extend the DM with new matrices, basically indicating whether transition groups can enable each other. More precisely, one can exploit refined guard splitting: A new matrix indicates whether executing transition group t_ℓ could enable or disable guard g_i.

The good news is that extending PINS with information on enabling/disabling relations between transition groups, allows the full reduction power of stubborn-set POR method [47]. LTSmin comes up with a reasonable default for the new POR-related matrices. Language modules that take the effort to derive more precise transition dependencies are again rewarded with more effective state space reduction power. Thus, a partial-order reduction block can be provided, which is suitable for all specification language modules implementing PINS and potentially supports all model checking algorithms based on the PINS interface.

One may wonder if this provides effective partial-order reduction for symbolic model checking? Unfortunately, after partial order reduction all dependency information is lost, so symbolic model checking on the reduced state space would be correct, but not effective. Similarly, in the case of timed automata, all transitions involve manipulating the clocks, so partial-order reduction of TA is correct, but not effective. Positive cases, where POR is effective, are the explicit multi-core model checking algorithms, both for safety and LTL properties, applied to mCRL2, Promela, DVE, PNML, or B models.

6   Application Examples

This section shows how the variants of the modular approach (library-based or language-based) can be instantiated in real situations.

6.1   PROB to LTSmin API: Linking High-Level Languages with Other Model Checkers

In [10] we have presented a first integration of PROB with LTSmin. We thereby managed to keep the full power of the constraint solving of PROB's Prolog interpreter to compute successor states for complicated events (see Sect. 3). But we also gained access to the symbolic model checking engine of LTSmin, to construct a symbolic BDD-style representation of the reachable states. For some experiments, this resulted in the reduction of the model checking time of an order of magnitude or more. The crux lies in the fact that through the greybox API, LTSmin gains information about read/write dependencies of events, which is crucial to build up the symbolic representation of the state space. Note that PROB's representation of B's datastructures are hidden to LTSmin: LTSmin does not need to know about higher-order sets and relations, nor about symbolic representations for infinite B functions, just to mention a few possible data values.

All LTSmin needs to know is the variables of the B model and the read-write dependencies. For example, suppose we have a state $\langle x = 10, y = \{\{2\}, \{4\}\}\rangle$ (where the variable y is a set of sets) and the event inc produces the single successor state $\langle x = 11, y = \{\{2\}, \{4\}\}\rangle$. Given the information that inc reads and writes only x, LTSmin knows, without having to query PROB, that the only successor of $\langle x = 10, y = \{\{1, 2\}\}\rangle$ is $\langle x = 11, y = \{\{1, 2\}\}\rangle$.

On a technical side, the communication was achieved by ZeroMQ. In ongoing work [44] the bridge has been extended to support partial order reduction and parallel LTL model checking, again with sometimes impressive speedups compared to PROB's internal explicit state model checker.

6.2   Analysis of Timed Automata

Uppaal's networks of timed automata are the de facto standard for the high-level specification of real time systems, with a well-integrated tool support in the Uppaal tool suite. For this reason, Uppaal is also used as a target of model transformation, as an IVL. Uppaal's efficient solver is based on zone based abstraction with subsumption. However, due to its tight integration, Uppaal uses a monolithic approach (Fig. 7a): all algorithms are tightly connected to Uppaal models, and not available as open source components, except the DBM library, which offers zone abstraction through Difference Bound Matrices.

We discuss two approaches to analyze Uppaal models using the API approach (linking Uppaal to LTSmin) or the IVL approach (translating Uppaal models to GAL specifications as in ITS-Tools).

LTSmin Approach.   A bridge between Uppaal and LTSmin was devised, cf. Fig. 7b, which supports full multi-core LTL model checking of Uppaal networks of timed automata [46]. The advantage of this approach is that it maximizes code reuse. It uses OPAAL to generate C-code from Uppaal models, which was adapted to implement the PINS interface. Furthermore, the next-state function directly calls the DBM-library. For LTSmin's multi-core algorithms, a state vector just contains an opaque pointer to a DBM to represent a symbolic time zone. In

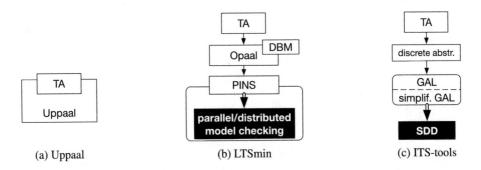

(a) Uppaal   (b) LTSmin   (c) ITS-tools

Fig. 7. Three architectures for TA model checkers.

this way, Uppaal users obtain a scalable multi-core LTL model checker in a transparent manner.

Two issues arise, however: First, timed automata based on timed zones have abstract states, which require subsumption for efficient state space reduction. This was solved by (again) extending the PINS interface with an extra function (to reuse the DBM-library for checking subsumption of symbolic states). Another issue is that time manipulation happens in every transition group, which leads to a dense dependency matrix. Hence symbolic model checking and partial-order reduction are not effective on timed automata.

ITS-Tools. The support for TA uses discrete time assumptions to be able to model the semantics using GAL, as in Fig. 7c. Fortunately, analysis in the discrete setting has been shown to be equivalent to analysis in a dense time setting provided all constraints in the automata are of the form $x \leq k$ but not $x < k$ [37]. We thus can build a transition that represents a one time unit delay and updates clocks appropriately. This transition is in fact a sequence of tests for each clock, checking if an urgent time constraint is reached (time cannot elapse), if the clock is active (increment its counter) or if it is inactive either because it will be reset before being read again, or because it has reached a value greater than any it could be tested against before a reset (do nothing). This test for inactive clocks corresponds to an abstraction that preserves observable behaviors, but prevents clock values from growing indefinitely, yielding an infinite state space.

Strengths. This discrete time approach is very effective to deal with systems where the number of concurrently enabled locations or clocks grows, since in such cases the classic explicit state with zones represented as DBM does not scale well. However, when the maximum bounds on clocks grow, even decision diagrams have trouble dealing with the state space explosion in the discrete setting. The two approaches thus have good complementarity, allowing to address different kinds of systems.

Weaknesses. Overall the main difficulty when developing support for timed automata is that the classical dense time semantics of TA cannot be feasibly encoded just using GAL which have discrete semantics. The correctness of switching to discrete semantics was fortunately already established [37], but in general mapping of arbitrary semantics to GAL is not always possible. It is much easier to map arbitrary semantics to a language such as Prolog (see Sect. 3.2) but this comes at the cost of verification power and efficiency. The discrete time models have a very large state space, and cannot feasibly be analyzed using non symbolic solution engines, so despite the pivot language approach, the choice of this path limits the choice of the solution engine. However explicit state approaches are of course still available on TA using the Uppaal verifier or LTSmin.

7   Discussion

This paper summarizes the evolution of modern model checking tools in terms of their architecture and usage to solve typical industrial-like problems, which are more and more stated using high-level, domain specific languages instead of the "traditional" specification languages. Moreover, complementary techniques are often used to solve particular situations. For example, explicit techniques may scale less but algorithms to compute counter-examples are simpler. On the contrary, symbolic techniques usually scale better but computation of a counter example is not trivial.

To cope with such situations, an intermediate level has been introduced, the pivot representation, which provides a modular architecture to link high-level specifications with a backend for verification. This pivot representation can be either a library offering an API, or a language itself. Both approaches co-exist today and show their own advantages and drawbacks. This is of interest to enable transparent activation of a given technique. This can be seen as a configuration issue (choice of a technique/algorithm at a given stage of the verification process) or to some preprocessing phase. It is thus particularly important to benefit from a large portfolio of techniques available in a given environment, and linked to the pivot representation. Such a situation is observed in the Model Checking Contest [43] where some tools concurrently operate several techniques and retrieve results from the first that finishes. Let us also refer to CIL that is used as an entry in the software competition to operate various tools and techniques (or PNML that has a similar role in the model checking contest).

In both approaches, the problem of translating counter examples back to the user level exists. Due to their tight integration, monolithic architectures can also offer an integrated user experience, which can be viewed as an advantage. For modular approaches, it takes some effort to link between transformations (this is typically supported by MDE-based approaches) but this is more difficult when there are several translations (e.g. optimization phases).

Embedding external code is possible within the API-approach, as long as one respects the absence of side effects. This is an attractive feature for verifying systems using complex data structures or libraries. The API approach also allows to reuse existing implementations of the operational semantics of specification languages. As a consequence, the transition relation is more opaque, isolating verification algorithms from the actual representation. This possibly disables some abstraction opportunities. We demonstrated how greybox API solutions (PINS) disclose sufficient structural information to enable some important optimizations, like state compression, partial-order reduction and decision-diagram representations.

The use of a reified intermediate verification language as a pivot preserves the semantics completely. This means that more solution engines remain available, such as SMT solvers for encoding data abstractions. The translation needs to be complete and true to the original semantics. This requires more effort, which may be hard or impossible in some cases due to the semantic gaps in expressivity when source and target languages differ too much (i.e., the translation of B to SMV in fact generates the full state space during the translation). Potential loss of the modular structure of specifications during the translation could also be a drawback, since this structure contains useful information that can in general be exploited by model checking heuristics.

The field of model checking is moving fast: new algorithms, improved data structures and high-performance implementations are emerging all the time. This also leads to new application domains, with their own domain-specific, high-level modeling languages. Within these dynamics, intermediate representations provide some stability, by decoupling verification algorithms from high-level specifications. This paper presents a decade of research in sophisticated intermediate representations, either as intermediate verification languages, or as on-the-fly greybox interfaces. Despite an improved understanding of the relationship between verification capabilities and features of the intermediate representation, a "golden standard API", or a "holy grail IVL" has not yet emerged. On the contrary, the building blocks of model checking architectures are also still in development. Fortunately, the approaches that we have reported combine very well from a methodological point of view. Several language translations and optimisations can be composed; the resulting "flattened" specification is easily adapted to an API; and several building blocks can be combined through plug-and-play with the API. We demonstrated that through these successful combinations one can obtain very efficient model checkers for high-level specification languages.

Acknowledgements. We would like to thank the many people who have worked on the various verification tools such as LTSMin and ProB. In particular, we want to thank Jens Bendisposto, Philipp Körner, Jeroen Meijer, Helen Treharne, Jorden Whitefield for their work on the ProB to LTSmin API described in Sect. 6.1.

We also thank Stefan Blom, Michael Weber, Elwin Pater for setting up the architecture of LTSmin and Alfons Laarman, Tom van Dijk, Jeroen Meijer for recent developments on multicore and symbolic LTSmin.

On the ProB side we are grateful to many researchers and developers who have contributed to the tool or its underlying techniques, notably Michael Butler, Joy Clark, Ivaylo Dobrikov, Marc Fontaine, Fabian Fritz, Dominik Hansen, Sebastian Krings, Thierry Massart, Daniel Plagge, David Schneider, Joshua Schmidt, Corinna Spermann.

We finally thank the many colleagues who contributed to the development and algorithms for ITS-Tools, in particular, Béatrice Bérard, Denis Poitrenaud, Maximilien Colange, Yann Ben Maïssa, and many master students.

The third author has been partially funded from the 4TU NIRICT.BSR project on Big Software on the Run.

References

1. Abrial, J.R.: The B-Book. Cambridge University Press, Cambridge (1996)
2. Abrial, J.R.: Modeling in Event-B: System and Software Engineering. Cambridge University Press, Cambridge (2010)
3. Alur, R., Henzinger, T.A.: Reactive modules. Formal Methods Syst. Des. **15**(1), 7–48 (1999)
4. Alur, R., Henzinger, T.A., Mang, F.Y.C., Qadeer, S., Rajamani, S.K., Tasiran, S.: MOCHA: modularity in model checking. In: Hu, A.J., Vardi, M.Y. (eds.) CAV 1998. LNCS, vol. 1427, pp. 521–525. Springer, Heidelberg (1998). https://doi.org/10.1007/BFb0028774

5. Arnold, A., Point, G., Griffault, A., Rauzy, A.: The altarica formalism for describing concurrent systems. Fundam. Inform. **40**(2–3), 109–124 (1999)
6. Barnett, M., Chang, B.-Y.E., DeLine, R., Jacobs, B., Leino, K.R.M.: Boogie: a modular reusable verifier for object-oriented programs. In: de Boer, F.S., Bonsangue, M.M., Graf, S., de Roever, W.-P. (eds.) FMCO 2005. LNCS, vol. 4111, pp. 364–387. Springer, Heidelberg (2006). https://doi.org/10.1007/11804192_17
7. Barrett, C., Fontaine, P., Tinelli, C.: The SMT-LIB standard: version 2.6. Technical report, Department of Computer Science, The University of Iowa (2017). www. SMT-LIB.org
8. Barrett, C., Stump, A., Tinelli, C.: The SMT-LIB standard: version 2.0. In: Gupta, A., Kroening, D. (eds.) Proceedings of the 8th IW on Satisfiability Modulo Theories, Edinburgh, UK (2010)
9. Behrmann, G., David, A., Larsen, K.G., Håkansson, J., Pettersson, P., Yi, W., Hendriks, M.: UPPAAL 4.0. In: QEST, pp. 125–126. IEEE Computer Society (2006)
10. Bendisposto, J., Körner, P., Leuschel, M., Meijer, J., van de Pol, J., Treharne, H., Whitefield, J.: Symbolic reachability analysis of B through PROB and LTSMIN. In: Ábrahám, E., Huisman, M. (eds.) IFM 2016. LNCS, vol. 9681, pp. 275–291. Springer, Cham (2016). https://doi.org/10.1007/978-3-319-33693-0_18
11. Berthomieux, B., Bodeveix, J.P., Filali, M., Lang, F., Le Botland, D., Vernadat, F.: The syntax and semantic of fiacre. Technical report 7264, CNRS-LAAS (2007)
12. Bjørner, N., Gurfinkel, A., McMillan, K., Rybalchenko, A.: Horn clause solvers for program verification. In: Beklemishev, L.D., Blass, A., Dershowitz, N., Finkbeiner, B., Schulte, W. (eds.) Fields of Logic and Computation II. LNCS, vol. 9300, pp. 24–51. Springer, Cham (2015). https://doi.org/10.1007/978-3-319-23534-9_2
13. Blom, S., Lisser, B., van de Pol, J., Weber, M.: A database approach to distributed state-space generation. J. Log. Comput. **21**(1), 45–62 (2011)
14. Blom, S., van de Pol, J., Weber, M.: LTSMIN: distributed and symbolic reachability. In: Touili, T., Cook, B., Jackson, P. (eds.) CAV 2010. LNCS, vol. 6174, pp. 354–359. Springer, Heidelberg (2010). https://doi.org/10.1007/978-3-642-14295-6_31
15. Bordini, R.H., Fisher, M., Visser, W., Wooldridge, M.: Verifying multi-agent programs by model checking. Auton. Agent. Multi-Agent Syst. **12**(2), 239–256 (2006)
16. Borges, R.M., Mota, A.C.: Integrating UML and formal methods. Electron. Notes Theor. Comput. Sci. **184**, 97–112 (2007). 2nd Brazilian Symposium on Formal Methods (SBMF 2005)
17. Butler, M., Leuschel, M.: Combining CSP and B for specification and property verification. In: Fitzgerald, J., Hayes, I.J., Tarlecki, A. (eds.) FM 2005. LNCS, vol. 3582, pp. 221–236. Springer, Heidelberg (2005). https://doi.org/10. 1007/11526841_16
18. Butler, M.J., Colley, J., Edmunds, A., Snook, C.F., Evans, N., Grant, N., Marshall, H.: Modelling and refinement in CODA. In: Derrick, J., Boiten, E.A., Reeves, S. (eds.) Proceedings 16th International Refinement Workshop, Refine@IFM 2013, Turku, Finland, 11 June 2013. EPTCS, vol. 115, pp. 36–51 (2013)
19. Cimatti, A., Clarke, E., Giunchiglia, E., Giunchiglia, F., Pistore, M., Roveri, M., Sebastiani, R., Tacchella, A.: NuSMV 2: an opensource tool for symbolic model checking. In: Brinksma, E., Larsen, K.G. (eds.) CAV 2002. LNCS, vol. 2404, pp. 359–364. Springer, Heidelberg (2002). https://doi.org/10.1007/3-540-45657-0_29
20. Clarke, E.M., Emerson, E.A., Sifakis, J.: Model checking: algorithmic verification and debugging (turing award 2007). Commun. ACM **52**(11), 74–84 (2009)

21. Correa, T., Becker, L.B., Farines, J., Bodeveix, J., Filali, M., Vernadat, F.: Supporting the design of safety critical systems using AADL. In: 15th IEEE International Conference on Engineering of Complex Computer Systems, ICECCS, pp. 331–336. IEEE Computer Society (2010)
22. Cousot, P., Cousot, R., Feret, J., Mauborgne, L., Miné, A., Monniaux, D., Rival, X.: The ASTREÉ analyzer. In: Sagiv, M. (ed.) ESOP 2005. LNCS, vol. 3444, pp. 21–30. Springer, Heidelberg (2005). https://doi.org/10.1007/978-3-540-31987-0_3
23. Delzanno, G., Podelski, A.: Model checking in CLP. In: Cleaveland, W.R. (ed.) TACAS 1999. LNCS, vol. 1579, pp. 223–239. Springer, Heidelberg (1999). https://doi.org/10.1007/3-540-49059-0_16
24. Delzanno, G., Podelski, A.: Constraint-based deductive model checking. STTT 3(3), 250–270 (2001)
25. van Dijk, T., van de Pol, J.: Sylvan: multi-core decision diagrams. In: Baier, C., Tinelli, C. (eds.) TACAS 2015. LNCS, vol. 9035, pp. 677–691. Springer, Heidelberg (2015). https://doi.org/10.1007/978-3-662-46681-0_60
26. Duret-Lutz, A., Lewkowicz, A., Fauchille, A., Michaud, T., Renault, É., Xu, L.: Spot 2.0 — a framework for LTL and ω-automata manipulation. In: Artho, C., Legay, A., Peled, D. (eds.) ATVA 2016. LNCS, vol. 9938, pp. 122–129. Springer, Cham (2016). https://doi.org/10.1007/978-3-319-46520-3_8
27. Eclipse Project: Model-to-Model Transformation MMT, subproject of Eclipse Modeling (2017). https://projects.eclipse.org/projects/modeling.mmt
28. Efftinge, S., et al.: XText (2017). http://www.eclipse.org/Xtext/
29. Fioravanti, F., Pettorossi, A., Proietti, M.: Verifying CTL properties of infinite-state systems by specializing constraint logic programs. In: Proceedings of VCL 2001, Florence, Italy, September 2001
30. Garavel, H.: OPEN/CÆSAR: an open software architecture for verification, simulation, and testing. In: Steffen, B. (ed.) TACAS 1998. LNCS, vol. 1384, pp. 68–84. Springer, Heidelberg (1998). https://doi.org/10.1007/BFb0054165
31. Garavel, H.: Nested-unit petri nets: a structural means to increase efficiency and scalability of verification on elementary nets. In: Devillers, R., Valmari, A. (eds.) PETRI NETS 2015. LNCS, vol. 9115, pp. 179–199. Springer, Cham (2015). https://doi.org/10.1007/978-3-319-19488-2_9
32. Garavel, H., Lang, F., Mateescu, R.: Compositional verification of asynchronous concurrent systems using CADP. Acta Inf. 52(4–5), 337–392 (2015)
33. Girault, C., Valk, R.: Petri Nets for Systems Engineering - A Guide to Modeling, Verification, and Applications. Springer, Heidelberg (2003). https://doi.org/10.1007/978-3-662-05324-9
34. Groote, J.F., Ponse, A., Usenko, Y.S.: Linearization in parallel pcrl. J. Log. Algebr. Program. 48(1–2), 39–70 (2001)
35. Havelund, K., Pressburger, T.: Model checking java programs using java pathfinder. Int. J. Softw. Tools Technol. Transf. 2(4), 366–381 (2000). https://doi.org/10.1007/s100090050043
36. Hayes, I., Jones, C.B.: Specifications are not (necessarily) executable. Softw. Eng. J. 4(6), 330–338 (1989)
37. Henzinger, T.A., Manna, Z., Pnueli, A.: What good are digital clocks? In: Kuich, W. (ed.) ICALP 1992. LNCS, vol. 623, pp. 545–558. Springer, Heidelberg (1992). https://doi.org/10.1007/3-540-55719-9_103
38. Hoare, C.A.R.: Communicating sequential processes. Commun. ACM 21(8), 666–677 (1978)
39. Holzmann, G.: Spin Model Checker, The: Primer and Reference Manual. Addison-Wesley Professional, Boston (2003)

40. Hopcroft, J.E., Ullman, J.D.: Introduction to Automata Theory, Languages and Computation. Addison-Wesley, Boston (1979)
41. Iliasov, A., Lopatkin, I., Romanovsky, A.: The SafeCap platform for modelling railway safety and capacity. In: Bitsch, F., Guiochet, J., Kaâniche, M. (eds.) SAFE-COMP 2013. LNCS, vol. 8153, pp. 130–137. Springer, Heidelberg (2013). https://doi.org/10.1007/978-3-642-40793-2_12
42. Kant, G., Laarman, A., Meijer, J., van de Pol, J., Blom, S., van Dijk, T.: LTSmin: high-performance language-independent model checking. In: Baier, C., Tinelli, C. (eds.) TACAS 2015. LNCS, vol. 9035, pp. 692–707. Springer, Heidelberg (2015). https://doi.org/10.1007/978-3-662-46681-0_61
43. Kordon, F., Garavel, H., Hillah, L.M., Paviot-Adet, E., Jezequel, L., Rodríguez, C., Hulin-Hubard, F.: MCC'2015 – the fifth model checking contest. In: Koutny, M., Desel, J., Kleijn, J. (eds.) Transactions on Petri Nets and Other Models of Concurrency XI. LNCS, vol. 9930, pp. 262–273. Springer, Heidelberg (2016). https://doi.org/10.1007/978-3-662-53401-4_12
44. Körner, P.: An integration of ProB and LTSmin. Master's thesis, Universität Düsseldorf, February 2017
45. Kroening, D., Tautschnig, M.: CBMC – C bounded model checker. In: Ábrahám, E., Havelund, K. (eds.) TACAS 2014. LNCS, vol. 8413, pp. 389–391. Springer, Heidelberg (2014). https://doi.org/10.1007/978-3-642-54862-8_26
46. Laarman, A., Olesen, M.C., Dalsgaard, A.E., Larsen, K.G., van de Pol, J.: Multicore emptiness checking of timed Büchi automata using inclusion abstraction. In: Sharygina, N., Veith, H. (eds.) CAV 2013. LNCS, vol. 8044, pp. 968–983. Springer, Heidelberg (2013). https://doi.org/10.1007/978-3-642-39799-8_69
47. Laarman, A., Pater, E., van de Pol, J., Hansen, H.: Guard-based partial-order reduction. STTT 18(4), 427–448 (2016)
48. Laarman, A., van de Pol, J., Weber, M.: Multi-core LTSMIN: marrying modularity and scalability. In: Bobaru, M., Havelund, K., Holzmann, G.J., Joshi, R. (eds.) NFM 2011. LNCS, vol. 6617, pp. 506–511. Springer, Heidelberg (2011). https://doi.org/10.1007/978-3-642-20398-5_40
49. Lamport, L.: Specifying Systems, The TLA+ Language and Tools for Hardware and Software Engineers. Addison-Wesley, Boston (2002)
50. Leuschel, M., Butler, M.: ProB: a model checker for B. In: Araki, K., Gnesi, S., Mandrioli, D. (eds.) FME 2003. LNCS, vol. 2805, pp. 855–874. Springer, Heidelberg (2003). https://doi.org/10.1007/978-3-540-45236-2_46
51. Leuschel, M., Fontaine, M.: Probing the depths of CSP-M: a new FDR-compliant validation tool. In: Liu, S., Maibaum, T., Araki, K. (eds.) ICFEM 2008. LNCS, vol. 5256, pp. 278–297. Springer, Heidelberg (2008). https://doi.org/10.1007/978-3-540-88194-0_18
52. Leuschel, M., Massart, T.: Infinite state model checking by abstract interpretation and program specialisation. In: Bossi, A. (ed.) LOPSTR 1999. LNCS, vol. 1817, pp. 62–81. Springer, Heidelberg (2000). https://doi.org/10.1007/10720327_5
53. Liu, Y., Sun, J., Dong, J.S.: PAT 3: an extensible architecture for building multidomain model checkers. In: IEEE 22nd International Symposium on Software Reliability Engineering, ISSRE 2011, Hiroshima, Japan, 29 November–2 December 2011, pp. 190–199 (2011)
54. Lowe, G.: Casper: a compiler for the analysis of security protocols. J. Comput. Secur. 6(1–2), 53–84 (1998)
55. Lynch, N.A., Tuttle, M.R.: Hierarchical correctness proofs for distributed algorithms. In: PODC, pp. 137–151. ACM (1987)

56. Margaria, T., Nagel, R., Steffen, B.: jETI: a tool for remote tool integration. In: Halbwachs, N., Zuck, L.D. (eds.) TACAS 2005. LNCS, vol. 3440, pp. 557–562. Springer, Heidelberg (2005). https://doi.org/10.1007/978-3-540-31980-1_38

57. Meijer, J., Kant, G., Blom, S., van de Pol, J.: Read, write and copy dependencies for symbolic model checking. In: Yahav, E. (ed.) HVC 2014. LNCS, vol. 8855, pp. 204–219. Springer, Cham (2014). https://doi.org/10.1007/978-3-319-13338-6_16

58. Meyer, R., Faber, J., Hoenicke, J., Rybalchenko, A.: Model checking duration calculus: a practical approach. Formal Asp. Comput. 20(4–5), 481–505 (2008)

59. Păsăreanu, C.S., Dwyer, M.B., Huth, M.: Assume-guarantee model checking of software: a comparative case study. In: Dams, D., Gerth, R., Leue, S., Massink, M. (eds.) SPIN 1999. LNCS, vol. 1680, pp. 168–183. Springer, Heidelberg (1999). https://doi.org/10.1007/3-540-48234-2_14

60. Ramakrishnan, C.R., Ramakrishnan, I.V., Smolka, S.A., Dong, Y., Du, X., Roychoudhury, A., Venkatakrishnan, V.N.: XMC: a logic-programming-based verification toolset. In: Emerson, E.A., Sistla, A.P. (eds.) CAV 2000. LNCS, vol. 1855, pp. 576–580. Springer, Heidelberg (2000). https://doi.org/10.1007/10722167_48

61. Roscoe, A.W.: The Theory and Practice of Concurrency. Prentice-Hall, Upper Saddle River (1999)

62. Roscoe, A.W., Gardiner, P.H.B., Goldsmith, M.H., Hulance, J.R., Jackson, D.M., Scattergood, J.B.: Hierarchical compression for model-checking CSP or how to check 10^{20} dining philosophers for deadlock. In: Brinksma, E., Cleaveland, W.R., Larsen, K.G., Margaria, T., Steffen, B. (eds.) TACAS 1995. LNCS, vol. 1019, pp. 133–152. Springer, Heidelberg (1995). https://doi.org/10.1007/3-540-60630-0_7

63. Samia, M., Wiegard, H., Bendisposto, J., Leuschel, M.: High-level versus low-level specifications: comparing B with Promela and ProB with spin. In: Proceedings TFM-B 2009, pp. 49–61. APCB, June 2009

64. Schröter, C., Schwoon, S., Esparza, J.: The model-checking kit. In: van der Aalst, W.M.P., Best, E. (eds.) ICATPN 2003. LNCS, vol. 2679, pp. 463–472. Springer, Heidelberg (2003). https://doi.org/10.1007/3-540-44919-1_29

65. Snook, C., Butler, M.: UML-B: a plug-in for the Event-B tool set. In: Börger, E., Butler, M., Bowen, J.P., Boca, P. (eds.) ABZ 2008. LNCS, vol. 5238, p. 344. Springer, Heidelberg (2008). https://doi.org/10.1007/978-3-540-87603-8_32

66. Spivey, J.M.: The Z Notation: A Reference Manual. Prentice-Hall, Upper Saddle River (1992)

67. Stefanescu, A., Wieczorek, S., Schur, M.: Message choreography modeling. Softw. Syst. Model. 13(1), 9–33 (2014)

68. Steffen, B., Claßen, A., Klein, M., Knoop, J., Margaria, T.: The fixpoint-analysis machine. In: Lee, I., Smolka, S.A. (eds.) CONCUR 1995. LNCS, vol. 962, pp. 72–87. Springer, Heidelberg (1995). https://doi.org/10.1007/3-540-60218-6_6

69. Steffen, B., Margaria, T., Braun, V.: The electronic tool integration platform: concepts and design. STTT 1(1–2), 9–30 (1997)

70. Steinberg, D., Budinsky, F., Paternostro, M., Merks, E.: EMF: Eclipse Modeling Framework 2.0, 2nd edn. Addison-Wesley Professional, Boston (2009)

71. Thierry-Mieg, Y.: Symbolic model-checking using ITS-tools. In: Baier, C., Tinelli, C. (eds.) TACAS 2015. LNCS, vol. 9035, pp. 231–237. Springer, Heidelberg (2015). https://doi.org/10.1007/978-3-662-46681-0_20

72. Valmari, A.: A stubborn attack on state explosion. Formal Methods Syst. Des. 1(4), 297–322 (1992)

73. Voelter, M., et al.: DSL Engineering - Designing, Implementing and Using Domain-Specific Languages (2013). dslbook.org

74. Woodcock, J., Cavalcanti, A., Freitas, L.: Operational semantics for model checking Circus. In: Fitzgerald, J., Hayes, I.J., Tarlecki, A. (eds.) FM 2005. LNCS, vol. 3582, pp. 237–252. Springer, Heidelberg (2005). https://doi.org/10.1007/11526841_17

75. Ye, K., Woodcock, J.: Model checking of state-rich formalism Circus by linking to CSP ∥ B. STTT **19**(1), 73–96 (2017)

76. Yu, Y., Manolios, P., Lamport, L.: Model checking TLA$^+$ specifications. In: Pierre, L., Kropf, T. (eds.) CHARME 1999. LNCS, vol. 1703, pp. 54–66. Springer, Heidelberg (1999). https://doi.org/10.1007/3-540-48153-2_6

77. Zhu, H., Sun, J., Dong, J.S., Lin, S.: From verified model to executable program: the PAT approach. ISSE **12**(1), 1–26 (2016)

The 10,000 Facets
of MDP Model Checking

Christel Baier[1], Holger Hermanns[2], and Joost-Pieter Katoen[3,4](✉)

[1] TU Dresden, Dresden, Germany
[2] Saarland University, Saarbrücken, Germany
[3] RWTH Aachen University, Aachen, Germany
katoen@cs.rwth-aachen.de
[4] University of Twente, Enschede, The Netherlands

Abstract. This paper presents a retrospective view on probabilistic model checking. We focus on Markov decision processes (MDPs, for short). We survey the basic ingredients of MDP model checking and discuss its enormous developments since the seminal works by Courcoubetis and Yannakakis in the early 1990s. We discuss in particular the manifold facets of this field of research by surveying the verification of various MDP extensions, rich classes of properties, and their applications.

1 Introduction

Markov decision processes (MDPs) have their roots in operations research and stochastic control theory. They are frequently used for stochastic and dynamic optimization problems and are widely applicable, see e.g., [151]. For instance, in 1957 Bellman [23] introduced MDPs by considering the following problem: a machine can produce either perfect or defective items and can breakdown requiring repair. Breakdowns and producing defective items are random phenomena, e.g., depending on the machine's age. When to decide whether to inspect the machine for a failure, or to just wait until a defective item is produced? If a defective item is produced, does one repair, inspect other sources of failure, or order new machine parts? These decisions depend amongst other on the costs of repair, inspection, and producing defective parts. This setting is naturally modelled as an MDP: the number of items produced so far is the state, breakdowns and producing defective or perfect items are probabilistic moves, inspections and repairs are decisions (a.k.a.: actions), and costs are modelled as rewards associated to actions in a given state.

The central problem for MDPs [74] is to find a policy (or strategy) required to determine what action to take in the light of what is known about the system at the time of choice. The typical aim is to optimize a given objective, such as minimizing expected cost until a given number of repairs, maximizing the probability of a system being operational for a large number of steps or minimizing the long-run average costs. The former two are known as finite horizon objectives, the latter as infinite time horizon objectives. These optimization problems

B. Steffen and G. Woeginger (Eds.): Computing and Software Science, LNCS 10000, pp. 420–451, 2019.
https://doi.org/10.1007/978-3-319-91908-9_21

can be cast as dynamic programming problems—Bellman equations—that are typically solved by value or policy iteration [133], or reinforcement learning [142].

This paper surveys approaches to tackle MDP problems from the perspective of *probabilistic model checking* (PMC) [17,107,113]. It determines for an MDP $\mathcal{M}$ and a property specification φ, typically expressed as a formula in mathematical logic or as a finite-state automaton, whether $\mathcal{M}$ satisfies φ. Under the hood, it uses graph algorithms, value or policy iteration, compact data structures, etc. so as to achieve a *fully automated* procedure. The use of logics enables to express the classical finite and infinite time-horizon MDP objectives, but also (new) intricate and complex objectives, or even mixtures thereof.

The power of PMC is that no matter how complex the logical guarantee, it is automatically checked which states in the MDP satisfy it. Neither manual manipulations of MDPs (or their high-level descriptions) are needed, nor expertise on any of its analysis techniques is required. Effective abstraction, reduction, and symbolic techniques curb the "curse of dimensionality" problem. Diagnostic feedback is provided in case $\mathcal{M}$ does not satisfy φ, giving useful insight in the reason of the refutation. More importantly though, is that PMC automatically obtains an optimal policy for the specification φ as a by-product of the verification procedure. PMC thus offers a flexible and powerful framework for MDP analysis.

In addition to the original application areas of MDP analysis such as operations research and stochastic control theory, MDP model checking is employed in several areas of computer science. Examples are randomized distributed algorithms, robotics, security and communication protocols, dynamic resource management, multimedia protocols and many more. We briefly give an idea for the first two.

For the class of randomized distributed algorithms, randomization provides an elegant way to break the symmetry between identical processes. This is perhaps best illustrated by the consensus problem: how to get a distributed network of processors to agree on a common bit. In the setting where processors communicate in an asynchronous manner and only one processor might crash, there is no distributed algorithm that solves this problem. This is the well-known FLP impossibility result [77]. If, however, a process can make a decision based on its internal state, its messages, and some coin-flip mechanism, consensus in this setting is almost surely possible [24]. Randomized mutual exclusion and leader-election algorithms naturally can be modelled as MDPs in which non-determinism naturally models the concurrent evolution of processes [147].

Another emerging application area of MDP model checking is the field of *robotics*. Robots have to perform tasks in uncertain environments (possibly involving humans) and may operate with errors in their sensing and actuation resulting in uncertainty when detecting and responding to its current state. Robot movements are modelled as being non-deterministic, and planning amounts to find an optimal control policy such that the robot achieves certain tasks (like picking up objects in a given order) while traversing a safe trajectory. A specification φ formally specifies which tasks are to be executed. In contrast to simulation, PMC offers formal guarantees about robot behaviour by providing bounds on how likely the robot satisfies its specification. As a by-product of the model checking, an optimal robot strategy is synthesized that can be used to construct controllers. PMC is applied in this context e.g., to analyze the probabilistic behavior of a robot operating with errors in its sensing and actuation [103] or to check whether robot swarms indeed behave as required [112]. More advanced applications of PMC include the analysis and repair of control policies using parametric probabilistic models [131] and the generation of policies using multi-objective model checking that ensure to achieve several objectives in a given order of priority: maximize the probability of finishing a task; maximize progress towards completion, if this is not possible; and minimize the expected time or cost required [119].

Purpose and Organization of This Paper. This paper reflects on the developments in MDP model checking and surveys its state-of-the-art. It is impossible to give a complete treatment of all works and developments on MDP model checking; this paper reflects the main directions and achievements from the perspective of the authors. The paper is written in an informal manner; numerous citations are provided to more detailed literature.

Section 2 introduces MDPs and the central problem in MDP model checking: determining reachability probabilities. Section 3 discusses several facets of MDPs such as costs, parametric probabilities, MDPs with intervals, MDPs with random delays, and MDPs whose state is only partially observable. Section 4 presents the kind of property specifications that can be treated by MDP model checking. Section 5 gives some insight in the techniques in tackling the state-space explosion problem in MDP model checking. Finally, Sect. 6 concludes this survey paper.

2   MDP Model Checking in a Nutshell

2.1   What are MDPs?

Markov decision processes (MDPs [102, 133]) are transition systems in which in any state a non-deterministic choice between a finite set of probability distributions exists. On reaching a state s in an MDP, non-deterministically a distribution $\mu \in \mathcal{D}(s)$ is selected, where $\mathcal{D}(s)$ is the set of available distributions (over the MDP's state space) in s. The next state is determined according to μ. That is, state s' is selected with probability $\mu(s')$. It is assumed that $\mathcal{D}(s) \neq \emptyset$ for each state s. Every MDP for which $|\mathcal{D}(s)| = 1$ in every state s, is a Markov chain (MC, for short). Paths in an MDP are infinite alternating sequences of pairs of states and distributions: (s_i, μ_i) where $\mu_i \in \mathcal{D}(s_i)$ and $\mu_i(s_{i+1}) > 0$, for each i. A probability measure Pr on such paths can be defined using the cylinder set construction provided for each state s_i it is known which distribution μ_i has been selected. This decision maker is a *policy*, also referred to as scheduler or adversary, that in state s_i selects a distribution $\mu \in \mathcal{D}(s_i)$. Several types of policies do exist. Two ingredients are relevant: on the basis of which information does a policy make a decision, and does it use randomization to do so, or not. Positional policies decide solely on the current state s_i and not on the history, i.e., the prefix of the path until reaching s_i. Randomized positional policies select $\mu \in \mathcal{D}(s_i)$ with a certain probability. Deterministic policies select a fixed distribution from $\mathcal{D}(s_i)$. History-dependent policies base their decision on the prefix $s_0 \mu_0 s_1 \mu_1 \cdots \mu_{i-1} s_i$. Such policies may thus depend on e.g., the states visited so far, the actions taken so far, the frequency of visiting states, and the order in which states have been visited. As a policy resolves the non-determinism in an MDP, it yields an (possibly infinite-state) MC.

2.2 Reachability

One of the elementary questions in MDP analysis is whether a certain set T of target states can be reached almost surely, i.e., with probability one. As the likelihood to reach T depends on how the non-determinism is resolved, one considers minimal, or dually, maximal probabilities. Let $\Pr_s^{\max}(\lozenge T)$ denote the maximal probability to reach some state in T starting from s. That is, $\Pr_s^{\max}(\lozenge T)$ is the supremum over all possible policies to reach T under such policy. A graph analysis suffices to determine all states s for which this probability equals one. It does so by iteratively eliminating all states for which $\Pr_s^{\max}(\lozenge T) < 1$. First all states that cannot reach T are removed as well as their incoming transitions. All states without outgoing transitions are then deleted. This is repeated as long as no change is possible anymore. Also all states for which $\Pr_s^{\max}(\lozenge T) = 0$ can be obtained by a polynomial-time graph analysis, and similar applies to minimal reachability probabilities. Graph algorithms also suffice for checking whether any ω-regular property holds almost surely [147].

Quantitative reachability amounts to check whether the probability to reach T exceeds a threshold different from one, like $4/7$. For a finite-state MDP, let variable $x_s = \Pr_s^{\max}(\lozenge T)$ for state s. The following recursive characterization will be helpful. If T is not reachable from s, then $x_s = 0$; if $s \in T$, then $x_s = 1$. For all other cases:

$$ x_s = \max \left\{ \sum_{t \in S} \mathbf{P}(s, \mu, t) \cdot x_t \mid \mu \in \mathcal{D}(s) \right\} $$

where $\mathbf{P}(s, \mu, t)$ denotes the probability to move from state s to t when selecting distribution μ in s. This is an instance of the Bellman equation. It is well known that for every finite MDP, a deterministic positional policy does exist that attains $\Pr_s^{\max}(\lozenge T)$. Value or policy iteration, and linear programming are computational techniques to obtain these policies. Linear *in*equation systems are thus key for reachability objectives in finite-state MDPs. Value iteration can be mildly amended such that it halts at the correct moment, i.e., when the iteratively computed probabilities truly converge [88].

Example 1. Consider the following stochastic job scheduling problem: complete n jobs on k identical processors under a pre-emptive scheduling policy. Once a job completes, all k processors can be assigned any of the m remaining jobs.

Pre-empted jobs need to be started from scratch. When $n - m$ jobs are finished, this yields $\binom{m}{k}$ non-deterministic choices. A property of interest is: what is the minimal expected time to complete all jobs? Or: what is the maximal probability to complete all jobs within 10,000 steps? We consider the scenario as given in [40] where the service time of job i is given by a negative exponential distribution with rate λ_i. (Here, we do not consider the timing yet; only the branching probabilities induced by these dealsy matter.) This job-shop scheduling problem can be naturally modelled as an MDP, where a state corresponds to the jobs that still need to be executed, scheduling decisions are actions, and the discrete probability distributions $\mathcal{D}(s)$ in state s are determined by the rates of the service times of the jobs that are being scheduled. The MDP for four jobs and two machines is indicated in Fig. 1. The initial state (left) contains all jobs, the rightmost state represents the completion of all four jobs. Each transition corresponds to a selection of two jobs that are scheduled. Probabilities are determined as follows. If one of the scheduled jobs, say job i, finishes in a situation where m jobs have not been processed yet, an event that happens with probability $p_{i,j} = \frac{\lambda_i}{\lambda_i + \lambda_j}$ (where j is the number of the other selected, but unfinished job), $m - 1$ jobs remain, and a new selection is made. It is known that the largest-expected-service-time-first-policy is optimal to minimize the expected time to complete all jobs [40].

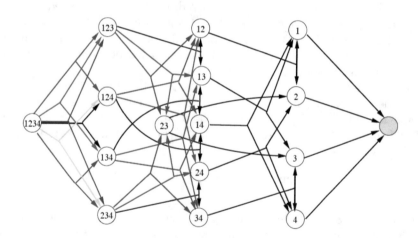

Fig. 1. Possible schedules for 4 jobs on 2 machines, modelled as an MDP.

3   The Manifold Facets of MDPs

This section considers several features of MDPs: costs (where each transition incurs a certain cost), parameters (where probabilities are unknowns and given as e.g., polynomials over a set of variables), partial observability (where the state of an MDP is only partially visible), and continuous time (where state residence times are governed by negative exponential distributions).

3.1 Costs

Already in Bellman's treatment [23], MDPs have been equipped with rewards (a.k.a.: gains), or dually costs. Costs are associated to transitions and are constant non-negative real values that are incurred on taking a transition. Thus, on selecting distribution μ in state s a reward $c(s, \mu)$ is earned. The cumulative reward of a finite path fragment in an MDP is the sum of all transition costs of the transitions on that path fragment. Typical MDP objectives are the maximal expected cost to reach a state in T (provided T can almost surely be reached), the maximal long-run average cost, and so forth. These objectives can be easily cast as Bellman equations and can be achieved by deterministic positional policies. If a constraint is imposed on the cumulative cost, e.g., what is the minimal probability to reach a bad state with a cumulative reward below a given threshold, finite-memory policies that keep track of the cumulative cost up to the decision point, i.e., the current state, are needed. A simple cost function associates cost one to each transition; in fact, the property "what is the maximal probability to complete all jobs within 10,000 steps?" in Example 1 refers to the cumulative cost in that case.

3.2 Parameters

In various circumstances, certain system quantities such as failure probabilities, packet loss ratios, etc. are often not—or at the best partially—known. In that setting, *parametric* MDPs where transition probabilities are specified as polynomials over real-valued parameters are useful. The problem of *parameter synthesis* is: Given a finite-state parametric MDP, what are all the parameter values for which a given property exceeds (or is below) a given fixed threshold? For the job-shop scheduling problem, an example of a synthesis problem is to determine the unknown job durations such that all jobs can be completed with a total expected duration of two days, say. Parameter synthesis typically amounts to partition the parameter space into safe and unsafe regions. A safe region contains all parameter valuations for which the property-of-interest is satisfied, while the unsafe region is its complement. In practise, typically not a full coverage can be achieved, but a large (say, >95%) coverage is aimed for. Existing parameter synthesis techniques use heuristics and sampling [89], or obtain over-approximations by replacing parametric transitions by non-deterministic choices over extremal parameter values resulting in a two-player stochastic game that is analyzed using standard means [134]. If for certain parameter regions, the result is inconclusive, the region is refined, and the procedure is repeated until a certain coverage is achieved. Parameter synthesis for parametric MDP models of about 100,000 states and two to four parameters have been reported [134]. Recently, geometric programming has been proposed to treat parameter synthesis for multi-objective parametric MDPs [51]; this provides a polynomial-time algorithm to obtain approximations that are arbitrarily close. Several instances of parametric Markovian models have been discussed in the literature, such as bounded-parameter MDPs [83] and interval MDPs [96,98], MDPs where the transition probabilities are known to lie within certain upper and lower bounds. This model is rooted in interval Markov chains introduced by Jonsson and Larsen [104] in the context of a specification theory for probabilistic systems.

3.3 Partial Observability

Partially observable MDP (POMDPs, for short) models generalize MDPs by relaxing the assumption that the state of the system is completely observable. POMDPs play an important role in, e.g., mobile robot navigation, probabilistic planning and multi-agent systems where each agent can access its own variables, but cannot view the variables and locations of the other agents. A POMDP models a decision process in which it is assumed that the system dynamics are determined by an MDP, but the policy cannot directly observe the underlying state. Instead a policy considers equivalence classes of states, states for which the observations are equal, and base their decision on these equivalence classes rather than on the states themselves. A POMDP thus is an MDP $\mathcal{M}$ equipped with an equivalence relation over its states. de Alfaro [59] has shown that checking whether for some policy the POMDP stays within a set T of target states is positive, is EXPTIME-complete. Many other model-checking problems for POMDPs have shown to be undecidable using reductions from the emptiness (or other undecidable problems) for probabilistic language acceptors, which can be seen as "fully blind" POMDPs where all states have the same observable [6, 12, 123]. Let us give some simple examples for undecidable problems for POMDPs. Checking the existence of a policy where the expected cost until reaching a goal state exceeds some threshold is undecidable, and so are other policy-existence problems for alternative expected cost criteria such as discounted or long-run average cost objectives [123]. These results have been shown using reductions from the emptiness problem for probabilistic finite automata. The inapproximability results for probabilistic finite automata carry over to POMDPs with expected total or long-run average costs [123]. However, there are several algorithms for the analysis of POMDPs under finite-horizon objectives as well as approximation algorithms for infinite-horizon discounted cost objectives [122] or expected cost objectives for POMDPs with positive cost functions [46]. The decidability of the value 1 problem that asks whether there are policies under which a reachability property holds with probability arbitrarily close to 1, has been established for a subclass of POMDPs [81].

Qualitative verification problems for MDPs, such as the problem to decide the existence of a policy ensuring that a goal state will be visited infinitely often almost surely, only depend on the graph structure of the MDP, but not on the precise transition probabilities. This facilitates efficient graph algorithms for checking qualitative verification problems in MDPs, possibly in combination with automata-based approach to represent complex path properties. The situation in POMDPs is different as such qualitative properties can depend on the transition probabilities. Indeed, the policy-existence problem for qualitative repeated reachability properties where the task is to check whether for some policy some state in T is visited infinitely often with positive probability is undecidable. This has been shown using reductions from the emptiness problem for probabilistic Büchi automata [6,12]. However, decidability and EXPTIME-completeness has been established for qualitative verification problems against ω-regular specifications when restricting to finite-memory policies [47].

3.4 Exponential Delays

Continuous-time MDPs [85] (CTMDPs, for short) are MDPs in which the state residence time is governed by a negative exponential distribution. The rate of this exponential distribution depends on the current state and the probability distribution μ that is used to determine the next state. Accordingly, the average residence time in state s under taking distribution μ is given by $1/r(s,\mu)$. Rate $r(s,\mu)$ thus determines the random residence time in state s provided distribution μ is selected in s by the policy. Paths in CTMDPs are infinite sequence of triples (s_i, t_i, μ_i) where t_i denotes the residence time in state s_i given that distribution μ_i has been selected. Policies in CTMDPs can decide on the basis of the states visited and the selected distributions so far, but may also exploit the elapsed time (in every state). This gives rise to uncountably many policies. It for instance, makes a difference whether a policy decides on entering a state (early) or on leaving a state (late) after delaying in that state. A categorisation of the class of policies for CTMDPs is given in [127]. Costs can be added to CTMDPs in the same vein as for MDPs except that the incurred cost linearly depends on the state residence time. That is, on selecting action μ after residing t time units in state s with cost rate $c(s,\mu)$, the cost $c(s,\mu)\cdot t$ is incurred.

Example 2. Consider the stochastic job scheduling problem again (see Example 1). Rather than considering time-abstract properties such as minimizing the expected completion time, we are now interested in: what is the maximal/minimal probability to finish all jobs within a given deadline. This requires to considering the timing behaviour of the job scheduling. Note that if jobs i and j are currently being scheduled, and i finishes first, then the elapsed time is determined by the rate λ_i. Due to the memoryless property of the exponential distribution, the remaining execution time of the pre-empted job j remains exponentially distributed with rate λ_j.

Other Forms of Stochastic Delays. Probabilistic extensions of timed automata exist [129]; they are known as probabilistic timed automata (PTA). Their edges are discrete probability distributions over states. PTA are finite symbolic representations of uncountable MDPs—as clock valuations are real values. Nondeterminism is inherited from timed automata. Computing reachability probabilities in PTA is decidable via a region graph-like construction. Whereas in PTA clocks are deterministic, stochastic timed automata [25] (STA) provide a stochastic interpretation to clocks. In STA, unbounded clocks are interpreted as negative exponential distributions, whereas bounded clocks obey a uniform distribution. Stochastic interpretations of TA are also used in statistical model checking [55].

4   The Manifold MDP Properties

This section considers a spectrum of properties that can be addressed by MDP model checking: probabilistic CTL, various variations of reachability objectives (expected cost until reaching a target state, total cost until reaching such state, quantiles, reachability with time deadlines, repeated reachability etc.), multiple objectives that need to be fulfilled simultaneously, mean payoff and long-run objectives, as well as energy/weight objectives, conditional probabilities. We also briefly discuss obtaining permissive policies, and counterexample generation.

4.1   Probabilistic CTL

PCTL [27,93] is a variant of the well-known computation tree logic (CTL). It replaces the universal and existential quantification over paths by an operator that expresses a bound on the probability of all paths satisfying a path-formula. In the setting for MDPs, the formula $\Phi = \mathbb{P}_{>p}(\varphi)$ asserts that regardless of the resolution of the non-determinism, the likelihood of the set of paths satisfying φ exceeds p. Formally, $s \models \mathbb{P}_{>p}(\varphi)$ if and only if for all policies it holds that $\Pr_s^\sigma(\varphi) > p$, where $\Pr^\sigma$ refers to the probability measure under the policy σ at hand. Stated differently, PCTL-formula $\mathbb{P}_{>p}(\varphi)$ holds in state s whenever $\Pr_s^{\min}(\varphi)$ exceeds p. Here, $\Pr_s^{\min}(\varphi)$ denotes the infimum of the probability of the set of φ-paths under all policies. For finite MDPs, this corresponds to the minimum over all policies, as a finite-memory policy suffices. A dual formulation holds for $\mathbb{P}$-formulas that have a probability upper bound. The model checking of a finite MDP against a PCTL-formula Φ can be done using a recursive descent over the parse tree of Φ. For each sub-formula of Φ the set of states is determined that satisfy this sub-formula. For reachability objectives, and until-formulas— reach a Φ_2-state via Φ_1-states only—this can be done using solving a linear equation system whose size is proportional to the number of states in the MDP. This yields a model-checking algorithm that is polynomial in the size of the MDP $\mathcal{M}$ and linear in the size of the PCTL-formula Φ; for details we refer to [17, Chap. 10.6].

4.2   Expected Costs Until Reaching a Target

For an MDP equipped with costs, a natural objective is to consider the expected cost until reaching some target state in T. For an infinite path through an MDP, let the cumulative cost until reaching T be defined as the sum of all costs until reaching some state in T for the first time, and undefined in case such state does not exist, i.e., the path does never reach T. A policy σ is said to be proper if T will be reached almost surely under σ, i.e., $\Pr_s^\sigma(\lozenge T) = 1$ for all states s. The expected reward for a state s under a given proper policy σ from which T will almost surely be reached is then the weighted sum over all σ-paths from s to T of their cumulative cost up to reaching T times their probability. If there is at least one proper policy and all costs are non-negative, the minimal expected cumulative costs are achieved by a deterministic positional policy and are computable in much the same way as extremal reachability probabilities by linear programming techniques, policy or value iteration [26,58]. The supremum of the expected cumulative costs until reaching T over all proper policies might be infinite. If the costs are non-negative then the latter can be checked in polynomial time. If the supremum is finite then a deterministic positional policy maximizing the expected cumulative costs until reaching T exist and is computable again using similar techniques as for extremal reachability probabilities [58].

4.3   Cost-Bounded Reachability

Whereas positional policies suffice for reachability (and long run) objectives, step- or cost-bounded reachability objectives require finite-memory policies [97]. The same applies to ω-regular properties. For $\Diamond^{\leq k} T$, i.e., can a state in T be reached while the accumulated costs are bounded by k, this can be intuitively understood as follows. Consider a state with two choices: one that almost surely leads to T but with high costs, and one that may lead to T directly with low costs, but with a certain probability ends up in a state from which T can never be reached. Then, depending on the cost bound left to reach T, an optimal policy will decide for the (first) safe choice, whereas the remaining cost bound to reach T is small, it picks the (second) unsafe strategy. Computing policies maximizing the probability for a cost-bounded event $\Diamond^{\leq k} T$ is known to be computationally hard, namely PSPACE-hard even for acyclic MDPs [86]. An exponential-time algorithm is obtained by using an iterative approach that successively computes the values $p_{s,i}$ for the maximal probability to reach T with cost-bound i from state s for $i = 0, 1, \ldots, k$. For this, we can rely on a variant of the Bellman equations

$$p_{s,i} = \max\left\{ \sum_{t \in S} \mathbf{P}(s, \mu, t) \cdot p_{t, \max\{i - c(s, \mu), 0\}} \;\middle|\; \mu \in \mathcal{D}(s) \right\}$$

for $s \notin T$ and T reachable from s. If $0 < c(s, \mu)$ is positive then the values $p_{t, \max\{i - c(t, \mu), 0\}}$ have been computed in a previous iteration. Zero-cost actions can be treated using linear programming techniques [9].

4.4   Quantiles

In quantile objectives, one considers computing the minimal cost bound k such that with probability at least p the target set T will be reached before the cumulative costs exceeds k. Qualitative quantile objectives (i.e., $p = 0$ or $p = 1$) can be determined in polynomial time, whereas an exponential-time algorithm for quantitative quantile objectives (where p belongs to the open interval $(0, 1)$) exists that relies on the successive computation of cost-bounded reachability probabilities [9,146]. Quantile objectives for MDPs with multiple cost functions for several pay-off criteria have been considered in [137].

4.5   Timed Reachability

In CTMDPs, policies that base their decision on the current state as well as the total cumulative time so far, the so-called total-time positional deterministic policies are optimal for timed reachability objectives—given a set T of target states and a deadline d, what is the maximal probability to reach T within d? This is the continuous counterpart of a policy in MDPs for bounded reachability $\Diamond^{\leq k} T$ where the total number of steps taken so far is needed to achieve optimality. PMC algorithms for timed reachability determine ϵ-close approximations of the optimal total-time positional deterministic policy. Timed reachability objectives can be tackled via a discretization yielding an MDP on which a corresponding step-bounded reachability problem is solved using value iteration. The smallest number of steps needed in the discretized MDP to guarantee an accuracy of ϵ is $\frac{\lambda^2 \cdot d^2}{2\epsilon}$, where λ is the largest rate of a state residence time in the CTMDP at hand [128]. In a similar way, minimal timed reachability probabilities can be obtained as well as their corresponding policies. Tighter bounds with slightly different discretization techniques have been obtained in [42,136]. A comparative empirical study shows that a simple greedy algorithm, originally developed for uniform models [16], can be lifted to the general setting, where it often outperforms all other approaches [44]. The duality between costs (at states) and time is discussed in [15] thereby enabling the use of algorithms for timed reachability for the purpose of computing cost-bounded reachability. Optimal policies for multi-cumulative cost reachability properties in CTMDPs are treated in [79].

Example 3. Consider timed reachability for the job-shop scheduling problem of Example 1 with exponential service times. That is, we focus on what is the probability to complete all jobs within a given deadline d? The results of applying this discretization on the example with 4 jobs and two machines is shown in Fig. 2 where the deadline d is given on the x-axis and the reachability probability on the y-axis. For equally distributed job durations, the maximal and minimal probabilities coincide. Otherwise, the probabilities depend on the scheduling policy. It turns out that the ϵ-optimal policy that maximizes the reachability probabilities adheres to the SEPT (shortest expected processing time first) strategy; moreover, the optimal ϵ-policy for the minimum probabilities obeys the LEPT (longest expected processing time first) strategy.

4.6   Beyond Reachability

Repeated reachability events or persistence probabilities can be obtained by considering maximal end-components [50,56], the MDP counterpart to bottom strongly connected components in Markov chains. An end component $\mathcal{E}$ of an MDP $\mathcal{M}$ is a sub-MDP of $\mathcal{M}$ whose induced graph is strongly connected. $\mathcal{E}$ is called maximal if there is no other end component $\mathcal{E}'$ that contains $\mathcal{E}$. A crucial observation made by de Alfaro [56] is that under each policy σ, the limit of almost all σ-paths constitutes an end component. Here, the limit of an infinite path π is the set of state-distribution pairs that occur infinitely often in π. Thus,

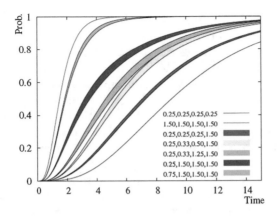

Fig. 2. Minimal and maximal reachability probabilities for finishing 4 jobs on 2 machines under a pre-emptive scheduling strategy.

maximal probability for a repeated reachability condition $\Box\Diamond T$ ("infinitely often T") is computable as the maximal probability to reach a maximal end component containing at least one T-state.

Determining the maximal probability of an ω-regular property φ in an MDP $\mathcal{M}$ amounts to determining the maximal probability to reach an accepting end component in the product of $\mathcal{M}$ with a deterministic ω-automaton for φ [21,50,56]. An accepting end component is an end component that satisfies the acceptance condition of the deterministic ω-automaton at hand. This procedure involves a double-exponential blow-up caused by (1) transforming an LTL formula into an ω-automaton, and (2) determinizing this automaton. In fact, no algorithm of lower complexity can be expected as the question, whether $\mathrm{Pr}_{\mathcal{M},s_0}^{\max}(\varphi) = 1$ for a given MDP $\mathcal{M}$ with initial state s_0 and LTL-formula φ, is 2EXPTIME-complete [50]. Recent practical advancements on converting LTL, an important temporal logic for expressing a large class of ω-regular properties, into deterministic ω-automata have been reported in [70].

4.7   Fairness

When using MDPs as an interleaving model for systems composed by several probabilistic processes, establishing liveness properties often requires fairness assumptions for the resolution of nondeterministic choices that rule out pathological cases where, e.g., one process never performs an action. In this context, one considers only fair policies, i.e., policies where a certain fairness assumption holds almost surely. The analysis of MDPs under fair policies has been considered in the context of LTL and PCTL-like logics [14,21,148]. Suppose *fair* is a realizable fairness assumption in the sense that there exists a fair policy τ such that *fair* holds with probability 1 from each state under this policy τ. Then, a fair policy maximizing the probability to reach a target T under all fair policies is obtained by first computing a positional (possibly unfair) policy σ maximizing the probability for $\Diamond T$ from each state where the maximum is taken over all policies. We then modify σ to a fair policy ν that behaves as σ until reaching T, in which case it switches mode and behaves as τ from then on. Thus, $\sup_{\sigma \text{ fair}} \Pr_s^\sigma(\Diamond T) = \max_{\sigma \text{ fair}} \Pr_s^\sigma(\Diamond T) = \Pr_s^{\max}(\Diamond T)$, which shows that realizable fairness is irrelevant for maximizing reachability probabilities. This does not hold when the task to find a fair policy minimizing the probability for reaching T. Consider, for example, an MDP with a state s that has two nondeterministic alternatives: either stay in s via action α or to move to a target state $t \in T$ via action β (both with probability one). If we suppose strong fairness for action β, i.e., each fair policy that visits s infinitely often with positive probability needs to take eventually action β in state s. Then, the probability to reach T from s is one under each fair policy, while $\Pr_s^{\min}(\Diamond T) = 0$. However, a fair policy minimizing the probability for reaching T can be obtained using the following fact (again we suppose realizability of the fairness condition):

$$\min_{\sigma \text{ fair}} \Pr_s^\sigma(\Diamond T) = 1 - \Pr_s^{\max}(\neg T \cup F)$$

where F denotes the set of states u such that $\Pr_u^\sigma(\Diamond T) = 0$ for some fair policy σ and where $\cup$ denotes the until operator. This set F is computable using an analysis of the end components of the MDP and PCTL model-checking techniques. Notions of fairness have also been used as an approximation of probabilistic executions and used in the context of proof systems for establishing qualitative linear-time properties for MDP-like models [132].

4.8   Mean Payoff and Other Long-Run Averages

Given a weighted MDP, i.e., an MDP with a cost function assigning (possibly negative) integers, called weights, to the state-distribution pairs (s, μ) with $\mu \in \mathcal{D}(s)$, the mean payoff $\text{MP}(\pi)$ of an infinite path π is defined as the limit superior of the sequence $wgt(\pi, n)/n$ where $wgt(\pi, n)$ denotes the accumulated weight of the first n state-distribution pairs in π. In finite-state MDPs, minimal and maximal expected mean payoff always exist and are achieved by deterministic positional policies. The minimal and maximal expected mean payoff are computable in polynomial-time using linear programming techniques that encode the long-run frequencies of the state-distribution pairs in randomized positional policies [106, 133]. MDPs with multiple mean-payoff objectives have been studied in [34]. Other forms of long-run averages have been proposed by de Alfaro [57] where finite-state automata serve to trigger so-called experiments that monitor finite fragments of the paths generated by the MDP and evaluate them in terms of a reward value. He presents polynomial-time algorithms to check whether there is a policy σ ensuring that almost all σ-paths satisfy a threshold condition for the long-run average reward, defined as the mean payoff, but the limit average is taken over the number of experiments rather than the number of transitions. These concepts have been further developed for reasoning about long-run ratios in MDPs and related synthesis problems using standard and fractional linear programming techniques [56, 149].

4.9   Multiple Objectives

The properties discussed so far focused on single objectives such as reachability, timed/bounded reachability, expected costs, and long-run averages. In practice, a system is subject to multiple objectives that are mutually influencing each other, like quickly reaching a target is more costly. Multi-objective model checking aims at achieving multiple objectives on MDPs at once and to facilitate *trade-off analysis* by obtaining Pareto curves. Multi-objective decision making for MDPs with discounting and long-run objectives has been well investigated; for a recent survey, see [138]. Etessami *et al.* [72] consider verifying finite MDPs with multiple ω-regular objectives. Other multiple objectives include expected rewards under worst-case reachability [41,78], quantiles, long-run ratio objectives, and conditional probabilities [10], multiple discounted rewards [49], mean payoffs and stability [38], long-run objectives [33] and total average discounted rewards under PCTL [143]. Combinations of safety properties and expected cost objectives have been considered for MDPs with unknown cost function [105].

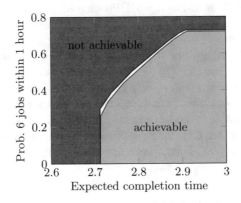

Fig. 3. Approximate Pareto curve for stochastic job scheduling.

Example 4. Consider again the job-shop scheduling problem. In addition to requiring that all jobs need to be completed within a given deadline with a high probability, let us impose *extra* constraints, e.g., requiring a high probability to finish a batch of c jobs within a tight deadline (to accelerate their post-processing), or having a low average waiting time. Figure 3, e.g., shows the results of CTMDP multi-objective model checking for 12 jobs and 3 processors. It approximates the set of points (t, p) for schedules achieving that (1) the expected time to complete all jobs is at most t and (2) the probability to finish half of the jobs within an is at least p. The red area indicates the set of points (t, p) that cannot be attained by any policy, whereas the green area indicates the set of points that are achievable by some policy; the white area is the "unknown" area, due to the ϵ-approximation. Whereas for MDP model checking [72], the set of achievable points is a convex area with finitely many corner points, for

CTMDPs the convex area may have infinitely many corner points [135]. This is why approximations of Pareto curves are obtained. Novel techniques for multi-objective model checking and robust strategy synthesis of MDPs with uncertain transition probabilities have also been discussed recently [91,139].

4.10   Energy and Other Weight Objectives

There is a close relation between the mean payoff and the energy objective, which again is closely related to the termination condition in one-counter systems. The energy condition imposes the constraint that the total cumulative weight never drops below 0 (or another constant) and is typically considered in conjunction with other ω-regular or weight conditions. In the case of MDPs the task is then to find a policy σ such that almost all σ-paths satisfy both the energy condition and the additional ω-regular or weight conditions. Energy-parity objectives in MDPs are solvable in pseudo-polynomial time and the decision problem is in NP $\cap$ coNP [48,125]. Even the pure energy objective is known to be reducible to (non-probabilistic) two-player mean-payoff games [32], for which no polynomial-time algorithms are known. Energy-MDPs with other side conditions have been studied, e.g., in [39] where multiple expected mean payoff constraints have been considered.

MDPs with the energy condition can also be seen as infinite-state MDPs that operate with a counter [36], or equivalently, with stacks over an unary stack alphabet, which again is closely related to the model of recursive MDPs [35,73]. Although reasoning about temporal properties with weight constraints is in general undecidable, even in the non-probabilistic case [29], the maximal or minimal probabilities for LTL formulas with constraints for the weight accumulated in windows of a fixed length are computable using a reduction to standard LTL [19].

4.11   Conditional Probabilities

Reasoning about conditional probabilities (rather than unconditional ones) is natural when the task is to analyze a system in specific (possibly rare) scenarios. For example, to analyze the impact and cost of error-handling mechanisms, selected error scenarios can be used as conditions. For another example, conditional probabilities and expectations are used to define the semantics of probabilistic programs in terms of weakest pre-expectations or to define conditional termination times [108]. They have also been used to formalize a notion of anonymity [3] by the requirement that the probability for an observable does not depend on the secret.

In purely probabilistic models, such as MC, conditional probabilities are computable directly by their definition $\Pr(\varphi|\psi) = \Pr(\varphi \wedge \psi)/\Pr(\psi)$ as quotient of "standard" probabilities. Such a simple approach is, however, not applicable in MDPs when the task is to find a policy maximizing the probabilities for φ, under the condition of a temporal property ψ. Suppose, e.g., that $\varphi = \Diamond T$ and $\psi = \Diamond A$ are reachability properties. A crucial observation to construct an optimal policy is that after having reached T (resp. A), optimal policies maximize the probability to reach A (resp. T) [4,18]. This observation allows to transform the given MDP $\mathcal{M}$ into a normal form MDP, which allows to assume that $T \subseteq A$. Suppose now s_0 is the initial state of $\mathcal{M}$. By adding "reset transitions" $s \to s_0$ for all states s in $\mathcal{M}$ with $\Pr_{\mathcal{M},s}^{\min}(\lozenge A) = 0$ as additional nondeterministic alternatives, we obtain an MDP $\mathcal{N}$ such that the maximal conditional probability for $\lozenge T$, given $\lozenge A$, in $\mathcal{M}$ from s_0 equals $\Pr_{\mathcal{N},s_0}^{\max}(\lozenge T)$. Intuitively, the reset transition serve to "discard" all paths violating the condition $\lozenge A$ and "re-distributing" their probability mass to the paths satisfying $\lozenge A$. Thus, maximal conditional reachability probabilities are reducible to maximal (unconditional) reachability probabilities. This approach can be generalized for the case where the objective φ and the condition ψ are ω-regular properties using deterministic ω-automata for φ and ψ.

The techniques for maximal or minimal expected costs until reaching target states sketched above seek for the optimum under all proper policies, i.e., policies under which the target will be reached almost surely. However, such policies need not to exist. Computing maximal conditional expected costs until reaching a target under the condition that the target will indeed be reached is more involved as positional policies are no longer powerful enough. [20] presents an exponential-time algorithm to compute maximal conditional expected costs until reaching a target and proves PSPACE-completeness for the threshold problem in acyclic MDPs that asks whether the maximal conditional expectation meets a given lower or upper bound.

4.12   Permissive Policies

Whereas MDP model checking typically generates a single policy that is optimal with respect to a given objective, recently this has been extended to obtaining multi-policies [66]. Such multi-policies specify multiple possible actions rather than a single possible action. The aim is to synthesize multi-policies that are as permissive as possible, which one can quantify by assigning penalties to actions. These are incurred when a multi-policy disallows (does not make available) a given action. Permissive controller synthesis aims to generate a multi-policy that minimises these penalties, whilst guaranteeing the satisfaction of a specified property φ. Randomised multi-policies are strictly more powerful than deterministic ones, and the permissive controller synthesis problem is NP-hard for either class with upper bounds in NP and PSPACE, respectively. Practical methods for synthesising multi-policies exploit mixed integer linear programming (MILP).

4.13   Counterexamples

If model checking MDP $\mathcal{M}$ against specification φ with upper bound p, say, yields an affirmative result, then a formal guarantee is obtained that $\mathcal{M}$ satisfies φ with probability at most p, regardless of how the non-determinism is resolved. As a by-product, most model checkers offer the possibility to obtain a policy that maximizes the likelihood of ensuring φ. If however, the model checking procedure yields a negative answer, then some diagnostic feedback would be useful. PMC techniques have been therefore extended with the possibility to obtain counterexamples. Such techniques obtain a sub-MDP of $\mathcal{M}$ whose maximal probability to satisfy φ exceeds p. Whereas obtaining such sub-MDP of minimal size is computationally hard (the corresponding decision problem is NP-hard [45]) for ω-regular properties, good practical results have been obtained using MILP [154].

5 Curbing State-Space Explosion

The often excessive size of the state space spanned by a concrete verification problem is a major impediment to practicality across the entire spectrum of verification methods, see e.g. [2,92]. This problem of state-space explosion also affects negatively the basic probabilistic model checking procedures we discussed thus far. A recent approach circumvents it by nevertheless explicitly enumerating all states and transitions, but keeping only a minor portion thereof in main memory at any time of the computation, storing the remainder almost exclusively in secondary storage (usually an attached hard disk) [94]. Other, more conceptual approaches consider abstraction and compression techniques for MDP models. They indeed form an important area of probabilistic model checking research. We can only present an abridged survey here, more detailed accounts can be found for instance in [62]. Abstraction and compression techniques remove details from concrete models provided these are not relevant to the property of interest. In many cases, only this makes the analysis of the model feasible or at least speeds up verification considerably. For real-world problems, abstraction and compression is a prerequisite for successful verification.

5.1 Compress

Bisimulation Minimization. A popular compression technique is bisimulation minimization [31]. Here, the states of the compressed system represent equivalence classes with respect to a bisimulation equivalence, ensuring that the compressed system, the quotient, is guaranteed to preserve all relevant properties. The basis thereof is an algorithm to decide the respective relation, which in the MDP setting is probabilistic bisimulation, a concept introduced by Larsen and Skou [120] in the early nineties, and adapted to MDPs by Segala [141]. Probabilistic bisimulation can be decided in polynomial time [11], and this extends to interval MDPs [96,98] with bounded nondeterminism, as well as to weak variations of bisimulation, i.e., to variations where internal steps are considered compressable [145]. Minimality of the quotient construction requires some care in the presence of probability, depending on the particular strong or weak bisimulation employed [68].

Compositional Minimization. The relevant bisimulations are congruence relations, in the sense that they are compatible with the usual variants of parallel composition and other composition operators. This enables the application of bisimulation minimization to components, which can turn out to be extremely effective. Non-trivial examples are known where state spaces with 1.6 billion states and 7 billion transitions can be compressed to a very small minimal MDP [76] prior to model checking.

Distribution-Based Bisimulation. Weaker equivalences lead to better model compression since they induce coarser partitions of the state space, but might come with higher algorithmic complexity. Weak distribution bisimulation is coarser than the aforementioned relations [69]. It is not defined as a relation between states, but instead between probability distributions on states. Exponential-time algorithms deciding distribution-based bisimulations have been proposed [67,99,140].

Symmetry. On the other hand, strong bisimulation equivalence is often induced by symmetries in the model, which in turn are generally easier to identify directly [65,115] instead of running a dedicated decision algorithm, albeit at the price of a possibly non-minimal result.

5.2   Be Symbolic

In non-probabilistic systems, symbolic data structures such as binary decision diagrams (BDDs) have been investigated successfully [43] to mitigate the state explosion phenomenon. For probabilistic systems, multi-terminal binary decision diagram (MTBDDs) [80], also called algebraic decision diagrams [5], have been introduced as a data structure for representing and manipulating functions from a finite set to values in an algebraic structure. In the context of probabilistic systems, they have been first used for computing steady-state probabilities [87] and PCTL model checking [8] for Markov chains and later extended for MDPs [60]. Among others, [60] demonstrate that model construction and reachability-based model checking is possible in a matter of seconds for certain classes of systems consisting of up to 10^{30} states. While [60] follows a purely symbolic approach, which causes the problem that the MTBDD-representation of the probability vector can degenerate to a tree-like structure, [114,130] introduces a hybrid approach using an MTBDD-representation of the MDP and an explicit representation of the probability vector.

Symblicit Analysis. For certain problems, the benefits of explicit and of symbolic analysis steps can be exploited in carefully crafted combinations, so-called symblicit analysis approaches [28,90,153].

Tool Support. The probabilistic model checkers PRISM [114,116] and storm [63] both support the hybrid approach, but also offer a purely symbolic MTBDD-based engine, a purely explicit engine, as well as a sparse engine that generates the model symbolically, but carries out the numerical computations using sparse data structures. The storm model checker [63] also implements bisimulation-based minimization algorithms applicable to MDPs.

5.3   Abstract Safely

Most abstraction schemes are based on grouping states that are not necessarily bisimilar. Abstract and original models are then no longer bisimilar but they are related by a *simulation* relation. Abstraction is typically conservative in the sense that affirmative verification results for abstract models carry over to concrete models. That is to say, if the abstract model satisfies a property, the concrete one does so too. Probabilistic simulation preserves a safe fragment of PCTL [100]. The converse does not apply, as spurious negative results may occur due to over-approximation in the abstraction. This however can be detected by checking the result on the concrete model, which in turn can be exploited for refining the abstract model.

Abstraction-Refinement. The use of abstraction-refinement for probabilistic systems has been pioneered by D'Argenio and coworkers [52,53]. In this approach a first attempt is made to prove a reachability property on the coarsest imaginable abstraction of the system. If that verification fails, the system is successively refined until a conclusive answer can be given.

Predicate and Game-Based Abstraction. The above concept has been taken up in combination with predicate abstraction and counterexample guided refinement [45,101], so as to form probabilistic counterexample-guided abstraction-refinement. Another important variation of this concept employs game-based abstraction [110,150]. Here, one player is representing the non-determinism that is inherent in the MDP, while the other player controls the non-determinism introduced by the abstraction, i.e., by the grouping of states into sets. The analysis of the resulting two-player stochastic game yields lower and upper bounds for the reachability properties of the MDP. The tightness of these bounds indicate the quality of the abstraction and form the basis of refinement. This typically relies on disagreeing strategies for the individual players to make the abstraction more precise when required. Magnifying-lens abstraction [61] uses a similar scheme, but rather considers the concrete states contained in an abstract state in each step, thereby magnifying the state as needed.

Three-Valued Abstraction. Three-valued semantics, i.e., an interpretation in which a formula evaluates to either true, false, or indefinite may help out. In this setting, abstraction is conservative for both positive and negative verification results. Only if the verification of the abstract model yields an indefinite answer ("don't know"), the validity in the concrete model is unknown. This has been adopted to interval MDPs [109]. For a queueing system from performance evaluation, (hand-crafted) three-valued abstraction shows that 10^{278} concrete states (calculated analytically) can be reduced to 1.2 million states, while preserving six decimals accuracy for timed reachability probabilities [111].

Other Approaches. A prominent technique to construct safe abstractions while possibly working with an explicit-state representation is partial-order reduction. This has effectively been lifted to the probabilistic setting [13,54,82] where it exhibits similarities with confluence reduction approaches [95]. Another approach to perform abstraction for probabilistic automata [64] uses may and must modalities, inspired by modal transition systems [121].

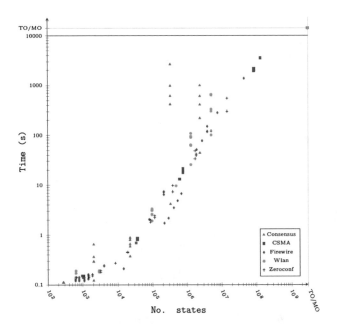

Fig. 4. Explicit MDP model checking

Example 5. We provide a glimpse of the effectiveness of several of the approaches mentioned above, especially symbolic representations and bisimulation-based compression.

Figure 4 provides a log-log scale plot of the total time (i.e., MDP construction from a high-level description plus the MDP model checking time) against the number of MDP states. It indicates the maximal size of the MDP that can be constructed and solved within 10,000 s when using an explicit engine, i.e., sparse matrix representations of the MDP. The results are obtained for all MDP case studies taken from the PRISM benchmark [117] suite. All MDPs model randomized distributed algorithms as indicated in the legend. The largest solved MDP instance within 10,000 s has about $130 \cdot 10^6$ states. The specifications are (minimal and maximal) reachability probability and expected reward objectives. Figure 5 provides a similar plot when carrying out the MDP model checking in a fully symbolic manner using MTBDDs. All experimental results are obtained using the storm model checker with accuracy 10^{-6} [63].

For most cases, the best results are obtained using a mixture of symbolic and explicit engines—this is also referred to as hybrid or symblicit. In that case, operations that can be done more efficiently using an explicit representation are done explicitly, whereas remaining operations are done on a symbolic representations. Figure 6 indicates the model sizes that can be treated within 10,000 s.

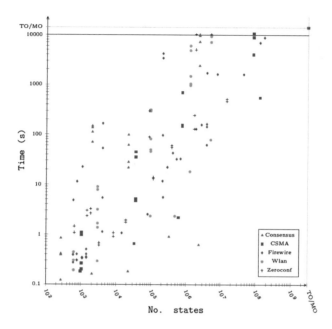

Fig. 5. Symbolic MDP model checking

The hybrid engine solves the largest problem instance of $2 \cdot 10^9$ states within 26 min.

As mentioned before, another important technique to curb the state-space explosion problem is bisimulation minimization. The effect of this technique on the MDP benchmark is indicated in Fig. 7. The reduction factor depends on the specification φ. For some qualitative specifications even models of one state remain. Reductions up to factor 10,000 are obtained. As indicated, for various MDPs the minimization could not be completed within 10,000 s (TO) and 16 GB RAM (MO).

6   Epilogue

The previous sections surveyed various techniques for the analysis of MDPs and related policy synthesis questions. This survey is by far not complete and there are many other research directions addressing the analysis of MDP-like models. Let us mention a few more recent developments.

A promising new direction is to *combine verification and learning* techniques. On the one hand, model checking examines all possible behaviours, in particular, certain corner cases are detected. An interesting question is if this information can be leveraged to *train* AI models in the sense that these corner cases are considered for the observed data. On the other hand, employing learning techniques could improve PMC's scalability. Initial results are promising. For instance, [37] exploits reinforcement learning so as to avoid treating fragments of the state

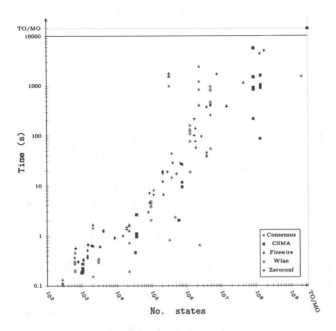

Fig. 6. Hybrid MDP model checking

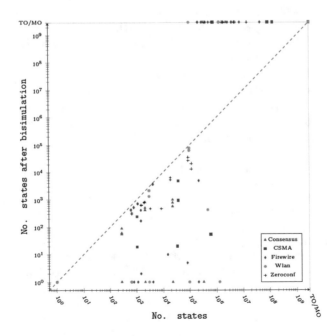

Fig. 7. MDP reduction by bisimulation

space that do almost not contribute to the probability of interest. For a mutual exclusion protocol with 10^{13} states only less than 2,000 are visited by the method ensuring a precision of 10^{-6}. Another example is the iterative combination of PMC and reinforcement learning to synthesize a safe policy whose expected cost is low for an MDP with unknown costs [105] as well as in the context of the compositional analysis of MDPs [75]. Learning has also been applied to continuous-time MDP (using gradient ascent) [22]. The use of automata learning techniques for probabilistic models [124] is also an interesting future direction.

Another future direction is the use of *parallelization* to exploit the presence of multiple cores in modern computers for MDP model checking. It is fair to say that this is still at its infancy. So far, determining maximal end components in MDPs has been parallelized on GPGPUs [152], but apart from some initial investigations in the setting of Markov chains [30], probabilistic computations on MDPs seem not yet to be parallelized.

The treatment in this paper has primarily focused on finite-state MDPs. A large variety of generalizations of infinite-state MDPs have been (and still are) investigated. Timed automata equipped with discrete branching probabilities give rise to uncountably large MDPs due to real-valued clocks. Using the region construction technique from timed automata [1], the standard algorithms for finite MDPs suffice for the analysis [118]. Model checking of (discrete-time) uncountable MDPs is treated in [144]. Countably infinite variants of MDPs include probabilistic lossy channel systems [7] where message losses have a probabilistic behavior while the component finite-state processes behave nondeterministically, one-counter MDPs [36], MDPs equipped with counters that can be arbitrarily negative or positive, and recursive MDPs [71,73] (that subsume one-counter MDPs). Recursive MDPs are equivalent to push-down MDPs. Deciding whether there is a policy that yields termination probability one is undecidable for recursive MDPs. Whereas in the finite-state setting, the least fixed point (least non-negative) solution to a monotone system of linear equations is key to MDP model checking, for termination probabilities of recursive MDPs these equations are polynomial. Infinite MDPs are a natural operational model for probabilistic programming with non-determinism [84,126].

Acknowledgement. The authors thank Matthias Volk (RWTH Aachen) for providing the scatter plots in this paper and Daniel Gburek (TU Dresden), Ernst Moritz Hahn (University of Liverpool), and Vahid Hashemi (Saarland University) for various useful comments. This work has been supported by the Excellence Initiative of the German federal and state government through the cluster of excellence cfaed, the Distinguished Professorship project APPA, the ERC Advanced Investigators Grant 695614 (POWVER), the CDZ project CAP (GZ 1023), the German Research Foundation (DFG) through the CRC 912 (HAEC), the RTG 2236 UnRAVeL and the projects BA 1679/11-1 and BA 1679/12-1.

References

1. Alur, R., Dill, D.L.: A theory of timed automata. Theor. Comput. Sci. **126**(2), 183–235 (1994)
2. Alur, R., Giacobbe, M., Henzinger, T., Larsen, K., Mikucionis, M.: Continuous-time models for system design and analysis. In: Steffen, B., Woeginger, G. (eds.) Computing and Software Science. LNCS, vol. 10000, pp. 452–477. Springer, Cham (2018)
3. Andrés, M.E., Palamidessi, C., van Rossum, P., Sokolova, A.: Information hiding in probabilistic concurrent systems. Theor. Comput. Sci. **412**(28), 3072–3089 (2011)
4. Andrés, M.E., van Rossum, P.: Conditional probabilities over probabilistic and nondeterministic systems. In: Ramakrishnan, C.R., Rehof, J. (eds.) TACAS 2008. LNCS, vol. 4963, pp. 157–172. Springer, Heidelberg (2008). https://doi.org/10.1007/978-3-540-78800-3_12
5. Bahar, I.R., Frohm, E.A., Gaona, C.M., Hachtel, G.D., Macii, E., Pardo, A., Somenzi, F.: Algebraic decision diagrams and their applications. Form. Methods Syst. Des. **10**(2/3), 171–206 (1997)
6. Baier, C., Bertrand, N., Größer, M.: On decision problems for probabilistic Büchi automata. In: Amadio, R. (ed.) FoSSaCS 2008. LNCS, vol. 4962, pp. 287–301. Springer, Heidelberg (2008). https://doi.org/10.1007/978-3-540-78499-9_21
7. Baier, C., Bertrand, N., Schnoebelen, P.: Verifying nondeterministic probabilistic channel systems against ω-regular linear-time properties. ACM Trans. Comput. Log. **9**(1), 5 (2007)
8. Baier, C., Clarke, E.M., Hartonas-Garmhausen, V., Kwiatkowska, M., Ryan, M.: Symbolic model checking for probabilistic processes. In: Degano, P., Gorrieri, R., Marchetti-Spaccamela, A. (eds.) ICALP 1997. LNCS, vol. 1256, pp. 430–440. Springer, Heidelberg (1997). https://doi.org/10.1007/3-540-63165-8_199
9. Baier, C., Daum, M., Dubslaff, C., Klein, J., Klüppelholz, S.: Energy-utility quantiles. In: Badger, J.M., Rozier, K.Y. (eds.) NFM 2014. LNCS, vol. 8430, pp. 285–299. Springer, Cham (2014). https://doi.org/10.1007/978-3-319-06200-6_24
10. Baier, C., Dubslaff, C., Klüppelholz, S.: Trade-off analysis meets probabilistic model checking. In: CSL-LICS, pp. 1:1–1:10. ACM (2014)
11. Baier, C., Engelen, B., Majster-Cederbaum, M.E.: Deciding bisimilarity and similarity for probabilistic processes. J. Comput. Syst. Sci. **60**(1), 187–231 (2000)
12. Baier, C., Größer, M., Bertrand, N.: Probabilistic ω-automata. J. ACM **59**(1), 1 (2012)
13. Baier, C., Größer, M., Ciesinski, F.: Partial order reduction for probabilistic systems. In: QEST, pp. 230–239. IEEE Computer Society (2004)
14. Baier, C., Groesser, M., Ciesinski, F.: Quantitative analysis under fairness constraints. In: Liu, Z., Ravn, A.P. (eds.) ATVA 2009. LNCS, vol. 5799, pp. 135–150. Springer, Heidelberg (2009). https://doi.org/10.1007/978-3-642-04761-9_12
15. Baier, C., Haverkort, B.R., Hermanns, H., Katoen, J.-P.: Reachability in continuous-time Markov reward decision processes. In: Logic and Automata History and Perspectives. Texts in Logic and Games, vol. 2, pp. 53–72. Amsterdam University Press (2008)
16. Baier, C., Hermanns, H., Katoen, J.-P., Haverkort, B.R.: Efficient computation of time-bounded reachability probabilities in uniform continuous-time Markov decision processes. Theoret. Comput. Sci. **345**(1), 2–26 (2005)

17. Baier, C., Katoen, J.-P.: Principles of Model Checking. The MIT Press, Cambridge (2008)
18. Baier, C., Klein, J., Klüppelholz, S., Märcker, S.: Computing conditional probabilities in markovian models efficiently. In: Ábrahám, E., Havelund, K. (eds.) TACAS 2014. LNCS, vol. 8413, pp. 515–530. Springer, Heidelberg (2014). https://doi.org/10.1007/978-3-642-54862-8_43
19. Baier, C., Klein, J., Klüppelholz, S., Wunderlich, S.: Weight monitoring with linear temporal logic: complexity and decidability. In: CSL-LICS, pp. 11:1–11:10. ACM (2014)
20. Baier, C., Klein, J., Klüppelholz, S., Wunderlich, S.: Maximizing the conditional expected reward for reaching the goal. In: Legay, A., Margaria, T. (eds.) TACAS 2017. LNCS, vol. 10206, pp. 269–285. Springer, Heidelberg (2017). https://doi.org/10.1007/978-3-662-54580-5_16
21. Baier, C., Kwiatkowska, M.Z.: Model checking for a probabilistic branching time logic with fairness. Distrib. Comput. **11**(3), 125–155 (1998)
22. Bartocci, E., Bortolussi, L., Brázdil, T., Milios, D., Sanguinetti, G.: Policy learning for time-bounded reachability in continuous-time Markov decision processes via doubly-stochastic gradient ascent. In: Agha, G., Van Houdt, B. (eds.) QEST 2016. LNCS, vol. 9826, pp. 244–259. Springer, Cham (2016). https://doi.org/10.1007/978-3-319-43425-4_17
23. Bellman, R.: A Markovian decision process. J. Math. Mech. **38**, 679–684 (1957)
24. Ben-Or, M.: Another advantage of free choice: completely asynchronous agreement protocols (extended abstract). In: PODC, pp. 27–30. ACM (1983)
25. Bertrand, N., Bouyer, P., Brihaye, T., Menet, Q., Baier, C., Größer, M., Jurdzinski, M.: Stochastic timed automata. Log. Methods Comput. Sci. **10**(4) (2014)
26. Bertsekas, D.P., Tsitsiklis, J.N.: An analysis of stochastic shortest path problems. Math. Oper. Res. **16**(3), 580–595 (1991)
27. Bianco, A., de Alfaro, L.: Model checking of probabilistic and nondeterministic systems. In: Thiagarajan, P.S. (ed.) FSTTCS 1995. LNCS, vol. 1026, pp. 499–513. Springer, Heidelberg (1995). https://doi.org/10.1007/3-540-60692-0_70
28. Bohy, A., Bruyère, V., Raskin, J.-F.: Symblicit algorithms for optimal strategy synthesis in monotonic Markov decision processes. In: SYNT. EPTCS, vol. 157, pp. 51–67 (2014)
29. Boker, U., Chatterjee, K., Henzinger, T.A., Kupferman, O.: Temporal specifications with accumulative values. ACM Trans. Comput. Log. **15**(4), 27:1–27:25 (2014)
30. Bosnacki, D., Edelkamp, S., Sulewski, D., Wijs, A.: Parallel probabilistic model checking on general purpose graphics processors. STTT **13**(1), 21–35 (2011)
31. Bouajjani, A., Fernandez, J.-C., Halbwachs, N.: Minimal model generation. In: Clarke, E.M., Kurshan, R.P. (eds.) CAV 1990. LNCS, vol. 531, pp. 197–203. Springer, Heidelberg (1991). https://doi.org/10.1007/BFb0023733
32. Bouyer, P., Fahrenberg, U., Larsen, K.G., Markey, N., Srba, J.: Infinite runs in weighted timed automata with energy constraints. In: Cassez, F., Jard, C. (eds.) FORMATS 2008. LNCS, vol. 5215, pp. 33–47. Springer, Heidelberg (2008). https://doi.org/10.1007/978-3-540-85778-5_4
33. Brázdil, T., Brozek, V., Chatterjee, K., Forejt, V., Kucera, A.: Markov decision processes with multiple long-run average objectives. Log. Methods Comput. Sci. **10**(1) (2014)
34. Brázdil, T., Brozek, V., Chatterjee, K., Forejt, V., Kucera, A.: Two views on multiple mean-payoff objectives in Markov decision processes. Log. Methods Comput. Sci. **10**(1) (2014)

35. Brázdil, T., Brozek, V., Etessami, K., Kucera, A.: Approximating the termination value of one-counter MDPs and stochastic games. Inf. Comput. **222**, 121–138 (2013)
36. Brázdil, T., Brozek, V., Etessami, K., Kucera, A., Wojtczak, D.: One-counter Markov decision processes. In: SODA, pp. 863–874. SIAM (2010)
37. Brázdil, T., Chatterjee, K., Chmelík, M., Forejt, V., Křetínský, J., Kwiatkowska, M., Parker, D., Ujma, M.: Verification of Markov decision processes using learning algorithms. In: Cassez, F., Raskin, J.-F. (eds.) ATVA 2014. LNCS, vol. 8837, pp. 98–114. Springer, Cham (2014). https://doi.org/10.1007/978-3-319-11936-6_8
38. Brázdil, T., Chatterjee, K., Forejt, V., Kucera, A.: Trading performance for stability in Markov decision processes. J. Comput. Syst. Sci. **84**, 144–170 (2017)
39. Brázdil, T., Kučera, A., Novotný, P.: Optimizing the expected mean payoff in energy Markov decision processes. In: Artho, C., Legay, A., Peled, D. (eds.) ATVA 2016. LNCS, vol. 9938, pp. 32–49. Springer, Cham (2016). https://doi.org/10.1007/978-3-319-46520-3_3
40. Bruno, J.L., Downey, P.J., Frederickson, G.N.: Sequencing tasks with exponential service times to minimize the expected flow time or makespan. J. ACM **28**(1), 100–113 (1981)
41. Bruyère, V., Filiot, E., Randour, M., Raskin, J.-F.: Meet your expectations with guarantees: beyond worst-case synthesis in quantitative games. In: STACS. LIPIcs, , vol. 25, pp. 199–213. Schloss Dagstuhl - Leibniz-Zentrum fuer Informatik (2014)
42. Buchholz, P., Hahn, E.M., Hermanns, H., Zhang, L.: Model checking algorithms for CTMDPs. In: Gopalakrishnan, G., Qadeer, S. (eds.) CAV 2011. LNCS, vol. 6806, pp. 225–242. Springer, Heidelberg (2011). https://doi.org/10.1007/978-3-642-22110-1_19
43. Burch, J.R., Clarke, E.M., McMillan, K.L., Dill, D.L., Hwang, L.J.: Symbolic model checking: $10^{\wedge}20$ states and beyond. Inf. Comput. **98**(2), 142–170 (1992)
44. Butkova, Y., Hatefi, H., Hermanns, H., Krčál, J.: Optimal continuous time Markov decisions. In: Finkbeiner, B., Pu, G., Zhang, L. (eds.) ATVA 2015. LNCS, vol. 9364, pp. 166–182. Springer, Cham (2015). https://doi.org/10.1007/978-3-319-24953-7_12
45. Chadha, R., Viswanathan, M.: A counterexample-guided abstraction-refinement framework for Markov decision processes. ACM Trans. Comput. Log. **12**(1), 1:1–1:49 (2010)
46. Chatterjee, K., Chmelik, M., Gupta, R., Kanodia, A.: Optimal cost almost-sure reachability in POMDPs. Artif. Intell. **234**, 26–48 (2016)
47. Chatterjee, K., Chmelik, M., Tracol, M.: What is decidable about partially observable Markov decision processes with ω-regular objectives. J. Comput. Syst. Sci. **82**(5), 878–911 (2016)
48. Chatterjee, K., Doyen, L.: Energy and mean-payoff parity Markov decision processes. In: Murlak, F., Sankowski, P. (eds.) MFCS 2011. LNCS, vol. 6907, pp. 206–218. Springer, Heidelberg (2011). https://doi.org/10.1007/978-3-642-22993-0_21
49. Chatterjee, K., Majumdar, R., Henzinger, T.A.: Markov decision processes with multiple objectives. In: Durand, B., Thomas, W. (eds.) STACS 2006. LNCS, vol. 3884, pp. 325–336. Springer, Heidelberg (2006). https://doi.org/10.1007/11672142_26
50. Courcoubetis, C., Yannakakis, M.: The complexity of probabilistic verification. J. ACM **42**(4), 857–907 (1995)

51. Cubuktepe, M., Jansen, N., Junges, S., Katoen, J.-P., Papusha, I., Poonawala, H.A., Topcu, U.: Sequential convex programming for the efficient verification of parametric MDPs. In: Legay, A., Margaria, T. (eds.) TACAS 2017. LNCS, vol. 10206, pp. 133–150. Springer, Heidelberg (2017). https://doi.org/10.1007/978-3-662-54580-5_8

52. D'Argenio, P.R., Jeannet, B., Jensen, H.E., Larsen, K.G.: Reachability analysis of probabilistic systems by successive refinements. In: de Alfaro, L., Gilmore, S. (eds.) PAPM-PROBMIV 2001. LNCS, vol. 2165, pp. 39–56. Springer, Heidelberg (2001). https://doi.org/10.1007/3-540-44804-7_3

53. D'Argenio, P.R., Jeannet, B., Jensen, H.E., Larsen, K.G.: Reduction and refinement strategies for probabilistic analysis. In: Hermanns, H., Segala, R. (eds.) PAPM-PROBMIV 2002. LNCS, vol. 2399, pp. 57–76. Springer, Heidelberg (2002). https://doi.org/10.1007/3-540-45605-8_5

54. D'Argenio, P.R., Niebert, P.: Partial order reduction on concurrent probabilistic programs. In: QEST, pp. 240–249. IEEE Computer Society (2004)

55. David, A., Larsen, K.G., Legay, A., Mikucionis, M., Poulsen, D.B.: Uppaal SMC tutorial. STTT 17(4), 397–415 (2015)

56. de Alfaro, L.: Formal verification of probabilistic systems. Ph.D. thesis, Department of Computer Science, Stanford University (1997)

57. de Alfaro, L.: How to specify and verify the long-run average behavior of probabilistic systems. In: LICS, pp. 454–465. IEEE Computer Society (1998)

58. de Alfaro, L.: Computing minimum and maximum reachability times in probabilistic systems. In: Baeten, J.C.M., Mauw, S. (eds.) CONCUR 1999. LNCS, vol. 1664, pp. 66–81. Springer, Heidelberg (1999). https://doi.org/10.1007/3-540-48320-9_7

59. de Alfaro, L.: The verification of probabilistic systems under memoryless partial-information policies is hard. In: Proceedings of 2nd International Workshop on Probabilistic Methods in Verification (ProbMiV 1999), Research Report CSR-99-9, pp. 19–32. Birmingham University (1999)

60. de Alfaro, L., Kwiatkowska, M., Norman, G., Parker, D., Segala, R.: Symbolic model checking of probabilistic processes using MTBDDs and the Kronecker representation. In: Graf, S., Schwartzbach, M. (eds.) TACAS 2000. LNCS, vol. 1785, pp. 395–410. Springer, Heidelberg (2000). https://doi.org/10.1007/3-540-46419-0_27

61. de Alfaro, L., Roy, P.: Magnifying-lens abstraction for Markov decision processes. In: Damm, W., Hermanns, H. (eds.) CAV 2007. LNCS, vol. 4590, pp. 325–338. Springer, Heidelberg (2007). https://doi.org/10.1007/978-3-540-73368-3_38

62. Dehnert, C., Gebler, D., Volpato, M., Jansen, D.N.: On abstraction of probabilistic systems. In: Remke, A., Stoelinga, M. (eds.) ROCKS 2012. LNCS, vol. 8453, pp. 87–116. Springer, Heidelberg (2014). https://doi.org/10.1007/978-3-662-45489-3_4

63. Dehnert, C., Junges, S., Katoen, J.-P., Volk, M.: A storm is coming: a modern probabilistic model checker. In: Majumdar, R., Kunčak, V. (eds.) CAV 2017. LNCS, vol. 10427, pp. 592–600. Springer, Cham (2017). https://doi.org/10.1007/978-3-319-63390-9_31

64. Delahaye, B., Katoen, J.-P., Larsen, K.G., Legay, A., Pedersen, M.L., Sher, F., Wasowski, A.: Abstract probabilistic automata. Inf. Comput. 232, 66–116 (2013)

65. Donaldson, A.F., Miller, A., Parker, D.: Language-level symmetry reduction for probabilistic model checking. In: QEST, pp. 289–298. IEEE Computer Society (2009)

66. Dräger, K., Forejt, V., Kwiatkowska, M.Z., Parker, D., Ujma, M.: Permissive controller synthesis for probabilistic systems. Log. Methods Comput. Sci. 11(2) (2015)

67. Eisentraut, C., Hermanns, H., Krämer, J., Turrini, A., Zhang, L.: Deciding bisimilarities on distributions. In: Joshi, K., Siegle, M., Stoelinga, M., D'Argenio, P.R. (eds.) QEST 2013. LNCS, vol. 8054, pp. 72–88. Springer, Heidelberg (2013). https://doi.org/10.1007/978-3-642-40196-1_6

68. Eisentraut, C., Hermanns, H., Schuster, J., Turrini, A., Zhang, L.: The quest for minimal quotients for probabilistic automata. In: Piterman, N., Smolka, S.A. (eds.) TACAS 2013. LNCS, vol. 7795, pp. 16–31. Springer, Heidelberg (2013). https://doi.org/10.1007/978-3-642-36742-7_2

69. Eisentraut, C., Hermanns, H., Zhang, L.: On probabilistic automata in continuous time. In: LICS, pp. 342–351. IEEE CS (2010)

70. Esparza, J., Kretínský, J., Sickert, S.: From LTL to deterministic automata - a safraless compositional approach. Form. Methods Syst. Des. **49**(3), 219–271 (2016)

71. Etessami, K.: Analysis of probabilistic processes and automata theory. In: Handbook of Automata Theory. European Mathematical Society (2016, to appear)

72. Etessami, K., Kwiatkowska, M.Z., Vardi, M.Y., Yannakakis, M.: Multi-objective model checking of Markov decision processes. Log. Methods Comput. Sci. **4**(4) (2008)

73. Etessami, K., Yannakakis, M.: Recursive Markov decision processes and recursive stochastic games. J. ACM **62**(2), 11:1–11:69 (2015)

74. Feinberg, E.A., Shwartz, A.: Methods and applications. In: Handbook of Markov Decision Processes. Kluwer (2002)

75. Feng, L., Han, T., Kwiatkowska, M., Parker, D.: Learning-based compositional verification for synchronous probabilistic systems. In: Bultan, T., Hsiung, P.-A. (eds.) ATVA 2011. LNCS, vol. 6996, pp. 511–521. Springer, Heidelberg (2011). https://doi.org/10.1007/978-3-642-24372-1_40

76. Fioriti, L.M.F., Hashemi, V., Hermanns, H., Turrini, A.: Deciding probabilistic automata weak bisimulation: theory and practice. Form. Asp. Comput. **28**(1), 109–143 (2016)

77. Fischer, M.J., Lynch, N.A., Paterson, M.: Impossibility of distributed consensus with one faulty process. J. ACM **32**(2), 374–382 (1985)

78. Forejt, V., Kwiatkowska, M., Norman, G., Parker, D., Qu, H.: Quantitative multi-objective verification for probabilistic systems. In: Abdulla, P.A., Leino, K.R.M. (eds.) TACAS 2011. LNCS, vol. 6605, pp. 112–127. Springer, Heidelberg (2011). https://doi.org/10.1007/978-3-642-19835-9_11

79. Fu, H.: Maximal cost-bounded reachability probability on continuous-time Markov decision processes. In: Muscholl, A. (ed.) FoSSaCS 2014. LNCS, vol. 8412, pp. 73–87. Springer, Heidelberg (2014). https://doi.org/10.1007/978-3-642-54830-7_5

80. Fujita, M., McGeer, P.C., Yang, J.C.-Y.: Multi-terminal binary decision diagrams: an efficient data structure for matrix representation. Form. Methods Syst. Des. **10**(2/3), 149–169 (1997)

81. Gimbert, H., Oualhadj, Y.: Deciding the value 1 problem for ♯-acyclic partially observable Markov decision processes. In: Geffert, V., Preneel, B., Rovan, B., Štuller, J., Tjoa, A.M. (eds.) SOFSEM 2014. LNCS, vol. 8327, pp. 281–292. Springer, Cham (2014). https://doi.org/10.1007/978-3-319-04298-5_25

82. Giro, S., D'Argenio, P.R., Ferrer Fioriti, L.M.: Partial order reduction for probabilistic systems: a revision for distributed schedulers. In: Bravetti, M., Zavattaro, G. (eds.) CONCUR 2009. LNCS, vol. 5710, pp. 338–353. Springer, Heidelberg (2009). https://doi.org/10.1007/978-3-642-04081-8_23

83. Givan, R., Leach, S.M., Dean, T.L.: Bounded-parameter Markov decision processes. Artif. Intell. **122**(1–2), 71–109 (2000)
84. Gretz, F., Katoen, J.-P., McIver, A.: Operational versus weakest pre-expectation semantics for the probabilistic guarded command language. Perform. Eval. **73**, 110–132 (2014)
85. Guo, X., Hernandez-Lerma, O.: Continuous-Time Markov Decision Processes: Theory and Applications. Stochastic Modelling and Applied Probability, vol. 62. Springer, Heidelberg (2009). https://doi.org/10.1007/978-3-642-02547-1
86. Haase, C., Kiefer, S.: The odds of staying on budget. In: Halldórsson, M.M., Iwama, K., Kobayashi, N., Speckmann, B. (eds.) ICALP 2015. LNCS, vol. 9135, pp. 234–246. Springer, Heidelberg (2015). https://doi.org/10.1007/978-3-662-47666-6_19
87. Hachtel, G.D., Macii, E., Pardo, A., Somenzi, F.: Markovian analysis of large finite state machines. IEEE Trans. CAD Integr. Circ. Syst. **15**(12), 1479–1493 (1996)
88. Haddad, S., Monmege, B.: Reachability in MDPs: refining convergence of value iteration. In: Ouaknine, J., Potapov, I., Worrell, J. (eds.) RP 2014. LNCS, vol. 8762, pp. 125–137. Springer, Cham (2014). https://doi.org/10.1007/978-3-319-11439-2_10
89. Hahn, E.M., Han, T., Zhang, L.: Synthesis for PCTL in parametric Markov decision processes. In: Bobaru, M., Havelund, K., Holzmann, G.J., Joshi, R. (eds.) NFM 2011. LNCS, vol. 6617, pp. 146–161. Springer, Heidelberg (2011). https://doi.org/10.1007/978-3-642-20398-5_12
90. Hahn, E.M., Hermanns, H., Wimmer, R., Becker, B.: Transient reward approximation for continuous-time Markov chains. IEEE Trans. Reliabil. **64**(4), 1254–1275 (2015)
91. Hahn, E.M., Hashemi, V., Hermanns, H., Lahijanian, M., Turrini, A.: Multi-objective robust strategy synthesis for interval Markov decision processes. In: Bertrand, N., Bortolussi, L. (eds.) QEST 2017. LNCS, vol. 10503, pp. 207–223. Springer, Cham (2017). https://doi.org/10.1007/978-3-319-66335-7_13
92. Hähnle, R., Huisman, M.: Deductive software verification: from pen-and-paper proofs to industrial tools. In: Steffen, B., Woeginger, G. (eds.) Computing and Software Science. LNCS, vol. 10000, pp. 345–373. Springer, Cham (2018)
93. Hansson, H., Jonsson, B.: A logic for reasoning about time and reliability. Form. Asp. Comput. **6**(5), 512–535 (1994)
94. Hartmanns, A., Hermanns, H.: Explicit model checking of very large MDP using partitioning and secondary storage. In: Finkbeiner, B., Pu, G., Zhang, L. (eds.) ATVA 2015. LNCS, vol. 9364, pp. 131–147. Springer, Cham (2015). https://doi.org/10.1007/978-3-319-24953-7_10
95. Hartmanns, A., Timmer, M.: Sound statistical model checking for MDP using partial order and confluence reduction. STTT **17**(4), 429–456 (2015)
96. Hashemi, V., Hermanns, H., Song, L., Subramani, K., Turrini, A., Wojciechowski, P.: Compositional bisimulation minimization for interval Markov decision processes. In: Dediu, A.-H., Janoušek, J., Martín-Vide, C., Truthe, B. (eds.) LATA 2016. LNCS, vol. 9618, pp. 114–126. Springer, Cham (2016). https://doi.org/10.1007/978-3-319-30000-9_9
97. Hashemi, V., Hermanns, H., Song, L.: Reward-bounded reachability probability for uncertain weighted MDPs. In: Jobstmann, B., Leino, K.R.M. (eds.) VMCAI 2016. LNCS, vol. 9583, pp. 351–371. Springer, Heidelberg (2016). https://doi.org/10.1007/978-3-662-49122-5_17

98. Hashemi, V.: Decision algorithms for modelling, optimal control and verification of probabilistic systems. Ph.D. thesis, Saarland University, Saarbrücken, Germany (2017)

99. Hermanns, H., Krčál, J., Křetínský, J.: Probabilistic bisimulation: naturally on distributions. In: Baldan, P., Gorla, D. (eds.) CONCUR 2014. LNCS, vol. 8704, pp. 249–265. Springer, Heidelberg (2014). https://doi.org/10.1007/978-3-662-44584-6_18

100. Hermanns, H., Parma, A., Segala, R., Wachter, B., Zhang, L.: Probabilistic logical characterization. Inf. Comput. **209**(2), 154–172 (2011)

101. Hermanns, H., Wachter, B., Zhang, L.: Probabilistic CEGAR. In: Gupta, A., Malik, S. (eds.) CAV 2008. LNCS, vol. 5123, pp. 162–175. Springer, Heidelberg (2008). https://doi.org/10.1007/978-3-540-70545-1_16

102. Howard, R.A.: Dynamic Probabilistic Systems: Semi-Markov and Decision Processes, vol. 2. Wiley, New York (1972)

103. Johnson, B., Kress-Gazit, H.: Analyzing and revising synthesized controllers for robots with sensing and actuation errors. Int. J. Robot. Res. **34**(6), 816–832 (2015)

104. Jonsson, B., Larsen, K.G.: Specification and refinement of probabilistic processes. In: LICS, pp. 266–277. IEEE Computer Society (1991)

105. Junges, S., Jansen, N., Dehnert, C., Topcu, U., Katoen, J.-P.: Safety-constrained reinforcement learning for MDPs. In: Chechik, M., Raskin, J.-F. (eds.) TACAS 2016. LNCS, vol. 9636, pp. 130–146. Springer, Heidelberg (2016). https://doi.org/10.1007/978-3-662-49674-9_8

106. Kallenberg, L.C.M.: Linear programming and finite Markovian control problems. Math. Center Tracts **148** (1983)

107. Katoen, J.-P.: The probabilistic model checking landscape. In: LICS, pp. 31–45. ACM (2016)

108. Katoen, J.-P., Gretz, F., Jansen, N., Kaminski, B.L., Olmedo, F.: Understanding probabilistic programs. In: Meyer, R., Platzer, A., Wehrheim, H. (eds.) Correct System Design. LNCS, vol. 9360, pp. 15–32. Springer, Cham (2015). https://doi.org/10.1007/978-3-319-23506-6_4

109. Katoen, J.-P., Klink, D., Leucker, M., Wolf, V.: Three-valued abstraction for probabilistic systems. J. Log. Algebr. Program. **81**(4), 356–389 (2012)

110. Kattenbelt, M., Kwiatkowska, M.Z., Norman, G., Parker, D.: A game-based abstraction-refinement framework for Markov decision processes. Form. Methods Syst. Des. **36**(3), 246–280 (2010)

111. Klink, D., Remke, A., Haverkort, B.R., Katoen, J.-P.: Time-bounded reachability in tree-structured QBDs by abstraction. Perform. Eval. **68**(2), 105–125 (2011)

112. Konur, S., Dixon, C., Fisher, M.: Analysing robot swarm behaviour via probabilistic model checking. Robot. Auton. Syst. **60**(2), 199–213 (2012)

113. Kwiatkowska, M.Z.: Model checking for probability and time: from theory to practice. In: LICS, p. 351. IEEE Computer Society (2003)

114. Kwiatkowska, M.Z., Norman, G., Parker, D.: Probabilistic symbolic model checking with PRISM: a hybrid approach. STTT **6**(2), 128–142 (2004)

115. Kwiatkowska, M., Norman, G., Parker, D.: Symmetry reduction for probabilistic model checking. In: Ball, T., Jones, R.B. (eds.) CAV 2006. LNCS, vol. 4144, pp. 234–248. Springer, Heidelberg (2006). https://doi.org/10.1007/11817963_23

116. Kwiatkowska, M., Norman, G., Parker, D.: PRISM 4.0: verification of probabilistic real-time systems. In: Gopalakrishnan, G., Qadeer, S. (eds.) CAV 2011. LNCS, vol. 6806, pp. 585–591. Springer, Heidelberg (2011). https://doi.org/10.1007/978-3-642-22110-1_47

117. Kwiatkowska, M.Z., Norman, G., Parker, D.: The PRISM benchmark suite. In: QEST, pp. 203–204. IEEE Computer Society (2012)
118. Kwiatkowska, M.Z., Norman, G., Segala, R., Sproston, J.: Automatic verification of real-time systems with discrete probability distributions. Theoret. Comput. Sci. **282**(1), 101–150 (2002)
119. Lacerda, B., Parker, D., Hawes, N.: Optimal policy generation for partially satisfiable co-safe LTL specifications. In: IJCAI, pp. 1587–1593. AAAI Press (2015)
120. Larsen, K.G., Skou, A.: Bisimulation through probabilistic testing. Inf. Comput. **94**(1), 1–28 (1991)
121. Larsen, K.G., Thomsen, B.: A modal process logic. In: LICS, pp. 203–210. IEEE Computer Society (1988)
122. Lovejoy, W.S.: A survey of algorithmic methods for partially oberserved Markov decision processes. Ann. Oper. Res. **28**(1), 47–65 (1991)
123. Madani, O., Hanks, S., Condon, A.: On the undecidability of probabilistic planning and related stochastic optimization problems. Artif. Intell. **147**(1–2), 5–34 (2003)
124. Mao, H., Chen, Y., Jaeger, M., Nielsen, T.D., Larsen, K.G., Nielsen, B.: Learning deterministic probabilistic automata from a model checking perspective. Mach. Learn. **105**(2), 255–299 (2016)
125. Mayr, R., Schewe, S., Totzke, P., Wojitczak, D.: MDPs with energy-parity objectives. In: LICS, pp. 1–12. IEEE Computer Society (2017)
126. McIver, A., Morgan, C.: Abstraction, Refinement and Proof for Probabilistic Systems. Monographs in Computer Science. Springer, New York (2005). https://doi. org/10.1007/b138392
127. Neuhäußer, M.R., Stoelinga, M., Katoen, J.-P.: Delayed nondeterminism in continuous-time Markov decision processes. In: de Alfaro, L. (ed.) FoSSaCS 2009. LNCS, vol. 5504, pp. 364–379. Springer, Heidelberg (2009). https://doi.org/10. 1007/978-3-642-00596-1_26
128. Neuhäußer, M.R., Zhang, L.: Time-bounded reachability probabilities in continuous-time Markov decision processes. In: QEST, pp. 209–218. IEEE Computer Society (2010)
129. Norman, G., Parker, D., Sproston, J.: Model checking for probabilistic timed automata. Form. Methods Syst. Des. **43**(2), 164–190 (2013)
130. Parker, D.: Implementation of symbolic model checking for probabilistic systems. Ph.D. thesis, University of Birmingham (2002)
131. Pathak, S., Pulina, L., Tacchella, A.: Evaluating probabilistic model checking tools for verification of robot control policies. AI Commun. **29**(2), 287–299 (2016)
132. Pnueli, A., Zuck, L.D.: Verification of multiprocess probabilistic protocols. Distrib. Comput. **1**(1), 53–72 (1986)
133. Puterman, M.: Markov Decision Processes: Discrete Stochastic Dynamic Programming. Wiley, New York (1994)
134. Quatmann, T., Dehnert, C., Jansen, N., Junges, S., Katoen, J.-P.: Parameter synthesis for Markov models: faster than ever. In: Artho, C., Legay, A., Peled, D. (eds.) ATVA 2016. LNCS, vol. 9938, pp. 50–67. Springer, Cham (2016). https:// doi.org/10.1007/978-3-319-46520-3_4
135. Quatmann, T., Junges, S., Katoen, J.-P.: Markov automata with multiple objectives. In: Majumdar, R., Kunčak, V. (eds.) CAV 2017. LNCS, vol. 10426, pp. 140–159. Springer, Cham (2017). https://doi.org/10.1007/978-3-319-63387-9_7
136. Rabe, M.N., Schewe, S.: Finite optimal control for time-bounded reachability in CTMDPs and continuous-time Markov games. Acta Inf. **48**(5–6), 291–315 (2011)

137. Randour, M., Raskin, J.-F., Sankur, O.: Percentile queries in multi-dimensional Markov decision processes. In: Kroening, D., Păsăreanu, C.S. (eds.) CAV 2015. LNCS, vol. 9206, pp. 123–139. Springer, Cham (2015). https://doi.org/10.1007/978-3-319-21690-4_8

138. Roijers, D.M., Vamplew, P., Whiteson, S., Dazeley, R.: A survey of multi-objective sequential decision-making. J. Artif. Intell. Res. **48**, 67–113 (2013)

139. Scheftelowitsch, D., Buchholz, P., Hashemi, V., Hermanns, H.: Multi-objective approaches to Markov decision processes with uncertain transition parameters. In: Casale, G., Marin, A., Petriu, D., Rossi, S., Van Houdt, B. (eds.) 11th International Conference on Performance Evaluation Methodologies and Tools, VALUETOOLS 2017, Venice, Italy (2017)

140. Schuster, J., Siegle, M.: Markov automata: deciding weak bisimulation by means of non-naïvely vanishing states. Inf. Comput. **237**, 151–173 (2014)

141. Segala, R., Lynch, N.A.: Probabilistic simulations for probabilistic processes. Nord. J. Comput. **2**(2), 250–273 (1995)

142. Sutton, R.S., Barto, A.G.: Reinforcement Learning: An Introduction. The MIT Press, Cambridge (1998)

143. Teichteil-Königsbuch, F.: Path-constrained Markov decision processes: bridging the gap between probabilistic model-checking and decision-theoretic planning. In: ECAI. Frontiers in AI and Applications, vol. 242, pp. 744–749. IOS Press (2012)

144. Tkachev, I., Mereacre, A., Katoen, J.-P., Abate, A.: Quantitative model-checking of controlled discrete-time Markov processes. Inf. Comput. **253**, 1–35 (2017)

145. Turrini, A., Hermanns, H.: Polynomial time decision algorithms for probabilistic automata. Inf. Comput. **244**, 134–171 (2015)

146. Ummels, M., Baier, C.: Computing quantiles in Markov reward models. In: Pfenning, F. (ed.) FoSSaCS 2013. LNCS, vol. 7794, pp. 353–368. Springer, Heidelberg (2013). https://doi.org/10.1007/978-3-642-37075-5_23

147. Vardi, M.Y.: Automatic verification of probabilistic concurrent finite-state programs. In: FOCS, pp. 327–338. IEEE (1985)

148. Vardi, M.Y., Wolper, P.: An automata-theoretic approach to automatic program verification (preliminary report). In: LICS, pp. 332–344. IEEE Computer Society Press (1986)

149. von Essen, C., Jobstmann, B., Parker, D., Varshneya, R.: Synthesizing efficient systems in probabilistic environments. Acta Inf. **53**(4), 425–457 (2016)

150. Wachter, B., Zhang, L.: Best probabilistic transformers. In: Barthe, G., Hermenegildo, M. (eds.) VMCAI 2010. LNCS, vol. 5944, pp. 362–379. Springer, Heidelberg (2010). https://doi.org/10.1007/978-3-642-11319-2_26

151. White, D.J.: A survey of applications of Markov decision processes. J. Oper. Res. Soc. **44**(11), 1073–1096 (1993)

152. Wijs, A., Katoen, J.-P., Bosnacki, D.: Efficient GPU algorithms for parallel decomposition of graphs into strongly connected and maximal end components. Form. Methods Syst. Des. **48**(3), 274–300 (2016)

153. Wimmer, R., Braitling, B., Becker, B., E., Hahn, M., Crouzen, P., Hermanns, H., Dhama, A., Theel, O.E.: Symblicit calculation of long-run averages for concurrent probabilistic systems. In: QEST, pp. 27–36. IEEE Computer Society (2010)

154. Wimmer, R., Jansen, N., Ábrahám, E., Katoen, J.-P., Becker, B.: Minimal counterexamples for linear-time probabilistic verification. Theor. Comput. Sci. **549**, 61–100 (2014)

Continuous-Time Models for System Design and Analysis

Rajeev Alur[1], Mirco Giacobbe[2], Thomas A. Henzinger[2], Kim G. Larsen[3], and Marius Mikučionis[3(✉)]

[1] Department of Computer and Information Science,
University of Pennsylvania, Philadelphia, USA
[2] Institute of Science and Technology Austria, Klosterneuburg, Austria
[3] Department of Computer Science, Aalborg University, Aalborg, Denmark
marius@cs.aau.dk

Abstract. We illustrate the ingredients of the state-of-the-art of model-based approach for the formal design and verification of cyber-physical systems. To capture the interaction between a discrete controller and its continuously evolving environment, we use the formal models of timed and hybrid automata. We explain the steps of modeling and verification in the tools UPPAAL and SPACEEX using a case study based on a dual-chamber implantable pacemaker monitoring a human heart. We show how to design a model as a composition of components, how to construct models at varying levels of detail, how to establish that one model is an abstraction of another, how to specify correctness requirements using temporal logic, and how to verify that a model satisfies a logical requirement.

1 Introduction

A *cyber-physical system* consists of computing devices communicating with one another and interacting with the physical world via sensors and actuators. Increasingly, such systems are everywhere, from smart buildings to medical devices to autonomous cars. Model-based design offers a promising approach for assisting developers to build cyber-physical systems in a systematic manner [2,18,26]. In this methodology, a designer first constructs a model, with mathematically precise semantics, of the system under design, and performs extensive analysis with respect to correctness requirements before generating the implementation from the model.

Models of cyber-physical systems need to capture both the controller—the system under design, and the plant—the environment with continuously evolving physical activities in which the system operates. This typically means a combination of block diagrams, state machines, and differential equations. Furthermore, we need to define models *formally*, that is, in a mathematically precise manner. The formal semantics allows us to answer questions such as, "what are the possible behaviors of a component" and "what does it mean to compose two

© Springer Nature Switzerland AG 2019
B. Steffen and G. Woeginger (Eds.): Computing and Software Science, LNCS 10000, pp. 452–477, 2019.
https://doi.org/10.1007/978-3-319-91908-9_22

components" rigorously, and forms the basis for analysis tools. In this article we do not attempt a survey of the rich literature on formal models and analysis tools for cyber-physical systems, but aim to give an introduction to the subject using a case study (see [13] for some recent surveys).

Medical devices offer an ideal test-bed for exploring the applications of formal methods in system design due to their safety-critical nature, which demands higher levels of reliability and rapidly growing complexity due to increased autonomous operation [27]. We use a dual chamber implantable pacemaker to illustrate the process of model construction and verification [10,22,28,30]. The first step in modeling is to choose a modeling formalism depending on what aspects of the system a designer wants to focus on. The control algorithm of the pacemaker is best modeled as a composition of *timed automata* [5], while the relevant features of the heart can be described as a network of *hybrid automata* [4]. We introduce these two formal models using the modeling tools UPPAAL [8,25] and SPACEEX [17], respectively.

To check that the design works correctly as intended, the designer first needs to express the requirements capturing correctness in a mathematically precise manner. We explain two common ways of formalizing requirements using the pacemaker case study. The automata-based approach corresponds to designing a *monitor* that observes the input/output behavior of the system and enters an error state if an undesirable pattern is detected [29]. The temporal-logic-based approach corresponds to writing down a formula in a specialized formal logic—TCTL (Timed Computation Tree Logic) in our case [3], which captures the desired correctness requirement. A *model checker* is then tasked with the job of automatically checking that the system model satisfies the requirement, and produce feedback in the form of a *counterexample* if this is not the case [12]. Model checkers for continuous-time systems need to symbolically explore the infinitely many reachable states of the model. While symbolic algorithms have been developed for both timed and hybrid automata, the existing technology is more scalable for timed automata [7]. Hence, we construct a timed-automaton-based model of the heart by suppressing many details of the hybrid model, and show how the model checker UPPAAL can then be used to verify requirements of the pacemaker.

Since we created a simplified heart model for the purpose of verifying requirements of the pacemaker, we are faced with a new analysis problem, namely, establishing a rigorous relationship between the two versions of the heart models. Showing that one model is a *refinement* or *abstraction* of another model is another key step in model-based design, and is essential if we want to infer properties of the more complex model based on the analysis of the simpler one [6,11].

Related Work. In this paper, we use a dual chamber implantable pacemaker to illustrate the modeling of control software and the physical world it interacts with. Analyzing the behavior of the heart using formal methods was first proposed in [30], and our modeling of a heart cell is based on the HH model with linear differential equations from that paper. The modeling and model checking of the control algorithm within a pacemaker first appears in [22], and we use the pacemaker model as well as abstracted heart model from that paper for our case study. Note that there has been considerable research on formal modeling and verification of the pacemaker. For instance, [10] develops a more precise SIMULINK model of the heart cell from [30] with non-linear differential equations, and [28] describes a translator from UPPAAL to SIMULINK/STATEFLOW for this purpose.

Organization of the Paper. We begin with an overview of the heart and pacemaker models in Sect. 2. Then, in Sect. 3, we use SPACEEX to construct an abstraction of the heart, and, in Sect. 4, we use UPPAAL to verify the whole heart-pacemaker system. We conclude with future challenges in Sect. 5.

2   The Pacemaker Case Study

The human heart is an excellent example of a naturally occurring timed system. It spontaneously generates electrical impulses that organize the sequence of muscle contractions during each heart beat. The underlying timing pattern of these impulses is key to the proper functioning of the heart. The implantable cardiac pacemaker is a rhythm management device that monitors these patterns and corrects them via external means when needed.

Controlled by the nervous system, a specialized tissue, called the *sinoatrial node*, at the top of the right atrium periodically generates electrical pulses. These pulses cause both atria to contract, forcing blood into the ventricles. The electrical conduction gets delayed at the *atrioventricular node*, allowing the ventricles to fill fully, but then spreads rapidly across the ventricular muscles, resulting in their coordinated contraction, which pumps the blood out of the heart.

A common heart disease, called *bradycardia*, is due to failures in either impulse generation or impulse propagation and results in slow heart rate, leading to insufficient pumping of blood. Bradycardia can be treated by an implantable pacemaker that monitors the heart rate and delivers timely external electrical pulses to maintain an appropriate heart rate as well as atrio-ventricular coordination. Such a pacemaker usually has two leads fixed on the wall of the right atrium and the right ventricle. Activation of local tissue is sensed by these leads, and these sensing events act as inputs to the pacemaker. If these sensed events do not occur in a timely manner, then the pacemaker responds by producing pacing events that trigger electrical stimuli to the heart.

Figure 1 shows the pacemaker controller connected to a heart by two leads (black lines) attached to the walls of the right atrium and the right ventricle (blue area) from the inside. The sinoatrial pulses are propagated through the neural cells (blue lines), which can both be measured and stimulated by the pacemaker.

A modern pacemaker responds to a variety of heart conditions and can operate in different modes. We focus on two modes DDD and VDI and switching between them. In the mode DDD, the pacemaker is pacing both the atrium and the ventricle, both chambers are being sensed, and the pacemaker software

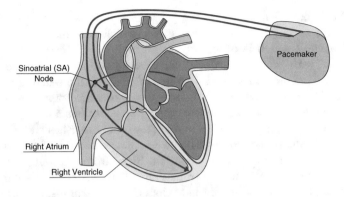

Fig. 1. A heart connected to a pacemaker.

responds to sensing by both activating and inhibiting further pacing, while in the mode VDI, the pacemaker paces only the ventricle, senses both chambers, and sensing causes inhibition of pacing.

2.1 Hybrid Automata: Modeling the Heart

To analyze the functionality of the pacemaker at design time, we need a model that captures how a human heart generates the sensory events. We can view the heart tissue as a network of cardiac cells, where the electric wave propagates along neighbouring cells assuring coordinated contraction. At the cellular level, the electrical signal is a change in the potential across the cell membrane, and is caused by the flow of ions, such as sodium and potassium, between the inside and outside of the cell. Mathematical modeling of the ionic processes corresponding to cell excitation has been studied extensively in computational systems biology. Typically, such a model is described using nonlinear differential equations, and consists of multiple continuous state variables corresponding to quantities such as voltage and ion concentrations and a large number of parameters.

A first step in modeling is to decide what level of detail is appropriate for the analysis task. For the purpose of this case study, we use the model proposed by [30], which is derived from the well-accepted Hodgkin-Huxley (HH) model of cell excitation. It is based on the observation that change in voltage with time that describes the cell excitation upon stimulation can be clearly separated in distinct phases, namely, upstroke, repolarization and resting, such that in each phase the dynamics can be captured by linear differential equations. This behavior can then be described using hybrid automata.

Hybrid automata offer a formal model for systems that exhibit both discrete and continuous behavior, such as the combination of heart cells (continuous behavior) and a pacemaker (discrete behavior). Continuous state change can be described by guarded differential equations, while discrete state change can be specified by guarded difference equations. The guard (or "invariant") of a differential equation is a state predicate that specifies the condition under which the differential equation is active; the guard of a difference equation is a state predicate that specifies the condition under which the difference equation is enabled. Formally, a hybrid automaton is a graph whose vertices (or "modes") are annotated with sets of guarded differential equations, and whose edges (or "mode transitions") are annotated with sets of guarded difference equations [19]. A behavior of a hybrid automaton is a sequence of trajectory segments, where each trajectory segment satisfies one of the mode equations and its invariant for the duration of the segment, the last state of a segment satisfies one of the guards of a transition equation, and together with the first state of the subsequent segment, it satisfies the transition equation. Since from any initial state, there may be several mode equations and transition equations to choose from, a hybrid automaton can have many different behaviors ("nondeterminism"). Two or more hybrid automata can be composed by using, in addition, synchronization labels on the transitions.

Figure 2 shows the hybrid automaton describing the behavior of a heart cell. It has two variables v_x and v_y for voltages over cell membrane, four modes resting, stimulus, upstroke, and repolarization, and five synchronization labels in0, in1, out0, out1, and get. The difference $v_x - v_y$ models the transmembrane voltage potential of the cell, the labels in1 and in0 model rising and falling edges of an input stimulus, and out1 and out0 of an output stimulus, respectively. The label get indicates a spike peak of the cell voltage. The parameters a_x, a_y, i_{st}, b_y, c_x, c_y, d_x, d_y, V_R, V_T, and V_O are constants and are defined according to the specific cell instance. Initially, the cell is in resting mode and v_x and v_y have any values that satisfy the invariant of resting, which is $0 \leq v_x - v_y \leq V_R$. Afterwards, the values of v_x and v_y continuously evolve according to the differential equation of resting which is given by $\dot{v}_x = a_x v_x$ and $\dot{v}_y = a_y v_y$. The parameters a_x and a_y are such that $a_x < a_y < 0$ therefore the voltage drops when in resting, and the continuous evolution progresses as long as the variables satisfy the invariant $0 \leq v_x - v_y \leq V_R$. At any time, the

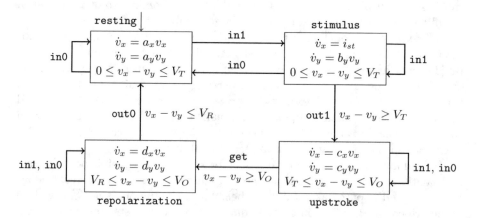

Fig. 2. Hybrid automaton for the Hodgkin-Huxley model of a heart cell.

automaton can either take a transition labelled by in0 and stay in resting or a transition labelled by in1 and switch to stimulus. In stimulus, the dynamics is governed by the flow $\dot{v}_x = i_{st}$ and $\dot{v}_y = b_y v_y$ for the parameters $b_y < 0 < i_{st}$ and satisfies the invariant $0 \leq v_x - v_y \leq V_T$, thus making the voltage rise up to V_T. As long as the values satisfy the invariant $0 \leq v_x - v_y \leq V_T$ the automaton can either execute the transition labelled with in1 and stay in stimulus or take in0 and switch back to resting, while as soon as the variable values satisfy the guard $v_x - v_y \geq V_T$ it can take out1 and switch to upstroke. The trajectory of the potential continues to progress in this manner, namely it evolves continuously in modes and discontinuously on transitions. In the remaining modes upstroke and repolarization the parameters are such that $c_x > c_y > 0 > d_y > d_x$. As a result, we show in Fig. 3 a sample trajectory demonstrating how invariants and guards relate to the automaton modes.

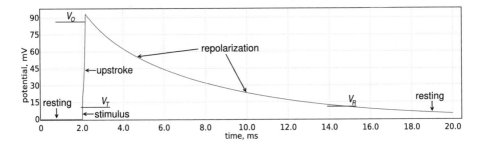

Fig. 3. Heart cell electrical potentials and modes (locations) over time.

The model of the whole heart consists of a composition of cells, which synchronize according to their output and input stimuli. Figure 4 shows such an example. The cells are organized in a linear fashion, where the labels out1 and out0 of a cell synchronize with the input labels in1 and in0 of the next cell. At the top of the network, we have the sinoatrial (SA) node, which is the cell that takes through in1 and in0 the input stimulus of the heart, which can come from its natural pacing or from the actuator of the pacemaker. The output labels out1 and out0 of the SA node then trigger the input labels of a second cell. The output of the second cell triggers the input of a third, and so on, creating a chain of stimuli. The whole chain can be seen as divided in two main groups, namely atrium and ventricle. The output of the cell at the boundary of the atrium then produces the output of the whole atrium, which is connected to the cell at the top of the ventricle, which is called atrioventricular (AV) node. The AV node may take the pacing coming from the atrium or from the second actuator of the pacemaker.

Hybrid automata synchronize transitions according to their labels, namely, transitions whose labels are shared fire synchronously, while transitions whose labels are not shared fire asynchronously. Figure 4 shows our naming scheme for the synchronization of output and input simili between cells. In particular, we

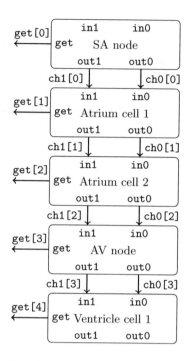

Fig. 4. Interface of a composition of heart cells.

obtain synchronization between the transition labeled by out1 and in1 (resp. out0 and in0) by renaming both to ch1[i] (resp. ch0[i]), where i is the index of the upstream cell. Complementarily, we prevent the synchronization between the transitions labeled by get by renaming each of them to get[i], where i is the index of the respective cell. Figure 5 shows part of the reachable configurations in the composition of two cells. Initially, both automata are in resting (Fig. 5, top left). In the initial configuration, the first automaton can execute all its available transitions (labeled by in1 and in0), while the second cannot execute any (labeled by ch1 and ch0). This is because ch1 and ch0 are shared between the two automata, and therefore can be executed only if both automata can. On the other hand, in1 and in0 appear only in the first automaton, and therefore they can be executed. As a result, in0 and in1 label asynchronous transitions, where the first makes a self loop to the initial configuration, and the second switches the first automaton to stimulus. The latter configuration (Fig. 5, top right) enables a transition labeled by ch1, which is synchronous and switches the first automaton to upstroke and the second to stimulus (Fig. 5, bottom right). In its turn, this configuration enables an asynchronous transition labeled by getA, and so on. The rest of the composition continues similarly.

Hybrid automata can be classified according to the generality of their guards, differential equations, and difference equations. The more restrictive these equations are, the more feasible the analysis of the resulting behaviors. Assume that

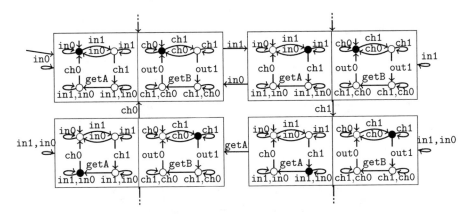

Fig. 5. Some configurations of a composition of two heart cells, where the events out1 and out0 of the left and in1 and in0 of the right cell are renamed, resp., to ch1 and ch0, and get to getA and getB. The active modes in each configuration of two cells are depicted by the black circles. The effect of an enabled transition is shown as a transition between configurations.

x is a state vector. A hybrid automaton has *piece-wise affine dynamics* if all mode invariants and transition guards have the form $x \in U$, all mode equations have the form $\dot{x} = Ax + v$ with $v \in V$, and all transition equations have the form $x' = Bx + w$ with $w \in W$, for matrices A and B, and polyhedra U, V, and W. The hybrid automaton has *piece-wise constant dynamics* if $A = 0$. It is a *timed automaton* if $A = 0$ and $V = 1$. In a timed automaton, all state components always advance at the rate of time; they represent "clocks".

2.2 Timed Automata: Modeling the Pacemaker

The pacemaker monitors the pattern of events emitted by the heart and corrects them via external means when needed. The pacemaker itself is composed of a number of components, each of which is essentially a simple state-machine producing output events triggered by timing constraints. This makes the formalism of timed automata ideal for the description of these components.

Figure 6 shows the architecture block diagram of the entire model. The pacemaker senses the voltage peaks of one cell from the atrium and one cell of the ventricle through the events Aget and Vget (which are renaming of the respective get labels), and controls the heart by sending stimuli to the SA node and the VA node though the labels AP and VP. In particular, upon the occurrence of AP the timed automaton AP-to-A generates a pulse by sending an event i1 to the SA node and after some fixed time sending i0 indicating the end of the stimulus pulse. Similarly, VP triggers VP-to-V which in its turn stimulates the VA node. The events AP and VP are generated by the internals of the pacemaker, which we introduce in this section.

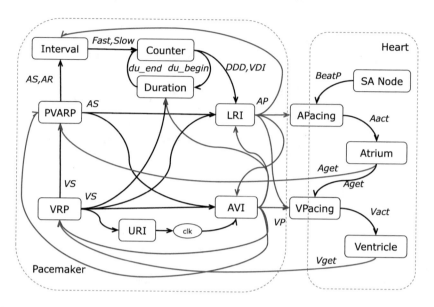

Fig. 6. Overview of the modeled processes: red arrows indicate pacing inputs to the heart, and blue arrows are monitored output events from the heart.

To first informally explain the formalism of timed automata and how they are modelled in the tool UPPAAL, we will use the **VRP** process shown in Fig. 7. UPPAAL timed automaton consists of locations and edges modeling its discrete states and discrete transitions respectively. Locations and edges have labels. For example, process **VRP** has an *initial* location with a circle O inscribed, which has a name label Idle. The location **VRP** has an invariant label

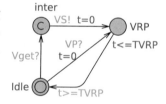

Fig. 7. Ventricular refractory period (**VRP**).

t<=TVRP meaning that the automaton may stay in **VRP** only while the clock t value is less or equal to the value of the **TVRP** constant. Process **VRP** may stay in location Idle for arbitrary amount of time because there is no invariant forcing it to move, it also listens for synchronizations over channels **Vget** and **VP**. The reception over channel **Vget** transitions it to inter, while the reception over **VP** switches it directly to location **VRP** and reset the clock t. The location inter has C inscribed to denote that it is *committed* and the automaton's progress cannot be interrupted neither by the time delay nor any other process, therefore it has to move immediately by taking an edge transition to location **VRP** which is labeled with synchronization VS! and update t=0 meaning that it emits a message on channel **VS** and resets the clock t so the time is counted from zero in location **VRP** up to the bound of **TVRP**. Then process **VRP** may move from location **VRP** back to Idle but only when the guard t>=TVRP is satisfied, i.e. only after spending at least the amount **TVRP** of time in location **VRP**. As a result, the state of a timed automaton consists of its location and variable values, and there are two kinds of transitions between states: delay (when clock values increase while satisfying the current invariant) and edge-transitions when clock values satisfy the guards, synchronize, update the value and satisfy the target location invariant.

In addition to theoretical definition of timed automata UPPAAL implements a number of practical extensions which make the modeling task easier and more succinct:

Integer variables. Apart from constants, most programming and modeling languages use variable value manipulations. Likewise UPPAAL allows bounded integer variables to be used and combined with clock constraints. On one hand, the value of an integer variable becomes an integral part of the state of the system. On the other hand, the integer variable value can be used as a constant in clock constraints because the integer variable value may change only upon edge-transitions between the timed automata states. An example of such integer use is demonstrated by `TPVARP` in Fig. 8d, where the bound `t<=TPVARP` is changed by transition from `PVARP` to `Idle`. Interestingly, the bounded integer variables do not increase the theoretical expressiveness of timed automata, therefore all theoretical results still apply. For example, we have compressed the representation of `Counter` and `Duration` in Fig. 8g and f by encoding the `fast?` and `slow?` counting into local integer variables `i` (originally [22] enumerated into a number of distinct locations).

Input-output synchronization. In contrast to non-directed multi-label synchronizations in SPACEEX hybrid automata, the synchronizations between UPPAAL processes are directed in the sense that one process is sending with exclamation mark (e.g. `VS!`) and the receiving process is listening with question mark (`VS?` respectively). By default, channel synchronizations are handshake, meaning that both sender and receiver must mutually agree for the transition to take place. Handshake synchronizations happen only in pairs of processes, i.e. only two processes may participate in the synchronization at a time, and all possible pairs are considered non-deterministically when multiple receivers are available.

Broadcast synchronization. In addition UPPAAL supports broadcast synchronization where one sender may synchronize with multiple receivers. In contrast to handshake synchronization, the broadcast synchronization is non-blocking in a sense that the sender is not required to wait for any receivers and only the ready receivers participate in the synchronization. While the broadcast synchronization can be emulated by adding receiving self-loops in locations where the process does not implement the reception part, but in practice it is more succinct way of modeling, allows partial order reduction and verification is more efficient as the tool does not need to consider the extra edges. All the synchronizations in the pacemaker study use broadcast channels because non-blocking behavior is closer to how the independent processes communicate and it is easier to include additional processes without modifying the original behavior, which is useful in adding extra monitors for diagnostics and verification.

Urgency. Sometimes the modeled process needs to execute several transitions without delaying in the locations between. We call such locations *urgent* and draw a letter U inside to mark that time cannot progress in them.

Atomicity. The process in urgent location may still be interrupted by a transition in another process even though the time is not allowed to pass. UPPAAL implements a *committed* location with C inscribed in case an uninterrupted ("atomic") sequence of transitions is needed. Committed locations are useful in connecting multiple channel synchronizations at the same time which would be very cumbersome to model otherwise.

We have reconstructed the pacemaker model from [22] shown in Fig. 8. The overview block diagram of the processes is shown in Fig. 6 where the heart is represented by SA Node cell, two atrium and two ventricle cells. The cells can be stimulated by ch1* and ch0* channels synchronizations denoting the start and ending of the stimulus. The heart can be self-stimulating by a SA Node cell or by a pacemaker by a signal over channel AP (Atrium Pulse). Normally the atrium cells relay the signal to ventricle cells, but if the stimulus is too weak (or too short), then the ventricle is stimulated by the pacemaker over VP (Ventricle Pulse) channel. The pacemaker monitors the activity of the atrium and ventricle by receiving from the signals over the corresponding channels Aget and Vget. All channels used in Fig. 8 are of broadcast type, meaning that one sending event can be sensed by zero or more receivers at once and the sending process is not blocked by the absence of receivers.

Low Rate Interval (LRI, Fig. 8a) maintains the minimum heart rate by providing pulses to the heart (AP! in DDD mode and VP! in VDI mode) if there was no signal from atrium (AS?) after the last ventricle pulse for longer than TLRI−TAVI time interval. The time interval is measured by the clock t which is reset after the last ventricle pulse (by sensing either VS? or VP?). The LRI also monitors the mode switching by reacting to inputs VDI? and DDD? and starts pacing the ventricle (VP!) instead of atrium (AP!).

Atrioventricular Interval (AVI, Fig. 8c) maintains the maximum interval between the atrium and ventricle activation by issuing ventricle pacing VP! if no ventricular event received VS? within TAVI time after the last atrial event (AS? or AP?). The interval is measured by the clock clk shared with **Upper Rate Interval** (URI, Fig. 8b) which prevents pacing the ventricle too fast by resetting clk upon ventricular event (VS? or VP?).

Postventricular Atrial Refractory Period (PVARP, Fig. 8d) converts atrium events A_act? and Aget? into sensed event AS! and filters the sensed noise during the blanking period (t<=PVAB) after the ventricular event followed by a refractory period (t<=PVARP). The blocked events are converted to ABlock! and AR! for advanced diagnostics.

Ventricular Refractory Period (VRP, Fig. 7) similarly translates the ventricle peak events over Vget? into sensed events over VS! and filters out by not re-transmitting for a time interval t<=TVRP after the last event.

We use the same set of constants as in the original publication [22]: TAVI = 150, TLRI = 1000, TPVARP = 100, TVRP = 150, TURI = 400, TPVAB = 50.

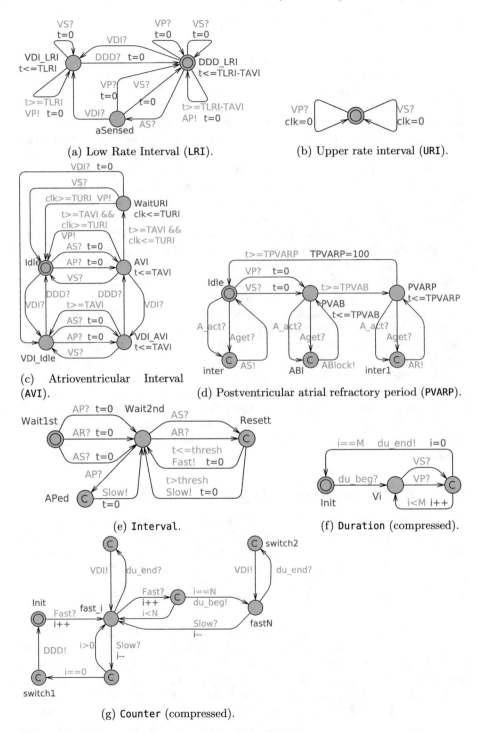

(a) Low Rate Interval (LRI).

(b) Upper rate interval (URI).

(c) Atrioventricular Interval (AVI).

(d) Postventricular atrial refractory period (PVARP).

(e) Interval.

(f) Duration (compressed).

(g) Counter (compressed).

Fig. 8. Timed automata model of the pacemaker.

3   Relating and Combining Models

Hybrid automata can be numerically simulated, or formally analyzed. While simulation generates one behavior at a time, formal analysis can answer questions about all possible behaviors of a hybrid automaton. The most basic behavioral analysis question about a hybrid automaton is the reachability question. The bounded reachability question asks, given two state sets S and T, and a time bound t, if there is a behavior from a state in S to a state in T of total duration no more than t. The unbounded reachability question asks, given two sets S and T, if there is a behavior of any duration from a state in S to a state in T. In general, both the bounded and unbounded reachability questions are formally undecidable even for hybrid automata with piece-wise constant dynamics [21]. However, methods and tools have been developed for solving many interesting instances of these problems [17,20]. Moreover, both questions can always be answered algorithmically for the special case of timed automata [5].

Unfortunately, the heart-pacemaker model is not a timed automaton, as heart cells fall in the class of hybrid automata with piece-wise affine dynamics, and so does their composition with the pacemaker. On the other hand, if each cell model was a timed automaton, the whole system would be a timed automaton, and therefore the verification answer solvable. Can we model each cell with timed automata, so that by verifying the resulting system we verify the original system too? To this aim, we exploit the notion of *abstraction*: if the timed automaton abstracts the original cell model, then any negative answer for the reachability question in the abstract composed system implies the same negative answer in the original composed system. In the following, we construct such a timed automaton, we explain its relation with the original hybrid automaton, and we demonstrate how to use SPACEEX to mechanically prove that the former abstracts the latter.

3.1   A Timed Abstraction of the Heart Cell Model

We construct a timed automaton A with the same discrete structure of the heart cell model in Fig. 2 and one clock variable. In the abstract model, the clock is reset upon entering each mode, and the transition guards out of a mode are chosen based on the duration of time spent in that mode. Figure 9 shows such construction. The clock variable is t and the times T_{out1}, T_{out0}, and T_{get} bound respectively the duration before the occurrence of the symbols out1, out0, and get.

The abstraction has been constructed manually, by making the following observations about the original model in Fig. 2. Initially the cell is in resting mode, where $v_x - v_y$ drops towards 0, therefore the invariant $0 \leq v_x - v_y \leq V_T$ is always satisfied. In mode resting the events in1 and in0 can occur at any time, where in0 is ignored and in1 switches to stimulus. In stimulus the automaton is also driven by the difference $v_x - v_y$ which may increase and force automaton to move to upstroke. The time bound T_{out1} models the largest time where $v_x - v_y$ hits V_T and satisfies the guard for out1, i.e., $v_x - v_y \geq V_T$. The symbol out1 may

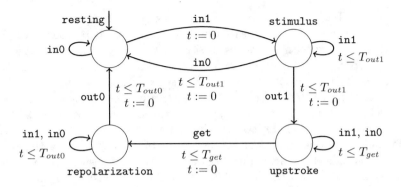

Fig. 9. Timed abstraction of the hybrid automaton in Fig. 2.

occur any time before T_{out1}, as well as in1 and in0 which may happen as long as the invariant $0 \le v_x - v_y \le V_T$ of stimulus is satisfied. Upon the occurrence of out1 the value of $v_x - v_y$ is exactly V_T, the process switches to upstroke in which it stays until the value of $v_x - v_y$ hits exactly V_O, whose time is modeled by V_O. Similarly, upon get the process switches to repolarization and stays until it takes out0 when $v_x - v_y$ hits V_R, which must happen no later than T_{out0} time.

Whether the timed automaton in Fig. 9 is an abstraction of the heart cell model in Fig. 2 requires us to first rigorously define what we mean by abstraction, namely, what are the features of the original system that are to be conserved by the abstract system. Second, we need to instantiate the parameters T_{out0}, T_{out1}, and T_{get} and prove that the so obtained timed automaton abstracts the original hybrid automaton. We discuss these points in Sects. 3.2 and 3.3. For the time being, the construction of the timed abstraction relies on the intuition and the expertise of the designer. In this phase, the only formal requirement is that the timed automaton needs to *deterministic*, so that in the next phase we can construct its complement. A timed automaton is deterministic if at every mode every pair of transitions with common symbol have disjoint guards [5]. The timed abstraction of Fig. 9 is deterministic simply because at every mode each symbol has at most one switch.

3.2   The Timed Language of Hybrid Automata

A hybrid automaton A abstracts a hybrid automaton B when all observable behaviors of the latter are also observable behaviors of the former. The observable behaviors are the features of the system dynamics that we need to observe in order to decide whether a specification is satisfied. The more detailed the observable behaviors, the harder is constructing an abstraction, but the more sophisticated are the properties that we can verify. For verifying properties such as Tachycardia, Bradycardia, and so on, we want to observe sequences of labels $\sigma = \sigma_0\sigma_1\ldots$ with the exact times $\tau = \tau_0\tau_1\ldots$ at which each of these events has occurred. Each of such pairs of sequences (σ, τ) is called a timed word. For instance, the word that repeats the pattern in1, out1, get, out0 is a timed word when coupled with the times of staying respectively in modes resting, stimulus, upstroke, and repolarization, repeatedly. The set of all the timed words of the hybrid automaton H is called its *timed language* $\mathcal{L}_H$.

Abstraction with respect to timed languages can be phrased as timed language inclusion, that is to say that the timed automaton A abstracts the hybrid automaton H if $\mathcal{L}_H \subseteq \mathcal{L}_A$. Alternatively, one can prove that A abstracts H by saying that there does not exist a timed word of H that is not a timed word of A. This is indeed a reachability question for the composition of H with the complement of A, which can be tackled by SPACEEX. To this aim, we first construct the complement automaton for A, i.e., the timed automaton for which all timed words from language $\mathcal{L}_A$ end up in accepting mode (corresponding to modes in the original automaton) and any other word end up hitting some auxiliary rejecting mode. Then, we use SPACEEX to search for any timed word of H that is rejected by the complement automaton of A, namely a word of their composition that hits a rejecting mode of the latter. If no such word is found, then we can conclude that A abstracts H.

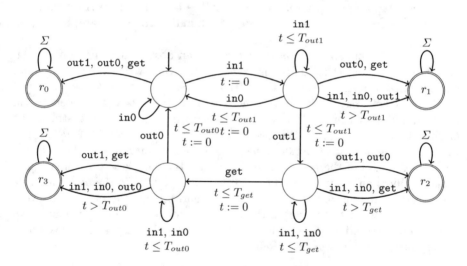

Fig. 10. Complement of the timed abstraction in Fig. 9.

The timed abstraction A is deterministic. To complement a deterministic timed automaton we need first to add dummy transitions so to make the automaton accept any timed word (on the same alphabet $\Sigma = \{$in0, in1, out0, out1, get$\}$), yet remaining deterministic. Figure 10 shows the result. From mode resting only in1 and in0 can be received, therefore we add a dummy transition, i.e., a transition to a dummy mode, which receives any other symbol, i.e., out1, out0, and get. From stimulus, in1, in0, and out1 can be received and can be received as long as $t \leq T_{out1}$, therefore we add a dummy transition with guard $t > T_{out1}$ that receives such events, so as to ensure all guards of transitions with common symbol to be disjoint and maintain the automaton deterministic. The symbols out0 and get cannot be received at all from stimulus, therefore we add a dummy transition with unconstrained guard. Similarly, we make the same construction on modes upstroke and repolarization. Finally, one can observe that every trajectory that ends in any dummy mode corresponds to a timed word that is not in $\mathcal{L}_A$. The dummy modes are those that recognise the complement language, thus we mark them as rejecting modes.

In summary, we formulate the question of whether the timed abstraction in Fig. 9 abstracts the heart cell model in Fig. 2 by asking SPACEEX whether the composition of the heart cell model in Fig. 2 with the complement automaton in Fig. 10 can reach any of the rejecting modes. The result is a reachability question on hybrid automata with affine dynamics.

3.3 Verifying the Abstraction Using SPACEEX

SPACEEX is a modeling framework for the composition of hybrid automata that collects several reachability analysis techniques, which are called *scenarios*. We can divide the currently available scenarios in three main categories: simulation based, support function based, and the polyhedra based scenarios. The simulation based scenario generates time-bounded sample trajectories, and can be used to reject an abstraction, but not to verify one. The support function and the polyhedra based scenarios perform reachability analysis by generating sequences of polyhedra that over-approximate the whole space of reachable states and both are possibly suitable for verifying an abstraction. In fact, when they answer that all rejecting modes are unreachable, then the rejecting modes are actually unreachable, and the abstraction is proven. The converse is not necessarily true and, moreover, termination is not guaranteed either. For this reason, successfully concluding an abstraction proof requires several trial and error attempts in tuning the parameters and the multiple heuristic options of SPACEEX.

We use the polyhedral based scenario which is also know as the PHAVER scenario. The PHAVER scenario over-approximates the continuous flow of every mode by piece-wise constant differential inclusions [16]. In other words, it turns affine dynamics of the form $\dot{x} = Ax + v$ with $v \in V$ into differential inclusions of the form $\dot{x} \in U$, where U is a set the contains all values that the derivative $\dot{x}$ can possibly take. Both such transformation and the symbolic reachability analysis on the so obtained hybrid automaton are then done by quantifier elimination, e.g., by the Fourier Motzkin algorithm [4].

The main challenge is then to choose the time bounds T_{out1}, T_{out0}, and T_{get}. Indeed, if we let v_x and v_y take arbitrary negative values it is impossible to find finite bounds, therefore we add the extra invariant $v_x, v_y \geq 0$ to all modes of the heart cell. Then, we proceed as follows. First, we set all constants using a set of values the original article [30], which we show in Table 1 (except for i_{st}, which is not specified there). Second, we decide a value for i_{st} and third, we

Table 1. The heart cell model parameters [30].

a_x	a_y	b_y	c_x	c_y	d_x	d_y	V_R	V_T	V_O
-0.98	-0.16	-0.16	15	1.4	-0.98	-0.16	10	10	83

search for tight enough values for T_{out1}, T_{out0}, and T_{get} until SPACEEX concludes that all rejecting modes are unreachable. Table 2 shows a few attempts to prove reachability of any of the rejecting modes r_0, r_1, r_2, or r_4. The parameters were chosen manually, and SPACEEX converged on each of these proofs in less than a second. The parameters for which none of the rejecting modes are reachable are parameters for which the abstraction is verified.

Table 2. Attempts of proving that the timed automaton of Fig. 9 abstracts the hybrid automaton of Fig. 2. The answer indicates the set of reachable rejecting modes in the complement automaton of Fig. 5.

i_{st}	T_{out1}	T_{out0}	T_{get}	Answer	i_{st}	T_{out1}	T_{get}	T_{out0}	Answer
10	1	1	1	$\{r_3\}$	1	1	0.5	7.5	$\{r_1\}$
10	1	1	10	$\emptyset$	1	10	0.5	7.5	$\emptyset$
10	0.1	0.1	1	$\{r_1, r_2, r_3\}$	100	10	0.5	7.5	$\emptyset$
10	1	0.5	10	$\emptyset$	100	0.01	0.5	7.5	$\{r_1\}$
10	1	0.5	7.5	$\emptyset$	100	0.1	0.5	7.5	$\emptyset$

3.4   Abstraction Refinement

An abstraction captures specific aspects of the original model while it may ignore others, and in some cases, an abstraction may be too coarse for proving a property. For instance, the timed automaton of Fig. 9 captures the upper bounds of the transition times for the labels out1, out0, and get, while it ignores the lower bounds. Without a lower bound for the duration of an output stimulus, properties such as the efficient propagation of a signal through cells (see Sect. 4.3) cannot be proven. In fact, often an abstraction requires to be adapted to the property of interest. This is usually done incrementally, by adding a few important details at a time, through a process of *abstraction refinement*. In the following, we show how to refine our abstraction by exploiting the compositionality of hybrid and timed automata.

The timed automaton of Fig. 11 captures the requirement that output stimulus of a heart cell should last at least time T_{stim}. As previously, we compute its complement, and we use SPACEEX to prove that for certain parameters of the heart cell model, certain lower bounds are satisfied (see Table 3), in this way obtaining a second abstraction for the original heart cell. We use the new abstraction B to refine the previous abstraction A by composing them, obtaining

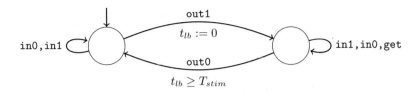

Fig. 11. Abstraction for the lower bound between out1 and out0.

the timed automaton in Fig. 12, which is again an abstraction of the original system. Table 3 shows the proven parameters. In particular, for the original model (parameters from Table 1, first line in Table 3) we cannot prove any lower bound unless we reduce V_R and additionally specify the global invariant that x and y do not exceed a maximum voltage V_{max}. For instance, with $V_{max} = 100$ and $V_R = 5$, we have a lower bound of 0.86. The lower bound for the stimulus length depends on V_{max}, V_R, and the coefficient d_x, e.g., with $d_x = -0.83$, we have $T_{stim} = 1.001$.

In summary, we construct a sequence of time abstractions for a heart cell and formally proved that they indeed abstract its timed language. The abstraction question turns out to be a reachability question on a heart cell composed with the complement of its timed abstraction, which is a rather small system. We employ SPACEEX on this problem, and then we modify the heart-pacemaker model by replacing each cell with the abstraction. The whole model is now a timed automaton, which can be verified by UPPAAL.

4   Verifying Temporal Requirements

Several behavioural properties of (composite) timed and hybrid automata models may be expressed as simple reachability properties. This is already illustrated previously in Sect. 3.2, where we saw that language inclusion between the "exact" hybrid automaton model H of a heart cell and a proposed timed automaton abstraction A could be stated as a simple reachability property of rejecting locations in a product between H and the complement of A. However, it may often be more convenient to express desired properties of a timed or hybrid automaton directly as formulas of temporal logic, thus permitting properties to be combined using boolean connectives. In fact the whole spectrum of temporal-logic has been extended to the setting of timed labelled transition systems, with

Table 3. Proven parameters for upper and lower bound abstractions (Figs. 9 and 11) w.r.t. different versions of a heart cell.

a_x	a_y	b_y	c_x	c_y	d_x	d_y	V_R	V_T	V_O	V_{max}	$i_s t$	T_{out1}	T_{get}	T_{out0}	T_{stim}
−0.98	−0.16	−0.16	15	1.4	−0.98	−0.16	10	10	83	∞	10	1	0.5	7.5	0
−0.98	−0.16	−0.16	15	1.4	−0.98	−0.16	5	10	83	100	10	1	0.5	7.5	0.86
−0.98	−0.16	−0.16	15	1.4	−0.83	−0.16	5	10	83	100	10	1	0.5	19	1.001

model checking suitably extended to timed automata, see e.g. [9]. In this section we demonstrate how timed automata verification using UPPAAL may be used in establishing key properties of the pace-maker.

4.1   Timed Automaton of a Heart Cell in UPPAAL

Figure 12 shows the UPPAAL version of the heart cell timed automaton abstract model of Fig. 9. The locations in the timed automaton match their corresponding modes in the hybrid automaton and the timings are taken from Table 3 and converted into microseconds as shown in Fig. 12b. Note that Tstim was determined as a minimum delay between out1! and out0! events, therefore we use an extra clock t_lb to enforce this constraint. This lower bound on the repolarization time turned out to be important to ensure a successful signal handover as verified in Sect. 4.3.

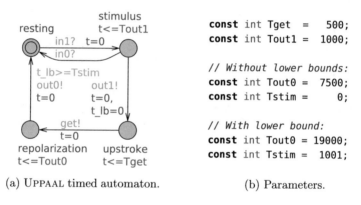

(a) UPPAAL timed automaton.   (b) Parameters.

Fig. 12. Abstract model of a heart cell.

4.2   Requirement Specifications

The model checker UPPAAL supports verification of requirements expressed within a fragment of *Timed Computation Tree Logic* (TCTL). Among TCTL properties we consider here the following:

- $\mathbf{A}\square\varphi$, which is satisfied if any reachable state satisfies φ (*Invariance*),
- $\mathbf{A}\square_{\leq T}\varphi$, which is satisfied if any state reachable within T time-units satisfies ϕ (*Time-bounded Invariance*),
- $\mathbf{A}\Diamond\varphi$, which is satisfied if on any path the properties φ is (eventually) satisfied at some point (*Eventual*),
- $\mathbf{A}\Diamond_{\leq T}\varphi$ which is satisfied if on any path the property φ is satisfied within T time-units φ (*Time-Bounded Eventual*),

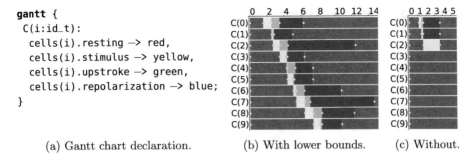

```
gantt {
  C(i:id_t):
    cells(i).resting -> red,
    cells(i).stimulus -> yellow,
    cells(i).upstroke -> green,
    cells(i).repolarization -> blue;
}
```

(a) Gantt chart declaration.   (b) With lower bounds.   (c) Without.

Fig. 13. Gantt chart of state evolution of 10 cell automaton from Fig. 12.

- $\varphi \rightsquigarrow_{\leq T} \psi$, which requires than whenever a state is reached satisfying φ, then any path from this state must eventually satisfy ψ – and within a total of T time-units. Logically, the (time-bounded) leads-to property is equivalent to $\mathbf{A}(\varphi \Rightarrow \mathbf{A}\Diamond_{\leq T}\psi)$ (*Time-Bounded Leads-to*).

For deterministic timed labelled transition systems, it may easily be shown that all of the above properties – as they all quantify universally over execution sequences out of a state – are preserved by language inclusion. Thus, if $\mathcal{L}_H \subseteq \mathcal{L}_A$ and A has been verified to satisfy a TCTL property φ of the above type, then it may readily be concluded that the "exact" model H also satisfies φ.

Moreover, as demonstrated in [1] all of the above properties may be expressed directly as a reachability property—i.e. invariance properties—of the given timed automaton composed with a monitor corresponding to the property.

4.3 Healthy Heart Requirements

Figure 13 shows the state evolution of 10 heart cell timed automata connected in series. In the beginning all cells are in `resting` (red bar), then the first cell is stimulated and moves to `stimulus` (yellow bar). After a short while the first cell stimulates the second one and moves to `upstroke` (green bar), then it moves to `repolarization` (blue bar) and back to `resting` (red bar). The second cell then stimulates the third and so on.

A healthy heart should propagate the signal all the way from SA node to atrium and then ventricle. This requirement can be formulated as the following *leads-to* property:

$$\mathbf{A}\Box(\text{ch1[0]!} \rightarrow \mathbf{A}\Diamond\,\text{ch1[N]!})$$

which says that for every stimuli of the first cell (`ch1[0]!`) we should eventually observe the signal at the end of the chain (`ch1[N]!`), where `N` is the number of cells. UPPAAL verifies that this property holds when `Tstim>Tout1`, i.e. the lower bound of being in repolarization is greater than the time spent in `stimulus`, and the signal propagates successfully just like in the Gantt chart in Fig. 13b. It takes 0.2 s to verify an instance of four cells, 6.8 s for five and 28 min for six, which shows signs of the state space explosion in terms of the number of processes due to non-deterministic behavior. Interestingly the property is not satisfied if the cell stays in repolarization longer than in stimulus, i.e. Tstim>Tout1, because the signaling cell may go from upstroke to repolarization, stop the stimulus and bring the next cell back to resting, thus disrupting the signal. One such particular scenario is visualized in Fig. 13c: the stimulus of cell(2) is interrupted by cell(1) by a quick move back to resting before cell(2) reaches upstroke, hence cell(3) stays in resting and the signal is lost. We conclude that the relation between maximum delay in stimulus and total delay in upstroke and repolarization is crucial for correct signal propagation through heart cell network.

In addition to checking the signal propagation we can also estimate the minimum and maximum delay time between the start and end of the signal by using the duration monitor automaton and queries shown in Fig. 14. The infimum and supremum queries instruct UPPAAL to record the minimum and maximum values of clock t when the automaton in the corresponding locations Min and Max. Note that the automaton always stays in location Max in between the from! and till! events, therefore the supremum of t corresponds to the time duration between those events. And the automaton visits Min when t has its maximum value, therefore the infimum of t in Min corresponds to the shortest observed duration between events.

In case of our chain of heart cell timed automata – using the above pattern – the duration between ch1[0]! and ch1[N]! is found to be bounded by the interval of $[0, N]ms$, where N is the number of cells in series. Due to congruence properties of abstraction, this bound is guaranteed to be valid also for the composition of hybrid heart cells in Fig. 5.

4.4   Abstraction of Cell Composition

Once we have estimated the duration of a signal travel through the chain of cells, we can model the entire chain as one automaton re-transmitting the signal with a delay. By replacing a chain of cells with one process we reduce the verification effort significantly without losing the precision. We model the atrium and the ventricle as separate processes representing a sequence of individual heart cells. Figure 15a shows a healthy atrium which relays its activation signal

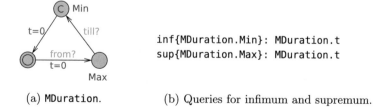

(a) MDuration.   (b) Queries for infimum and supremum.

Fig. 14. Estimating the delay between from! and till! events.

to the recipient (ventricle and pacemaker) by delaying 150 ms. We model an atrium which may loose a signal by taking an extra transition without notifying the recipient in Fig. 15a to reflect abnormal behavior. The ventricle part of the heart is modeled likewise. The sinoatrial node is responsible for triggering the heart beating process and is modelled in Fig. 15b. In principle, healthy SANode may beat with interval of 500–2000 ms (30–120 bpm), but a faulty one may beat more or less frequently or stop beating altogether, thus we do not put any constraints to allow all possible (healthy and faulty) behavior to allow a pacemaker to do its job, there the verification will cover all possible scenarios (failure may occur at any time, in SANode, atrium or ventricle). The result is a sequence of signals: the SANode stimulates atrium and atrium stimulates ventricle, but atrium and ventricle may also be stimulated by a pacemaker, thus we also add a pacing process which multiplexes the pacing events (`AtrioP` and `VentriP`) with heart events (`BeatP` and `Aget`) into atrium (`Aact`) and ventricle (`Vact`) stimuli as shown in Fig. 15c.

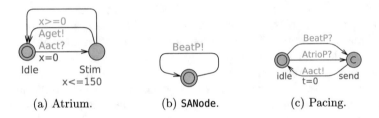

(a) Atrium.   (b) SANode.   (c) Pacing.

Fig. 15. Abstract heart model.

4.5 Pacemaker Requirements

The pacemaker is required not to issue ventricle pace events (`VP!`) for at least `TURI` time units since the last ventricle pulse (`VP!`) or the ventricle sense (`VS!`) events. This requirement can be formulated into the following TCTL property:

$$\mathbf{A}\square((\mathsf{VS!} \vee \mathsf{VP!}) \rightarrow \mathbf{A}\square_{\leq \mathsf{TURI}} \neg \mathsf{VP!})$$

This property expresses that the action `VP!` may only occur after a time-separation of at least `TURI` time-units from a previous `VP!` of `VS!` action. Dually, the requirement that the interval between two ventricular events (either `VP!` or `VS!`) should be less than `TLRI` can be expressed as the following property:

$$(\mathsf{VS!} \vee \mathsf{VP!}) \rightsquigarrow_{\leq \mathsf{TLRI}} (\mathsf{VS!} \vee \mathsf{VP!})$$

which says that the actions `VP!` and `VS!` must occur with at most a time-separation of `TLRI` time-units.

Table 4. Resources used by UPPAAL to verify properties from Fig. 16.

Pacemaker model	URL			LRL		
	Time	Memory	Result	Time	Memory	Result
Basic DDD	0.01 s	5.37 MB	OK	0.01 s	5.37 MB	OK
DDD-VDI	129.57 s	248.26 MB	OK	148.58 s	267.78 MB	Not OK

UPPAAL implements TCTL referring to system states rather than synchronization events, therefore the above properties are converted into the event-monitoring automata (Fig. 16a and b respectively) and the requirements are reformulated in terms of monitoring automata locations and clock values. The monitor transitions are labeled with VP? and VS? synchronizing with the corresponding events VP! and VS!, and the local clocks t are reset accordingly, so that the value of the local clock t in locations interval and two_a corresponds to the time duration between two successive events. The property then verifies that the duration is within bounds U.t>=TURI and L.t<=TLRI.

The model with abstracted heart cell chain had too large state space to verify due too many non-deterministic processes in the heart. Interestingly the unrestricted "random" heart model (as described in [22]) takes much less resources as it does not need to remember the complex heart state. We used a heart model with arbitrary rate $(0, \infty)$ which may beat at any time or not at all. Such heart captures all possible heart behaviors and hence verification provides a much stronger safety guarantee than with the more realistic and detailed heart model. Table 4 shows that the basic DDD pacemaker model is simple enough that it hardly takes any time to verify (0.01 s, 5.37 MB). The DDD-VDI pacemaker includes counters and thus the behavior is much more complicated leading to more verification effort (129.57 s, 248.26 MB). We found that the lower rate limit property does not hold with TLRI bound on more complex DDD-VDI pacemaker (the result is "Not OK"), but the basic DDD satisfies the lower rate limit with twice as large 1500 bound, meaning that the pacemaker may delay longer before pacing, but the bound is still reasonable (one pulse per 1.5 s).

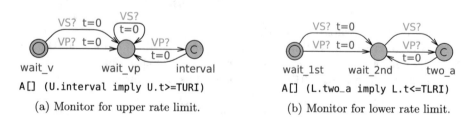

A[] (U.interval imply U.t>=TURI)   A[] (L.two_a imply L.t<=TLRI)

(a) Monitor for upper rate limit.   (b) Monitor for lower rate limit.

Fig. 16. Automata and queries for timed properties from [22].

5   Future Directions and Challenges

As illustrated by the case study presented in this paper, model-based design and verification is a promising approach to the development of cyber-physical systems in a principled manner, and the foundations of this methodology lie in cross-fertilization of ideas from mathematical modeling and algorithmic analysis. As systems keep getting more and more complex, and society increasingly relies upon the internet of things, advances in tools for designing such systems are crucial to ensuing the safe and reliable operation of systems. This calls for continued research in core areas of formal methods such as identification of analyzable design abstractions, analysis techniques, and scalability of tools. We conclude this paper by highlighting some directions for future research.

Scalability: Given the computational intractability of the computational problems in formal verification, developing tools that can analyze real-world systems will always remain a challenge. The experience with tools such as UPPAAL demonstrates that small steps in advancing the scalability collectively contribute towards impressive results over the long haul. For the verification of hybrid systems, tools based on robustness analysis offer promising opportunities [14,15]. Robust analysis means that results obtained should not be too sensitive with respect to the actual quantities (timing, voltages, energy, etc.) used in the underlying model. Efforts on identifying metrics that will ensure "continuity" of various behavioral properties are currently being researched for a number of quantitative modeling formalisms. As illustrated in Sect. 3, abstraction is an effective way of reducing the complexity of a system, and developing techniques for constructing abstractions automatically remains a challenge.

Quantitative Analysis: Traditionally, models and techniques used for establishing correctness and for evaluating performance have been disjoint. In our pacemaker case study, beyond functional correctness of the control algorithm, we are also interested in estimating, for instance, the average energy used by the pacemaker. A promising new direction in formal methods research these days is the development of probabilistic models, with associated tools for quantitative evaluation of system performance along with correctness (see [23]).

Applications: Given the scalability challenges, formal methods for the design and analysis of cyber-physical systems are not yet widely applicable. Thus, identifying application domains and problems where the current techniques and tools can be applied effectively is itself a challenge that requires an understanding of formal methods as well as the application domains. As our example of pacemaker suggests, medical cyber-physical systems is a promising domain, and other interesting recent case studies include an infusion pump and an artificial pancreas [27]. Another promising domain of application is ensuring the safety of controllers used in autonomous vehicles [24].

Data-Driven Models: As our case study illustrates, a key step is the construction of the heart model. Mathematical models of physical systems are hard to obtain, but increasingly, due to the rapid proliferation of sensors, lots of data is available. This leads to a new research question: given the pacemaker algorithm and the property that we want to verify, can we construct a patient-specific model of the heart derived from the sensory data obtained from a patient? Deriving models suitable for formal analysis from data is a challenging, and relatively unexplored, research area.

Acknowledgements. This research was supported in part by the Austrian Science Fund (FWF) under grants S11402-N23(RiSE/SHiNE) and Z211-N23 (Wittgenstein Award). This research has received funding from the Sino-Danish Basic Research Centre, IDEA4CPS, funded by the Danish National Research Foundation and the National Science Foundation, China, the Innovation Fund Denmark centre DiCyPS, as well as the ERC Advanced Grant LASSO.

References

1. Aceto, L., Bouyer, P., Burgueño, A., Larsen, K.G.: The power of reachability testing for timed automata. In: Arvind, V., Ramanujam, S. (eds.) FSTTCS 1998. LNCS, vol. 1530, pp. 245–256. Springer, Heidelberg (1998). https://doi.org/10.1007/978-3-540-49382-2_22
2. Alur, R.: Principles of Cyber-Physical Systems. MIT Press, Cambridge (2015)
3. Alur, R., Courcoubetis, C., Dill, D.: Model-checking in dense real-time. Inf. Comput. **104**(1), 2–34 (1993)
4. Alur, R., Courcoubetis, C., Halbwachs, N., Henzinger, T., Ho, P.-H., Nicollin, X., Olivero, A., Sifakis, J., Yovine, S.: The algorithmic analysis of hybrid systems. Theoret. Comput. Sci. **138**, 3–34 (1995)
5. Alur, R., Dill, D.L.: A theory of timed automata. Theoret. Comput. Sci. **126**(2), 183–235 (1994)
6. Alur, R., Henzinger, T., Lafferriere, G., Pappas, G.: Discrete abstractions of hybrid systems. Proc. IEEE **88**(7), 971–984 (2000)
7. Behrmann, G., David, A., Larsen, K., Pettersson, P., Yi, W.: Developing uppaal over 15 years. Softw. - Pract. Exp. **41**(2), 133–142 (2011)
8. Behrmann, G., David, A., Larsen, K.G.: A tutorial on UPPAAL. In: Bernardo, M., Corradini, F. (eds.) SFM-RT 2004. LNCS, vol. 3185, pp. 200–236. Springer, Heidelberg (2004). https://doi.org/10.1007/978-3-540-30080-9_7
9. Bouyer, P., Fahrenberg, U., Larsen, K.G., Markey, N., Ouaknine, J., Worrell, J.: Model checking real-time systems. In: Clarke, E., Henzinger, T., Veith, H. (eds.) Handbook of Model Checking. Springer, Heidelberg (2017)
10. Chen, T., Diciolla, M., Kwiatkowska, M., Mereacre, A.: Quantitative verification of implantable cardiac pacemakers over hybrid heart models. Inf. Comput. **236**, 87–101 (2014). Special Issue on Hybrid Systems and Biology
11. Clarke, E., Grumberg, O., Long, D.: Model checking and abstraction. In: Proceedings of 19th ACM Symposium on Principles of Programming Languages, pp. 343–354 (1992)
12. Clarke, E., Grumberg, O., Peled, D.: Model Checking. MIT Press, Cambridge (2000)
13. Derler, P., Lee, E.A., Sangiovanni-Vincentelli, A.L.: Modeling cyber-physical systems. Proc. IEEE **100**(1), 13–28 (2012)

14. Duggirala, P.S., Fan, C., Mitra, S., Viswanathan, M.: Meeting a powertrain verification challenge. In: Kroening, D., Păsăreanu, C.S. (eds.) CAV 2015. LNCS, vol. 9206, pp. 536–543. Springer, Cham (2015). https://doi.org/10.1007/978-3-319-21690-4_37

15. Fainekos, G.E., Sankaranarayanan, S., Ueda, K., Yazarel, H.: Verification of automotive control applications using S-TaLiRo. In: IEEE American Control Conference, pp. 3567–3572 (2012)

16. Frehse, G.: PHAVer: algorithmic verification of hybrid systems past HyTech. In: Morari, M., Thiele, L. (eds.) HSCC 2005. LNCS, vol. 3414, pp. 258–273. Springer, Heidelberg (2005). https://doi.org/10.1007/978-3-540-31954-2_17

17. Frehse, G., et al.: SpaceEx: scalable verification of hybrid systems. In: Gopalakrishnan, G., Qadeer, S. (eds.) CAV 2011. LNCS, vol. 6806, pp. 379–395. Springer, Heidelberg (2011). https://doi.org/10.1007/978-3-642-22110-1_30

18. Henzinger, T.A., Sifakis, J.: The embedded systems design challenge. In: Misra, J., Nipkow, T., Sekerinski, E. (eds.) FM 2006. LNCS, vol. 4085, pp. 1–15. Springer, Heidelberg (2006). https://doi.org/10.1007/11813040_1

19. Henzinger, T.A.: The theory of hybrid automata. In: Inan, M.K., Kurshan, R.P. (eds.) Verification of Digital and Hybrid Systems, vol. 170, pp. 265–292. Springer, Heidelberg (2000). https://doi.org/10.1007/978-3-642-59615-5_13

20. Henzinger, T.A., Ho, P.-H., Wong-Toi, H.: HyTech: a model checker for hybrid systems. In: Grumberg, O. (ed.) CAV 1997. LNCS, vol. 1254, pp. 460–463. Springer, Heidelberg (1997). https://doi.org/10.1007/3-540-63166-6_48

21. Henzinger, T.A., Kopke, P.W., Puri, A., Varaiya, P.: What's decidable about hybrid automata? J. Comput. Syst. Sci. **57**(1), 94–124 (1998)

22. Jiang, Z., Pajic, M., Moarref, S., Alur, R., Mangharam, R.: Modeling and verification of a dual chamber implantable pacemaker. In: Flanagan, C., König, B. (eds.) TACAS 2012. LNCS, vol. 7214, pp. 188–203. Springer, Heidelberg (2012). https://doi.org/10.1007/978-3-642-28756-5_14

23. Kwiatkowska, M.: Quantitative verification: models, techniques, and tools. In: Proceedings of ACM SIGSOFT Symposium on Foundations of Software Engineering, pp. 449–458 (2007)

24. Larsen, K.G., Mikučionis, M., Taankvist, J.H.: Safe and optimal adaptive cruise control. In: Meyer, R., Platzer, A., Wehrheim, H. (eds.) Correct System Design. LNCS, vol. 9360, pp. 260–277. Springer, Cham (2015). https://doi.org/10.1007/978-3-319-23506-6_17

25. Larsen, K.G., Pettersson, P., Yi, W.: Uppaal in a nutshell. Int. J. Softw. Tools Technol. Transf. **1**(1–2), 134–152 (1997)

26. Lee, E.A.: What's ahead for embedded software. IEEE Comput. **33**, 18–26 (2000)

27. Lee, I., Sokolsky, O., Chen, S., Hatcliff, J., Jee, E., Kim, B., King, A., Mullen-Fortino, M., Park, S., Roederer, A., Venkatasubramanian, K.: Challenges and research directions in medical cyber-physical systems. Proc. IEEE **100**(1), 75–90 (2012)

28. Pajic, M., Jiang, Z., Lee, I., Sokolsky, O., Mangharam, R.: Safety-critical medical device development using the UPP2SF model translation tool. ACM Trans. Embed. Comput. Syst. **13**(4), 127:1–127:26 (2014)

29. Vardi, M., Wolper, P.: Reasoning about infinite computations. Inf. Comput. **115**(1), 1–37 (1994)

30. Ye, P., Entcheva, E., Grosu, R., Smolka, S.A.: Efficient modeling of excitable cells using hybrid automata. In: Proceedings of Computational Methods in System Biology, pp. 216–227 (2005)

Statistical Model Checking

Axel Legay[1], Anna Lukina[2(✉)], Louis Marie Traonouez[1], Junxing Yang[3],
Scott A. Smolka[3], and Radu Grosu[2]

[1] Inria Rennes – Bretagne Atlantique, Rennes, France
anna.lukina@tuwien.ac.at
[2] Cyber-Physical Systems Group, Technische Universität Wien, Vienna, Austria
[3] Department of Computer Science, Stony Brook University, Stony Brook, USA

Abstract. We highlight the contributions made in the field of *Statistical Model Checking* (SMC) since its inception in 2002. As the formal setting, we use a very general model of *Stochastic Systems* (an SS is simply a family of time-indexed random variables), and *Bounded LTL* (BLTL) as the temporal logic. Let S be an SS and φ a BLTL formula. Our survey of the area is centered around the following five main contributions.

Qualitative approach to SMC: Is the probability that S satisfies φ greater or equal to a certain threshold?

Quantitative approach to SMC: What is the probability that S satisfies φ? Typically this results in a confidence interval being computed for this probability.

Rare Events: What happens when the probability that S satisfies φ is extremely small, i.e. it is a rare event? To make the SMC approach viable in this setting, rare-event estimation techniques *Importance Sampling* and *Importance Splitting* are deployed to great advantage.

Optimal Planning: Motivated by the success of Importance Sampling and Importance Splitting in rare-event SMC, we explore the use of these techniques in the context of optimal planning. In particular, we consider ARES, an optimal-planning approach based on a notion of adaptive receding-horizon planning. We illustrate the utility of ARES on the planning problem of bringing a flock of birds (autonomous agents) from a random initial configuration to a *V-formation*, an energy-conservation formation deployed by migrating geese. Somewhat ironically, the performance of ARES can be evaluated using (quantitative) SMC, as the problem to be solved is of the form $F(J \leq \theta)$; i.e. does an ARES-generated plan eventually bring the flock to a configuration where the flock-wide cost function J is below a given threshold θ?

Optimal Control: We show that the techniques we presented for optimal planning in the form of ARES carry over to the control setting in the form of *Adaptive-Horizon Model-Predictive Control* (AMPC). We again use the V-formation problem for evaluation purposes. We also introduce the concept of *V-formation games*, and show how the power of AMPC can be used to ward off cyber-physical attacks.

B. Steffen and G. Woeginger (Eds.): Computing and Software Science, LNCS 10000, pp. 478–504, 2019.
https://doi.org/10.1007/978-3-319-91908-9_23

1   Introduction

Quantitative models of computer systems include *stochastic systems*, whose state transitions are equipped with a probability distribution. Stochastic systems in turn include both discrete- and continuous-time Markov Chains. Our main interest will be in computing the probability by which a stochastic system S satisfies a given temporal-logic property φ. In contrast to the Boolean version of the model checking problem, this *quantitative model checking* (QMC) problem allows one to precisely determine how well S satisfies φ. When φ is a linear temporal logic (LTL) formula, QMC serves as a way to measure the number of paths that satisfy the formula.

The QMC problem is typically solved by a numerical approach that, like state-space exploration, iteratively computes (or approximates) the exact measure of paths satisfying relevant subformulas. The algorithm for computing such measures depends on the class of stochastic systems being considered as well as the logics used for specifying the correctness properties. QMC algorithms for a variety of such contexts have been discovered [1,8,9] and there are mature tools (see e.g. [7,28]) that have been used to analyze a variety of systems in practice.

Despite the great strides made by numerical QMC algorithms, there are many challenges. Numerical algorithms work only for systems that have certain structural properties. Further, these algorithms have significant time and space requirements, and thus scaling to large systems is a challenge. Also, the temporal logics supported by these QMC algorithms are extensions of classical temporal logics that are not particularly popular among engineers. Finally, numerical techniques do not easily scale to extended stochastic models whose semantics also depends on other quantities such as real-time or energy.

Another approach to QMC is to *simulate* the system for finitely many runs, and use techniques from the area of statistics to infer whether the samples provide a *statistical* evidence for the satisfaction or violation of the specification [41]. The crux of this approach is that since sample runs of a stochastic system are drawn according to the distribution defined by the system, they can be used to obtain estimates of the probability measure on executions. These techniques are known under the name of *Statistical Model Checking* (SMC).

The SMC approach enjoys many advantages. First, these algorithms only require the system to be simulatable (or rather, sample executions be drawn according to the measure space defined by the system). Thus, it can be applied to a larger class of systems than numerical QMC algorithms, including black-box systems and infinite-state systems. Second, the approach can be generalized to a larger class of properties, i.e., Fourier transform-based logics [2,3]. Finally, the algorithm is easily parallelizable, which can help scale to large systems. In cases where the model-checking problem is undecidable or too complex, SMC is often the only viable solution. As we shall see, SMC has been the subject of intensive research. SMC algorithms have been implemented in a series of tools, including Ymer [39], Prism [29], and UPPAAL [10]. Recently, we have implemented a series of SMC techniques in a flexible and modular toolset called Plasma Lab [4].

Despite the successes SMC has enjoyed, a serious obstacle in its application is its poor performance in predicting the satisfaction of properties holding with very low probability, so-called *rare events* (REs). In such cases, the number of samples required to attain a high confidence ratio and a low error margin explodes [16,42]. Two sequential Monte-Carlo techniques, *importance sampling (ISam)* [12] and *importance splitting (ISpl)* [15], originally developed for statistical physics [25], promise to overcome this obstacle. We discuss the important role these techniques have come to play in the SMC arena and beyond, in particular, for the purposes of optimal planning and control of controllable MDPs, a popular strategy-based probabilistic modeling formalism [14].

With this background in place, the following discussion summarizes the main contributions of this chapter. It also serves as a guide to how the chapter is organized.

- Section 2 provides definitions of the two basic ingredients of the SMC problem. It presents a very general definition of stochastic system as a family of time-indexed random variables, and it also introduces the temporal logic Bounded LTL (BLTL), which is often used in the SMC setting.
- Section 3 describes SMC-based approaches to both the qualitative and quantitative stochastic verification problems [33,39]. The qualitative version is of the form "How is the probability of property satisfaction related to a given threshold?", whereas the quantitative version asks the question "What is a confidence interval for this probability?"
- Section 4 considers the impact of *rare events* on the performance of SMC. As discussed above, we show how *importance sampling* and *importance splitting* can be successfully used for the statistical model checking of rare-event properties. In particular, we consider *command-based importance sampling* which is intended to reduce the computational burden imposed by ISam. Instead of reiterating the process of choosing a good distribution, the command-based approach considers parametrization over the syntax of stochastic guarded commands. We thereafter investigate the application of importance splitting with fixed and adaptive levels for rare-event probability estimation. These approaches are implemented in the Plasma toolset, thereby allowing for a thorough evaluation of their performance.
- Section 5 shows how the rare-event approach to SMC can be exploited for the purpose of optimal plan synthesis for controllable MDPs. Specifically, we present ARES, an efficient approximation algorithm for generating optimal plans (action sequences) that take an initial state of an MDP to a state whose cost is below a specified (convergence) threshold [30]. ARES uses Particle Swarm Optimization (PSO), with *adaptive sizing* for both the receding horizon and the particle swarm. Inspired by Importance Splitting, the length of the horizon and the number of particles are chosen such that at least one particle reaches a *next-level* state, that is, a state where the cost decreases by a required delta from the previous-level state.
- Section 6 demonstrates the utility of importance splitting and PSO in the context of control, where we present a new formulation of model-predictive

control called *Adaptive-Horizon MPC* (AMPC). We show that under certain controllability conditions, an AMPC controller can bring a system to an optimal state (WRT a given cost function) with probability 1. Somewhat ironically, we provide statistical guarantees of the performance of AMPC and ARES using SMC, the same approach that inspired our use of rare-event techniques in the first place.

– Section 7 draws our conclusions and discusses future work in the area.

2   Formal Definitions

In this section, we introduce several formal definitions that will be used in the rest of the chapter. We consider a set of states S and a time domain $T \subseteq \mathbb{R}$. We first introduce the general definition of a stochastic system.

Definition 1 (Stochastic system). *A stochastic system over S and T is a family of random variables $\mathcal{X} = \{X_t \mid t \in T\}$, each random variable X_t having range S.*

The definition of a stochastic system as a family of random variables is quite general and includes systems with both continuous and discrete dynamics. In this work, we will focus our attention on a limited, but important, class of stochastic system: stochastic discrete event systems, which we note $\mathcal{S} = (S, T)$. This class includes any stochastic system that can be thought of as occupying a single state for a duration of time before an event causes an instantaneous state transition to occur. An *execution* for a stochastic system is any sequence of observations $\{x_t \in S \mid t \in T\}$ of the random variables $X_t \in \mathcal{X}$. It can be represented as a sequence $\omega = (s_0, t_0), (s_1, t_1), \ldots, (s_n, t_n) \ldots$, such that $s_i \in S$ and $t_i \in T$, with time stamps monotonically increasing, e.g. $t_i < t_{i+1}$. Let $0 \leq i \leq n$, we denote $\omega^i = (s_i, t_i), \ldots, (s_n, t_n)$ the suffix of ω starting at position i. Let $\bar{s} \in S$, we denote $Path(\bar{s})$ the set of executions of $\mathcal{X}$ that starts in state $(\bar{s}, 0)$ (also called initial state) and $Path^n(\bar{s})$ the set of executions of length n.

In [39], Younes showed that the set of executions of a stochastic system is a measurable space, which defines a probability measure μ over $Path(\bar{s})$. The precise definition of μ depends on the specific probability structure of the stochastic system being studied.

Properties over traces of $\mathcal{S}ys$ are defined via the so-called Bounded Linear Temporal Logic (BLTL). BLTL restricts Linear Temporal Logic by bounding the scope of the temporal operators. The syntax of BLTL is defined as follows:

$$\phi = \phi \vee \phi \mid \phi \wedge \phi \mid \neg \phi \mid \mathrm{F}^{\leq t} \phi \mid \mathrm{G}^{\leq t} \phi \mid \phi \, \mathrm{U}^{\leq t} \phi \mid \mathrm{X}\phi \mid \alpha$$

$\vee, \wedge$ and $\neg$ are the standard logical connectives and α is a Boolean constant or an atomic proposition constructed from numerical constants, state variables and relational operators. X is the *next* temporal operator: $\mathrm{X}\phi$ means that ϕ will be true on the next step. F, G and U are temporal operators bounded by time interval $[0, t]$, relative to the time interval of any enclosing formula. We refer to this as a *relative interval*. F is the *finally* or *eventually* operator: $\mathrm{F}^{\leq t}\phi$

means that ϕ will be true at least once in the relative interval $[0, t]$. G is the *globally* or *always* operator: $G^{\leq t}\phi$ means that ϕ will be true at all times in the relative interval $[0, t]$. U is the *until* operator: $\psi U_{\leq t}\phi$ means that in the relative interval $[0, t]$, either ϕ is initially true or ψ will be true until ϕ is true. Combining these temporal operators creates complex properties with interleaved notions of *eventually* (F), *always* (G) and *one thing after another* (U).

3   On Verifying Requirements: The SMC Approach

Consider a stochastic system (S, T) and a property ϕ. *Statistical model checking* refers to a series of simulation-based techniques that can be used to answer two questions: (1) **Qualitative:** Is the probability that (S, T) satisfies ϕ greater or equal to a certain threshold? and (2) **Quantitative:** What is the probability that (S, T) satisfies ϕ? Contrary to numerical approaches, the answer is given up to some correctness precision. As we shall see later, SMC solves those problems with two different approaches, while classical numerical approaches only solve the second problem, which implies the first one, but is harder.

In the rest of the section, we overview the two first statistical model checking techniques that were proposed in the literature. Let B_i be a discrete random variable with a Bernoulli distribution of parameter p. Such a variable can only take 2 values 0 and 1 with $Pr[B_i = 1] = p$ and $Pr[B_i = 0] = 1 - p$. In our context, each variable B_i is associated with one simulation of the system. The outcome for B_i, denoted b_i, is 1 if the simulation satisfies ϕ and 0 otherwise. The latter is decided with the help of a monitoring procedure [18]. The objective of an SMC algorithm is to generate simulations and exploit the Bernoulli outcomes to extract the global confidence on the system.

In the next subsections, we present three algorithms used in the early works on SMC to solve both the quantitative and the qualitative problems. Extension of those algorithms to unbounded temporal operators [17,34] and to nested probabilistic operators exist [39]. As shown in [19] those extensions are debatable and often slower. Consequently, we will not discuss them.

3.1   Qualitative Analysis Using Statistical Model Checking

The main approaches [33,39] proposed to answer the qualitative question are based on *hypothesis testing*. Let $p = Pr(\phi)$, to determine whether $p \geqslant \theta$, we can test $H : p \geqslant \theta$ against $K : p < \theta$. A test-based solution does not guarantee a correct result but it is possible to bound the probability of making an error. The *strength* (α, β) of a test is determined by two parameters, α and β, such that the probability of accepting K (respectively, H) when H (respectively, K) holds, called a Type-I error (respectively, a Type-II error), is less or equal to α (respectively, β).

A test has *ideal performance* if the probability of the Type-I error (respectively, Type-II error) is exactly α (respectively, β). However, these requirements make it impossible to ensure a low probability for both types of errors simultaneously (see [39] for details). A solution to this problem is to relax the test by working with an *indifference region* (p_1, p_0) with $p_0 \geqslant p_1$ ($p_0 - p_1$ is the *size of the region*). In this context, we test the hypothesis $H_0 : p \geqslant p_0$ against $H_1 : p \leqslant p_1$ instead of H against K. If the value of p is between p_1 and p_0 (the indifference region), then we say that the probability is sufficiently close to θ so that we are indifferent with respect to which of the two hypotheses K or H is accepted. The thresholds p_0 and p_1 are generally defined in terms of the single threshold δ, e.g., $p_1 = \theta - \delta$ and $p_0 = \theta + \delta$. We now need to provide a test procedure that satisfies the requirements above. In the next two subsections, we recall two solutions proposed by Younes in [39,40].

Single Sampling Plan. This algorithm plays more a historical role rather than to be used directly. However, it is still exploited in subsequent algorithms. To test H_0 against H_1, we specify a constant c. If $\sum_{i=1}^{n} b_i$ is larger than c, then H_0 is accepted, else H_1 is accepted. The difficult part in this approach is to find values for the pair (n, c), called a *single sampling plan (SSP in short)*, such that the two error bounds α and β are respected. In practice, one tries to work with the smallest value of n possible so as to minimize the number of simulations performed. Clearly, this number has to be greater if α and β are smaller but also if the size of the indifference region is smaller. This results in an optimization problem, which generally does not have a closed-form solution except for a few special cases [39]. In [39], Younes proposes a binary search based algorithm that, given p_0, p_1, α, β, computes an approximation of the minimal value for c and n.

Sequential Probability Ratio Test (SPRT). The sample size for a single sampling plan is fixed in advance and independent of the observations that are made. However, taking those observations into account can increase the performance of the test. As an example, if we use a single plan (n, c) and the $m > c$ first simulations satisfy the property, then we could (depending on the error bounds) accept H_0 without observing the $n - m$ other simulations. To overcome this problem, one can use the *sequential probability ratio test (SPRT in short)* proposed by Wald [36]. The approach is briefly described below.

   In SPRT, one has to choose two values A and B ($A > B$) that ensure that the strength of the test is respected. Let m be the number of observations that have been made so far. The test is based on the following quotient:

$$\frac{p_{1m}}{p_{0m}} = \prod_{i=1}^{m} \frac{Pr(B_i = b_i | p = p_1)}{Pr(B_i = b_i | p = p_0)} = \frac{p_1^{d_m}(1 - p_1)^{m - d_m}}{p_0^{d_m}(1 - p_0)^{m - d_m}}, \tag{1}$$

where $d_m = \sum_{i=1}^{m} b_i$. The idea behind the test is to accept H_0 if $\frac{p_{1m}}{p_{0m}} \geq A$, and H_1 if $\frac{p_{1m}}{p_{0m}} \leq B$. The SPRT algorithm computes $\frac{p_{1m}}{p_{0m}}$ for successive values of m until either H_0 or H_1 is satisfied; the algorithm terminates with probability 1 [36]. This has the advantage of minimizing the number of simulations. In [39], Younes proposed a logarithmic based algorithm SPRT that given p_0, p_1, α and β implements the sequential ratio testing procedure.

SPRT has been largely used in the formal methods area. In this paper, we shall show that the approach extends to a much larger class of problems than the one originally foreseen.

3.2   Quantitative Analysis Using Statistical Model Checking and Estimation

In the case of estimation, existing SMC algorithms rely on classical Monte Carlo estimation. More precisely, they calculate a priori the required number of simulations according to a Chernoff bound [31] that allows the user to specify an error ε and a probability δ that the estimate $\hat{p}$ will not lie outside the true value $\pm\varepsilon$. Given that a system has true probability p of satisfying a property, the Chernoff bound ensures $P(|\hat{p} - p| \geqslant \varepsilon) \leqslant \delta$. Parameter δ is related to the number of simulations N by $\delta = 2e^{-2N\varepsilon^2}$ [31], giving

$$N = \lceil (\ln 2 - \ln \delta)/(2\varepsilon^2) \rceil . \tag{2}$$

4   Rare Events

SMC is a Monte Carlo method that takes advantage of robust statistical techniques to bound the error of the estimated result (e.g., [31,36]). To quantify a property, it is necessary to observe the property, where increasing the number of observations generally increases the confidence of the estimate. Rare properties are often highly relevant to system performance (e.g., bugs and system failures are required to be rare) but pose a problem for statistical model checking because they are difficult to observe. Fortunately, rare-event techniques such as *importance sampling* [24,26] and *importance splitting* [25,26,32] may be successfully applied to statistical model checking.

Importance sampling and importance splitting have been widely applied to specific simulation problems in science and engineering. Importance sampling works by estimating a result using weighted simulations and then compensating for the weights. Importance splitting works by reformulating the rare probability as a product of less rare probabilities, conditioned on the levels that must be achieved.

In this section, we summarize our contributions in terms of applying importance sampling and importance splitting to the SMC problem. We then discuss their implementation within the Plasma toolset.

4.1   Command-Based Importance Sampling

Importance sampling works by simulating a probabilistic system under a weighted (*importance sampling*) measure that makes a rare property more likely to be seen [23]. It then compensates the results by the weights, to estimate the probability under the original measure. When simulating Markov Chains, this compensation is typically performed on the fly, with almost no additional overhead.

Given a set of finite traces $\omega \in \Omega$ and a function $z : \Omega \to \{0, 1\}$ that returns 1 iff a trace satisfies some property, the importance sampling estimator is given by

$$\sum_{i=1}^{N} z(\omega_i) \frac{\mathrm{d}f(\omega_i)}{\mathrm{d}f'(\omega_i)}.$$

N is the number of simulation traces ω_i generated under the importance sampling measure f', while f is the original measure. $\frac{\mathrm{d}f}{\mathrm{d}f'}$ is the *likelihood ratio*.

For importance sampling to be effective it is necessary to define a "good" importance sampling distribution: (i) the property of interest must be seen frequently in simulations and (ii) the distribution of the simulation traces that satisfy the property in the importance sampling distribution must be as close as possible to the normalized distribution of the same traces in the original distribution. Failure to consider both (i) and (ii) can result in underestimated probability with overestimated confidence.

Since the main motivation of importance, sampling is to reduce the computational burden, the process of finding a good importance sampling distribution must maintain the scaling advantage of SMC and, in particular, should not iterate over all the states or transitions of the system. We, therefore, consider parameterized importance sampling distributions, where our parametrization is over the syntax of stochastic *guarded commands*, a common low-level modeling language of probabilistic systems[1].

Each command has the form (*guard, rate, action*). The *guard* enables the command and is a predicate over the state variables of the model. The *rate* is a function from the state variables to $\mathbb{R}_{>0}$, defining the rate of an exponential distribution. The *action* is an update function that modifies the state variables. In general, each command defines a set of semantically linked transitions in the resulting Markov chain.

The semantics of a stochastic guarded command is a Markov jump process (has discrete movements with random arrival times, i.e., a Poisson process). The semantics of a parallel composition of commands is a system of concurrent Markov jump processes. Sample execution traces can be generated by discrete-event simulation. In any state, zero or more commands may be enabled. If no commands are enabled the system is in a halting state. In all other cases, the enabled commands "compete" to execute their actions: sample times are drawn from the exponential distributions defined by their rates and the shortest time "wins". As showed in [20], this optimization can be performed, e.g., with the cross-entropy method. The techniques also extend to real-time stochastic systems (see [22]).

4.2   Importance Splitting

The earliest application of importance splitting is perhaps that of [24, 25], where it is used to calculate the probability that neutrons pass through certain shielding

---

[1] http://www.prismmodelchecker.org/manual/ThePRISMLanguage/.

materials. This physical example provides a convenient analogy for the more general case. The system comprises a source of neutrons aimed at one side of a shield of thickness T. The distance traveled by a neutron in the shield defines a monotonic sequence of levels $\ell_0 = 0 < \ell_1 < \ell_2 < \cdots < \ell_n = T$, such that reaching a given level implies having reached all the lower levels. While the overall probability of passing through the shield is small, the probability of passing from one level to another can be made arbitrarily close to 1 by reducing the distance between levels. Denoting the abstract level of a neutron as ℓ, the probability of a neutron reaching level ℓ_i can be expressed as $P(\ell \geqslant \ell_i) = P(\ell \geqslant \ell_i \mid \ell \geqslant \ell_{i-1})P(\ell \geqslant \ell_{i-1})$. Defining $\gamma = P(\ell \geqslant \ell_m)$ and $P(\ell \geqslant \ell_0) = 1$, we obtain

$$\gamma = \prod_{i=1}^{m} P(\ell \geqslant \ell_i \mid \ell \geqslant \ell_{i-1}). \tag{3}$$

Each term of (3) is necessarily greater than or equal to γ, making their estimation easier.

The general procedure is as follows. At each level, a number of simulations are generated, starting from a distribution of initial states that corresponds to reaching the current level. It starts by estimating $P(\ell \geqslant \ell_1 \mid \ell \geqslant \ell_0)$, where the distribution of initial states for ℓ_0 is usually given (often a single state). Simulations are stopped as soon as they reach the next level; the final states becoming the empirical distribution of initial states for the next level. Simulations that do not reach the next level (or reach some other stopping criterion) are discarded. In general, $P(\ell \geqslant \ell_i \mid \ell \geqslant \ell_{i-1})$ is estimated by the number of simulation traces that reach ℓ_i, divided by the total number of traces started from ℓ_{i-1}. Simulations that reached the next level are continued from where they stopped. To avoid a progressive reduction of the number of simulations, the generated distribution of initial states is sampled to provide additional initial states for new simulations, thus replacing those that were discarded.

Score Function. The concept of levels can be generalized to arbitrary systems and properties in the context of SMC, treating ℓ and ℓ_i in (3) as values of a score function over the model-property product automaton. Intuitively, a score function discriminates good paths from bad, assigning higher scores to paths that more nearly satisfy the overall property. Since the choice of levels is crucial to the effectiveness of importance splitting, various ways to construct score functions from a temporal logic property are proposed in [20].

Formally, given a set of finite trace prefixes $\omega \in \Omega$, an ideal score function $S : \Omega \to \mathbb{R}$ has the characteristics $S(\omega) > S(\omega') \iff P(\models \varphi \mid \omega) > P(\models \varphi \mid \omega')$, where $P(\models \varphi \mid \omega)$ is the probability of eventually satisfying φ given prefix ω. Intuitively, ω has a higher score than ω' iff there is more chance of satisfying φ by continuing ω than by continuing ω'. The minimum requirement of a score function is $S(\omega) \geq s_\varphi \iff \omega \models \varphi$, where s_φ is an arbitrary value denoting that φ is satisfied. Any trace that satisfies φ must have a score of at least s_φ and any trace that does not satisfy φ must have a score less than s_φ. In what follows we assume that (3) refers to scores.

The Fixed-Levels Algorithm. The fixed-levels algorithm follows the general procedure previously presented. Its advantages are that it is simple, it has low computational overhead, and the resulting estimate is unbiased. Its disadvantage is that the levels must often be guessed by trial and error, adding to the overall computational cost.

In Algorithm 1, $\tilde{\gamma}$ is an unbiased estimate (see, e.g., [11]). Furthermore, from Proposition 3 in [5], we can deduce the following $(1 - \alpha)$-confidence interval:

$$CI = \left[\hat{\gamma} / \left(1 + \frac{z_\alpha \sigma}{\sqrt{n}} \right), \hat{\gamma} / \left(1 - \frac{z_\alpha \sigma}{\sqrt{n}} \right) \right] \qquad \text{with} \qquad \sigma^2 \geqslant \sum_{i=1}^{m} \frac{1 - \gamma_i}{\gamma_i}. \qquad (4)$$

Confidence is specified via z_α, the $1 - \alpha/2$ quantile of the standard normal distribution, while n is the per-level simulation budget. We infer from (4) that for a given γ the confidence is maximized by making both the number of levels m and the simulation budget n large, with all γ_i equal.

Algorithm 1. Fixed levels

Let $(\tau_k)_{1 \leq k \leq m}$ be the sequence of thresholds with $\tau_m = \tau_\varphi$
Let *stop* be a termination condition
$\forall j \in \{1, \ldots, n\}$, set prefix $\tilde{\omega}_j^1 = \epsilon$ (empty path)
for $1 \leq k \leq m$ **do**
  $\forall j \in \{1, \ldots, n\}$, using prefix $\tilde{\omega}_j^k$, generate path ω_j^k until $(S(\omega_j^k) \geq \tau_k) \vee stop$
  $I_k = \{\forall j \in \{1, \ldots, n\} : S(\omega_j^k) \geq \tau_k\}$
  $\tilde{\gamma}_k = \frac{|I_k|}{n}$
  $\forall j \in I_k, \tilde{\omega}_j^{k+1} = \omega_j^k$
  $\forall j \notin I_k$, let $\tilde{\omega}_j^{k+1}$ be a copy of ω_i^k with $i \in I_k$ chosen uniformly randomly
$\tilde{\gamma} = \prod_{k=1}^{m} \tilde{\gamma}_k$

In general, however, score functions will not equally divide the conditional probabilities of the levels, as required by (4) to minimize variance. In the worst case, one or more of the conditional probabilities will be too low for the algorithm to pass between levels. Finding good or even reasonable levels by trial and error may be computationally expensive and has prompted the development of adaptive algorithms that discover optimal levels on the fly [6,20,21]. Instead of pre-defining levels, the user specifies the proportion of simulations to retain after each iteration. This proportion generally defines all but the final conditional probability in (3).

Adaptive importance splitting algorithms first perform a number of simulations until the overall property is decided, storing the resulting traces of the model-property automaton. Each trace induces a sequence of scores and a corresponding maximum score. The algorithm finds a level that is less than or equal to the maximum score of the desired proportion of simulations to retain. The simulations whose maximum score is below this current level are discarded. New

simulations to replace the discarded ones are initialized with states corresponding to the current level, chosen at random from the retained simulations. The
new simulations are continued until the overall property is decided and the procedure is repeated until a sufficient proportion of simulations satisfy the overall
property.

4.3   Rare Events: Comparison of Methods

In this section, we compare the two rare-event approaches with the Monte Carlo
approach.

Model. We consider a chemically reacting system that consists of a set of three
chemical reactions between five molecular species (A, B, C, D, E). These reactions are the following:

$$A + B \rightarrow C \tag{5}$$
$$C \rightarrow D \tag{6}$$
$$D \rightarrow E \tag{7}$$

Initially, the system only contains species A and B. Then reactions start
according to a rate that depends on the number of reactants. We model this
system as a continuous time Markov chain (CTMC) using the Reactive Module
Language (RML), the input language of the tools Prism and Plasma Lab. The
code of the model, presented in Fig. 1, contains a single module component with
three transitions to model the three reactions. The quantities of each element
are modeled as an integer variable from 0 to 1000. A and B start with 1000
elements, while C, D, and E start at zero. A transition that models a chemical
reaction is composed of a guard, that is always true, a rate, e.g., a $*$ b, and a set
of updates, e.g., $(a' = a - 1)$. The rate of the transition defines the speed of the
reaction as the rate of an exponential distribution: the higher it is the faster will
be the reaction. An example of a simulation of this system is presented in Fig. 2.
It shows how the quantities of each species may evolve over time, where time is
presented as the number of steps (chemical reaction) performed by the system.

Property. We consider a bounded linear temporal logic formula as the property
of this system to be verified:

$$\varphi := F \leqslant 3000(d > 470)$$

It checks if a level of 471 for species D can be reached within 3000 steps. We
would like to estimate the probability of satisfying this formula. As we can see
in a typical simulation run of this system in Fig. 2, species D tends to reach a
maximum of 400 before being transformed into species E.

Model Checking. The first approach to compute the probability of φ would be
to use a probabilistic model checker like PRISM to compute its exact value.
However, this model checking problem is intractable due to the size of its state
space (10^{15}).

ctmc

```
module chem
    a : [0..1000] init 1000;
    b : [0..1000] init 1000;
    c : [0..1000] init 0;
    d : [0..1000] init 0;
    e : [0..1000] init 0;
    [] true -> a*b :
       (a'=a-1) & (b'=b-1) & (c'=c+1)
       ;
    [] true -> c :
       (c'=c-1) & (d'=d+1);
    [] true -> d :
       (d'=d-1) & (e'=e+1);
endmodule
```

Fig. 1. CTMC model of chemical reactions written in the Reactive Module Language

Fig. 2. Simulation of the evolution of chemical species through time (in number of steps)

Monte Carlo. Consider next the Monte Carlo statistical model checking approach. We used Plasma Lab to run 1,000,000 simulations on an 8-core 2.6 GHz computer. It took 839 s, but we were not able to find even one trace that satisfies the formula. To have an idea of the evolution of the probability according to maximum value of species D checked by the property, we plot in Fig. 3 the results of Monte Carlo analyses with 100,000 simulations for several values of the maximum value from 350 to 450. As one can see, the probability to reach a maximum greater than 400 of species D is very low. To estimate the probability of reaching 471 we need to use statistical techniques for rare events.

Importance Splitting. Importance splitting works by splitting the verification of a rare property into a sequence of less rare properties. For instance, in our problem, any trace that eventually satisfies the formula φ, satisfies the formulas $F <= 3000(d > 460)$, $F <= 3000(d > 450)$, $F <= 3000(d > 440)$, etc. Therefore, the maximum value of d reached by a trace defines a natural notion of a level that can be used to split the rare property into a sequence of less-rare properties. We implement this decomposition in Plasma Lab by writing an observer that computes the score of a trace, i.e., the maximum value of d along the trace.

We can then use the adaptive importance splitting of Plasma Lab to estimate the probability of φ. The results are summarized in Table 1. We performed three experiments of the algorithm with a different number of simulations (100, 200, 500). Each experiment is repeated 20 times and we report the average value of the estimated probability, number of levels, and computation time. We also report the standard deviation of the probability and the relative standard deviation (quotient of standard deviation and average probability).

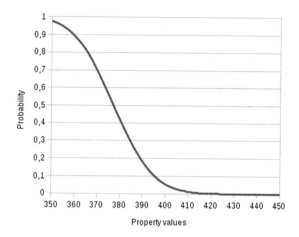

Fig. 3. Probability estimation with Monte Carlo for a maximum value on D that ranges from 350 to 450

Using this technique we are able to find traces that satisfy the property in 5 s with 1 core of a 2.6 GHz computer, using only a budget of 100 simulations. However, we were not able to run the adaptive algorithm with a budget of 1000 as we ran out of memory. Indeed this algorithm is more memory-intensive than classical Monte Carlo as it needs to keep in memory all the traces.

The relative standard deviation is a good measure of the performance of the estimator. A reliable estimator should have a relative standard deviation lower than 0.3. As can be seen, the relative standard deviation of our adaptive estimator is much higher. It tends to decrease when increasing the number of simulations, but using this algorithm we are limited by the memory.

Table 1. Results of the adaptive importance splitting algorithm

Nb. simulations	100	200	500
Nb. levels	116.6	121.2	127.9
Probability	6.02×10^{-11}	9.46×10^{-11}	2.07×10^{-10}
Std. deviation	1.44×10^{-10}	1.76×10^{-10}	4.51×10^{-10}
Relative std. deviation	2.39	1.86	2.18
Time (s)	5	14.6	55

The original importance-splitting algorithm uses a fixed number of levels. This algorithm is less memory intensive because it only keeps in memory the final states of the simulations. However, we must specify by hand the intermediate levels that we want to reach. To minimize the variance of the estimator, we should select as much as possible a set of levels whose conditional probabilities are equal. We selected 32 levels of d between $[380, 471]$ and ran the importance-splitting algorithm for a different number of simulations. We report the results in Table 2. They show that when increasing the number of simulations, we improve the relative deviation of the results.

Table 2. Results of the fixed levels importance splitting algorithm

Nb. simulations	1000	2000	5000
Probability	1.35×10^{-10}	1.28×10^{-10}	9.83×10^{-11}
Std. deviation	1.74×10^{-10}	9.07×10^{-11}	6.44×10^{-11}
Relative std. deviation	1.28	0.706	0.655
Time (s)	30.7	47.3	114

Importance Sampling. In Plasma Lab, we implemented the importance sampling algorithm for the Reactive Module Language. It requires adding sampling parameters to the model in order to modify the rate of some transitions. To produce a good result, the sampling parameters should have optimal values. This is determined using the minimum cross-entropy algorithm. This algorithm iteratively determines the values of the sampling parameters by running Monte Carlo experiments and counting the number of times each transition is used.

To use importance sampling on our model, we replace it by the one in Fig. 4. The three sampling parameters are named lambda. They are each associated with a counter variable nb_lambda. Parameters are initialized such that every simulation satisfied the rare property φ.

We then use the minimum cross-entropy algorithm to determine the optimal values of the parameters. In a run of the algorithm, we use 50 iterations to determine the final values of the parameters. Fig. 5 illustrates the evolution of the three parameters during a run of the algorithm. We ran the algorithm 10 times with 50 iterations and 1000 at each iteration. We report the results in Fig. 6. In this problem, the algorithm provides the best results, with a relative standard deviation lower than 0.3.

5   Importance Splitting/Sampling for Optimal Planning

In this section, we demonstrate how the incorporation of importance splitting and importance sampling into SMC for the treatment of rare-event properties has inspired planning algorithms for Markov decision processes (MDPs), a popular modeling formalism for policy-based stochastic systems. The goal of Sect. 6 is similar, but in this case for control algorithms. Planning and control often go hand-in-hand, with planning focused on long-term system objectives (e.g., how can an autonomous system get from point A to point B by following a sequence of so-called waypoints), and with control focused on the sub-second decisions the system must make in order to realize the planning objectives in question.

ctmc sampling

```
const double lambda1 = 2;
const double lambda2 = 1;
const double lambda3 = 0.1;
global nb_lambda1 : int init 0;
global nb_lambda2 : int init 0;
global nb_lambda3 : int init 0;

module test
a : [0..1000] init 1000;
b : [0..1000] init 1000;
c : [0..1000] init 0;
d : [0..1000] init 0;
e : [0..1000] init 0;
[] true -> {lambda1} a*b : (a'=a-1)&(b'=b-1)&(c'=c+1)
                           & (nb_lambda1'=nb_lambda1+1);
[] true -> {lambda2} c : (c'=c-1)&(d'=d+1)
                           & (nb_lambda2'=nb_lambda2+1);
[] true -> {lambda3} d : (d'=d-1)&(e'=e+1)
                           & (nb_lambda3'=nb_lambda3+1);
endmodule

label "rate_lambda1" = a*b;
label "rate_lambda2" = c;
label "rate_lambda3" = d;
```

Fig. 4. CTMC model of chemical reactions with sampling parameters

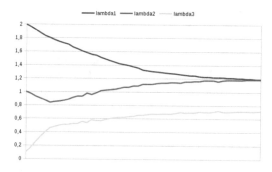

Nb. sims.	1000
Prob.	1.50×10^{-10}
Std. dev.	$4,03 \times 10^{-11}$
Rel. std. dev.	$0,269$
Time(s)	118

Fig. 5. Evolution of the three sampling parameters during a run of the minimum cross-entropy algorithm

Fig. 6. Results of the importance sampling algorithm with minimum cross-entropy

Definition 2. *A **Markov decision process (MDP)** $\mathcal{M}$ is a sequential decision problem that consists of a set of states S (with an initial state s_0), a set of actions A, a transition model T, and a cost function J. An MDP is **deterministic** if for each state and action, $T : S \times A \to S$ specifies a unique state.*

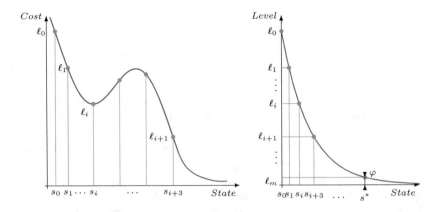

Fig. 7. Left: If state s_0 has cost ℓ_0 and its successor-state s_1 has cost less than ℓ_1, then a horizon of length 1 is appropriate. If, however, s_i has a local-minimum cost ℓ_i, one has to pass over the cost ridge in order to reach level ℓ_{i+1}, and therefore ARES has to adaptively increase the horizon to 3. Right: The cost of the initial state defines ℓ_0 and the given threshold φ defines ℓ_m. By choosing m equal segments on an asymptotically converging (Lyapunov) function (where m is empirically determined), one obtains on the vertical cost-axis the levels required for ARES to converge.

The particular planning and control problems addressed here are concerned with V-formation in a flock of birds, a quintessential example of emergent behavior in a distributed stochastic system. V-formation brings numerous benefits to the flock. It is primarily known for being energy-efficient due to the upwash benefit a bird in the flock enjoys from its frontal neighbor. It also offers each bird a clear frontal view, unobstructed by any flockmate. Moreover, the collective spatial mass of a V-formation can be intimidating to potential predators.

5.1   The Optimal Plan Synthesis Problem

In [30] we presented ARES, a general *adaptive, receding-horizon synthesis algorithm* that given an MDP and one of its initial states, generates an optimal plan (action sequence) taking that state to a state whose cost is below a desired threshold. To improve the probability of reaching a V-formation in a bird flock via ARES-based planning, we considered this phenomenon as a rare event and incorporated importance splitting into the core of the ARES algorithm. This level-based approach allows ARES to steer the. We then use SMC system towards the desired configuration to estimate this reachability probability.

Definition 3. *The **optimal plan synthesis problem** for an MDP $\mathcal{M}$, an arbitrary initial state s_0 of $\mathcal{M}$, and a threshold φ, is to synthesize a sequence of actions $\boldsymbol{a}^i$ of length $1 \leqslant i \leqslant m$ taking s_0 to a state s^* such that cost $J(s^*) \leqslant \varphi$.*

ARES uses the particle swarm optimization (PSO) algorithm [27] at each time step to incrementally generate a plan. Each particle in a PSO swarm is a realization of a random variable that is taken as a candidate optimal action (acceleration) sequence which can be used to simulate $\mathcal{M}$. The model is cloned into $\mathcal{M}_k$ instances, $k = 1, \ldots, n$, and a PSO swarm is assigned to each clone. These clones are later considered as independent simulation runs in the fashion of importance sampling.

This incremental approach to optimal-plan construction is in principle unnecessary, as one could generate an optimal plan in its entirety by calling PSO only once and running it until the global optimum is found or time bound is reached. Such an approach, however, is impractical, as each (transition-based) unfolding of the MDP adds a number of new dimensions to the search space. Consequently, to obtain adequate coverage of the monolithic optimal-plan search space, one needs a very large number of particles, a number that is either going to exhaust available memory or require a prohibitive amount of time to find an optimal plan.

A simple solution to this problem is to use a short horizon, typically of size two or three. This is indeed the current practice in model-predictive control (MPC) [13]. This approach, however, has at least three major drawbacks. First, and most importantly, it does not guarantee convergence and optimality, as one may oscillate or become stuck in a local optimum. Second, in some of the steps, the window size is unnecessarily large thereby negatively impacting performance. Third, in other steps, the window size may not be large enough to guide the optimizer out of a local minimum; see Fig. 7(left). One would therefore like to find the proper window size adaptively, but the question is how can one do this?

5.2   Adaptive Receding-Horizon Synthesis of Optimal Plans

Inspired by the SMC-based *importance splitting* technique (ISp) described in Sect. 4.2, we introduce the notion of a *level-based horizon*, where level ℓ_0 equals the cost of the initial state, and level ℓ_m equals the target threshold φ. By using an asymptotic cost-convergence function ranging from ℓ_0 to ℓ_m, and dividing its graph into m equal segments, we can determine on the vertical axis a sequence of levels ensuring convergence. See Fig. 7(right).

The asymptotic function ARES implements is essentially $\ell_i = \ell_0 (m - i)/m$, but specifically tuned for each simulation of $\mathcal{M}$. Formally, if simulation k, $k = 1, \ldots, n$, has previously reached level $J_k(s_{i-1})$, then its next target level is within the distance $\Delta_k = J_k(s_{i-1})/(m-i+1)$. After passing the thresholds assigned to the simulations, the values of the cost function in the current state s_i are sorted in ascending order $\{\widehat{J}_k\}_{k=1}^n$. The lowest cost $\widehat{J}_1$ should be at least Δ_1 apart from the previous level ℓ_{i-1} for the algorithm to proceed to the next level $\ell_i := \widehat{J}_1$.

The levels serve two purposes. First, they implicitly define a Lyapunov function, which guarantees convergence. If desired, this function can be explicitly generated for all states, up to some topological equivalence. Second, the levels ℓ_i help PSO overcome local minima; see Fig. 7(left). If reaching the next level requires PSO to pass over a state-cost ridge, then ARES incrementally increases the size of the horizon h, up to a maximum size h_{max}. For simulation k, passing the thresholds Δ_k means that it reaches a new level, and the definition of Δ_k ensures a smooth degradation of its threshold.

Another idea imported from the statistical model checking of rare-event properties is *importance sampling* (IS). In our context, it means that we maintain n clones $\{\mathcal{M}_k\}_{k=1}^n$ of the MDP $\mathcal{M}$ (and its initial state) at any time t, and run PSO for prediction horizon h on each h-unfolding $\mathcal{M}_k^h$ of $\mathcal{M}$. This results in an action sequence $\boldsymbol{a}_k^h$ of length h (see Algorithm 2). This approach allows us to call PSO for each simulation and desired horizon, with a very small number p of particles per simulation.

To check which simulations have overcome their associated thresholds, we sort the simulation traces according to their current cost, and split them into two sets: the successful set, having the indexes $\mathcal{I}$ and whose costs are lower than the median among all clones; and the unsuccessful set with indexes in $\{1,\ldots,n\}\setminus\mathcal{I}$, which are discarded. The unsuccessful ones are further replenished, by sampling uniformly at random from the successful set $\mathcal{I}$ (see Algorithm 3).

The number of particles in PSO is increased to $p = p + p_{inc}$ if no simulation trace reaches the next level, for all horizons chosen. When this happens, we reset the horizon to one, and repeat the process. In this way, we adaptively focus our resources on escaping from local minima. From the last level, we choose the state s^* with the minimal cost, and traverse all of its predecessor states to find an optimal plan comprised of actions $\{\boldsymbol{a}^i\}_{1\leqslant i\leqslant m}$ that led MDP $\mathcal{M}$ to the optimal state s^*. In our running example, we select a flock in V-formation and traverse all its predecessor flocks. The overall ARES procedure is shown in Algorithm 4.

Proposition 1 (Optimality and Minimality). *(1) Let $\mathcal{M}$ be an MDP. For any initial state s_0 of $\mathcal{M}$, ARES is able to solve the optimal-plan synthesis problem for $\mathcal{M}$ and s_0. (2) An optimal choice of m in function Δ_k, for some simulation k, ensures that ARES also generates the shortest optimal plan.*

Proof (Sketch; see [30] for the details). (1) The dynamic-threshold function Δ_k ensures that the initial cost in s_0 is continually decreased until it falls below φ. Moreover, for an appropriate number of clones, by adaptively determining the horizon and the number of simulations needed to overcome Δ_k, ARES always converges, with probability 1, to an optimal state, given enough time and memory. (2) This follows from convergence property (1), and from the fact that ARES always gives preference to the shortest horizon while trying to overcome Δ_k.

Algorithm 2. Simulate $(\mathcal{M}, h, i, \{\Delta_k, J_k(s_{i-1})\}_{k=1}^n)$

---

foreach $\mathcal{M}_k \in \mathcal{M}$ **do**
    $[\boldsymbol{a}_k^h, \mathcal{M}_k^h] \leftarrow \texttt{particleswarm}(\mathcal{M}_k, p, h)$; // *use PSO to determine best next action sequence for MDP $\mathcal{M}_k$ with RPH (receding prediction horizon) h*
    $J_k(s_i) \leftarrow \texttt{Cost}(\mathcal{M}_k^h, \boldsymbol{a}_k^h, h)$; // *calculate cost function if applying the sequence of optimal actions of length h*
    if $J_k(s_{i-1}) - J_k(s_i) > \Delta_k$ **then**
        $\lfloor\ \Delta_k \leftarrow J_k(s_i)/(m-i)$; // *new level-threshold*

Algorithm 3. Resample ($\{\mathcal{M}_k^h, J_k(s_i)\}_{k=1}^n$)

$\mathcal{I} \leftarrow$ Sort ascending $\mathcal{M}_k^h$ by their current costs; // *find indexes of MDPs whose costs are below the median among all the simulations*
for $k = 1$ **to** n **do**
 if $k \notin \mathcal{I}$ **then**
  | Sample r uniformly at random from $\mathcal{I}$; $\mathcal{M}_k \leftarrow \mathcal{M}_r^h$;
 else
  | $\mathcal{M}_k \leftarrow \mathcal{M}_k^h$; // *Keep more successful MDPs unchanged*

Algorithm 4. ARES

Input : $\mathcal{M}, \varphi, p_{start}, p_{inc}, p_{max}, h_{max}, m, n$
Output: $\{a^i\}_{1 \leqslant i \leqslant m}$ // *synthesized optimal plans*

Initialize $\ell_0 \leftarrow \inf$; $\{J_k(s_0)\}_{k=1}^n \leftarrow \inf$; $p \leftarrow p_{start}$; $i \leftarrow 1$; $h \leftarrow 1$; $\Delta_k \leftarrow 0$;
while $(\ell_i > \varphi) \vee (i < m)$ **do**
 // *find and apply best actions with RPH h*
 $[\{a_k^h, J_k(s_i), \mathcal{M}_k^h\}_{k=1}^n] \leftarrow$Simulate$(\mathcal{M}, h, i, \{\Delta_k, J_k(s_{i-1})\}_{k=1}^n)$;
 $\widehat{J}_1 \leftarrow sort(J_1(s_i), \ldots, J_n(s_i))$; // *find minimum cost among all simulations*
 if $\ell_{i-1} - \widehat{J}_1 > \Delta_1$ **then**
  | $\ell_i \leftarrow \widehat{J}_1$; // *new level has been reached*
  | $i \leftarrow i+1$; $h \leftarrow 1$; $p \leftarrow p_{start}$; // *reset adaptive parameters*
  | $\{\mathcal{M}_k\}_{k=1}^n \leftarrow$ Resample$(\{\mathcal{M}_k^h, J_k(s_i)\}_{k=1}^n)$;
 else
  if $h < h_{max}$ **then**
   | $h \leftarrow h+1$; // *improve time exploration*
  else
   if $p < p_{max}$ **then**
    | $h \leftarrow 1$; $p \leftarrow p + p_{inc}$; // *improve space exploration*
   else
    | break;

Take a clone in the state with minimum cost $\ell_i = J(s_i^*) \leqslant \varphi$ at the last level i;
foreach i **do**
 | $\{s_{i-1}^*, a^i\} \leftarrow Pre(s_i^*)$; // *find predecessor and corresponding action*

We assess the rate of success in generating optimal plans in form of an (ε, δ)-approximation scheme, for the desired error margin ε, and confidence ratio $1 - \delta$. Moreover, we can use the state-action pairs generated during the assessment (and possibly some additional new plans) to construct an explicit (tabled) optimal policy, modulo some topological equivalence. Given enough memory, one can use this policy in real time, as it only requires a table lookup.

To experimentally validate our approach, we have applied ARES to the problem of V-formation in a flock of birds (with a deterministic MDP) as described in [37,38]. The cost function to be optimized is defined as a weighted sum of the (flock-wide) clear-view (CV), velocity alignment (VA), and upwash benefit (UB) metrics. CV means that no bird's frontal view is obstructed by a flockmate, whereas VA is essential for maintaining formation (like V-formation) once it has been reached. Regarding UB, by flapping its wings, a bird generates a trailing upwash region off its wing tips; a bird flying in this region (left or right) can save energy. Note that in V-formation, all birds but one (the leader) enjoy UB.

We ran ARES on 8000 initial states chosen uniformly at random, such that they are packed closely enough to benefit from UB, but not too close to colliding. We succeeded to generate a V-formation 95% of the time, with an error margin of 0.05 and a confidence ratio of 0.99 computed using SMC. These statistics improve significantly if we consider all generated states as independent initial states. The fact that each state within a plan is independent of the states in all other plans allows us to do this.

6   Importance Splitting for Optimal Control

As in Sect. 5 where our focus was on optimal planning, in this section, we show how SMC-style importance splitting can be brought to bear on the problem of optimal control. In particular, we present the AMPC algorithm, short for level-based Adaptive-horizon Model-Predictive Control. We also consider stochastic two-player reachability games on MDPs (between a controller and an attacker) and demonstrate resiliency of AMPC control in this setting. As in Sect. 5, we consider the problem of V-formation in a flock of B birds as a motivating example.

6.1   Adaptive-Horizon Model-Predictive Control

The AMPC algorithm performs step-by-step control of a given MDP $\mathcal{M}$ by looking h steps ahead and predicting the next best state to move to [35]. We use PSO to identify the potentially best actions a^h in the current state achieving the optimal value of the fitness function in the next state. The fitness function, Fitness($\mathcal{M}, a^h, h$) of a^h is defined as the minimum fitness metric J obtained within h steps by applying a^h on $\mathcal{M}$. Formally, we have

$$\text{Fitness}(\mathcal{M}, a^h, h) = \min_{1 \leq \tau \leq h} J(s_{a^h}^\tau) \tag{8}$$

where $s_{a^h}^\tau$ is the state after apply the τth action of a^h on $\mathcal{M}$. For horizon h, PSO searches for the best sequence of 2-dimensional acceleration vector of length h, thus having $p = 2Bh$ parameters to be optimized. The number of particles used in PSO is proportional to the number of parameters, i.e., $p = 2\beta Bh$.

The pseudocode for the AMPC algorithm is given in Algorithm 5. A novel feature of AMPC is that, unlike classical MPC that uses a fixed horizon h, AMPC adaptively chooses an h depending on whether it is able to reach a fitness value that is lower than the current fitness by our chosen quanta $\Delta_i, \forall i \in \{0, \ldots, m\}$.

AMPC is hence an adaptive MPC procedure that uses level-based horizons introduced in Sect. 5, which was in turn inspired by the importance-splitting technique introduced in Sect. 4.2. It employs PSO to identify the potentially

---

Algorithm 5. AMPC: Adaptive Model-Predictive Control

Input : $\mathcal{M}, \varphi, h_{max}, m, B, \texttt{Fitness}$
Output: $\{a^i\}_{1 \leq i \leq m}$ // *optimal control sequence*

Initialize $\ell_0 \leftarrow J(s_0)$; $\widehat{J} \leftarrow \inf$; $p \leftarrow 2\beta Bh$; $i \leftarrow 1$; $h \leftarrow 1$; $\Delta_0 \leftarrow (\ell_0 - \varphi)/m$;

while $(\ell_{i-1} > \varphi) \wedge (i < m)$ **do**
  | // *find and apply first best action out of the horizon sequence of length h*
  | $[a^h, \widehat{J}] \leftarrow \texttt{particleswarm}(\texttt{Fitness}, \mathcal{M}, p, h)$;
  | **if** $\ell_{i-1} - \widehat{J} > \Delta_i \vee h = h_{max}$ **then**
  | | // *if a new level or the maximum horizon is reached*
  | | $a^i \leftarrow a^h_1$; $\mathcal{M} \leftarrow \mathcal{M}^{a^i}$; // *apply the action and move to the next state*
  | | $\ell_i \leftarrow J(s(\mathcal{M}))$; // *update ℓ_i with the fitness of the current state*
  | | $\Delta_i \leftarrow \ell_i/(m - i)$; // *update the threshold on reaching the next level*
  | | $i \leftarrow i + 1$; $h \leftarrow 1$; $p \leftarrow 2\beta Bh$; // *update parameters*
  | **else**
  | | $h \leftarrow h + 1$; $p \leftarrow 2\beta Bh$; // *increase the horizon*

---

best next actions. If the chosen actions improve (decrease) the fitness of the next state $J(s_{k+h})$, $\forall\ k \in \{0, \ldots, m \cdot h_{max}\}$, in comparison to the fitness of the previous state $J(s_k)$ by the predefined Δ_i, the controller considers these actions to be worthy of an optimal solution.

In this case, the controller applies the actions to each agent (bird) and transitions to the next state of the MDP. The threshold Δ_i determines the next level $\ell_i = J(s_{k+\widehat{h}})$ of the algorithm, where $\widehat{h} \leq h$ is the horizon with the best fitness. The prediction horizon h is increased iteratively if the fitness has not been decreased enough. Upon reaching a new level, the horizon is reset to one (see Algorithm 5). Having the horizon $\widehat{h} > 1$ means it will take multiple transitions in the MDP in order to reach a solution with improved fitness. However, when finding such a solution with $\widehat{h} > 1$, we only apply the first action to transition the MDP to the next state. This is explained by the need to allow the other player (environment or an adversary) to apply their action before we obtain the actual next state. If no new level is reached within h_{max} horizons, the first action of the best a^h using horizon h_{max} is applied.

The dynamic threshold Δ_i is defined as in [30]. Its initial value Δ_0 is obtained by dividing the fitness range to be covered into m equal parts, that is, $\Delta_0 = (\ell_0 - \ell_m)/m$, where $\ell_0 = J(s_0)$ and $\ell_m = \varphi$. Subsequently, Δ_i is determined by the previously reached level ℓ_{i-1}, as $\Delta_i = \ell_{i-1}/(m - i + 1)$. This way AMPC advances only if $\ell_i = J(s_{k+\widehat{h}})$ is at least Δ_i apart from $\ell_{i-1} = J(s_k)$.

This approach allows us to force PSO to escape from a local minimum, even if this implies passing over a fitness-function ridge (see also Fig. 7(left)), by gradually increasing the exploration horizon h. We assume that the MDP is controllable and that the set G of goal states is nonempty, which means that from any state, it is possible to reach a state whose fitness decreased by at least Δ_i. Algorithm 5 presents our approach.

Theorem 1 (AMPC Convergence). *Let* $\mathcal{M} = (S, A, T, J)$ *be an MDP with a positive and continuous fitness function J, and let $G \subset S$ be a nonempty set of target states with $G = \{s \mid J(s) < \varphi\}$. If the transition relation T is controllable with actions in A, then there is a finite maximum horizon h_{max} and a finite number of execution steps m such that AMPC is able to find a sequence of actions $a_1, \ldots, a_m$ that brings a state in S to a state in G with probability one.*

Proof. In each (macro-)step of horizon length h, from level $\ell_{i-1} = J(s_k)$ to level $\ell_i = J(s_{k+\hat{h}})$, AMPC decreases the distance to φ by $\Delta_i \geq \Delta$, where $\Delta > 0$ is fixed by the number of steps m chosen in advance. Hence, AMPC converges to a state in G in a finite number of steps for a properly chosen m. AMPC is able to decrease the fitness in a macro step by Δ_i by the controllability assumption and the fairness assumption about the PSO algorithm. Since AMPC is a randomized algorithm, the result is probabilistic.

Note that AMPC is a general procedure that performs adaptive MPC using PSO for dynamical systems that are controllable, come with a fitness metric, and have at least one optimal solution.

6.2   Resiliency of the AMPC Algorithm

Inspired by the emerging problem of CPS security, we introduced the concept of *controller-attacker games* [35]. A controller-attacker game is a two-player stochastic game, where the two players, a controller and an attacker, have antagonistic objectives. A controller-attacker game is formulated in terms of an MDP, with the controller and the attacker jointly determining the transition probabilities.

Definition 4. *Let* $\mathcal{M} = (S, A, T, J, I)$ *be an MDP. A **randomized strategy** σ over $\mathcal{M}$ is a function of the form $\sigma : S \mapsto PD(A)$, where $PD(A)$ is the set of probability distributions over A. That is, σ takes a state s and returns an action consistent with the probability distribution $\sigma(s)$.*

Definition 5. *A **controller-attacker game** is an MDP $\mathcal{M} = (S, A, T, J, I)$ with $A = C \times D$, where C and D are action sets of the controller and the attacker, respectively. The transition probability $T(s, c \times d, s')$ is jointly determined by actions $c \in C$ and $d \in D$.*

We also introduced a class of controller-attacker games we call V-formation games, where the goal of the controller is to maneuver the plant (a simple model of flocking dynamics) into a V-formation, and the goal of the attacker is to prevent the controller from doing so.

Let $x_i(t), v_i(t), a_i(t)$, and $d_i(t)$ respectively denote the position, velocity, acceleration, and displacement of the i-th bird at time t, $1 \leqslant i \leqslant B$. The behavior of bird i in discrete time is modeled as follows:

$$x_i(t+1) = x_i(t) + v_i(t+1) + d_i(t)$$
$$v_i(t+1) = v_i(t) + a_i(t) \tag{9}$$

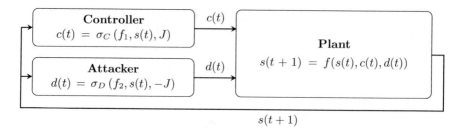

Fig. 8. Controller-Attacker Game Architecture. The controller and the attacker use randomized strategies σ_C and σ_D to choose actions $c(t)$ and $d(t)$ based on dynamics $f_1 = f(s(t), c(t), 0)$ and $f_2 = f(s(t), 0, d(t))$, respectively, where $s(t)$ is the state at time t, and f is the dynamics of the plant model. The controller tries to minimize the cost J, while the attacker tries to maximize it.

The next state of the flock is jointly determined by the accelerations and the displacements based on the current state following Eq. 9.

Controllers in V-formation games utilize AMPC, giving them extraordinary power: we prove that under certain controllability conditions, an AMPC controller can attain V-formation with probability 1.

Definition 6. *A **V-formation game** is a controller-attacker game $\mathcal{M} = (S, A, T, J, I)$, where $S = \{s \mid s = \{\boldsymbol{x}_i, \boldsymbol{v}_i\}_{i=1}^{B}\}$ is the set of states for a flock of B birds, $A = C \times D$ with the controller choosing accelerations $\boldsymbol{a} \in C$ and the attacker choosing displacements $\boldsymbol{d} \in D$, T and J are given in Eqs. 9 and 8, respectively.*

We define several classes of attackers, including those that in one move can remove a small number R of birds from the flock, or introduce random displacement (perturbation) into the flock dynamics, again by selecting a small number of victim agents. We consider both *naive attackers*, whose strategies are purely probabilistic, and *AMPC-enabled attackers*, putting them on par strategically with the controller. The architecture of a V-formation game with an AMPC-enabled attacker is shown in Fig. 8.

While an AMPC-enabled controller is expected to win every game with probability 1, in practice, it is *resource-constrained*: its maximum prediction horizon and the maximum number of execution steps are fixed in advance. Under these conditions, an attacker has a much better chance of winning a V-formation game.

In Sect. 5, we presented a procedure for synthesizing plans (sequences of actions) that take an MDP to a desired set of states (defining a V-formation). The procedure adaptively varied the settings of various parameters of an underlying optimization routine. Since we did not consider any adversary or noise, there was no need for a control algorithm. Here we consider V-formation in the presence of attacks, and hence we developed a generic adaptive control procedure, AMPC, and evaluate its resilience to attacks.

Our extensive performance evaluation of V-formation games uses statistical model checking to estimate the probability that an attacker can thwart the controller. Our results show that for the bird-removal game with 1 bird being removed, the controller almost always wins (restores the flock to a V-formation). When 2 birds are removed, the game outcome critically depends on which two birds are removed. For the displacement game, our results again demonstrate that an intelligent attacker, i.e. one that uses AMPC in this case, significantly outperforms its naive counterpart that randomly carries out its attack.

Traditional feedback control is, by design, resilient to noise, and also certain kinds of attacks; as our results show, however, it may not be resilient against smart attacks. Adaptive-horizon control helps to guard against a larger class of attacks, but it can still falter due to limited resources. Our results also demonstrate that statistical model checking represents a promising approach toward the evaluation of CPS resilience against a wide range of attacks.

7 Conclusions

The field of Statistical Model Checking (SMC) is now more than 15 years old, and has experienced significant theoretical and practical development during this time. In this chapter, we have presented a review of SMC as an efficient technique for the model checking of stochastic systems, and presented three algorithms representing both the quantitative and qualitative versions of SMC. We also discussed one of the major challenges facing the SMC approach, namely the treatment of rare events. Taking advantage of sequential Monte Carlo methods, we presented efficient procedures for rare-event probability estimation, and illustrated their utility via our implementation in Plasma. We further demonstrated the applicability of the SMC-inspired rare-event approach to tackling plan- and control-synthesis problems for stochastic systems. Looking forward, there are a wealth of challenges facing the SMC community, such as the verification of cyber-physical systems, where SMC can play a crucial role in developing robust and efficient algorithms.

References

1. Baier, C., Haverkort, B.R., Hermanns, H., Katoen, J.-P.: Model-checking algorithms for continuous-time Markov chains. IEEE Trans. Softw. Eng. **29**(6), 524–541 (2003)
2. Basu, A., Bensalem, S., Bozga, M., Caillaud, B., Delahaye, B., Legay, A.: Statistical abstraction and model-checking of large heterogeneous systems. In: Hatcliff, J., Zucca, E. (eds.) FMOODS/FORTE - 2010. LNCS, vol. 6117, pp. 32–46. Springer, Heidelberg (2010). https://doi.org/10.1007/978-3-642-13464-7_4
3. Basu, A., Bensalem, S., Bozga, M., Delahaye, B., Legay, A., Sifakis, E.: Verification of an AFDX infrastructure using simulations and probabilities. In: Barringer, H., et al. (eds.) RV 2010. LNCS, vol. 6418, pp. 330–344. Springer, Heidelberg (2010). https://doi.org/10.1007/978-3-642-16612-9_25
4. Boyer, B., Corre, K., Legay, A., Sedwards, S.: PLASMA-lab: a flexible, distributable statistical model checking library. In: Joshi, K., Siegle, M., Stoelinga, M., D'Argenio, P.R. (eds.) QEST 2013. LNCS, vol. 8054, pp. 160–164. Springer, Heidelberg (2013). https://doi.org/10.1007/978-3-642-40196-1_12

5. Cérou, F., Del Moral, P., Furon, T., Guyader, A.: Sequential Monte Carlo for rare event estimation. Stat. Comput **22**, 795–808 (2012)
6. Cérou, F., Guyader, A.: Adaptive multilevel splitting for rare event analysis. Stoch. Anal. Appl. **25**, 417–443 (2007)
7. Ciesinski, F., Baier, C.: Liquor: a tool for qualitative and quantitative linear time analysis of reactive systems. In: Proceedings of 3rd International Conference on Quantitative Evaluation of Systems (QEST), pp. 131–132. IEEE (2006)
8. Ciesinski, F., Größer, M.: On probabilistic computation tree logic. In: Baier, C., Haverkort, B.R., Hermanns, H., Katoen, J.-P., Siegle, M. (eds.) Validation of Stochastic Systems. LNCS, vol. 2925, pp. 147–188. Springer, Heidelberg (2004). https://doi.org/10.1007/978-3-540-24611-4_5
9. Courcoubetis, C., Yannakakis, M.: The complexity of probabilistic verification. J. ACM **42**(4), 857–907 (1995)
10. David, A., Larsen, K.G., Legay, A., Mikučionis, M., Wang, Z.: Time for statistical model checking of real-time systems. In: Gopalakrishnan, G., Qadeer, S. (eds.) CAV 2011. LNCS, vol. 6806, pp. 349–355. Springer, Heidelberg (2011). https://doi.org/10.1007/978-3-642-22110-1_27
11. Del Moral, P.: Feynman-Kac Formulae: Genealogical and Interacting Particle Systems with Applications. Probability and Its Applications. Springer, New York (2004). https://doi.org/10.1007/978-1-4684-9393-1
12. Doucet, A., de Freitas, N., Gordon, N.: Sequential Monte Carlo Methods in Practice. Springer, New York (2001). https://doi.org/10.1007/978-1-4757-3437-9
13. Garca, C.E., Prett, D.M., Morari, M.: Model predictive control: theory and practice - a survey. Automatica **25**(3), 335–348 (1989)
14. Gimbert, H.: Pure stationary optimal strategies in Markov decision processes. In: Thomas, W., Weil, P. (eds.) STACS 2007. LNCS, vol. 4393, pp. 200–211. Springer, Heidelberg (2007). https://doi.org/10.1007/978-3-540-70918-3_18
15. Glasserman, P., Heidelberger, P., Shahabuddin, P., Zajic, T.: Multilevel splitting for estimating rare event probabilities. Oper. Res. **47**(4), 585–600 (1999)
16. Grosu, R., Smolka, S.A.: Monte Carlo model checking. In: Halbwachs, N., Zuck, L.D. (eds.) TACAS 2005. LNCS, vol. 3440, pp. 271–286. Springer, Heidelberg (2005). https://doi.org/10.1007/978-3-540-31980-1_18
17. Younes, H.L.S., Clarke, E.M., Zuliani, P.: Statistical verification of probabilistic properties with unbounded until. In: Davies, J., Silva, L., Simao, A. (eds.) SBMF 2010. LNCS, vol. 6527, pp. 144–160. Springer, Heidelberg (2011). https://doi.org/10.1007/978-3-642-19829-8_10
18. Havelund, K., Roşu, G.: Synthesizing monitors for safety properties. In: Katoen, J.-P., Stevens, P. (eds.) TACAS 2002. LNCS, vol. 2280, pp. 342–356. Springer, Heidelberg (2002). https://doi.org/10.1007/3-540-46002-0_24
19. Jansen, D.N., Katoen, J.-P., Oldenkamp, M., Stoelinga, M., Zapreev, I.: How fast and fat is your probabilistic model checker? An experimental performance comparison. In: Yorav, K. (ed.) HVC 2007. LNCS, vol. 4899, pp. 69–85. Springer, Heidelberg (2008). https://doi.org/10.1007/978-3-540-77966-7_9
20. Jegourel, C., Legay, A., Sedwards, S.: Importance splitting for statistical model checking rare properties. In: Sharygina, N., Veith, H. (eds.) CAV 2013. LNCS, vol. 8044, pp. 576–591. Springer, Heidelberg (2013). https://doi.org/10.1007/978-3-642-39799-8_38
21. Jegourel, C., Legay, A., Sedwards, S.: An effective heuristic for adaptive importance splitting in statistical model checking. In: Margaria, T., Steffen, B. (eds.) ISoLA 2014. LNCS, vol. 8803, pp. 143–159. Springer, Heidelberg (2014). https://doi.org/10.1007/978-3-662-45231-8_11

22. Jégourel, C., Legay, A., Sedwards, S.: Command-based importance sampling for statistical model checking. Theoret. Comput. Sci. **649**, 1–24 (2016)

23. Kahn, H.: Stochastic (Monte Carlo) attenuation analysis. Technical report P-88, Rand Corporation, July 1949

24. Kahn, H.: Random sampling (Monte Carlo) techniques in neutron attenuation problems. Nucleonics **6**(5), 27 (1950)

25. Kahn, H., Harris, T.E.: Estimation of particle transmission by random sampling. In: Applied Mathematics. Series 12, vol. 5. National Bureau of Standards (1951)

26. Kahn, H., Marshall, A.W.: Methods of reducing sample size in Monte Carlo computations. Oper. Res. **1**(5), 263–278 (1953)

27. Kennedy, J., Eberhart, R.: Particle swarm optimization. In: Proceedings of 1995 IEEE International Conference on Neural Networks, pp. 1942–1948 (1995)

28. Kwiatkowska, M.Z., Norman, G., Parker, D.: Prism 2.0: a tool for probabilistic model checking. In: QEST, pp. 322–323. IEEE (2004)

29. Kwiatkowska, M., Norman, G., Parker, D.: PRISM 4.0: verification of probabilistic real-time systems. In: Gopalakrishnan, G., Qadeer, S. (eds.) CAV 2011. LNCS, vol. 6806, pp. 585–591. Springer, Heidelberg (2011). https://doi.org/10.1007/978-3-642-22110-1_47

30. Lukina, A., Esterle, L., Hirsch, C., Bartocci, E., Yang, J., Tiwari, A., Smolka, S.A., Grosu, R.: ARES: adaptive receding-horizon synthesis of optimal plans. In: Legay, A., Margaria, T. (eds.) TACAS 2017. LNCS, vol. 10206, pp. 286–302. Springer, Heidelberg (2017). https://doi.org/10.1007/978-3-662-54580-5_17

31. Okamoto, M.: Some inequalities relating to the partial sum of binomial probabilities. Ann. Inst. Stat. Math. **10**, 29–35 (1959)

32. Rosenbluth, M.N., Rosenbluth, A.W.: Monte Carlo calculation of the average extension of molecular chains. J. Chem. Phys. **23**(2), 356–359 (1955)

33. Sen, K., Viswanathan, M., Agha, G.: Statistical model checking of black-box probabilistic systems. In: Alur, R., Peled, D.A. (eds.) CAV 2004. LNCS, vol. 3114, pp. 202–215. Springer, Heidelberg (2004). https://doi.org/10.1007/978-3-540-27813-9_16

34. Sen, K., Viswanathan, M., Agha, G.: On statistical model checking of stochastic systems. In: Etessami, K., Rajamani, S.K. (eds.) CAV 2005. LNCS, vol. 3576, pp. 266–280. Springer, Heidelberg (2005). https://doi.org/10.1007/11513988_26

35. Tiwari, A., Smolka, S.A., Esterle, L., Lukina, A., Yang, J., Grosu, R.: Attacking the V: on the resiliency of adaptive-horizon MPC. In: D'Souza, D., Narayan Kumar, K. (eds.) ATVA 2017. LNCS, vol. 10482, pp. 446–462. Springer, Cham (2017). https://doi.org/10.1007/978-3-319-68167-2_29

36. Wald, A.: Sequential tests of statistical hypotheses. Ann. Math. Stat. **16**(2), 117–186 (1945)

37. Yang, J., Grosu, R., Smolka, S.A., Tiwari, A.: Love thy neighbor: V-formation as a problem of model predictive control. In: LIPIcs-Leibniz International Proceedings in Informatics, vol. 59. Schloss Dagstuhl-Leibniz-Zentrum fuer Informatik (2016)

38. Yang, J., Grosu, R., Smolka, S.A., Tiwari, A.: V-formation as optimal control. In: Proceedings of Biological Distributed Algorithms Workshop 2016 (2016)

39. Younes, H.L.S.: Verification and planning for stochastic processes with asynchronous events. Ph.D. thesis, Carnegie Mellon University (2005)

40. Younes, H.L.S.: Error control for probabilistic model checking. In: Emerson, E.A., Namjoshi, K.S. (eds.) VMCAI 2006. LNCS, vol. 3855, pp. 142–156. Springer, Heidelberg (2005). https://doi.org/10.1007/11609773_10

41. Younes, H.L.S., Simmons, R.G.: Probabilistic verification of discrete event systems using acceptance sampling. In: Brinksma, E., Larsen, K.G. (eds.) CAV 2002. LNCS, vol. 2404, pp. 223–235. Springer, Heidelberg (2002). https://doi.org/10.1007/3-540-45657-0_17

42. Zuliani, P., Baier, C., Clarke, E.M.: Rare-event verification for stochastic hybrid systems. In: Proceedings of 15th ACM International Conference on Hybrid Systems: Computation and Control, HSCC 2012, pp. 217–226. ACM, New York (2012)

Automated Software Test Generation: Some Challenges, Solutions, and Recent Advances

George Candea[1] and Patrice Godefroid[2(✉)]

[1] Ecole Polytechnique Fédérale de Lausanne (EPFL), 1015 Lausanne, Switzerland
[2] Microsoft Research, One Microsoft Way, Redmond, WA 98052, USA
`pg@microsoft.com`

Abstract. The automation of software testing promises to delegate to machines what is otherwise the most labor-intensive and expensive part of software development. The past decade has seen a resurgence in research interest for this problem, bringing about significant progress. In this article, we provide an overview of automated test generation for software, and then discuss recent developments that have had significant impact on real-life software.

Keywords: Software testing · Program analysis · Symbolic execution

1 Introduction

Software testing is generally used to assess the quality of a program, where "quality" can mean reliability, performance, usability, compliance, etc. depending on context. The purpose of this assessment can be to debug the program, because testing points out programming errors and ways to reproduce the program failure they induce. Another purpose can be assessing whether the program is acceptable to a client, because tests can reveal not only bugs but also gaps between what the client wanted and what the developer thought she wanted. All in all, software testing is a method for critiquing a program rather than demonstrating its correctness. In Dijkstra's words, "testing shows the presence, not the absence of bugs" [45].

Testing a program consists of executing the program with a given set of inputs and observing its behavior. *Test automation* entails running several tests in an automated fashion, such as every night or every time a major change is made to the program. Such automation requires one or more *test cases*, each consisting of specific inputs to the program, and an automated means of validating the outcome, often called a *test oracle*. Test cases can be written in a black-box manner (where the test developer chooses scenarios solely based on knowledge of what the program is supposed to do) or a white-box manner (where internal knowledge of the program source code supplements the external knowledge in choosing test scenarios). There exist many types of testing (e.g., unit, feature,

© Springer Nature Switzerland AG 2019
B. Steffen and G. Woeginger (Eds.): Computing and Software Science, LNCS 10000, pp. 505–531, 2019.
https://doi.org/10.1007/978-3-319-91908-9_24

functional, system, regression) that fulfill various goals. Testing is complementary to other non-dynamic methods for checking program correctness, such as visual code inspection or static program analysis.

The outcome of running tests is measured in various ways. For example, counting how many tests succeed vs. fail is often a proxy metric for the program's code quality. Another example is test coverage, which measures the rigorousness of testing, e.g., by computing what fraction of the program's instructions were executed during a test suite.

The fundamental challenge in thoroughly testing a program is that the number of possible inputs is large. For example, consider a program that takes four 64-bit integers and adds them up: there exist 2^{256} different combinations of integers that could be provided to this program. In contrast, scientists estimate that the observable Universe has on the order of 2^{240} atoms [115]. A naive approach of trying all inputs one by one would therefore not complete, so one must be clever about picking test inputs.

This brings us to *test generation*, i.e., producing "interesting" inputs to test software. There is an inherent trade-off between how long it takes to choose the inputs vs. how long it takes to run the corresponding test and measure outcomes. For example, if executing a program takes a long time, it makes sense to spend time on smartly choosing inputs, so as to minimize the number of times the program must execute during testing. However, if running the program is quick, then taking a long time to choose inputs can be detrimental compared to running the program many times with many inputs.

A good way to reduce the time spent choosing test inputs is to automate the process. This observation gave rise to the field of *automated test generation*, which is the subject of this article. We discuss the spectrum of techniques used for automated test generation (Sect. 2) along with some of the challenges they face when applied in practice (Sect. 3). We highlight two recent advances in the engineering and application of these techniques: SAGE (Sect. 4) and S2E (Sect. 5). While this article is by no means a survey of automated test generation techniques, we do mention many approaches, techniques and tools throughout, as well as in Sect. 6. We conclude with a few thoughts on future directions in this field of research (Sect. 7).

2   Automated Test Generation: An Overview

Techniques for automatically generating test inputs lay along a spectrum that has at one end blackbox random testing (Sect. 2.1) and at the other end whitebox symbolic execution (Sect. 2.2). We now describe these two end-points.

2.1   Random Testing and Input Fuzzing

Perhaps the simplest form of automated test generation is to select program inputs at random [92]. Various input probability distributions can be used, either uniform or biased towards some specific values believed to lead to interesting corner cases, like 0, −1 or MAXINT for integer input values.

A more evolved form, called *fuzz testing*, consists of starting with well-formed inputs and repeatedly modifying them, more or less at random, to produce new inputs—this preserves the benefit of blackbox testing while increasing the probability of inputs found in this way being "interesting" (e.g., capable of getting past the first layer of input parsing). This proved to be an effective way to find crashes and security vulnerabilities in software, with some of the most notorious security vulnerabilities having been found this way [27]. Fuzz testing (or "fuzzing" for short) has become a standard fixture in most commercial software testing strategies [1, 75, 91].

Key to the effectiveness of fuzzing is test *quantity*, i.e., the ability to generate and try out new inputs at high rate. Large-scale fuzzing efforts (such as ClusterFuzz [5] that tests the Chromium web browser) test software round the clock, using as many machines as are available. The number of bugs found is limited by the number of CPU resources given to the fuzzer—intuition suggests that the more tests the fuzzer gets to run, the more likely it is to find bugs.

The other key ingredient is test *quality*. First, testing many random inputs in a blackbox fashion can at best discover shallow bugs, whereas picking inputs smartly can penetrate deeper into the program code and reduce the number of executions needed to find a bug. To improve the quality of generated inputs, modern fuzzers use feedback from prior executions to steer input generation toward those inputs that are more likely to uncover bugs. Second, detecting anomalous behaviors automatically during the test runs increases the chances of detecting the manifestation of a bug. Therefore, fuzzers check for a wide range of "illegal behaviors," with memory safety violations being the most popular. The premise is that higher-quality tests are more likely to find bugs.

Most modern blackbox fuzzers, like AFL [119] or LibFuzzer [84], have moved away from the initial "random testing" end-point of the spectrum: they operate in a feedback loop, as shown in Fig. 1. They rely on instrumentation to detect program features triggered by tests, e.g., a basic block being executed or a buffer overflow. Whenever a feature is seen for the first time, the fuzzer reacts: it adds the test to its corpus of interesting testcases, or reports a bug.

Different types of instrumentation can detect various features of interest. For example, *coverage bits* detect when a particular edge in the control-flow graph of the program is executed. When a coverage bit fires, the fuzzer knows that it has found new code. A *coverage counter* similarly detects how often an edge has been executed, and can signal to the fuzzer that it made progress when exploring a loop. *Safety checks* detect abnormal conditions, alerting the fuzzer that a bug has been found. Such checks can be either added by developers in the form of assertions, or done automatically by tools such as Purify, AppVerifier, Valgrind, UndefinedBehaviorSanitizer, ThreadSanitizer, AddressSanitizer, FORTIFY_SOURCE, AFL's libdislocator, stack-protector, and others [34, 44, 52, 78, 108, 109]. Using safety checks increases the quality of tests, and thus the number of bugs that fuzzers can detect. Without them, developers

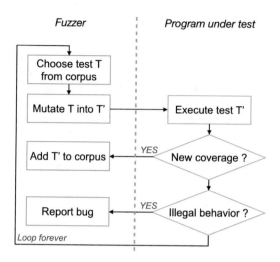

Fig. 1. Typical workflow of a fuzzer driven by coverage feedback

need to hope that illegal behavior leads to a segmentation fault or other visible exception. This does not always happen, particularly for tricky cases such as use-after-free or buffer over-read bugs.

Ideally, a fuzzer should simultaneously have high test throughput and high test quality, but unfortunately these two requirements conflict: obtaining good feedback comes at the cost of throughput. Both detecting program misbehavior and collecting code coverage information is done using program instrumentation, which competes for CPU cycles with the actual instructions of the program being tested. It is in fact not unusual for fuzzers to invest less than half of their resources into executing code of the target program, and spend the rest on improving test quality.

2.2   Test Generation with Symbolic Execution

At the other end of the spectrum, the most precise form of automatic code-driven test generation known today is dynamic test generation with symbolic execution.

Symbolic execution is a program analysis technique that was introduced in the 70s (e.g., see [14, 37, 76, 79, 103]). Symbolic execution means executing a program with symbolic rather than concrete values. Assignment statements are represented as functions of their (symbolic) arguments, while conditional statements are expressed as constraints on symbolic values. Symbolic execution can be used for many purposes, such as bug detection, program verification, debugging, maintenance, and fault localization [38].

Symbolic execution can be used to symbolically explore the tree of all computations the program exhibits when all possible value assignments to input parameters are considered [79]. As an example, consider the simple program on the left of

Fig. 2 and its computation tree on the right. This program takes an integer value
rpm as input. The set of possible values for program variable *rpm* is represented by
a *symbolic* value λ that can initially take on any integer value: this is represented
by the constraint $\lambda \in Z$. During symbolic execution of that program, whenever a
branch depending on λ is encountered, a new constaint is generated to capture how
to make that input-dependent branch condition evaluate to true (e.g., $\lambda > 1000$)
or false (e.g., $\lambda \leq 1000$) respectively. By repeating this process going down the
tree, we obtain an execution tree annotated with conjunctions of input constraints
which characterize what input values are required in order to reach what parts of
the program. Those conjunctions of constraints are called *path constraints*, or *path
conditions*, and are shown in grey on the right of Fig. 2.

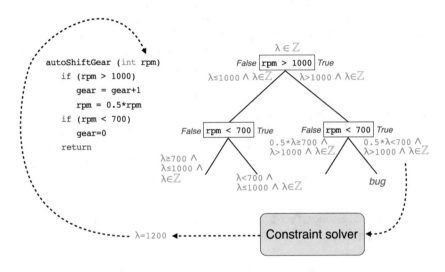

Fig. 2. Test generation for a simple program using symbolic execution.

In other words, for each *control path* p, that is, a sequence of control locations of the program, a *path constraint* ϕ_p is constructed that characterizes the
input assignments for which the program executes along p. All the paths can be
enumerated by a search algorithm that explores all possible branches at conditional statements. The paths p for which ϕ_p is satisfiable are *feasible* and are
the only ones that can be executed by the actual program. The solutions to ϕ_p
characterize the inputs that drive the program through p. This characterization
is *exact* provided symbolic execution has *perfect precision*. Assuming that the
theorem prover used to check the satisfiability of all formulas ϕ_p is sound and
complete, this analysis amounts to a kind of exhaustive symbolic testing of all
feasible control paths of a program.

Work on automatic code-driven test generation using symbolic execution can
roughly be partitioned into two groups: *static* versus *dynamic* test generation.
Static test generation (e.g., [79]) consists of analyzing a program P statically, by
using symbolic execution techniques to attempt to compute inputs to drive P

along specific execution paths or branches, *without ever executing the program*. In contrast, dynamic test generation (e.g., [22,23,31,62,68,80,98,107]) consists of executing the program P starting with some concrete inputs, while performing symbolic execution *dynamically*, collecting symbolic constraints on inputs gathered from predicates in branch statements along the execution, and then using a constraint solver to infer variants of the previous inputs in order to steer the next execution of the program towards an alternative program branch.

The key practical advantage of dynamic test generation compared to static test generation is that the entire program does not need to be executed symbolically for test generation. Imprecision in dynamic symbolic execution can easily be alleviated using concrete values: whenever dynamic symbolic execution does not know how to generate a constraint for a program statement depending on some inputs, one can always simplify this constraint using the current concrete values of those inputs. One can prove [60] that dynamic test generation is more precise than static test generation mainly because of its ability to observe concrete values and record those in path constraints.

In practice, the key strength of symbolic execution is that it can generate quality test inputs that exercise program paths with much better precision than random testing or other blackbox heuristic-based test-generation techniques. However, symbolic execution does not have perfect precision, constraint solvers are typically not sound and complete, and programs can have (infinitely) many control paths due to loops or recursion. Moreover, symbolic execution is complex to engineer properly. We discuss these challenges in the next section.

3   Symbolic Execution Meets Practice: Challenges and Solutions

In practice, automatic test generation using symbolic execution suffers from several important limitations. This section discusses these challenges and various solutions.

Fortunately, approximate solutions are sufficient in practice. To be useful, symbolic execution does not need to be perfect, it must simply be "good enough" to drive the program under test through program branches, statements and paths that would be difficult to exercise with simpler techniques like random testing. Even if a systematic search cannot typically explore all the feasible paths of large programs in a reasonable amount of time, it usually does achieve better coverage than pure random testing and, hence, can find new program bugs.

3.1   Exploring New Program Paths

Dynamic symbolic execution is used to systematically explore the execution tree of a program. These paths are discovered incrementally and can be explored independently "in parallel": each inner node is a branching decision, and each leaf is a program state that contains its own address space, program counter, and set of constraints on program variables. In order to exercise a new program path during such a systematic search, the path constraint for this new path is solved with a constraint solver. If the constraint is satisfiable, the solver returns a satisfying assignment for every symbolic variable in the constraint, which is then mapped to new program inputs. There are two main ways to explore new program paths of a program.

One approach consists of running the program with some fixed concrete inputs and performing dynamic symbolic execution along that execution (using runtime instrumentation) until the program terminates or a specific limit is reached. In this approach, exploring a different execution path requires re-running the target program from the beginning with new concrete inputs. This is the approach used in, e.g., [62,64,107].

A second approach consists in literally "forking" (using the fork system call) the program state before branch decisions. This way, a new address space is created for a copy of the program that now explores an alternate path through the tree. Copy-on-write techniques can be used to efficiently deduplicate these address spaces. This is the approach used in, e.g., [23,31].

The two approaches present different trade-offs. The first approach (DART-style concolic execution) presents, on the one hand, the benefit of not having to solve constraints at runtime to determine feasibility of execution paths and requires less memory. On the other hand, it requires re-running the program from scratch for every explored path. The second approach (KLEE-style symbolic execution), on the one hand is able to efficiently explore paths in parallel, without re-running the program, and enables flexible search strategies for deciding which program paths to explore next (e.g., in the presence of loops) based on a broad number of factors. On the other hand, it requires more CPU (in particular for solving constraints to determine path feasibility) and memory, which limits scalability.

3.2   Interacting with the Environment

In theory, symbolic execution does not use abstraction and is therefore fully precise with respect to predicate transformer semantics [46]: it generates "per-path verification conditions" whose satisfiability implies the reachability of a particular statement, so it generally does not produce false positives.

In practice, to test real-world programs, a symbolic execution engine must mediate between the program and its runtime environment, i.e., external libraries, the operating system, the thread and process scheduler, I/O interrupt events, etc. Thus symbolic execution engines need to minimize the time they spend executing the environment, while of course ensuring correct behavior of the program.

Existing solutions roughly fall into two categories: they either concretize calls to the environment and thus avoid symbolic execution of the environment altogether, or they abstract the environment as much as possible using models with varying degrees of completeness. We now discuss those two options.

Concrete Environment. The first modern symbolic execution engines [24,62, 107] executed the program concretely, and maintained the symbolic execution state only during the execution of the program code itself. Whenever symbolic execution is not possible, such as inside external library calls (possibly executed in kernel-mode or on some other machine or process) or when facing program instructions with unknown symbolic semantics, the program execution can still proceed. This approach turns the conventional stance on the role of symbolic execution upside-down: symbolic execution is now an adjunct to concrete execution. As a result, a specific concrete execution can be leveraged as an automatic fall back for symbolic execution [62]. This avoids altogether symbolic execution of the environment.

A benefit of this approach is that it can be implemented incrementally: only some program statements can be instrumented and interpreted symbolically, while others can simply be executed concretely natively. A tool developer can improve the precision of symbolic execution over time, by adding new instruction handlers in a modular manner.

The main drawback is that program behaviors that correspond to environment behaviors other than the ones seen in the concrete executions are not explored.

Modeled Environment. This drawback can be addressed with another approach: model the environment during symbolic execution. For example, KLEE [23] redirects calls to the environment to small functions that understand the semantics of the desired action well enough to generate reasonable responses. With about 2,500 lines of code, they modeled roughly 40 Linux system calls, such as `open`, `read`, and `stat`. These models are hand-written abstractions of actual implementations of the system calls. Subsequently, [18] expanded the models for KLEE to a full POSIX environment.

The benefit of this approach is that target programs can now be exposed to more varied behaviors of the environment, and their reaction can be evaluated. For instance, what does the program do whenever a `write` operation to a file fails due to a full disk? A suitably written model for `write` can have a symbolic return value, which will vary depending on success or failure of that operation. In fact, one can write models that return different error codes for different failures, and a symbolic execution engine can automatically test the program under all these scenarios.

This approach has two main drawbacks. First, by definition, the model is an abstraction of the real code, and it may or may not model all possible behaviors of that code. (If the model was fully precise, it would be equivalent to the actual implementation.) Second, writing models by hand is labor-intensive and prone to error.

To mitigate these drawbacks, selective symbolic execution [31] does not employ models but instead automatically abstracts the environment. In doing so, it is guided by consistency models that govern when to over-approximate and when to under-approximate. More details on this system appear in Sect. 5.

3.3   Path Explosion

Symbolically executing all feasible program paths does not scale to large programs, because the number of feasible paths in a program can be exponential in the program size, or even infinite if the program, such as a network server, has a single loop whose number of iterations may depend on some unbounded input, such as a stream of network packets. A program like the Firefox web browser has more than 500,000 `if` statements; if just one thousandth of them were to have both a `then` and an `else` branch that are feasible for some inputs, then Firefox could be expected to have on the order of 2^{500} paths, which still far exceeds the number of atoms in the observable Universe [115]. We now discuss solutions to this path explosion problem.

A Generic Symbolic Execution and Search Algorithm. In order to present different trade-offs, we describe the operation of a symbolic execution engine in a more precise manner using the worklist-style Algorithm 1.

The algorithm is parameterized by a function *pickNext* for choosing the next state to expand in a worklist, a function *follow* that returns a decision on whether to follow a branch, and a relation $\sim$ that controls whether program states should be merged or kept separate (more on this later). A program state is a triple (ℓ, pc, s) consisting of a program location ℓ, the path condition pc, and the symbolic store s that maps each variable to either a concrete value or an expression over input variables. In line 1, the worklist w is initialized with a state whose symbolic store maps each variable to itself (we ignore named constants, for simplicity). Here, $\lambda x.e$ denotes the function mapping parameter x to an expression e, with $\lambda(x_1, \ldots x_n).e$ mapping multiple parameters. In each iteration, the algorithm picks a new state from the worklist (line 3).

On encountering an assignment $v := e$ (lines 5–6), the algorithm creates a successor state at the fall-through successor location $succ(\ell)$ of ℓ by updating the symbolic store s with a mapping from v to a new symbolic expression obtained by evaluating e in the context of s, and adds the new state to the set S. At every branch (lines 7–11), the algorithm first checks whether to follow either path and, if so, adds the corresponding condition to the successor state, which in turn is added to S. A symbolic execution engine can decide to not follow a branch if the branch is infeasible or would exceed a limit on loop unrolling. For assertions (line 12–13), the path condition, the symbolic store, and the negated assertion are put in conjunction and checked for satisfiability. Halt statements terminate the analyzed program, so the algorithm just outputs the path condition—a satisfying assignment of this condition can be used to generate a test case for the execution leading to the halt.

In lines 16–21, the new states in S are merged with any matching states in the worklist before being added to the worklist themselves. Two states match if they share the same location and are similar according to relation $\sim$. Merging creates a disjunction of the two path conditions and builds the merged symbolic store from ite expressions that assert one or the other original value, depending on the path taken (line 19).

Input: Choice function *pickNext*, similarity relation $\sim$, branch checker *follow*, and initial location ℓ_0.

Data: Worklist w and set of successor states S.

```
 1   w := {(ℓ₀, true, λv.v)};
 2   while w ≠ ∅ do
 3   │   (ℓ, pc, s) := pickNext(w); S := ∅;
     │   // Symbolically execute the next instruction
 4   │   switch instr(ℓ) do
 5   │   │   case v := e                                    // assignment
 6   │   │   │   S := {(succ(ℓ), pc, s[v ↦ eval(s, e)])};
 7   │   │   case if(e) goto ℓ'                             // conditional jump
 8   │   │   │   if follow(pc ∧ s ∧ e) then
 9   │   │   │   │   S := {(ℓ', pc ∧ e, s)};
10   │   │   │   if follow(pc ∧ s ∧ ¬e) then
11   │   │   │   │   S := S ∪ {(succ(ℓ), pc ∧ ¬e, s)};
12   │   │   case assert(e)                                 // assertion
13   │   │   │   if isSatisfiable(pc ∧ s ∧ ¬e) then abort else S := {(succ(ℓ), pc, s)}
14   │   │   case halt                                      // program halt
15   │   │   │   print pc;
     │   // Merge new states with matching ones in w
16   │   forall (ℓ'', pc', s') ∈ S do
17   │   │   if ∃(ℓ'', pc'', s'') ∈ w : (ℓ'', pc'', s'') ∼ (ℓ'', pc', s') then
18   │   │   │   w := w \ {(ℓ'', pc'', s'')};
19   │   │   │   w := w ∪ {(ℓ'', pc' ∨ pc'', λv.ite(pc', s'[v], s''[v]))};
20   │   │   else
21   │   │   │   w := w ∪ {(ℓ'', pc', s')};
22   print "no errors";
```

Algorithm 1. Generic symbolic execution of programs written in a simple input language with assignments, conditional **goto** statements, assertions, and **halt** statements. For simplicity, this algorithm is just intraprocedural; function calls must be inlined. It can generate precise symbolic function summaries, if invoked per procedure and with a similarity relation that merges all states when the function terminates.

Search Heuristics for Program Loops. Bounded model checkers [36] and extended static checkers [7,54,118] unroll loops up to a certain bound, which can be iteratively increased if an injected unwinding assertion fails. Such unrolling is usually performed by statically rewriting the control-flow graph, but can be fit into Algorithm 1 by defining *follow* to return false for branches that would unroll a loop beyond the bound. By default, symbolic execution explores loops as long as it cannot prove the infeasibility of the loop condition; in the case of an unbounded loop, this can lead to an infinite number of unrollings.

Modern symbolic execution typically performs loop unrolling and aims to be smart about choosing which program state to explore next. Dynamic test generation as implemented in DART [62] starts with an arbitrary initial unrolling of the loop (driven by an original concrete input) and explores different unrollings in subsequent tests, driven by follow-on concrete inputs chosen by DART. In other words, it implements *pickNext* to follow concrete executions, postponing branch alternatives to be covered by a subsequent concrete execution. Simple techniques like bounding the number of constraints injected at each program location are effective practical solutions to limit path explosion [64]. Dynamic test generation as implemented in KLEE [23] employs a search strategy implemented in the function *pickNext* that biases the choice of program states from the worklist against states that perform many repetitions of the same loop. For example, a search strategy optimized for line coverage selects states close to unexplored code and avoids states in deep loop unrollings.

While these code-coverage-based search heuristics do not change the number of execution paths through a target program, they focus the search on different parts of the program. In practice, these heuristics are important to explore diverse parts of the program, to avoid being stuck in specific parts of the search space, and hence to try to maximize code coverage and the number of bugs found given a limited time and space budget.

Summaries and State Merging. In addition to search heuristics, one can also *reduce* the number of paths to be explored by *memoizing and merging* program states reached by different program paths. This general idea of analyzing programs *compositionally* (e.g., [105]) is well-known in interprocedural static program analysis and is key to make it scale to large programs (e.g., [21, 29, 43, 70]). In the context of static analysis, a merged state typically *over*-approximates the individual states that are merged [43, 88]; even if the resulting imprecision can be reduced, it cannot be eliminated, thus leading to false positives (i.e., infeasible executions). In contrast, in the context of symbolic execution for test generation, as a matter of principle, a merged state must precisely represent the information from *all* execution paths subsumed by that state *without any* over-approximation. In other words, while compositional static analysis typically computes and memoizes *"may"* over-approximate function summaries, compositional test generation computes *"must"* under-approximate summaries [59].

For test generation, symbolic summaries can be computed at the block, method, function or procedure level, or at arbitrary program points. These can be computed incrementally, one interprocedural path at a time, and then bundled together using disjunctions as shown in lines 17–22 of Algorithm 1. The advantage of this approach is that, instead of being symbolically re-executed over and over again in different calling contexts, each intraprocedural path is symbolically executed only once, and the results of that symbolic execution are memoized using local input-preconditions and output post-conditions. A symbolic summary for a procedure is then simply defined as the disjunction of the summaries of its intraprocedural paths. Whenever a higher-level procedure `foo` calls an already-summarized procedure `bar`, the summary for `bar` is re-used and included in the current path condition of foo. The effect of re-using a symbolic summary is thus to *merge* all the states that can be reached when the summarized procedure returns. Such summaries can be computed in various ways, e.g., in an inner-most-first order [59] or lazily on-demand [3], and can also be used together with "may" summaries generated with static analysis (e.g., [67]).

Unfortunately, the main drawback of using summaries and state merging is that both symbolic execution and constraint solving become more complex and expensive: summaries (i.e., disjunctions of sub-program paths) need to be computed and memoized, which makes the path conditions (which now have more disjunctions) harder to solve.

Therefore, various trade-offs have been proposed. Two extreme trade-offs are (i) no state merging at all, i.e., complete separation of paths [23,24,62], and (ii) complete static state merging, as implemented by verification condition generators [7,36,77,118]. Static state merging combines states at join points after completely encoding all subpaths, i.e., it defines *pickNext* to explore all subpaths leading to a join point before picking any states at the join point, and it defines ∼ to contain all pairs of states. In search-based symbolic execution engines with no state merging, *pickNext* can be chosen freely according to the search goal, and ∼ is empty.

Some approaches adopt intermediate merging strategies. In the context of bounded model checking (BMC), Ganai and Gupta [56] investigate splitting the verification condition along subsets of paths; this moves BMC a step into the direction of symbolic execution, and corresponds to partitioning the ∼ relation. Hansen et al. [72] describe an implementation of static state merging in which they modify the exploration strategy to effectively traverse the control-flow graph in topological order and merge all states that share the same program location. Alas, for two of their three tested examples, the total solving time increases with this strategy due to the added load placed on the constraint solver by the increased complexity of the merged path conditions.

Indeed, the challenge in state merging is that, while merging two program states on the one hand may reduce the number of execution paths by an exponential factor, it could also increase the time the symbolic execution engine spends solving the more complex constraints. The net effect can be positive or negative. [82] proposes a technique for deciding when merging two program states is expected to be benefical vs. not. The approach uses a query count estimation algorithm to compute, during symbolic execution, whether the performance benefit resulting from the reduction in number of execution paths would outweigh the increase in constraint solver time. Experiments showed that this approach consistently achieved several orders of magnitude speedup over the then state of the art.

An alternative to implementing state merging inside the symbolic execution engine is to present this same engine with an equivalent variant of the target program that is easier to symbolically execute. Whereas a usual compiler translates programs into code that executes as quickly as possible on a target CPU, taking into account CPU-specific properties, Overify [116] instead compiles programs to have the simplest possible control flow, using techniques like jump threading, loop unswitching, transforming conditionally executed side-effect-free statements into speculative branch-free versions, splitting objects into smaller ones to reduce opportunities for pointer aliasing, and others. The net effect is that compiling a program with the `-Overify` option reduces the time of exhaustive symbolic execution by up to almost two orders of magnitude.

3.4   Efficient Constraint Solving

Another key component is the constraint solver being used to solve path constraints. Over the last decade, several tools implementing dynamic test generation for various programming languages, properties and application domains have been developed. Examples of such tools are DART [62], EGT [22], PathCrawler [117], CUTE [107], EXE [24], SAGE [64], CatchConv [93], PEX [113], KLEE [23], CREST [20], BitBlaze [111], Splat [87], Apollo [4], YOGI [67], Kudzu [106], S2E [31], and JDart [85]. The above tools differ by how they perform dynamic symbolic execution (for languages such as C, Java, x86, .NET), by the type of constraints they generate (for theories such as linear arithmetic, bit-vectors, arrays, uninterpreted functions, etc.), and by the type of constraint solvers they use (such as lp_solve, CVClite, STP, Disolver, Yikes, Z3). Indeed, like in traditional static program analysis and abstract interpretation, these important parameters are determined in practice depending on which type of program is to be tested, on how the program interfaces with its environment, and on which properties are to be checked. Moreover, various cost/precision tradeoffs are also possible while generating and solving constraints.

Fortunately, and driven in part by the test generation applications reported in this article, the science and engineering of automated theorem proving has made a lot of progress over the last decade as well. Notably, the last decade witnessed the birth and rise of so-called Satisfiability-Modulo-Theories (SMT) solvers [2,10,16,49,57,95], which can efficiently check satisfiability of complex constraints expressed in rich domains. Such solvers have also become computationally affordable in recent years thanks to the increasing computational power available on modern computers.

3.5   Parallelization and Testing as a Cloud Service

An orthogonal approach to speed up symbolic execution is *parallelization* of path exploration on a cluster of machines, harnessing its aggregate CPU and memory capabilities (alternatively, one could imagine running a symbolic execution engine on a supercomputer). One way to parallelize symbolic execution is by statically dividing up the task among nodes and have them run independently. However, when running on large programs, this approach leads to high workload imbalance among nodes, making the entire cluster proceed at the pace of the slowest node—if this node gets stuck, for instance, while symbolically executing a loop, the testing process may never terminate. In [18], a method is described for parallelizing symbolic execution on shared-nothing clusters in a way that scales well. Without changing the exponential nature of the problem, parallel symbolic execution harnesses cluster resources to make it feasible to run automated testing on larger systems than would otherwise be possible.

In essence, software testing reduces to exercising as many paths through a program as possible and checking that certain properties hold along those paths (no crashes, no buffer overflows, etc.). The advances in symbolic execution lead naturally to the "testing as a service" (TaaS) vision [26,66] of (1) offering software testing as a competitive, easily accessible online service, and (2) doing fully automated testing in the cloud, to harness vast, elastic resources toward making automated testing practical for real software. A software-testing service allows users and developers to upload the software of interest, instruct the service what type of testing to perform, click a button, and then obtain a report with the results. For professional uses, TaaS can integrate directly with the development process and test the code as it is written. TaaS can also serve as a publicly available certification service that enables comparing the reliability and safety of software products [25].

Having seen some key challenges in automated test generation and possible solutions, we now describe two recent systems that employ many of these techniques: SAGE (Sect. 4) and S2E (Sect. 5).

4   Whitebox Fuzzing with SAGE

Whitebox fuzzing of file parsers [64] is a "killer app" for automatic test generation using dynamic symbolic execution and constraint solving. Many security vulnerabilities are due to programming errors in code for parsing files and packets that are transmitted over the Internet. For instance, the Microsoft Windows operating system includes parsers for hundreds of file formats. A security vulnerability in any of those parsers may require the deployment of a costly, visible security patch to more than a billion PCs, i.e., millions of dollars [65]. Because of the magnitude of this problem, Microsoft has invested significant resources to hunt security vulnerabilities in its products, and provided the right environment for whitebox fuzzing to mature to an unprecedented level.

Whitebox fuzzing extends dynamic test generation from unit testing to whole-program security testing in three main ways: First, inspired by blackbox fuzzing [55], whitebox fuzzing performs dynamic test generation starting from one or several *well-formed* inputs, which is a heuristic to increase code coverage quickly and give the search a head-start. Second, again like blackbox fuzzing, the focus of whitebox fuzzing is to find *security vulnerabilities*, like buffer overflows, not to check functional correctness; finding such security vulnerabilities can be done fully automatically and does not require an application-specific test *oracle* or functional specification. Third, and more importantly, the main technical novelty of whitebox fuzzing is *scalability*: it extends the scope of dynamic test generation from (small) units to (large) whole programs. Whitebox fuzzing scales to large file parsers embedded in applications with millions of lines of code and execution traces with hundreds of millions of machine instructions.

Since whitebox fuzzing targets large applications, it must scale to long program executions, and such symbolic execution is expensive. For instance, a single symbolic execution of Microsoft Excel with 45,000 input bytes executes nearly a billion x86 instructions. In this context, whitebox fuzzing uses a novel directed search algorithm, dubbed *generational search*, that maximizes the number of new input tests generated from each symbolic execution. Given a path constraint, *all* the constraints in that path are systematically negated one-by-one, placed in a conjunction with the prefix of the path constraint leading to it, and attempted to be solved by a constraint solver. This way, a single symbolic execution can generate thousands of new tests. (In contrast, a standard depth-first or breadth-first search would negate only the last or first constraint in each path constraint, and generate at most one new test per symbolic execution.)

Whitebox fuzzing was first implemented in the tool SAGE, short for Scalable Automated Guided Execution [64]. SAGE was the first tool to perform dynamic symbolic execution at the x86 binary level, which allows it to be used on any program regardless of its source language or build process. It also ensures that "what you fuzz is what you ship," as compilers can perform source-code changes which may impact security.

SAGE uses several optimizations that are crucial for dealing with huge execution traces with billions of machine instructions. To scale to such execution traces, SAGE uses several techniques to improve the speed and memory usage of constraint generation: *symbolic-expression caching* ensures that structurally equivalent symbolic terms are mapped to the same physical object; *unrelated constraint elimination* reduces the size of constraint solver queries by removing the constraints which do not share symbolic variables with the negated constraint; *local constraint caching* skips a constraint if it has already been added to the path constraint; *flip count limit* establishes the maximum number of times constraints generated from a particular program branch can be flipped; using a cheap syntactic check, *constraint subsumption* eliminates constraints logically implied by other constraints injected at the same program branch (mostly likely due to successive iterations of an input-dependent loop) [64].

Since 2008, SAGE has been running in production on hundreds of machines, automatically fuzzing hundreds of applications in Microsoft security testing labs. This is over 500 machine-years and the "largest computational usage ever for any Satisfiability-Modulo-Theories (SMT) solver" according to the authors of the Z3 SMT solver [95], with over four billion constraints processed to date [13].

During this fuzzing, SAGE found many new security vulnerabilities (buffer overflows) in many Windows parsers and Office applications, including image processors, media players, file decoders, and document parsers. Notably, SAGE found roughly one third of *all* the bugs discovered by file fuzzing during the development of Microsoft's Windows 7 [65], saving millions of dollars by avoiding expensive security patches for nearly a billion PCs worldwide. Because SAGE was typically run last, those bugs were missed by everything else, including static program analysis and blackbox fuzzing.

In 2015, SAGE and other popular blackbox fuzzers used internally at Microsoft were packaged into Project Springfield [91], the first commercial cloud fuzzing service (renamed Microsoft Security Risk Detection in 2017). Customers who subscribe to this service can submit fuzzing jobs targeting their own software and benefit from the technology described in this article. No source code or symbols are required. Springfield fuzzing jobs are easy to set up by non-experts, and are processed using the same tools used for over a decade inside Microsoft, for automatic job validation, seed minimization, fuzzing on many machines (leveraging the cloud) each running different fuzzing tools and configurations, and then automatic analysis, triage and prioritization of the bugs found, with results available directly on the Springfield web-site.

5   Selective Symbolic Execution with S2E

When the target of testing is not individual applications but *systems* code (e.g., device drivers) or *full system stacks* (i.e., the operating system kernel with drivers, libraries, and applications all together), the dominant considerations become the interaction between the tested software and its environment (Sect. 3.2) and scaling beyond a single application. These challenges motivated the development of the S2E system [31].

S2E is a symbolic execution engine for x86 and ARM binaries. It is built around a modified version of the QEMU [12] virtual machine, and it dynamically dispatches guest machine instructions either to the host CPU for native execution or to a symbolic execution engine (KLEE [23]) embedded inside S2E. Most instructions do not access symbolic state, so they can run natively, while the rest are interpreted symbolically.

The original use case for S2E was testing full system stacks with complex environments (proprietary OS kernel, many interdependent libraries, etc.). An accurate assessment of program behavior requires taking into account every *relevant* detail of the environment, but making *a priori* the choice of what is relevant is hard. So S2E offers "in-vivo" symbolic execution, in which the environment is automatically abstracted on-the-fly, as needed. This is in contrast to "in-vitro" symbolic execution, as done by symbolic execution engines and model checkers that use stubs or models [8, 23, 97]).

Such in-vivo symbolic execution was used both in industrial and academic settings. Engineers at Intel used S2E to search for security vulnerabilities in UEFI BIOS implementations [11]. DDT [81] used S2E to test closed-source proprietary Microsoft Windows device drivers, without access to the driver source code or inside knowledge of the Windows kernel. DDT found memory leaks, segmentation faults, race conditions, and memory corruption bugs in drivers that had been shipping with Windows for many years. Network researchers used S2E to verify the dataplane of software network routers [47] by using a form of exhaustive symbolic execution on specific elements in the router without having to model the rest of the router.

The key design choice that enables in-vivo symbolic execution is to carefully maintain a unified global state store that simultaneously captures both symbolic and concrete execution state. An execution can thus alternate between concrete and symbolic execution multiple times during the same run, without losing desired correctness and precision. For example, when symbolically executing a driver in-vivo, the initial execution starts out concrete from userspace, is concrete in the kernel, then switches to symbolic when entering the driver, then back to concrete when the driver calls into the kernel, back to symbolic when execution returns inside the driver, and so on. In this way, "interesting" program paths are explored in the software of interest (the driver, in this example) without symbolically executing the rest of the real environment.

The unified state store consists of machine state (memory, CPU registers and flags, system clock, devices, etc.) that is shared between the symbolic execution engine and the virtual machine. S2E is responsible for the transparent conversions of concrete state to symbolic state and vice versa, governed by an *execution consistency model*. For example, under a so-called "locally consistent execution" model, when a driver calls `kmalloc` with a symbolic argument λ to allocate kernel memory, S2E automatically picks a concrete value that satisfies the path constraint, say 64, and executes `kmalloc` concretely in the kernel. Once the kernel returns the concrete 64-byte memory buffer, S2E returns to the driver a symbolic two-valued pointer $p = 0 \mid \&buffer$ capturing the two possible outcomes of the `kmalloc` call. S2E then augments the path constraint with $\lambda = 64$ and continues symbolic execution in the driver. Depending on consistency model, if λ is later involved in a branch condition with one of the branches made infeasible by the $\lambda = 64$ constraint, S2E can return to the original `kmalloc` call site to re-concretize λ to an additional value that enables that branch, and repeat the call.

Execution consistency models in S2E are analogous to memory consistency models [94]. The traditional assumption about system execution is that the state at any point in time is consistent, i.e., there exists a feasible concrete-execution path from the system's start state to the system's current state. This is what S2E calls "strictly consistent concrete execution," and this is the strongest of all execution consistency models. Relaxing this assumption results in the definition of five additional consistency models [32], each offering different trade-offs. For example, "strictly consistent unit-level execution" corresponds to the consistency model that governs how DART [62] and EXE [24] handle the environment. The "locally consistent execution" mentioned above is the one DDT [81] employed for the interface between device drivers and the OS kernel.

An interesting concept in S2E is that of *symbolic hardware*. It corresponds to "overapproximately consistent execution," and allows virtualized hardware to return unconstrained symbolic values. DDT [81] and SymDrive [104] used this execution consistency model for the hardware interface, in order to test drivers for hardware error paths that are difficult to exercise, and to make up for the all-together absence of the hardware.

One of S2E's optimizations is *lazy concretization*: concretize symbolic values on-demand, only when concretely-running code is about to branch on a condition that depends on that value. This makes it possible to carry a lot of data through the layers of the system stack without conversion. For example, when a program writes a buffer of symbolic data to the filesystem, there are usually no branches in the kernel or the disk device driver that depend on the data per se, so S2E can pass the buffer through unconcretized and write it in symbolic form to the virtual disk, from where it can later be read back in its symbolic form, thus avoiding the loss of precision inherent in concretization.

Over time, S2E turned into a general platform for software analysis, and saw a number of surprising use cases. For example, RevNIC [30] employed "overap-proximately consistent execution" to automatically reverse-engineer proprietary Windows device drivers and produce equivalent drivers for different platforms. In [32], S2E was used to develop a comprehensive performance profiler to mea-sure instruction count, cache misses, TLB misses, and page faults for arbitrary memory hierarchies along all paths of a program. A side effect of S2E's design as a virtual machine is that it can be used not only for proprietary software but also for self-modifying, JITed, and/or obfuscated and packed/encrypted binaries. This made S2E well suited for malware analysis in a commercial setting [41]. It was also used to develop Chef [17], a tool for turning the vanilla interpreter of a dynamically interpreted language (like Python) into a sound and complete symbolic execution engine for that language. As a final example, two of the seven systems competing in the finals of DARPA's Cyber Grand Challenge in 2016 were based on S2E. This competition was an all-machine computer secu-rity tournament, where each competing machine had to autonomously analyze computer programs, find security vulnerabilities, fix them, and launch attacks on other competitors. As part of Galactica (one of the DARPA competitors), S2E launched 392 successful attacks during the competition, twice as many as the competition's all-around winner.

S2E is currently an open-source project [51] and is also at the heart of several commercial cybersecurity products. S2E illustrates how automated test genera-tion can morph into a variety of other forms of program analysis.

6   Other Approaches to Automated Test Generation

As mentioned in the introduction, this paper is not a survey on automatic test generation. We do mention briefly here some other notable test-generation tech-niques.

Model-Based Testing. Given an abstract representation of the program, called *model*, model-based testing consists of generating tests by analyzing the model in order to check the *conformance* of the program with respect to the model (e.g., [114]). Such models are usually program specifications written by hand, but they can also be generated automatically using machine-learning techniques (e.g., see [69,102] and the article on automata learning in this volume [74]). In contrast, the code-driven test-generation techniques discussed in this article do not use or require a model of the program under test. Instead, their goal is to generate tests that exercise as many program statements as possible, including assertions inserted in the code.

Grammar-Based Fuzzing. Most popular blackbox random fuzzers for security testing support some form of grammar representation to specify the input format of the application under test, e.g., Peach [99] and SPIKE [100], among many others [112]. Such grammars are typically written by hand, and this process is laborious, time consuming, and error-prone. Nevertheless, grammar-based fuzzing is the most effective fuzzing technique known today for fuzzing applications with complex structured input formats, like web-browsers which must take as inputs web-pages including complex HTML documents and JavaScript code. Work on grammar-based test input generation started in the 1970's [71,101]. Test generation from a grammar is usually either random [40,89,110] or exhaustive [83]. Imperative generation [33,42] is a related approach in which a custom-made program generates the inputs (in effect, the program encodes the grammar). Grammar-based fuzzing can also be combined with whitebox fuzzing [61,86].

Search-Based Test Generation. Test generation can be viewed as a search and optimization problem (e.g., how to maximize code coverage), and various heuristics and search techniques have been proposed, for instance, using genetic algorithms and simulated annealing (e.g., [90]). The fuzzing heuristics using code-coverage feedback mentioned earlier are related to these techniques. These techniques have also been applied to other software engineering problems, including other testing-related problems such as test case minimization and test case prioritization [90].

Exploit Generation. A targetted form of security testing is exploit generation: given a program, automatically find vulnerabilities and generate exploits for them. Systems like Mayhem [28] have used pre-conditioned symbolic execution to find and exploit zero-day security bugs [6], and work prior to that augmented such test generation with knowledge from security patches in order to reverse-engineer the exploits against which those patches were defending [15].

Combinatorial Testing. Given a program and a set of input parameters, combinatorial testing aims at generating efficiently a set of test inputs which cover all pairs of input parameters (e.g., [39]). Generalizations from pairs to arbitrary k-tuples have also been proposed. In practice, these techniques are used provided the number of input parameters is sufficiently small, e.g., for configuration parameters [39].

Concurrency Testing. Systematic testing techniques and algorithms have also been proposed for concurrent software (e.g., [50,53,58,96]). Such techniques explore the possible interleavings of multiple processes or threads using a runtime scheduler with the goal of finding concurrency-related bugs such as deadlocks and race conditions.

Runtime Verification. Runtime verification tools (e.g., [48,73]) monitor at run-time the behavior of a program and compare this behavior against a high-level specification, typically represented as a finite-state automaton or a temporal-logic formula. These tools can be viewed as extensions of runtime checking tools mentioned earlier (like Purify and AddressSanitizer), and are complementary to test generation.

Program Verification. Over the past few decades, symbolic execution, constraint generation and automated theorem proving have also been developed further in various ways for program verification, such as verification-condition generation (e.g., [9,46]), symbolic model checking [19] and bounded model checking [35]. Program verification aims at proving the absence of program errors, while test generation aims at generating concrete test inputs that can drive the program to execute specific program statements or paths. A detailed technical comparison can be found in [63]. In practice, symbolic execution, constraint generation and solving are typically not sound and complete, and *fully automatic* program verification remains elusive for large complex software.

7 Conclusion

This article presented an introduction and overview of automated test generation for software. We discussed how test generation using dynamic symbolic execution can be more precise than static test generation and other forms of test generation such as random, taint-based and coverage-heuristic-based test generation. This test generation approach is also more sophisticated, requiring the use of automated theorem proving for solving path constraints. This machinery is more complex and heavy-weight, but may exercise more program paths, find more bugs and generate fewer redundant tests covering the same path. Whether this better precision is worth the trouble depends on the application domain.

Research on automatic test generation has been carried out over many years and is still an active area of research. The techniques described in this article have been implemented in tens of tools. The application of those tools has, collectively, found thousands of new bugs, many of them critical from a reliability or security point of view, in many different application domains.

While this progress is significant and enoucouraging, there is room for further improvements. Automated test generation tools have been successfully applied to several application domains so far, but they are not being used routinely yet by most software developers and testers. New application domains are arising for which the techniques described here need significant rethinking. For example the models automatically learned by machine-learning algorithms (e.g., used in self-driving vehicles) are unlike regular programs, and so testing them automatically requires new approaches. More work is required to further lower the cost of automated test generation (e.g., in terms of computation and memory) while increasing the value it provides (e.g., by providing actionable information on how to fix the bugs instead of just providing test cases). Automated testing can benefit from human insights (both in terms of providing test criteria and in prioritizing test case search), and the potential of combining human intelligence with fuzzing and symbolic execution has yet to be realized. We also see opportunities for machine learning in automated testing, such as in learning input grammars from examples and leveraging these grammars for generating tests. Finally, the goal of automated test generation is to enable software engineers to produce better software faster, and further research is required on how best to integrate testing tools in software development processes, in particular modern agile processes and continuous integration, and how to tighten the feedback loop for fixing bugs.

References

1. Aizatsky, M., Serebryany, K., Chang, O., Arya, A., Whittaker, M.: Announcing OSS-Fuzz: Continuous fuzzing for open source software (2016). https://testing. googleblog.com/2016/12/announcing-oss-fuzz-continuous-fuzzing.html
2. Alberti, F., Ghilardi, S., Sharygina, N.: Decision procedures for flat array properties. In: Ábrahám, E., Havelund, K. (eds.) TACAS 2014. LNCS, vol. 8413, pp. 15–30. Springer, Heidelberg (2014). https://doi.org/10.1007/978-3-642-54862-8_2
3. Anand, S., Godefroid, P., Tillmann, N.: Demand-driven compositional symbolic execution. In: Ramakrishnan, C.R., Rehof, J. (eds.) TACAS 2008. LNCS, vol. 4963, pp. 367–381. Springer, Heidelberg (2008). https://doi.org/10.1007/978-3-540-78800-3_28
4. Artzi, S., Kiezun, A., Dolby, J., Tip, F., Dig, D., Paradkar, A.M., Ernst, M.D.: Finding bugs in web applications using dynamic test generation and explicit-state model checking. IEEE Trans. Softw. Eng. 36(4), 474–494 (2010)
5. Arya, A., Neckar, C.: Fuzzing for security (2012). https://blog.chromium.org/2012/04/fuzzing-for-security.html
6. Avgerinos, T., Cha, S.K., Hao, B.L.T., Brumley, D.: AEG: automatic exploit generation. In: Network and Distributed System Security Symposium (2011)
7. Babic, D., Hu, A.J.: Calysto: scalable and precise extended static checking. In: International Conference on Software Engineering (2008)
8. Ball, T., Bounimova, E., Levin, V., Kumar, R., Lichtenberg, J.: The static driver verifier research platform. In: Touili, T., Cook, B., Jackson, P. (eds.) CAV 2010. LNCS, vol. 6174, pp. 119–122. Springer, Heidelberg (2010). https://doi.org/10.1007/978-3-642-14295-6_11
9. Barnett, M., Chang, B.-Y.E., DeLine, R., Jacobs, B., Leino, K.R.M.: Boogie: a modular reusable verifier for object-oriented programs. In: de Boer, F.S., Bonsangue, M.M., Graf, S., de Roever, W.-P. (eds.) FMCO 2005. LNCS, vol. 4111, pp. 364–387. Springer, Heidelberg (2006). https://doi.org/10.1007/11804192_17
10. Barrett, C., et al.: CVC4. In: Gopalakrishnan, G., Qadeer, S. (eds.) CAV 2011. LNCS, vol. 6806, pp. 171–177. Springer, Heidelberg (2011). https://doi.org/10.1007/978-3-642-22110-1_14
11. Bazhaniuk, O., Loucaides, J., Rosenbaum, L., Tuttle, M.R., Zimmer, V.: Symbolic execution for BIOS security. In: USENIX Workshop on Offensive Technologies (2015)
12. Bellard, F.: QEMU, a fast and portable dynamic translator. In: USENIX Annual Technical Conference (2005)
13. Bounimova, E., Godefroid, P., Molnar, D.: Billions and billions of constraints: whitebox fuzz testing in production. In: International Conference on Software Engineering (2013)

14. Boyer, R.S., Elspas, B., Levitt, K.N.: SELECT - a formal system for testing and debugging programs by symbolic execution. SIGPLAN Not. **10**, 234–245 (1975)
15. Brumley, D., Poosankam, P., Song, D., Zheng, J.: Automatic patch-based exploit generation is possible: techniques and implications. In: IEEE Symposium on Security and Privacy (2008)
16. Brummayer, R., Biere, A.: Boolector: an efficient SMT solver for bit-vectors and arrays. In: Kowalewski, S., Philippou, A. (eds.) TACAS 2009. LNCS, vol. 5505, pp. 174–177. Springer, Heidelberg (2009). https://doi.org/10.1007/978-3-642-00768-2_16
17. Bucur, S., Kinder, J., Candea, G.: Prototyping symbolic execution engines for interpreted languages. In: International Conference on Architectural Support for Programming Languages and Operating Systems (2014)
18. Bucur, S., Ureche, V., Zamfir, C., Candea, G.: Parallel symbolic execution for automated real-world software testing. In: ACM EuroSys European Conference on Computer Systems (2011)
19. Burch, J., Clarke, E., McMillan, K., Dill, D., Hwang, L.: Symbolic model checking: 10^{20} states and beyond. In: Symposium on Logic in Computer Science (1990)
20. Burnim, J., Sen, K.: Heuristics for scalable dynamic test generation. In: International Conference on Automated Software Engineering (2008)
21. Bush, W., Pincus, J., Sielaff, D.: A static analyzer for finding dynamic programming errors. Softw. Practice Exp. **30**(7), 775–802 (2000)
22. Cadar, C., Engler, D.: Execution generated test cases: how to make systems code crash itself. In: Godefroid, P. (ed.) SPIN 2005. LNCS, vol. 3639, pp. 2–23. Springer, Heidelberg (2005). https://doi.org/10.1007/11537328_2
23. Cadar, C., Dunbar, D., Engler, D.R.: KLEE: unassisted and automatic generation of high-coverage tests for complex systems programs. In: Symposium on Operating System Design and Implementation (2008)
24. Cadar, C., Ganesh, V., Pawlowski, P.M., Dill, D.L., Engler, D.R.: EXE: automatically generating inputs of death. In: Conference on Computer and Communication Security (2006)
25. Candea, G.: A software certification service. In: Symposium on Operating System Design and Implementation (2008). "Research Vision" talk session
26. Candea, G., Bucur, S., Zamfir, C.: Automated software testing as a service. In: Symposium on Cloud Computing (2010)
27. CERT: CERT database of security vulnerabilities (2017). http://www.cert.org/vulnerability-analysis/knowledgebase/
28. Cha, S.K., Avgerinos, T., Rebert, A., Brumley, D.: Unleashing Mayhem on binary code. In: IEEE Symposium on Security and Privacy (2012)
29. Chen, H., Dean, D., Wagner, D.: Model checking one million lines of C code. In: Network and Distributed System Security Symposium (2004)
30. Chipounov, V., Candea, G.: Reverse engineering of binary device drivers with RevNIC. In: ACM EuroSys European Conference on Computer Systems (2010)
31. Chipounov, V., Kuznetsov, V., Candea, G.: S2E: a platform for in-vivo multi-path analysis of software systems. In: International Conference on Architectural Support for Programming Languages and Operating Systems (2011)
32. Chipounov, V., Kuznetsov, V., Candea, G.: The S2E platform: design, implementation, and applications. ACM Trans. Comput. Syst. **30**(1), 2 (2012). Special issue: Best papers of ASPLOS
33. Claessen, K., Hughes, J.: QuickCheck: a lightweight tool for random testing of Haskell programs. In: ACM SIGPLAN International Conference on Functional Programming (2000)

34. Clang Users Manual: Undefined behavior sanitizer (2017). http://clang.llvm.org/docs/UsersManual.html

35. Clarke, E.M., Biere, A., Raimi, R., Zhu, Y.: Bounded model checking using satisfiability solving. Formal Methods Syst. Des. **19**(1), 7–34 (2001)

36. Clarke, E., Kroening, D., Lerda, F.: A tool for checking ANSI-C programs. In: Jensen, K., Podelski, A. (eds.) TACAS 2004. LNCS, vol. 2988, pp. 168–176. Springer, Heidelberg (2004). https://doi.org/10.1007/978-3-540-24730-2_15

37. Clarke, L.A.: A program testing system. In: ACM Annual Conference (1976)

38. Clarke, L.A., Richardson, D.J.: Applications of symbolic evaluation. J. Syst. Softw. **5**(1), 15–35 (1985)

39. Cohen, D.M., Dalal, S.R., Parelius, J., Patton, G.C.: The combinatorial design approach to automatic test generation. IEEE Softw. **13**(5), 83–88 (1996)

40. Coppit, D., Lian, J.: Yagg: an easy-to-use generator for structured test inputs. In: International Conference on Automated Software Engineering (2005)

41. Cyberhaven Inc: Cyberhaven product line. http://cyberhaven.io/

42. Daniel, B., Dig, D., Garcia, K., Marinov, D.: Automated testing of refactoring engines. In: Symposium on the Foundations of Software Engineering (2007)

43. Das, M., Lerner, S., Seigle, M.: ESP: path-sensitive program verification in polynomial time. In: International Conference on Programming Language Design and Implementation (2002)

44. Dhurjati, D., Kowshik, S., Adve, V.: Safecode: enforcing alias analysis for weakly typed languages. In: International Conference on Programming Language Design and Implementation (2006)

45. Dijkstra, E.W.: Notes on Structured Programming. In: Structured Programming. Academic Press, Cambridge (1972)

46. Dijkstra, E.W.: Guarded commands, nondeterminacy and formal derivation of programs. Commun. ACM **18**(8), 453–457 (1975)

47. Dobrescu, M., Argyraki, K.: Software dataplane verification. In: Symposium on Networked Systems Design and Implementation (2014)

48. Drusinsky, D.: The temporal rover and the ATG rover. In: Havelund, K., Penix, J., Visser, W. (eds.) SPIN 2000. LNCS, vol. 1885, pp. 323–330. Springer, Heidelberg (2000). https://doi.org/10.1007/10722468_19

49. Dutertre, B., de Moura, L.: A fast linear-arithmetic solver for DPLL(T). In: Ball, T., Jones, R.B. (eds.) CAV 2006. LNCS, vol. 4144, pp. 81–94. Springer, Heidelberg (2006). https://doi.org/10.1007/11817963_11

50. Edelstein, O., Farchi, E., Goldin, E., Nir, Y., Ratsaby, G., Ur, S.: Framework for testing multi-threaded Java programs. Concurrency Comput.: Practice Exp. **15**(3–5), 485–499 (2003)

51. EPFL and Cyberhaven Inc: S2E software distribution. http://s2e.systems/

52. Etoh, H.: Propolice: GCC extension for protecting applications from stack-smashing attacks (2000). https://www.researchgate.net/publication/243483996_GCC_extension_for_protecting_applications_from_stack-smashing_attacks

53. Flanagan, C., Godefroid, P.: Dynamic partial-order reduction for model checking software. In: Symposium on Principles of Programming Languages (2005)

54. Flanagan, C., Leino, K.R.M., Lillibridge, M., Nelson, G., Saxe, J.B., Stata, R.: Extended static checking for Java. In: International Conference on Programming Language Design and Implementation (2002)

55. Forrester, J.E., Miller, B.P.: An empirical study of the robustness of windows NT applications using random testing. In: USENIX Windows System Symposium (2000)

56. Ganai, M.K., Gupta, A.: Tunneling and slicing: towards scalable BMC. In: Design Automation Conference (2008)
57. Ganesh, V., Dill, D.L.: A decision procedure for bit-vectors and arrays. In: Damm, W., Hermanns, H. (eds.) CAV 2007. LNCS, vol. 4590, pp. 519–531. Springer, Heidelberg (2007). https://doi.org/10.1007/978-3-540-73368-3_52
58. Godefroid, P.: Model checking for programming languages using VeriSoft. In: Symposium on Principles of Programming Languages (1997)
59. Godefroid, P.: Compositional dynamic test generation. In: Symposium on Principles of Programming Languages (2007)
60. Godefroid, P.: Higher-order test generation. In: International Conference on Programming Language Design and Implementation (2011)
61. Godefroid, P., Kiezun, A., Levin, M.Y.: Grammar-based whitebox fuzzing. In: International Conference on Programming Language Design and Implementation (2008)
62. Godefroid, P., Klarlund, N., Sen, K.: DART: directed automated random testing. In: International Conference on Programming Language Design and Implementation (2005)
63. Godefroid, P., Lahiri, S.K.: From program to logic: an introduction. In: LASER Summer School (2012)
64. Godefroid, P., Levin, M., Molnar, D.: Automated whitebox fuzz testing. In: Network and Distributed System Security Symposium (2008)
65. Godefroid, P., Levin, M., Molnar, D.: SAGE: whitebox fuzzing for security testing. Commun. ACM 55(3) (2012)
66. Godefroid, P., Molnar, D.: Fuzzing in the cloud. Technical report MSR-TR-2010-29, Microsoft Research, March 2010
67. Godefroid, P., Nori, A., Rajamani, S., Tetali, S.: Compositional may-must program analysis: unleashing the power of alternation. In: Symposium on Principles of Programming Languages (2010)
68. Gupta, N., Mathur, A.P., Soffa, M.L.: Generating test data for branch coverage. In: International Conference on Automated Software Engineering (2000)
69. Hagerer, A., Hungar, H., Niese, O., Steffen, B.: Model generation by moderated regular extrapolation. In: Kutsche, R.-D., Weber, H. (eds.) FASE 2002. LNCS, vol. 2306, pp. 80–95. Springer, Heidelberg (2002). https://doi.org/10.1007/3-540-45923-5_6
70. Hallem, S., Chelf, B., Xie, Y., Engler, D.: A system and language for building system-specific static analyses. In: International Conference on Programming Language Design and Implementation (2002)
71. Hanford, K.: Automatic generation of test cases. IBM Syst. J. 9(4) (1970)
72. Hansen, T., Schachte, P., Søndergaard, H.: State joining and splitting for the symbolic execution of binaries. In: Bensalem, S., Peled, D.A. (eds.) RV 2009. LNCS, vol. 5779, pp. 76–92. Springer, Heidelberg (2009). https://doi.org/10.1007/978-3-642-04694-0_6
73. Havelund, K., Rosu, G.: Monitoring Java programs with Java PathExplorer. In: International Conference on Runtime Verification (2001)
74. Howar, F., Jonsson, B., Vaandrager, F.: Combining black-box and white-box techniques for learning register automata. In: Steffen, B., Woeginger, G. (eds.) Computing and Software Science. LNCS, vol. 10000, pp. 563–588. Springer, Heidelberg (2018)
75. Howard, M., Lipner, S.: The Security Development Lifecycle. Microsoft Press (2006)

76. Howden, W.: Symbolic testing and the DISSECT symbolic evaluation system. IEEE Trans. Softw. Eng. **3**(4) (1977)

77. Ivančić, F., Yang, Z., Ganai, M.K., Gupta, A., Shlyakhter, I., Ashar, P.: F-SOFT: software verification platform. In: Etessami, K., Rajamani, S.K. (eds.) CAV 2005. LNCS, vol. 3576, pp. 301–306. Springer, Heidelberg (2005). https://doi.org/10.1007/11513988_31

78. Jelinek, J.: Fortify_source: Object size checking to prevent (some) buffer overflows. https://gcc.gnu.org/ml/gcc-patches/2004-09/msg02055.html

79. King, J.C.: Symbolic execution and program testing. J. ACM **19**(7) (1976)

80. Korel, B.: A dynamic approach of test data generation. In: IEEE Conference on Software Maintenance (1990)

81. Kuznetsov, V., Chipounov, V., Candea, G.: Testing closed-source binary device drivers with DDT. In: USENIX Annual Technical Conference (2010)

82. Kuznetsov, V., Kinder, J., Bucur, S., Candea, G.: Efficient state merging in symbolic execution. In: International Conference on Programming Language Design and Implementation (2012)

83. Lämmel, R., Schulte, W.: Controllable combinatorial coverage in grammar-based testing. In: Uyar, M.Ü., Duale, A.Y., Fecko, M.A. (eds.) TestCom 2006. LNCS, vol. 3964, pp. 19–38. Springer, Heidelberg (2006). https://doi.org/10.1007/11754008_2

84. Libfuzzer–a library for coverage-guided fuzz testing. http://llvm.org/docs/LibFuzzer.html

85. Luckow, K., Dimjašević, M., Giannakopoulou, D., Howar, F., Isberner, M., Kahsai, T., Rakamarić, Z., Raman, V.: JDART: a dynamic symbolic analysis framework. In: Chechik, M., Raskin, J.-F. (eds.) TACAS 2016. LNCS, vol. 9636, pp. 442–459. Springer, Heidelberg (2016). https://doi.org/10.1007/978-3-662-49674-9_26

86. Majumdar, R., Xu, R.: Directed test generation using symbolic grammars. In: International Conference on Automated Software Engineering (2007)

87. Majumdar, R., Xu, R.-G.: Reducing test inputs using information partitions. In: Bouajjani, A., Maler, O. (eds.) CAV 2009. LNCS, vol. 5643, pp. 555–569. Springer, Heidelberg (2009). https://doi.org/10.1007/978-3-642-02658-4_41

88. Mauborgne, L., Rival, X.: Trace partitioning in abstract interpretation based static analyzers. In: Sagiv, M. (ed.) ESOP 2005. LNCS, vol. 3444, pp. 5–20. Springer, Heidelberg (2005). https://doi.org/10.1007/978-3-540-31987-0_2

89. Maurer, P.: Generating test data with enhanced context-free grammars. IEEE Softw. **7**(4) (1990)

90. McMinn, P.: Search-based software test data generation: a survey. Int. J. Softw. Test. Verification Reliab. **14**(2) (2004)

91. Microsoft: Project springfield. https://www.microsoft.com/springfield/

92. Miller, B., Fredriksen, L., So, B.: An empirical study of the reliability of UNIX utilities. Commun. ACM **33**(12) (1990)

93. Molnar, D., Wagner, D.: Catchconv: symbolic execution and run-time type inference for integer conversion errors. Technical report EECS-2007-23, U.C. Berkeley (2007)

94. Mosberger, D.: Memory consistency models. ACM SIGOPS Oper. Syst. Rev. **27**(1) (1993)

95. de Moura, L., Bjørner, N.: Z3: an efficient SMT solver. In: Ramakrishnan, C.R., Rehof, J. (eds.) TACAS 2008. LNCS, vol. 4963, pp. 337–340. Springer, Heidelberg (2008). https://doi.org/10.1007/978-3-540-78800-3_24

96. Musuvathi, M., Qadeer, S.: Iterative context bounding for systematic testing of multithreaded programs. In: International Conference on Programming Language Design and Implementation (2007)

97. Musuvathi, M., Qadeer, S., Ball, T., Basler, G., Nainar, P.A., Neamtiu, I.: Finding and reproducing Heisenbugs in concurrent programs. In: Symposium on Operating System Design and Implementation (2008)

98. Offutt, A.J., Jin, Z., Pan, J.: The dynamic domain reduction procedure for test data generation. Softw. Practice Exp. **29**(2) (1999)

99. Peach fuzzer (2017). http://www.peachfuzzer.com/

100. Spike fuzzer (2017). http://resources.infosecinstitute.com/fuzzer-automation-with-spike/

101. Purdom, P.: A sentence generator for testing parsers. BIT Numer. Math. **12**(3) (1972)

102. Raffelt, H., Merten, M., Steffen, B., Margaria, T.: Dynamic testing via automata learning. Int. J. Softw. Tools Technol. Transf. **11**(4) (2009)

103. Ramamoorthy, C., Ho, S.B., Chen, W.: On the automated generation of program test data. IEEE Trans. Softw. Eng. **2**(4) (1976)

104. Renzelmann, M.J., Kadav, A., Swift, M.M.: Symdrive: testing drivers without devices. In: Symposium on Operating System Design and Implementation (2012)

105. Reps, T., Horwitz, S., Sagiv, M.: Precise interprocedural dataflow analysis via graph reachability. In: Symposium on Principles of Programming Languages (1995)

106. Saxena, P., Akhawe, D., Hanna, S., Mao, F., McCamant, S., Song, D.: A symbolic execution framework for javascript. In: IEEE Symposium on Security and Privacy, pp. 513–528 (2010)

107. Sen, K., Marinov, D., Agha, G.: CUTE: a concolic unit testing engine for C. In: Symposium on the Foundations of Software Engineering (2005)

108. Serebryany, K., Bruening, D., Potapenko, A., Vyukov, D.: AddressSanitizer: a fast address sanity checker. In: USENIX Annual Technical Conference (2012)

109. Serebryany, K., Iskhodzhanov, T.: ThreadSanitizer - data race detection in practice. In: Workshop on Binary Instrumentation and Applications (2009)

110. Sirer, E., Bershad, B.: Using production grammars in software testing. In: Conference on Domain-Specific Languages (1999)

111. Song, D., et al.: BitBlaze: a new approach to computer security via binary analysis. In: Sekar, R., Pujari, A.K. (eds.) ICISS 2008. LNCS, vol. 5352, pp. 1–25. Springer, Heidelberg (2008). https://doi.org/10.1007/978-3-540-89862-7_1

112. Sutton, M., Greene, A., Amini, P.: Fuzzing: Brute Force Vulnerability Discovery. Addison-Wesley Professional, Boston (2007)

113. Tillmann, N., de Halleux, J.: Pex–white box test generation for .NET. In: Beckert, B., Hähnle, R. (eds.) TAP 2008. LNCS, vol. 4966, pp. 134–153. Springer, Heidelberg (2008). https://doi.org/10.1007/978-3-540-79124-9_10

114. Utting, M., Pretschner, A., Legeard, B.: A taxonomy of model-based testing approaches. Int. J. Softw. Test. Verification Reliab. **22**(5) (2012)

115. Villanueva, J.C.: How many atoms are there in the universe? (2015). http://www.universetoday.com/36302/atoms-in-the-universe/

116. Wagner, J., Kuznetsov, V., Candea, G.: -OVERIFY: optimizing programs for fast verification. In: Workshop on Hot Topics in Operating Systems (2013)

117. Williams, N., Marre, B., Mouy, P., Roger, M.: PathCrawler: automatic generation of path tests by combining static and dynamic analysis. In: Dal Cin, M., Kaâniche, M., Pataricza, A. (eds.) EDCC 2005. LNCS, vol. 3463, pp. 281–292. Springer, Heidelberg (2005). https://doi.org/10.1007/11408901_21
118. Xie, Y., Aiken, A.: Scalable error detection using Boolean satisfiability. In: Symposium on Principles of Programming Languages (2005)
119. Zalewski, M.: American Fuzzy Loop (2017). http://lcamtuf.coredump.cx/afl/

Runtime Verification Past Experiences and Future Projections

Klaus Havelund[1]([✉]), Giles Reger[2], and Grigore Roşu[3]

[1] Jet Propulsion Laboratory, California Institute of Technology, Pasadena, USA
klaus.havelund@jpl.nasa.gov
[2] University of Manchester, Manchester, UK
[3] University of Illinois at Urbana-Champaign, Urbana, USA

Abstract. The paper provides an overview of the work performed by the authors since the year 2000 in the field of *runtime verification*. Runtime verification is the discipline of analyzing program/system executions using rigorous methods. The discipline covers such topics as specification-based monitoring, where single executions are checked against formal specifications; predictive runtime analysis, where properties about a system are predicted/inferred from single (good) executions; fault protection, where monitors actively protect a running system against errors; specification mining from execution traces; visualization of execution traces; and to be fully general: computation of any interesting information from execution traces. The paper attempts to draw lessons learned from this work, and to project expectations for the future of the field.

1 Introduction

Runtime verification (RV) [10,32,41] has emerged as a field of computer science within the last couple of decades. RV is concerned with the rigorous monitoring and analysis of software and hardware system executions. The field, or parts of it, can be encountered under several other names, including, e.g., runtime checking, monitoring, dynamic analysis, and runtime analysis. Since only single executions are analyzed, RV scales well compared to more comprehensive formal methods, but of course at the cost of coverage. Nonetheless, RV can be useful due to the rigorous methods involved.

The first and last author's initial interest in RV started around 2000. We had at that time explored software model checking with the Java PathFinder tool [43,49]. Part of that work focused on exploring the spectrum from full formal verification to more scalable testing. That investigation led to our interest in RV. Our initial efforts were inspired by Doron Drusinky's Temporal Rover system [30] for monitoring temporal logic properties, and by the company Compaq's work on predictive data race and deadlock detection algorithms [36]. These algorithms can detect the *potential* for a data race or deadlock by analyzing a run that does

---

K. Havelund—The research performed by this author was carried out at Jet Propulsion Laboratory, California Institute of Technology, under a contract with the National Aeronautics and Space Administration.

B. Steffen and G. Woeginger (Eds.): Computing and Software Science, LNCS 10000, pp. 532–562, 2019.
https://doi.org/10.1007/978-3-319-91908-9_25

not necessarily encounter the error. This paper reports on our own RV work, with some references to related work that specifically inspired us or which we find closely related, and discusses the lessons learned and our perspective on the future of this field.

A particular software or hardware system to be monitored is from here on referred to as the System Of Interest (SOI). We shall, due to our own lack of experience in monitoring hardware systems, limit our focus to monitoring of software systems, although for the majority of the discussion this distinction is not important. An important part of RV is how to extract an execution trace from an SOI, for example through manual logging or automated code instrumentation. This touches on the combination of static and dynamic analysis. We are not dealing with how to obtain various executions, as in e.g. test case generation (another important topic covered e.g. in [18] in this volume). Runtime verification can be used prior to deployment for testing purposes, referred to as test oracles in [18], and during deployment for ensuring safety and security, e.g. as part of a fault protection strategy.

As a more formal account, assume an SOI S, and assume that an execution of S is captured as an execution trace $\sigma = \langle e_1, e_2, \ldots, e_n \rangle$, which is a sequence of observed events. Each event e_i captures a snapshot of S's execution state. Monitors can be deeply embedded in the running system, able to access the full state of the system, or they can observe from a "distance", receiving execution events (data records) from the running system. Assume the type $\mathbb{E}$ of events, then the RV problem can be formulated as constructing a program $M : \mathbb{E}^* \to D$, which when applied to a trace σ, as in $M(\sigma)$, returns some data value $d \in D$ in a domain D of interest. The problem can be generalized to computing a result from multiple traces (as e.g. done in learning and statistical model checking), giving M the type[1] $M : \mathcal{P}(\mathbb{E}^*) \to D$.

In specification-based RV, M can be generated from a formal specification given in e.g. temporal logic, state machine notation, regular expressions, and d is a value in the Boolean domain ($d \in \mathbb{B}$), or some extension of the Boolean domain as discussed in [12], indicating whether the trace conforms to the specification. However, the field should be perceived broadly, e.g. d can be a visualization of the execution trace, a learned specification (specification mining), statistical information about the trace, an action to perform on the running system S, etc.

The body of the paper is largely organized according to the time periods in which the research was performed. Section 2 describes the first systems we developed, starting with monitoring propositional events, and transitioning to monitoring of parametric events carrying data, focusing on expressive logics as well as efficient monitoring algorithms based on trace slicing. Section 3 describes our experiments with aspect-oriented programming as a natural way of combining RV and code instrumentation. Section 4 describes early rule-based systems, as well as systems developed specifically targeting space mission applications. Section 5 describes our experiments with internal DSLs defined as APIs in a programming language. Furthermore, trace slicing is yet again pursued for an

---

[1] For any set S, $\mathcal{P}(S)$ is the power set of S, containing all subsets of S as elements.

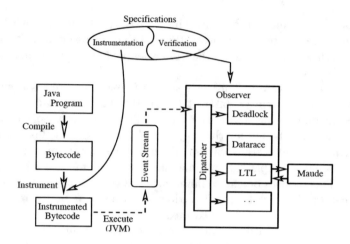

Fig. 1. The JPaX architecture.

expressive logic, and a system for Complex Event Processing (CEP) is developed, where the result of monitoring is a more complex data structure than just a Boolean value. Section 6 covers mostly the entire period, and describes efforts in predictive analysis, concerned with predicting anomalies in programs from successful observed executions. Finally, Sect. 7 reflects on the presented work, and provides thoughts on the future of the field of runtime verification.

2   2000–2005 - From Propositional to Parametric RV

2.1   Java PathExplorer

Architecture. Our first monitoring system, Java PathExplorer (JPaX) [47,48] was a general framework for analyzing execution traces. It supported three kinds of algorithms: propositional temporal logic conformance checking, data race detection, and deadlock detection. Figure 1 shows JPaX's architecture. A Java program is instrumented (at byte code level) to issue events to the monitoring side, which is customizable, allowing the addition of new monitors. The temporal logic monitoring module was originally based on a propositional future time linear temporal logic, but was later extended to also cover past time.

Future Time LTL. The future time LTL monitoring used Maude to rewrite formulas. Consider, e.g., the LTL formula $p \, \mathcal{U} \, q$, meaning q eventually becomes true and until then p is true. The implementation of JPaX was based on classical equational laws for temporal operators, such as:

$$p \, \mathcal{U} \, q = q \wedge \bigcirc(p \, \mathcal{U} \, q) \qquad \text{and} \qquad \Box p = p \wedge \bigcirc(\Box p) \tag{1}$$

Consider the sample formula $\Box(green \rightarrow \bigcirc(\neg red \, \mathcal{U} \, yellow))$. Upon encountering a *green* in a trace, the formula will be rewritten into the following formula, which must be true in the next state: $(\neg red \; \mathcal{U} \; yellow) \wedge \square(green \rightarrow (\neg red \; \mathcal{U} \; yellow))$. In Maude this was realized by a few simple rewrite rules, including the following two for the until operator (E is an event and T is a trace, the first rule handles the case of a trace consisting of only one event):

```
eq E |= X U Y = E |= Y .
eq E,T |= X U Y = E,T |= Y or E,T |= X and T |= X U Y .
```

Past Time LTL. Later, an efficient dynamic programming algorithm for monitoring *past time* logic was developed [47]. Consider the following past time formula: $red \rightarrow \blacklozenge green$ (whenever *red* is observed, in the past there has been a *green*). The algorithm for checking past time formulas like this uses two arrays, now and pre, recording the status of each sub-formula now and previously. Index 0 refers to the formula itself with positions ordered by the sub-formula relation. Then for this property, for each observed event the arrays are updated as follows.

```
bool pre [0..3],   now [0..3];

fun processEvent(e) {            // Sub−formula:
    now[3] := (event = red)      // red
    now[2] := (event = green)    // green
    now[1] := now[2] || pre [1]  // PREV green
    now[0] := !now[3] || now[1]  // red −> PREV green
    if !now[0] then output (" property violated ");
    pre := now;
}
```

Data Races and Deadlocks. When used for bug finding, the effectiveness of runtime verification depends on the choice of test suite. For concurrent systems this is critical, due to the many possible non-deterministic execution paths. *Predictive runtime analysis* approaches this problem by replacing a target property P with a stronger property Q such that there is a high probability that the program satisfies P iff a random trace of the program will satisfy Q. Some of the first such algorithms, which greatly inspired us, were implemented in Compaq's Visual Threads tool [36] for analyzing multi-threaded applications in C and C++. One such algorithm was the Eraser algorithm [68], for detecting *potentials* for data races (where two threads can access a shared variable simultaneously). It is often referred to as the *lock set* algorithm as each variable is associated with a set of locks protecting it. Alternatively, the *lock graph* algorithm, would detect "dining philosopher"-like deadlock potentials by building a simple lock graph where a cycle indicates a deadlock potential. We continued this line of work in a variety of ways. In [37] we explored the idea of letting a predictive analysis guide a model checker towards data race and deadlock potentials. In [15] we augment the original lock graph algorithm to reduce false positive in the presence of guard locks (locks that prevent cyclic deadlocks). Other forms of data races than those detected by Eraser are possible. In [3] is described a dynamic algorithm for detecting so-called high-level data races (races involving collections of variables). Section 6 goes into more detail with research on predictive analysis.

2.2 Eagle

JPaX had a number of limitations. The perhaps most important was the propositional nature of the temporal logics. One could not, for example, monitor parametric events carrying data, such as *openFile("data.txt")*. A second drawback of JPaX was the separation between past time and future time temporal logic, in two different logical systems. More generally, it seemed to us unfortunate that one had to pick a particular logic amongst the many existing for writing temporal properties, including past and future time temporal logic, extended regular expressions, state machines, interval logics, real-time logics, data constraint logics, and statistical logics. It would be very attractive if a user could define his/her own temporal logic from a small set of primitives. These thoughts lead, during 2003, to the work on Eagle, first documented in [6]. Eagle was a small and general logic having similarities with the μ-calculus.

The logic allowed the definition of new temporal operators which could be parameterized with formulas and primitive data such as integers. In addition to the standard Boolean operators, the logic includes: $\bigcirc f$ (next f), $\odot f$ (previous f), $f_1 \cdot f_2$ (concatenation: f_1 on part of the trace and f_2 on the remaining part of the trace), f (now f), and $\mathsf{N}(f_1, ..., f_n)$ (call N with arguments). A fundamental idea in Eagle was the option for a user to define temporal operators using recursion similar to the equations in (1) on page 3. Such user-defined temporal operators are defined as follows in Eagle:

min Until(**Form** f_1 , **Form** f_2) $= f_2 \vee (f_1 \wedge \bigcirc$ Until(f_1 ,f_2))
max Always(**Form** f) $= f \wedge \bigcirc$ Always(f)

Note how the different operators are defined as respectively minimal and maximal fixpoints, reflecting the definition of liveness and safety properties respectively. The difference in semantics appears at the boundaries of a trace where remaining minimal terms evaluate to false whereas maximal terms evaluate to true. These can now be used in writing monitors as follows:

mon M $=$ Always(x $> 0 \Rightarrow$ Eventually(y > 0))

Eagle handles data parameterized formulas through data parameterized rules. Consider the first-order temporal logic formula ("whenever $x > 0$, then if we name x's value k, then eventually $y = k$"): $\Box(x > 0 \to \exists k \, . \, (x = k \wedge \Diamond y = k))$. This can be formulated in Eagle using a data parameterized rule as follows.

min yBecomes(**int** k) $=$ Eventually(y $= k$)
mon M $=$ Always(x $> 0 \Rightarrow$ yBecomes(x))

The later Hawk system [27] was an attempt to tie Eagle to the monitoring of Java programs with automated code instrumentation using aspect-oriented programming, specifically AspectJ [57]. A similar (and simultaneous) integration of parametric runtime verification (with LTL) and AspectJ was presented in the J-LO tool [78]. Hawk supports two modal constructs inspired by dynamic logic: the construct <e> F means that e *can* occurand the proposition F is true thereafter. The construct [e] F means that *if* e occurs, then F is true thereafter. As a complete example, consider the following observer, monitoring that elements put into a buffer eventually get taken out of the buffer:

```
observer BufferObserver {
  var Buffer b ; var Object o ; var Object k ;

    mon B = Always ([b?.put(o?)]
               Eventually ( <b.get() returns k?> (o == k) )) .
}
```

2.3   JavaMOP

The same JPaX limitations that motivated the development of Eagle also stimulated the apparition of monitoring-oriented programming (MOP) [21–23]. MOP proposed that runtime monitoring be supported and encouraged as a fundamental principle of software development, where monitors are automatically synthesized from formal specifications and integrated at appropriate places in the program. Violations and/or validations of specifications can trigger user-defined code at any points in the program, in particular recovery code, outputting/sending messages, or raising exceptions. MOP has made three important early contributions. First, it proposed specification formalism independence, allowing users to insert their favorite or domain-specific requirements specification formalisms via *logic plugin* modules. Second, it proposed automated code instrumentation as a means to weave the monitoring checking code within the application; the first version in 2003 used Perl for instrumentation [22], while the subsequent versions starting with 2004 [21] used AspectJ [57]. Finally, it proposed a formalism-independent semantics and implementation for parametric specifications.

Parametric properties are properties with free variables, allowing us to describe behaviors of collections of related objects. Consider, for example, the following JavaMOP parametric property.

```
SafeLock(Lock l, Thread t)  {
  event acquire before(Lock l, Thread t):
    call ( * Lock.acquire ()) && target(l) && thread(t) {}
  event release before(Lock l, Thread t):
    call ( * Lock. release ()) && target(l) && thread(t) {}
  event begin before(Thread t):
    execution( * *.*(..)) && thread(t) && !within(Lock+) {}
  event end after(Thread t):
    execution( * *.*(..)) && thread(t) && !within(Lock+) {}

  cfg: S -> S begin S end | S acquire S release  |  epsilon
```

```
@fail { System.out.println ("Improper lock usage"); }
}
```

It has two parameters: a lock and a thread. The four event declarations declare the parametric events of interest, and the property, in this case formalized using the context-free grammar (CFG) plugin, states that each acquire and release event should be paired in the same method. Any mismatched acquire or release is considered to be a violation of the property. At violation we chose to report an error message, but any Java code can be executed, e.g., recovery code. Note that this property cannot be expressed using regular patterns or automata.

It is not trivial to monitor parametric properties efficiently. For the example it is not uncommon in a multi-threaded Java program execution to see thousands of threads created/terminated and thousands of synchronization locks acquired/released by such threads dynamically. Conceptually, execution traces are sliced according to each observed instance of the parameters, and each slice is checked by its own monitor instance in a manner that is independent of the employed specification formalism. The practical challenge is how to deal with the potentially huge number of monitor instances.

JavaMOP proposed several optimizations, presented in [66] together with the mathematical foundations of parametric monitoring. For example, we can ignore parameter instances that can never reach the target monitor states (e.g., not all threads use all locks). Also, some monitors can become unnecessary during execution because the objects that can generate the triggering events have died; such unnecessary monitors can and should be garbage collected.

A demo of JavaMOP is found at http://fsl.cs.uiuc.edu/JavaMOPDemo.html. The academic JavaMOP project has been migrated into the commercial RV-Monitor tool at http://runtimeverification.com/monitor. In addition to efficient support for simultaneous monitoring of multiple specifications, a major innovations of RV-Monitor is to separate instrumentation from the efficient monitoring data-structures. The former can be done either manually or using AspectJ (statically at compile time or dynamically as a Java agent), while the latter is automatically generated as a library from the parametric specifications.

3   2005–2006 - Further Experimentation with AOP

Whilst initial runtime verification frameworks targeted Java, the RMOR (Requirement Monitoring and Recovery) framework [38] targeted the monitoring of C programs against state machines using a homegrown aspect-oriented framework to perform program instrumentation. RMOR is implemented in OCaml using CIL (C Intermediate Language), a C program analysis and transformation system, itself written in OCaml. Consider as an example an application for uplinking data from a planetary rover to a space craft, and consider the property: *"It is illegal to have more than one connection opened at any time"*. This requirement can be formulated as follows.

```
monitor UplinkRequirement {
  event OPEN = after call(main.c:open_connection);
  event CLOSE = after call(main.c:close_connection);

  initial state Closed {
    when OPEN → Opened;
  }

  live state Opened {
    when CLOSE → Closed;
    when OPEN → error;
  }
}
```

The Opened state is a *live* state as indicated by the modifier keyword live, meaning a non-acceptance state. Other state modifiers include super states as in hierarchical state charts. It is possible to provide a call-back handler function to be called for each detected violation. However, RMOR is propositional.

In previous solutions (such as Hawk and MOP) we have seen monitors translated *to* aspects. A more radical approach is to take the view that monitors *are* aspects. Some of our experiments went in the direction of what today is called *state-full aspects* [1, 80]. We proposed this line of work already in [34]. An (non-finished) attempt in this direction was XspeC [50], designed to be an extension of ACC (an aspect-oriented programming framework for C) with data parameterized monitoring using state machines. As an example, consider the property of a C program that a file should be opened and eventually closed in that order. When an already opened file is re-opened the attempt should be logged and when the program terminates all opened files should be closed. The specification in XspeC becomes as follows.

```
xspec OpenClose(char *file) {
  pointcut open : call (void openfile (char*)) && args(file);
  pointcut close : call (void closefile (char*)) && args(file);

  state FileClosed {
    after : open( file ) → FileOpen;
    after : close ( file ) ⇒ error;
  }

  live state FileOpen {
    after : open( file ) ⇒ error { log( file ); }
    after : close ( file ) → FileClosed ;
    before : end { closefile ( file ); }
  }
}
```

The specification is parameterized with a file, meaning that it is intended to track the behavior of a file. The intended semantics is similar to the semantics of Tracematches [1] and MOP in that we consider a specification to denote an infinite set of monitors, one for each file as indicated by the parameter to the specification. The double arrow ($\Rightarrow$) denotes a transition that stays in the source state (for continued verification), in contrast to the single arrow ($\rightarrow$).

In [34] we discussed the idea (and similar work was proposed in HandlErr [74]), to extend aspect-oriented programming in two ways: vertically and horizontally. The pointcut languages originally supported, for example in AspectJ, have been limited, reducing to method calls and assignment to variables. A *vertical* extension consists of enriching the pointcut language to cover more concepts, such as e.g. branching on a conditional, cycling through a loop, or acquiring and releasing a lock. Some of the algorithms described in this paper analyzing multi-threaded programs for data races and deadlocks, for example, cannot use AspectJ for instrumentation since AspectJ does not support definition of pointcuts catching lock acquisitions and releases in the general case. In [17] we proposed extending AspectJ with new pointcuts: **lock**() and **unlock**(). A *horizontal* extension consists of changing the definition of advice to incorporate tracecuts. The ultimate extension of aspect-oriented programming is the product of a horizontal and a vertical extension. In addition, static analysis (theorem proving) can be invoked to prove stated properties. HandlErr e.g. allowed pre and post conditions, invariants in aspects.

A much later work presented in [73] is the InterAspect system, an aspect-oriented API in C for instrumenting C programs compiled with the GCC compiler infrastructure. InterAspect is implemented using the GCC plug-in API. The system allows for specification of tracecuts using regular expressions, much along the lines of MOP. InterAspect has access to GCC internals, which allows one to exploit static analysis during the weaving process. Consider the following file access property. Any access to a file object after the file has been closed is a memory error which might not manifest itself as incorrect behavior during testing. This can be formalized in InterAspect as the following "aspect" matching an execution as soon as any read is performed on a closed file.

```
tc = tc_create_tracecut (); tc_add_param(tc,"file", aop_t_all_pointer ());
tc_declare_call_symbol (tc,"open","(file)fopen()",AOP_AFTER);
tc_declare_call_symbol (tc,"read","fread(?,?,?,file)",AOP_BEFORE);
tc_declare_call_symbol (tc,"read_char","fgetc(file)",AOP_BEFORE);
tc_declare_call_symbol (tc,"close","fclose(file)",AOP_BEFORE);
tc_add_rule(tc,"open (read | read_char)* close (read | read_char)");
```

4 2006–2010 - Missions and Rules

4.1 Commanding and Monitoring

One project, described in [14], was driven by a collaboration between JPL and KSC (Kennedy Space Center) from where NASA's rocket launches take place.

The project had as a goal to develop a DSL for commanding and monitoring all aspects of a rocket launch platform in the moments up to a launch. The DSL was implemented as a Python API. A program would, through a publish-subscribe framework, command and monitor *items* distributed geographically across the KSC launch site. The state can be understood as a collection of *measurements*, representing data samples collected from sensors in the items, and distributed throughout the system on a message bus. Each measurement maps a variable name to a value. The DSL then provides a collection of functions for monitoring the state (collection of measurements) of the entire system as it evolves over time. From a temporal logic point of view, a trace is a sequence of collections of measurements. Some of these functions are shown below.

```
def verify (C, [R], [S]):  ...
def verify_within (C, D, [R], [S]):  ...
def verify_subset_within (N, C_list , D_list , [R], [S]):  ...
def assert_constraint (S, C, R, [D], [F]):  ...
def conditional_interrupt (S, C, R, [D], [F]):  ...
```

The following symbols are used for arguments: C stands for a condition to be verified and R stands for a reaction to be executed in case a condition gets violated. Both C and R are assumed to be parameter-less functions. D stands for a duration, expressed in seconds. S stands for a string, generally a name associated with the verification operation for documentation purposes. N stands for a natural number. Finally, F stands for a Boolean flag indicating whether verification should be repeated in case of property violations. Arguments in square brackets [...] denote optional arguments (this is not Python syntax).

The functions (the first three of which are blocking, waiting for the verification to terminate) have the following meaning. verify verifies that the condition is true now. verify_within verifies that the condition C eventually becomes true within the time duration D. verify_subset_within verifies that at least N of a list of conditions become true within given durations, provided as a separate list matching in length. assert_constraint verifies that the condition is continuously true throughout the duration. conditional_interrupt is a variant of assert_constraint where if the condition at some point evaluates to *true*, the calling application is interrupted (temporarily stopped) while the reaction is executed. The DSL also provides functions for commanding items and interacting with users at terminals. The team at KSC subsequently developed a tabular DSL using spreadsheets, which is a form of external DSL built on top of the (internal) Python DSL.

4.2   RuleR

RULER [9] started life as a low-level event-based rule system into which other temporal specification languages were supposed to be compiled for efficient trace checking. The work was directly inspired by the complexity of the Eagle implementation. However, it then assumed a life of its own as a specification language. RULER preserves the interest in monitoring data via parametric events but also achieves high expressiveness through the use of powerful low-level features. The flavor of specifications in RULER is different from those based on temporal logic seen earlier as they tend to be more *operational*. For example, to monitor the previous property $\Box(x > 0 \rightarrow \exists k \ . \ (x = k \ \wedge \ \Diamond y = k))$ we would monitor events x and y and whenever observing a relevant x event create an obligation to see a future y event with that value. This is captured by the following rule system.

```
ruler M {
  observes x( int ), y( int );
  always start { x(n: int ) & n>0 —> wait(n); }
  state wait(n: int ){ y(n) —> Ok; }
  forbidden wait;
  initials  start ;
}
```

This monitor declares a set of events being observed and then two rules. Rules are of the form

$$conditions \rightarrow obligations$$

and define *rewrite rules* on sets of *rule instances*. If the set of rule instances satisfy the conditions then the obligations should be applied to this set where an obligation may add or remove a rule instance from the set. Importantly, the only rules that can be applied are those that have a corresponding rule activation in the current set. This extends to data parameterization. If wait(1) is not in the current set then the event y(1) would not satisfy any conditions. Another aspect of a rule is its *modifier*. In the above example the **always** modifier means that a rule activation should be kept if its corresponding rule is applied to it, whilst the **state** modifier indicates that it should be removed. The following evaluation illustrates the above rule system applied to a sequence of events.

$$\{start\} \xrightarrow{x(5)} \underbrace{\{start, wait(5)\}}_{A} \xrightarrow{y(5)} \underbrace{\{start\}}_{B} \xrightarrow{x(1)} \{start, wait(1)\} \xrightarrow{end} \bot$$

The final result is failure ($\bot$) as the wait rule is in the **forbidden** set, which means that a trace ending with one of these rules in its set of rule activations is not accepted. RULER was given a finite-trace semantics with four verdicts. The verdicts STILL_TRUE and STILL_FALSE are given if the rule system would accept/reject the trace if it were to end at the current event, whilst the verdicts TRUE and FALSE were reserved for traces where every extension would be accepted/rejected. For the above example, the A set of rule instances would be given the verdict STILL_FALSE whilst the B set would be given STILL_TRUE. These multiple verdicts support various translations of finite-trace linear temporal logics.

A more realistic example is the following rule system checking the proper usage of Java iterators. Here the **assert** keyword requires that at least one of the given rules is applied on each step. This allows, for example, the rule system to detect failure on the event sequence consisting only of a next event.

```
ruler  SafeIteratorCheck{
  observes hasNext(obj), next(obj);
  always Start{ hasNext(i:obj) −> Next(i); }
  state Next(i:obj){ next(i) −> Ok; }
  assert Start, Next;
  initials  Start;
}
```

RULER allowed for very complex rule systems that could be *chained* together such that one rule system produced outputs for another rule system to consume as input events. Rule systems could be combined sequentially, in parallel, and conditionally. Another powerful feature was the use of non-determinism and rules as data. However, it was difficult to find a practical need for such features.

4.3   LogScope

A project solidly rooted in an actual space mission was the development of the LogScope temporal logic for log analysis [7]. The purpose of the project was to assist the team testing the flight software for JPL's Mars rover Curiosity, which successfully landed on Mars on August 6, 2012. The software produces rich log information. Traditionally, these logs are analyzed with complex Python scripts. The LogScope logic was developed to support notions more comprehensible to test engineers, including a very simple and convenient data parameterized temporal logic, which was translated to a form of data parameterized automata, which themselves can be used for specification of more complex properties that the temporal logic cannot express. LogScope was furthermore implemented in Python, allowing Python code fragments to be included in specifications, all in order to integrate with the existing Python scripting culture at JPL.

As an example, consider the property *"Whenever a flight software power command is issued, before the next flight software command there should follow a dispatch of that command on board, and then exactly one success of that command within 5 s. Before the dispatch there should be no dispatch failure, and in between the dispatch and the success there should be no execution failure"*. Commands have names x and numbers y. This property can be specified as follows in LogScope:

```
pattern Commands :
  COMMAND{Type:"FSW", Name:x, Num:y} where {: x.startswith("PWR") :} ⇒
      [
        !EVR{DispatchFailure:x, Num:y},
         EVR{Dispatch:x, Num:y, Time: t1},
        !EVR{Failure:x, Num:y},
         EVR{Success:x, Num:y, Time: t2} where {: t2 − t1 <= 5 :},
        !EVR{Success:x, Num:y}
      ] upto COMMAND{Type: "FSW"}
```

A specification consists of one or more specification units, each of which is either a temporal logic *pattern* (as above), or a parameterized *automaton*. A pattern has a name, and is triggered by an event. When the event is observed in the log, the consequence must be observed, optionally up to some other event, which then limits the scope of the pattern. The consequence can be that an event must eventually occur, or not occur, or it can be a list of consequences, enclosed in either square brackets (as here) indicating the consequences must occur in that order, or curly brackets (not shown) indicating that the consequences must occur but any order is allowed. Note the lack of temporal operators as found in classical LTL. The **where**-clauses can contain Python expressions inside {: ... :} brackets. The formula reflects the linear ordering of a time line [75], but textually presented. In general the user can define Python functions at the beginning of a specification file to be used in such predicates.

LogScope also allows testers to write properties as parameterized automata, to which the temporal patterns are also translated. Just as events can be parameterized with values, so can states. Automata can furthermore be visualized, which has shown to be useful for creators of patterns to confirm their meaning. The automaton for pattern Commands above is the following.

```
automaton Commands {
  always S1 {
    COMMAND{Type:"FSW", Name:x, Num:y}
      where {: x. startswith ("PWR") :} ⇒ S2(x,y)
  }
  hot state S2(x,y) {
    EVR{DispatchFailure:x, Num:y} ⇒ error
    EVR{Dispatch:x, Num:y, Time: t1} ⇒ S3(x,y,t1)
  }
  hot state S3(x,y,t1) {
    EVR{Failure:x, Num:y} ⇒ error
    EVR{Success:x, Num:y, Time:t2} where {: t2 − t1 <= 5 :} ⇒ S4(x,y)
  }
  state S4(x,y) {
    EVR{Success:x, Num:y} ⇒ error
  }
}
```

5   2010–2017 - Internal DSLs, Slicing, and CEP

5.1   TraceContract

TraceContract [8] is an internal Scala DSL (effectively an API) for monitoring, based on a mixture of temporal logic and state machines. TraceContract, although a research tool, was used for analysis of command sequences sent to NASA's LADEE (Lunar Atmosphere and Dust Environment Explorer) spacecraft throughout its mission. Consider the LogScope specification on page 12. In order to specify this property in TraceContract we first define the event kinds, for example as follows:

```scala
trait Event
case class Command(time:Int,kind:String,name:String,nr:Int) extends Event
case class DispatchFailure(time:Int,name:String,nr:Int) extends Event
case class Dispatch(time:Int,name:String,nr:Int) extends Event
case class Failure(time:Int,name:String,nr:Int) extends Event
case class Success(time:Int,name:String,nr:Int) extends Event
```

Events are commonly modeled as objects (instances) of **case** classes (A **case** class allows pattern matching against its objects), all extending the Event trait (similar to abstract class in Java). Each event type is parameterized with data (the constructor parameters), which must be provided when creating an object of the class. The following monitor corresponds to the LogScope monitor on page 12, but now expressed in the internal Scala DSL.

```scala
class Commands extends Monitor[Event] {
  require {
    case Command(_, "FSW", x, y) if x.startsWith("PWR") ⇒
      hot {
        case DispatchFailure(_, 'x', 'y') ⇒ error
        case Dispatch(t1, 'x', 'y') ⇒ hot {
          case Failure(_, 'x', 'y') ⇒ error
          case Success(t2, 'x', 'y') if t2 − t1 <= 5 ⇒
            state { case Success(_, 'x', 'y') ⇒ error }
        }
      } upto { case Command(_,"FSW",_,_) ⇒ true }
  }
}
```

Our property is defined as a class Commands extending the class Monitor, which is parameterized with the event type, and which defines all the TraceContract DSL functions (marked in blue) and constants (marked in red). The DSL functions in this example all take as argument a Scala partial function enclosed in curly brackets, and defined with **case** statements.

The call of the function require (when a Commands object is created) causes a side-effect, namely storing the property represented by the partial function. Note that quotes around names, as in 'x' means: match the value previously bound to x. The underscore '_' is the wildcard pattern that always matches. The monitor can be instantiated and applied to a trace (a list of events). TraceContract offers numerous additional constructs, including other kinds of anonymous states (e.g. strong next), state machines with named states, linear temporal logic, and the possibility to combine these with Boolean combinators (and, or, not). Mixed with general Scala programming this becomes a very powerful paradigm. A simpler version of TraceContract, but making states queryable facts (useful for expressing past time properties), is presented in [39].

A few other internal runtime verification DSLs/APIs have been developed. For example, a propositional Haskell DSL for linear temporal logic [79], and a Java API re-implementing MOP's trace slicing algorithms [16].

5.2 LogFire

Another example of an internal Scala DSL is LogFire [40]. LogFire is a rule-based system similar to RuleR, but based on the Rete algorithm implemented in several rule-based systems. LogFire was part of an investigation of the Rete algorithm's applicability for runtime verification. The algorithm maintains a network of facts to avoid re-evaluating all conditions in each rule's left-hand side each time the fact memory changes. We modified the Rete algorithm in a couple of ways to fit the runtime verification objective, including an indexing optimization and introducing the distinction between events and facts. As an example of a rule-system in LogFire consider safe use of Java iterators, where hasNext must be called before any call of next. This property can be formalized in LogFire as follows.

```
class HasNext extends Monitor {
    val hasNext, next = event
    val Safe = fact

    "r1" − hasNext('i) ↦ insert (Safe('i))
    "r2" − Safe('i) & next('i) ↦ remove (Safe)
    "r3" − next('i) & not(Safe('i)) ↦ error
}
```

As in TraceContract, a monitor is defined as an extension of a class Monitor, which defines the LogFire DSL features. The first two lines define the events that are observed and the facts (Safe) that the rules will generate. The monitor contains three named rules. Each rule has the form:

$$\text{"name"} − cond_1(...) \; \& \; ... \; \& \; cond_n(...) \mapsto action$$

starting with a name (a string value), a conjunction of conditions, and an action to execute (following the ↦ symbol) in case the conditions evaluate to true. The insert function adds a new fact to the fact database, and the function remove (id) removes the fact id referred to on the left-hand side of the rule. The specification should be self-explanatory. In [40] it is described how higher-level operators can be defined in a few lines of code, generating rules automatically.

5.3 QEA

Quantified event automata (QEA) [5] and the associated MarQ tool [65] were introduced to take advantage of the efficient trace slicing approach previously introduced in the JavaMOP tool [63] (see Sect. 2.3) whilst dealing with some of the limitations with respect to expressiveness. QEA consist of a list of quantifications and an automaton. Consider the following example specification of the command property given on page 12. The specification begins with universal quantification over the command name and number and then gives an automaton structure similar to that of the LogScope monitor but the underlying semantics are quite different.

```
qea(Commands){
  forall (name, number)
  accept skip(1){
    command(name,number) → 2
  }
  next(2){
    dispatchFailure (name,number) → Fail
    dispatch (name,number,t1) → 3
  }
  next(3){
    failure (name,number) → Fail
    success (name,number,t2) if t2−t1 ≤ 5 → 4
  }
  accept skip(4){
    success (name,number,t) → Fail
  }
}
```

The semantics is defined in terms of *slicing* with respect to the quantified variables. For a given name and number pair an input trace is projected to preserve only events relevant to those values, giving a so-called *trace slice*. This trace slice is checked with respect to the given automaton. This semantics allows for efficient indexing structures that lookup the relevant part of the monitoring data to update given an event. However, to make the above slicing framework work incrementally is non-trivial as the values with which the trace is to be sliced are being discovered as the slice is being observed. The QEA work formalizes the notion of acceptance using quantification and extends[2] the framework to allow for *existential quantification* and *local state* via *unquantified/free variables*. The two specifications below demonstrate these features.

```
qea(RoverCommand){
  forall (q) exists (s) forall (r)
  accept skip( start ) {
    declare (q,r) → inside
  }
  skip( inside ) {
    ping(r,s) → pinged
  }
  skip(pinged){
    ack(s,r) → Success
  }
}
```

```
qea(AuctionBidding) {
  forall ( i )
  accept next(start){
    list (i,r) do c := 0 → listed
  }
  accept next( listed ){
    bid (i,a)
      if a>c do c := a → listed
  }
}
```

---

[2] This is not a proper extension as some concepts expressible in the original framework are no longer expressible. For example, partial matches or multiple verdicts. The main reason is that the original framework was defined in terms of *matching* and triggering advise whilst this framework is defined in terms of *correctness*.

The specification on the left is a variation of a property given in [44] and demonstrates existential quantification. It specifies the property that for every quadrant q there exists a satellite s such that every rover r in q has pinged s and received an acknowledgement i.e. there is a known single point of contact in that quadrant. The specification on the right is from [5] and specifies that bids on an item placed for auction should be strictly increasing. To support local state in a useful way it was necessary to introduce the notion of variables that do not take part in slicing (called *free* variables in this work).

Like RULER, QEA has a four-valued semantics allowing for anticipatory results i.e. there are *false* and *true* verdicts if all extensions of a trace have the same verdict and *still-false* and *still-true* verdicts otherwise. An example where *false* may be returned is where a quantification is purely universal and slice enters a state from which no accepting state is reachable. Whilst the addition of local state and arbitrary actions and guards on transitions can theoretically make the expressiveness of QEA Turing-complete, overuse of such features can make QEA unreadable, arguably rendering the *usable* expressiveness almost regular. The automaton model means that specifications often capture low-level details. This can lead to less readable specifications than in, e.g., temporal logic [45] and a *plug-in* style approach as taken by JavaMOP may be beneficial in the future.

5.4 Nfer

Complex Event Processing (CEP) can be characterized as *event abstraction*, where a stream of low-level events are aggregated and transformed into higher-level events. CEP can be used for further analysis and/or human comprehension, e.g. through visualization. We here briefly describe nfer [56], in part influenced by our work on rule-based systems, and LogFire in particular. Consider the command example, where we monitor events such as Command(time,kind,name,nr), Distpatch(time,name,nr), and Success(time,name,nr). Assume further that an event Starvation indicates that a task on board the spacecraft is starved from executing. We now want to highlight the situation where a starvation warning is issued during a period where at the same time there is Earth communication activity and data-fetch (from the cameras) activity. The following nfer specification defines this scenario.

```
command :− Dispatch before Success
    where Dispatch.name = Success.name & Dispatch.nr = Success.nr
    map {name → Dispatch.name}
communication :− command where command.name = "COMM"
fetchdata :− command where command.name = "FETCH"
starvation  :− Starvation during (communication intersect fetchdata)
```

The result of a applying an nfer specification to an event stream is a set of intervals, tuples of the form (η, t_1, t_2, m) consisting of a name η, a start time t_1, an end time t_2, and a map m holding data. The specification consists of four interval-generating rules, each of the form: name :− body (a rule name followed by a rule body). The semantics is similar to that of Prolog (hence the :− symbol): when the body is true an interval is generated with that name. A difference from Prolog is that rule bodies contain temporal constraints. The first rule defines an interval describing the execution of a command as occurring between a command dispatch and a subsequent success where the command names and numbers match. The resulting command interval will also have an associated map that maps x to the command name. The next two rules named communication and fetchdata define the intervals where communication and data fetching commands are executed. The rule starvation captures the starvation occurring during the intersection of communication and data fetching. Other temporal operators (inspired by Allen temporal logic), include: **meet, coincide, start, finish**, and **overlap**. Rules can also access and explicitly reason about time values.

6   2003–2017 - Sound Predictive Runtime Analysis

An increasingly important class of runtime analysis algorithms are concerned with *predicting* anomalies in programs from *successful* observed executions. Two such early algorithms implemented in JPaX, one for predicting deadlocks and another for predicting data-races, were discussed in Sect. 2.1. Both of those algorithms are *unsound*, that is, they can and do report false positives. In contrast to static analysis, in predictive runtime analysis a sound algorithm is one which predicts only real errors, i.e., no false alarms. We discuss two categories of sound algorithms, one based on vector-clocks and another based on SMT solving.

6.1   Vector-Clock Based Algorithms: From JMPaX to jPredictor

A series of sound predictive runtime analysis algorithms and tools have been proposed for multi-threaded systems about a decade ago, based on *vector clocks* [33,62] and on techniques proposed by the distributed systems debugging community, e.g., [19,26,76]. The main idea is to instrument the multi-threaded program to emit events timestamped by vector clocks, thus enabling the observer to extract a partial order reflecting the causal dependency on memory accesses. If any linearization of that inferred partial order leads to a violation of the desired property then an error is reported to the user, with the meaning that there are (likely different from the observed one, but definitely feasible) executions of the multithreaded program which violate the requirements.

Our first vector-clock-based predictive runtime verification tool was Java MultiPathExplorer (JMPaX) [70], briefly explained below. Consider the following multi-threaded program (in pseudocode) over shared variables x, y and z,

$$\text{Initially: } x = -1; \ y = 0; \ z = 0;$$

thread $T_1\{$	*thread $T_2\{$*
$x{+}{+};$	$z = x + 1;$
$y = x + 1;$	$x{+}{+};$
$\}$	$\}$

together with a desired property "if $(x > 0)$, then $(x = 0)$ has been true in the past, and since then $(y > z)$ was always false." Note that the shared variables may correspond to physical actions and thus violations of this property may result in potentially catastrophic system failures. This safety property can be formally specified using a past-time LTL formalism (similar to that used for JPaX in Sect. 2.1) but we keep the discussion informal here. A possible execution of the program can yield the sequence of states $(-1, 0, 0)$, $(0, 0, 0)$, $(0, 0, 1)$, $(0, 1, 1)$, $(1, 1, 1)$, where the tuple $(-1, 0, 0)$ denotes the state in which $x = -1$, $y = 0$, $z = 0$. This execution does *not* violate the desired property, so a normal runtime monitor would not report a violation. However, JMPaX' vector-clock based algorithm will infer, from the same execution above and without access to the actual code, that two other executions are possible (without false alarms) and that one of them in fact violates the property, namely $\{x = -1, y = 0, z = 0\}$, $\{x = 0\}$, $\{y = 1\}$, $\{z = 1\}$, $\{x = 1\}$, which corresponds to the sequence of states $(-1, 0, 0)$, $(0, 0, 0)$, $(0, 1, 0)$, $(0, 1, 1)$, $(1, 1, 1)$.

The vector-clock technique employed in JMPaX essentially implements a variant of Lamport's happens-before causality adapted to multi-threaded systems. Our colleagues have extended the technique in various ways, essentially demonstrating that increasingly more complex, yet more relaxed but still sound causal models can be considered, this way improving the predictive capability without reporting any false alarms; due to space constraints, we refer the reader to [52, 72] for a literature review. We have ourselves contributed by further extending the technique to consider various kinds of Java-like synchronization and communication primitives [69]. Finally, we noticed that in multi-threaded systems one can go beyond the usual happens-before causality [71]: a write event can be atomically grouped with all its corresponding subsequent read events, and that such groups of events can be permuted atomically; similarly, blocks of events in different threads protected by the same lock can be permuted atomically. As shown in [69, 71], these improvements led to significant increases in prediction capability without jeopardizing soundness. However, without taking into account information about the code of the program that generated the trace, that is without static analysis, we were not able to improve the vector-clock-based predictive runtime analysis algorithms any further.

jPredictor [25] was, to our knowledge, the first sound predictive runtime analysis system which combined static and dynamic analyses. Specifically, it implemented *sliced causality* [24], a happen-before causality drastically but soundly sliced by removing irrelevant causalities using semantic information about the program obtained with an a priori static analysis. Consider, e.g., a simple and common safety property for a shared resource, that any access should be authenticated, and consider the following buggy program executed as shown:

```
Main Thread {                        Task Thread {
  1. resource.authenticate();
  2. flag = true;                       3. if(!flag) Thread.yield();
                                        4. resource.access();
}                                     }
```

The main thread authenticates and then the task thread uses the authenticated resource. They communicate via the `flag` variable. Synchronization is unnecessary, since only the main thread modifies `flag`. However, the developer makes a common mistake, using `if` instead of `while` in the task thread. Suppose now that we observed a successful run of the program, as shown above. Techniques based on traditional happen-before will not be able to find this bug, due to the causality induced by the write/read on `flag`. But since `resource.access()` is not controlled by `if`, sliced-causality techniques will correctly predict this error from the successful execution. When the bug is fixed replacing `if` with `while`, `resource.access()` is controlled by `while` (since it is a potentially non-terminating loop), so no violation is reported.

jPredictor is also implemented using vector clocks, but as discussed in [25], we were not able to obtain a faithful implementation. The vector-clock implementation was stronger than the sliced causality, thus maintaining soundness but potentially failing to report violations that were theoretically possible. In spite of the limitation, [25] experimentally showed that the combination of static and dynamic information cut, on average, about 50% of the dependencies, thus increasing the predictive capability of the technique exponentially. Unfortunately, probably due to the complex nature of resulting technique and its implementation, to our knowledge nobody continued to work in that direction. On the positive side, a new and appealing direction took shape, discussed below.

6.2   Maximal Causality and SMT-Based Algorithms: RV-Predict

As mentioned above, the runtime verification community has developed increasingly more complex and more relaxed sound causal models of multithreaded system computations. A question naturally had arisen: is there an end to this quest? That is, is there a *maximal* causal model that we can extract from an observed trace, which cannot be surpassed? We answered this question positively for sequentially consistent systems [67,72], essentially proposing a constructive causal model and showing the following: (1) all programs which can produce the observed execution can generate all traces in the model; and (2) for any trace t not in the model there exists a program generating the observed trace which cannot generate t. In other words, any sound and purely dynamic predictive runtime analysis technique can only detect a subset of the violations that the maximal causal model comprises (but albeit more efficiently). This result is foundationally very important, because on the one hand it draws a line in the sand w.r.t. how much sound predictive runtime analysis can go, and on the other hand it shows that the limit can be achieved.

Consider, for example, an execution of the program in Fig. 2. The program contains a race between lines (3,10) that may cause an authentication failure of resource z at line 12, which in consequence causes an error to occur when z is used at line 15. Supposing the execution follows an order denoted by the line numbers, however, previous sound causal models cannot detect this race because line 3 causally-precedes line 10, because the two lock regions contain conflicting accesses to y. While how to best use static analysis to further enhance

$$\textit{initially} \quad x=y=0 \quad \text{resource } z=0$$

Thread $t1$	Thread $t2$

Thread $t1$

1. *fork t2*
2. *lock l*
3. $x = 1$
4. $y = 1$
5. *unlock l*

Thread $t2$

6. { //*begin*
7. *lock l*
8. $r1 = y$
9. *unlock l*
10. $r2 = x$
11. $if(r1 == r2)$
12. $z = 1$ (**auth**)
13. } //*end*

14. *join t2*
15. $r3 = z$ (**use**)
16. $if(r3 == 0)$
17. *Error*

Fig. 2. An example program with a race (3,10).

$$\textit{initially} \quad x=y=0 \quad y \text{ is } \textit{volatile}$$

Thread $t1$ Thread $t2$

1. $x = 1$
2. $y = 1$

3. ① $r1 = y$ ② *while*$(y == 0)$;
4. $r2 = x$

Fig. 3. The two cases ① and ② produce the same read/write trace. However, (1,4) is a race in case ① but not in case ②.

the maximal causal model is a valid question and worth pursuing, we found that the maximal causal model can already elegantly deal with information flow information if execution traces are enriched to also emit control-flow-changing (or branching) events [52]. Consider the scenario in Fig. 3 where y is volatile and line 3 has two cases: ① $r1 = y$ and ② *while*$(y == 0)$. For case ①, (1,4) is a race on x; while for case ②, it is not, because line 4 is control-dependent on the while loop at line 3. However, without considering the control dependence between operations, the dynamic execution traces for these two cases are identical. But using the control flow information we can tell that, in case ①, line 4 is not control-dependent on line 3. In other words, regardless of what value line 3 reads, line 4 will always be executed. Therefore, we can safely drop the happens-before edge from line 2 to line 3, which enables detecting the race (1,4). Similarly, we are able to detect the race (3,10) in Fig. 2 by dropping the happens-before edge from line 4 to line 8, because there is no control flow from line 8 to line 10 and hence no need to ensure line 8 should read value 1 (written by line 4).

$$O_1 < O_2 < \ldots < O_5 \wedge O_{14} < \ldots < O_{16}$$

A. Happens-before (Φ_{hb})
$$O_6 < O_7 < \ldots < O_{13}$$
$$O_1 < O_6 \wedge O_{13} < O_{14}$$

B. Locking (Φ_{lock})
$$O_5 < O_7 \vee O_9 < O_2$$

C. (3,10)Race (Φ_{race})
$$O_{10} = O_3$$

Fig. 4. Constraint modeling of the example execution in Fig. 2.

The maximal causal model is more mathematically involved than the previous causal models, and it is still unknown whether it can be implemented using vector clocks. However, as Said et al. [67] first noticed, it is not very difficult to represent the maximal causal model as a mathematical formula. Specifically, we can associate to each event e in the trace one integer variable O_e, called its *order variable*, and then use the semantics of the various concurrent objects and control flow events to generate constraints over the order variables. For example, all the events emitted by the same thread must follow the same order as emitted (but can have other events interleaved), blocks protected by the same lock cannot overlap, and so on. Finally, one adds constraints for the property one is interested in; for a data-race, e.g., one says that the two involved events occur at the same time. Figure 4 shows the constraints for the execution in Fig. 2.

The formula generated for a given trace therefore encodes all the ordering constraints that must be satisfied by any permutations of the events in the same trace in order to maintain soundness, as well as all the constraints that must be satisfied in order for the property of interest to be matched by the predicted trace. All is left now is to check the satisfiability of the resulting formula (e.g. with a SMT solver). If not satisfiable, then we can conclude that the observed execution trace has no evidence in it that the property is matched. If satisfiable, then a solution of it is a counter-example showing that there indeed exists a feasible execution of the system that match the property.

One might think that it is not practical to solve large formulae that can result from large traces. However, with some additional engineering and optimizations, the commercial RV-Predict tool (https://runtimeverification.com/predict) [52] has demonstrated not only that it can detect concurrency errors that no other predictive runtime analysis tools can, but also that it can do it at a relatively acceptable performance.

7   Reflections and Future Perspectives on RV

Logics. The move from the early propositional temporal logics (such as JPaX) to parametric temporal logics (such as Eagle and MOP) was important, leading to an impressive community effort in researching logics and algorithms. The spectrum of specification logics has spanned many standard logics, such as automata, regular expressions, (future as well as past) linear temporal logics, context-free grammars, variations of the μ-calculus, process algebras, stream processing, and rule-based systems. Most of these standard logics have had to be extended with first-order features to handle the parametric case [46]. In addition to the first-order trend, another trend has been the attempts to extend state machine notations with special states (such as the distinction between skip and next-states). Several attempts have been made in combining logics, specifically regular expressions and linear temporal logic, as in e.g. SALT [13]. These logics combine sequencing (adopted from regular expressions) with temporal operators. The LogScope language provided a formalism resembling a textual version of time lines and without explicit temporal operators such as *eventually*. The MOP system took a different view by providing a collection of different logics, such that each property is written in "the logic that fits" that property. An interesting logic framework is the modal μ-calculus, which e.g. is the basis for Eagle, where temporal properties and recursion can be combined with "named states". One particular promising aspect of Eagle was the support for user-defined temporal operators. Rule systems appear to be an interesting alternative to automata for the data parameterized case. However, traditional rule programs are in many cases not as readable as e.g. temporal logic. To improve this situation, they can be extended with syntactic sugar, e.g. state machine concepts, as done in RuleR. Rule systems can be powerful; for example, RuleR rules can take rules as arguments as a way of modeling context-free grammars. In RuleR, rule programs can be chained together with facts produced by one rule program becoming input to another rule program. This is related to stream processing. The idea of an event stream resulting in a set of facts/data can be viewed as Complex Event Processing (CEP), and is especially realized in the nfer system. This is an interesting avenue for future research. When formalizing a temporal property it can be useful to first to draw a time-line on a piece of paper, and then plot in events. This suggests that tool support for such a graphical time line approach might lower the barrier for writing temporal properties. Timelines have been studied in the context of model checking [75].

External versus Internal DSLs. Whether to develop a DSL as external or internal is a non-trivial decision. An external DSL is usually cleaner and more directly tuned towards the immediate needs of the user. In addition, they are easier to process and therefore optimize for efficiency. However, the richer the DSL becomes (moving towards Turing-completeness) the harder the implementation effort becomes. An internal DSL can be very fast to implement and augment with new (even user-defined) operators, and can provide an expressiveness that would require a major effort to support in an external DSL. One also gains the advantage of IDEs etc. for the host language. However, some concepts may not be easily representable as an internal DSL. Also, a user will have to be a programmer in the host language. In this respect, some programming languages seem to be less of a barrier than others, e.g. Python is considered easy to learn.

A hypothesis is that monitoring logics used in practice will need to support very expressive expression languages to process data, such as strings and numbers that are part of the observed events. TraceContract is a shallow DSL in contrast to LogFire, which is (mostly) a deep DSL. As a shallow DSL, TraceContract relies on Scala's type system. In contrast, for LogFire such a type system would have to be implemented from scratch. Also, in LogFire names have to be symbols or strings, which is somewhat annoying. LogScope was a compromise where the core DSL was external but with "holes" where one could write Python code, much like how parser generators such as `yacc` function. This was only possible due to Python's capabilities for evaluating a text string as a program (the `eval`-function), and would not, e.g. be possible in Java or Scala.

Programming Languages. Temporal logic could become part of a programming language assertion language. This could be seen as part of a design-by contract approach also supporting pre/post conditions and class invariants. Libraries can come equipped with such temporal assertions verifying their correct use. The paper [20] in this volume discusses what to expect from future programming languages, and specifically likewise mentions support for "richer specifications" supported by stronger static and dynamic analysis. Adding such concepts to a programming language would be easier if the language came equipped with syntax extension/meta programming frameworks, a need we have often experienced in our work.

Aspect-Oriented Programming. Aspect-oriented programming has been a popular way of instrumenting Java programs for runtime verification. Although research in aspect-oriented programming seems to have slowed down, we do believe that the ideas of vertical (enriching pointcut language) and horizontal (stateful aspects) extensions of AOP are interesting, and should be part of a programming language's meta-programming environment. AOP is a natural host for RV. That is, rather than using AOP to instrument for RV, RV can be considered as a natural extension of AOP. Note, however, that not all RV solutions require such a close integration with a programming language; e.g. web service monitoring does not require this form of integration.

RV Oriented Requirements Engineering. An intriguing thought is an approach to requirements engineering where at least *events* become part of the formal vocabulary, and where the implementation of the designed system is obliged to generate logs of such events, which can then be monitored. Logging (and monitoring) should become part of programming larger systems.

Algorithms. Concerning monitoring algorithms, the slicing-based algorithms, as found in Tracematches, MOP, and QEA, have so far shown to be the most efficient, initially at the cost of limited expressiveness, but in QEA extended to allow for improved expressiveness. Experiments such as the use of the Rete algorithm in LogFire, or the use of SMT [29] in MMT (Monitoring Modulo Theories) have not shown the same degree of performance. We still think, however, that new algorithms for parametric monitoring are of interest, especially since the original limitations wrt. expressiveness can be considered a major issue. In [42] we e.g. experiment with the use of BDDs for monitoring first-order past time temporal logic, with interesting performance results.

Predictive Monitoring. The earliest examples of predictive algorithms for dead-lock and data race detection from Compaq were very promising, and showed to be exceptionally effective in practice. Later results using SMT have shown tremendous potential.

Beyond Boolean. Specification-based runtime verification approaches tend to be Boolean valued algorithms: determining whether a sequence of events satisfies a temporally oriented specification. That is, $M(\sigma) \in \mathbb{B}$ (or some simple extension $\mathbb{B}^+$ of $\mathbb{B}$). However, as stated in Sect. 1, runtime verification in its generality can be considered as computing any kind of value, $M(\sigma) \in D$, for any domain D. We already encountered the nfer system which computes intervals (D is the set of intervals). In [35], a very early approach to computing values from a trace driven by temporal formulas is described. In other approaches, the result is a probability for a property to be satisfied, as in [77] (see discussion below). In statistical model checking [58], see also [60] in this volume, a stochastic system is executed multiple times, monitoring each execution against a temporal formula, computing either the probability that the system satisfies a formula (quantitative SMC), or determining whether the probability is greater than or equal to a certain treshold (qualitative SMC).

Specification Mining and Inference. We consider the 'mining' or 'learning' of specifications from traces to be a very promising field. Here we consider some work in this area (including our own e.g. [59,64,77]) but do not make an attempt to be complete. There exist general introductions to the topic [2,28,61]. In [77], an approach named *Runtime Verification with State Estimation* (RVSE) is described, which uses learning to estimate the probability that a trace with missing events (gaps in the trace) satisfies a given temporal property. This idea can, for example, be applied when monitoring overhead is reduced by sampling. The strategy is to learn the nominal behavior (without gaps) of the system as a Hidden Markov Model (HMM), and the later use this model to "fill in" sampling-induced gaps in an observed trace. Two approaches have attempted to use parametric trace slicing to learn parametric specifications. In [59], a probabilistic automata learning algorithm was applied to trace slices to build a hypothesis specification which was then heuristically refined. In [64] many pre-defined patterns were checked against trace slices and then combined to form ranked hypothesis specifications. Further work in both directions, and in specification mining in general, seems important to the field of runtime verification as the lack of specifications is sometimes cited as a barrier to application of RV. The above work was *passive* in the sense that it took as an input a given set of traces. Another promising direction is the area of *active* automata learning where queries may be given to build a (in some contexts) complete specification of behavior. One of the more advanced instances of this approach [53] is the learning of *register automata* – an extension of finite automata where data values may be communicated, stored and manipulated. In this sense, this work corresponds to the parametric approaches mentioned above. Additionally, an approach is described in the paper [51] in this volume for combining black-box (no access to code) and white-box (access to code) techniques. These active learning techniques are implemented in the well-known LearnLib tool [55]. Recent work [54] has adapted the framework to handle the long traces encountered in RV.

Trace Visualization. Execution trace visualization is a subject that in our opinion has promising potential, although our own work in this direction is limited to [4] and nfer (where the intent is to visualize event hierarchies). The advantage of visualization is that it can provide a free-of-charge abstract view of the trace, from which a user potentially may be able to conclude properties about the program, or at least the execution, without having to explicitly formulate these properties. We can distinguish between two forms of trace visualization: *still visualization*, where all events are visualized in one view, and *animated visualization*. In [4], an extension of UML sequence diagrams with symbols is described for representing still visualizations of the execution of concurrent programs. There appears to be a relationship between still visualization and automated specification mining. For example, a state machine learned from several runs can be regarded as a still visualization, as well as a specification of its behavior during those runs.

Combining Static and Dynamic Analysis. Full verification is of course preferred over partial verification performed by a monitor. The combination of static and dynamic verification can provide the best of both worlds: prove as much as is feasible and verify the remaining proof obligations during runtime.

Runtime Enforcement and Fault Protection. In runtime enforcement [31], one uses a monitor as a filter in front of a system, the target, receiving events from another system, the source. In this preventive approach, only events satisfying the property defined by the monitor will be let through to the target. In fault-protection strategies, the goal is to recover the system once it has failed; see e.g. [11] where this is called *adaptive runtime verification*. Here, two versions of the program being monitored exist: the complex version (running by default) and the simple version, and in case of a property violation the simple version overtakes the complex version. The general problem of how to recover from a bad program state is interesting and quite challenging. The ultimate solution to this problem can be found in planning and scheduling systems, where a planner creates a plan (straight-line program) to execute for a limited time period, an executive executes the plan, and a monitor monitors the execution. Upon failure detected by the monitor, a new plan (program) is generated online.

Summary. Searching for the most efficient monitoring algorithms, balanced with expressiveness of logics, is an ongoing research topic. The field has studied and produced an interesting set of temporal logics, that differ from logics produced by the field of e.g. model checking, in part due to the different application scenario, such as focus on single traces with data carrying events. This includes the distinction between external and internal DSLs, AOP, and logics for computing data (beyond the Boolean domain) from traces. Avoiding writing specifications, as pursued in specification mining and predictive monitoring, is an interesting line of research with a lot of potential. The integration of static and dynamic analysis is another important line of research, that is in its infancy as well. Finally, it would be interesting to pursue an integration of temporal logic in programming languages as part of the assertion language.

References

1. Allan, C., Avgustinov, P., Christensen, A.S., Hendren, L., Kuzins, S., Lhoták, O., de Moor, O., Sereni, D., Sittampalam, G., Tibble, J.: Adding trace matching with free variables to AspectJ. SIGPLAN Not. **40**, 345–364 (2005)
2. Ammons, G., Bodík, R., Larus, J.R.: Mining specifications. ACM Sigplan Not. **37**(1), 4–16 (2002)
3. Artho, C., Havelund, K., Biere, A.: High-level data races. Softw. Test. Verification Reliab. **13**(4), 207–227 (2004)
4. Artho, C., Havelund, K., Honiden, S.: Visualization of concurrent program executions. In: 31st Annual International Computer Software and Applications Conference (COMPSAC 2007), vol. 2, pp. 541–546, July 2007
5. Barringer, H., Falcone, Y., Havelund, K., Reger, G., Rydeheard, D.: Quantified event automata: towards expressive and efficient runtime monitors. In: Giannakopoulou, D., Méry, D. (eds.) FM 2012. LNCS, vol. 7436, pp. 68–84. Springer, Heidelberg (2012). https://doi.org/10.1007/978-3-642-32759-9_9
6. Barringer, H., Goldberg, A., Havelund, K., Sen, K.: Rule-based runtime verification. In: Steffen, B., Levi, G. (eds.) VMCAI 2004. LNCS, vol. 2937, pp. 44–57. Springer, Heidelberg (2004). https://doi.org/10.1007/978-3-540-24622-0_5
7. Barringer, H., Groce, A., Havelund, K., Smith, M.: Formal analysis of log files. J. Aerospace Comput. Inf. Commun. **7**(11), 365–390 (2010)
8. Barringer, H., Havelund, K.: TraceContract: a Scala DSL for trace analysis. In: Butler, M., Schulte, W. (eds.) FM 2011. LNCS, vol. 6664, pp. 57–72. Springer, Heidelberg (2011). https://doi.org/10.1007/978-3-642-21437-0_7
9. Barringer, H., Rydeheard, D.E., Havelund, K.: Rule systems for run-time monitoring: from Eagle to RuleR. J. Logic Comput. **20**(3), 675–706 (2010)
10. Bartocci, E., Falcone, Y., Francalanza, A., Reger, G.: Introduction to runtime verification. In: Bartocci, E., Falcone, Y. (eds.) Lectures on Runtime Verification. LNCS, vol. 10457, pp. 1–33. Springer, Cham (2018). https://doi.org/10.1007/978-3-319-75632-5_1
11. Bartocci, E., Grosu, R., Karmarkar, A., Smolka, S.A., Stoller, S.D., Zadok, E., Seyster, J.: Adaptive runtime verification. In: Qadeer, S., Tasiran, S. (eds.) RV 2012. LNCS, vol. 7687, pp. 168–182. Springer, Heidelberg (2013). https://doi.org/10.1007/978-3-642-35632-2_18
12. Bauer, A., Leucker, M., Schallhart, C.: The good, the bad, and the ugly, but how ugly is ugly? In: Sokolsky, O., Taşiran, S. (eds.) RV 2007. LNCS, vol. 4839, pp. 126–138. Springer, Heidelberg (2007). https://doi.org/10.1007/978-3-540-77395-5_11
13. Bauer, A., Leucker, M., Streit, J.: SALT—structured assertion language for temporal logic. In: Liu, Z., He, J. (eds.) ICFEM 2006. LNCS, vol. 4260, pp. 757–775. Springer, Heidelberg (2006). https://doi.org/10.1007/11901433_41
14. Bennett, M., Borgen, R., Havelund, K., Ingham, M., Wagner, D.: Prototyping a domain-specific language for monitor and control systems. J. Aerospace Comput. Inf. Commun. **7**(11), 338–364 (2010)

15. Bensalem, S., Havelund, K.: Dynamic deadlock analysis of multi-threaded programs. In: Ur, S., Bin, E., Wolfsthal, Y. (eds.) HVC 2005. LNCS, vol. 3875, pp. 208–223. Springer, Heidelberg (2006). https://doi.org/10.1007/11678779_15

16. Bodden, E.: MOPBox: a library approach to runtime verification. In: Khurshid, S., Sen, K. (eds.) RV 2011. LNCS, vol. 7186, pp. 365–369. Springer, Heidelberg (2012). https://doi.org/10.1007/978-3-642-29860-8_28

17. Bodden, E., Havelund, K.: Aspect-oriented race detection in Java. IEEE Trans. Softw. Eng. **36**(4), 509–527 (2010)

18. Candea, G., Godefroid, P.: Automated software test generation: some challenges, solutions, and recent advances. In: Steffen, B., Woeginger, G. (eds.) Computing and Software Science. LNCS, vol. 10000, pp. 505–531. Springer, Heidelberg (2018)

19. Chase, C.M., Garg, V.K.: Detection of global predicates: techniques and their limitations. Distrib. Comput. **11**(4), 191–201 (1998)

20. Chatley, R., Donaldson, A., Mycroft, A.: The next 7000 programming languages. In: Steffen, B., Woeginger, G. (eds.) Computing and Software Science. LNCS, vol. 10000, pp. 250–282. Springer, Heidelberg (2018)

21. Chen, F., D'Amorim, M., Roşu, G.: A formal monitoring-based framework for software development and analysis. In: Davies, J., Schulte, W., Barnett, M. (eds.) ICFEM 2004. LNCS, vol. 3308, pp. 357–372. Springer, Heidelberg (2004). https://doi.org/10.1007/978-3-540-30482-1_31

22. Chen, F., Roşu, G.: Towards monitoring-oriented programming: a paradigm combining specification and implementation. In: Proceedings of the 3rd International Workshop on Runtime Verification (RV 2003). Electronic Notes in Theoretical Computer Science, vol. 89, no. 2, pp. 108–127. Elsevier Science Inc. (2003)

23. Chen, F., Roşu, G.: MOP: an efficient and generic runtime verification framework. In: Object-Oriented Programming, Systems, Languages and Applications (OOPSLA 2007), pp. 569–588. ACM (2007). ACM SIGPLAN Notices

24. Chen, F., Roşu, G.: Parametric and sliced causality. In: Damm, W., Hermanns, H. (eds.) CAV 2007. LNCS, vol. 4590, pp. 240–253. Springer, Heidelberg (2007). https://doi.org/10.1007/978-3-540-73368-3_27

25. Chen, F., Serbanuta, T.F., Rosu, G.: jPredictor: a predictive runtime analysis tool for Java. In: ICSE (2008)

26. Cooper, R., Marzullo, K.: Consistent detection of global predicates. ACM SIGPLAN Not. **26**(12), 167–174 (1991). Proceedings of the ACM/ONR Workshop on Parallel and Distributed Debugging

27. d'Amorim, M., Havelund, K.: Event-based runtime verification of Java programs. ACM SIGSOFT Softw. Eng. Notes **30**(4), 1–7 (2005)

28. De la Higuera, C.: Grammatical inference: learning automata and grammars. Cambridge University Press, Cambridge (2010)

29. Decker, N., Leucker, M., Thoma, D.: Monitoring modulo theories. In: Ábrahám, E., Havelund, K. (eds.) TACAS 2014. LNCS, vol. 8413, pp. 341–356. Springer, Heidelberg (2014). https://doi.org/10.1007/978-3-642-54862-8_23

30. Drusinsky, D.: The temporal rover and the ATG rover. In: Havelund, K., Penix, J., Visser, W. (eds.) SPIN 2000. LNCS, vol. 1885, pp. 323–330. Springer, Heidelberg (2000). https://doi.org/10.1007/10722468_19

31. Falcone, Y., Fernandez, J.-C., Mounier, L.: What can you verify and enforce at runtime? Int. J. Softw. Tools Technol. Trans. **14**(3), 349–382 (2012)

32. Falcone, Y., Havelund, K., Reger, G.: A tutorial on runtime verification. In: Broy, M., Peled, D., Kalus, G. (eds.) Engineering Dependable Software Systems. NATO Science for Peace and Security Series - D: Information and Communication Security, vol. 34, pp. 141–175. IOS Press (2013)

33. Fidge, C.J.: Partial orders for parallel debugging. In: Proceedings of the 1988 ACM SIGPLAN and SIGOPS Workshop on Parallel and Distributed debugging, pp. 183–194. ACM (1988)

34. Filman, R., Havelund, K.: Source-code instrumentation and quantification of events. In: Foundations of Aspect-Oriented Languages (FOAL 2002), Enschede, The Netherlands, April 2002

35. Finkbeiner, B., Sankaranarayanan, S., Sipma, H.: Collecting statistics over runtime executions. Formal Methods Syst. Des. **27**(3), 253–274 (2005)

36. Harrow, J.J.: Runtime checking of multithreaded applications with visual threads. In: Havelund, K., Penix, J., Visser, W. (eds.) SPIN 2000. LNCS, vol. 1885, pp. 331–342. Springer, Heidelberg (2000). https://doi.org/10.1007/10722468_20

37. Havelund, K.: Using runtime analysis to guide model checking of Java programs. In: Havelund, K., Penix, J., Visser, W. (eds.) SPIN 2000. LNCS, vol. 1885, pp. 245–264. Springer, Heidelberg (2000). https://doi.org/10.1007/10722468_15

38. Havelund, K.: Runtime verification of C programs. In: Suzuki, K., Higashino, T., Ulrich, A., Hasegawa, T. (eds.) FATES/TestCom -2008. LNCS, vol. 5047, pp. 7–22. Springer, Heidelberg (2008). https://doi.org/10.1007/978-3-540-68524-1_3

39. Havelund, K.: Data automata in Scala. In: Proceedings of the 8th International Symposium on Theoretical Aspects of Software Engineering (TASE 2014). IEEE Computer Society (2014)

40. Havelund, K.: Rule-based runtime verification revisited. Int. J. Softw. Tools Technol. Trans. **17**(2), 143–170 (2015)

41. Havelund, K., Goldberg, A.: Verify your runs. In: Meyer, B., Woodcock, J. (eds.) VSTTE 2005. LNCS, vol. 4171, pp. 374–383. Springer, Heidelberg (2008). https://doi.org/10.1007/978-3-540-69149-5_40

42. Havelund, K., Peled, D.A., Ulus, D.: First order temporal logic monitoring with BDDs. In: Formal Methods in Computer Aided Design (FMCAD), pp. 116–123. IEEE (2017)

43. Havelund, K., Pressburger, T.: Model checking Java programs using Java PathFinder. Int. J. Softw. Tools Technol. Transf. **2**(4), 366–381 (2000)

44. Havelund, K., Reger, G.: Specification of parametric monitors. In: Drechsler, R., Kühne, U. (eds.) Formal Modeling and Verification of Cyber-Physical Systems, pp. 151–189. Springer, Wiesbaden (2015). https://doi.org/10.1007/978-3-658-09994-7_6

45. Havelund, K., Reger, G.: Runtime verification logics - a language design perspective. In: Aceto, L., Bacci, G., Bacci, G., Ingólfsdóttir, A., Legay, A., Mardare, R. (eds.) Models, Algorithms, Logics and Tools. LNCS, vol. 10460, pp. 310–338. Springer, Cham (2017). https://doi.org/10.1007/978-3-319-63121-9_16

46. Havelund, K., Reger, G., Thoma, D., Zălinescu, E.: Monitoring events that carry data. In: Bartocci, E., Falcone, Y. (eds.) Lectures on Runtime Verification. LNCS, vol. 10457, pp. 61–102. Springer, Cham (2018). https://doi.org/10.1007/978-3-319-75632-5_3

47. Havelund, K., Roşu, G.: An overview of the runtime verification tool Java PathExplorer. Formal Methods Syst. Des. **24**(2), 189–215 (2004)

48. Havelund, K., Rosu, G.: Monitoring programs using rewriting. In: Proceedings of the 16th IEEE International Conference on Automated Software Engineering (ASE 2001), pp. 135–143 (2001)

49. Havelund, K., Visser, W.: Program model checking as a new trend. STTT **4**(1), 8–20 (2002)

50. Havelund, K., Wyk, E.V.: Aspect-oriented monitoring of C programs. In: The Sixth IARP-IEEE/RAS-EURON Joint Workshop on Technical Challenges for Dependable Robots in Human Environments, Pasadena, CA, 17–18 May 2008
51. Howar, F., Jonsson, B., Vaandrager, F.: Combining black-box and white-box techniques for learning register automata. In: Steffen, B., Woeginger, G. (eds.) Computing and Software Science. LNCS, vol. 10000, pp. 563–588. Springer, Heidelberg (2018)
52. Huang, J., Meredith, P., Rosu, G.: Maximal sound predictive race detection with control flow abstraction. In: Proceedings of the 35th Annual ACM SIGPLAN Conference on Programming Language Design and Implementation (PLDI 2014), pp. 337–348. ACM, June 2014
53. Isberner, M., Howar, F., Steffen, B.: Learning register automata: from languages to program structures. Mach. Learn. **96**(1–2), 65–98 (2014)
54. Isberner, M., Howar, F., Steffen, B.: The TTT algorithm: a redundancy-free approach to active automata learning. In: Bonakdarpour, B., Smolka, S.A. (eds.) RV 2014. LNCS, vol. 8734, pp. 307–322. Springer, Cham (2014). https://doi.org/10.1007/978-3-319-11164-3_26
55. Isberner, M., Howar, F., Steffen, B.: The open-source LearnLib. In: Kroening, D., Păsăreanu, C.S. (eds.) CAV 2015. LNCS, vol. 9206, pp. 487–495. Springer, Cham (2015). https://doi.org/10.1007/978-3-319-21690-4_32
56. Kauffman, S., Havelund, K., Joshi, R.: nfer − a notation and system for inferring event stream abstractions. In: Falcone, Y., Sánchez, C. (eds.) RV 2016. LNCS, vol. 10012, pp. 235–250. Springer, Cham (2016). https://doi.org/10.1007/978-3-319-46982-9_15
57. Kiczales, G., Hilsdale, E., Hugunin, J., Kersten, M., Palm, J., Griswold, W.G.: An overview of AspectJ. In: Knudsen, J.L. (ed.) ECOOP 2001. LNCS, vol. 2072, pp. 327–354. Springer, Heidelberg (2001). https://doi.org/10.1007/3-540-45337-7_18
58. Larsen, K.G., Legay, A.: Statistical model checking: past, present, and future. In: Margaria, T., Steffen, B. (eds.) ISoLA 2016. LNCS, vol. 9952, pp. 3–15. Springer, Cham (2016). https://doi.org/10.1007/978-3-319-47166-2_1
59. Lee, C., Chen, F., Rosu, G.: Mining parametric specifications. In: Proceedings of the 33rd International Conference on Software Engineering, ICSE 2011, 21–28 May 2011, Waikiki, Honolulu, HI, USA, pp. 591–600 (2011)
60. Legay, A., Lukina, A., Traonouez, L.M., Yang, J., Smolka, S.A., Grosu, R.: Statistical model checking. In: Steffen, B., Woeginger, G. (eds.) Computing and Software Science. LNCS, vol. 10000, pp. 478–504. Springer, Heidelberg (2018)
61. Lo, D., Khoo, S.-C., Han, J., Liu, C.: Mining Software Specifications: Methodologies and Applications. CRC Press, Boca Raton (2011)
62. Mattern, F.: Virtual time and global states of distributed systems. In: Cosnard, M., et al. (eds.) Parallel and Distributed Algorithms: Proceedings of the International Workshop on Parallel and Distributed Algorithms, pp. 215–226. Elsevier Science (1989)
63. Meredith, P., Jin, D., Griffith, D., Chen, F., Roşu, G.: An overview of the MOP runtime verification framework. J. Softw. Tools Technol. Transf. **14**, 249–289 (2011)
64. Reger, G., Barringer, H., Rydeheard, D.: A pattern-based approach to parametric specification mining. In: 2013 IEEE/ACM 28th International Conference on Automated Software Engineering (ASE), pp. 658–663, November 2013
65. Reger, G., Cruz, H.C., Rydeheard, D.: MarQ: monitoring at runtime with QEA. In: Baier, C., Tinelli, C. (eds.) TACAS 2015. LNCS, vol. 9035, pp. 596–610. Springer, Heidelberg (2015). https://doi.org/10.1007/978-3-662-46681-0_55

66. Roşu, G., Chen, F.: Semantics and algorithms for parametric monitoring. Logical Methods Comput. Sci. **8**(1), 1–47 (2012)
67. Said, M., Wang, C., Yang, Z., Sakallah, K.: Generating data race witnesses by an SMT-based analysis. In: Bobaru, M., Havelund, K., Holzmann, G.J., Joshi, R. (eds.) NFM 2011. LNCS, vol. 6617, pp. 313–327. Springer, Heidelberg (2011). https://doi.org/10.1007/978-3-642-20398-5_23
68. Savage, S., Burrows, M., Nelson, G., Sobalvarro, P., Anderson, T.: Eraser: a dynamic data race detector for multithreaded programs. ACM Trans. Comput. Syst. **15**(4), 391–411 (1997)
69. Sen, K., Roşu, G., Agha, G.: Online efficient predictive safety analysis of multithreaded programs. In: Jensen, K., Podelski, A. (eds.) TACAS 2004. LNCS, vol. 2988, pp. 123–138. Springer, Heidelberg (2004). https://doi.org/10.1007/978-3-540-24730-2_9
70. Sen, K., Rosu, G., Agha, G.: Runtime safety analysis of multithreaded programs. In: Proceedings of ESEC/FSE 2003: European Software Engineering Conference and ACM SIGSOFT International Symposium on the Foundations of Software Engineering. ACM, Helsinki, September 2003
71. Sen, K., Roşu, G., Agha, G.: Detecting errors in multithreaded programs by generalized predictive analysis of executions. In: Steffen, M., Zavattaro, G. (eds.) FMOODS 2005. LNCS, vol. 3535, pp. 211–226. Springer, Heidelberg (2005). https://doi.org/10.1007/11494881_14
72. Şerbănuţă, T.F., Chen, F., Roşu, G.: Maximal causal models for sequentially consistent systems. In: Qadeer, S., Tasiran, S. (eds.) RV 2012. LNCS, vol. 7687, pp. 136–150. Springer, Heidelberg (2013). https://doi.org/10.1007/978-3-642-35632-2_16
73. Seyster, J., Dixit, K., Huang, X., Grosu, R., Havelund, K., Smolka, S.A., Stoller, S.D., Zadok, E.: InterAspect: aspect-oriented instrumentation with GCC. Formal Methods Syst. Des. **41**(3), 295–320 (2012)
74. Smith, D.R., Havelund, K.: Toward automated enforcement of error-handling policies. Technical report number: TR-KT-0508, Kestrel Technology LLC, August 2005
75. Smith, M.H., Holzmann, G.J., Etessami, K.: Events and constraints: a graphical editor for capturing logic requirements of programs. In: 21st IEEE International Requirements Engineering Conference (RE), Toronto, Canada, August 2001
76. Stoller, S.D.: Detecting global predicates in distributed systems with clocks. In: Mavronicolas, M., Tsigas, P. (eds.) WDAG 1997. LNCS, vol. 1320, pp. 185–199. Springer, Heidelberg (1997). https://doi.org/10.1007/BFb0030684
77. Stoller, S.D., Bartocci, E., Seyster, J., Grosu, R., Havelund, K., Smolka, S.A., Zadok, E.: Runtime verification with state estimation. In: Khurshid, S., Sen, K. (eds.) RV 2011. LNCS, vol. 7186, pp. 193–207. Springer, Heidelberg (2012). https://doi.org/10.1007/978-3-642-29860-8_15
78. Stolz, V., Bodden, E.: Temporal assertions using AspectJ. In: Proceedings of the 5th International Workshop on Runtime Verification (RV 2005). Electronic Notes in Theoretical Computer Science, vol. 144, no. 4, pp. 109–124. Elsevier Science Inc. (2006)
79. Stolz, V., Huch, F.: Runtime verification of concurrent Haskell programs. In: Proceedings of the 4th International Workshop on Runtime Verification (RV 2004). Electronic Notes in Theoretical Computer Science, vol. 113, pp. 201–216. Elsevier Science Inc. (2005)
80. Walker, R., Viggers, K.: Implementing protocols via declarative event patterns. In: Taylor, R., Dwyer, M. (eds.) ACM Sigsoft 12th International Symposium on Foundations of Software Engineering (FSE-12), pp. 159–169. ACM Press (2004)

Combining Black-Box and White-Box Techniques for Learning Register Automata

Falk Howar[1]([⊠]), Bengt Jonsson[2], and Frits Vaandrager[3]

[1] Dortmund University of Technology and Fraunhofer ISST, Dortmund, Germany
falk.howar@tu-dortmund.de
[2] Department of Information Technology, Uppsala University, Uppsala, Sweden
[3] Institute for Computing and Information Sciences,
Radboud University, Nijmegen, The Netherlands

Abstract. Model learning is a black-box technique for constructing state machine models of software and hardware components, which has been successfully used in areas such as telecommunication, banking cards, network protocols, and control software. The underlying theoretic framework (active automata learning) was first introduced in a landmark paper by Dana Angluin in 1987 for finite state machines. In order to make model learning more widely applicable, it must be further developed to scale better to large models and to generate richer classes of models. Recently, various techniques have been employed to extend automata learning to extended automata models, which combine control flow with guards and assignments to data variables. Such techniques infer guards over data parameters and assignments from observations of test output. In the black-box model of active automata learning this can be costly and require many tests, while in many application scenarios source code is available for analysis. In this paper, we explore some directions for future research on how black-box model learning can be enhanced using white-box information extraction methods, with the aim to maintain the benefits of dynamic black-box methods while making effective use of information that can be obtained through white-box techniques.

1 Introduction

Model learning, also known as active automata learning, is a black-box technique which constructs state machine models of software and hardware components from information obtained by providing inputs and observing the resulting outputs. Model learning has been successfully used in several different application domains, including

- generating conformance test suites of software components, a.k.a. *learning-based testing* (e.g., [38,39]),
- finding mistakes in implementations of security-critical protocols (e.g., [3,16, 28–30,62]),

© Springer Nature Switzerland AG 2019
B. Steffen and G. Woeginger (Eds.): Computing and Software Science, LNCS 10000, pp. 563–588, 2019.
https://doi.org/10.1007/978-3-319-91908-9_26

- learning interfaces of classes in software libraries (e.g., [42]),
- checking that a legacy component and a refactored implementation have the same behavior (e.g., [63]).

Active automata learning techniques are partly based on a landmark paper by Angluin [6] showing that finite automata can be learned in the so-called *Minimally Adequate Teacher* (MAT) framework [6], using two types of queries. A *membership* (or *I/O*) *query* asks what the output is in response to an input sequence. An *equivalence query* asks whether a hypothesized state machine is equivalent to the sought finite automaton; it is answered by *yes* if this is the case, otherwise by a *counterexample* that distinguishes the hypothesized and sought state machines.

Steffen et al. [38] made the important observation that the MAT framework can be used for black-box learning of abstract and concise state machine models of software components. They assume a software component, called the *System Under Learning (SUL)*, whose behavior can be described by (an unknown) state machine, and which can always be brought back to its initial state. An I/O query can now be implemented by bringing the SUL to its initial state and then observing the outputs generated in response to the given input sequence. Equivalence queries can be approximated using a conformance testing tool [9,52, 68] via a finite number of *test queries* to the SUL. Peled et al. [37,60] observed that learning models can be used as a basis for model checking of black-box components.

The most widely known algorithm for model learning of finite automata is L^* [6], which has, e.g., been implemented in the LearnLib framework [48]. A key strength of model learning is that it aims to produce succinct models of the externally observable behavior of the SUL. This allows it to extract simple models of complex software, especially if we choose the right perspective (e.g., focus on a subset of a component's functionality) and apply appropriate abstractions. Examples are implementations of network protocols, which typically consist of many thousands of lines of code, but after appropriate abstraction induce state diagrams with at most a few dozen states, see e.g. [29,62].

There is certainly a large potential for application of model learning to many different aspects of software development, maintenance and refactoring, especially when it comes to handling legacy software. We survey examples of existing such applications in Sect. 3. To realize this potential, two major challenges must be addressed: (1) currently, techniques do not scale well, and (2) they are not yet satisfactorily developed for richer classes of models. Let us elaborate on these challenges.

1. Concerning scaling, we note that the complexity of the currently most efficient algorithm for active learning of finite-state models [50] has a cubic worst-case time complexity in the size of the learned model. Another expensive component of model learning is that sufficiently precise approximation of equivalence queries in a black-box setting may require a number of membership queries that is exponential in the number of states of the SUL.

2. Concerning richness of models, in many situations it is crucial for models to also be able to describe *data flow*, i.e., constraints on data parameters that are passed when the component interacts with its environment, as well as the mutual influence between control flow and data flow. For instance, models of protocol components must describe how different parameter values in sequence numbers, identifiers, etc. influence the control flow, and vice versa. Such models often take the form of *extended finite state machines* (EFSMs). Recently, various techniques have been employed to extend automata learning to EFSM models, which combine control flow with guards and assignments to data variables [3,15]. Such techniques either rely on manually constructed mappers that abstract the data aspects of input and output symbols into a finite alphabet, or otherwise infer guards and assignments from observations of test outputs. The latter can be costly, especially for models where control flow depends on test on data parameters in input: in this case, learning an exact guard that separates two control flow branches may require a large number of queries. For instance, to infer that a branch is taken if an input parameter is greater than 42 may take a number of membership queries.

One way to address these challenges is to augment model learning with white-box information extraction methods, which are able to obtain information about the SUL at lower cost than black-box techniques. When dealing with computer-based systems, there is a spectrum of how much information we have about the code. For third party components that run on separate hardware, we may not have access to the code at all. Frequently we will have access to the executable, but not anymore to the original code. Or we may have access to the code, but not to adequate tools for analyzing it (this often happens with legacy components). If we can construct a good model of a component using black-box learning techniques, we do not need to worry about the code. However, in cases where black-box techniques do not work and/or the number of queries becomes too high, it makes sense to exploit information from the code during model learning.

In this article, we explore how existing approaches for model learning can be improved by effective use of available white-box information about the SUL (the full code, the executable,..), with the aim to maintain the benefits of black box methods.[1] We will develop three promising directions for future research:

1. In a black-box setting equivalence queries are approximated using a finite number of test queries to the SUL. This is time consuming and often constitutes a major bottleneck in model learning [65]. Moreover, the approximation may be incorrect because, as Dijkstra observed, testing can be used to show the presence of bugs, but never to show their absence. We have no guarantees that a learned model is correct. In Sect. 6.1, we review a number of techniques

---

[1] Of course, dynamic white-box techniques (for instance, based on symbolic execution) or other static analysis white-box techniques can also be used to generate models directly from code without using any active learning. Such models, however, will typically depend heavily on the internal structure of the SUL's program, and programs with the same observale behavior do not necessarily induce equivalent models.

that use white-box information about the SUL to reduce the time required to find discrepancies in a hypothesis model, or to prove the absence of such discrepancies.

2. In Sect. 6.2, we discuss extensions of Angluin's MAT framework with new types of queries. A learner may for instance ask which previous values and operations have been used by the SUL to compute some output value. Or she may ask if some previous input value may subsequently be tested or output by the SUL. Such queries may dramatically simplify the task for the learner, but can often be simply answered by the teacher using off-the-shelf code analysis tools. An example would be a query about which registers are needed in a specific state or location.

3. Finally, access to the source code of a program or component can be used to compute information about the component that can help saving queries during learning. Information about which methods access internal variables and read or write those variables, e.g., can be used to decide whether queries can be reduced or even skipped. We discuss possible use cases for static code analysis in Sect. 6.3.

In order to make the discussion of the paper concrete, we will place it in a simple setting that is well-understood, namely *register automata*. Register automata (and the related *nominal automata*) constitute an extension of finite automata in which data values may be communicated, stored and manipulated. Recently, black-box learning algorithms have been generalized from finite automata to register automata [1,15,57].

Outline. We start by giving a brief overview to the field of model learning: In the next section, we provide a short introduction to the underlying learning setting and the practical challenges that arise when using automata learning for generating models of program behavior. Section 3 discusses related work and highlights cases in which learning has been applied successfully in practice. In the second half of the paper we develop several proposals for leveraging white-box analysis techniques in the concrete setting of learning register automaton models: We introduce register automata in Sect. 4 and we discuss existing learning algorithms for register automata in Sect. 5. We conclude by presenting our proposals in Sect. 6.

2   Inferring Models of Program Behavior

The general setting that we consider is illustrated in Fig. 1. We assume a SUL that execute some program in the set Programs. The semantics of programs is given by a function *beh* : Programs → Behaviors that describes the external, observable behavior of the SUL when it runs a program. Two programs $P, P' \in$ Programs are deemed equivalent if they induce the same behavior: $P \equiv P' \Leftrightarrow beh(P) = beh(P')$. We postulate that each program $P \in$ Programs can be described by a model $model(P)$ from some universe Models. In general, a program can be described by several models. The semantics of models is specified by a

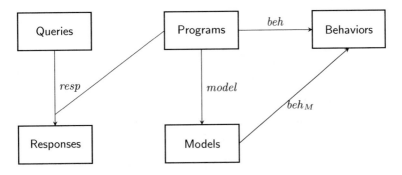

Fig. 1. Learning setting.

function beh_M : Models $\rightarrow$ Behaviors and we assume $beh(P) = beh_M(model(P))$. Within the area of model-based testing, this assumption is commonly referred to as the *test hypothesis* [11,31]. Two models M and M' are equivalent if they induce the same observable behavior: $M \equiv M' \Leftrightarrow beh_M(M) = beh_M(M')$.

Many instantiations of this general framework are possible. In the case of reactive systems, for instance, the set Behaviors may consist of functions λ : $\Sigma^* \rightarrow \Omega^*$ from sequences of inputs to sequences of outputs that preserve the prefix ordering (here denoted $\leq$) and the length of sequences, that is, for all $w, w' \in \Sigma^*$, $w \leq w' \Rightarrow \lambda(w) \leq \lambda(w')$ and $\mid \lambda(w) \mid = \mid w \mid$. In this case, the set Models naturally consists of (deterministic) Mealy machines with inputs Σ and outputs Ω. For reactive systems in which inputs and outputs do not alternate strictly, Behaviors may be defined as the class of prefix closed sets of *suspension traces* and Models as the class of *I/O transition systems* [69,72].[2]

2.1 Model Learning

Model learning is relevant in situations where we do not know $model(P)$, either because we do not even know P, or because we know P but are somehow unable to compute $model(P)$ from P. In order to learn a model M with $M \equiv model(P)$, we postulate a collection Queries of *queries* that can be applied to the SUL. A function $resp$: Queries $\times$ Programs $\rightarrow$ Responses specifies the result of applying a query to the SUL that is running some program. In the setting of Mealy machines, for instance, Angluin's MAT framework uses I/O queries and equivalence queries. An I/O query consists of a sequence of inputs $w \in \Sigma^*$ and the response is given by

$$resp(w, P) = beh(P)(w).$$

---

[2] In fact, in the case of nondeterministic reactive systems, instantiations of our framework may be defined for each equivalence from the linear time—branching time spectrum of Van Glabbeek [33]. However, as far as we know, such instantiations have not yet been studied in the literature on model learning.

An equivalence query consists of an hypothesis $H \in \mathsf{Models}$ and the response satisfies

$$resp(H, P) = \begin{cases} \text{yes} & \text{if } beh_M(H) = beh(P) \\ \text{no}, w & \text{otherwise, where } w \in \varSigma^* \text{ and } beh_M(H)(w) \neq beh(P)(w). \end{cases}$$

The queries of the MAT framework are *extensional*: in order to answer them we do not need access to the program, but only to its observable behavior. Formally, for all programs P and P' and queries Q,

$$P \equiv P' \Rightarrow resp(Q, P) = resp(Q, P').$$

2.2   Abstraction

As stated in the introduction, the strength of model learning is that it can produce simple models of complex systems. This, of course, depends on the application of an appropriate abstraction. In the above description of model learning, such an abstraction is hidden in functions beh and beh_M. While in practice, beh_M usually is the semantics associated with the class of models that is inferred by some learning algorithm, the function beh abstracts the actual observable behavior of a program to the level of this semantics. Angluin's MAT framework, e.g., has been implemented for Mealy machine models over finite sets of inputs and outputs [46], where beh_M is a mapping from sequences of inputs to outputs. On the other hand, learning Mealy machine models of realistic software components requires a test harness which translates the abstract sequences of inputs to concrete seqeuences of method invocations on the component interface, and abstracts concrete return values of invocations to abstract outputs.

The choice of a class of models requires the existence of a learning algorithm for this class of models as well as the definition of a function beh that abstracts concrete program executions to traces in the semantics of this class of models. Defining such an appropriate abstraction beh oftentimes is not trivial as it is required to be deterministic and determines the aspects of a component's behavior that becomes observable.

The extension of learning algorithms to richer classes of models is an effort that has two positive impacts in this scenario: On the one hand, using more expressive classes of models can help representing more interesting aspects of a component's behavior in a model. On the other hand, using more expressive models can mitigate the laborious and often error-prone burden of defining appropriate functions beh.

This has led to multiple lines of works that extend Angluin's MAT framework to richer classes of models — most notably classes that can describe control-flow as well as data-flow or timing information. Extensions require finding right-congruences for more expressive classes of automata. One principal challenge that all these works face is that in a black-box setting, models can only be learned from observable behavior. Inferring complex causal relations like data manipulations or timed behavior quickly requires many queries and often has principle

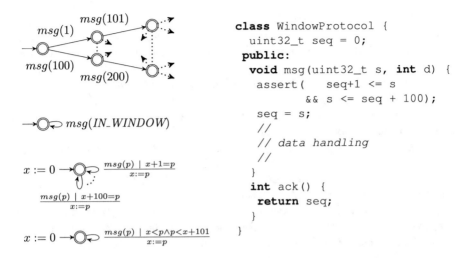

Fig. 2. Models (left) and code (right) for a fictitious protocol component

limitations (e.g., the absence of a right-congruence) as has been shown for learning timed automata [36] models which cannot in general be determinized.

White-box access to a component can be beneficial for defining adequate *beh* functions, for reducing the number of required tests as well as for alleviating limitations on the expressivity of inferred models.

2.3   Example: A Protocol Component

We illustrate the above concepts using a small fictitious protocol component as an example. The C-code for the component is shown in the right half of Fig. 2. The component has two methods msg(uint32_t s, int d) and ack(), and one internal field seq that is initialized to 0. The msg method is guarded to accept only sequence numbers s in a certain window relative to seq. If the guard is satisfied, the internal field seq is updated to the value of s. The method then performs some operation on the payload data d that is not observable from the outside of the component (values of d are not stored and no observable error can occur while operating on d). The ack method returns the current value of seq.

When inferring a model of the behavior of the WindowProtocol component, a class of models and a corresponding function *beh* has to be fixed that abstracts the observable behavior of the component to the semantics of this class. The left half of Fig. 2 shows four models of the behavior of this component at different levels of abstraction, i.e., for different classes of models and different functions *beh*. For the purpose of illustration, the models only cover the behavior of the component under the msg(uint32_t s, int d) method. In each model, we consider a behavior to be a sequence of calls to the msg(uint32_t s, int d) method (at some level of abstraction), which does not trigger any failing assertion. The model itself represents the set of such behaviors.

The first model is the (huge) finite state automaton that results from using (abstract) inputs $msg(i)$ for all `ints` i and translating those to calls `msg(i,d)` with some random fixed `d`. Each state of the model represents one concrete valuation of the variable `seq` of the component. All states can be distinguished since they accept pairwise different sets of invocations of $msg(i)$ for Integer data values i. Only accepting locations are shown. While this model is finite and faithful to the behavior of the component, it is expensive to infer (due to the size) and of limited explanatory value.

The second model is a much more concise finite state machine that can be obtained by using the same learning algorithm as for the first model but with a much more involved function *beh* that basically models the implementation of the `msg` method and can concretize sequences of abstract $msg(IN\_WINDOW)$ inputs to consecutive concrete method invocations with sequence numbers in the accepted respective windows. While the model is a perfect and concise documentation of the behavior of the component, it can only be inferred and interpreted with the help of an involved and state-dependent *beh* function.

The third model is a register automaton that can encode storing of method parameters (p) in registers (x) and compares parameters and sums of registers and constants for equality. We define register automata formally in Sect. 4. For this preliminary discussion, please note that the register automaton has a single accepting location that corresponds to all concrete accepting states in the first model. The model has one hundred transitions that loop from this location for all guards $x + i = p$ where $1 \le i \le 100$. Current learning algorithms for register automata models [15] would need two inputs for producing such a model: a grammar for terms allowed in equalities, e.g., $t ::= x + c \mid p$, and the set of allowed constants c.

Finally, in the fourth model, the one hundred transitions of the third model are merged into a single transition with a slightly more expressive guard, using inequalities instead of equalities and the single constant 101. As in the above case, a learning algorithm would need to be capable of inferring guards with inequalities and receive the constant as an input.

The example shows the potential for application of white-box information during model inference. Access to the source code of the component can be used, e.g., to identify methods that do not change the state of the component, to identify the required expressivity of guards or the necessary constants in an automated fashion. White-box analyses can also be used to determine, which parameters are stored in fields or to compute symbolic guards with fewer executions.

3   Related Work and Applications

Active automata learning gained a lot of traction over the past few years as a technique for inferring models of software components. One indication of the growing attention is a recent article on model learning in the Communications of the ACM [70]. In fact, the field and its applications have grown and diversified to an extent that makes it impossible to provide a complete and comprehensive overview here. Instead, we try to sketch the lines of work that target increased expressivity of inferred models or the integration of white-box approaches. Additionally, we provide some examples of works that have shown positive results of using learned models for the (formal) analysis of components and systems.

From DFA to More Expressive Models. Dana Angluin presented the MAT model and a first learning algorithm (named L^*) in her seminal 1987 paper [6]. The L^* algorithm infers deterministic finite automata models of unknown regular languages. Hungar et al. presented the first learning algorithm for Mealy machine models in the MAT model [46]. Their work was motivated by the goal of producing more natural models of input/output behavior as well as reducing the cost of learning models.

Learning algorithms for Mealy machine models have been the basis for a line of works that construct beh_P functions (so-called *mappers*) for inferring models of infinite-state components. This approach is described explicitly for the generation of models from protocol entities in [3].

However, defining mappers is an error-prone and laborious manual effort. In [44] automated alphabet abstraction refinement is integrated with active learning to overcome this problem. More recent works extend this approach and combine automata learning with learning symbolic descriptions of transition structures, e.g., for models with large or infinite structured alphabets [56], or for alphabets that expose an algebraic structure [25].

The above approaches essentially still infer finite state machine models. Another different line of work aims at extending model learning to infinite state models in which states are defined over sets of variables. The authors of [10] present a technique for inferring *symbolic Mealy machines*, i.e., automata with guarded transitions and state-local sets of registers. The presented technique learns a Mealy machine over a large enough finite domain. In a post-processing step, from this Mealy machine a symbolic version is constructed.

Howar et al. extend active automata learning in the MAT model to register automata, which model control-flow as well as data-flow between data parameters of inputs, outputs, and a set of registers [43]. Registers and data parameters can be compared for equality. The authors demonstrate the effectiveness of their approach by inferring models of data structures [42] and extend the expressivity to allow for arbitrary data relations that meet certain learnability criteria [14,15]. Aarts et al. develop a slightly different approach for inferring register automata models that can compare registers and data parameter for equality [1,5]. The two approaches are compared in [2].

A more in-depth overview of works that extend active automata learning to infinite state models is provided in [49].

Applications. After Peled et al. suggested active automata learning for making black-box systems amenable to the application of formal methods [60], Hagerer et al. pioneered the application of active automata learning for generating models of components; components of a computer telephony system in their particular case [38,39]. The models were used as a basis for testing the system. In recent years, generating models for testing has been continued by different authors for several types of systems, e.g., for Event-B models [23,24], for graphical user interfaces of android applications [18,19], and for integration testing [64] of automotive components. Meinke and Sindhu present LBTest, a tool for learning-based testing for reactive systems, integrating model checking, active automata learning, and random testing [55].

Other applications target generating behavioral specifications of Web applications [61], the new biometric European passport [4], bot nets [12], and enterprise applications [73]. Margaria et al. showed that model learning may help to increase confidence that a legacy component and a refactored implementation have the same behavior [53]. Inspired by this work, Schuts et al. use inferred specifications and equivalence checking to assist re-engineering of legacy software in an industrial context at Philips [63]. Sun et al. use active automata learning in combination with automated abstraction refinement and random testing for finding abstract behavioral models of Java classes [67].

An emerging area of applications is the learning-based analysis of safety or security of components and systems: De Ruiter and Poll use active automata learning for inferring models of TLS implementations and discover previously unknown security flaws in the inferred models [62]. Xue et al. use active automata learning for inferring behavioral models of JavaScript malware [74]. Fiterau et al. use learning and model checking to analyze the behavior of different implementations of the TCP protocol stack and document several instances of implementations violating RFC specifications [29]. Using a similar approach, Fiterau et al. show that also three different implementations of the SSH protocol violate the RFC specifications [30]. Khalili et al. [51] use active automata learning to obtain behavioral models of the middleware of a robotic platform. The models are used during verification of control software for this platform.

Integration of White-Box Techniques. In [54], Margaria et al. investigate the potential of what they call "domain-specific knowledge" for reducing the cost of learning models. Their domain-specific knowledge, e.g., assumptions about prefix-closedness of an unknown target language or the independence of inputs, is a first example of the kind of information about a system that can be computed by white-box techniques.

The first works that actually used white-box techniques to implement more powerful queries explore combinations of active automata learning and different forms of symbolic execution for producing expressive models of components. Giannakopoulou et al. develop an active learning algorithm that infers safe interfaces of software components with guarded actions. In their model, the teacher is implemented using concolic execution [32]. Cho et al. present MACE an approach for concolic exploration of protocol behavior. The approach uses active automata learning for discovering so-called deep states in the protocol behavior. From these states, concolic execution is employed in order to discover vulnerabilities [17]. Botinčan and Babić present a learning algorithm for inferring models of stream transducers that integrates active automata learning with symbolic execution and counterexample-guided abstraction refinement [13]. They show how the models can be used to verify properties of input sanitizers in Web applications. Their work is the first in this line of works that produces infinite-state models that can store data values in a set of registers. Finally, Howar et al. extend the work of [32] and integrate knowledge about the potential effects of component method invocations on a component's state to improve the performance during symbolic queries [45]. The knowledge is obtained through static code analysis.

Another (earlier) line of work uses active learning in model-checking contexts. The moderate style of exploration that achieved by learning is used to mitigate the problem of state space explosion (e.g. [22]). Recent advances in this area have been made by finding active automata learning for expressive classes of models. Learning algorithms are usually based quite directly on the classic L^* algorithm. The required extensions in expressivity of models are usually realized through powerful teachers. For instance, Feng et al. present an algorithm for inferring assumptions for probabilistic assume/guarantee reasoning [26,27].

4   Register Automata

In order to make the discussion of the paper concrete, we will place it in a setting that is well-understood, namely *register automata*. These extend finite automata with data values that may be communicated, stored and manipulated. In this section, we introduce basic definitions of data languages and register automata that generalize corresponding concepts for languages and finite automata.

In our setting, data languages and register automata are parameterized on a vocabulary that determines how data can be examined, which in our setting is called a *theory*. A *theory* is a pair $\langle \mathcal{D}, \mathcal{R} \rangle$ where $\mathcal{D}$ is an unbounded domain of *data values*, and $\mathcal{R}$ is a set of *relations* on $\mathcal{D}$. The relations in $\mathcal{R}$ can have arbitrary arity. Known constants can be represented by unary relations.

Examples of simple theories include

- $\langle \mathbb{N}, \{=\} \rangle$, the theory of natural numbers with equality; instead of the set of natural numbers, we could consider any other unbounded domain, e.g., the set of strings (representing passwords or usernames).
- $\langle \mathbb{R}, \{<\} \rangle$, the theory of real numbers with inequality: this theory also allows to express equality between elements.

Operations, such as increments, addition and subtraction, can in this framework be represented by relations. For instance, addition can be represented by a ternary relation $p_1 = p_2 + p_3$. In the following, we assume that some theory $\langle \mathcal{D}, \mathcal{R} \rangle$ has been fixed.

Data Languages. We assume a set Σ of *actions*, each with an arity that determines how many parameters it takes from the domain $\mathcal{D}$. For notational convenience, we will here assume that all actions have arity 1. A *data symbol* is a term of form $\alpha(d)$, where α is an action and $d \in \mathcal{D}$ is a data value. A *data word* is a sequence of data symbols. The concatenation of two data words w and w' is denoted ww'. Two data words $w = \alpha_1(d_1) \ldots \alpha_n(d_n)$ and $w' = \alpha_1(d_1') \ldots \alpha_n(d_n')$ are $\mathcal{R}$-*indistinguishable*, denoted $w \approx_{\mathcal{R}} w'$, if they have the same sequence of actions, and $R(d_{i_1}, \ldots, d_{i_j}) \Leftrightarrow R(d_{i_1}', \ldots, d_{i_j}')$ whenever R is a j-ary relation in $\mathcal{R}$ and $i_1, \cdots, i_j$ are indices among $1 \ldots n$, i.e., the sequence of data values cannot be distinguished by any of the relations in $\mathcal{R}$.

A *data language* $\mathcal{L}$ is a set of data words that respects $\mathcal{R}$ in the sense that $w \approx_{\mathcal{R}} w'$ implies $w \in \mathcal{L} \leftrightarrow w' \in \mathcal{L}$. We will often represent data languages as mappings from the set of data words to $\{+, -\}$, where $+$ stands for ACCEPT and $-$ for REJECT.

Register Automata. We assume a set of *registers* $x_1, x_2, \ldots$. A *parameterized symbol* is a term of form $\alpha(p)$, where α is an action and p a formal parameter. A *guard* is a conjunction of negated and unnegated relations (from $\mathcal{R}$) over the formal parameter p and registers. An *assignment* is a simple parallel update of registers with values from registers or the formal parameter p. We represent an assignment which updates the registers $x_{i_1}, \ldots, x_{i_m}$ with values from the registers $x_{j_1}, \ldots, x_{j_n}$ or p as a mapping π from $\{x_{i_1}, \ldots, x_{i_m}\}$ to $\{x_{j_1}, \ldots, x_{j_n}\} \cup \{p\}$, meaning that the value of the register or formal parameter $\pi(x_{i_k})$ is assigned to the register x_{i_k}, for $k = 1, \ldots, m$. Using multiple-assignment notation, this would be written as $x_{i_1}, \ldots, x_{i_m} := \pi(x_{i_1}), \ldots, \pi(x_{i_m})$.

Definition 1 (Register automaton). *A register automaton (RA) is a tuple $\mathcal{A} = (L, l_0, \mathcal{X}, \Gamma, \lambda)$, where*

- *L is a finite set of* locations, *with $l_0 \in L$ as the* initial location,
- *$\mathcal{X}$ maps each location $l \in L$ to a finite set $\mathcal{X}(l)$ of registers, and*
- *Γ is a finite set of* transitions, *each of form $\langle l, \alpha(p), g, \pi, l' \rangle$, where*
  - *$l \in L$ is a source location,*
  - *$l' \in L$ is a target location,*
  - *$\alpha(p)$ is a parameterized symbol,*
  - *g is a guard over p and $\mathcal{X}(l)$, and*
  - *π (the* assignment*) is a mapping from $\mathcal{X}(l')$ to $\mathcal{X}(l) \cup \{p\}$, and*
- *λ maps each $l \in L$ to $\{+, -\}$.* □

Register automata are required to be *completely specified* in the sense that for each location $l \in L$ and action α, the disjunction of the guards on the α-transitions from l is equivalent to *true*.

A restriction of register automata, as defined by Definition 1, is that transitions do not allow to assign arbitrary expressions to registers, only the value of a formal parameter or a register. A main reason for this restriction is to limit the number of possibilities for inferring guards and assignments that match the result of membership queries. As an example, suppose that a SUL accepts sequences with increasing parameter values, e.g., $offer(4)\ offer(5)\ offer(6)\ offer(7)$. We could then learn a RA if the theory includes, e.g., the relation *issucc*, defined by $issucc(x, y)$ iff $x + 1 = y$. If assignments to registers would allow expressions that include e.g. the $+1$ operator, or even arbitrary addition, then the learning algorithm would have to choose between a potentially large number of different guards and assignments on each transition, This would complicate the design of a learning algorithm. On the other hand, we do not foresee any fundamental difficulty in extending the theory for learning RAs in order to produce more expressive classes of RAs; we conjecture that this could be done by making the implementation of tree queries more advanced and extending the Nerode equivalence (cf. Sect. 5.2). However, in order to focus on the conceptual extensions needed to learn RAs, we have so far excluded expressions in assignments of RAs.

The semantics of register automata is defined in the standard way. Let $\mathcal{A}$ be an RA $\mathcal{A} = (L, l_0, \mathcal{X}, \Gamma, \lambda)$. A *state* of $\mathcal{A}$ is a pair $\langle l, \nu \rangle$ consisting of a location l and a *valuation* $\nu : \mathcal{X}(l) \to \mathcal{D}$ of the registers $\mathcal{X}(l)$ of that location. A *step* of $\mathcal{A}$, denoted $\langle l, \nu \rangle \xrightarrow{\alpha(d)} \langle l', \nu' \rangle$, transfers $\mathcal{A}$ from state $\langle l, \nu \rangle$ to state $\langle l', \nu' \rangle$ on input of the data symbol $\alpha(d)$ if $\mathcal{A}$ has a transition $\langle l, \alpha(p), g, \pi, l' \rangle \in \Gamma$, whose guard is satisfied by d under valuation ν (i.e., $\nu \models g[d/p]$), and whose assignment produces the updated valuation ν' (i.e., $\nu'(x_i) = \nu(x_j)$ if $\pi(x_i) = x_j$, otherwise $\nu'(x_i) = d$ if $\pi(x_i) = p$). A *run* of $\mathcal{A}$ over a data word $w = \alpha(d_1)\ldots\alpha(d_n)$ is a sequence of steps of $\mathcal{A}$

$$\langle l_0, \nu_0 \rangle \xrightarrow{\alpha_1(d_1)} \langle l_1, \nu_1 \rangle \quad \ldots \quad \langle l_{n-1}, \nu_{n-1} \rangle \xrightarrow{\alpha_n(d_n)} \langle l_n, \nu_n \rangle$$

for some initial valuation ν_0. The run is *accepting* if $\lambda(l_n) = +$ and *rejecting* if $\lambda(l_n) = -$. The word w is *accepted (rejected) by $\mathcal{A}$ under ν_0* if $\mathcal{A}$ has an accepting (rejecting) run over w which starts in $\langle l_0, \nu_0 \rangle$.

Existing techniques for active learning of register automata only consider RAs that are *determinate*, meaning that there is no data word over which it has both accepting and rejecting runs. A nondeterministic but determinate RA can be easily transformed into a deterministic RA by strengthening its guards. Note that, unlike for finite automata, nondeterministic (and nondeterminate) RAs are strictly more expressive than deterministic RAs (for instance, the universality problem for nondeterministic RAs is undecidable [59]).

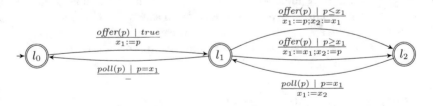

Fig. 3. Priority queue with capacity 2.

Example. As a simple example of a determinate register automaton, let us consider a priority queue with capacity two. A priority queue stores a set of keys from some totally ordered set. We will use the set of rational numbers as the set of keys. We abstract from values that are stored along with keys. The interface of the priority queue supports two operations:

- *offer* inserts a given key into the priority queue. It succeeds if the queue is not full;
- *poll* asks for the smallest key in the queue; the operation returns that key and removes it; if the queue contains several copies of the smallest key only one is removed. If the queue is empty, the operation does not succeed.

The interface consists of operations with input parameters and return values. In order to represent it as a data language, we model sequences of successful operations as data words. A successful *offer* is represented by the data symbol *offer*(d), where d is the inserted key. A successful *poll* operation is represented by the data symbol *poll*(d), where d is the returned value. A valid sequence of operations is represented by the sequence of data symbols that represent its successful operations.

The RA in Fig. 3 accepts the language which models a priority queue with capacity two. The two keys are stored in registers x_1 and x_2, respectively, with $x_1 \leq x_2$, so that a successful *poll* operation always returns the value of x_1.

For conciseness, we have omitted nonaccepting locations. Thus the RA in Fig. 3 should be extended with a terminal non-accepting location; from each location, there should be transitions to the non-accepting location for data symbols that do not satisfy any of the existing guards. For instance, from l_1 there is a transition to the non-accepting location for *poll*(p) symbols where $p \neq x_1$.

5   Black-Box Learning of Register Automata

In this section, we summarize some of the proposed algorithms for learning register automata. A number of such algorithms have been proposed, which generalize the classical L^* algorithm in some way. The obvious challenge for such algorithms is that register automata is a much richer formalism than finite automata. It is a challenge to devise techniques that can infer all the features of an RA, including locations, registers, guards, and assignments, in a black-box context, using only membership queries and counterexamples returned by equivalence queries. The only *a priori* information available is the static interface of the SUL, i.e., the set of actions that it can process, and a theory (i.e., set of relations on the data domain) which is assumed to be expressive enough to model the behavior of the SUL.

5.1   Learning Symbolic Automata

Let us first consider the subclass of *symbolic automata*, which are essentially register automata without registers and assignments. Symbolic automata have been studied in recent years as a tool for string processing, where transitions are guarded by predicates of various theories [40,71]. They allow automata over large or infinite alphabets to be expressed compactly.

For large finite domains of data values, symbolic automata are equivalent to ordinary finite automata. However, a naive application of L^* to such automata will lead to an excessive number of membership queries, since queries must be performed for each data value in the data domain. More efficient approaches have been presented by Isberner et al. [47] and by Mens and Maler [56]. A main idea is to associate to each transition a *representative* data value which satisfies its guard. The hypothesis is that all data values that satisfy the guard induce the same behavior in the SUL; formally this means that they lead to the same residual languages. When such a hypothesis is refuted, typically as a result of an equivalence query (i.e., two data values that satisfy the guard lead to different residual languages), the algorithm splits the guard accordingly. In [47,56], some predefined structure for splitting guards by need is assumed. For instance, when the data domain is the set of integers, the algorithm could prescribe that all membership queries initially be performed using a specific integer (e.g., 0). If later, it turns out that different behavior is induced by a negative number, a transition may be split into two, one for nonnegative and one for negative numbers.

The approach of [47] has been shown to improve over naive L^* by several orders of magnitude on a set of benchmarks of moderate size. So far, the approach has not been applied to learn symbolic automata of the form considered in, e.g., [40,71] with its rich collection of predicates.

5.2   Learning Register Automata: The SL^* Algorithm

The class of register automata with registers and assignments brings additional challenges to the design of learning algorithms. For symbolic automata, which do not have registers, the learning algorithm can still be based on the classical definition of Nerode congruence for identifying locations. That is, two data words are Nerode congruent if they induce the same future behavior (i.e., residual language), and each congruence class corresponds to a location. In this case, the main problem is to infer, for each state, a suitable partitioning of data symbols that processed as input in that state, and map the partitioning onto guards on outgoing transitions. For register automata, the future behavior from a location (i.e., its residual language) depends also on the data values assigned to its registers. A learning algorithm must thus infer both (i) which registers are needed in a location, and (ii) how to partition the set of data values in input data symbols to produce guards on different outgoing transitions, in a way that depends on the register valuation. Thus, the concept of residual language must be generalized to a mapping from register valuations to future behaviors. Furthermore, since assignments can permute registers, the concept of Nerode congruence must be defined in such a way that it allows permutations of registers: different permutations will result in different assignments to registers on incoming transitions.

As an illustration, the future behavior from location l_2 in Fig. 3 depends on two data values. A learning algorithm will infer that a word leading to l_2 has two *memorable* data values; intuitively, an input value d is memorable if it has an impact on the future behavior of the SUL: either d occurs in a future output, or a future output depends on d (e.g., if d appears in a guard). A learning algorithm will therefore create two registers: x_1 and x_2. Assume that location l_1 is represented by the word *offer*(3). Initially, a learning algorithm may assume that all outgoing *offer*-transitions from l_1 can be represented by a single symbol, say *offer*(5), and generate a single outgoing transition from l_1 with the guard *true*. A subsequent counterexample, e.g., of form, *offer*(3)*offer*(1)*poll*(1) will make the learning algorithm realize that the future behavior after *offer*(3)*offer*(1) is equivalent to that after *offer*(3)*offer*(5), if we are allowed to adapt the contents of registers so that x_1 is assigned the smaller value and x_2 the larger value. The learning algorithm will therefore split the transition guarded by *true* into two different transitions, with a guard that compares the parameter of the current data symbol to the value of the register, as in Fig. 3, and equip each transition with a different assignment.

The above concepts are a basis for the SL^* algorithm for learning register automata [15]. In extends predecessor algorithms such as [6,47,56] by the concept of *tree queries*, which are used in place of membership queries. The arguments of a tree query is a prefix data word, and a set of so-called *symbolic suffixes*, i.e., data words with uninstantiated data parameters. The tree query returns a so called *symbolic decision tree* (SDT), which has the form of an "RA-fragment" which accepts/rejects suffixes obtained by instantiating data parameters in one of the symbolic suffixes.

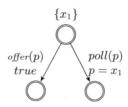

Fig. 4. Symbolic decision tree returned by tree query for prefix *offer*(3) and symbolic suffixes $\{offer(p), poll(p)\}$

Let us illustrate this on the priority queue example for the prefix *offer*(3) and the set of symbolic suffixes $V = \{offer(p), poll(p)\}$. The acceptance/rejection of suffixes obtained by instantiating data parameters in V after *offer*(3) can be represented by the SDT in Fig. 4. In the initial location, the value 3 from *offer*(3) is stored in a register. We use the convention that register x_i stores the ith data value from the prefix. Thereafter, suffixes of form *poll*(d) are accepted if the data value d equals the value stored in the register, and rejected otherwise (for each action there is an implicit transition to a rejecting location with a guard that is the conjoined negations of all accepting transitions). Suffixes of form *offer*(d) are always accepted.

Tree queries can be implemented by performing several membership queries and combining their results. A straightforward implementation of a tree query for a prefix u and an uninstantiated suffix of form $\alpha(p)$ produces a set of maximally refined but still satisfiable guards over registers x_i, storing values from u, and suffix parameter p without introducing additional constraints between registers. For each such maximally refined satisfiable guard in the theory a membership query for the concatenation of u and $\alpha(d)$ for some d that satisfies the guard is sufficient to characterize the behavior for all data values satisfying this guard. For instance, the SDT of Fig. 4 can be formed by combining the results of the membership queries $offer(3)offer(1)$ for guard $(x_1 > p)$, $offer(3)offer(3)$ for guard $(x_1 = p)$, $offer(3)offer(5)$ for guard $(x_1 < p)$, and analogous membership queries for suffix $poll(p)$.

One reason for using the tree queries instead of simple membership queries is that they allow to properly approximate a Nerode equivalence under which words can be equivalent after permutation of data values. Suppose, for instance, that we would only pose the membership query $offer(3)offer(5)poll(3)$, which is accepted; we then use the principles of [47,56] to infer that after $offer(3)offer(5)$ all symbols of form $poll(p)$ are accepted. If then the membership query $offer(3)offer(1)poll(3)$ is rejected, we infer that after $offer(3)offer(1)$ all symbols of form $poll(p)$ are rejected. We would then conclude that the prefixes $offer(3)offer(5)$ and $offer(3)offer(1)$ are not Nerode equivalent and represent different locations, although in the final automaton (see Fig. 3) they are represented by the same location. Thus, our preliminary approximation of the Nerode equivalence would *not* overapproximate the "actual" Nerode equivalence. This would destroy the partition-refinement structure of the L^* algorithm, which in turn is the basis for establishing convergence guarantees of the learning algorithm.

5.3 Limitations and Extensions

Section 5.2 outlined the principles of a framework for extending active automata learning to register automata [15]. This framework has been implemented in RAlib [14], and used to infer register automata and register mealy machines with simple theories, such as theories of numbers with equality and inequality. In order to make it more generally usable, some limitations must be overcome, of which we list some here.

- **Richer theories with structured data types:** The simple framework outlined in the preceding sections can be used to infer register automata models, whose registers are assigned scalar values, such as the priority queue model in Fig. 3. Obviously, this model structure does not scale to modeling priority queues of arbitrary size. For this, we need to work with theories that can describe structure data, such as sequences, and operations on such sequences. It remains to be seen whether the overall framework for learning RAs outlined in this section will also function well with such structured data type.
- **Scalability:** The realization of the ideas is still somewhat naive. For instance, the number of membership queries used to realize a tree query is exponential in the length of the prefix (and suffix) of the query. As explained in Sect. 5.2 this is motivated by the desire to stay within a partition refinement framework, but there is still much room for optimizing this aspect of the algorithm.

One way to address these limitations is to augment the learning algorithms with white-box information extraction methods. Some directions will be discussed in the next section.

6   Exploiting White-Box Techniques

We have discussed the potentially positive impact of exploiting white-box techniques in automata learning in previous sections and have sketched the current limitations and open questions when learning register automata models. We conclude the paper by discussing directions for future research with a particular focus on using white-box techniques to improve learning of expressive register automata models while retaining the benefits of the black-box approach, i.e., concise and abstract models.

6.1   Improving the Equivalence Oracle

Black-box learning approaches, although effective in constructing hypothesis models for finite state machines, typically have difficulties to find counterexamples for hypotheses with a large number of states and events [65]. If we have direct access to the code or binary of the SUL, several additional techniques become available to discover counterexamples for hypothesis models. There is a range of white-box symbolic execution techniques, such as veritesting [7], concolic testing [35], and white-box fuzz testing [34] that can be adapted to find counterexamples for hypothesis models. We survey some works that exploit this idea.

Smetsers et al. [66] used American fuzzy lop (AFL)[3] to efficiently obtain counterexamples for hypothesis models. AFL is a fuzzer that uses compile-time instrumentation and genetic algorithms to automatically discover test cases that trigger new internal states in the targeted binary. By combining model learning with AFL, Smetsers et al. were successful in the RERS 2016 challenge[4], which aims to compare verification techniques and tools.

The PSYCO tool integrates active automata learning and dynamic symbolic execution for generating component interfaces [32]. Recent work explores the potential of using symbolic search on a component's state space [58] for estimating an upper bound on the length of counterexamples that can be found during learning by PSYCO. Fully symbolic and synchronized exploration of a SUL and a conjectured model, i.e., checking the conjecture against the SUL, would allow it to decide equivalence (assuming decidability of the corresponding SMT encoding). The white-box learning algorithm Σ^* [13] uses predicate abstraction to construct models that overapproximate stream processing code in order to answer equivalence queries.

---

[3] http://lcamtuf.coredump.cx/afl/.
[4] http://www.rers-challenge.org/2016.

6.2   Introducing New Queries

In a black-box setting, one important reason why many membership queries are needed is that the learner cannot see directly whether a value is stored by the SUL, or whether it is compared to other values in the guard of a transition. The task of the learner is to figure this out using black-box experiments only. In [15], learning algorithms are presented that accomplish this task for some simple theories with equality and/or inequality. These algorithms have a high query complexity, however, and it is not clear how they can be generalized to richer theories. Consider, for instance, a trace $offer(2)$ $offer(3)$ $offer(4)$ $offer(4)$ in a setting with equality, successor and addition. What guard was used on the last transition? Is the last value required to be equal to the previous one? Or is it the successor of the second value $(3 + 1 = 4)$? Or has it been obtained by addition from the first value $(2 + 2 = 4)$? A number of works use forms of symbolic execution for making symbolic constraints on execution paths visible when performing tests on a component during membership queries. In this way, a learner can observe directly which values are stored and which predicates are tested in a trace. The idea is to replace membership queries (is word w in the language?) by a symbolic version in which the reply consists not only of a yes/no answer but also includes the complete symbolic run induced by input word w. The white-box learning algorithm Σ^* [13] is an example of an approach in which the learner may pose "symbolic" membership queries.

A lightweight alternative for the use of symbolic executions is provided by taint analysis. Dynamic taint analysis (also referred to as dynamic information flow tracking) [8,20,21,41] is a technique in which code is instrumented in order to mark and track data in a program at run time. Inputs to a program are "tainted", i.e. labeled with a tag. When the program executes, these tagged values are propagated such that any new values derived from a tagged value also carry a tag derived from these source input tags. Dynamic tainting, as implemented for instance in Autogram [41], allows to precisely identify which program inputs are stored, tested, or processed at any point in time.

In order to see how a learner may use tainting information, consider the priority queue example of Fig. 3. Suppose the learner is using the SL^* algorithm of Sect. 5.2 and needs to construct a symbolic decision tree for the prefix $offer(3)$ and the set of symbolic suffixes $V = \{offer(p), poll(p)\}$. Suppose that taint analysis reveals that the parameter of a call to $offer$ is stored in some variable, say x_1, and that the return value of a subsequent call to $poll$ is equal to the value of this variable. Based on this information, the learner may deduce the right branch of Fig. 5. After calls $offer(3)$ $offer(4)$, taint analysis tells that the first parameter is stored in x_1, the second parameter is compared with x_1 in a test $p > x_1$, and then stored in x_2. Based on this, the learner deduces the left branch of Fig. 5, and infers that the tree is still incomplete. In order to complete the tree, the learner performs calls $offer(3)$ $offer(2)$, where 2 is an arbitrary value less than 3. Using taint analysis, the learner can now infer the third and final branch in the tree.

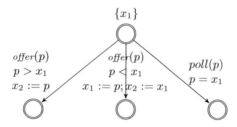

Fig. 5. Symbolic decision tree constructed using dynamic taint analysis

It is interesting to compare the SDTs of Figs. 4 and 5. Whereas a black-box tree query initially returns the incorrect decision tree of Fig. 4 for prefix *offer*(3), and several additional tree queries (and even an equivalence query) are required before a correct decision tree is found, a white-box tree query produces the correct decision tree of Fig. 5 right away. This benefit comes at a price, as application of taint analysis requires instrumentation of the code. According to [41], their tainting framework for Java programs (which is not yet optimized) runs approximately 100 times slower than the original, uninstrumented code.

A key benefit of taint analysis is that it enables the application of the SL^* algorithm in settings with richer theories. The SL^* algorithm crucially depends on an oracle that answers tree queries. In [15] it is shown how a tree oracle can be implemented via (black-box) membership queries for some commonly occurring theories: the theory of equalities, the theory of equality and inequality over rational (or real) numbers, and the theory of equality and inequality over integers. Every single tree query is mapped to an exponential number of membership queries (in the number of data values in a queried word w) that identify relevant relations between data values in w. Moreover, these tree oracle implementations are nontrivial and their correctness proofs are involved. Computation of decision trees and counterexample analysis becomes harder (or even impossible) when more relations are added to the theory.

6.3   Computing Domain-Specific Information

The state of a component is usually maintained as valuations of internal variables. A static code analysis that produces, e.g., for a Java class, which methods write internal variables, can help identifying methods that cannot alter the state of a component before actually learning a model of the component. A comparative analysis (reads and writes) can identify pairs of independent methods for which the order of execution is irrelevant. Information of this kind can be used to reduce the number of membership queries as has been shown in [45,54].

When inferring register automata, static code analysis can reveal important information about a component.

Live Variables. Knowing about live variables can help deciding if values have to become memorable or not in certain states without performing extensive testing or expensive symbolic analysis.

Tests and Computations on Variables. Knowing that only certain tests are performed on a variable can help when determining the theory that is used for learning the behavior that is possibly associated with this variable. This can help reducing the number of tests that have to performed when learning models. On the other hand, knowledge about the set of computations that can be used on parameters or register contents may enable learning more expressive models that, e.g., describe application of cryptographic primitives on parameters or internal fields.

Independent Parameters/Fields. If there are subsets of parameters and fields that are independent, a learning algorithm does not have to perform tests for inferring potential relations between these sets. The typing mechanism that is presented in [14] allows to exploit this information during learning. Static code analysis could be used to compute it in a fully automated approach.

The above list is not exhaustive but rather a starting point for future research.

In all three directions, initial positive results exist and indicate the potential that lies in the application of white-box techniques for the implementation of more performant learning algorithms, inferring more expressive classes of models.

7 Conclusion

We have outlined current techniques and applications for model learning, a.k.a. active automata learning, and pointed at challenges for improving its scalability and applicability to richer models. We then outlined proposals for exploiting white-box techniques in order to overcome these limitations. We indicated some approaches that have started in these directions, and we expect a significant body of techniques to be developed over the next years.

References

1. Aarts, F., Fiterau-Brostean, P., Kuppens, H., Vaandrager, F.: Learning register automata with fresh value generation. In: Leucker, M., Rueda, C., Valencia, F.D. (eds.) ICTAC 2015. LNCS, vol. 9399, pp. 165–183. Springer, Cham (2015). https://doi.org/10.1007/978-3-319-25150-9_11
2. Aarts, F., Howar, F., Kuppens, H., Vaandrager, F.: Algorithms for inferring register automata. In: Margaria, T., Steffen, B. (eds.) ISoLA 2014. LNCS, vol. 8802, pp. 202–219. Springer, Heidelberg (2014). https://doi.org/10.1007/978-3-662-45234-9_15
3. Aarts, F., Jonsson, B., Uijen, J., Vaandrager, F.W.: Generating models of infinite-state communication protocols using regular inference with abstraction. Formal Methods Syst. Des. **46**(1), 1–41 (2015)
4. Aarts, F., Schmaltz, J., Vaandrager, F.: Inference and abstraction of the biometric passport. In: Margaria, T., Steffen, B. (eds.) ISoLA 2010. LNCS, vol. 6415, pp. 673–686. Springer, Heidelberg (2010). https://doi.org/10.1007/978-3-642-16558-0_54

5. Aarts, F., Heidarian, F., Vaandrager, F.: A theory of history dependent abstractions for learning interface automata. In: Koutny, M., Ulidowski, I. (eds.) CONCUR 2012. LNCS, vol. 7454, pp. 240–255. Springer, Heidelberg (2012). https://doi.org/10.1007/978-3-642-32940-1_18

6. Angluin, D.: Learning regular sets from queries and counterexamples. Inf. Comput. **75**(2), 87–106 (1987)

7. Avgerinos, T., Rebert, A., Cha, S.K., Brumley, D.: Enhancing symbolic execution with veritesting. In: Proceedings of the 36th International Conference on Software Engineering, ICSE 2014, pp. 1083–1094. ACM, New York (2014)

8. Bell, J., Kaiser, G.: Phosphor: illuminating dynamic data flow in commodity JVMs. In: Proceedings of the 2014 ACM International Conference on Object Oriented Programming Systems Languages & Applications, OOPSLA 2014, pp. 83–101. ACM, New York (2014)

9. Berg, T., Grinchtein, O., Jonsson, B., Leucker, M., Raffelt, H., Steffen, B.: On the correspondence between conformance testing and regular inference. In: Cerioli, M. (ed.) FASE 2005. LNCS, vol. 3442, pp. 175–189. Springer, Heidelberg (2005). https://doi.org/10.1007/978-3-540-31984-9_14

10. Berg, T., Jonsson, B., Raffelt, H.: Regular inference for state machines using domains with equality tests. In: Fiadeiro, J.L., Inverardi, P. (eds.) FASE 2008. LNCS, vol. 4961, pp. 317–331. Springer, Heidelberg (2008). https://doi.org/10.1007/978-3-540-78743-3_24

11. Bernot, G., Gaudel, M.C., Marre, B.: Software testing based on formal specifications: a theory and a tool. Softw. Eng. J. **6**(6), 387–405 (1991)

12. Bossert, G., Hiet, G., Henin, T.: Modelling to simulate botnet command and control protocols for the evaluation of network intrusion detection systems. In: Proceedings of the 6th Conference on Network and Information Systems Security, SAR-SSI 2011, pp. 1–8. IEEE Computer Society (2011)

13. Botinčan, M., Babić, D.: Sigma*: symbolic learning of input-output specifications. In: Proceedings of the 40th Annual ACM SIGPLAN-SIGACT Symposium on Principles of Programming Languages, POPL 2013, pp. 443–456. ACM, New York (2013)

14. Cassel, S., Howar, F., Jonsson, B.: RALib: a LearnLib extension for inferring EFSMs. In: International Workshop on Design and Implementation of Formal Tools and Systems, DIFTS 2015, Austin, Texas (2015). http://www.faculty.ece.vt.edu/chaowang/difts2015/papers/paper_5.pdf

15. Cassel, S., Howar, F., Jonsson, B., Steffen, B.: Active learning for extended finite state machines. Formal Asp. Comput. **28**(2), 233–263 (2016)

16. Chalupar, G., Peherstorfer, S., Poll, E., de Ruiter, J.: Automated reverse engineering using Lego. In: Proceedings of 8th USENIX Workshop on Offensive Technologies (WOOT 2014), San Diego, California, Los Alamitos, CA, USA, August 2014. IEEE Computer Society (2014)

17. Cho, C.Y., Babić, D., Poosankam, P., Chen, K.Z., Wu, E.X., Song, D.: Mace: model-inference-assisted concolic exploration for protocol and vulnerability discovery. In: Proceedings of the 20th USENIX Conference on Security, SEC 2011, Berkeley, CA, USA, p. 10. USENIX Association (2011)

18. Choi, W.: Automated testing of graphical user interfaces: a new algorithm and challenges. In: Proceedings of the 2013 ACM Workshop on Mobile Development Lifecycle, MobileDeLi 2013, pp. 27–28. ACM, New York (2013)

19. Choi, W., Necula, G., Sen, K.: Guided GUI testing of android apps with minimal restart and approximate learning. SIGPLAN Not. **48**(10), 623–640 (2013)

20. Clause, J., Li, W., Orso, A.: Dytan: a generic dynamic taint analysis framework. In: Proceedings of the 2007 International Symposium on Software Testing and Analysis, ISSTA 2007, pp. 196–206. ACM, New York (2007)

21. Clause, J., Orso, A.: Penumbra: automatically identifying failure-relevant inputs using dynamic tainting. In: Proceedings of the Eighteenth International Symposium on Software Testing and Analysis, ISSTA 2009, pp. 249–260. ACM, New York (2009)

22. Cobleigh, J.M., Giannakopoulou, D., Pasareanu, C.S.: Learning assumptions for compositional verification. In: Garavel, H., Hatcliff, J. (eds.) TACAS 2003. LNCS, vol. 2619, pp. 331–346. Springer, Heidelberg (2003). https://doi.org/10.1007/3-540-36577-X_24

23. Dinca, I., Ipate, F., Mierla, L., Stefanescu, A.: Learn and test for event-B – a rodin plugin. In: Derrick, J., Fitzgerald, J., Gnesi, S., Khurshid, S., Leuschel, M., Reeves, S., Riccobene, E. (eds.) ABZ 2012. LNCS, vol. 7316, pp. 361–364. Springer, Heidelberg (2012). https://doi.org/10.1007/978-3-642-30885-7_32

24. Dinca, I., Ipate, F., Stefanescu, A.: Model learning and test generation for event-B decomposition. In: Margaria, T., Steffen, B. (eds.) ISoLA 2012. LNCS, vol. 7609, pp. 539–553. Springer, Heidelberg (2012). https://doi.org/10.1007/978-3-642-34026-0_40

25. Drews, S., D'Antoni, L.: Learning symbolic automata. In: Legay, A., Margaria, T. (eds.) TACAS 2017. LNCS, vol. 10205, pp. 173–189. Springer, Heidelberg (2017). https://doi.org/10.1007/978-3-662-54577-5_10

26. Feng, L., Han, T., Kwiatkowska, M., Parker, D.: Learning-based compositional verification for synchronous probabilistic systems. In: Bultan, T., Hsiung, P.-A. (eds.) ATVA 2011. LNCS, vol. 6996, pp. 511–521. Springer, Heidelberg (2011). https://doi.org/10.1007/978-3-642-24372-1_40

27. Feng, L., Kwiatkowska, M., Parker, D.: Automated learning of probabilistic assumptions for compositional reasoning. In: Giannakopoulou, D., Orejas, F. (eds.) FASE 2011. LNCS, vol. 6603, pp. 2–17. Springer, Heidelberg (2011). https://doi.org/10.1007/978-3-642-19811-3_2

28. Fiterău-Broştean, P., Howar, F.: Learning-based testing the sliding window behavior of TCP implementations. In: Petrucci, L., Seceleanu, C., Cavalcanti, A. (eds.) FMICS/AVoCS -2017. LNCS, vol. 10471, pp. 185–200. Springer, Cham (2017). https://doi.org/10.1007/978-3-319-67113-0_12

29. Fiterău-Broştean, P., Janssen, R., Vaandrager, F.: Combining model learning and model checking to analyze TCP implementations. In: Chaudhuri, S., Farzan, A. (eds.) CAV 2016. LNCS, vol. 9780, pp. 454–471. Springer, Cham (2016). https://doi.org/10.1007/978-3-319-41540-6_25

30. Fiterău-Broştean, P., Lenaerts, T., Poll, E., de Ruiter, J., Vaandrager, F., Verleg, P.: Model learning and model checking of SSH implementations. In: Proceedings of the 24th ACM SIGSOFT International SPIN Symposium on Model Checking of Software, SPIN 2017, pp. 142–151. ACM, New York (2017)

31. Gaudel, M.-C.: Testing can be formal, too. In: Mosses, P.D., Nielsen, M., Schwartzbach, M.I. (eds.) CAAP 1995. LNCS, vol. 915, pp. 82–96. Springer, Heidelberg (1995). https://doi.org/10.1007/3-540-59293-8_188

32. Giannakopoulou, D., Rakamarić, Z., Raman, V.: Symbolic learning of component interfaces. In: Miné, A., Schmidt, D. (eds.) SAS 2012. LNCS, vol. 7460, pp. 248–264. Springer, Heidelberg (2012). https://doi.org/10.1007/978-3-642-33125-1_18

33. van Glabbeek, R.J.: The linear time – branching time spectrum I. The semantics of concrete, sequential processes. In: Bergstra, J.A., Ponse, A., Smolka, S.A. (eds.) Handbook of Process Algebra, pp. 3–99. North-Holland, Amsterdam (2001)

34. Godefroid, P., Levin, M.Y., Molnar, D.A.: Automated whitebox fuzz testing. In: Proceedings of the Network and Distributed System Security Symposium, NDSS 2008, 10th February - 13th February 2008, San Diego, California, USA. The Internet Society (2008)
35. Godefroid, P., Klarlund, N., Sen, K.: DART: directed automated random testing. SIGPLAN Not. **40**(6), 213–223 (2005)
36. Grinchtein, O., Jonsson, B., Leucker, M.: Learning of event-recording automata. Theoret. Comput. Sci. **411**(47), 4029–4054 (2010)
37. Groce, A., Peled, D., Yannakakis, M.: Adaptive model checking. Logic J. IGPL **14**(5), 729–744 (2006)
38. Hagerer, A., Hungar, H., Niese, O., Steffen, B.: Model generation by moderated regular extrapolation. In: Kutsche, R.-D., Weber, H. (eds.) FASE 2002. LNCS, vol. 2306, pp. 80–95. Springer, Heidelberg (2002). https://doi.org/10.1007/3-540-45923-5_6
39. Hagerer, A., Margaria, T., Niese, O., Steffen, B., Brune, G., Ide, H.-D.: Efficient regression testing of CTI-systems: testing a complex call-center solution. Ann. Rev. Commun. Int. Eng. Consortium (IEC) **55**, 1033–1040 (2001)
40. Hooimeijer, P., Veanes, M.: An evaluation of automata algorithms for string analysis. In: Jhala, R., Schmidt, D. (eds.) VMCAI 2011. LNCS, vol. 6538, pp. 248–262. Springer, Heidelberg (2011). https://doi.org/10.1007/978-3-642-18275-4_18
41. Höschele, M., Zeller, A.: Mining input grammars from dynamic taints. In: Proceedings of the 31st IEEE/ACM International Conference on Automated Software Engineering, ASE 2016, pp. 720–725. ACM, New York (2016)
42. Howar, F., Isberner, M., Steffen, B., Bauer, O., Jonsson, B.: Inferring semantic interfaces of data structures. In: Margaria, T., Steffen, B. (eds.) ISoLA 2012. LNCS, vol. 7609, pp. 554–571. Springer, Heidelberg (2012). https://doi.org/10.1007/978-3-642-34026-0_41
43. Howar, F., Steffen, B., Jonsson, B., Cassel, S.: Inferring canonical register automata. In: Kuncak, V., Rybalchenko, A. (eds.) VMCAI 2012. LNCS, vol. 7148, pp. 251–266. Springer, Heidelberg (2012). https://doi.org/10.1007/978-3-642-27940-9_17
44. Howar, F., Steffen, B., Merten, M.: Automata learning with automated alphabet abstraction refinement. In: Jhala, R., Schmidt, D. (eds.) VMCAI 2011. LNCS, vol. 6538, pp. 263–277. Springer, Heidelberg (2011). https://doi.org/10.1007/978-3-642-18275-4_19
45. Howar, F., Giannakopoulou, D., Rakamarić, Z.: Hybrid learning: interface generation through static, dynamic, and symbolic analysis. In: Proceedings of the 2013 International Symposium on Software Testing and Analysis, ISSTA 2013, pp. 268–279. ACM, New York (2013)
46. Hungar, H., Niese, O., Steffen, B.: Domain-specific optimization in automata learning. In: Hunt, W.A., Somenzi, F. (eds.) CAV 2003. LNCS, vol. 2725, pp. 315–327. Springer, Heidelberg (2003). https://doi.org/10.1007/978-3-540-45069-6_31
47. Isberner, M., Howar, F., Steffen, B.: Inferring automata with state-local alphabet abstractions. In: Brat, G., Rungta, N., Venet, A. (eds.) NFM 2013. LNCS, vol. 7871, pp. 124–138. Springer, Heidelberg (2013). https://doi.org/10.1007/978-3-642-38088-4_9
48. Isberner, M., Howar, F., Steffen, B.: The open-source LearnLib. In: Kroening, D., Păsăreanu, C.S. (eds.) CAV 2015. LNCS, vol. 9206, pp. 487–495. Springer, Cham (2015). https://doi.org/10.1007/978-3-319-21690-4_32
49. Isberner, M., Howar, F., Steffen, B.: Learning register automata: from languages to program structures. Mach. Learn. **96**(1–2), 65–98 (2014)

50. Isberner, M., Howar, F., Steffen, B.: The TTT algorithm: a redundancy-free approach to active automata learning. In: Bonakdarpour, B., Smolka, S.A. (eds.) RV 2014. LNCS, vol. 8734, pp. 307–322. Springer, Cham (2014). https://doi.org/10.1007/978-3-319-11164-3_26
51. Khalili, A., Natale, L., Tacchella, A.: Reverse engineering of middleware for verification of robot control architectures. In: Brugali, D., Broenink, J.F., Kroeger, T., MacDonald, B.A. (eds.) SIMPAR 2014. LNCS (LNAI), vol. 8810, pp. 315–326. Springer, Cham (2014). https://doi.org/10.1007/978-3-319-11900-7_27
52. Lee, D., Yannakakis, M.: Principles and methods of testing finite state machines – a survey. Proc. IEEE **84**(8), 1090–1123 (1996)
53. Margaria, T., Niese, O., Raffelt, H., Steffen, B.: Efficient test-based model generation for legacy reactive systems. In: Proceedings of the 2004 Ninth IEEE International High-Level Design Validation and Test Workshop, HLDVT 2004, Washington, DC, USA, pp. 95–100. IEEE Computer Society (2004)
54. Margaria, T., Raffelt, H., Steffen, B.: Knowledge-based relevance filtering for efficient system-level test-based model generation. Innov. Syst. Softw. Eng. **1**(2), 147–156 (2005)
55. Meinke, K., Sindhu, M.A.: LBTest: a learning-based testing tool for reactive systems. In: Sixth IEEE International Conference on Software Testing, Verification and Validation, ICST 2013, Luxembourg, Luxembourg, 18–22 March 2013, pp. 447–454 (2013)
56. Mens, I.-E., Maler, O.: Learning regular languages over large ordered alphabets. Log. Methods Comput. Sci. **11**(3), 1–22 (2015)
57. Moerman, J., Sammartino, M., Silva, A., Klin, B., Szynwelski, M.: Learning nominal automata. In: Castagna, G., Gordon, A.D. (eds.) Proceedings of the 44th ACM SIGPLAN Symposium on Principles of Programming Languages, POPL 2017, 18–20 January 2017, Paris, France, pp. 613–625. ACM (2017)
58. Mues, M., Howar, F., Luckow, K., Kahsai, T., Rakamaric, Z.: Releasing the PSYCO: using symbolic search in interface generation for Java. ACM SIGSOFT Softw. Eng. Notes **41**(6), 1–5 (2016)
59. Neven, F., Schwentick, T., Vianu, V.: Finite state machines for strings over infinite alphabets. ACM Trans. Comput. Logic **5**(3), 403–435 (2004)
60. Peled, D., Vardi, M.Y., Yannakakis, M.: Black box checking. J. Automata Lang. Comb. **7**(2), 225–246 (2002)
61. Raffelt, H., Merten, M., Steffen, B., Margaria, T.: Dynamic testing via automata learning. STTT **11**(4), 307–324 (2009)
62. de Ruiter, J., Poll, E.: Protocol state fuzzing of TLS implementations. In: 24th USENIX Security Symposium (USENIX Security 2015), Washington, D.C., pp. 193–206. USENIX Association, August 2015
63. Schuts, M., Hooman, J., Vaandrager, F.: Refactoring of legacy software using model learning and equivalence checking: an industrial experience report. In: Ábrahám, E., Huisman, M. (eds.) IFM 2016. LNCS, vol. 9681, pp. 311–325. Springer, Cham (2016). https://doi.org/10.1007/978-3-319-33693-0_20
64. Shahbaz, M., Groz, R.: Analysis and testing of black-box component-based systems by inferring partial models. Softw. Test. Verif. Reliab. **24**(4), 253–288 (2014)
65. Smeenk, W., Moerman, J., Vaandrager, F., Jansen, D.N.: Applying automata learning to embedded control software. In: Butler, M., Conchon, S., Zaïdi, F. (eds.) ICFEM 2015. LNCS, vol. 9407, pp. 67–83. Springer, Cham (2015). https://doi.org/10.1007/978-3-319-25423-4_5
66. Smetsers, R., Moerman, J., Janssen, M., Verwer, S.: Complementing model learning with mutation-based fuzzing. CoRR, abs/1611.02429 (2016)

67. Sun, J., Xiao, H., Liu, Y., Lin, S.W., Qin, S.: TLV: abstraction through testing, learning, and validation. In: Proceedings of the 2015 10th Joint Meeting on Foundations of Software Engineering, ESEC/FSE 2015, pp. 698–709. ACM, New York (2015)

68. Tretmans, J.: A formal approach to conformance testing. Ph.D. thesis, University of Twente, December 1992

69. Tretmans, J.: Model-based testing and some steps towards test-based modelling. In: Bernardo, M., Issarny, V. (eds.) SFM 2011. LNCS, vol. 6659, pp. 297–326. Springer, Heidelberg (2011). https://doi.org/10.1007/978-3-642-21455-4_9

70. Vaandrager, F.W.: Model learning. Commun. ACM **60**(2), 86–95 (2017)

71. Veanes, M., Hooimeijer, P., Livshits, B., Molnar, D., Bjørner, N.: Symbolic finite state transducers: algorithms and applications. In: POPL, pp. 137–150. ACM (2012)

72. Volpato, M., Tretmans, J.: Active learning of nondeterministic systems from an ioco perspective. In: Margaria, T., Steffen, B. (eds.) ISoLA 2014. LNCS, vol. 8802, pp. 220–235. Springer, Heidelberg (2014). https://doi.org/10.1007/978-3-662-45234-9_16

73. Windmüller, S., Neubauer, J., Steffen, B., Howar, F., Bauer, O.: Active continuous quality control. In: Proceedings of the 16th International ACM Sigsoft Symposium on Component-based Software Engineering, CBSE 2013, pp. 111–120. ACM, New York (2013)

74. Xue, Y., Wang, J., Liu, Y., Xiao, H., Sun, J., Chandramohan, M.: Detection and classification of malicious JavaScript via attack behavior modelling. In: Proceedings of the 2015 International Symposium on Software Testing and Analysis, ISSTA 2015, pp. 48–59. ACM, New York (2015)

Author Index

Printed in the United States
By Bookmasters